THE LIFE OF ST. FRANCIS OF ASSISI

St. France Marries Lady Poverty. —Andrea Sacchi

THE LIFE OF ST. FRANCIS OF ASSISI

The Rev. Candide Chalippe, OFM

In a New Edition
by:

MEDIATRIX PRESS

MMXIV

ISBN: 9780692243374

Cover Art: *Pope Innocent III approves the rule of St. Francis.* Giotto Bondone (atributed). Detail from the Basilica of St. Francis of Assisi.

Mediatrix Press
607 E. 6th Ave.
Post Falls, ID 83854
www.mediatrixpress.com

TABLE OF CONTENTS

THE LIFE OF ST. FRANCIS OF ASSISI
BOOK I

CHAPTER I
EARLY LIFE AND CONVERSION

His birth—Prediction of his future greatness—His studies—He applies himself to commerce—His purity, and affection for the poor—He is taken prisoner—He falls sick—His charity increases towards the poor—He has a mysterious dream—He wishes to go to the war—Jesus Christ dissuades him—He is rapt in spirit—His conversion—He kisses a leper—Jesus Christ crucified appears to him—Salutary effects of this apparition—He goes to Rome—Mingles with the poor—Is tempted by the devil—A voice from heaven commands him to restore the Church of St. Peter Damian—His devotion to the passion of Jesus Christ—He takes some pieces of cloth from his father's house, and sells them, to restore the Church of St. Damian—He escapes from the anger of his father, and retires to a cave—He appears in Assisi, where he is ill-treated—His father confines him—His mother delivers him, and he returns to St. Damian—He manifests his intention to his father, who appeals to justice, and cites him before the Bishop of Assisi—He renounces his inheritance, and gives back his clothes to his father... 1

CHAPTER II
FOUNDATION OF THE ORDER

Retires to a monastery—They give him a hermit's habit—He devotes himself to the leprous—Receives the gift of healing, and returns to Assisi, where he searches for stone to restore the Church of Assisi—He lives on alms—His father and brother exercise his patience—The victories he gains over himself—People begin to esteem and honor him—He restores the Church of St. Peter and that of St. Mary of the Angels, or the Portiuncula—Dwells at St. Mary of the Angels, and is favored therewith heavenly apparitions—He is called to the apostolical life—Renounces money, and goes discalced—His poor and humble habit—God inspires him to preach—He weeps bitterly over the sufferings of Jesus Christ—Receives three disciples, and retires with them to a deserted cottage—He makes them beg for alms—He predicts to the Emperor Otho the short duration of his glory—It is revealed to him that his sins are remitted—He is rapt in ecstasy, and predicts the extension of his Order—He proposes a new mission to his disciples—The address he makes them on their preparation for, and

CHAPTER III

ST. MARY OF THE ANGELS

THE LIFE OF ST. FRANCIS OF ASSISI
BOOK II

CHAPTER I

APOSTOLIC PREACHING

CHAPTER II

A LIGHT FOR A VAST SPACE

CHAPTER III

SPAIN—AFRICA—BROTHER WOLF'S LAYER

CHAPTER IV

COUNCIL OF THE LATERAN—APPROVAL OF THE RULE

THE LIFE OF ST. FRANCIS OF ASSISI
BOOK III

CHAPTER I

THE GENERAL CHAPTER

THE LIFE OF ST. FRANCIS OF ASSISI
BOOK V

CHAPTER VI

ST. FRANCIS DE SALES said, that while many saints should be imitated, some of the saints are to be admired more than imitated. The life of St. Francis gives us some of both. On the one hand, his extraordinary love of God, his humility, his penance, his charity, his prudence and his detachment from and loathing for the world, are all virtues that every Christian should seek to emulate throughout his life. On the other hand, his discernment of spirits, his miracles, his extraordinary fasting and mortification of his body, his ecstasies and the stigmata are all things God performed in St. Francis for our wonderment, to give glory to Him for what He brought about in his servant.

Today, however, there is a false Francis, a Francis who, far from being the man of penance, warning of the danger of sin, is presented as an advocate for the environment who loved everyone for their sins, and preached a worldly peace. The reality of Francis is quite different. Therefore, we have provided a spiritual classic, Fr. Candide Chalippe's *Life of St. Francis,* translated by the Oratorians of London into English. The value of Chalippe's narrative, having compiled all of the sources available at the time of his writing (1727) is that he balances the narrative between the two different elements which made Francis one of the greatest saints in the history of the Church. Chalippe's work is not only a spiritual *tour de force,* but is also a great work of theology, as he unfolds the life of St. Francis with respect to the subsequent theology of the Church through St. Bonaventure, St. Thomas, the Council of Trent and St. Robert Bellarmine. He quotes frequently not only from the Franciscan sources, but also from the Holy Scripture, the Fathers, and the great Theologians of the Middle Ages and the early modern period.

Chalippe's work has been reprinted several times already, but what makes this edition distinctive is the conservative editing which leaves in tact the original text but for a slight revision of archaic language and spelling. Moreover, we have retained all of the footnotes of the author, which reflect the faith and devotion of a writer in an age where men were not afraid to speak the truth lest they might tread upon the sensibilities of a post-Christian age. Furthermore, at the time in which Chalippe's work was written, it was common place to divide it into "Books" without chapters which continue for a hundred pages at a time. To make things easier for the modern reader, we have divided each book into chapters. Lastly, we have added numerous works of art to elucidate and illustrate the work. These are drawn from the frescoes attributed to the great painter Giotto di Bondone, which are found in the Basilica of St. Francis in Assisi, as well as other painters (for the purposes of this work, we simply attribute and do not take up the debate over whether Giotto did paint them, which is an insoluble problem). Giotto, however, occupies the principal place. He is often credited with beginning the Renaissance, and in some ways he did, though he can scarcely be identified with the humanist goals of Petrarch, or the classicism of Michelangelo or Raphael. Giotto is firmly within the Byzantine tradition of Iconography, but as he progressed in his career added elements of perspective and three dimensional painting, while presenting an essentially iconographic depiction of the life of St. Francis. The Frescoes reproduced here are filled with theological depth which bring out in pictures (in an age prior to the printing press when literacy was not accessible to the masses due to technological limitations) the spiritual depth of the events in St. Francis' momentous life. In like manner, the oil paintings from other artists are theologically rich as they are faithful in the depiction of the events in St. Francis' life.

In fine, Francis is a simulacrum of Christ Himself, and many of the events of his life were brought about by Providence, in order to conform the life of the Saint to his own. His is an epoch, of great emperors, sultans, and Popes such as Innocent III, one of the most able Popes in history. His is the age of St. Dominic, the Crusades, the Reconquista, and a great period of reform in the life of the Church, as well as a font of subsequent renewal in subsequent centuries.

The life of Francis is also a model of reform in our age, when the crisis in the Church is not only of the secular state on the outside, but the corruption on the inside, which can only be cleansed and renewed by the qualities which allowed Francis to perform miracles and enter the depths of transforming union; he possessed true faith, penance, reverence for the Mass and the Eucharist, forming him as an apostle of divine charity. May this work be a benefit to everyone in the Church, that they will seek to be one with Christ as completely as St. Francis.

Mediatrix Press, 2014

AUTHOR'S PREFACE

WHEREIN THE PREJUDICES OF CERTAIN PERSONS AGAINST MIRACLES WHICH ARE RECORDED IN THE LIVES OF THE SAINTS ARE SHOWN TO BE BOTH UNREASONABLE AND DANGEROUS, AND THAT THE MIRACLES ATTRIBUTED TO SAINT FRANCIS ARE VERY WELL AUTHENTICATED.

 VERY COMMON failing amongst men is to adopt one extreme in the endeavor to avoid another, and sometimes not to perceive that the extreme into which they fall is greater than that from which they attempted to flee. To insure themselves against weak incredulity, some have imbibed such prejudice against the miracles in the Lives of the Saints, that they cannot endure to hear of them. The very ideas of miracles, revelations, ecstasies, visions, apparitions, are hateful and disgusting to them; all that is said on these subjects they look upon as fabulous and incredible. They call in question the most undeniable evidence, or attribute these wonders to natural and unknown causes. The wonders which are recorded in the Life of St. Francis, afford an opportunity of grappling with these prejudices.

In the first place, no man using his right reason will reject the wonders recorded in the Lives of the Saints, because of their impossibility. Miracles are extraordinary events, which break through the laws of nature, and exceed the force of all natural causes; it is only necessary to make use of our reason to be aware that God, whose power is infinite, having freely established these laws, may, whenever He thinks fit, break through them Himself by the ministry of His creatures, whom He makes use of as He pleases. That these suspensions may enter into the external designs of His wisdom and providence, and that they occur by successive acts, without there having been any change in Him, because it is an act of His will which causes them, as it does every other thing. Now this proves that miracles are possible, and that there is no impossibility in the wonders recorded in the Lives of the Saints.

In the second place, these wonders ought not to cause an incredulous surprise in any sensible person who pays due attention to the wonders of nature. "Man," says St. Augustine, "sees extraordinary things happen, and he admires them, while he himself, the admirer, is a great wonder, and a much greater miracle than any things which are done by the intervention of man. There is nothing more marvelous done in the world, which is not less wonderful than the world itself. All nature is full of what is miraculous; we seem unconscious of it, because we see those things daily, and because this daily repetition lowers them in our eyes. And this is one reason why God has reserved to Himself other things out of the common course of nature, on which He shows His power from time to time, in order that their novelty may strike us; but when we consider attentively, and with reflection, the miracles we constantly see, we find that they are far greater than others, however surprising and uncommon these may be."[1]

The holy doctor admits that the prodigies which are out of the common course of nature, and which are properly called miracles, are to be viewed with astonishment, since they are works of God, worthy of admiration; he only requires that the surprise they cause shall be qualified by a consideration of the wonders of nature, to which he likewise gives the name of miracles, in a more extended sense: on the same principle, and *a fortiori,* what there is surprising in them should not make them appear to us incredible. An enlightened mind does not believe in miracles which are communicated to him, unless due proof of them is adduced; but it is not because what is wonderful in them renders him incredulous, because he sees more marvelous things in the universe and in himself. If men who apply themselves to the study of nature, are pertinacious in refusing to believe in the miracles of the saints, it is because they do not make use of the light they have received, and do not reason deductively; they have only sought to gratify their curiosity, or to gain credit for their discoveries; and do not some of them lose themselves in their speculations, and become impious, even so as to recognize no other God than nature itself?

In the third place, faith in the great mysteries of religion must incline us to believe in the wonders we read in the Lives of the Saints. Are we, then, not called upon to say to those whose prejudices we oppose: "As you belong to the society of the faithful, you not only believe that three Persons make only one God; that the Son of God was made man; that the dead shall rise again; but also, that Jesus Christ becomes every day present on our altars, under the species of bread and wine, at the words of consecration; and you believe all the other astonishing wonders that are proposed to you in our holy religion: why, then, do you find such repugnance in believing those of the Lives of the Saints, which are far inferior to the former"?

It is useless to say in answer, that these last are only based on human testimony, which we are not obliged to receive; that the mysteries are propounded to us by Divine authority, to which we are bound to submit; for this is not the question before us. We only compare one wonder with another, and we maintain that the belief in the one should facilitate the belief in the other. In fact, if we believe with a firm and unshaken faith what God, in His goodness, has been pleased to effect for the salvation of all men, and what He continues daily to effect in the Eucharist, may we not easily convince ourselves that He may have given extraordinary marks of His affection for his

---

[1] Vide homo insolita et miratur, cum sit ipse mirator magnum miraculum. -Serm. 126 et alias 32, ex homil. 50. Omni miraculo quod fit per hominem majus miraculum est homo. -De Civ. Dei, 1, 10, c. 12. Quidquid mirabile fit in hoc mundo, profecto minus est quam totus hic mundus. - *Ibid.* Omnis natura rerum plena miraculis. - Epist. 102, alias 49, n. 5. Trin. 24; *in Joan.* n. 1, et alibi. -Quamvis miracula visibilium naturarum videndi assiduatate viluerint; tamen cum ea sapienter intuemur inusitatissimis rarissimisque majora sunt. -De Civ. Dei, sup.

most faithful servants?

In the fourth place, similar wonders to those which are found in the Lives of the Saints are also found in the Holy Scriptures. Raptures, ecstasies, frequent visions and apparitions, continual revelations, an infinity of miracles, miraculous fasts of forty days, are things recorded in the Old and New Testaments. We believe all these wonderful circumstances, and we are obliged to believe them, although they far surpass our understanding; on what, then, shall we rely for maintaining that the wonders recorded in the Lives of the Saints are improbable, and that we may reasonably call them in question? Reason, on the contrary, marks them as so much the more probable and worthy of credit, as we know and believe similar ones which we may not doubt of. Christians should be accustomed to what is marvelous, and require nothing but proofs for the most unusual prodigies.

In the fifth place, the promise which Jesus made that the power of working miracles should be given to true believers, gives authority to the belief in miracles in the Lives of the Saints. "Amen, amen, I say to you, he that believeth in me, the works that I do he shall do also, and greater than these shall he do; because I go to the Father. And whatsoever you ask the Father in my name, that will I do."[2] "And these signs shall follow them that believe: In my name they shall cast out devils; they shall speak with new tongues; they shall take up serpents; and if they shall drink any deadly thing, it shall not hurt them; they shall lay their hands upon the sick, and they shall recover."[3]

Our Savior, according to the doctrine of the Holy Fathers,[4] has promised the gift of miracles, not to each one of the faithful in particular, but to the Church in general; and His promise is for all times, when the good of religion requires its accomplishment. Heretics pretend that it only related to the days of the apostles, and that miracles were only required for the establishment of the faith. What right have they to limit the words of the Son of God? Do they imagine that they understand the Scriptures better than the holy doctors? How will they prove that since the time of the apostles there have been no combinations of circumstances in which the good of religion shall have required that miracles should be performed? They were required for the infidels, to whom the Gospel has been preached in different centuries, as well as for the Greek and Roman idolaters, to whom it was first announced. The Church has required them to silence the heretics who have successively endeavored to impugn her dogmas, and to strengthen the faith of her own children. They have been always useful for manifesting the eminence of virtue, for the glory of God, for the conversion of sinners, for reanimating piety, for nourishing and strengthening the hopes of the good things of another life. We

---

[2] John 14: 12, 13.

[3] Mark 16: 17,18.

[4] S. Chrys. *De S. Babyla contra Gent.*, no. 12, ed. Nov. S. August. *De Civit. Dei*, lib 22, c 8; et *Retract.* Lib 1, C. 13 et 14; S. Greg. *Moral,* lib. 34, n. 7, edit. nov.

are, therefore, justified in saying that the promise of Jesus Christ is for all times, in certain occasions, and that the belief in the miracles in the Lives of the Saints is authorized thereby.

In the sixth place, that there have been miracles in the Lives of the Saints are facts, the proofs of which are unquestionable. The Acts of the Martyrs, which have always been read in the Church, and the genuineness[5] of which has been admitted by the most talented critics, contain recitals of the most wonderful events: the confessors of the faith instantaneously cured, after having undergone the most cruel tortures; wild beasts tamed and crouching at their feet; lights and celestial voices, apparitions of Jesus Christ and His angels, and many other wonderful circumstances.

In the first six centuries there are scarcely any ecclesiastical writers and Holy Fathers who do not record miracles worked by the servants of God, and by their relics; and they speak of them as of things which they have either seen with their own eyes, or were of public notoriety.

Saint Justin Martyr, in the second century, speaking of the power of Jesus Christ over the demons, in his Apology, addressed to the Emperors Marcus Aurelius and Lucius Verus, and to the Roman Senate, says: "You have proofs of what passes before your eyes, and in your city, and in all the rest of the world; for you know that many of those possessed, not having been able to be delivered by your exorcists, enchanters, and magicians, have been so by the Christians who have exorcized them in the name of Jesus Christ, who was crucified under Pontius Pilate."[6]

Saint Irenaeus assures us that in the same century some true disciples of Jesus Christ had received supernatural gifts, which they made use of advantageously for other men: "Some," says he, "drive away devils; and this is certain, that often those who have been delivered embrace the faith, and join the Church. To others it is given to know the future, and to have prophetic visions. Others cure the sick by the imposition of hands, and restore them to perfect health. Very often, even in every place, and for some requisite cause, the brethren solicit, by fasting and fervent prayers, the resurrection of a dead person, and obtain it; these dead, thus revived, have lived with us for several years afterwards. What shall I say further? It is not possible to enumerate the extraordinary gifts which the Church receives from God, and what she operates in every part of the world, in favor of the nations, in the name of Jesus Christ crucified."[7]

"We can," says Origen, writing against Celsus, "show an immense multitude of Greeks and barbarians who believe in our Lord Jesus Christ; there are some who prove their faith by the power of working miracles. They cure

---

[5] See Dom. Thierri Ruynard, Praefat. *In Acta Martyrum*; and Father Honore de Sainte Marie, *Reflexions sur les Regies et sur l'Usage de la Critique,* Dissert. 4, Art. 1, et sequ.

[6] S. Justin, *Apol.* 2, sec. 1, p. 45.

[7] S. Iren. Cont Haeres., lib. 2, c. 32, alias 57, n. 4 and 5, c. 31, alias 66; lib. 5, c. 6, n. 1.

the sick by invoking their God, the Creator and the Sovereign Lord of all things, and the name of Jesus Christ, our Savior, of whose Gospel they recite a part. We ourselves have seen several sick persons delivered from the most formidable maladies, and the cured are too numerous to be counted."[8]

Tertullian, in his Apology, and in another work, records plainly the miraculous fall of rain which was obtained from heaven by the prayers of the Christian soldiers, which saved the army of the Emperor Marcus Aurelius, which was reduced to the last extremity. He proves the truth of this fact by the very letter of the emperor.[9] We have also authentic proofs of this event in the authors and records of paganism itself. Tertullian, likewise, tells us that the pagans received extraordinary graces by means of the Christians, some of which he quotes, and he adds: "How many persons of distinction, without mentioning other people, have been thus delivered from the devil, and cured of their evils!"

St. Cyprian upbraided an idolater in the following terms, while refuting him: "The gods whom you adore we exorcize in the name of the true God, and they are compelled to leave the bodies which they possessed. Oh, if you chose to see and hear them, when suffering under the power of our words, as if they were spiritual scourges, and feeling the secret operation of the Divine Mastery! They howl terrifically, entreat of us to spare them, declare, in presence of their adorers, whence they came, and confess a future judgment. Come and be convinced of the truth of what we say, to be at least moved. Those whom you adore, fear us; those to whom you pray, entreat of us to spare them; those whom you revere as sovereigns, are as prisoners in our hands, and tremble as so many slaves. We interrogate them, and in your presence they declare what they are; they cannot dissemble the impostures which they make use of to deceive you."[10]

Such are the miracles which many of God's servants operated in the second and third centuries, and which cannot be called in question. How many different kinds are recorded in subsequent times by St. Basil, and by St. Gregory of Nyssa, in the life of St. Gregory Thaumaturgus; by St. Athanasius in the life of St. Anthony; by Sulpicius Severus, in the life of St. Martin; by St. Chrysostom, St. Jerome, St. Ambrose, St. Augustine, St. Paulinus, in many parts of their works; by Theodoret, in his religious history; by Pope St. Gregory, in his dialogues; by St. Hilary of Arles, St. Ouen, and very many others worthy of credit!

The saintly and learned Bishops, Avitus, Metropolitan of Vienne, and Stephen of Lyons, Eon of Arles, conferring with the Arians, in presence of Gondebauld, King of the Burgundians, after having proved the consubstantiality of the Word, by the testimony of the Scripture, and by

---

[8] Orig. cont. Cels. Lib 3, p. 124, and lib. 1, p. 5, lib 2. p. 62, lib 8, p. 337. Edit. Cantabrig, 1658.

[9] See S. de Tillemon, Histoire des Empereurs, tom. 2, p. 407, et sequ. Lib. ad Scapul, supra.

[10] S. Cypr. Ad Demet., p. 201, et de Idol. Var., p. 206, edit. Rigalt, et alibi.

powerful arguments, offered to give additional proof thereof by miracles, if the heretics would promise to acquiesce in consequence, and quoted the example of St. Remigius, Apostle of the French, who was then living, and setting up the faith on the ruins of idolatry by a multitude of prodigies.

The miracles operated by means of relics are neither less well authenticated, nor less celebrated; they were known to the whole world. St. Augustine was an eyewitness of them, being at Milan when St. Ambrose discovered, by means of a revelation, the spot where the bodies of SS. Gervasius and Protasius reposed.[11] He saw a great many miracles performed in Africa by the relics of St. Stephen, of which he makes mention in his book of the *City of God*, written for the confutation of the most learned of the pagans, wherein he says that, to quote only those operated in the Dioceses of Calame and Hippo, several books would not suffice.[12] Nicetius, Bishop of Treves, writing to Clodosvinda, or Glotinda, Queen of the Lombards, to exhort her to solicit the conversion of King Alboin, her husband, advised her to make use of the visible miracles which were operated at the tomb of St. Martin, and by the invocation of St. Germanus, St. Hilary, St. Lupus, St. Remigius, and St. Medardus.[13] They were so evident, that the heretics dared not call them in question, and could not deprive them of their splendor. God made use of these for the conversion of kings, and of the entire nations.

In all ages after the six first centuries, the prodigies of the Lives of the Saints are noticed by numerous authors of all countries, whose talents, learning, probity, holiness, and dignity, render them respectable to the most searching critics. They are supported by incontrovertible evidence, by juridical depositions, by authentic acts, and by splendid monuments which have been erected to their memory by bishops, princes, magistrates, cities and kingdoms to perpetuate the recollections of these splendid achievements. We find that the saints have made numerous predictions, which have been justified by the event; and that, either moved by the Spirit of God, or compelled by obedience, they have admitted the supernatural operations which they felt in their souls. Finally, the prodigies which are found in the Lives of the Saints have always been considered as indubitable facts amongst the faithful; the Church recognizes them, and they form one of the objects of their piety and devotion; no one is placed in the catalogue of saints whose sanctity has not been attested from heaven, by means of miracles; and she takes such rigorous precautions, and carries their strictness so far, that, according to all human prudence, it is impossible she should be deceived.

We now ask whether it can be permitted to think and to say that such facts are absolutely false, and should only be looked upon as fables unworthy of credence? In such case it would be necessary to abrogate the rule judiciously

---

[11] S. Aug. *Confess.*, lib 9, cap. 7.

[12] *De Civ. Dei*, lib 22, cap 8.

[13] *Concil. General* Labb., tom. 5, p. 835.

and universally received in the world, that facts which have nothing incredible in themselves are not to be controverted when duly proved; it would be also necessary to refuse credence to all that is related in sacred and profane history, to lay down as a maxim to believe nothing but what we see, and to refuse to receive the testimony of the honorable people with whom we live. Now, this is what is requisite to prove and convince every man of good sense that the prejudice against the miracles of the Lives of the Saints is quite unreasonable; but this does not point out its quality sufficiently; it is senseless and ridiculous, it is rash, and, what is more, it is dangerous.

The Protestants are opposed to these marvels, as indeed, they are to almost everything that is religious. They do not call in question the evidence: on the contrary, they produce it, and we find it correctly set forth by the Centuriators of Magdeburg[14], in each century; but because it was confirmatory of the truth of the Catholic Church and its dogmas, which they did not choose to believe, they affected to say that the narratives were fabulous, or delusions of the devil. They were even daring enough to say that the fathers of the Church were either imposed upon, or impostors; they cast aside all tradition; the saints were considered as visionaries, and they turned into ridicule canonizations grounded on miracles.

Catholics ought to be cautious in adopting anything coming from heretics; their opinions are almost always contagious. This is apparent in systems which, so to express it, border on theirs, and lead, in a course of reasoning, to erroneous conclusions, which indeed are denied, but without being able to show that they are inconsistent. We admit that all those who are prejudiced against the marvels in the Lives of the Saints, do not go so far as the Protestants do: the excesses of the latter, however, are the natural, necessary, and almost immediate consequences of such prejudices.

Whoever denies what the Fathers of the Church attest as having seen, or having been authentically informed of, must conclude that they were either very credulous, or deceived the people. To refuse to believe the marvels which have reached us by a uniform and universal tradition, is to call in question all tradition, to render all its channels suspicious, and to cause it to be looked upon as a questionable proposition. What can be thought of the saints, if the miraculous graces, which they certify that they have received from God, are to be treated as chimeras; if the accomplishment of what they have foretold, is to be attributed to chance? What even can be thought of their most heroic victims? What opinion will be formed of their acts? Will they be deemed more trustworthy in other matters? When it is asserted that there have been no

---

[14] *The Centuries of Magdeburg* was an early historical work by Protestants in the 16th century to show that their religion was the religion of the early Church. Cardinal Baronius, in his *Annales,* shows from clear documentary evidence why this is not the case, and today, the *Centuries of Magdeburg* is considered little more than a polemical work, even by Protestant historians. —Editor's note.

miracles since the days of the apostles, it must be said, by a necessary consequence, that the Church, which grounds canonization on miracles, makes use of falsehood in that most solemn and religious act, and that the public worship which the Church directs is uncertain. Now this very much resembles heresy; for the great principles of religion teach us[15] that on these occasions the Church receives peculiar enlightenment from the Holy Spirit, by which she can neither be deceived herself, nor can she deceive others.

These miracles, it is said, are not articles of faith, and the Church does not oblige us to believe them. As if nothing was believed in the world but such things as are of faith; as if it was not dangerous obstinately to reject those things which are sanctioned by the authority of the Holy Fathers, by reason and by piety, by tradition and by the Church, and which cannot be rejected without fatal consequences!

This incredulity attacks, moreover, one of the proofs of the divinity of Jesus Christ, which the fathers adduced against the pagans. St. Chrysostom having asserted, on the subject of the miracles of the martyr, St. Babylas, that our Savior, on the night of His Passion, had promised to those who should believe in Him, the power of working these miracles, adds: "It had been antecedently seen that many had taken upon themselves the character of masters, who had disciples, and who boast of performing wonders; nevertheless, we do not hear of any who had ventured to promise their disciples the same power. The insolence of their impostures did not go so far, because they knew that no one would believe them, all the world being convinced that it is only given to God to make a similar promise, and to fulfill it."[16] On this principle the holy doctor proves that Jesus Christ is God, since He has given to those who believe in Him the power of working miracles, which His disciples actually did, and which His servants now do. St. Augustine makes use of the same proofs, in his book of the City of God. Thus the miracles of the saints have in all ages been adduced as proofs of the Divinity of our Savior; and this is what those endeavor to do away with, who, without reflection, consider them as fables.[17]

Another danger is, that they speak of these marvels according to their own prejudices. They openly say that they do not believe them, and that persons ought not to have the weakness to believe them; they speak contemptuously of the books in which they are recorded; they cannot endure that they should form part of panegyrics of the saints. They make use of impious derisions, and turn into ridicule the faithful who credit them, and they censure the conduct of the Church which consecrates them. Such discourse sanctions heresy and licentiousness; worldlings and the undevout applaud it, the tepid seem to

---

[15] Melchior Cano, *De Locis Theologicis*, Lib 5, quaest. 5, concl. 3.; M. Tournely, *De Eccles.* Tom 2., pp. 586, 587, et alii.

[16] S. Aug. *De Civit. Dei*, lib 22, cap. 10.

[17] S. Chyrs., lib. *In S. Babyl. Et contra Gen.*, tom. 2, p. 536, n. 1 and 12.

consent to it, and the falsely devout approve it; it is a scandal to the weak, and a dishonor to religion.

It is also to be feared that prejudices against what is wonderful in the Lives of the Saints may spread to other subjects, if we only judge from the principles which are the cause of them. For, in what do these principles consist? They are not grounded on reason or religion; they must, therefore, have a basis of incredulity for everything which they do not understand: the foolish vanity of being thought singular; ignorance, which boldly repudiates what it knows nothing of; keeping company with libertines; a conformity of feeling with heretics, and the spirit of the world, which is the enemy of all piety. Such calamitous causes give room to fear the most fatal effects.

In general, the liberty only to believe those things which we choose, on points in which religion is concerned, is very dangerous; it often makes a destructive progress, for its first attempts embolden it. Persons are easily persuaded that all miraculous narratives are false, though the Church guarantees the truth of many; and when this same Church pronounces on dogmatical facts, declaring: such and such propositions to be heretical which are in such and such a book, and exacts an interior submission[18] of heart and mind, do these doubters show more docility? Do they not cloak their disobedience by a respectful silence, always ill kept and finally broken through by open rebellion? Do we not see persons in the world speaking irreverently of relics, purgatory, indulgences, and even of the holy mysteries, after having treated contemptuously the marvels of the Lives of the Saints?

Certain critics admit these marvels, but have imbibed the idea that falsehood is so mixed up with the truth, that they cannot be separated but by using certain rules, which they take upon themselves to lay down. This prejudice is not less dangerous, nor less unreasonable than the other.

Because some inconsiderate writers, who cannot be too severely censured, have given scope to their imagination in certain legends, and have employed fiction for the embellishment of their narratives, the doubters pretend that the whole history of the saints is full of impostures. Nevertheless, pure sources have been the basis of their authentic acts, in the works of the Fathers, and in an infinity of authors well worthy of credit, and in the Bulls of Canonization. An Asiatic priest, as related by St. Jerome, who quotes Tertullian[19], composed false acts of St. Thecla through an ill-understood sentiment of devotion: does it

---

[18] The interior deference of mind and heart which the Church requires for the decision of dogmatic facts, must be extended so far as to consider this decision as infallible and irreclaimable. It is what the Abbé Tournely invincibly established, by the proofs which he brings to this conclusion: "Ecclesia accepit a Christo auctoritatem judicandi de sensu seu doctrina propositionum librorum et auctorum, ac fideles ad suam subscribendam sententiam compelendi: cui proinde tenentur illi acquiescere interna mentis et judicii adhaesione, non solo, ut vocant religioso silentio: atque certum est nec errori obnoxium hujuscemodi Ecclesiae judicium." — *De Eccles.*, tom. ii., art 5, p. 533, et sequ., p. 446, et seq.

[19] St. Hieron., *de Script. Ecles.* In Luca. 15

follow from that, that the truth of many other acts which were there read, and which we still possess, is to be set aside?

Moreover, the Church has remedied the evil; she has rejected the false prodigies; she has expunged from the legends the indiscreet additions; a new edition has been long since placed in the hands of the faithful, which only contains the well-authenticated and certain miracles.

A learned man[20] has demonstrated that the rules of these critics for the elucidation of these miracles are not judicious; that they are extravagant, and that it would be risking too much to follow them; that they are contradictory, and not in unison with each other; that it often happens that they reject or admit miracles against their own principles. If they find splendid ones, and many of them in the same legend, they hold them to be suppositions or altered, although, the oldest and most authentic documents contain similar ones; they reject them as false, without assigning any reason in proof of their having been falsified; they pretend that the authors who have recorded them were too credulous, though they received other articles on the testimony of these same authors. In order to believe them, they require perfect certainty, although they give credit to many circumstances in ecclesiastical and profane history on mere probabilities. One of them professes not to omit a single miracle which is vouched for by good authority, nevertheless, he suppresses many of the most considerable; and many of those which he feels compelled to bring forward, he does so in terms which mark doubtfulness, to say nothing more.

Thus, the ultra-critics while admitting the wonders of the Lives of the Saints, reduce them to nothing by rules, which they invent for separating truth from falsehood, as those who profess to believe an infallible authority in the Church make that infallibility to depend on so many conditions, that they may always maintain that the Church, dispersed or assembled, has never come to any decision in opposition to their errors.

It is, they say, the love of truth which induces them to examine most scrupulously the miracles of the saints; nothing should be believed, or be proposed to belief, but what is true. But Based said of bad critics: "They are content, provided they can pass for more subtle observers than others, and they find themselves sharper, in not giving credit to so many wonders." The love of truth does not consist in denying its existence, where so many persons of first-rate genius have found it; it does not depend on rendering obscure the light it sheds, nor in giving to the public Lives of Saints accompanied by a dry, bitter, and licentious criticism, calculated to throw doubt on all that is extraordinary in them, and thereby to give scandal. The learned Jesuits, the continuators of Bollandus, show, by the precision of their researches, that they are sincere lovers of truth, but we do not see that they endeavor to diminish

---

[20] Father Honore de Sainte Marie, a barefooted Carmelite, in his "Reflexions sur les Regies et sur l'Usage de la Critique," tom I., Dissert., art 3, 4 and 5, and in other parts of that work, condemns everywhere all ultra-criticism.

the number of miracles: "They have no idea of taking them for fictions; nothing astonishes them in the lives of the friends of God, provided it be well attested." Father Thomassen, of the Oratory, in his treatise on the Celebration of Festivals, speaks of a miraculous event which occurred in the sixth century, and which is reported by Bollandus, and he adds: "These sorts of miracles are by no means articles of faith, but nevertheless, they are not to be rejected by sage and considerate persons.

"Upon reading the works of St. Cyprian, St. Augustine, St. Ambrose, and St. Jerome, and those of St. Gregory of Nyssa, of St. Basil, and St. Athanasius, we can have no doubt that these fathers had no difficulty in believing similar occurrences, similarly attested. St. Augustine, indeed, has related several much more incredible; and it is greatly to be feared that to set one's self above the Augustines, the Jeromes, the Gregories, and the most learned Fathers of the Church, must be the effect of a most dangerous pride."

It is objected that the multitude is credulous; that it likes the marvelous, and should not be exposed to believe untruths. But credulity is far less dangerous than incredulity; the one admits of cure much easier than the other; the former, in proper limits, may be very useful, the latter engenders nothing but evil. Some one has said,[21] that the love of the marvelous is the ancient malady of mankind; it would, perhaps, be more accurate to say, that it is a remainder of their original greatness; and that, being created to witness the marvels of the Divinity, they are impelled, by an interior impulse, to believe whatsoever seems to them to approach to them, until such time as their visions shall be fully gratified. This impulse only becomes a malady when it receives wonderful things which are absurd, or without any foundation.

Aversion from the marvelous, which has its origin in the weakness of a mind oppressed by sin, is a much greater malady, and may have most dangerous consequences, in a wholly marvelous religion which we must love. These marvels are displeasing in pious narratives, where they are fully proved, and they are sought for in theatrical compositions, where they are mere fictions: the distinction is dishonorable to Christians. Finally, as to the falsehood: What risk does the pious multitude run, in believing the miracles of the Lives of the Saints? They find nothing in them which is not proved, or worthy of belief; nothing but what may very prudently be believed; nothing but what is edifying; and this, according to St. Augustine,[22] is a sufficient guarantee from falling into any dangerous credulity.

We should be very dangerously credulous, if we put our faith in false and deceitful miracles, which only tend to seduce the mind, and corrupt our belief. We are warned in the Gospel, that "there shall arise false christs and false prophets, and shall show great signs and wonders, insomuch as to deceive (if it

---

[21] M. de la Fontaine. 17

[22] *De Utilit. Cred.* Cap. 11, no. 25.

be possible) even the elect;"[23] and St. Paul teaches us that Antichrist, "that man of perdition, will come according to the working of Satan in all power, and signs, and lying wonders."[24] The father of lies has often inspired the heretics to produce miracles, which they have asserted to have been performed by persons of their party, living or dead, from whence they inferred that God authorized the doctrines they taught. Ecclesiastical history furnishes many examples of this, and there are some very recent ones.

But Jesus Christ has furnished us with a sure and infallible rule to avoid the contagion: it is to hear the Church;[25] it is to consider those only as true miracles of which she approves, and of which she sanctions the publication; it is to believe firmly that no one who is in revolt against the Church will ever perform a miracle favorable to his sect, whatever appearance of austerity, piety, charity, or sanctity, he may put on; which St. Thomas bases[26] mainly on this principle: that it is impossible that God, who alone can give the power of working a true miracle, shall ever communicate that power to confirm a false doctrine; from whence it follows, that all the miracles produced by sectarians, notwithstanding all their evidence, and all their pretended attestations, must neither be examined nor listened to, and must only be looked upon as purely natural effects, or as impostures, or as delusions and diabolical operations. This is the way in which St. Augustine[27] expresses himself on the subject of the miracles which the Donatists claimed to have performed, and claimed as evidence in favor of their schism. Let Catholics, therefore, reject with horror the false prodigies of sectarians, but let them piously give credit to the miracles of the saints, without paying attention to the ultra-criticism which strives to throw doubts upon them; and let them be intimately persuaded that the Church, which approves of them, has founded that approval on evidence irreproachable.

The marvels which are found in the Life of St. Francis are perfectly well attested.[28] That Life was first written by Thomas de Celano, one of his companions, who was directed by Pope Gregory DC to compile it, and who afterwards added a second part on additional memoirs.[29] John or Thomas de Ceperano, Apostolic Notary, who was a staunch friend of the Saint, published at the same time what he knew of his actions. Crescentius de Jesi, General of the Order of the Friars Minors, gave directions, by circular letters, to collect and transmit to him whatever had been seen or learnt, relative to the sanctity

---

[23] Matt. 24: 24.

[24] 2 Thessal. 2: 7.

[25] Matt. 18: 17; Luke 10: 16.

[26] 1 Part, quaest. 110, art. 4 et 2, quaest. 178, Acts ii, iii.

[27] *De Unit. Eccl.* c. 19, n. 49, and Tract 13 in Joan., n. 17.

[28] Wading, *Annal. Min.* ad ann. 1230, n. 7, ad ann. 1244, n. 8, 9, and 10.

[29] His first work was called "The Legend of Gregory IX," and the second, "The Ancient Legend."

and miracles of the blessed Father. He addressed himself particularly to three of his twelve first companions: Leo, his secretary and his confessor; Angelus and Rufinus: all three joined in compiling what is called "The Legend of the Three Companions." The others noted separately what they had themselves seen, and the things which they had learnt from others. Saint Bonaventure, being at the head of the Order, was urgently entreated, by the general chapter, to write the life of their holy Patriarch. With the intention of learning, with certainty, the truth of the facts, he went expressly to Assisi. "There," he says, in the preface to his work, "I had frequent and serious conferences with those who had been in the confidence of the great man, and who were still living; and principally with those who were most intimately consociated with him, and who have become the most faithful imitators of his holy life, to whose testimony we must undoubtedly give credit, because their acknowledged sanctity assures us that they have spoken truth." Now, what can the most exact and severe criticism wish more, in order to give warranty to the marvels in the Life of St. Francis, than contemporaries, ocular witnesses, holy persons, his own companions, who lived with him and enjoyed his confidence?

The legend of Saint Bonaventure was spread everywhere, as soon as it appeared, and was everywhere highly approved: there are many manuscripts of it. Lipoman, Bishop of Verona, caused it to be printed in 1556. No one ever attempted to call its accuracy in question. Octavian quoted it, in his petition to Pope Sixtus IV for the canonization of the holy doctor, in 1482.

The first legends have been preserved in manuscript; the celebrated annalist of the Order of Friars Minors, Luke Wading, saw them and made use of them. He was one of the most learned men of his time,[30] and all other learned men have been loud in his praise, not only on account of his profound erudition, but because he was so ardent a lover of truth, which he sought for with great care, and having developed it, nothing could hinder him from publishing it and committing it to writing.

The uprightness of his heart was conspicuous on a certain occasion, which is too honorable to him for us to pass it over in silence. He had been one of the examiners nominated by Pope Innocent X to inquire into the writings of Jansenius, Bishop of Ypres, and he had convinced himself that the five propositions which appeared to be censurable in those writings might be tolerably explained in a certain theological sense. Those who are themselves upright are not easily brought to think ill of others, particularly in difficult affairs, and they sometimes endeavor to justify them, through charitable feelings, which are praiseworthy in principle, but which may have evil consequences, when a doctrine is in question which has been widely spread, and which is supported by a cabal. Wading, seeing that the five propositions

---

[30] He lived in the 16th and 17th centuries, when erudition and criticism were in their prime.

were censured by various constitutions of the Pope, made a report[31] on the whole affair, with the following beautiful declaration, worthy of a truly Catholic Doctor: "If, before this decision, any one shall have been of a different opinion (as to the five propositions) on whatever reasonings, or whatsoever authority of doctrine, he is now obliged to bend his mind to the yoke of faith, according to the advice of the apostle. I declare it to be what I do with all my heart, condemning and anathematizing all the aforesaid propositions, in all and every sense in which His Holiness has proposed to condemn them, although, before this decision, I thought they might have been maintained in a certain sense, in the manner I have explained in the suffrage which has been just seen."

We may feel assured that a man of this upright character, such a lover of truth, and, moreover, one of such eminent talents, would not have made use of the two Legends of Thomas de Celano and that of the Three Companions, without having ascertained their correctness. Moreover, the critics of his time, who were particular, and in great numbers, had it in their power to examine them as those of our times have, also, since they are still extant in the convent of St. Isidore at Rome.

The first, which was composed under the Pontificate of Gregory IX, was quoted by Luke, Bishop of Tuy, when he wrote against the Albigenses, in 1231. It is to be found in the Abbey of Longpont, of the Order of Citeaux, in the diocese of Soissons, and in the Abbey of Jouy, of the same order, in the Diocese of Sens. The Legend of the Three Companions is in the king's library, at the Recollets of Louvain, and in their convent at Malines.

These are the principal sources which were consulted by Wading for writing the Life of St. Francis, which forms part of the first tome of his Annals. He also consulted the acts and public monuments, the constant tradition, and some manuscripts of the thirteenth century, which contain other testimonials from the companions of St. Francis, and were published by contemporaries who lived with them, who collected their very words, and who are worthy of credence. But the most marvelous thing which he relates, relative to the actions of the Saint, he has taken from the legends, as well as a great number of the splendid miracles which were operated by his intercession after his death, and of which Pope Gregory IX was fully informed, as he declares in the Bull of Canonization.

All modern authors who have given the Life of St. Francis in various languages, have adhered mostly to Wading; in this work, also, we have made a point of following him; and the learned, who have so much esteem for that great man, will agree that we could not have taken a better guide. Baillet admits that, among the writers of the Life of St. Francis, Luke Wading is one of

---

[31] See "Defense de l'Eglise contre Leyddecher," y Pere Quesnel, second edition, p. 427. "L'Histoire de Cinq repositions," by the Abbé du Mas, tom 1, lib. 1, p. 79, of the edition of Trevoux, 1702. The Abbé of Tournely, tom. 1, *De Gratia*, quaest. 3, epoch. 2, p. 382.

the most careful and most accurate; and yet he taxes him with not having written methodically, when he adds: "After all the labors of so many persons, who have been zealous for his glory, we are still compelled to wish for a methodical history of his life." Whoever may read the Annals of Wading, and his notes on the works of St. Francis, will find in them as much method as research and accuracy; but according to some ultra-critics, it is not considered writing methodically, when marvels which they dislike are permitted to find their way into history.

Baillet might have said that it has been long a subject of complaint that we have not in our language a complete and methodical Life of St. Francis. This complaint[32] is the more just, as the saint had a particular liking for France; he had learned the language with so much facility, and spoke it so readily, that they gave him the name of Francis, although he was baptized John. Paris was one of the first objects of his zeal; he would even have gone thither, if a cardinal had not detained him in Italy for reasons which related to his Order. Not having it in his power to undertake this mission, which he had much at heart, he destined for it some of his principal followers.

Some of the wise of the world would have wished that, in order to meet the prejudices of those who dislike the marvelous, some part at least of them should have been suppressed in this Life of St. Francis; but, having clearly shown that these prejudices are unreasonable and dangerous, it would not have been proper to have paid attention to them; besides which, the Life of the venerable patriarch is chiefly written for his children, and for persons of piety, who would not have tolerated such a curtailment.

There are some who affect to think that, in the Lives of the Saints, their example should alone be proposed to the public, imagining that the miracles they have performed can nowise contribute to the edification of souls; and two authors[33] of this century have ventured to suppress all miracles in the Lives of Saints which they have published. The Church, nevertheless, causes them to be recited in the Divine Office, and they are carefully related by the holy fathers; neither does any author of repute, of the centuries preceding, fail to bring them forward. In fact, no one can deny that they add great resplendency to the merits of the saints, and, consequently, give great weight to the example they afford us. They uphold and increase the idea we have of the power of God, of

---

[32] Those which have been heretofore published, are seldom met with; they are full of piety, but it must be admitted that they are neither methodical nor complete, and they would not now be received as they probably were in former times.

[33] In the beginning of this century [the 18th], M. Echard de Commanville published a *Nouvelle Vie des Saints,* in which he only admitted miracles recorded in Scripture. See on this subject the "Memoirs de Tervoux." May and June; 1701, p. 64, et seq. An anonymous writer has also omitted the miracles, on pretense of not increasing the size of the volume, in the Lives of the Saints for every day in the year, etc., printed in 1722, by W. Despreg and J. Desesarts, but he has found sufficient room for introducing many pernicious things in points of doctrine, as we may perceive from the work itself, or by faithful extracts in the "Memoirs de Trevoux." Oct 5th, 1722, Art. 107.

His providence, His justice, His bounty, and His mercy, by which they excite us to glorify, love, and serve Him; and, in showing His special good-will to His servants, they induce us to invoke their mediation with confidence. Moreover, miracles strengthen the faithful in their faith, because, being performed in the bosom of the Catholic Church, they confirm the truth she teaches. Now, it is not of less consequence to strengthen faith, than to propose that which tends to the correction of morals, particularly when incredulity makes as much progress as licentiousness. Moreover, the miraculous actions of the saints frequently contain most salutary instructions, and are always accompanied by virtues which may be imitated, which will be very apparent in the Life of St. Francis.

Some may, perhaps, think that his virtues are too transcendent for imitation, and content themselves with admiring them, without gathering any fruit from them. A celebrated heresiarch admired them in this manner, in the last century. Based remarks, in his excellent "History of the Variations,"[34] that "Luther reckoned among the saints not only St. Bernard, but also St. Francis, St. Bonaventure, and others of the thirteenth century; and that St. Francis, amongst all the rest, appeared to him to be an admirable character, animated with wonderful fervor of mind." But the faithful in admiring his virtues, must not think them not to be imitated, for they consisted in following the Gospel; and they are all obliged to live according to the precepts of the Gospel.

REV. CANDIDE CHALIPPE, O.F.M.

---

[34] *Histoire de Variations*, tom. 1, lib. 3, n. 50.

THE LIFE OF ST. FRANCIS OF ASSISI

BOOK I

CHAPTER I
EARLY LIFE AND CONVERSION

His birth—Prediction of his future greatness—His studies—He applies himself to commerce—His purity, and affection for the poor—He is taken prisoner—He falls sick—His charity increases towards the poor—He has a mysterious dream—He wishes to go to the war—Jesus Christ dissuades him—He is rapt in spirit—His conversion—He kisses a leper—Jesus Christ crucified appears to him—Salutary effects of this apparition—He goes to Rome—Mingles with the poor—Is tempted by the devil—A voice from heaven commands him to restore the Church of St. Peter Damian—His devotion to the passion of Jesus Christ—He takes some pieces of cloth from his father's house, and sells them, to restore the Church of St. Damian—He escapes from the anger of his father, and retires to a cave—He appears in Assisi, where he is ill-treated—His father confines him—His mother delivers him, and he returns to St. Damian—He manifests his intention to his father, who appeals to justice, and cites him before the Bishop of Assisi—He renounces his inheritance, and gives back his clothes to his father.

E HERE OFFER, to the pious reflections of the faithful, the life of a man who proposed to himself to practice literally the precepts of the Gospel, and to conform entirely to Jesus Christ crucified, and to inspire the whole world with His love; who became a singular model of penance, whom God favored with the most precious gifts of His grace, whom He honored with favors until then unheard of, whom he constituted the Head of an Apostolical Order, founded solely on His Providence, and which was wonderfully spread for the services of His Church.

Such a purpose must seem great to all those who can appreciate true grandeur by the light of religion. In its contempt of the goods of the world, it manifests an elevation of mind far above the ostentation of the ancient philosophers; in its deep humiliations, an heroical courage; in its extreme simplicity, the most exalted sentiments; in its weakness, and in the apparent foolishness of the cross, the strength and wisdom of God. The infidels themselves admired all this, and it will be not less meet to revive the fervor of Christians, and to increase the veneration they have always entertained for St. Francis.

He was born at Assisi, a town of Umbria, in Italy, in the year 1182, under the Pontificate of Lucius III. Peter Bernardo,[1] his father, was a rich merchant,

---

[1] Ottavio, Bishop of Assisi, says in a book entitled, "Lumi Serafici di Portiuncula," printed at Venice, 1701, pp. 6 and 7, that when he was preaching during Lent in the cathedral church of Luca, in Tuscany, in the year 1689, a canon named Morican, showed him an old memorial, in which he read these words: "There were at Luca two brothers, merchants, named Morican. The one remained in his own country, the other, called Bernard, established himself at Assisi where he was called

whose principal commercial transactions were with France. His mother, whose name was Pica, had only two sons, Francis and Angelo. The latter married at Assisi, and some of his descendants were still at Assisi in 1534.

God, who has often condescended to usher in His Saints by portents, was pleased, at the birth of Francis, to give signs of what he would be during his life. For some days Pica had suffered great pains, without her confinement having been the result; when a man, dressed as a pilgrim, came to tell her that she would only be delivered of her infant in a stable, who would be born on straw. Although this communication appeared most strange, they, nevertheless, acted upon it. The patient was removed to the nearest stable, where she was successfully delivered; an event which may well be looked upon, as in the intention of Providence, thereby to mark the conformity of the holy man to Jesus Christ, poor and humble; as much, at least, as the creature can be in conformity with the Creator, and the servant with the Master of the universe.

This stable has been turned into a chapel, called in Italian, "San Francesco il piccolo", "St. Francis the little." There is over the door the following Latin inscription, in very old writing:

HOC ORATORIUM FUIT BOVIS ET ASINI STABULUM, IN QUO NATUS EST FRANCISCUS, MUNDI SPECULUM.

THIS CHAPEL WAS THE STABLE OF THE OX AND THE ASS, WHERE FRANCIS WAS BORN, THE MIRROR OF THE WORLD.

His mother had the name of John given to him at his baptism, his father being then absent in France. A stranger presented himself as his godfather, and he was accepted as such, whether it was that something extraordinary was perceived in this person, or that they had been struck with astonishment at the first event. The uniform tradition at Assisi is, that this stranger disappeared after the ceremony, and that he left the impression of his knees on a marble step of the altar, which is shown in the cathedral church, with the baptismal font, on which these words in Italian are engraved: "Questi e il Fonte, dove fu battezzato il Serafico Padre San Francesco."

At the return from the baptismal ceremony, a man, who seemed to have

---

Bernardon. He married and had a son called Peter; who, being already wealthy, married a girl called Pica of a noble family. St. Francis, who was their son, called himself out of humility, son of Peter Bernardon; not choosing to take his family name, which was Morican."

It is probably of this origin that Thomas Washington, a Benedictine, said that Francis was a Tuscan; which is also noticed in an old Flemish chronicle. The Bishop of Assisi adds, that the branch of the Morican family, which remained at Luca, was there in his time, and was in the number of its nobles.

been sent by God, as well as the other two, or rather an angel in human form, came to beg that he might be allowed to see the child and hold it. He took it in his arms, caressed it a good deal, and impressed upon its right shoulder a well-formed cross, as a mark of his consecration, recommending the nurse to take particular care of the child, not to expose him to the snares of the devils, who had a foresight that he would one day wage a severe war against them. One of these evil spirits was obliged to confess by the mouth of one possessed, whom they were exorcizing, that the princes of darkness, alarmed at the birth of Francis, had tried various ways to take away his life; and it was the Saint himself who expelled this devil afterwards. These portents,[2] marvelous as they are, are less surprising, when we consider the singular and marked favors which heaven destined for him.

His parents brought him up with great care, and he was put to study with the clergy of the Parish of St. George. After he had acquired some knowledge of letters, he was initiated in commercial affairs, the correspondence of which necessitated his learning the French language; he acquired it with so much ease, that his father gave him the name of Francis, a name which he bore ever after.

Bernardo and Francis pursued their avocation in a very different manner. The first, with no other object than his worldly interest, thought of nothing but his profits, and had no other care than that of accumulating. Francis, who had not a particle of avarice, and had less thought of his profit than of dealing with honor, traded with nobler and more elevated feelings. But he loved the world, he frequented society, and spent a good deal in dress, festivities, and parties of pleasure. His father frequently reprimanded him on the subject of his expenses, but his remonstrances had little effect, because he had no consideration of the value of money, and he wished to be distinguished amongst his young companions, who always considered him as their leader.

His mother, who was tender and generous, had more patience with him; and she said to those who spoke to her of his profusion, that from what she remarked in his conversation, in his actions, and even in his amusements, she had reasons to hope something great when he should come to maturer years.

Indeed, in all his demeanor, excellent prospects for the future were observable: his temper was exquisite, mild, and condescending, his manners were agreeable and very polite; he was lively, and had great good sense: he

---

[2] Prophecies of the celebrated Abbot Joachim are also noticed, relative to St. Francis, St. Dominic and their orders, made long before the birth of either. They are admitted as authentic by the learned Jesuits of Antwerp, the continuators of the Acts of the Saints of Bollandus. But they assign reason for not believing that this Abbot placed portraits of the two Saints in the church of St. Mark at Venice, as some writers assert. Act. SS. tom. 7, Mai die 29, § 8, p. 141.

Wading, and others, believed that he was the first who bore the name of Francis. But Mabillon found this name without any surname in the Cartulary of Chateaudun, written at the beginning of the twelfth century, and he remarks that it was the first time. We see also, in the *Italia Sacra,* that the Bishop of Arezzo, in 1188, was called Francis.

was brave, and had a strong inclination to be generous, even to give beyond his means. Although he plunged into the vain amusements of the world, there was nothing blamable in his moral conduct. By the special protection of heaven, he avoided the rocks on which youth is too often wrecked; he preserved the inestimable treasure of purity; it was also remarked that he was distressed at any licentious expressions, and never made any reply to them.

God had imprinted in his heart great feelings of compassion for the poor, which increased from his infancy, and which induced him to afford them liberal aid, so that, following the Gospel precept, "Give to every one that asks you,"[3] he made a resolution to give to all who should ask alms of him, and principally if they should solicit it for the love of God. This feeling for the love of God had its effect upon him, even then, notwithstanding his dissipation; he could seldom hear the expression made use of, as he has since admitted, without being sensibly affected. It having once happened to him, in the hurry of business, to turn away a poor person who had asked a charity for the love of God, his conscience smote him immediately, and he ran after the poor man, relieved him amply, and made a promise to God that he would never refuse a single individual as long as it was in his power, when an alms should be asked for His love, a promise which he faithfully kept to his death, and which, as St. Bonaventure remarks, was of essential service in increasing the grace and love of God in his heart. What is there more likely to bring down the grace of conversion and sanctification, and increase the love of God, than the practice of works of mercy?

The amiable qualities of Francis rendered him a favorite throughout the town, where he was looked up to as the flower of the youth, and great hopes were entertained for the future in his regard. A man of simple manners, but enlightened from above, caused a still greater esteem to be entertained for him. When he met him in the streets, he spread his cloak on the ground before him, and as a reason for showing him so unusual a mark of respect, "This young man," he said, "will soon do great things; he will deserve all sorts of honors, and will be revered by the faithful." Francis, who was unconscious of the designs of God, did not understand the meaning of this prediction. He knew not that these honors were to be rendered him only after severe humiliations according to the words of the Gospel.[4] Engrossed by the affairs of the world, and attached to its vanities, he thought little of this divine truth, and he had less taste for it; nevertheless he hoped that he should some day receive the honors which others foretold, and which God permitted him likewise to predict of himself in an affliction which came upon him.

The towns of Assisi and Perugia were at war with each other;[5] he was

---

[3] Luke 6: 30.

[4] Matt. 23:12.

[5] These two towns may have taken opposite sides when Marcuald or Marcomald laid waste the lands of the Church. Rayn. an. 1188-89.

taken prisoner with some of his fellow-citizens: whether it was that he had taken up arms in the service of his country, or that he was beyond the limits of the town on his commercial affairs. His captivity, however, did not affect his spirits; he preserved his cheerfulness and good humor. His companions, who were dejected and cast down, were offended at this, and upbraided him with it, saying that he might, at least out of feeling for them, disguise them, disguise his satisfaction. "I am very sorry for you," he replied, "but as to myself, my mind is at ease, and I am thankful that it is so. You see me now a prisoner, but at a future period, you will see me honored by the whole world." There was one among the prisoners whose quarrelsome temper and extreme ill humor caused him to be shunned by the others. Francis entreated them to draw a distinction between his person and his defects, and to bear with him: not being able to induce them to do so, he had the charity to keep him company himself, and by his good advice, he rendered him more gentle. All were so delighted with his goodness of heart, that they sought his friendship.

Liberated from captivity, he returned to Assisi, where God visited him with a long and severe illness, which reduced him to a state of great weakness. This was to prepare his soul for the influence of grace. As soon as he could walk, he wished to enjoy the beauty and air of the country; but he failed to be pleased therewith, and was even disgusted with what he had previously liked the most; he felt contempt for what he had before esteemed, and his own conduct appeared to him to be senseless. This change surprised him much, but it did not as yet make any alteration in his heart. The return of health renewed his attachment to the world, his ambition and vanity revived; he entertained fresh hopes of greatness, and paid once more great attention to his dress. Thus it frequently happens that when God sends illness to worldly persons with a view to their conversion, these have no other effect than momentary reflections and promises, which are soon forgotten on the return of strength.

However, Francis became more and more charitable, and gave to all the poor either money or his clothes. Having met a poor and ill-clad officer who was of a noble family, he saw in him the poverty of Jesus Christ, the King of kings, and being moved to pity, he gave him the new suit of clothes he had on.

The following night God showed him in his sleep a great and magnificent palace, full of warlike arms, all marked with the sign of the cross, to give him an idea of the reward his charity was to receive. He asked who all that belonged to; and he was answered, that the arms were for his soldiers.

Not as yet understanding the meaning of mysterious dreams, he took this as a token of the success he was to have in warlike achievements, without suspecting that the crosses he had seen had a totally different signification. At that time Walter, Count of Brienne, in Champagne, was waging active war against the emperor, in the kingdom of Naples, on the subject of the claims of his wife Alberia, the eldest daughter of Tancred, King of Sicily, who had been some years dead. Francis resolved to offer him his services, in the hope of gaining military honors. He attached himself to an officer of distinction, who belonged to the count's army, and he set out with a good retinue, after having assured his friends that he was sure of acquiring great renown.[6]

He first went to Spoleto, and there Jesus Christ addressed these benevolent words to him during the night: "Francis, which of the two, think you, can be of the greatest service to you: the master or the servant, the rich or the poor?" "It is the master and the rich," he answered without any hesitation. "Why then," continued our Lord, "do you leave God who is master and rich, to seek man, who is the servant and poor?" "O Lord!" exclaimed Francis, "what is it your pleasure I should do?" Jesus Christ then said to him, "Return to your town; what you have seen signifies nothing but what is spiritual. It is from God, and not from man, that you will receive their accomplishment." The very next morning he retraced his steps towards Assisi, to await the orders of the Lord, without troubling himself as to what the world should say as to this precipitate return.

His friends came as usual to propose a party of pleasure. He received them, as was his custom, with great politeness, and feasted them magnificently, to bid them, thus honorably, an eternal adieu. On parting from them, he found himself suddenly struck with the vanity of all terrestrial things, and with the grandeur of all that is heavenly, by a communication from the Spirit of God, full of mildness, but so internal, and so forcible, that his senses were brought into a state of inaction, and he himself remained motionless. He afterwards told his confessor, that, if he had been torn to pieces in this state of rapture, he would not have felt it; that, in that moment, he could only feel at the bottom of his soul. The company, quite alarmed, drew near him; and when he had recovered his usual serenity, they enquired of him, laughing, what had occasioned his extraordinary reserve; if, perhaps, he was not thinking of taking a wife? "It is so," he replied: "I shall take one, but one so noble and so beautiful, that such another will not be found in the whole world." Evangelical poverty, which he afterwards embraced, was the spouse to which the Holy Spirit inspired him to allude.

After this divine favor he disembarrassed himself as much as possible of his commercial affairs, to beg of God to know what He would have him do; and he usually went to pray in a grotto with a confidential friend, who left him there in entire liberty. The frequent recourse to prayer excited in his heart so ardent a desire for the celestial country, that he already looked upon everything that was earthly as nothing. He felt that this happy disposition contained a treasure, but he did not as yet know how to possess himself of the hidden prize. The spirit of God merely insinuated to him that the spiritual life, under the idea of a traffic, must begin by a contempt of the world, and under the idea of a warfare, by a victory over self. All spirituality not based upon these two divine lessons, will never have anything solid in it.

---

[6] Maimb. *Hist. Des Crois.* Tom 2, lib. 9.

Francis had soon occasion to put these lessons in practice. As he was riding across the plains of Assisi, he perceived a leper coming straight to him. At first he felt horror-stricken, but calling to mind that he had formed a resolution to labor to attain perfection, and that, in order to be a soldier of Jesus Christ, it was necessary to begin, by obtaining a victory over self, he dismounted, kissed the leper, and gave him an alms. When he again mounted his horse, he no longer saw any one, though he looked all round the plain. Filled with astonishment, and transported with joy, he began to sing the praises of God, and formed a firm resolution to aim at still greater perfection. This is the effect of generous and courageous efforts, they draw down fresh graces, and reanimate our courage. He acquired also more inclination for retirement; he had no longer any liking but for solitude, for those places which were adapted to the holy sorrow of penance, where he unceasingly addressed himself to God in fervent prayer, accompanied by lamentations, which cannot be described: God at length favorably heard him.

His fervor daily increasing, insomuch that he was wholly absorbed in God, Jesus Christ appeared to him as if attached to the cross. His soul, at this stupendous scene, was wholly penetrated, and, as it were, dissolved, and the image of his crucified Savior became from that time so strongly and intimately imprinted on his heart, that every time it recurred to his mind, he had a difficulty in restraining his sobs and tears. This is what some, who were in his confidence, learnt from him towards the close of his life.

In this marvelous apparition he was made aware that these words of the Gospel were personally addressed to him: "If any man will come after Me, let him deny himself, and take up his cross and follow Me."[7] He received from them that foretaste of poverty and humility which became his characteristics, and so ardent a charity inflamed his heart, that he had the courage to devote himself to the service of the lepers. Before this day they were so much his horror, that, far from allowing them to be in his presence, as soon as he saw them, at whatever distance, he turned away from them, and if they were near he passed on quickly, holding his nose. But for the love of Jesus crucified, who was pleased to represent Himself to the prophet Isaiah[8] under the despised figure of a leper, he lowered himself to attending upon them in their hospitals, where, having abundantly supplied them with alms, he made their beds, dressed their sores, and performed for them the most abject services; he often even kissed their hands and their faces with great feelings of commiseration. The words which our Savior one day addressed to him while at prayer, stimulated him to continue this charitable exercise, notwithstanding his natural repugnance: "Francis, if you desire to know My will, you must despise and hate all that you have loved and wished for till now. Let not this new path alarm you, for, if the things which now please you must become bitter and

---

[7] Matt. 16: 24.

[8] Isaiah, 53: 4.

distasteful, those which now displease you, will become sweet and agreeable." Shortly before his death he declared that what had seemed to him most bitter in serving the lepers, had been changed into what was pleasing both for soul and body; and all those who strive to overcome themselves for the love of God feel, as he did, that the severest practices are soon softened down by the unction of grace.

The sight of Jesus Christ fastened to the cross made him feel the misery of the poor so intensely, that he would have wished to employ all he had, and his own person, in their relief. Sometimes he did strip himself to clothe them; and when he had not enough to satisfy them all, he unsewed or tore his clothes to divide among them. In the absence of his father he caused much more bread to be brought to table at their meals than was necessary; and when his mother asked the reason, he said, "that it was in order to give more quickly to those who came to ask, for I cannot bear their complaints; they pierce my heart with grief." This pious mother saw with pleasure the charity of her son and far from endeavoring to check it, she was not displeased at his leaving her alone at table, while he took to the neighboring sick the viands of which he stinted himself. An equally lively and respectful zeal induced him to come to the aid of such priests as were in want; he took particular care to provide for the decoration of the altars, in order the better to assist at the divine service. He bought the finest linen, and distributed it to the poor country churches to be employed at the sacrifice of the mass; and when this August sacrifice was about to be celebrated, if anything was wanting, or if the altar was not properly found in everything he would offer himself to the officers of the church, in order to supply what was required either from his purse or by his assistance.

But all these good works did not come up to what he had figured to himself as requisite for perfection. He could have wished to withdraw into some distant country, there to practice voluntary poverty, which had already inflamed his heart. At first he resolved to go to Rome, to visit the tomb of St. Peter, by that movement of devotion which God has often inspired in His Saints, and which has been so frequent from the fourth century. He also proposed to himself to solicit from the Almighty, by the intercession of the Prince of the Apostles, the grace to carry out the resolution he had come to of leading an Apostolic life. After having put up his prayer in this holy place, he noticed that in the crowd of people some made but a slender offering, while others made no donation whatever. "What then," said he, "is devotion grown so cold? How is it that men do not offer all they have, and do not even offer themselves on a spot where the ashes of the Prince of the Apostles reposed? How does it happen that they do not decorate with all possible magnificence this Peter, on which Jesus Christ has founded his Church?" He contributed to the best of his power, leaving a considerable sum for that purpose; and what he had wished was subsequently executed. The Sovereign Pontiffs, and in particular Sixtus V, who was a religious of his order, have rendered the Basilica of St. Peter so sumptuous and magnificent, that it is become the admiration of the universe.

On going out of the church, he saw a multitude of poor, whom he immediately joined, as much for the affection he had for them, as for the love of poverty. He gave his clothes to him who appeared the most necessitous, and took his rags himself, and he remained the rest of the day in their company, with extraordinary satisfaction to himself; and thus he trod under foot the pride of life, and raised himself up by degrees to evangelical perfection. The following day, having dressed himself with propriety, he set out on his return to Assisi, praying God to guide him in the ways of holy poverty.

The devil, who was sensible that the young man would become confirmed in his intention if he persevered in prayer, appeared to him under a most terrific form, and threatened him, if he persisted, to render him a dreadful deformity like unto an old woman of the town, who was so hideous that he would not even look at her. But the newly-enlisted soldier of Jesus Christ, who began to be inured to warfare, laughed at the threats of the tempter, and was more urgent in his prayers, for which purpose he chose underground places, where he could better defend himself against the snares of his enemy. The fruit of these holy exercises was a lively sorrow for the use he had made of the first years of his youth, and a great perseverance in the mortification of his senses, in order to bear the cross of Jesus Christ in his body, as he bore it in his heart, and to consecrate himself wholly to God. Assiduity in prayer, joined to the practice of mortifications, are two excellent means for advancement in virtue and arriving at a state of sanctity.

It was thus that Francis acted before having changed his habit, or quitted the world. St. Bonaventure, says that he had then no other master from whom he received instructions than Jesus Christ; nevertheless, an author quoted by Wading, assures us that he sometimes consulted the Bishop of Assisi. We may here say, in order that there may be no seeming contradiction between the two, that he received instructions from Jesus Christ only because he was inspired by Him, but that he communicated with the Bishop on the points on which he had been inspired; and we may be the more assured of this, as we shall see hereafter that this prelate had his confidence, and that there is reason to think that he was his spiritual Father.

The servant of God, walking and meditating one day out of Assisi, near the church of St. Damian, which was very old and falling into ruin, was moved by the Holy Spirit to enter it to pray. There, prostrated before the crucifix, he repeated three times the following beautiful words, which gave him great interior consolation, and which he subsequently made frequent use of "Great God, full of glory, and You, my Lord Jesus Christ! I entreat you to enlighten me and to dispel the darkness of my mind, to give me a pure faith, a firm hope, and an ardent charity. Let me have a perfect knowledge of You, O God! so that

I may in all things be guided by Your light, and act in conformity to Your will." He cast his eyes, filled with tears, upon the crucifix, when a voice came forth from it, and he heard distinctly these words repeated three times, not interiorly, but loudly pronounced: "Francis, go and repair my house, which you see is falling into ruin." So wonderful a voice, in a place where he was alone, alarmed him greatly, but he felt immediately the salutary effects of it, and he was transported with joy.

The sense of these words chiefly related to the state of the Church which Jesus Christ had purchased at the price of His blood, which the holy man was to repair in all its defects by his ministry and the labors of his disciples, according to the explanation which the Holy Spirit gave to him of them subsequently, which he communicated to his brethren, as St. Bonaventure tells us.

Nevertheless, the powerful protection which he received from heaven for the repair of the church of St. Damian, was an indication that the same words were to be understood to relate to that building also: as the sacred oracles had a twofold literal sense in the mouths of the Prophets, one of which related to events which were at hand, and the other to a distant time, and to mysteries wholly spiritual.

Francis came to himself; he left the church fully resolved to undertake its repair, and left money in the hands of a priest named Peter, who did the parochial duties of it, to keep a lamp burning before the crucifix, promising to give more, and to employ all he had for the use of this holy place.

The voice which had issued from the crucifix renewed in his mind and heart the impression of the mystery of the Passion. He felt himself interiorly wounded through the wounds of Jesus Christ, and he shed such burning tears, that his eyes were quite inflamed, and, as it were, full of blood, when he returned from prayer. To make his body participate in the sufferings which penetrated his very soul, and to punish himself for the levities of his youth, he imposed on himself a very rigorous abstinence, with various other kinds of mortification.

The eagerness he felt to commence the repair of St. Damian's church, suggested to him means by which the work might be begun. After having fortified himself by the sign of the cross, he took from his father's stores several pieces of cloth, which he sold at Foligno, together with his horse. He came back on foot, and offered the money respectfully to the priest of St. Damian for the repair of the church, and in aid of the poor, humbly entreating him to allow him to remain some time with him. The priest consented to receive Francis, but refused the money, fearing the displeasure of his father; and Francis, who had utter contempt for money, not valuing it more than so much dust, when it was of no use for good works, threw it upon one of the windows of the church.[9]

---

[9] This church is still extant: and they show the window into which the money was thrown.

The heretics of the last century, who calumniated the Saint for many things, have deemed it criminal in him to have taken these pieces of cloth from his father's stores. St. Bonaventure is of a different way of thinking; he has not thought that this action required justification; on the contrary, he calls the sale of the cloth and of the horse a fortunate bargain. And, indeed, without going into the right which the son may have had in the commercial affairs of his father, in consequence of their partnership, and of his age of twenty-five, had he not reason to think that, having received orders from heaven to repair a church, God, who is the Master and Dispenser of all goods, permitted him to employ a proportion of those which were under his paternal roof, since he had no other means of obeying the injunction? But it is an extraordinary case, which must not be drawn into precedent. The general rule of Christian morality is, that children may not dispose of anything without the permission of their parents even under the pretext of piety.[10]

Bernardo on his return from a journey, having heard what his son had done, came in great wrath to St. Damian's with several members of his family; and Francis, who had not yet sufficient strength of mind to encounter the storm, and wished to avoid the first ebullition, went and hid himself in the priest's room. Three contemporary authors assure us that, having placed himself behind the door, and pressing himself against the wall, when the door was opened he was miraculously let into the wall, so that he was not seen by those who were looking for him.[11]

When his father was gone, he retired secretly into a cavern, which was known only to one servant, from whom he received what was necessary for his immediate sustenance, and where he occupied himself in continual prayer, shedding abundance of tears, in order that he might be delivered from those

---

[10] The conduct of the Saint on this occasion may seem at first sight opposed to the ordinary rules of right and wrong; for how could he, it may be objected, in justice dispose of property which did not belong to him? However, the blessing which rested upon the action, and the testimony which God has since borne to the sanctity of His servant, oblige us to inquire whether he may not have acted in obedience to some higher rule, namely, to the direct inspiration of the Holy Spirit It is certainly quite contrary to the ordinary law of justice for one man to take for himself the property of another; but if Almighty God, to whom all things ultimately belong, and for whom we are only stewards, is pleased to dispense with this His own law in a particular case, and to bestow what He has hitherto given to one upon another, He confers at the same time a valid title to the gift, and it is no robbery in him who has received it to act upon that title.

We but apply to the Saint the same principle which is used to exculpate the seeming injustice of the Israelites in spoiling the Egyptians, the sacrifice of Isaac, and the indiscriminate slaughter of the Chanaanites. The event justifies or condemns the act in the eyes of the world at large; while for those who feel impelled to actions opposed to ordinary laws, there are rules laid down in classical theology by which they may discern whether their impulse is a movement of the Holy Spirit, or a delusion of the evil one. Perhaps the anecdote in the text may also be explained on the supposition that St. Francis was in partnership with his father, as is suggested in the text, and therefore had a right to a portion of his property.

[11] This wall was preserved, when a convent of his order was built in the place in his life-time, and the hollow place is seen in it (Wading.)

who pursued him, and be able to accomplish the work which God had inspired him to undertake.

After having passed a month in this place, he considered that it was in God alone that he ought to hope, without putting any confidence in his own exertions, and this thought filled him with interior joy, and raised his depressed spirits. Reproaching himself, therefore, with his pusillanimity, he left his cavern and went straight to the town, as a soldier, who, feeling ashamed of having fled, returns intrepidly to the charge. Of what is not he capable, who is fully persuaded that he can do nothing of himself towards his salvation, but that he can do all through Him who imparts strength to him? On these two principles the Saints have undertaken, and carried into execution, the greatest things.

The inhabitants of Assisi, who saw his face all pale and wan, and who remarked how changed were his conversation and opinions, thought that his mind was disturbed. He was called a madman, they threw mud and stones at him, and followed him, hooting and calling after him. But, without paying attention to these insults, and being on the contrary well pleased to bear these marks of the holy folly of the cross, the servant of God continued his way as if he had been deaf and insensible.

Bernardo being told that his son had returned, and was made the object of public derision, went immediately in pursuit of him, reproached him bitterly with his conduct, seized him and dragged him to his house, where he beat him severely, and confined him in a hole under the staircase.[12] This severity had no effect in shaking the resolution of the holy prisoner; he even acquired more firmness, and encouraged himself to suffer by the words of the Gospel: "Blessed are they that suffer persecution for justice sake, for theirs is the kingdom of heaven."[13]

A short time after, when his father was on a journey, his mother, who did not approve of the severity with which he was treated, and who moreover had no hope of overcoming his constancy, set him at liberty. He gave thanks to God for it, and made use of it, to return to the church of St. Damian. Bernardo, not finding him in his confinement at his return, was not content with upbraiding his wife in the severest terms, but went off to St. Damian's to drive him out of the country if he should not succeed in bringing him back. Francis, to whom God had given strength, presented himself boldly to his Father, and told him decidedly that he cared not for his blows, nor for his shackles, for that he was prepared willingly to suffer all sorts of evils for the name of Jesus Christ. His father, seeing that there was nothing more to hope in his case thought of nothing further than to get back the money for the cloth and the horse, and he found the whole in the window where Francis had thrown it,

---

[12] This sort of prison is still seen. It was preserved in 1615, when the house was turned into a church and convent, at the request of Philip the Third, King of Spain. — Wading. App. 6 3.

[13] Matt. 5: 10.

when the priest refused to take it; and then his wrath was somewhat appeased.

Avarice, which is never satisfied, induced Bernardo that his son had other money, and he had him summoned before the city magistrates, to account for it. Francis appeared before their tribunal and told them that he had changed his state of life, that God had delivered him from the slavery of the world, and that he had nothing more to do with its affairs. The magistrates, who knew his conversion and his perseverance, saw something grand in his demeanor, and told his father, who urged them to put interrogatories to his son, that this affair ought to be carried into the bishop's court. Bernard addressed himself to that authority, not only to compel his son to give up what money he had, but to force him to renounce his claims to any paternal inheritance. Francis, who was a sincere lover of poverty, cheerfully consented to all that was required of him, and said that he would willingly appear before the bishop, who was the pastor and father of his soul. As soon as he was there, without waiting for his father to make his demand, and without saying anything himself, he gave up what money he still had, and then stripped off his clothes, even to his shirt, under which it was seen that he wore a hair-shirt, and gave them up to his father, addressing him in the following beautiful words: "Until this time I have called you father on earth; but from henceforward I may boldly say, Our Father who art in Heaven, in whom I have placed all my treasure, and all my confidence."

The prelate, who was a man of great worth, admiring this excess of fervor, and moved even to tears, rose up, and embracing the servant of God, covered him with his cloak, and ordered his servants to bring such clothing as was necessary for him. It was no doubt by a dispensation of Divine Providence that a bishop pressed to his bosom him who was to combat so strenuously for the service of the Church. They brought an old cloak belonging to a laborer, who was in the employ of the bishop, which Francis received with great satisfaction, and with which he clothed himself, making on it a cross with some mortar which he met with accidentally; thus manifesting what he wished to be, a half-naked poor one, and a crucified man. This occurred in the year 1206, when he was in his twenty-fifth year. St. Bonaventure, who gives the name of spiritual intoxication to the admirable fervor with which he stripped himself entirely in order to be able to follow Jesus Christ naked on the cross, says that, moreover, in order to avoid the shipwrecks of the world, he fortified himself with the representation of the wood which was the instrument of our salvation.

CHAPTER II
FOUNDATION OF THE ORDER

Retires to a monastery—They give him a hermit's habit—He devotes himself to the leprous—Receives the gift of healing, and returns to Assisi, where he searches for stone to restore the Church of Assisi—He lives on alms—His father and brother exercise his patience—The victories he gains over himself—People begin to esteem and honor him—He restores the Church of St. Peter and that of St. Mary of the Angels, or the Portiuncula—Dwells at St. Mary of the Angels, and is favored therewith heavenly apparitions—He is called to the apostolical life—Renounces money, and goes discalced—His poor and humble habit—God inspires him to preach—He weeps bitterly over the sufferings of Jesus Christ—Receives three disciples, and retires with them to a deserted cottage—He makes them beg for alms—He predicts to the Emperor Otho the short duration of his glory—It is revealed to him that his sins are remitted—He is rapt in ecstasy, and predicts the extension of his Order—He proposes a new mission to his disciples—The address he makes them on their preparation for, and conduct during, the mission—He returns near to Assisi, where he receives four more disciples—He assembles all his disciples—Composes a Rule, and goes to obtain the Pope's approval—He knows miraculously what will happen to him at Rome—He is at first repulsed by Pope Innocent III, but is afterwards received favorably—Difficulties on the approbation of his Rule—He overcomes them by an address he makes the Pope—The Pope approves his Rule, and accumulates favors on it.

 MANCIPATED from the ties of worldly desires, as he had wished to be, he now sought for some sequestered spot, where alone and in silence he might listen to the voice of God. In a wood, through which he was passing, singing the praises of God in the French language, some thieves surrounded him and asked him who he was. "I am the herald of the great King," he replied, in a prophetical sense, with perfect confidence in God. On receiving this answer, they beat him cruelly, threw him into a hole that was full of snow, and ridiculed the title he gave himself. When they had left him, he again began to sing the praises of God in a louder voice than before, delighted to have had an opportunity of suffering. At a neighboring monastery, where he implored alms, which he received as a contemptible beggar, they employed him for some days in the vilest affairs of the scullery. But seeing that this interfered too much with his spiritual exercises, he came to Gubbio, where one of his friends, having recognized him, gave him, in order that he might be more decently clad, a hermit's dress,[1] a short tunic, a leathern girdle, shoes, and a staff.

In this penitential habit, he subjected his body to additional austerities; and in order to fulfill all the functions of humility, to which he was much attached, he devoted himself to the service of the lepers. He was constantly seen in their hospitals, moving about in all directions to aid them, preventing all their wants, showing the greatest compassion for them, washing their feet, cleansing their sores, removing the matter, and, by a wonderful effort of charity, kissing their disgusting ulcers. He received from God in reward the gift of healing; and this was a figure of the evangelical cures, which he was soon to apply to the diseases of the soul.

Among many proofs which St. Bonaventure adduces of his having the gift of healing miraculously, he mentions that of a man of the Duchy of Spoleto, whose mouth and cheeks were eaten away by a dreadful cancer, and for whom all sorts of remedies had been fruitlessly employed. This man met Francis returning from Rome (whither he had been to implore the assistance of the blessed Apostles), who, out of great respect, wished to kiss his feet; this the humble Francis prevented, but kissed the cancerous face, which was instantaneously cured. The same Saint remarks: "I know not which is most to be admired, such a kiss, or such a cure!"

The servant of God, who now acknowledged no other country than heaven, and who was fearful of being the cause of some of his father's violences, proposed to himself to take up his abode in Gubbio and devote himself to the exercises of charity, without returning to Assisi; but calling to mind the order which had been given him by the voice which came from the crucifix, to repair the Church of St. Damian, he thought himself bound to obey it, at least by "questing" for what was requisite for working at it. The profound humility which he had acquired by the degradations he had subjected himself to, gave him the courage he required for begging in his native town, where he had been known to have possessed everything in plenty. Having cast aside all bashfulness for the love of Jesus Christ poor and crucified, he went through the center of Assisi as one inspired, publishing the glories of God, and soliciting stones for the repair of the church; addressing his fellow-citizens with simplicity, thus: "Whosoever will give me a stone, shall have a reward; whoever will give two shall have a double reward; and he who gives three shall be rewarded threefold."

Many treated him with contempt, and turned him into ridicule. Others could not understand how a young man of a good and opulent family, with excellent prospects, hitherto considered as the model of the young men of the

---

[1] Three centuries later, some persons pretended that he then adopted, not a hermit's dress, but that of the Augustinians, from the hands of a religious of that order, and that he had made profession of that rule. Wading has proved unanswerably, that this opinion is incorrect, and it has been given up.

place, could demean himself to such a degree as to beg in his native town. Some thought that such a change could only come from God, and were greatly moved by it. But the new-made pauper, having no respect for the opinions of men, and receiving cheerfully the insults put upon him, after the example of Jesus Christ, thought of nothing but the church of St. Damian, for which he quested so successfully, that many persons, moved by his exhortations, furnished sufficient for its repair. He himself worked at it daily, and carried the materials on his shoulders as a common laborer, without any regard for his body, which was emaciated by the rigors of penance and fasting.

The priest of St. Damian took compassion on the pious workman, and took care to provide him with a substantial meal when he came in from work. Francis having received this charitable succor for some days running, reflected on his situation, and said to himself, as he afterwards told his disciples; "Will you find everywhere a priest who has so much consideration for you? This is not the sort of life you have chosen: go, then, henceforward from door to door, as a poor man, and solicit food for the love of God, with an empty plate, on which you will put whatever may be given you. For it is thus you must live for the love of Him who was born poor, who lived poorly, whom they affixed naked to the cross, and who was put after His death into another man's tomb." One must be very dead to self, have great contempt of the world, and a sincere love of God, to entertain such feelings and carry them out.

The following day he took a plate, and went begging from door to door, and sat down in the street to eat. At the first mouthful he took of this disgusting mess, he felt a nausea at his stomach, which made him recoil. Animated at the same instant by the love of poverty, he became ashamed of his weakness, and reproached himself for the feeling; after which, he ate the remainder without reluctance, and with so much relish, that he thought he had never eaten a better meal. He also felt an interior joy and strength in his body, which enabled him to bear with pleasure, for God's sake, whatever might be most severe or bitter. After having returned fervent thanks to the Father of the poor, who had given him so wonderful a taste, he went to the priest and entreated him to take no further trouble with respect to his nourishment, "because," he said, "I have found an excellent purveyor, and a very able cook, who can season his dishes in a superior way." He had often these jocose expressions, which were as much the effect of the spiritual joy he felt, as of his natural lively and joyous turn of mind.

Bernardo, vexed in the greatest degree at seeing his son begging and exposed to the jeers of the public, was inflamed with anger, and either turned from him when he met him, or cursed him. Francis admitted that these curses affected him more than any other suffering he endured, and he hit upon a method of protecting himself from him. It was to take another poor and miserable man with him, who should be as father to him, whom he engaged to bless him, making the sign of the cross on him whenever his father cursed him; and then he said to Bernardo: "Believe me, my father, that God can give me, and indeed has given me, another father, from whom I receive blessings for your curses."

His brother Angelo, a young man full of the love of the world, also mocked him, and turned him into ridicule. Seeing him one day in church shivering with cold in his poor hermit's dress, and praying devoutly, he said to one of his friends: "Go and ask him to sell you a little of his sweat." Francis replied, "I do not choose to sell my sweat to men; I can sell it at a better price to God." If all Christians thought thus, they would not take so much pains for the world, which pays so ill, and they would do much for God, who rewards so magnificently.

The pauper of Jesus Christ gained many other victories over himself in the quest he had taken upon himself for the building of St. Damian. He suffered with admirable patience the persecution of some worldly persons, who treated him as a fool, and insulted him in a thousand ways. Every time that it happened to him to blush when he met any of his acquaintances or friends, he reprimanded himself as if he had committed some great fault; he humbled himself the more, and begged for alms more submissively, to take down all influence of pride. One day when he was begging for oil for two lamps which he wished to keep constantly burning before the crucifix, from which the miraculous voice had been heard, he went into a house where some persons of his acquaintance were collected together for gaming. Their sight struck him, and gave him a feeling of shame which induced him to retire. He had scarcely left the door, when, thinking on what he had done, he considered himself guilty of a great want of firmness, and he immediately returned to the place where they were at play, he acknowledged his fault before all present, and begged boldly for the lamps of the church in the French language, which set the company into an immoderate fit of laughter. Such efforts show the truth of the remark of St. Ambrose: that the saints were no less liable than ourselves to fall into faults; but that they had greater care to practice virtue, and to correct the faults into which they fall.[2]

Pious and well-thinking persons remarked that the conduct of Francis was maintained with an equality of fervor, and they found a high degree of wisdom in what appeared to the generality of the world to be littleness of mind and folly. These opinions gradually spread and brought over many to esteem and venerate him; even those who had despised and insulted him, came forward to solicit his forgiveness. The prior of the monastery where he had served in the kitchen, who was then at Assisi, and who there became acquainted with his rare virtues, showed him great respect, begged him to pardon the treatment he had received, and excused himself, by saying, that he could not then be known under the miserable disguise under which he had hid himself. The man who had foretold that he would do great things, added to this prediction, while

---

[2] *Lib. de Joseph. Patriarch*, cap. I, n. 4.

applauding himself: "You know what I before said to you of this young man; you only see the beginning of his holiness, but you will see the continuation. Jesus Christ will do wonders through him, which all the world will admire."

The dispositions which were now entertained in his regard, procured for him the means of completing the repairs of St. Damian towards the close of the year 1206. In the course of this work, it was remarked that he said to those who passed by, "Assist me in finishing this building; there will be a monastery here some day of poor females of holy fife, whose reputation will tend to glorify our heavenly Father throughout His holy Church." This was a real prophecy, the accomplishment of which was witnessed five years afterwards, when he established the holy virgin Clare and her companions, whom he had consecrated to Jesus Christ, as will be recorded in its place; and this prophecy was so well known, that Saint Clare inserted its very words in the will she made in the year 1253.[3]

At the beginning of the year 1207, Francis, not to remain idle, undertook a new work. He proposed to restore the church of St. Peter, which was at a little distance from the town, in consequence of the devotion with which the purity of his faith inspired him towards the Prince of the Apostles; and this intention was soon put in force, because, it having been seen how usefully he had made use of the donations he had received for his first work, he was now furnished with what he required, more readily and more abundantly. He now was desirous of effecting some essential repairs to a third church or chapel, about a mile from Assisi, which was very ancient, but so deserted and in such a state of ruin, that it only served as a refuge for herdsmen in bad weather: its name was St. Mary of the Angels, and Ottavio, Bishop of Assisi, thus describes its foundation:

"In the year of 352, a year after the appearance in the heavens of a luminous cross on the 7th of May, in broad daylight, over the city of Jerusalem, which extended from Mount Calvary to the Mountain of Olives, a cross which was more brilliant than the sun, as St. Cyril, then bishop of that city, and one of the eye-witnesses of the phenomenon, relates in his letter to the Emperor Constantius, four holy hermits came from Palestine into Italy, and obtained from Pope Liberius leave to remain in the valley of Spoleto, and settled themselves in the vicinity of Assisi, with the permission of the authorities of the town. There they built a chapel which was called St. Mary of Josaphat,[4] because they placed in it a relic of the sepulcher of the Blessed Virgin,[5] and because the altar was consecrated by the title of her glorious Assumption. In

---

[3] This will is given at full length by Wading, in the Annals of the Friars Minor, in the year 1255.

[4] It is usually believed that the sepulcher of the B. Virgin was in the village of Gethsemani, at the part of Mount Olivet from whence the Valley of Josaphat extends to Jerusalem.

[5] Baronius thinks that the tomb of the B. Virgin was covered with the ruins of Jerusalem, when sacked by the Romans, and was found in the fifth century; but the hermits may have had a relic of the sepulcher from the first faithful.

the sixth century it was given to the religious of the Order of St. Benedict, who enlarged and strengthened it; and it was afterwards called St. Mary of the Angels." We shall soon explain the reason for this. It was also called Portiuncula, because of some portions of ground which the Benedictines of Mount Saubazo possessed in the vicinity.

The same author adds that, at the close of the twelfth century, pious persons were accustomed to visit this chapel, although it was deserted; and that the mother of St. Francis, after having implored the protection of the Blessed Virgin, had had this first child who was destined to repair the very place in which she had made her request. He labored at it also, in consequence of his fervent devotion to the Blessed Virgin, and he had equal success to what he had for the other two churches.

We can easily understand that a man without any property, who was poor and a beggar, could not have accomplished these works without assistance from above; but St. Bonaventure finds in it a still further mystery. He says that divine Providence, which guided Francis in all his actions, preordained things in such manner, that he repaired three churches previous to instituting there his orders, in order that the material temples should be the types of the three spiritual edifices which he was to raise up; and that passing from what is perceptible to the senses, to what is only apparent to the mind, and rising gradually to what is still more elevated, he was enabled to give to the Church of Jesus Christ three descriptions of soldiery able to combat for the reformation of morals, and worthy to triumph gloriously in heaven. We may add, that the austerities, labors, and humiliations of the servant of God had been for the two previous years as so many strokes of the hammer, which rendered him a chosen and living foundation-stone on which might be based these sacred edifices. Such is the method which is adopted by our Lord. He prepares all things, and brings them successively to perfection; instead of which, men are always hurried, and often endeavor in the way to perfection to advance faster than the grace which directs them.

Of the three churches which Francis had repaired, he chose that of St. Mary of the Angels for his residence, in order to honor the Mother of God and the celestial Intelligences. St. Bonaventure says that he was often favored by visits from Angels, on account of the frequent apparitions of these blessed spirits there. The man of God passed days and nights there in fervent prayer, when he entreated the Blessed Virgin, that as she had conceived and brought forth the Word of the Father, full of grace and truth, she would have the goodness to obtain for him a participation therein it was there also, that, by the merits of this powerful advocate, he had the happiness to conceive and bring forth, if it may be so expressed, his evangelical life, the precious fruit of grace and truth, which the Son of God had come to bring upon earth.

One day when he was assisting in this church at a mass of the Apostles, which he had requested the priest of St. Damian to say he listened attentively to the Gospel,[6] where this form of fife is prescribed by our Savior for the mission of His Apostles: "Do not possess gold, nor silver, nor money in your purses; nor scrip for your journey, nor two coats, nor shoes, nor a staff."[7] After mass, he asked the priest to explain these words to him; he understood the sense of them well, and impressed them well on his heart, finding in them the image of that poverty which he loved: "This is what I seek for," he exclaimed, quite overjoyed; "this is what I desire with my whole heart." At the same instant he threw away his purse with a feeling of horror for money, he took off his shoes, he replaced his leather girdle by a cord, and devoted his thoughts to putting in practice what he had just heard, and to conforming himself in all things to the evangelical rule. It is a vocation similar to that of St. Anthony, of whom St. Athanasius relates, that having heard in the church these words of Jesus Christ, "If you will be perfect, go sell what you have, and give it to the poor,"[8] he went immediately to put this counsel in practice, in order to attain perfection.

The hermit's tunic, which Francis still retained, appeared to him too delicate; he therefore got one coarse and rough, of an ash gray, which came down to the feet, and the sleeves of which reached to the fingers; to this he added a hood, which covered sufficiently the head and face. This description of dress he continued to wear during the remainder of his life,[9] except that the tunic and hood had sometimes more or less length or breadth, as is seen in his habits which are preserved with great veneration at Assisi, at Mount Alvernia, and at Florence. Seeking nothing but poverty and humility, he chose the dress that was the plainest, the most despicable, and the most likely to make himself despised by the world, whose vanities he held in utter contempt; it was also the dress most like to that of the shepherds, and other country peasants, who chose it to protect them from the weather; or rather he imitated the prophets, who only covered themselves with a sack, to which he afterwards added a short cloak.

What we have been speaking of happened in the year 1208, which is reckoned the first year of the Order of St. Francis, because it is the one in which he took the habit, which he gave in the following year to such as chose

---

[6] This Gospel is not now read either at the feasts of the Apostles or Evangelists, nor at their votive masses; it is only read on the Thursday of the Octave of Pentecost, which shows that the Gospels have been differently placed in the Missals.

[7] Matt. 10: 9 and 10.

[8] Sanct. Athan. tom. 5, part 2, p. 796. Ed. Nov.; Matt. 19: 21.

[9] It is similar to the one which he gave subsequently to his religious, and which is still retained in his order. At the general chapter held at Narbonne in 1260, St. Bonaventure thought proper to add to the hood sufficient material to cover the breast and shoulders; this is called Mozetta from the Italian, which is used for a small cloak for bishops. Some of the children of St. Francis do not wear it, and differ from the others in some points; but all those who call him Father need have no difficulty on this head. It is by their poverty and humility that he will acknowledge them for his true children.

to imitate him, and in which the first stone was laid which served as a foundation for this spiritual edifice.

Then God inspired him to preach, to exhort sinners to repentance, and to cause evangelical perfection to be loved in the world. Although he expressed himself in a very plain manner, his discourses had nothing in them that was low; they were solid and animated with the Spirit of God, and so effectually penetrated the hearts of his hearers, that every one was surprised at it. He always began them by the following salutation, which he afterwards declared had been revealed to him by God; "May the Lord grant you His peace." It was noticed that a very pious man, who was in the habit of addressing the following words to all whom he met, "Pax et bonum — Pax *et bonum*", that is: "Peace and weal[10], — Peace and weal!" was not seen in Assisi after Francis began to preach; as if he wished it to be understood that his mission had ended by the presence of him whose precursor he was. In fact, this new preacher was in truth an angel of peace sent from heaven to reconcile a great number of sinners with Jesus Christ, and to draw down on them all sorts of benefits.

He joined to the ministry of the word the exercise of every sort of virtue, and applied himself particularly to prayer, where the sufferings of our Blessed Savior made such impression on his soul that he groaned and sobbed aloud, when he found himself at liberty. One of his friends, passing by the church of St. Mary of the Angels, having heard him, went in, and seeing him bathed in tears, reproached him with it as of a weakness unbecoming in a man. "I weep for the Passion of my Lord Jesus Christ," answered Francis, "and I ought not to be ashamed of weeping openly before the whole world." This enviable emotion was in the heart of St. Augustin, when he said to his people: "The Passion of Jesus Christ, which the Church puts every year before us, moves and affects us as if we saw Him personally stretched on the cross; there are none but the impious who can be insensible to it.

"As for me, I wish to lament with you in considering this affecting spectacle. This is the time in which to weep, to acknowledge ourselves criminals, and to pray for mercy. Which of us would have it in his power to shed a sufficiency of tears to equal the merit of so great and so worthy a subject of grief?"[11] Every Christian ought to blush, if he is wanting in these sentiments of gratitude and love.

The words and actions of Francis soon became noised abroad. Some became converted, and embraced the penitential course he preached. Others formed the resolution of leaving all and joining him. The first was Bernard da Quintavalle, a rich and discreet man, of one of the best families in Assisi, who had great influence in the town, and guided it by his advice. This respectable man, as St. Bonaventure called him, considering the contempt with which Francis viewed all the things of this world, was desirous of ascertaining

---

[10] "Weal" is an old English word meaning "well", or what is good for you. — Editor's note.

[11] D. August, *in Ps. XXI. Enarr*, 2. n. 1.

whether it was in truth an effect of sanctity, or of littleness of mind. He invited him, therefore, to supper and to sleep at his house, and had a bed prepared for him in his room. While he feigned to sleep soundly, he saw by the light of a lamp Francis get up, fall on his knees, melt into tears, his eyes raised to heaven, his arms crossed, pronounce slowly these words: *"Deus meus et omnia,"* — "My God, and my all," which he repeated during the whole night. So ardent and so tender an expression is quite convincing that he was then in an exalted state of contemplation, where interior communications made him sensible that the Lord was especially his God, and filled the whole soul. Happy he who can with truth say, *Deus meus et omnia.* For this it is requisite that he should belong wholly interiorly to God, and that the world should be nothing to him.

Bernard did not interrupt Francis in his holy exercise, but, filled with devotional feelings, he said to himself, "Truly this is a man of God." After having put him to other proofs, he resolved to give all his goods to the poor and follow him, and he put this question to him: "If a man had received from his master a certain portion for several years, and then wished no longer to make use of it, what do you think it would be best for him to do?" Francis said in answer, that he ought to return it to the master from whom he had received it. "It is I," replied Bernard "who have received a great deal from God, and much more than I have deserved; I return it willingly into His hands, and place it at your disposal; for I mean to attach myself to you." At these words, Francis, delighted to find that God began the accomplishment of his works by so worthy a personage: "Your intention," he said, "is one of great importance; you must consult God upon it, to learn from Him how you are to put it in execution. Early tomorrow morning we will ask the Curate of St. Nicholas, who is known to be a most worthy man, to say a mass for us, and after having heard it, we will continue in prayer till the hour of Terce." We see in this the mode of acting of one who has the spirit of God; he hurries nothing, he has recourse to prayer, and he makes use of the ordinary practices of the Church.

The following day they did what they had proposed; after which, Francis, who had great devotion to the three Persons of the Blessed Trinity, opened three times in their honor the book of the Gospels,[12] entreating the Almighty to confirm, by the testimony of their texts, Bernard's holy resolution.[13] At the first opening they found the following: "If you will be perfect, go sell all you have, and give it to the poor."[14] At the second: "Take nothing for the

---

[12] Some authors say that it was the curate who opened the book, and this seems to coincide with the great respect he had for priests.

[13] This mode, which he took to ascertain the will of God, was accompanied by all the conditions requisite, according to St. Thomas, to make it legitimate; and we cannot reasonably doubt that God inspired him to make use of it, as Ecclesiastical history shows us that He so inspired other Saints.

[14] Matt. 19:21.

journey."[15] At the third: "If any man will come after Me, let him deny himself, and take up the cross, and follow Me."[16] Then Francis, addressing himself to Bernard, said: "There is the life we must lead, the rule we must follow, you and I, and all those who shall desire to join us. Go and put in execution what you have just heard."

The new disciple, intimately convinced that his design came from God, sold, as fast as he could, all his effects, from which he got a considerable sum, which he had carried to the Square of St. George, and distributed it entirely among the poor whom he could collect. Francis then gave him a habit similar to his own; he called him his eldest son, and was always tenderly attached to him: he was indeed a most holy man.

Peter of Catania, canon of the church of St. Ruffinus, the cathedral of Assisi, edified by the self-denial and charity of Bernard, was disposed to become a disciple of the same master, and received the penitential habit on the same day, which was the 16th of April. All three retired to a hut which had been deserted, near to a rivulet called Rivo Torto, on account of its winding so very much.

Seven days after that, a very pious man called Giles, who was greatly looked up to in Assisi, on his return from the country, learned what his two fellow-citizens had done, which had excited the admiration of the whole town, and felt an ardent wish to imitate them, and thus carry out an intention he had entertained of devoting himself to the service of God. He passed the following night in prayer, when he was inspired to offer himself to Francis, for whom he had already great esteem, on account of the extreme contempt of the world and of himself, which was remarked in the whole of his conduct. In the morning he went to the church of St. George, whose festival it was, there to implore the saint's intercession, that he might find him whom he was seeking, of whose abode he was ignorant. Seeing out of the town three roads, without knowing which to take, he addressed the following prayer to God: "O Lord, most holy Father, I entreat You by Your mercy, if I am to persevere in this holy vocation, so to guide my steps that I may arrive at the place where Your servant lives whom I am seeking." He took one of the three roads as God inspired him; and as he walked full of his holy project, Francis, who was at prayer in a neighboring wood, came out to meet him.

As soon as Giles saw him, he went to him, and threw himself at his feet, and begged the favor of being received into his society. The holy man, who was at once satisfied of the faith and piety of the postulant, replied: "My brother, your request is that God would receive you as His servant and soldier. This is no small favor. It is as if the emperor were to come to Assisi, and wish to make choice of a favorite; each one would say, 'I wish to God it may be me.' Thus it is that God has made choice of you." He assured him that his vocation

---

[15] Mark 6: 8.

[16] Matt. 13:24.

came from heaven, and exhorted him to persevere. Then presenting him to Bernard and Peter, he said: "Here is a good brother, whom God has sent us."[17] And when he was alone with them, he told them that that man would one day excel in sublime virtue.

After a slender meal, and a spiritual conference, Francis set out with his new postulant for Assisi, to procure what was requisite for clothing. On the way, a woman having asked charity of them, the Saint turned to Giles, and with an angelic countenance, said: "My dear brother, let us give this poor woman the cloak you have on for the love of God." Giles gave it immediately, and it seemed to him that this alms ascended to heaven, which filled him with great joy. They begged at Assisi for some very coarse cloth, with which Francis clothed his third disciple, in the small hut where he instructed him in the religious exercises of a religious life with the other two.

St. Bonaventure[18] bears witness in his Life of St. Francis, that the holy Father Giles (for it is thus he calls him) was a man full of God, and worthy, by the excellence of his virtues, of undying remembrance, according to the testimony of this saintly patriarch; that during a great number of years he had his mind ever raised to heaven, and that he had been often seen lifted up in ecstasy, and that he seemed to live a life more angelical than human. "I myself," he adds, "have seen him with my own eyes raised up in ecstasy." He, moreover, gave thanks to God for having permitted him to live at a time when he had an opportunity of seeing this most holy brother Giles, and converse with him. There is extant a collection of his axioms, which are of the highest wisdom, force, and unction.[19]

Francis did not permit his disciples long to enjoy the sweetness of a life of retirement. Having informed them that they were bound to go forth to instruct their neighbors by unstudied words and an edifying life, he sent Bernard and Peter into Emilia,[20] and set out himself with Giles for the March of Ancona.

These apostolic men preached everywhere the grandeur and goodness of God, the obligation of each one to love Him, to obey His love, and to do penance. When they wanted the necessaries of life, they rejoiced, as if it were a treasure that they had purchased at the price of all they had possessed. Some persons received them obligingly, and did them good offices; but the singularity of their dress, and the rigor of their mode of life, shocked most of those who saw them. They were even frequently insulted, covered with mud,

---

[17] He was of the number of lay-brothers.

[18] He wrote the Life of St. Francis in 1261, and he speaks in it of the B. Giles as of one defunct; from which we assume that he died in 1260, as some writers assert, and not in 1262, as others have recorded; unless we suppose that the holy doctor, who only published his work in 1263, at the general chapter held at Pisa, may then have added the article relative to this holy person, after the 23rd of April, 1262, which was the time of his death.

[19] They are mentioned in his Life, written by the continuators of Bollandus for the 23d of April. A translation of it would be very acceptable.

[20] A province which formed part of Lombardy and Romagna.

dragged by their hood, and severely beaten this they joyfully bore, judging from the interior profit which they derived from it, that it was greatly to their advantage.

Their virtue, nevertheless, caused them to be treated at times with respect, and honors were even rendered to them. This mortified them, Giles in particular, who only gloried in the mortifications which he suffered for Jesus Christ's sake, and could not bear to be so honored. He said to his father: "When men honor us, we lose our glory." He also expressed to him his dissatisfaction that the mode of greeting which he had taught them, "May the Lord grant you His peace," was ill received by the men of the world. "Pardon them," replied Francis, "for they know not what they do. I verily assure you that hereafter there will be many nobles and princes who will respect you and your brethren, when you shall address those words to them." He foretold to him likewise that his Institute would spread, and that it might aptly be compared to a net which a fisherman casts into the river, with which he catches a multitude of fish.

The pious missionaries having gone through several towns, and given great satisfaction, returned to the hut at Rivo Torto, when a fourth disciple offered himself: his name was Sabbatin.

Morique, a religious of the order of Crosiers, or cross-bearers,[21] was the fifth. Being sick, and in extremity, given over and abandoned by the medical men of the hospital of St. Savior of Assisi, where all strangers were received, he got himself recommended to the prayers of Francis, who willingly prayed for him, and mixed a little crumb of bread with the oil of the lamp which burnt before the altar of St. Mary of the Angels, which he sent him by two of his brethren, saying to them: "Take this to our dear brother Morique. The power of Jesus Christ will not only restore him to perfect health, but will cause him to become a generous soldier, who will enter into our militia, and will persevere in it." The sick man had hardly swallowed the remedy when he was quite cured, and he soon after entered the Institute of his charitable physician, in which he lived in prodigious austerity during a long life, and enjoyed perfect health.

A sixth disciple, called John, and surnamed De Capella, began well, but finished ill.[22] He was employed to distribute to his brethren what was given to them in alms, and he took willingly the trouble of procuring for them what was wanted. But by little and little he got attached to temporal things, went too much abroad, and was very much relaxed from the regular discipline. The

---

[21] It was of the congregation of Italy which Pope Alexander VII suppressed in 1666. The Order of the religious of the Holy Cross, of which Clair Lieu, near Hui, is the chief place, still exists in France and in the Low Countries.

[22] This surname was given him because he wore on his head a sort of hat or capulary not worn by the rest, which was called in Umbria, *Capella*, from the Latin *capellus*, in low Latin. The religious of abbeys wore a hood or capulary, according to the remark in Menage in his Etymological Dictionary.

holy founder, having frequently reprimanded him severely, and without effect, he threatened him for his contumacy with a severe illness and a miserable death. In fact, this unworthy religious was stricken with a horrible leprosy, which he had not patience to endure. He forsook the poor of Jesus Christ, his companions, and, letting himself fall into despair, he hanged himself, as Judas had done.

St. Antoninus remarks that the life of St. Francis was in conformity with that of Jesus Christ, even in the circumstance of having had an unworthy disciple.[23] He only became such by his depraved will; but God in His wisdom made him serve as an example to show that we may be lost even in the most holy states of life if we cease to labor with fear and trembling for our salvation. Peter Rodulphus, bishop of Sinigaglia, in the Duchy of Urbino, adds, that the loss of one of the first children of St. Francis, and still more that of Judas in the Apostolic college, should induce those who are inclined to think ill and contemptibly of a whole order, on account of the ill-behavior of some individual, to reform their method of forming their opinions.[24]

Among the instructions which Francis gave to his disciples, he laid great stress on poverty, the practice of which might appear to them to be very severe. In order to render them wise herein by experience, and to make them feel that their subsistence depended on the charity of the faithful, he took them all into Assisi, and made them beg from door to door. This voluntary mendicity, which seemed new, and which had hardly been seen till then, drew down upon them derision, contempt, rebuffs, and angry words. In one place they were treated as sluggards and idlers, and turned away with curses; in another they were told they were fools to have given up their own property to go begging from other people. The parents and relatives of those who were thus begging, asserted that their families were dishonored by these practices, and made loud complaints. There were, however, some who respected their poverty, and aided them with good will. Such was the feeling of the public of those times in regard to evangelical poverty, which differs but little from what it is in our own days.

After this quest, Francis went to report to the bishop of Assisi the proceedings of his new soldiers. This worthy prelate, who greatly valued him, and gave him his support on all occasions, could not help telling him then, that he thought the sort of life he had chosen, in which they gave up all possessions whatsoever, hard and grievous. "As to me," replied the holy man, "I find it still harder and more grievous to possess anything; for one cannot take care of what one possesses without much solicitude and embarrassment. It gives rise to lawsuits, which must be undertaken; sometimes people are obliged to take up arms to protect it; and all this extinguishes the love of God and of our neighbor." The bishop approved of his remarks, and once more promised him

---

[23] S, Anton. *Chron.* part. 3, tit. 24, cap. 7.

[24] Rudolph. *Hist. Script. Relig.* lib, I fol. 67.

his protection. It is true that the state of voluntary poverty in which a person possesses nothing whatever, has its inconveniences; and where does human corruption fail to find such? But it cannot be denied that the state in question is very favorable to salvation, since it is based upon the counsel of Jesus Christ; and that, on the contrary, the possession of property is dangerous for salvation, since He Himself has said emphatically: "How hardly shall they that have riches enter into the kingdom of God."[25]

While the evangelical poor continued at Rivo Torto, the Emperor Otho IV, who was on his way to Rome with a great train in order to be consecrated and crowned by Innocent III, passed by their hut.[26] They were too mortified to pay any attention to the pomp of his retinue; but Francis ordered one of them to go to the emperor and tell him that all the glory which surrounded him would be but of short duration. The religious obeyed, and boldly told the emperor what he had been desired. The prediction displeased the prince, who, nevertheless, admitted from the event that it was well founded.[27] For, having violated his coronation oath, and committed various injustices towards the Church, he was excommunicated the following year by the same Pope, and afterwards deprived of his empire, and abandoned by the whole world.[28] It is thus that the greatness of the world, so fickle in itself, and always put an end to by death, falls sometimes even before that, by misconduct, and by the just judgments of God.

Zeal for the salvation of souls induced Francis to move his small troop into the Valley of Rieti. He halted at an abandoned hermitage on a large rock, which he thought to be a convenient place for entering into conversation with God, and where he came to pass the nights, after having been preaching and asking charity in the neighborhood with the other six during the day, principally at Poggio Bastone, a town in the vicinity.[29]

Being at prayer one day on this rock, and ruminating in the bitterness of his soul on his past years, he was assured, by a fresh inspiration of the Holy Spirit, that his sins were forgiven him, which filled him with joy. We cannot doubt but that his sins had been remitted him at the period of his conversion, by sincere contrition and the sacrament of penance. But in this happy moment he received the assurance thereof by revelation, and he learnt at the same time that the remission was entire, that is to say, that all the temporal punishment due to his sins had been remitted.

St. Bridget,[30] whose revelations are sanctioned and respected by the

---

[25] Luke XVII:24.

[26] The ceremony took place 27th Sept., 1209.; cf. Bernard. *Cor. Hist. Mediolan.* part 2. V. Bellov. *Hist,* lib. 30.

[27] Godef. *Monac. ad ann.* 1209.

[28] Chron. Foss. Nov. ad ann. 1211 and 1212.

[29] In Latin, *Oppidum Podii Bosconis.*

[30] She was a princess of the blood royal of Sweden.

Church, relates that she learned from our Savior that, when Francis retired from the world to enter on the way of perfection, he obtained from God a lively sorrow for his sins, which enabled him to say: "There is nothing on earth which I am not heartily willing to give up; nothing so laborious and so toilsome that I would not joyfully endure, nothing that I would not undertake, according to the strength of my body and soul, for the glory of my Lord Jesus Christ; and I will, as far as is possible, excite and induce all others to love God with their whole hearts, and above all other things." Such beautiful sentiments, well lived up to and exemplified by actions and conduct, would give us, not an entire assurance as to the remission of our sins, but a firm and well-founded confidence thereof.

The holy penitent received with this plenary indulgence the grace of an ecstasy, wherein, by a bright illumination from on high, God communicated to him what was to occur to his order. When he returned to join his disciples: "Take courage, my dear children," he said, "rejoice in the Lord. Be not cast down at the smallness of your numbers. Let not my simplicity nor yours alarm you, for God has shown me clearly that, by His blessing, He will spread this family of which He is the Father, into all parts of the world. I could wish to be silent on all that I have seen, but charity compels me to communicate it to you. I saw a great multitude coming to us to take a similar habit, and to lead the same life. I saw all the roads filled with men who walked hither, and hastened themselves very much. They came in great numbers, French, Spaniards, Germans, English, and from almost all nations. The noise of such as come and go, to execute the orders of holy obedience, still sounds in my ears."

So magnificent a prediction reminds us of the prophet Isaiah on the establishment of the Church: "Jerusalem, who says, 'I am barren'! lift up your eyes and look all around you. All this vast multitude surrenders itself up to you. I see them coming from afar; some from the North, others from the West, others from the land of the South; a thousand will come forth from the smallest among them, and from the very least a great people."[31]

The event has verified, in the eyes of the universe, the prophecy of the holy Patriarch. There was in a very short time a great number of religious; his order extended itself to all parts with astonishing rapidity, and it has multiplied itself so wonderfully for more than five centuries, that it may be looked upon as a representation of the birth and progress of the Church.

The disciples, greatly comforted by what they had just heard, and persuaded that their master had the spirit of prophecy, entreated him to inform them what would in future be the situation of his order. He explained to them in parables the good which would be effected by it, and at the same time the relaxations which would be introduced into its discipline, in order that the graces of God, which were to be bestowed on it, might excite their utmost gratitude, and that the fear of their weakness and want of fervor might

---

[31] Isaiah, chap. 49 and 50.

render them vigilant and humble.

The odor of sanctity which issued through the environs of the hermitage, and the holiness of their lives, brought many persons to them for instruction, and to profit from the edification they would receive. A very worthy person, whose name was Philip the Long, was desirous of entering the state of evangelical poverty. Francis made him his seventh disciple, and he brought them all back to the hut at Rivo Torto. In this holy retreat he spoke to them frequently of the kingdom of God, of the contempt of the world, of renouncing of their own will, of the mortification of the senses, and other maxims of a spiritual life. He opened to them also his intention of sending them into the four parts of the world; for, with the seven children which evangelical poverty and simplicity had given him, it was his wish to bring all the faithful to penance, and to generate them in some measure anew by the word of truth, to give them, or rather to restore them, to Jesus Christ. In fine, he told all his disciples openly, but with great humility, that the Divine Majesty had, in His wisdom, decided to employ them, and the companions they should aggregate to their community, to renew the face of the earth, by their preaching and their example, in order that the losses the Church had sustained by the corruption of morals, might be made good; and that it was for this purpose that grace had put it in their power so promptly to exercise the holy ministry. In order to prepare them for this mission, he made them the following discourse, which is worthy of being recorded at full length, in the words in which it has been preserved by his companions, to whom it was addressed:

"Let us consider, my dear brethren, what our vocation is. It is not only for our own salvation that God has called us by His mercy, but it is for the salvation of many others. It is in order that we should exhort all the world, more by example than by words, to do penance and to keep the Divine precepts. We are looked upon as senseless and contemptible, but let not this depress you; take courage, and be confident that our Lord, who conquered the world, will speak efficaciously through you. Let us be cautious, after having given up all, not to lose the kingdom of heaven for a trifling gain. If we find money anywhere, let us consider it as valueless as the dust which we tread under our feet. Let us not judge and despise the rich who five in luxury and wear the ornaments of vanity. God is their Lord, as He is ours; He may call them and justify them; we must honor them as our brethren, and as our masters. They are our brethren, because we have all the same Maker; and they are our masters, because they befriend the good by the assistance they afford them. Go then, and exhort men to do penance for the remission of their sins, and for peace. You will find some among the faithful mild and good, who will receive you with pleasure and willingly listen to you. Others, on the contrary, people without religion, proud and violent, will censure you, and be very hostile to you. But make up your minds to bear all this with humble patience, and let nothing alarm you. In a very short time many learned and noble persons will join themselves to you, to preach to kings, to princes, and to nations. Be therefore patient in tribulations, fervent in prayer, and fearless in labor. Be unassuming in speech, be grave in your manner, and grateful for the favors and benefits you may receive. The kingdom of God, which is eternal, will be your reward. I entreat the one and only God, who lives and reigns in Three Persons, to grant it to us, as He doubtless will grant it to us, if we are faithful to fulfill all that we have voluntarily promised."

This discourse filled them with fresh ardor. They threw themselves at the feet of the holy man, and joyfully received the orders he gave them, in addressing to each one of them these words of the Psalmist, which he was accustomed to repeat when he gave those instructions which required obedience: "Cast your care upon the Lord, and He shall sustain you."[32] Having divided the routes they were to take, by forming a cross which pointed to the four quarters of the globe, and knowing that he was to be the model for his brethren, he took one side for himself with a companion, and sent the other six, two and two, to the other sides. Wherever they found a church, they prostrated and made use of this formula, which they had learnt from their Father: "We adore You, O most holy Lord Jesus Christ here and in all Your churches which are in the whole world, and we bless You for having redeemed the world by Your holy cross." They had a great veneration for all chapels, for all crosses, and for all that had any relation to the worship of God. As soon as any one addressed them, they wished him peace, and instructed him in the way to gain it. If any one appeared to them to have strayed from the way of salvation, they endeavored to bring him back in a mild and humble manner. In their sermons they spoke ingenuously whatever was inspired them by the Holy Spirit, pointed out the true way to heaven, showed what were the duties of charity, and endeavored to bring all to love and fear the Creator and keep His holy commandments.

When they were asked from what country they came, and to what profession they belonged, they replied: "We are penitents come from Assisi;" for they would not as yet give the name of religion to their society. There were worthy people who received them with pleasure; but there were many others who disapproved of their habit, their institute, their discourses, imagining also that it was dangerous to give them house-room, and that alms ought not even to be given to them; so that these poor of Jesus Christ, cast off on all sides, had often to pass the nights under porticos.

Bernard and Giles went as far as Florence. A pious individual named Guy offered them some money, which they refused, and when it was wished to know from them, why, being so poor, they would not take it, they made this answer: "We have left all that we possessed, according to the evangelical counsel. We have voluntarily embraced poverty, and we have renounced the use of money." So perfect a detachment, joined to an ardent zeal for the

---

[32] Ps. 54 (55): 25.

salvation of souls, and to sublime virtues, and particularly a patience full of meekness and charity in the midst of insults and injurious treatment, caused them to be looked upon in the town as holy personages; they were consulted in cases of conscience, and dwellings were offered them.

While these Apostolic men continued their mission, Francis, guided by the spirit of God, returned to the hut at Rivo Torto, where he received four additional disciples: Constantius, or John of St. Constantius; Barbarus; Bernard of Viridant, or Vigilantius; and Sylvester, who was a priest. He was the first in the order, and his vocation was marvelous, of which the following are the circumstances.

He had sold some stones to St. Francis for the church of St. Damian, and had received the payment of their value. When he saw him preside over the distribution of the property of Bernard de Quintavalle, he complained of having been injured in the sale of the stones, and demanded a compensation. The servant of God, who did not choose to have any dispute with him on the subject, taking a bag full of money, gave him handfuls, saying: "Take this for the payment you demand from me, but which I do not owe you." He offered him some a second time, but Sylvester would not take it, but left him well satisfied with what he had got. At night the injustice of what he had done occurred to him; he conceived a sincere sorrow for it, asked pardon of God, and promised to restore what he had extorted to the prejudice of the poor.

Nevertheless, he formed his opinion of Francis according to the ideas of the world, and he looked with disgust on his mode of life. God was pleased to will that he should be cured of this prejudice, which was dangerous for his salvation, and that he should surrender himself to the saint as one of his disciples, which was effected by means of a mysterious dream. During the night he saw a horrible dragon, which surrounded the town of Assisi, as if about to destroy it, together with the entire country. Francis immediately came forth, and from his mouth there came forth a golden cross, which reached up to heaven, and the arms of it extended to the extremities of the earth, and its splendor put the dragon to flight. Having had this dream three successive nights, he perceived in it something divine, and he went and related it to Francis, with the minutest exactness. This humble servant of Jesus Christ, far from having the least complacency at it, only made use of it to admire the goodness of God who grants such favors, and to animate himself to combat the infernal dragon with renovated energy, and publish the glory of the cross of our Savior. But Sylvester, profiting by the grace attached to the vision, was not satisfied with restoring what he had unjustly extorted; he resolved, moreover, to leave all that he possessed, to embrace poverty under the guidance of Francis, which his affairs did not permit him to carry into execution till the end of the year 1209. St. Bonaventure says, that an authentic proof of the truth of the vision was the holiness of the life he led when in the order. In fact, he undertook so sincerely to walk in the footsteps of Jesus Christ, and made such vast progress in prayer, that, according to the account of this blessed Father, he conversed with God in a manner nearly similar to what is written of Moses: "That the Lord spoke to him as a man is accustomed to speak to his friend."[33]

Francis, full of the tenderest feelings for his children, was desirous of having them all assembled together. He entreated the Lord, who had in former times congregated the people of Israel dispersed among the nations, to do him a similar favor in regard to his small family, and his prayer was heard.[34] The six who were out on missions returned to Assisi from various places, as if they had acted in concert, without having any notice given them. The pleasure which their return gave him was greatly increased by the sincere and modest recital which they made him of all that had passed in their travels for the glory of God and the benefit of their neighbor. They gave an account, with evident joy, of the outrages and blows they had endured and suffered, pleased to have been found worthy to undergo those trials in the service of Jesus Christ. The last comers envied them, and were only consoled by the thought and hope that a time would come when they would be employed in this holy warfare, and, should an opportunity be given them, of displaying equal courage; the seniors embraced the latter, and congratulated them on having chosen this holy estate of life: they all exhorted each other to perseverance.

Their common Father brought them up in the practice of the most rigorous penances, but with the utmost mildness and kindness. He did not impose upon them any considerable number of prayers because he was not desirous of compelling devotion, and rather wished that these exercises of piety should be spontaneous. He only then prescribed to them to say daily, for each part of the Divine Office, the Lord's Prayer three times, and to hear Mass, at which he desired they should employ themselves in meditating on the mystery. It is, in fact, the very best way of assisting at the Holy Sacrifice, and the faithful should be advised to practice it. But those are not to be censured who make use of vocal prayer during Mass, provided they do so with attention and piety in the very spirit of the mystery; since there is nothing in that but what is good, and because, moreover, every one has not the talent of meditation.

The servant of God, considering that the number of his brethren increased, thought seriously of forming a Rule for them, and having assembled the eleven, the number they then were, he said to them: "I see, my dear brethren, that God, in His infinite goodness, proposes to extend our society; it is therefore necessary that we should prescribe for ourselves a Rule of Life, and go and give an account thereof to the most holy Roman Pontiff; for I am persuaded that in matters of faith, and in such as concern Religious Orders, nothing can be done which is pure and stable without his consent and

---

[33] Exod. 33:55.

[34] Ps. 146:2.

approbation.[35] Let us then go and find our Mother, the Holy Roman Church. Let us make known to our Holy Father the Pope, what God has deigned to begin through our ministry, in order that we may pursue our course according to his will, and under his orders."

A celebrated Bishop of France said, in an assembly of his Clergy:[36] "Paul, having returned from the third heaven, came to see Peter, in order to give a form to all future ages, and that it be established forever, that, however learned or holy we may be, were any of us another St. Paul, we must see Peter." These sentiments are in entire accordance with those of St. Francis, and contain an important principle, from which it is easy to deduce the consequence.

All the disciples applauded the proposal of their master, declaring that they were ready to receive the rule that he would give them, and to go to Rome to solicit its confirmation. Francis betook himself to prayer, and composed,[37] in a plain, unadorned style, in twenty-three chapters, a Rule of Life, the immovable basis of which was the observance of the Gospel; to which he added some exercises, which he considered necessary for the sake of uniformity. Besides the three vows of Poverty, Chastity, and Obedience, they renounced all possessions whatsoever, and they bound themselves to live on charity without ever receiving money. Clerks and laymen were alike admitted to embrace this Institute, under the name of Friars Minor. There were also some regulations relative to the Divine Office, prayer, the practice of virtue, fasts, the bareness of the feet, preaching, and the missions, which will be noticed when we come to speak of the second rule which the Patriarch gave in the year 1223, which they keep in his Order, and which is nothing more than an abridgment of the first. This last having been read and accepted, Francis with his brethren set out for Rome, to which, through humility, he chose that Bernard de Quintavalle should lead them.

They pursued their journey with great simplicity, only speaking of God and of things calculated for edification; they often retired to some byplace for the purpose of praying, without troubling themselves where they should pass the night; and God raised up persons who received them hospitably. By an effect of His Providence, they went out of their way to go to Rieti, where they remained two days. Francis met in one of the streets an officer of the army,

---

[35] He spoke this in 1210, when there was no ecclesiastical law which obliged them to solicit this approbation. This was only required for all religious establishments by the fourth Lateran Council, in 1255, and it was renewed at the General Council of Lyons in 1274. Thus the sole motives of the Saint on this occasion were, the purity of his faith, and the inviolable attachment he bore to the Holy See.

[36] Based, Bishop of Meaux, in 1632, in his opening discourse to his clergy.

[37] A Flemish chronicle states that some of the most learned of his disciples worked at this with him. But the oldest writers of his Life assure us that it was his own composition, enlightened by the Holy Spirit; and the second rule proves this decisively, as well as the testimony he gives of it himself in his will.

whose name was Angelo Tancred.[38] He was quite unknown to him, but, nevertheless, he accosted him by his name, and said: "Angelo, you have worn long enough your spurs, your sword, and your belt; it is time that you should have a thick cord instead of a belt; the Cross of Jesus Christ instead of a sword; and mud and dust instead of spurs. Follow me, therefore, and I will make you a soldier of Jesus Christ." At the very moment the officer quitted all things, followed Francis, took his poor habit, and became his twelfth disciple, who now by their number resembled the twelve Apostles, whose lives they revered. This wonderful conversion shows that God sometimes moves sinners by his active and powerful grace; as when He said to Matthew, "Follow me," and Matthew followed Him.[39] But it must also make us reflect that, in the ordinary course of things, He invites to repentance by graces, the impressions of which upon the mind are not so active, and which have only progressive advances, each of which requires being faithfully responded to.

The holy Patriarch continued his route, placing his entire confidence in God; but the others became alarmed at their own simplicity, they were fearful that it would impede their design; but God removed their fears by a vision which their holy Father had. It seemed to him that he was walking along a way where there was a very high tree. Coming near it, he went under it to admire it, when all on a sudden he felt himself raised up in the air by divine power, so that he had reached the top of the tree, and that from thence he easily made the tallest branches bend quite to the ground. The Holy Spirit pointed out to him that this was a presage of the favorable issue of his application to the Apostolic throne. This filled him with joy, and his recital of it to his brethren renovated their courage.

The Bishop of Assisi, whom they found at Rome, received them with great kindness. The sight of them at first gave him some uneasiness, being apprehensive that it was their intention to leave his diocese, and that his people would be deprived of the examples of these holy men. But having learned from them the motive of their journey, he promised them to use his influence in their favor, and gave them hopes of succeeding through the intervention of Cardinal John of St. Paul, Bishop of Sabina, who was his intimate friend.

This prelate was of the Colonna family; he was the friend of the poor, and of all worthy persons; he was respected for his many eminent qualities, and had great authority at the Roman court. What the Bishop of Assisi had already told him of Francis and his companions, of their holy life, and of the singularity of their institute, had excited in him a great wish to see them. As soon as he had heard of their arrival, he had them brought to his palace, received them with great honor, and was so pleased with their conversation,

---

[38] He relates himself the circumstances of his conversion in a work he composed on the actions of St. Francis in the Valley of Rieti.

[39] Matt. 9: 10.

that, after having assured them of his favor, he begged them to consider him from thenceforward as one of themselves. And he declared himself their protector, and by his interference he soon procured for them the friendship of the principal persons in the Sacred College, and particularly that of Cardinal Ugolino, nephew to the Pope, and subsequently Pope by the name of Gregory IX.

Francis, who was anxious to get his affairs expeditiously brought to a termination, got himself introduced to the Pope by an officer of his acquaintance. The Pope, who was walking at that moment in a place called the Mirror,[40] and being deeply engaged respecting some difficult affairs of the Church, would not so much as listen to him, but repulsed him rudely as a stranger of no very respectable appearance. The servant of God humbly withdrew; and it is recorded that he then restored to sight a blind man who had had his eyes torn out. The Holy Father saw in his sleep a palm-tree grow slowly at his feet and become a fine large tree.[41] Pleased with what he saw, but not understanding its meaning, he learnt by a divine inspiration that the palm-tree represented the poor man whom he had ungraciously repulsed the day before. As soon as it was day, he gave directions that the poor man should be sought for. He was found in the hospital of St. Anthony, and came to the feet of the Pope, and laid before him the rule of life he followed, with energetic though humble solicitations for his Holiness' approval thereof.

Innocent III, a Pontiff of great wisdom, acknowledged the candor and the admirable courage and zeal of the servant of God. He received him into his favor as one truly poor in Jesus Christ, and he was inclined to comply with his request; however, he postponed doing so, because his mode of life appeared novel to some of the Cardinals, and so much beyond what human strength could endure; the evil times, and the coldness of charity, making them think it very difficult and almost impossible for an order to subsist without possessing any effects whatever.

Cardinal John of St. Paul was indignant at these obstacles, and he expressed himself with great warmth to the other Cardinals in presence of the Pope. "If you reject the prayers of this poor man, on the pretense that his rule is novel, and too austere, let us take care that we do not reject the Gospel itself; since the rule of which he solicits the approval, is in conformity with what the Gospel teaches; for, to say that evangelical perfection, or the vow to practice it, contains anything unreasonable and impossible, is to blaspheme against Jesus Christ, the author of the Gospel." The Pope, struck with this reasoning, said to Francis: "My son, pray to Jesus Christ that He may make known His will to us, that so we may favor your wishes." The servant of God

---

[40] It was so called because it was an elevated spot exposed to the sun, commanding a beautiful view.

[41] He himself relates this vision to Cardinal Ugolini, his nephew; this Cardinal repeated it, and St Bonaventure published it. — Wading.

retired to pray, and soon after returned and set forth this parable.[42]

"Most Holy Father, there was a beautiful young girl, who was very poor, and who lived in a wilderness. The king of the country, who saw her, was so charmed with her beauty that he took her for his wife. He lived some years with her, and had children, who all resembled their father, and had, nevertheless, the beauty of their mother; he then came back to his court. The mother brought up her children with great care, and after some time said to them: 'My children, you are born of a great king, go and find him, tell him who you are, and he will give you all that is befitting your birth. As to myself, I will not leave this desert, and I even cannot.' The children went to the king's court, who, seeing their resemblance to himself, and that they had the beauty of their mother, received them with pleasure, and said to them: 'Yes, you are my true children, and I will support you as the children of a king; for, if I have strangers in my pay, if I maintain my officers with what is served at my table, how much more care should I not have for my own children, the offspring of so beautiful a mother? As I love the mother extremely, I will keep the children she has had by me at my court, and I will feed them at my table.'

"This king, most Holy Father," continued Francis, "is our Lord Jesus Christ. This beautiful girl is poverty, which, being everywhere despised and cast off, was found in this world as in a desert. The King of kings coming down from heaven, and coming upon earth, was so enamored of her, that He married her on the manger. He has had several children by her in the desert of this world, Apostles, Anchorites, Cenobites, and many others, who have voluntarily embraced poverty. This good mother sent them to their Father with the marks of royal poverty, as well as of her humility and obedience. This great King received them kindly, promising to maintain them, and saying to them: I who cause my sun to shine on the just and on sinners, who give my table and my treasures to pagans and to heretics, food, clothing, and many other things, how much more willingly shall I give to you what is necessary for you, for you, and all those who are born in the poverty of my much-cherished Spouse.

"It is to this celestial King, most holy Father, that this Lady, His spouse, sends her children whom you see here, who are not of a lower condition than those who came long before them. They do not degenerate; they have the comeliness both of their Father and their mother, since they make profession of the most perfect poverty. There is, therefore, no fear of their dying of poverty, being the children and heirs off the immortal King, born of a poor mother, of the image of Jesus Christ, by the virtue of the Holy Spirit; and being brought up in the spirit of poverty in a very poor order. If the King of heaven promises that such as imitate Him shall reign with Him eternally, with how much more confidence ought we not to believe that He will give them what He usually gives, and with so much liberality, to the good and to the bad."

---

[42] Three of his companions report the parable at length. St. Bonaventure only gives an abridgment, but which contains the gist.

The Pope listened very attentively to the parable and to its application. He was greatly pleased with it, and had no doubt but that Jesus Christ spoke by the mouth of Francis. He was also convinced by an interior light of the Holy Spirit, that in him a celestial vision which he had had some days before would be accomplished, and which, as St. Bonaventure informs us, he himself related. While he slept, he saw that the Lateran Church was on the point of falling, when a poor and miserable man supported it on his shoulders. On which he exclaimed: "Yes truly, it is that man who will support the Church of Jesus Christ by his works and by his doctrine." He thus foretold the great service Francis and his children would render to the universal Church, which indeed they have rendered, and, for the last six centuries, have not ceased to render; this was what was prefigured by the vision; although it has been remarked as something very singular, that the Lateran Church has been repaired, improved and ornamented by three Popes, the children of the blessed Patriarch, to wit, Nicholas IV, Sixtus IV, and Sixtus V.

Innocent III, moved and greatly affected by these celestial portents, conceived for Francis a most tender friendship, which he preserved ever after. He approved his rule verbally, granted him several other favors, and promised many more. After having received in his own hands the profession of the founder, and of those who accompanied him, he directed him to preach penance in all parts, and to labor for the extension of the Catholic faith. In order to enable them to employ themselves more freely in preaching, and to assist the priest with greater dignity in the performance of the holy mysteries, he directed that the lay brethren who were then with them, should receive the Tonsure, and wear small crowns;[43] he even conferred minor orders on them, and deacon's orders on Francis, whom he constituted Superior General of all the Religious of the Order of Friars Minor, present and to come.[44] Those who were present promised obedience to Francis, and Francis promised to obey the Pope. The pious Pontiff gave the new Patriarch, with paternal kindness, instructions in various matters which related to the well-being and strengthening of the Institution, and he assured him of his peculiar favor; and finally, having embraced each one of them, he gave them his blessing, and dismissed them filled with joy and consolation.

---

[43] It was a singular and personal favor, which this Pontiff and his successors did not extend, and which it was not necessary to extend; because, soon after, there were in the Order a great number of clerks. Moreover, it was necessary to adhere to the difference established by the general law of the Church, and by the special disposition of the rule, between the two states of clerks and lay-brethren who compose the Order of Friars Minor; although they are both religious and members of the Order.

[44] We cannot doubt but that St. Francis was a deacon. For, besides that his three companions who wrote his Life, state that Pope Innocent III gave him the deaconship, St. Bonaventure expressly says that Francis, the Levite of Jesus Christ, sang the Gospel at a solemn mass: "Celebrantes Missarum Solemnia. Levita Christi Francisco sacmm Evangelium decantante." [In Ecclesiastical Latin, *levita* is used for a deacon. — Editor]

We have witnessed these favors renewed in 1723 by Innocent XIII, of happy memory, the fifth Pope of the ancient and illustrious house of the Counts of Segni, to which Innocent III belonged. The Holy Father, assisted by four Cardinals, had the goodness to preside at the general chapter of the Order of St. Francis, held at Rome in the convent of Ara Cœli, making known to all Christendom on that splendid occasion, that he looked upon the Friars minor as his children, as much from family affection, as from his dignity of supreme Pontiff.

The illustrious author of the "Variations," who quotes the abbot of Ursperg, says that it was to give the Church true poor, more denuded and more humble than the false poor of Lyons, that Pope Innocent III approved the institution of the Friars Minor assembled under Francis, who was a model of humility, and the wonder of the age.[45] The false poor, who are also known by the name of Vaudois,[46] and are placed in the number of heretics by Pope Lucius III, assumed the exterior of poverty and humility, although they had none of the spirit of poverty and humility. They were filled with hatred of the Church and its ministers, whom they reviled in their secret assemblies. In 1212 they feigned submission, and had the daring to go to Rome, to solicit the approbation of the Holy See for their sect, but they were rejected by the Pope, and from that time were considered as obstinate and incorrigible heretics.

Conrad, abbot of Ursperg, who was at Rome when they came there in 1212 with Bernard their master, remarks that the Friars Minor[47] were very different from the false poor, practiced poverty with sincerity, and were free from all errors; that they went bare footed in winter, as well as in summer; that they received no money, and lived wholly on alms, and were in everything obedient to the Holy Apostolic See; an obedience which will ever be a mark by which true virtue may be distinguished from false. Moreover, the strongest ties must always invariably attach the Order of Friars Minor to the Holy See, which is the center of all the faithful. The Order was born there; is in immediate dependence on it; has received numberless benefits from it; and its blessed Patriarch engaged solemnly to obey Pope Innocent III and his successors.

---

[45] Hist, des Variations, tom. 2, lib. 2, n. 83 and 84.

[46] So called from Peter Valdo, a merchant of Lyons, born in the village of Vaud in Dauphiny, on the Rhone, the chief of the sect.

[47] The abbot of Ursperg says in the same place, that the Friars Minor took at first the name of "Poor Minors," which they afterwards dropped, lest the title of poverty, which they practiced, should appear ostentatious, and make them vanglorious. Nevertheless, no other author of the Order mentions this name; and in the sixth chapter of the rule, which was approved by Pope Innocent III, it was directed that those who should profess it, should call themselves Friars Minor. The other name may have been given them by some and the abbot may have thought that they had taken it.

CHAPTER III

ST. MARY OF THE ANGELS

He leaves Rome with his friars for the valley of Spoleto—God provides for his necessities—He stops at a deserted church—Consults God on his mission, and returns to the cottage of Rivo-torto—His sufferings there—The instructions he gives—God shows him to his brethren under a most marvellous aspect—The church of St. Mary of the Angels is given to him—He establishes himself there, with his Friars.

RANCIS, finding himself protected by the Almighty, and authorized by the Pope, acquired great confidence. He placed his most apostolical Order under the immediate protection of the holy Apostle, whose tomb he visited. He took leave of the Cardinals, John of St. Paul, and Ugolino, whom he made acquainted with his intentions, and to whom he expressed his great gratitude; then he took his departure from Rome with his twelve companions, and bent his steps to the Valley of Spoleto, there to practice and preach the Gospel.

On the way he conversed with them on the means of adhering faithfully to the rule, and relative to the manner in which they should strive to attain perfection, so that they might be examples to others. One day the conference lasted so long, that the hour for their meal passed by without their having stopped; finding himself tired, they went a little out of the way to rest. They were very hungry, but they had no means of satisfying their craving. There then came to them a man who brought them a loaf, and immediately disappeared, without their having had it in their power to notice from what side he had come, or which way he had gone from them. Then, says St. Bonaventure, divine Providence came to the aid of the poor of Jesus Christ, when all human assistance failed them. They were well aware that the company of their holy founder procured them this favor from Heaven; and the miraculous nourishment they had just received, which renovated the strength of their minds as well as that of their bodies, by the interior consolation they received from it, inspired them with a firm resolution never to swerve from the poverty to which they had devoted themselves, under any circumstances whatsoever.

Pursuing their route towards Orta, they came in the plain near that town to a Church which had been deserted, and where, having offered up their prayers, they agreed to stop, until such time as they should learn where it was

God's intention they should settle themselves. From thence they went, daily, to the town to preach penance in the public places; and it was with much fruit for the salvation of souls. The people began to feel attached to them; and as they saw that on their quest they refused everything but what was strictly necessary, they took them many things to the church in which they had retired, and those considered themselves fortunate who could make themselves useful to them. They even came in crowds to see them, and to listen to the discourses of these new men, whose actions and whose speech made them appear as persons descended from heaven.

But Francis, who found that this concourse of people interrupted and disturbed their spiritual exercises, determined to leave this place. The very beauty of it decided him to do so. It was a most agreeable spot; on one side there were meadows covered with beautiful flowers; on the other, a thick wood, where birds caroled the livelong day; near the church there was a fine spring and a rivulet, whose waters murmured pleasantly around them; the view of the whole plain, with that of the town beyond it on the heights, was all that could be wished. The holy man was fearful lest so delicious an abode should enervate the minds of his disciples, that the vigor of their intellect, so requisite for penitential reflections, should become relaxed when surrounded by objects so pleasant to the senses; and lest that which inspired gladsomeness should make them lose the seriousness necessary in prayer, and deprive them of the spiritual delight which is felt therein. Thus, as a skillful general who was the leader of the soldiers of Jesus Christ, and only followed His intentions, he made his little band raise their camp at the end of a fortnight, and resume their march towards the Valley of Spoleto.

In the way they counseled together whether they should communicate with the world, or whether they should retire into some solitary retreat. Francis, not choosing to trust either to his own fights or to those of his companions, had recourse with them to prayer, to ascertain what the will of God was on this head; and he learned by a revelation, St. Bonaventure says, that God had sent him expressly to gain souls which the devil was endeavoring to draw away from Jesus Christ. He therefore resolved to dedicate himself to this holy employment, and to five a fife which should be useful to his neighbor rather than to himself; being likewise animated thereto by the example of Him of whom St. Paul said: "One died for all."[1] With this view he continued his route to the Valley of Spoleto, and brought his brethren to the hut at Rivo Torto, near Assisi, where he had been before.

One must feel surprised that St. Francis, with all the assurances he had of his vocation, could have doubted for a single instant that he had been sent by God for the spiritual service of his neighbors. But his doubts only had their rise in the powerful attractions he had for contemplation, which the tenderness of his conscience made him fearful of resisting, by employing himself in the

---

[1] 2 Cor. 5: 14.

exercises of an active life; and it was this that lessened his inclination for the functions of Apostolicity; for, according to the doctrine of the Fathers, and of Saint Bernard in particular,[2] there are no more worthy ministers of the Gospel than such as devote themselves to conversation with God in retreat, and who leave that retreat to preach the doctrines of salvation only when they have reason to think that God calls upon them so to do. Our Lord, who thus in his wisdom permitted that His servant should labor under this uncertainty, revealed to him already that he was destined to labor for the salvation of souls, and we shall see, further on, that He assured him again by other revelations.

The hut in which these men devoted to evangelical poverty had retired was so small and so confined, that, far from being able to lie at full length in it, there was barely room for them to sit, insomuch so, that their Father was obliged to assign to each his place by writing his name on the beams, in order that they might pray and take their rest without being disturbed. They remained some time in this miserable habitation, which might be looked upon more as a tomb for the living, or rather for such as were dead to the world. They bore it for the love of God, with more fraternal charity and joy than can be described. The life they led there was so laborious, and so poor, that frequently, not having a morsel of bread, necessity compelled them to search the country for herbs and roots, which they ate with satisfaction; preferring to be nourished with tears rather than with any other food.

Their most frequent exercise was prayer, and that more mental than vocal, because they had not as yet books for saying the Divine Office. A wooden cross, of moderate size, which Francis had fixed in the middle of the hut, round which they prayed, served them instead of a book. They meditated on it unceasingly, and read in it with the eyes of faith, instructed by the example of their saintly chief, who often discoursed to them on the Passion and Cross of Jesus Christ.

However, they wished to learn from him what vocal prayers they ought to recite; and he told them, as our blessed Savior had told the Apostles:[3] This is the prayer that you will say: "Our Father, who art in heaven, hallowed be Thy name," etc. To which he added the Act of Adoration which he had before taught them: "Lord Jesus Christ, we adore You in all the churches in the whole world, and we bless You for having redeemed the world by Your holy Cross." He likewise taught them to praise God in all things, to make use of all creatures, to raise up their minds to Him, to have great respect for priests, to be inviolably attached to the true faith, which is believed and taught by the Holy Roman Church, and to confess it plainly. His faithful disciples put in practice all that he taught them, and conformed to all his maxims, which they did in still greater perfection after the marvel which we are about to relate.

Francis being one Saturday in Assisi, in order to preach on the Sunday

---

[2] Bern, *in Cant.* serm. 41 and 64.

[3] Matt 6: 2.

morning in the cathedral, as it was his custom to do, retired to a small shed in a garden belonging to the Canons of the Church, to pass the night in contemplation, which he usually did. About midnight, a fiery car of great brilliancy, on which there was a globe as bright as the sun, and which gave a light equal to that of noon, entered into the hut in which the brethren were collected, and moved round it three times. Some of them were watching and praying; the others, who were taking a little rest, awoke. It is not to be expressed what was their astonishment when they found themselves enlightened, as well interiorly as exteriorly, by this penetrating light, which manifested to them the state of their consciences.

St. Bonaventure remarks on the subject of this marvelous light, on the testimony of those who had been witnesses of it, that they understood that, by this luminous and burning figure, God represented to them the lively and holy flames which illuminated their Father, who, though absent in the body, was present with them in spirit, in order that, as true Israelites, like unto Eliseus,[4] they might look up to and imitate this new Elias, whom He had appointed the light and guide for spiritual men. Doubtless, he continues, the Lord, who opened the eyes of the servant of Eliseus, that he might see around that Prophet, that "the mountain was full of horses and chariots of fire,"[5] would also, at the prayer of Francis, open those of his disciples to show them the marvel which was operating in their favor.

At his return from Assisi, the Father conversed with his children on the prodigy which they had witnessed, and took occasion from it to confirm them in their vocation. He entered in detail as to the secret dispositions of their consciences; he foretold them many circumstances relative to the increase of his Order; he made known to them, in fine, so many sublime things beyond human ken, that they became perfectly aware that the Spirit of God rested fully on him, and that their greatest security would be in a conformity of themselves to his life and doctrine.

People were so greatly moved and affected by his virtues and his discourses, that many presented themselves to join his Order, but he declined as yet to receive them, because the hut was too small for the twelve he had; but he availed himself of the opportunity to say to these: "My dear brethren, God, in His goodness, has made known to me that He proposes to increase our poor family. I cannot receive those who wish to join us, until I have a place large enough to admit all. We require a larger habitation, as well as a church, where we may hear mass, say the Divine Office, and deposit in peace those of our society who may die. Let us therefore go to our Lord Bishop and the Canons. Let us earnestly entreat of them, for the love of God, to cede to us some church near the town, and to put our rising Order under cover in some part of their domain. If they cannot assist us, we will go and ask the same

---

[4] 4 Reg. 11:12.

[5] 4 Reg. 1:11.

favor of the Religious of Mount Soubazo."

The Bishop of Assisi and the Canons had it not in their power to promote their views, having no church at their disposal; but the Abbot of Mount Soubazo, with the consent of the community, granted him for himself and his brethren the chapel of St. Mary of the Angels, or of Portiuncula, which he had put into repair; but he added this condition, that, if the Institution became more extended, this church should be always considered the place of its origin, and the chief monastery.

Francis received the present, and accepted the condition with great thankfulness, and came and told his brethren of it, expressing the pleasure he felt, in having, for the first church of his Order, a church of the Blessed Virgin, very small and very poor, obtained by begging, and in which he had first taken upon himself the Apostolic life. On the same day he went to St. Mary of the Angels, where a pious ecclesiastic of Assisi was living, whose name was Peter Mazancoli, to whom the care of that church had been entrusted after it had been repaired. He communicated to him the cession which the Religious of Mount Soubazo had made to his Order, and begged him to come and live with his brethren.

As true piety, which is charity itself, is never jealous, and is delighted in what is of advantage to its neighbors, the ecclesiastic embraced Francis and assured him how desirous he was to see the Blessed Virgin honored and praised in this place, which she loved, where concerts by the Angelic host were constantly heard. As a proof of this, he called a laborer of the vicinity, who certified to have several times heard in the night melodious canticles, and to have seen a great light come forth from the windows.

The experience of Francis himself was an additional proof. For, being in prayer during the following night in order to recommend his family to the protection of the Blessed Virgin, he saw on the altar, by means of a splendid light, our Savior Jesus Christ, His holy Mother, and a multitude of angels, who cast upon him looks of great benignity. He adored, and recited these words: "O most holy Lord, King of heaven, Redeemer of the world, sweet Love! and thou, O Queen of angels! by what excess of goodness do you come down from heaven into this small and poor chapel?" He immediately heard this reply: "I am come with my Mother to settle you and yours in this place, which is very dear to us." All then disappeared, and Francis exclaimed: "Truly this place is holy, which ought to be inhabited by angels, rather than by men. As long as I possibly can, I will not leave it; it shall be, for me and mine, an eternal monument of the goodness of God!" It became, in fact, a great object of devotion and veneration for himself and his brethren, particularly after it had been revealed to him that, among all the temples consecrated under the name of the Blessed Virgin, this was the one for which she had the greatest attachment.

At break of day he sent for the other religious by his companions, with directions to bring with them the few pieces of furniture which they had in the hut at Rivo Torto, in order to place them in the house adjoining the church of St. Mary of the Angels, which the pious ecclesiastic willingly gave up to them.

He communicated to the new guests the sanctity of the place they were about to inhabit, and recommended them to live therein holily, never ceasing to praise the Lord. Then he said to them: "You must be very grateful to the Benedictine Fathers for the benefit they have conferred upon us. They have consecrated all the habitations we shall hereafter have, by this house of God, which is the model of the poverty which must be observed in gill the houses of our Order, and the precious germ of the holiness which we must seek for in it."

But, in order to show that he did not live there as on a property wholly his, as well as for a mark of his gratitude to his benefactors, he took care to have taken yearly to the abbey of Mount Soubazo, as a ground-rent, a basket of fish, a species of mullet, which is taken in quantities in the river Asi, or Chiascio, near the church of St. Mary of the Angels. The Friars Minor have always cherished the feelings of the blessed Patriarch for the Order of St. Benedict. They will ever manifest, with sincerest gratitude, that it is to this great Order, so ancient and so celebrated in the Church, that they are indebted for their first establishment, and for many other benefits.

St. Francis gives his cloak to a poor knight. —Giotto

Vision of the Palace. —Giotto

The Crucifix of San Damiano speaks to St. Francis. —Giotto

St. Francis renounces the goods and affairs of the world. —Giotto

Innocent III dreams that Francis will save the Church. —Giotto

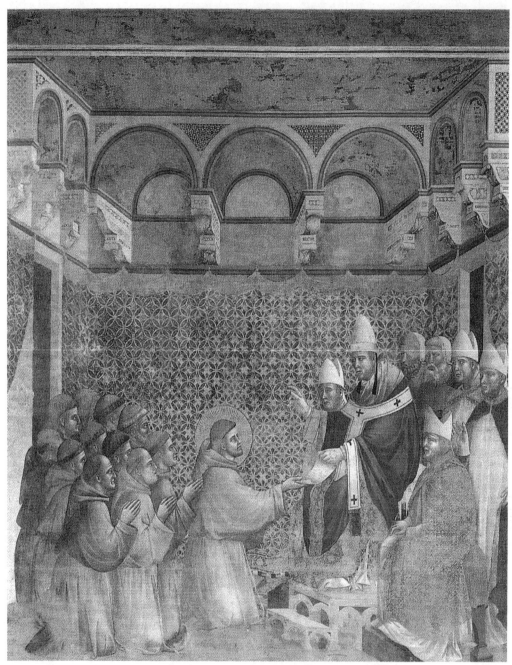

Pope Innocent III confirms the Rule and approves the order. —Giotto

Vision of St. Francis on a fiery chariot. —Giotto

THE LIFE OF ST. FRANCIS OF ASSISI

BOOK II

CHAPTER I
APOSTOLIC PREACHING

He receives many novices—Instructs and models them—Sends them to different provinces of Italy—What he says on this occasion—He departs for Tuscany, and passes by Perugia, where he makes a prediction which is accomplished—Many young men enter his Order—They build a house for him near Cortona—His miraculous fast during Lent—He commands the devils, and they obey him—He cures many miraculously—He preaches at Florence—Makes a prediction—Preaches in various places in Tuscany—What his friars are doing in other places.

A. D. 1210

IT WAS THEREFORE in the small church of St. Mary of the Angels, or of Portiuncula,[1] that Francis laid the foundations of the Order of Friars Minor, which spread over the whole earth with wonderful rapidity. This holy place was, as it were, the cradle of the Institute, and the nursery of the houses of the religious; the source which supplied a great river, which was divided into various channels; the citadel from whence numerous brave warriors went forth to encounter the enemies of the Church; the school which has produced a very great number of saints, and a multitude of learned men, whose doctrine and piety have been equally celebrated.

The new habitation, less confined than the hut of Rivo Torto, enabled the Patriarch to receive the postulants who had before presented themselves; among whom may be noticed, Leo, Rufino, Massé of Marigan, and Juniper—Leo, whom Francis chose for his confessor and secretary, and whom he generally called Pecorella di Dio (the sheep of God), on account of his admirable candor. Rufino, of whom he said: "I learnt, by a revelation, that he is one of the most faithful and of the most pure souls that there was in the world, and I should have no fear of giving him, though in a mortal body, the title of Saint, since he is already canonized in heaven." Massé, whom he often sent, instead of going himself, to converse with persons of piety, in order not to be

---

[1] Some persons have imagined that the Saint had given the name of Portiuncula to this church, as to the small part he had wished for, and had received for the shelter of his little flock; it is even recorded in the first lesson of the second Nocturn of the festival of the Portiuncula. However, St. Bonaventure expressly says that this chapel was called Portiuncula when St. Francis undertook to put it in repair. Both the one and the other are true. It had this name because of some portions of the land belonging to the Benedictines, as has been remarked, from the ancient legend; and St. Francis confirmed this name to it in consequence not only of the smallness of their numbers when it was given to them, but also from the title of Minors, which he gave his brethren, in order that they might always be the lowly and humble flock according to the Gospel.

interrupted in his own meditations, because this religious added great mildness and suavity of manner to a rare talent of speaking about heavenly things. Juniper, whom he found so valuable for his evangelical simplicity, for his contempt of himself, and for his great desire to attract upon himself the contempt of the world, that, alluding to his name, he used to say good-humoredly: "I wish to God we had a wood full of such Junipers."

The charitable father had all his children in his heart, and he brought them up with a tenderness truly maternal. He was the first to go from door to door, to ask charity to provide for their wants; sometimes he even went alone, to spare them the mortification of begging, under the impression that they might still retain the prejudices of the world on this head. But the weakness of his frame not admitting of his providing for all, and his religious being bound to subsist on charity alone, he resolved to teach them to solicit it for the love of God, and he made them the following exhortation, which they have recorded:

"My very dear brethren and well-beloved children, be not ashamed of soliciting alms, since our Lord became poor in this world for the love of us, and that, following His example, we have chosen this state of the most perfect poverty. For, if we have made this choice for the love of Jesus Christ, we must not blush at begging in our quality of poor. Heirs of the kingdom of God should not blush at what is a pledge of their heirship. Yes, we are heirs of heaven; this is a benefit which our Lord has obtained for us, to which He has given us a right, as He has to all those who choose to live in a state of holy poverty. I make known to you as a truth, that a great number of the most noble of the age will become members of the Order, who will consider it an honor to solicit alms, and who will look upon it as a favor to be permitted to do so. You, therefore, who are the very first of the Order, do this cheerfully; do not refuse to practice what you will have to teach these saintly personages. Go, then, and with the blessing of God solicit alms, full of confidence and joy, more than would be felt by him who should offer a hundred for one. For it is the love of God you offer in asking, when you say, 'For the love of God, bestow your charity on me'; and in comparison with this divine love, heaven and earth are as nothing."

To mitigate the reluctance still felt by some of them, he brought forward the two following motives: "The bread which holy poverty causes to be collected from door to door, is the bread of Angels, because it is the good Angels who inspire the faithful to bestow it for the love of God. It is thus that the words of the Prophet,[2] "Man ate the bread of Angels,"[3] are fulfilled in these holy poor ones. God has given the Friars Minor to the world in these latter times, that the elect may have it in their power to practice what will cause

---

[2] Ps. 77 (78): 29.

[3] This is literally understood of the manna which was prepared by the Angels; and, in the figurative sense, of the most holy Eucharist, which is called the Bread of Angels. The Saint in this place makes the application.

them to be glorified by the Supreme Judge, when He will address them in these mellifluous words: 'What you did to one of these, the least of My brethren, you did it to Me.'[4] It is pleasing to solicit charity in the capacity of a Friar Minor, whom our Master seemed to designate expressly by the appellation, the least of My brethren."[5]

The disciples, persuaded and moved by this appeal, went of their own accord to quest in the neighboring places, to get the better of the natural repugnance they felt to it. At their return they presented themselves to their father with satisfied countenances, which delighted him, and by a holy emulation they were proud of the things they had collected for the love of God. One of them returning one day with much cheerfulness, singing loudly the praises of the great Benefactor of men, Francis took from him the weighty wallet, which was full of bits of bread, placed it on his own shoulders, kissed the shoulders of him who had carried it, and came and said publicly: "So it is that I wish my brethren to go always on the quest, and return from it: ever joyful, and glorifying God for all the good which He does in our favor."

The blessed founder employed himself day and night unceasingly inspiring them with the love and practice of the most sublime virtues; he warned and exhorted each one of them in particular, and he made discourses to them when collected, on the most essential heads; and this again he enforced by his own good example, knowing that they were called by God to train up those who would embrace his rule in the different parts of the earth, and that on the instruction of the one depended that of the others. What he taught them on the subject of poverty, mortification, obedience, prayer, humility, and generally on all the means of acquiring religious perfection, will be noticed at the end of the Life.

Under such a master, with the powerful assistance which they received from Heaven, they made in a short time such considerable progress, that the latest corners were not less competent for the exercise of the evangelical ministry than the first. Altogether animated with the same spirit, watching, fasting, praying, penetrated with the fear of God, full of holy desires, they resembled in a great degree the primitive Church confined in the supper-room. Francis, who was perfectly acquainted with their most inward feelings, and with the intentions of Divine Providence, thought that he ought not to delay sending them forth on missions; according to the idea of St. Chrysostom,[6] who says that the Apostles, who were commissioned to labor in the conversion of the world, were necessarily separated, and that it would have been very prejudicial to the interests of the universe had they kept together longer.

But, as he had not yet heard them preach, he desired prudently to judge by

---

[4] Matt. 25: 40.

[5] He alludes in this to the name of Friars Minor, which is contained in these words of Jesus Christ: *"Quamdiu non fecistis uni de minoribus his, nec Mihi fecistis."*

[6] S. Chrysostom. *Homil 87. in Joan.* circ. med.

his own experience of their respective talents. Having assembled them together, he desired Bernard de Quintavalle to speak on the mysteries of religion. He immediately obeyed, and spoke beautifully on the several points. Peter of Catania was directed to set forth the greatness of God, which he did with as much facility and learning as if he had been long perfect in the art of preaching. A third was called upon to give an exhortation on avoiding sin, and practicing virtue, which he complied with in powerful language. In short, they all handled the subjects which were allotted to them, so as plainly to show that wisdom was given to them from on high.

After they had made this essay in preaching, or rather this masterpiece of eloquence, Jesus Christ, who had inspired their thoughts and words, appeared in the midst of them in the form of a very beautiful young man, and gave His blessing to each of them successively, with wonderful benignity. This astonishing vision threw them into a rapturous transport; after which, Francis addressed them as follows:

"My brethren, and dear children, give abundant thanks to God most powerful, and to His Son, our Lord Jesus Christ, for having deigned to have communicated celestial treasures through the speeches of the most simple of men; for it is God who causes infants to speak, who opens the mouths of little children, and makes the tongues of the most ignorant eloquent: His goodness renders Him compassionate to the world, which is loaded with crime. He has resolved to warn men of the woes into which they are plunging themselves; and in order to root out from amongst them the works of the devil, which are sins,[7] He has chosen vile and despicable preachers,[8] so that no one shall have reason to glorify himself before Him, and that every one shall acknowledge that all the good which is done comes from Him. Although there are few among you of whom it can be said that they have worldly wisdom, or are powerful or noble, yet it is you whom the Lord hath chosen for this important work. It is His will that you should go into all parts to honor Him by your actions and by your words, bringing to His fear and to His love such as have strayed into evil ways.

"Prepare yourselves therefore to set forth; gird your loins[9] according to the commands of Jesus Christ; be courageous; put on the armor of faith;[10] be devoted to the service of the Gospel; always prepared to let yourselves be carried away as clouds, whithersoever the Spirit of God may direct you, by the guidance of obedience, to shed the dew of the divine word on the dry and arid soil of hardened hearts.[11] For our Lord has not called you into this institute to think of nothing but saving your own souls quietly, without any fatigue, in the

---

[7] 1 John, 3: 8.

[8] 1 Cor. 1: 28, 29, and 26.

[9] Luke 12: 35.

[10] Ephes. 6: 11, 13, and 16.

[11] Isaiah 60:8.

hearts of your country, and in the bosom of your families; His intention is, that you carry His name and His faith into the nations, and before the kings of the earth.[12] Now, lest we should appear to be slow in carrying His will into execution, we will divide Italy amongst us; and soon after, we will make other missions into more distant countries."

To this discourse the disciples replied, that they were prepared for everything; that, having renounced their own will, they only waited the order to commence the journey; and that the distrust they had of themselves in consequence of their simplicity, was counterbalanced by the confidence they had in the assistance of the Almighty, which animated them.

The next morning Francis divided Italy among them, taking Tuscany for himself with Sylvester, who was the first priest in his Order, so that he might, by this arrangement, be at the shortest distance from St. Mary of the Angels, where he left some of the brethren to guide the novices whom he should send there.

Two reasons induced him to make his beginning in Italy. The first was, that it appeared to him to be just that the divine Word should be first spread in that country, of which the preachers were natives, as the Apostles had done in regard to the Jews. The second was, that he might judge from what they should effect among the Italians, what they were capable of effecting elsewhere: in which his judgment is to be admired.

He could not doubt but that the vocation of his children came from God; nevertheless, he used all the precautions which prudence dictated, because he knew that the Lord, who acts according to His good pleasure by secret and supernatural means, chooses that men on their part should pursue the ordinary course in all that depends on them. This is a sure ground-work, which is not only a rule in all that relates to salvation, but also is applicable to the affairs of this life.

The man of God, having commenced his route towards Tuscany, passed through Perugia, where he preached in the great Square, as is customary in Italy. Some young gentlemen, of the first families of the place, came also there for the exercises of the tournament, and made so much noise that the preacher could be no longer heard. As they continued their lance exercises, notwithstanding the remonstrance of the people, the Saint, turning to the side in which they were, addressed them in the following words with great animation:

"Pay attention, and learn what the Lord declares to you through me, who am His servant, and do not imagine to satisfy yourselves by saying, 'This is only a man from Assisi who speaks to you'" (A precaution he took because Perugia and Assisi, neighboring towns, were always opposed to each other). "What I tell you, I do not tell you as man. God has raised you above all the adjacent countries; in gratitude for which you should humble yourselves, not

---

[12] Acts 9: 15

merely in His eyes, but before all the world. But, on the contrary, your strength and your glory have so inflamed your pride, that you have pillaged and laid waste all that surrounds you, and you have killed no inconsiderable number. For which reason I declare to you that, unless you be speedily converted, and repair the damage you have done, the Lord, who suffers no evil to be committed with impunity, will take revenge on your sins. In order to create in you the greater dismay, He will suffer you to rise up one against the other, to excite a popular commotion, and to do yourselves much greater injury than any your neighbors could do to you."

He remained some time at Perugia, where they soon saw the effect of his threats. The nobles were irritated against the plebeians, the clergy joined the party of the nobles, and they came to blows; the people, who were the strongest, drove the others out of the town. The discomfited party, in order to be revenged, laid waste everything in the country which belonged to the people; who, by way of reprisals, pillaged the houses of the nobles, and massacred their servants and even their children. Indeed the disaster was so great, that, according to the prediction, armed neighbors could not have caused any greater.

The Perugians having thus, at their cost, discovered the holiness of the preacher, wished to retain him in their city, and entreated him to choose what place he pleased for his abode. Many young persons of pure morals joined his Order; one among others, whose vocation was very singular. As he was walking one day out of the town, his mind intent upon his wish to consecrate himself to God, Jesus Christ appeared to him, and said: "Man of desires, if you hope to be in the enjoyment of what you wish for, and to effect your salvation, take a religious habit and follow Me." He immediately asked into what Order he should enter. Our Lord answered him: "Join the new Order of Francis of Assisi." He then made this further inquiry: "Lord, when I shall have joined that Order, what mode of life shall I follow, to be more agreeable to You?" and this is the answer he received: "Lead the usual life; enter into no particular intimacies with your brethren; take no notice of the defects of others, and form no opinion to their disadvantage." These are admirable means for living holily and peaceably in a community. The young man came and offered himself to Francis, who knew that Jesus Christ had sent him, and admitted him immediately, and gave him the name of Brother Humble, on account of the humility he found in his heart.

At Cortona, to which place he next took the word of God, there was another young man named Guy, who, moved by his preaching, had invited him to dinner: "This young man," said Francis, "will enter our militia today, and will sanctify himself in this town." He was the oldest of his family, brought up in study and in virtue, and the excellence of whose conduct exceeded even that of his education. He frequented the churches and the sacraments, he gave great alms, and visited the sick to assist them; he wore a hair-shirt, and chastised his body severely, to enable him to preserve his virginal purity, which he had made a vow to do. After the dinner, he knelt down and petitioned for the habit of a Friar Minor, which he received in the principal church of the town, in the presence of a numerous concourse of people, after having first fulfilled two conditions which the father had prescribed for him: The first was, to give to the poor all that he had inherited by his right of primogeniture; the second was, to renounce all the rest of his fortune. It was in the same town that he lived a most holy life,[13] as had been foretold, honored by many miracles; and by permission of the Holy See, he is publicly invoked.

The love of prayer and retirement made Francis wish to find in the neighborhood of Cortona a fit place for building a house suitable for the education of his novices. Guy pointed one out to him in the valley, near a place called Celles. This location greatly pleased him, because it was solitary; and by the aid of some pious persons, he built a very poor dwelling, which he soon filled with novices, and where he received the celebrated Brother Elias, of whom we shall have much to say hereafter.

Having spent nearly two months in preaching at Cortona, and in forming his novices at the convent of Celles, he was inspired to pass over to a desert island in the middle of the lake of Perugia, for Lent was drawing near. He recommended the care of the house to Sylvester, without letting him know what his own intention was; and on Ash-Wednesday he caused himself to be taken to the island by a boatman, having with him only two loaves of bread. The boatman was a worthy man and his friend, and he begged him not to tell any one where he was, and only come to take him back on the Wednesday of Holy Week.

Having made himself there a sort of hut in one of the thickets, to preserve himself from the cold, he had his intercourse with God alone during two and forty days; and his fast was so rigorous, that of the two loaves he brought with him he only ate half a one. In the ecclesiastical history[14] we meet with examples of these miraculous fasts, of which the holy Fathers have had an assured knowledge, and which the weakness of human nature was enabled to sustain by virtue of the Spirit of God, which supported them. The fruit which they were to derive from it, was to animate the faithful to keep, with as much exactness as was in their power, the fasts prescribed by the Church, and particularly the fast of Lent, which many principal motives of religion render so venerable.[15]

On the Wednesday in Holy Week, the boatman went to fetch Francis and bring him back to Cortona. On the passage the Saint stilled a storm, by making the sign of the cross on the waves; and as soon as he had landed he went to the

---

[13] His life is given on the 12th of June, by the continuators of Bollandus.

[14] S. Greg. Naz. Carm. 47; Theodoret. *Rel. Hist.* cap. 26.

[15] S. Hierom. Epist. 21, ad Marcell; S. Aug. Epist. 36, ad Caful.

convent at Celles, where he passed the remainder of the Holy-Week with his brethren. His confidant did not think it necessary to keep the secret of the marvelous fast. The rumor spread, and many persons went to the island to see and venerate the hut in which he had lived. The miracles which were operated there by the merits of the Saint, induced some persons to build there; and gradually a small town arose, where later a church was built, with a convent of his Order, near a spring at which he had drunk, where sick were afterwards cured.

After the Easter solemnities, he placed a superior in the convent; then having tenderly embraced the religious, he made the sign of the cross on them, and separated himself from them to go to Arezzo.

This town was at that time greatly agitated by intestine dissensions, which were likely to bring on its entire ruin. Francis being lodged in the suburbs, where he had been hospitably received, saw over the town, with the penetrating sight which the Almighty had given him, devils who excited the citizens to massacre each other, and who appeared to be transported with joy. To put these evil spirits to flight, he sent Sylvester, as his herald, and gave him this command: "Go to the gate of the town, and standing before it, order the devils, in the name of the Almighty God, and in virtue of obedience, instantly to retire." Sylvester, who was a man of extraordinary simplicity, praising God beforehand for what was about to happen, went as fast as possible, and cried out with all his might "All you devils who are here, begone, go far from hence. It is in the name of God and of His servant, Francis, that I call upon you to go." At this very moment the citizens, who were on the point of flying to arms, came to an understanding on the points which were in dispute, and peace was restored to the town. On which St. Bonaventure remarks, that the obedience and humility of Francis had obtained for him that absolute power over the proud spirits who fear and fly from the sublime virtue of the humble.

It became known in Arezzo who the author was of so sudden a reconciliation, because the words which had been spoken by Sylvester had been heard. Francis was sought for and brought into the town in a sort of triumph, notwithstanding the efforts he made to escape from this honor. He preached in the great Square on the love of peace, and on the means of preserving it, pointing out to them that dissensions and quarrels came from, and are promoted by, the evil spirit. The magistrates entertained him at the town-house, and had a convent built for his Order according to his wishes, that is to say, according to holy poverty; in which he placed some worthy subjects who had presented themselves to him. A child was brought to him who was quite distorted; he took it into his arms, and it forthwith became straight. This miracle, and several others which he performed during his stay, proved that God had given him as much power over bodily complaints as over the evil spirits.

From Arrezo he bent his steps to Florence, preaching with great success throughout the route. The lords of Ganghereto received him with great respect, and were so pleased with the holiness of his life, that they begged his acceptance of a field and a small wood for the service of his religious. He set up a hut there, where his infirmities compelled him to remain some time. After preaching and prayer, to which he daily gave some time, one after the other, he employed himself in building a small wall round a spring of water which he got miraculously, and which still flows, the water of which God was pleased to render salutary.

As soon as his health was in some degree restored, he continued his way towards Florence, where he went to lodge in the hospital. The following day he preached in the town, and was listened to as a Saint. They gave him a small dwelling near the church of St. Gall, about five hundred paces from the city, in which he received several novices, who rendered themselves illustrious by their exalted virtues; among whom John Parent is particularly noticed, who was a native of Carmignano, near Pistoia, a lawyer of great note, first magistrate of Fescennia, or Citta Castellana, who, for his distinguished merit, had had granted to him the rights and privileges of Roman citizens.

His conversion was attributable to a very peculiar circumstance. As he was walking one evening in the environs of the town, he saw a swineherd who was endeavoring to drive his pigs into a stable, and who, being in a great passion because, instead of going in, they dispersed themselves in all directions, called out to them in his anger: "Swine, get into this stable as judges get into hell." He had scarcely said the words, when these animals went quietly in. That which might have appeared to this magistrate nothing but an impertinence, struck him, and made so strong an impression upon him, that, having seriously reflected on the dangers incurred by a judge (which are indeed very great) as to salvation he threw up his magistracy, and retired to Florence. There he saw Francis, examined his conduct, admired his virtues, and felt himself called by God to imitate him. An only son of his had a similar vocation. The father and the son divided their all among the poor, and became disciples of the Saint,[16] whose prophecy began thus to be fulfilled: that the wise and learned of the world would enter into his Order.

Such a conversion sets before us this important truth: that the Spirit breaths where He will;[17] that the Lord gives His grace sometimes to what is most common, most simple, and even most base, according to the notions of the world; that it is necessary to be attentive, that we may not receive the grace of God in vain;[18] and that, little as it may seem at first, by being carefully

---

[16] John Parent shone in the Order of S. Francis, by the holiness of his life, and by the splendor of his talents. He was elected General of the Order the year 1230, and governed it with great prudence. It has been noticed that he made all his visitations on foot and barefooted, in many parts Europe. —Wading ad ann. 1251, no. 25.

[17] John. 3: 8.

[18] 2 Cor. 6: 1.

attended to, it may have the most beneficial results. Not to be thankful for it, to neglect it, to resist it, is a heavy present loss, and running the risk of losing more.

While Francis was at St. Gall, he foretold a thing which the event justified a few years afterwards. Three men at Florence brought each a child to receive his blessing. As soon as he was apprised of it, he went into the garden and gathered five figs; then he came in, and gave one to the first of the children, one to the second, and three to the third, to whom he addressed the following words: "You will be my dear child." That one, when he had attained the proper age, took the habit of the Friars Minor, and was called Brother Angel, which he deserved by his angelic life, which was the fruit of his great devotion to the Blessed Virgin, from whom he received very marked favors.

From the month of October, 1211, to the beginning of the year 1212, the man of God visited the towns of Pescia, Pisa, San Miniato, Sarthiano, Cetona, and other places in Tuscany, where he made many wonderful conversions, and left some of his brethren to continue the work of God. We shall relate, at the end of his Life, the great honors which were publicly shown him; honors which he received with the greatest humility, and yet with the most generous sentiments.

The brethren whom he had dispersed in the other provinces of Italy, and who partook of his apostolic spirit, labored on their part with great zeal and success. They founded many establishments, and formed many disciples, whom they sent to the holy founder in order to their receiving the habit of the Order from him.

They mention particularly what happened at Bologna to Bernard de Quintavalle. As soon as he made his appearance, his extraordinary and very poor habit made him looked upon as a person not worthy of notice. He went to the great Square in order to preach the truth of salvation, and he went there several times without having collected an audience. Children and idle people surrounded him; some pulled him by the hood, others threw mud and stones at him; and he was daily assailed with fresh outrages, which he bore with exemplary patience.

A lawyer, having noticed this, made his reflections on it, and it occurred to him that his conduct might be attributed to virtue rather than insensibility. One day, then, he came up to Bernard and asked him who he was, and what he had come to do at Bologna. "You will know who I am," replied Bernard, "if you will take the trouble to read what I now offer you." It was the Rule of Francis, of which he had a copy, and which he placed in his hand. The lawyer having read it with astonishment, said to those who accompanied him: "I own I have never seen anything so perfect or so heroic as this mode of life. Those who ill-use this man are very criminal; he ought, on the contrary, to be loaded with honors, as a special friend of God." Then, addressing himself to Bernard, he said: "If you will follow me, I will give you a place in which you may serve the

Lord." Bernard, having accepted the offer, was taken to the house of his benefactor, who received him with affection, and gave him a house, which he furnished with everything necessary, and promised to protect him and his companions. After this, Bernard was so highly respected in Bologna, that people considered themselves fortunate if they could get near him, touch him, or even see him. This truly humbly man, mortified at the honor which was shown him, went to Francis, and said: "My Father, all is in good order in Bologna. But send any other religious thither rather than me, who may remain there; for I have no longer any hopes of being useful there: it is even to be feared that I may lose myself on account of the great honors I receive." This prudent mistrust of himself was as pleasing to the holy Father as the affection of the Bolognese, to which he responded by sending them several of his disciples, who subsequently spread the Order throughout all Romagna.

The holy Patriarch returned some time before Lent to St. Mary of the Angels, where his first care was to examine rigidly whether in his evangelical progress some worldly dust might not have adhered to him in consequence of his communications with seculars; and in those instances in which the extreme delicacy of his conscience gave him room for self-reproach, he purified Himself by very severe penitential observances. He then applied himself carefully to the formation of the novices, whom he had collected from various places, and he preached during the Lent at Assisi.

CHAPTER II

A LIGHT FOR A VAST SPACE

He preaches the Lent at Assisi, with great fruit—He consecrates, to Jesus Christ, Clare, and Agnes, her sister—Establishes Clare and Agnes in the Church of St. Damian—He erects a monastery there, the first one of his second Order, which he then instituted—He is troubled by a serious doubt, on which he consults his brethren—His doubt is cleared up by an oracle from heaven—He goes out to preach—He sighs for martyrdom—Asks permission of the Pope to preach to the infidels—Makes conversions at Rome, and establishes his Order there—Returns to Assisi, and leaves for the Levant—Embarks, but is obliged to put into a harbor in Sclavonia—Goes by sea to Ancona—A miracle which God performs in his favor— He converts a celebrated poet—Returns to Tuscany, and to St. Mary of the Angels—He falls sick—Wonderfully humbles himself—Tries a vocation.

IS DISCOURSES, backed by his example, and his prayers and exhortations, animated by an ardent zeal, were so efficacious, that in the town and county of Assisi a very great number of persons was converted, and the fire of divine love was kindled in every heart. "Then," says St. Bonaventure, using the words of the Holy Scriptures, "the vine of the Lord spread its branches[1] and bore flowers of a most agreeable odor, and produced fruits of glory in abundance." There were many young girls who made vows of perpetual virginity; amongst whom, says the same holy doctor, the Blessed Clare appeared as the most beautiful plant in the garden of the celestial Spouse, and as a star more brilliant than all the others.

This illustrious maiden was the daughter of a rich and noble family of Assisi.[2] The Cavaliere Favorine, or Favarone, her father, was descended from the ancient and powerful houses of Scifi and Fiumi. Her mother, of equal high birth and exalted piety, was called Hortulana. She had the talent of joining the care of her household to the practice of good works, and to regulate her time so well, that she found enough in which to visit, with the consent of her husband, many holy places: she even made a pilgrimage to the Holy Land. If this practice is no longer usual in these days, particularly as regards distant countries, it arises from the circumstances of the times being very different, and from there having been a great change in manners. But Christian piety does not permit us altogether to condemn (independently of abuses) voyages

---

[1] Is. 27:6, and 35:2; Eccl. 24: 23.

[2] It has been said that about the year 1487 there were still at Assisi some descendants of the family of St Clare.

or journeys of devotion, since they are sanctioned by the examples of the Saints, have been approved by the Fathers of the Church, and since at one time they were directed as sacramental penances for certain sinners.[3]

Hortulana had three daughters, Clare, Agnes, Beatrix. Being about to be confined for the first, and praying to God before a crucifix in a church for a safe delivery, she heard a voice, which said to her: "Woman, fear not, you will bring forth, without danger, a light which will illuminate a vast space."

This was the reason she gave the name of Clare[4] to the daughter to whom she gave birth, in the hopes of seeing the accomplishment of what it might signify.

Indeed, from her earliest years, her virtue shone as an Aurora, the prognostication of a fine day. She received with docility the instructions of her mother, and her whole conduct was the fruit thereof; the exercise of prayer became familiar to her; she every day recited the Lord's Prayer a number of times, which she marked with small stones,[5] in order to be exact in the daily number she had assigned for herself. In that she resembled the solitary of the desert of Seethe,[6] who kept an account of the number of his prayers, offering them to God three hundred times each day. Naturally tender and compassionate to the poor, she aided them voluntarily, and the opulence of her family enabled her to assist them abundantly. But, in order to render her charities more agreeable to God, she sent to the poor, by confidential persons, the nicest eatables which were served to herself. The love of God, with which these holy practices inflamed her heart, inspired her with a hatred of her own body, and showed her the vanity of all the things of this world. Under her own costly dresses, which her situation in society obliged her to wear, she constantly had a hair-shirt; and she cleverly refused a proposal of marriage which her parents wished her to accept, recommending to God her virginity, which she intended to preserve in entire purity. Although she was at that time confined in the bosom of her family, and solely intent on sanctifying herself in secret before the eyes of God, her virtue became the subject of admiration, without her being conscious of it, and drew down upon her the esteem and praise of the whole town.

The great celebrity which the sanctity of Francis gained in the world, could not be unknown to the young Clare. Aware that this wonderful man renewed a perfection in the earth which was almost forgotten, she wished much to see

---

[3] See P. Morin Comment. *Hist, de Poenit.*

[4] In Italian, *Chiara* (Clare) means light. —Editor's note.

[5] Heretics only, and bad Catholics can disapprove of the order and arrangement adopted for private and public prayers. The Church has regulated the Divine Office in number and time, and she causes the same words to be frequently repeated to honor God and His Saints. See on this subject the learned Mabillon, when treating of the Crown and of the Rosary or Beads (Chaplet), of the Blessed Virgin. -*Act. SS. Ord. S. Bened.* sec. 5, Praefet. no. 125, et seq. And Bellarmine, *de cultu Sanctorum,* lib. 3, cap. 8.

[6] *Hist. Lausiac.* cap. 23.

him and to have conversation with him. Francis also, having heard the reputation of Clare's virtues, had an equal desire to communicate with her, that he might tear her from the world and present her to Jesus Christ. They saw and visited each other several times. Clare went to St. Mary of the Angels with a virtuous lady, a relation of hers, whose name was Bona Guelfuccii; Francis also came to see her, but always taking the necessary precautions to have the pious secret kept. She placed herself entirely under his guidance, and he soon persuaded her to consecrate herself to God. An interior view of eternal happiness inspired her with such contempt for the vanities of the world, and filled her heart with such divine love, that she had a complete loathing for finery, which it was not as yet permitted her to throw aside; and from that time she entered into engagements to live in a state of perpetual virginity.

The holy director did not choose that so pure a soul should continue longer exposed to the contagion of the world. She had herself come to him some days before Palm Sunday to hasten the execution of her intention; he told her to assist at the ceremony of the delivery of palms dressed in her usual ornaments, to leave Assisi the following night, as our Blessed Savior had left Jerusalem to suffer on Mount Calvary, and to come to the church of St. Mary of the Angels, where she would exchange her worldly ornaments for a penitential habit, and the vain joys of the world for holy lamentations over the Passion of Jesus Christ.

On the 18th of March, being Palm Sunday, Clare, magnificently dressed, went with other ladies to the cathedral church, and as she remained in her place out of bashfulness while the others crowded forward to receive the palms, the bishop came down from the altar, and carried a palm branch to her, as a symbol of the victory she was about to gain over the world.

The following night, accompanied as propriety required, she arranged her flight as her spiritual Father had directed, and according to the earnest wish of her soul. Not being able to get out by the front door of which she had not the key, she had the courage and strength to break open a small door which had been blocked up with stones and wood, and she repaired to the church, where Francis and his brethren, who were saying their matins, received her with great solemnity, bearing lighted tapers in their hands. They cut off her hair before the altar, and after she had taken off her ornaments with the help of the females who accompanied her, she received the penitential habit, consecrating her virginity to Jesus Christ, under the protection of the Queen of virgins, while the religious chanted hymns and canticles.

It was a touching scene to see a young noble lady, only eighteen years of age, in solitude in the middle of the night, renounce all the advantages and allurements of the world, put on sackcloth and a cord, and devote herself to a rigorous system of penitential exercises, solely for the love of God. Similar sacrifices can only be made by a supernatural virtue; they prove that the religion which inspires them is divine; and justly does St. Ambrose consider them to be far above the most heroical pagan virtues.[7]

It must be remarked, moreover, that the church of St. Mary of the Angels, which was the cradle of the Order of the poor evangelical brethren which Francis had just established, was also the place where Clare made profession of the same poverty, that she subsequently prescribed to the Order of women, which she instituted together with the holy Patriarch. This gives to the two Orders the pleasing consolation of knowing that they belong to the Mother of God from their origin, and that she is specially their mother.

As soon as the ceremony was over, Francis, who was always guided by the spirit of wisdom, took the new bride of Jesus Christ, followed by her companions, to the monastery of Benedictines of St. Paul, there to remain until divine Providence should provide a dwelling for her.

When morning dawned, and her parents learnt what had occurred during the night, they were overwhelmed with grief. They equally disapproved of what Clare had done, and of the manner in which she had carried her intention into execution; and they went in great numbers to the monastery of St. Paul, to compel her to leave it. At first they spoke to her in mild and friendly terms; they represented to her that she was choosing a vile and contemptible state of life, which was disgraceful to her family, and that there was no precedent in the whole country of such an occurrence. After which they attempted by violence to force her from the monastery; which they might easily have done, because in those times the religious females did not keep strict enclosure, besides which her relations were all military men, accustomed to acts of violence.

Clare uncovered her head to show them that she was shorn; and she protested, clinging to the altar, that nothing in the world should tear her from Jesus Christ. Either because they had too much respect for religion to venture to violate so holy an asylum, or that God restrained them by His power, they molested her no farther. She had only to resist the fresh efforts they made to induce her to return to her father. But the love of God gave her courage to resist with such determined firmness, that, giving up all hopes of conquering her, they left her in peace.

A short time after, Francis removed her from the monastery of St. Paul to that of St. Angelo de Panso, of the same Order of St. Benedict, near Assisi, to which she drew her sister Agnes. The conformity of their inclinations and manners, which rendered them tenderly united, had made them sensibly feel their separation.

Clare was greatly grieved that Agnes, at so tender an age, should be exposed to the dangers of the world. She prayed fervently to the Almighty to cause her sister to feel the sweets of His grace, so that she might grow disgusted with the world, and become her companion in the service of Jesus Christ. Her prayer was soon favorably heard, for, a fortnight after her

---

[7] St. Ambrose lib. I, *de Virginibus*, cap. 4.

consecration, Agnes came to her, and declared that she was decided to give herself wholly to God. "I return Him thanks," replied Clare, "for that He has thus relieved me from the uneasiness I was in on your account."

The indignation of the family was extreme, when it became known that one sister had followed the other. On the morrow, twelve of its principal members hastened to the monastery of St. Angelo. At first they feigned to have come in a peaceful mood; but, having been admitted, they turned to Agnes, for they had no longer any hopes of Clare, and said: "What business have you here? Come immediately home with us." She replied that she did not choose to leave her sister, when one of the knights, forgetting himself altogether, attacked her furiously, struck her with his fist, kicked her, pulled her down by the hair, and the others carried her off in their arms. All that this innocent lamb could do, thus torn by the wolves, was to cry out, "My dear sister, come to my aid; do not let them separate me from Jesus Christ." Clare could give her no assistance, but by praying to God to render her steadfast, and to check the violence of her ravishers. This prayer was followed by a miraculous effect, similar to what the Church records in the Life of the illustrious virgin and martyr, St. Lucia.[8]

As the relations of Agnes dragged her down the mountain, tearing her clothes, and scattering her hair along the road, because she continued violently to resist, she became suddenly so heavy, that they were unable to raise her from the ground, even with the help of persons who flocked from the fields and the vineyards. They were blind to the finger of God in so extraordinary an event, and they even made a jest of it; for ill-disposed persons, like the Pharisees of the Gospel, do not submit to the evidence of miracles, but carry their impiety to the length of turning all miracles into ridicule. The one which God was pleased to operate in the person of Agnes, threw her uncle, whose name was Monaldi, into such a rage, that he raised his arm to strike her in such a manner as would have killed her, if the Divine power had not arrested the blow by bringing such an excessive pain into the limb as to disable it, and which lasted a considerable time. This is a grand lesson for those parents who prevent their children from consecrating themselves to God in a religious state. If they do not experience in this world the effects of His anger,[9] they ought to fear the consequences of the anathema in the next with which the Council of Trent menaces, not only them, but those also who compel their children to embrace a religious state.

Clare came to the field of battle, where she found her sister half dead. She entreated the relations to retire and to leave her in her care, which they regrettingly did. Agnes then rose with great ease, glad to have had a share in the cross of Jesus Christ. She returned to the monastery with her sister, to consecrate herself to God under the direction of Francis, who cut off her hair

---

[8] Offic. S. Luciae, Surius, cap. 3, Dec. n. 9.

[9] Conc. Trid. sess. 23, de Regul. cap. 13.

with his own hands, and instructed her in the duties of the state she was about to enter. Clare, not having her mind quite at ease in the monastery of St. Angelo, removed to the house which adjoined the church of St. Damian, the first of the three which he had repaired, and where he had foretold that there would be one day a monastery of poor females, who should lead a sanctified life, and whose reputation would cause our Heavenly Father to be glorified.

Clare had scarcely fixed herself there, when the fame of her sanctity spread all around, and produced wonderful effects. The influence of grace was so great, that there were many persons of all sexes and all ages, of all states of life, nobles and rich, who took to a religious life. They mutually excited each other in families, as St. Jerome tells us that it occurred in all Africa, when the illustrious virgin, Demetrias, moved by the exhortation of St. Augustine, took the holy veil.[10] It was even seen that married persons separated by mutual consent, and entered separate convents: and those who could not do this, strove to sanctify themselves in the world. The virtues of the holy spouse of Jesus Christ, as a precious perfume, attracted pure and innocent souls, who made the house of St. Damian a numerous monastery, and the origin of the Order of the Poor Sisters, or of St. Clare, the second of the three which were established by St. Francis. He appointed Clare abbess of St. Damian, although her humility made her wish to be the servant of the others, and he only overcame her repugnance by enforcing that obedience which she had promised him.

It was there that this holy abbess was enclosed during a period of forty-two years in the practice of the most eminent perfection, and which we shall have an opportunity of referring to, when we come to speak of her rule.

After Francis had regulated the spiritual exercises of these nuns, provided for the enclosure, and placed the house in good order, he turned in his mind what was personal to himself, and was for several days in great perplexity as to what his future way of life should be. In order to come to a decision, he consulted those of his brethren with whom he was in habits of familiar intercourse, and proposed to them his difficulties as follows:

"My brethren, what do you advise me? Which of the two do you think best: that I shall give myself to prayer, or that I shall go forth to preach? To me it seems that prayer is what is most advantageous to me, for I am a simple person, who am not a good speaker, and I have received the gift of prayer, rather than that of speech: moreover, we gain much by prayer; it is the source of graces; but, in preaching, we only distribute to others what God has communicated. Prayer purifies the heart and the affections; it unites us to the sole true and sovereign good, and strengthens us in virtue. Preaching renders the feet of the spiritual man dusty; it is an employment which dissipates and distracts, and which causes regular discipline to be relaxed. In fine, in prayer we speak to God, and we listen to Him; we converse with the angels, as if we

---

[10] Div. Hieronym. Epist. 97, ad Demetriad.

lived an evangelic life. In preaching, we must have much condescension towards men, and, living with them, we must hear and see, speak and think, in some measure as they do, in a human way. But there is one thing which seems to prevail over all this before God, which is, that the only Son, who is in the bosom of His Father, and is the sovereign wisdom, came down from heaven to save souls, to instruct mankind by His example and by His word, to redeem them by His blood, and to make of this precious blood a bath and a celestial beverage: all that He had He gave up liberally and without reserve for our salvation. Now, having bound ourselves to do all things according to the model given us in His person, it seems more in conformity to the will of God, that I should give up my own repose in order to labor for the benefit of others."

After all these reflections, he continued in an anxious state of uncertainty as to the course he ought to take; and this man, who had wonderful knowledge through the spirit of prophecy, had no light thrown on his doubts by prayer: God permitting at that time that he should not be sensible to the evident proofs he had, that he was called to the apostolic life.

We have already seen that powerful attractions to a contemplative life had given rise to similar difficulties arising in his mind. As he wished in all things to act faithfully and perfectly, his principal care was to apply himself to the virtues which he knew, by the inspiration of the Holy Spirit, to be most agreeable to God.

St. Bonaventure says that this was the ground of his doubt, and he gives two reasons why God permitted that the saint should not have been able to solve the difficulty, the solution of which appeared so easy. The first is, in order that the heavenly oracles which had announced that Francis was destined to preach the Gospel, should give a more exalted idea of the merits of that ministry; to this may be added, that it was of consequence that it should be known with certainty that the holy founder and his disciples were destined by Heaven to labor for the salvation of souls, since in after times it has been found that some of their adversaries have contested it. Secondly, the doubt of the servant of God was useful in preserving his humility and rendering it still greater. In the capacity of a Friar Minor, he was not ashamed of seeking the advice of the least of his brethren, he who had been taught such elevated things from the sovereign Master. It was likewise one of his maxims throughout his whole life, and of the principles of the sacred philosophy, of which he made profession, to address himself to the simple as well as to the learned, to the imperfect as well as to the perfect, to the young as to the old, with the ardent desire to find from intercourse with them in what way and by what means he could best serve God according to His good pleasure, and raise himself to the greatest perfection.

Finally, we must not be surprised that he entreated God to grant him additional proofs of his vocation, after having received such convincing ones by revelations, by miracles, and from the mouth of the vicar of Jesus Christ, when we see in the sacred Scriptures,[11] that Gideon, having been chosen by God to fight the enemies of His people, and this choice having been manifested by the apparition of an angel, by a miracle and by a revelation, he nevertheless begged the Lord to give other miraculous signs, in order to be still further assured of it, and his prayer was granted. Would to God, that, without asking for miracles and without expecting them, all vocations, particularly those for the holy ministries, and other affairs of conscience, were examined on such sound principles, and weighed by means as likely to deserve the light of Heaven.

In order to know how finally to decide, Francis sent two of his religious, Philip and Massé, to Brother Sylvester the priest, who was then on the mountain near Assisi, continually intent on prayer, begging him to consult the Lord on the subject of his doubt, and to let him know the result. He made a similar application to Clare, recommending her to put the same question to her sisters, and particularly to the one who should appear to her to be the most pure and most single-minded. The venerable priest and the consecrated virgin gave similar answers, and pronounced that it was the will of God that Francis should go forth to preach.

When the two religious returned, Francis received them with great respect and affection; he washed their feet, embraced them, and gave them their meal. He then took them into the wood, where he knelt bareheaded and inclined with his hands crossed upon his breast, and said to them: "Now tell me what my Lord Jesus Christ commands me to do?" "My very dear brother and my Father," replied Massé, "Sylvester and Clare received precisely the same answer from our Lord Jesus Christ, which is, that you set out to preach; because it is not for your salvation alone that He called you, but for the salvation of others also; and for them He will put His words into your mouth."

Then Francis, moved by the Spirit of God, as the prophets had been, and inflamed by the fire of charity, rose up, saying, "Let us then go in the name of the Lord;" and he set out with two of his companions, Massé of Marignan, and Angelo of Rieti. He walked so fast to obey the words of Heaven, that it was easy to see that the Lord acted upon him, and that he had received fresh strength from above for the ministry of preaching. His companions were the more convinced of this by the very extraordinary wonders which were worked by him on the route. As it pleased God to renew these often in his favor, they will be given altogether at the end of his life.

The apostolical preacher went first to Bevagna, where he pronounced an excellent discourse on the love of God; after which, in presence of the whole audience, he restored the sight of a blind girl by putting spittle three times on her eyes in the name of the Blessed Trinity. This miracle had a salutary effect on a number of sinners, who were converted; and many of them joined him who was the instrument of the Divine Power.

---

[11] Judic. 6: 12, 21, 25, 36, 39, 40.

So many souls garnered to Jesus Christ in one place, stimulated him to carry the faith into the Levant. The triumph of martyrs, whose charity could not be extinguished by the violence of persecutions, excited in him a holy jealousy. Burning with similar fire, he wished to offer himself, as they had done, a sacrifice, in order to mark his gratitude in some measure, by the effusion of his blood, for the goodness of Jesus Christ, who vouchsafed to die for our salvation, thus the better to excite others to love Him. But he desired to have the sanction of the Sovereign Pontiff for this undertaking, and therefore bent his steps to Rome, preaching as he went the truths of salvation, which God confirmed by miracles.

Arrived at Rome, he sought an audience of the Pope. Innocent III still filled the Papal throne; he first communicated to him the wonderful extension of his Order, the holy lives of his brethren, and the design which God had to bring about a reformation of morals in the world, which was growing old, and was visibly in a state of decay. Then he disclosed the project he had of transporting himself to the lands of the Muslims and Tartars, to endeavor to give them some knowledge of the Gospel. It must be remarked, that the Saint attributed to the world that decay which is the effect of old age, but he did not extend this to the Church, because he well knew that, although old, she was not infirm. St. Augustine says, that[12] her old age is always young, fresh, and vigorous, and that she bears fruit in abundance.[13] The Pope, who was very religious, was highly gratified at the fortunate success which he now learnt had attended the Saint's labors; he willingly granted the servant of God leave to preach to the infidels, and he affectionately gave him his blessing.

Two sermons which Francis preached at Rome procured him two disciples, Zachary and William; the one was a Roman, the other was an Englishman. John de Capella, of whom we have before spoken, having left the Order about this time, and having had a similar end to that of Judas. William was substituted for him, as St. Mathias had filled the place of the traitor in the apostolate, and he was afterwards always considered as the twelfth of the first companions of the Patriarch.

A Roman widow, very noble and very rich, called Jacqueline de Settesoli,[14] having heard the Saint preach, was very anxious to have an interview with

---

[12] These words differ greatly from those which were said to the venerable servant of God, Vincent de Paul, and which he heard with horror. See his *Life*, written by M. Abelly, Bishop of Rodez, in 1664, lib. 2, ch. II. And *La Vraie Defense de ses Sentimens*, which the same prelate wrote in 1668, in refutation of a libel entitled: *Defense de feu St. Vincent de Paul.*

[13] S. August, *in Psal. XXXVI*, serm. 3, n. 4, et *in Psal. XCI*, n. 11.

[14] Wading, not having found any traces of a family of that name, believes that the lady was so called from the part of Rome which she inhabited, which was called Septisolium, or Septemsolia, or Septasolis. Baronius says that this place was between Mount Palatine and the declivity of Scaurus; and that there were there several ruins on which were raised seven thrones, which had the appearance of a high tower. Ad ann. 1084, n. 5. A manuscript in the Vatican says that the temple of the Sun, which was in the same place, bears the same name. —Wading, ad ann. 1226, n. 28.

him. He agreed to it, although reluctantly, and he gave her such salutary instructions, that she committed the care of all her affairs to her two sons, who were afterwards senators, in order that she might apply herself to the sanctification of her soul, employing the gift of tears which God had given her, to weep incessantly the neglects of her past life. This lady and St. Clare were the only two persons of the female sex with whom the servant of Jesus Christ had any intimate relations on the subject of their salvation; which ought to serve as a caution for this sort of direction not to be too greatly multiplied, and to have care taken that it be always holy.

As there is no affection more solid or more effective than that which is grounded on charity, the pious widow rendered to Francis and his brethren all the good offices in her power. When they came to Rome she provided them with lodgings, she fed them, clothed them, and assisted them in their sicknesses with the tenderness of a mother. It was she who procured for them from the Benedictines of the abbey of St. Cosmas beyond the Tiber, a refuge in the hospital of St. Blaise; and this hospital with its church was entirely ceded to them by the same religious Order in the year 1229, at the request of Pope Gregory DC; it is at this day the convent of St. Francis of Ripa.[15] Thus the Friars Minor are indebted to the children of St. Benedict for the first establishment they had in Rome, as well as for that of St. Mary of the Angels, or Portiuncula, the first of the whole Order.

Francis, having terminated his business at Rome, returned to St. Mary of the Angels, where he communicated to his brethren his intention of proceeding to the Levant. He exhorted them in the strongest terms to perfect themselves in the exercises of a religious life; he left them Peter of Catania as superior during his absence, and set out with one companion for Ascoli. At that place they were extremely anxious to see and hear this admirable man, who was everywhere looked upon as a Saint: he was scarcely arrived in the town when all flocked to him; whichever way he went, a crowd followed him; every one was anxious to get near him, and they pressed upon each other in order only to be able to touch his miserable habit. His presence and preaching in this town procured him thirty disciples, some priests, and some laymen, whom he placed in different houses of the Order.

The desire of martyrdom which he aspired to from the infidels, did not admit of a longer stay at Ascoli; he therefore made for the sea-side, and embarked on board a vessel which was bound for Syria. But on the passage the winds became adverse, and they were obliged to come to anchor off Sclavonia, where he remained some days in hopes of finding some other vessel bound to the Levant. Not finding any, and perceiving that his intention had been foiled, he applied to some seamen who were about to sail to Ancona, to take him on

---

[15] It is on the borders of the Tiber. The cell of the Saint is visited out of devotion, which has been changed into a chapel, where several cardinals and prelates come to say Mass. —Wading, ad ann. 1229, n. 23.

board their vessel for the love of God. They refused obstinately to do so, because he had no money wherewith to pay his passage; notwithstanding this, the holy man contrived to slip secretly on board with his companion.

An unknown person came on board the vessel and brought provisions with him, saying to one of the passengers: "Worthy man, I confide these provisions to you, for the use of two poor religious who are secreted in the vessel; take care of them, and give them to them when required." Who could this charitable purveyor be? There is reason to think, with St. Bonaventure, that he was sent by God to the assistance of these two poor religious, who were only poor for love of Him. Stormy weather rendered the passage disastrous; they could neither carry sail, nor return to land. All the sailors' provisions were expended: there was nothing left but the provisions put on board for the two religious. Divine Providence was pleased to multiply these, inasmuch that they sufficed for all who were in the vessel for several days, during which they were still at sea, before they reached Ancona. The sailors, astonished at this miracle, were convinced that the poor man whom they had refused to receive on board, had, by his merits, saved their lives, and they returned thanks to God for the mercy.

After having landed, Francis went to several places, spreading the word of God as a precious seed, which produced an ample harvest. Many came to see him from afar, so greatly had his reputation been disseminated. A celebrated poet came amongst others, having heard his entire contempt for the things of this world spoken of. He was of the class of persons who were called in Provence *Troubadours,* who invented fables, and composed different pieces of poetry, which were sung in the houses of the nobles. The art of versifying in the vulgar tongue was uncommon in those times, and was only practiced by the nobility. The Italians imitated the people of Provence, and translated into their language the best compositions of the *Troubadours.* The poet of whom we are speaking excelled in this art, and the Emperor Frederic II had crowned him as the Prince of Poets, which caused him to be usually called "The King of Verse."

Coming then to see Francis, he passed through the borough town of San Severino, and entered the church of a monastery, where the servant of God was preaching on the mystery of the Cross. He listened to him at first without knowing him; but God disclosed him to him in the course of the sermon, by two shining swords pierced through him cross-wise from the head to the feet, and from one hand to the other through the breast; from this he became aware that the preacher was the holy man of whom so much was spoken. The first impression which the vision made upon him was, that he ought to live a better life; but the words of the preacher filled him with such compunction, that he felt as if he had been pierced by the sword of the spirit which came out of his mouth, and he went after the sermon to renounce in his hands all the vanities of the world, and to embrace his institute. Francis, seeing him pass so perfectly from the agitations of the world to the peace of Jesus Christ, gave him the name of Brother Pacificus.

St. Bonaventure adds, that he was a man of so much holiness that he received the additional favor from God of seeing on the forehead of his Blessed Father a great *Tau*,[16] painted in a variety of colors, which threw a remarkable softness on his countenance. This letter, which represents the cross, showed the interior comeliness which the love of the cross of the Son of God gave to his soul.

Watchfulness and affection inspired the Father with the wish to return into Tuscany, to visit the establishments he had founded there the preceding year, and to learn from his own inspection how they progressed in the ways of God. The family of the Ubaldini, which is among the most illustrious of Florence, gave him a convent which had been built and founded by their ancestors for the religious of the Order of St. Basil, in the sixth or seventh century, some leagues from the city, in the middle of a wood, and which had been since occupied by hermits. He put some of his companions into it, and returned towards the end of October to St. Mary of the Angels, preaching, as was his custom, in all the places he passed through. The repose he allowed himself after so much fatigue, was that of applying himself to the instruction of his disciples, and addressing discourses to them full of wisdom and prudence, an abridgment of which will be given at the end of this work.

At the end of this year he had an attack of ague,[17] which became quartan, and reduced him to a great state of languor. The bishop of Assisi, who was a most charitable prelate, and his particular friend, having heard of his illness, came to see him, and, notwithstanding his resistance, had him removed to the palace, where he attended to his recovery with the charity of a pastor and the affection of a parent. His religious came to him there to seek the lights they required. They also brought to him such postulants as presented themselves, and those who were recommended to him (thirty or forty at a time sometimes) by the missionaries he had in various parts of Italy; for none were there received who had not been examined by the founder himself. A young gentleman from Lucca came with tears in his eyes, to entreat him to give him the habit. "Unfortunate young man," said the Saint, "why do you attempt to show by your eyes what is not in your heart? You have, without due consideration, formed a plan which you will soon as lightly give up." In fact, a

---

[16] S. Jerome, on the ninth chapter of Ezechiel, says, that in his time they made use, in the Samaritan language, of the letter Tau, which is the last of the ancient Hebrew letters, and that it represented a cross. It is the Tau of the Greeks, and the large letter T of the Romans. It was God's pleasure, in the vision of the prophet, that this sign should be printed on the forehead of the faithful Jews, as the figure of the Cross on which Jesus Christ was to be immolated for our salvation. From the Apostolic times, the Christians made the sign of the Cross on themselves, and it was the sign of their profession. See Tertul. lib. 3, *adv. Marcian,* cap. 22; Corn, a Lapide et *Synops. crit.* in cap. 9, Ezech. et Palaeog. Graec. lib. 2, cap. 3. *Editor's note*: In Hebrew, ת, in Greek, τ.

[17] A medieval word for a Malarial type of infection. —Editor's note.

few days after he went home with two of his relations who had come in search of him, and he thought no more of becoming a religious.

The servant of God, having regained some portion of strength during his residence with the bishop, by relaxing in the severity of his abstinences, which were extreme, became irritated with his own body, and was inflamed with the desire of humbling himself: "It is not right," he said, "that people should think me austere, while I am pampered in secret." Upon which the spirit of humility suggested to him an act, which St. Bonaventure records, not as an example, but as a prodigy, to be compared only with those extraordinary things which God commanded the Prophets to perform.[18] He rose, and accompanied by a great number of his brethren, he went to the great Square of Assisi, assembled the people, and led them to the cathedral. Then he caused himself to be dragged by the vicar of his convent from the church to the place of execution, stripped, and with a cord round his neck, as the prophet Isaiah. There, weak as he still was, and shivering with cold, he addressed the assembly with surprising energy, and said in a loud voice: "I assure that I ought not to receive honor as if I were a spiritual man. I am a carnal, sensual, and greedy man, whom you ought thoroughly to despise." The hearers, who knew the austerity of his life, struck with such a scene, admitted that such extraordinary humility was more to be admired than imitated.

Nevertheless, the holy doctor, whom we have just named, finds in this some wholesome instruction. It teaches us, he says, that, in the practice of virtue, we must avoid with great care everything having any tendency to hypocrisy, repress the slightest approaches of vanity, and have a sovereign contempt for praise. The humble Francis, who strenuously labored for his interior sanctification, did many things with a view of rendering himself contemptible, endeavoring, above all, to prevent men from being deceived in the idea they might have formed of his sanctity. This is the characteristic of true devotion; it has no borrowed exterior; it is, or it endeavors to be, all that it seems.

The religious whom Francis had sent into Lombardy, fulfilled the mission in an admirable manner. They acquired so much esteem at Milan by their preaching and by their good example, that the archbishop of that city, Henry Satalas, gave them an establishment there, which became considerable later, by the liberality of the Milanese.

One of the fruits of their apostolic labors was the vocation of a young man of rank, who was rich and talented, and who solicited the habit of the Order. Upon their acquainting him that, to become a Friar Minor, it was requisite to renounce all temporal goods, he immediately disposed of all of which he was then master, and distributed the greater part to the poor, reserving the remainder to pay the expenses of his journey to Assisi, where he was told that it was necessary to present himself to the founder, who alone had the power of

---

[18] Isa. 20: 2, et seq, Jer. 27: 2, et 28: 13, Ezech. 4: 12 and 13.

receiving novices.

He induced some of his relations and friends to accompany him, and took with him a considerable number of servants; one of the religious was also requested to go with them, in order to introduce the postulant, and favor his reception. When they arrived at St. Mary of the Angels, Francis, seeing such a number of persons, and such an appearance of vanity, asked the religious who was with them, who these lords were, and what they wanted? He answered: "My father, this is a young man, learned and rich, of one of the first families of Milan, who wishes to become your disciple." Francis replied, before them all, smiling: "This young man does not seem to me to be fit for our Order, for, when people come with so much pomp, which is the mark of a proud spirit, to embrace a state of poverty, we are led to believe that they have not yet sufficient contempt and aversion for the world, and that they are not prepared wholly to relinquish it. But I will consult our brethren on the subject."

He assembled them all, and asked their opinion, which was not to receive him, because he had still a fund of pride, and because the love of the splendor of the world was not yet eradicated from his heart.

The young man who was present burst into tears; and Francis, who was moved with compassion, said: "My brethren, will you receive him if he consents to serve in the kitchen? It will be the means of inducing him to renounce the vanities of the world." They assented on this condition, which the postulant willingly agreed to, protesting that he was prepared to do anything that was required of him. The Father embraced him, after having returned to those who accompanied him his money and his equipage. He sent him to the hospital of St. Blasius of Rome, there to act as cook; and the young novice attained to such perfection in that humble employment, that Francis judged him worthy to be placed over others, and made him superior of the same place.

The line adopted in respect to this young man shows evidently, that for the religious profession neither birth nor riches nor talents are to be heeded, but that the essential qualifications principally to be considered for this holy state, are to be sincerely prepared to die to the world and to self. This is for the combined interest of those who have the admission of postulants, of the postulants themselves, and for that of the Order itself.

CHAPTER III

SPAIN—AFRICA—BROTHER WOLF'S LAYER

Falls sick again, and writes to all Christians—Writes a second letter to them—Departs for Spain and Africa, in search of martyrdom—His miracles, and other particulars of his journey— His profound humility—He raises the dead—Count Orlando gives him Mount Alverna—God miraculously protects him—He preaches in Piedmont, and passes into Spain—Works a miraculous cure there—The king, Alphonso IX, permits him to establish his Order there—He receives houses there—A violent sickness prevents him going to Morocco—His actions whilst he is delayed in Spain—He returns to Italy—His route thither—He arrives at St. Mary of the Angels, and disapproves a building there—He goes to Mount Alverna—Is beaten by devils—Mortifies his sense,, and taste—Makes water spring from a rock—Visits the mountain—Converts there a celebrated brigand.

AT THE BEGINNING of the year 1213, the fever of which Francis had been cured at the Bishop's palace of Assisi recurred; sometimes it was tertian, sometimes quartan, but always with great severity. He bore the suffering with great equanimity, because of the hatred he felt for his body, and from the patience taught by Jesus Christ. The violence of the fever which burned his body, was, in his opinion, a lesser evil than the fire of temptations which inflame the soul; his sufferings appeared to him a gain. All the Saints have had a like way of thinking, and the principles of Christianity admit of no other. The only uneasiness the sickness gave to the holy man, was its having prevented his putting in force the intentions he had in view for the salvation of souls. But charity, which is ever active, suggested to him to exhort the faithful in writing, as he could not do so in person; he therefore addressed them a short letter,[1] couched in the following terms:

---

[1] There are some similar letters written by an ancient solitary, and by St. Columban. They had for models the letters of the Apostles, and the circulars that the prelates often wrote on points of faith, morals, or discipline, to be communicated to the churches. It was an effect of the charity with which the hearts of these holy men were inflamed, and which extended to the whole world. —See Wading in Ep. 1, St. Fran.

To all Christian priests, religious laymen, men and women, over the whole Earth.

"O how happy are all those who love God, and who worthily practice all that Jesus Christ has taught in His holy gospel. You shalt love the Lord your God with your whole heart, and with your whole soul, and your neighbor as yourself.[2] Let us love and adore God with great purity of mind and heart; for that is what He seeks for above all things. He has said that the true adorers shall adore the Father in spirit and in truth, and that they who adore Him, must adore Him in spirit and truth.[3] 1 salute you in our Lord."

This short letter was still fresh from his hand, when an infinity of copies were made of it, so anxious were all people to see anything that came from the hand of so holy a person. In this simple and brief exhortation they admired the candor of his soul and the extent of his charity, and, in reading it, they were moved by a power which penetrated the soul; for the words of the Saints have a secret unction which is not found elsewhere. Many persons entreated him to write at greater length, and his zeal not permitting him to refuse so pious a request, he penned a second letter, of which we give an extract only here, because it is very long.

"To all Christian priests, religious, and laymen, as well women as men, in the whole earth; Brother Francis, their most humble servant, respectfully presents his services, wishing them the true peace which comes from heaven, and perfect charity in our Lord."

He remarks in the first place, that being the servant of all, and from his infirmities not having it in his power to preach the word of God in person, he has thought it his duty to supply for it by letters. He then proposes to them the incarnation, the institution of the Eucharist, and the death of Jesus Christ, who offered Himself for us on the cross, because it was His wish to save us all and who has left us an example that we may follow His footsteps. He urges the praising Him and keeping His commandments, which he enforces from motives of fear, of hope, and of love. He recommends frequenting churches, and having great respect for ecclesiastics. He exhorts to the use of prayer, of fasting, of almsgiving, of all works of penance, of confession and communion. He speaks of the love of our neighbor, of the administration of justice, of good government, of submission to legitimate authority, of Christian humility, and the duties of the religious states, and finally, after having pointed out the misery of the body, which is nothing but corruption, and the happiness of the soul, which has wonderful relations with the Three Divine Persons, he deplores the blindness of sinners, who permit themselves to be deceived by the

---

[2] Matt. 22: 37 and 39.

[3] John. 4: 23 and 24.

world, the flesh, and the devil, and pictures the death of one of the rich of this world, who has only become such by a series of injustices; the representation of this is too vivid and too natural not to be laid before the reader.

"A man of the world falls sick, death is at hand, and it must at length be said to him: 'Take order with your house, for you shall die and not live.' His wife, his children, his relatives, his friends, crowd around his bed, and affect to weep. He looks at them, and weeps also. 'See,' he says to them, 'what can be done for my soul, my body, for my property; I place all in your hands.' Woeful and accursed, according to the words of the prophet, is he who places his salvation and his confidence in such hands.[4] The family calls in a priest, who, knowing the life this man has led, asks him if he desires to confess his sins, and do penance for them, as much as may be in his power. The sick man replies in the affirmative. 'But,' continues the priest, 'will you make restitution of all you have unjustly taken from others, and give of your wealth to satisfy the justice of God?' 'Oh, as to that,' replies the sick man, 'it is impossible.' 'But why?' rejoins the priest. 'Because,' says the man, 'I will not do such an injury to my family; I leave to them the whole of my property.' While he thus argues, his malady grows worse, he loses the use of his speech, and dies in this deplorable state! Now all the world must know, that wherever, and in whatsoever manner, a man dies in a state of mortal sin, without having satisfied the justice of God, as he might have done, he is stripped of all he had, and the devil carries off his soul, with sufferings which can only be known to those who feel them; that soul is tormented in hell, while the worms consume his body; his family share the property he leaves, and curse him for not leaving more. Thus, the love of the transitory goods of this world is the cause of his losing body and soul for all eternity." The letter terminates in these word: "I, brother Francis, the meanest of your servants, sincerely ready to kiss your feet, entreat and conjure you, by that charity which is God Himself,[5] to receive and put in practice, humbly and with affection, these words of our Lord Jesus Christ, and all others which came from His mouth. May all those into whose hands they shall fall, and who shall understand their sense, send them to others, in order that they also may profit by them. If they persevere to, the end in the good use they ought to make of them, may they receive the blessing of the Father, the Son, and the Holy Spirit. Amen."

These spiritual services, and others which Francis rendered to his neighbor, with the continual instruction he gave to his brethren, were his occupations during his sickness, and until such time as returning health permitted him to do more. He was somewhat better in the spring, as is usually the case with those who have the quartan ague; but his extraordinary austerities had so weakened his constitution, that he never wholly recovered his health, and the remainder of his life was little else than a state of languor.

---

[4] Jeremiah 7: 5.

[5] I John 4: 16.

As soon as he could commence traveling, he committed the care of his Order to Peter of Cantania, and set out with Bernard of Quintavalle and some others, in order to go to Morocco, through Spain, to preach the gospel to the Miramolin and to his subjects, in the hopes of attaining by this means the crown of martyrdom, which was the great object of his wishes. Feeble as he was, his zeal enabled him to walk fast, and he got before his companions: by the example of Jesus Christ, who, in going to Jerusalem, when He was to be delivered up to death, advanced quicker than His disciples, urged on by the ardent love He bore us, and anxious as He was to be immolated for our redemption.[6]

The servant of God did not reach Spain till near the end of the year, because he had stopped in various places to preach, to visit the houses of his Order, and to receive accounts of others. His whole route was a succession of miracles, and other remarkable things, which contain admirable instructions.

At Foligno, the sign of the cross which he made on the house of his host, protected it from various accidents, and particularly from fire, which did no damage to that dwelling, although the adjoining houses were three or four times on fire: the flames were even seen to take a contrary direction. At Spoleto, knowing that a rich man thought ill of his institute, and refused his brethren alms, he asked him only to give him a loaf; and, having received it, he divided it among his religious, and directed them to say the Lord's Prayer and the evangelical salutation three times, for the person who had given it. Their scanty meal was scarcely finished, when this man came to ask forgiveness for the harshness he had shown them, and he was, after that, the best friend of their convent, so good an idea of their institution had the saint impressed upon him.

At Terni, the bishop who had listened to one of Francis' sermons, ascended the pulpit when he had done, and said to the people: "My brethren, the Lord, who has often enlightened His church by men illustrious for their science, has now sent you this Francis whom you have just heard, a poor illiterate man, and contemptible in appearance, in order that he may edify you by his word and his example. The less learned he is the more does the power of God shine in his person, who chooses those who are foolish according to the views of the world, to confound all worldly wisdom. The care which God takes of our salvation obliges us to honor and glorify Him; for He has not done the like to other nations."

Francis followed the prelate, fell on his knees, kissed his hand, and said: "My lord, in very truth, no one has ever done me so much honor as I have this day received from you. Some attribute to me a sort of sanctity, which noway belongs to me, and which ought to be referred to God alone, the author of every perfect gift.[7] But you, my lord, have wisely separated what is valuable

---

[6] Mark 10: 32.

[7] Jac. 1:17.

from what is vile, the worthy from the unworthy, the saint from the sinner;[8] giving the glory to God, and not to me, who am but a miserable mortal. It is, indeed, only to God, the King of Ages, immortal and invisible, that men should give honor and glory for ever and ever."[9] The bishop, even more pleased with this specimen of his humility than with his preaching, embraced him affectionately.

In the same city, by the sign of the cross he rendered some sour wine perfectly good, and that before persons who had tasted it in its acid state. But he performed a much greater miracle, which was universally admired, on a young lad who had been just crushed by the fall of a wall; having had him brought to him, he applied himself to prayer, and, extending himself on the corpse, as the prophet Eliseus had done on the child of the Sunamite,[10] he restored him to life.

In the county of Narni, he was lodged in the house of a worthy man who was in great affliction for the death of his brother, who had been drowned, and whose body could not be found, so that it might be buried. After having privately prayed for some time, he marked a spot in the river where he said that the body certainly was at the bottom, where it had been stopped by the entanglement of the clothes. They dived there, and the body was found, which he restored to life in the presence of the whole family.

The fever, and a severe stomach complaint, caused him to faint in a hermitage which had been given him near the borough of St. Urban, and he asked for some wine to recover from the weakness which had ensued. As there was none to be had there, he had some water brought to him, which he blessed, by making the sign of the cross over it, and it was instantly changed thereby into excellent wine. The little that he took of it renovated him so promptly, that it was a double miracle. Upon which St. Bonaventure remarks, that this wonderful change is a type of the change he had effected in his heart, in casting off the old man to put on the new.[11]

In the City of Narni, he cured a man who had lost the use of his limbs for five months from palsy, employing no other remedy than a sign of the cross, which he made over his whole body; this he did at the request of the bishop of the place, and by virtue of the same sign he restored the sight of a blind girl. Being at Orti, he straightened a child, who was so deformed that its head touched its feet. At San Gemini, he prayed, with three of his companions, for the wife of his host, whom the devil had possessed for a long while, and the evil spirit left her. Such evident miracles, publicly performed, and in great numbers, gave a wonderful splendor to his sanctity. In the archives of the Town of Poggibonsi, in Tuscany, the act of donation of a house given to him is

---

[8] Jer. 15:19.

[9] 1 Tim. 1:17.

[10] 4 Reg. 4: 34.

[11] 2 Col. 3: 9 and 10.

preserved, which commences thus: "We cede to a man named Francis, whom all the world considers as a saint," etc.

The discourses of so holy a man, of one so gifted with the power of miracles, had the greatest effect upon the hearts of his hearers, and made the people very anxious to have houses of his Order established among them. He settled some of his religious at Foligno, at Trevi, at San Gemini, at Sienna, and in several other places.

Fresh disciples joined him from all quarters, but he did not receive any until he had strictly examined their vocation. A young gentleman, having heard him preach at Monte Casale, a town in the Appennines, came to acquaint him with the design he had long formed of entering his Order. "You must think seriously of it," replied Francis; "for the kind of life we lead must appear very hard to those who have been tenderly brought up." The young man answered courageously: "My Father, are not you and yours of the same nature as I am, and formed of the same earth? I hope, with God's help, to bear without much inconvenience what my fellow-men can bear so willingly." These ideas were very pleasing to the Patriarch, and the postulant was received. It must be admitted that man has resources of strength which he might make use of to imitate the saints in many things, if he were not wanting in exertion and confidence in God.

From Monte Casale Francis passed over the Appennines, and went through the Valley of Marecchia to reach Monte Feltro, or St. Leo. He learnt on the road that the lord of that town was about to be knighted at his castle, where he was giving a grand feast, accompanied by games and theatricals, to a numerous assembly of the nobility, among whom was Count Orlando Catanio, lord of Chiusi Nuovo, and of all the Casentino. Being near the castle, and hearing the sound of the trumpets, which denoted that the revelry was about to begin: "Let us get hither also," he said to his companions, "and let us combat with all our might the devil, who never fails to lay his snares in these rejoicings, into which many fall; for it is our duty to labor everywhere and in all places for the salvation of souls." He went up to the castle, and heard the solemn mass with all those who accompanied the new knight. As soon as it was over, he took a position on a height near the church, in order to preach from thence, and the crowd gathered round him to listen.

He took the following Italian words for his text: *Tanto e il ben che aspetto, che d'ogni pena mi diletto* which means, "that the good which I hope for is so great, that to obtain it all suffering is pleasurable." He proved his text by this passage from St. Paul: "The sufferings of this life are not worthy to be compared with the glory to come;"[12] by the example of the apostles, who were filled with joy for having been found worthy to suffer for the Name of Jesus;[13] by the example of the martyrs, who willingly exposed themselves to torments

---

[12] Rom. 8: 18.

[13] Acts 5: 41.

and death, that they might obtain heaven; and, finally, by such cogent reasons, so pathetically set forth, that all the auditors admired the doctrine, and felt what he wished to inspire them with. They found in the preacher something divine, which commanded respect, and they fixed their looks upon his countenance as if it had been that of an angel.

Count Orlando, more impressed with what he had heard than the rest, went after the sermon to embrace the preacher, and he entreated him particularly to instruct him in the affairs of his salvation. Francis, who, in addition to his ardent zeal, had much discretion and suavity of manner, said: "Count, go now and do honor to your friends whom you have invited, and we will talk of this affair at a more convenient time." The count, complying with this advice, joined the nobility who waited for him, and did not forget to take care of the servants of God. The feast having ended, he returned to the prudent director, with whom he had a lengthened conversation, with which he was so much struck, that in order to have the comfort of seeing familiarly the religious of his institute, he offered him the mountain of Alvernia, which belonged to him, with a promise, if he agreed to it, of building there a convent for him.

As this was a lonely place, very fit for contemplation, Francis gladly accepted the offer, and promised to send two of his brethren to Chiusi, before he should leave Italy. He did in fact send them, and the count having received them as angels sent from heaven, he took them to Mount Alvernia, where they fixed upon a spot which appeared to them to be fit to build a church on. Fifty soldiers who had been brought thither began immediately to fell timber, and a place was cleared, where hutting was set up to lodge the religious, in which they dwelt until the church and convent were built. These are the circumstances under which the Friars Minor were settled on this mountain, which subsequently became so celebrated in the Christian world by the stigmata of St. Francis. The place was ceded to them by an authentic document which the count gave them, and which is preserved in the original in the archives of the convent. We shall speak further of this holy place when we come to relate the first visit the saint paid it on his return from Spain.

He continued his journey through Bologna, from whence, after having visited his brethren, he came to Imola. He first went to offer his respects to the bishop, and asked permission to preach to his people. "I preach," replied the bishop coldly, "and that is quite enough." Francis bowed humbly, and retired; but an hour afterwards he returned, and the bishop, surprised and angered at seeing him again, asked him what he could possibly want? To which he replied, in a tone of sincere humility: "My lord, if a father drives his son out of the house by one door, it is right that the son should return through another." The bishop, mollified by this mild address, embraced him with affection, and said: "From henceforth you and your brethren may preach in my diocese. I give you a general leave, it is what your humility has merited." Is there anything which can soften minds and obtain favors sooner than this virtue?

The humility of Francis was accompanied with great courage, which rendered him firm and confident in the most imminent dangers, which was owing to the great confidence he had in God. Night overtook him once when he was in company with Leo, between Lombardy and the Trevisan Marshes, on a road having on one side the Po, one of the most considerable rivers in Italy, and on the other a deep morass. Leo, much alarmed, exclaimed: "Father, pray to God to deliver us from the danger we are in." Francis, full of faith, replied: "God can, if it is His good pleasure, give us light to dissipate the darkness of the night." These words were hardly spoken, when they found themselves surrounded by a brilliant light, which not only made the way clear to them, but enabled them to see many things on either side of the way, although the darkness was very dense everywhere else. They pursued their route, singing the glories of God; the celestial torch served them as a guide till they reached the place where they were to be lodged, which was then very far off. This miraculous light was a notification to the Saint that it was God's pleasure that he should have a dwelling in the place to which His goodness had led him, and he told this to his companion. The inhabitants made no difficulty in assigning him one, after having heard him preach, and he gave the convent the name of The Holy Fire, as it is still called.

In Piedmont, where he was well received, his preaching, with the reputation of his sanctity, confirmed by many miracles, converted a considerable number of persons, and procured him several houses.[14] From thence he went into Spain, but the writers of his Life have not recorded by what route. But it is scarcely to be doubted that he went by land, and through France; ancient documents show that he entered Spain through Navarre, and that he arrived in the year 1213 at Logrono, a town of Old Castile, which had formerly belonged to Biscay.

On the road he came up with a poor and abandoned invalid, for whom he felt so much pity that he directed Bernard da Quintavalle, one of his companions, to stay with him and take care of him, which the other willingly undertook to do. At Logrono, he miraculously cured a young gentleman who was on the point of death; then he went on to Burgos, where Alphonso IX, (or VIII, according to some,) father of Blanche, Queen of France, and mother of St. Louis, then was. Francis presented himself before the king; he showed him the rules of his institute, and entreated him to receive the Friars Minor into his states. This monarch, who, in addition to his political and military talents, had a great fund of goodness and piety, received the holy man very favorably; he condescended to read the rules, and after having conversed with him for some

---

[14] Wading only says, that they gave him a house at Quiers, near Turin. But a learned Piedmontese author proves, not only from tradition, but from documents taken from the archives of Savoy, and from those of convents, of which Wading had no knowledge, that Francis placed some of his brethren at Cairo, Cortemiglia, Asti, Montcalier, Turin, Veillane, and Susa; and that he did various marvelous things in Piedmont.

time, he gave leave to build houses in Spain for the Order.[15]

The servant of God, fortified by the royal protection, procured a small church of St. Michael, near Burgos, where he dwelt for some time, and which he left in the care of two of the brethren, in order to continue his journey at the beginning of the year 1214. But Medrani, an officer of the army of the king of Castile, father of the young man whom he had cured at Logrono, knowing that the king had permitted him to establish himself at Burgos, induced him to return to Logrono, where he gave him his own house and gardens to turn into a convent. Francis had it altered properly for the accommodation of religious, and placed it in charge of one of his companions, leaving in it, under his guidance, some of his novices, whom his preaching and miracles had drawn to him. He did the same at Vittoria, in respect to a dwelling, which, together with a church, he received from the municipality.

He then turned his thoughts entirely to advancing towards the seaside in order to embark for Morocco, there to suffer martyrdom, for this was the great object of his wishes. If we only formed our opinion of things by the ordinary rules of prudence, we should be surprised, that a man, visibly sent by God for the institution of a new order of religious, should leave it so short a time after its birth, to seek for death among the infidels. But the Saints only thought of following the impulses which the Spirit of God suggested to them, with reference to the works which they had commenced by God's order. St. Anthony,[16] father of a great number of Cenobites, left his monastery, and followed at Alexandria certain confessors of the faith; he attended upon them in prison, and exhorted them under torment to procure for himself the palm of martyrdom. St. Dominic, animated by a similar spirit, had formed the intention of going among the Saracens, only two years after the institution of his order.[17] Francis, thus inspired from above, desired to meet death for Jesus Christ, and left to God the care of his rising family.

This disposition, which was the fruit of ardent charity, was very pleasing to God; it entered into the economy of His providence for the salvation of souls and for the aggrandizement of the new Order, for the Saint did not cease his labors when he took the route which was to lead to martyrdom. Nevertheless, God did not choose that his design should be carried into execution; and His will was made known to His servant by a violent illness,

---

[15] The translator of Mariana's History of Spain, which appeared in 1725, should have remarked that Mariana was in error when he said that St. Francis established his Order in Spain after that of St. Dominic, and after having had his institute approved by Honorius, and that in 1218. For it is certain that that Pope only gave his approval by Bull in 1225, to the Order of the Saint, which Innocent III had verbally approved in 1210 which, proves that the Order was introduced into Spain before that of St. Dominic; since the institute of this holy Patriarch was only approved by Innocent III at the Lateran Council, held in 1215, and not in 1212, as the translator inadvertently says, in a note, and was only approved by a Bull of Honorius in 1216.

[16] S. Athan. in vit. St. Anton, n. 45.

[17] *Vita S. Damin a Theod.* lib. 2, cap. 2.

which put it out of his power to embark for Morocco. Francis gave up his wishes, obeying what was thus signified to him, and came to the resolution to return to Italy for the guidance of his flock; however, he did not set out till the close of the year.

The authors of the Order are agreed in saying that he went to visit the tomb of the apostle St. James, at Compostela, the capital of Galicia, to which place devotion has attracted, for many centuries past, crowds of pilgrims, and that an angel appeared to him there, and assured him that it was God's will that he should return to Italy, after having founded some establishments in Spain. They also say that he went into Portugal,[18] where he raised to life the daughter of his host at Guimaraens, a town of the diocese of Braganza, which caused him to be considered as a Saint throughout the whole country; and that he went through nearly the whole of the kingdom of Arragon and the adjacent provinces. Finally, they relate a most extraordinary circumstance.

Francis being one evening on the banks of the river Orbego, with his companions, where there was no food, a young man of the town of Novia overtook them, and carried them over on some horses he had with him, and received them hospitably. The gratitude the Saint manifested, was by saying, "May the Lord reward you for the kindness you have shown us, when He rewards the just." Some short time after, this young man, having gone to Rome out of devotion, and having endeavored to put his conscience in a fit state, he prayed fervently to God, to take him out of this world before he should commit a mortal sin. His prayer was heard; he died. His father desired to have a funeral service said for him, and thirty Friars Minor attended it without having been asked; none knew from whence they came, nor whither they afterwards went, which made it thought that the assistance was miraculous; and as it was known what the holy man Francis had said to the deceased, it was understood that he had, by this means, procured the reward of the just for him whose hospitality he had received.

Gonzagues, Bishop of Mantua, who had been General of the Order of St. Francis, says, that it is held as certain in Spain, that he commenced the establishments of Gasta, Arevalo, Avila, Madrid, Tudela, and caused several other convents to be built. It is easily understood that in the eight or nine months in which he remained in Spain after his illness, he arranged much by himself and by his companions; the old inscriptions which are still seen on the tombs of many of them are an additional proof. What is quite certain is, that his holy life and his preaching were of the greatest benefit to souls, and that

---

[18] Some persons think that St. Francis saw Queen Urraqua, the wife of Alphonso II, in Portugal, and that he foretold to her, that Portugal would never be united to Spain. Wading proves that not to be true; and he adds, that had such a prediction been made, it could not be said up to this time that it was false, because the Spaniards had been masters of Portugal under Philip II. For besides that that occupation was temporary, there was never any true union between the two countries, even when the same king governed them. Portugal was subject to Spain, but not united. Philip II declares this in an assembly of the states, and the public documents prove it. Wading, ad aim. 1213.

his Order was received in Spain with an affection which has passed from age to age, from fathers to sons; so that Spain is one of the countries of the world in which there is the greatest veneration for St. Francis, and the greatest consideration for the Order of Friars Minor.

The same bishop tells us, on the testimony of universal and unvaried tradition, of many miracles performed by the Almighty, through the ministry of the holy man. We shall satisfy ourselves by relating one of them, which is warranted by manuscripts and documents.

Francis was lodged at Compostela, at the house of a poor dealer in charcoal, whose name was Cotolai, and he often went to pass the night in contemplation on a neighboring mountain. God made known to him, that it was His will that he should build a convent between two valleys, the one of which was commonly called the valley of God, and the other the valley of hell. He knew that this ground belonged to the Benedictines of Compostela, of the Abbey of St. Pay, or Pelagius, since transferred to that of St. Martin; and, bearing in mind the favors which the Religious of this holy Order had done him in the gifts of St. Mary of the Angels, and at Rome, he called upon the Abbot and asked him unhesitatingly permission to build a convent between the two valleys. "What will you give me in payment?" says the Abbot. Francis replied, "As I am very poor, and have neither money, nor anything else to give you, if you grant me what I ask, and what will be most precious to me, I will give you in quit rent yearly, a small basket of fish if they can be caught in the river." The Abbot who was a very pious man, admiring his simplicity and his confidence, granted him his request on the condition proposed, and an act to that effect was prepared and signed by both.

The holy man came to Cotolai and told him what had passed between the Abbot of St. Pay and himself, and added: "My dear host, it is God's will that you should build this convent; therefore prepare yourself for the work. "Oh, how shall I be able to do that," answered Cotolai, "I who am so poor, and who live by my daily labor?" "Take courage," said Francis, "take a pickaxe, and go to the spring which is close by; make a hole a little in front of it, and you will find a treasure which will enable you to execute the order of heaven." Cotolai, relying on the Saint's word, searched as he was desired, found the treasure, and built the convent, which is known by the name of St. Francis at this day. This fact is narrated in an authentic manuscript in the archives of the Abbey of St. Martin, from whence this is copied; and in two very old inscriptions, one of which is on the tomb of Cotolai and his wife, whose name was Mary de Bicos, and the other over the gate of the church of the convent in which their tomb is. The deed which was executed by Francis and the Abbot of St. Pay, is preserved in the original in the archives of the Abbey of St. Martin of Compostela. The Prince of Spain, Philip the Second, saw it in the year 1554, when he was about to embark at Corunna, to marry Mary, queen of England. However, the marvel has nothing in it which should be the cause of much surprise: our Savior, who made St. Peter find in the mouth of a fish wherewithal to pay the tribute for his Master and himself,[19] could easily cause a treasure of money to be found sufficient to build a house for his faithful servant Francis.

When the apostolical man had terminated his mission in Spain, he went to rejoin Bernard de Quintavalle, whom he had left on entering it, in charge of the poor sick man, who was perfectly cured, and he came through Aragon into Catalonia. The magistrates of Barcelona, where he stopped for a short time, were so pleased with his poverty, his humility, and his other virtues, that, for the sake of having some religious of his Order, they converted the hospital where he was lodged into a convent, the church and cloister of which are still extant, and are venerable from the remembrance of the Saint.

At San Saloni, a small town between Barcelona and Gerona, an adventure occurred to him which seemed purely accidental, but which God tinned to good. As he walked by the side of a vineyard, his companion gathered a bunch or two of grapes to refresh himself. He who had charge of the vineyard, perceiving it, came violently upon the religious, beat him and abused him in no measured terms, and took from him his poor cloak. Francis asked to have the cloak back, alleging mildly, that what had been taken had done no injury to the vineyard, and that good feeling required that this assistance should be given to a passer-by who needed it.[20] But, not having succeeded in procuring its restoration, he went to the proprietor of the vineyard, from whom he had no difficulty in getting it back, after having told him what had happened. He then conversed with him on heavenly things with such effect, that the man, devoting himself from that moment to his service, promised to receive hospitably all the Friars Minor who should pass through San Saloni, and furnish them with whatsoever they might require, as far as his means would allow; which he never failed to do as long as he lived. Francis, in return, granted him participation in all the spiritual merits of his Order, and gave him the name of father of the Friars Minor.

It is from this precedent that the superiors of the Order give letters of filiation, as they are called, in virtue of which the holders participate in the merits of all the practices of the community. This is grounded on the communion of saints, one of the articles of the apostolic symbol by which each member of the faithful who is not excommunicated, and principally if he be in a state of grace, participates in the good works of others.[21] Besides this general communication, the faithful may assist each other by their prayers, and their

---

[19] Matt. 17: 26.

[20] The law of Moses allowed grapes to be eaten in a neighboring vineyard, but not to be carried away; and we see in the Gospel that the disciples of Jesus Christ, being hungry, and passing through cornfields, gathered the ears and ate them. Deuter. XXIII: 24, 25, and Matt. XII: 1.

[21] S. Amb. *de Offic.* lib. I, c. 29. St. August, *in Joan.* Tract 32, n. 7 and 8,13. *Serm. 3, in Psalm* 103, n. 9.

own merits, as is done in confraternities and all pious associations. This is the way in which the Order of St. Francis, and all other religious orders, manifest their gratitude to their benefactors; in this they do that which St. Augustine says of the ministers of Jesus Christ in regard to the faithful who support them; "They give spiritual things, and only receive temporal ones; they give gold, and only receive grass."[22] Those who know what the communion of saints is, and who neglect nothing which can contribute to their salvation, have great esteem (as, indeed, they ought) for letters of filiation, and strive to live in a Christian-like manner in order to profit by them.

From Catalonia, Francis continued his route through Roussillon, and it is believed that he placed some of his religious at Perpignan, the capital. He then entered Languedoc, which the errors and arms of the Albigenses had alike tended to desolate. The Catholics[23] at that time enjoyed some calm by the valor of the illustrious Simon, Count of Montfort, who had just overthrown the heretics, principally by the celebrated victories obtained, at Muret, over Peter, king of Aragon, whom ill-understood interests had made protector of the Albigenses, to the detriment of religion, and who was killed in that battle. The saintly traveler did not make any stay in Languedoc; perhaps because it was the field destined by Providence to be cultivated by St Dominic, whose preaching and miracles had made an infinity of conversions, and who was then at Carcassonne, where he gave the nuptial benediction to the marriage of Amaury de Montfort, the son of Simon, with the Princess Beatrice, the daughter of the Dauphin, Count of Viennois. Francis arrived at Montpellier at the time when they were about to open the council, at which Simon of Montfort was loaded with praises, and chosen to be possessor of the city of Toulouse, and the other conquests of the Crusaders; he preached there, and foretold that a convent would be built there for his brethren in the hospital where he lodged, a prophecy which was fulfilled in the year 1220.

His bad health, the fatigues of his journey, and the rigor of the season, had brought him into a state of great languor, and compelled him to stop one day. His malady gave him a disgust for all sorts of meat, and he thought that he could only relish some wild fowl. As he was speaking of it to his companion Bernard, a well-appointed cavalier brought him one ready dressed, saying, "Servant of God, take what the Lord sends you," after which he disappeared. Francis, admiring the goodness of God, who fulfills the desires of those who fear Him,[24] ate willingly of this celestial food, and was so strengthened by it, that he rose up immediately and continued his journey through Dauphiny and Piedmont; from whence he went to St. Mary of the Angels, continuing to perform the functions of an apostle and Patriarch of the Order on his way, but

---

[22] Id. Serm. 3, in Psalm 103, n. 9.

[23] See the history of the Crusades against the Albigenses by Father Langlois of the Society of Jesus, 1703.

[24] Ps. 144: 19.

not without having to endure the honors which his miracles and the reputation of his sanctity procured him from all parts.

His return was the subject of great rejoicing to his children, to Clare in particular, and to a number of young men, among whom were many nobles and many learned persons who were waiting to be received into the Order.

He was surprised to find a building which Peter of Catania, his vicar, had had constructed during his absence; he inquired the reason of it, and Peter having replied, "that it was for the accommodation of their guests, where they might say the divine office more commodiously." "Brother Peter," he said, "this place is the rule and the model of the Order; I choose that those who come to it shall suffer, as well as those who live in it, the inconveniences of poverty, in order that they may tell others how poorly we live at St. Mary's of the Portiuncula; for if the guests see that they are provided with everything they can wish for, they will expect the same thing in their provinces, and will say, that they only do as they do at Portiuncula, which is the original place of the institution." He was desirous that the building should be pulled down, and he even directed it to be done; but, upon the representations of the need they had of it, he consented to let it stand. They could not do without room to lodge the number of people who were drawn thither by the rumor of his great virtues, and the multitudes of his religious who came from various parts to consult him.

Those whom he had destined for Mount Alvernia, having come with several others to congratulate him on his return, informed him that Count Orlando had loaded them with favors; that they were settled on the mountain, and that it was the place, of all others, proper for contemplation. This gave him a wish to go thither, and he set out with three companions, Leo, Massé, and Angelus of Rieti. It was his custom in traveling to name one of those who accompanied him as guardian and leader, and he obeyed him humbly in all things. On this occasion, he gave this commission to Massé, desiring him not to disquiet himself about their food, and giving no other instructions, except that the divine office should be punctually and piously recited, that silence should be rigidly observed, and that their deportment should be reserved. He preached, as usual, wherever he went, and performed many miracles, the principal of which will be spoken of hereafter.

One night he went into a church which was deserted, in order to pass the night in prayer, knowing from experience that the Spirit of God was communicated more freely to the soul in quiet solitary places. At the beginning of the night, the devils used every sort of artifice to interrupt his prayers and to disturb him. Then they attacked him in person, as St. Athanasius relates that they did St. Anthony,[25] so that they seemed to come to blows with him. The more they annoyed him, the more fervently he prayed, and the more strenuously he invoked Jesus Christ with confidence, in the words of the

---

[25] S, Athan. in vit. S. Anton, n. 5.

prophet: "Protect me under the shadow of your wings from these wicked ones who pursue me;"[26] and he said to the devils: "Spiteful and deceitful spirits, do all you can against me, for you can do nothing but what God permits, and here I am, ready to suffer with pleasure all the afflictions it is His pleasure to send me." Then the devils cast themselves upon him with still greater violence; they pushed him about on all sides, they dragged him along the ground and beat him severely. In the midst of his sufferings, he exclaimed: "My Lord Jesus Christ, I give You thanks for all Your benefits; this is not one of the least; it is an assured mark of the goodness You have for me. You punish my sins in this world to spare me in the next. My heart is ready, O my God, my heart is ready to suffer still more if such be Your holy will." St. Bonaventure says, that he was often tormented in this manner by demons; but that these proud spirits, not being able either to overcome him, or to bear his constancy, retired in confusion. Such a resistance would repress all the efforts of the tempter when he attacks us invisibly.

In the morning, he could not disguise from his companions what had happened to him, and the extreme weakness which it had brought on obliged him to desire his companions to go to the neighboring village, to procure him, for the love of God, some means of riding on with them. The farmer to whom they applied, having learnt that it was for Francis of Assisi, of whom he had heard so much good spoken, went to fetch his own ass to carry him on, on his mission.

On the way, Francis bethought himself of stopping for a short time at this farmer's to recruit his strength by some poultry and other delicacies of the country; but, wishing to punish himself for having merely listened to such a suggestion, he took up a half-rotten fowl from a dunghill, and smelt at it, saying to himself: "Here, glutton! here is the flesh of the poultry that you so anxiously wished for; satisfy your longing, and eat as much as you like." To support himself, he ate nothing but bread, on which he sprinkled ashes, and he drank nothing but water. He blessed the house of his host, and promised him very long lineage, who should be neither poor nor rich, and who should have conveniently all the necessaries of life. The remembrance of this prediction has been carefully preserved in this place, and the house still exists, bearing the name of St. Francis, where the religious of his Order are always charitably received. This is what is taught by the apostle: "That God, by His blessing, gives to charitable persons the means of continuing and multiplying their good works."[27] The invalid was replaced on the ass, and they took the road to Chiusi which they reached by noon. Count Orlando was greatly pleased to see them, and would have been but too glad to detain them, if only for that day; but Francis would go as soon as dinner was done to Mount Alvernia, whither the count accompanied him.

---

[26] Ps. XIV: 10.

[27] 2 Cor. 9: 8, et seq.

The mountain Alvernia is on the confines of Tuscany, not far from Camaldoli, and Val Ombrosa; it is part of the Apennines,[28] and it rises higher than the adjacent mountains from which it is separated: two rivers flow at its foot, the Tiber and the Arno. On their sides it has rocks so perpendicular and so smooth that they might be mistaken for walls; and on the side on which the top may be reached, no one would dare to attempt the ascent but for the number of beech trees and underwood which hide the precipices. These trees, which are very lofty, hide some extensive and beautiful pasturages. There was also there abundance of the plant called carline or Caroline,[29] which is a cure for the plague.

The farmer, who was their guide, made bold to address him as follows: "Brother, I hear much good spoken of you, and I understand that God has shown you great favors, for which you are greatly indebted to Him; strive, then, to be what it is said you are, and never to change, in order that those who have confidence in you may not be deceived; this is a piece of advice I give you." Francis, delighted at what he had heard, dismounted, kissed the man's feet, thanked him, acknowledging the great mercy of God, who had been pleased to cast His eyes on the lowliness of His servant. Although this advice came from a poor countryman, it was nevertheless the very best that could be given to a saint. So true it is that no one should be despised, and that the most simpleminded persons often say more sensible and more spiritual things than men of the greatest genius.

The same man being very thirsty at the steepest part of the mountain, exclaimed loudly: "I shall die, if I cannot get something to drink." Francis immediately alighted, threw himself on his knees, raised his hands to heaven, and prayed until he knew that he had been heard. Then, pointing out a large stone to the man, he said, "Go there quickly, and you will find some living water: it is Jesus Christ who, out of His great mercy, makes it spring from this rock that you may drink." The man ran directly, found water, and drank as much as he required. No spring had ever been known to be in that place, and no water was ever found there afterwards. Wonderful goodness of the Almighty, exclaims St. Bonaventure, who thus with so much benevolence grants the prayers of His servants.

At length they reached the top of Mount Alvernia, where the religious resided. The father was well pleased with their dwelling, because everything was on a small scale and poor. Count Orlando returned in the evening and came back next day, bringing something for their dinner. After they had

---

[28] Apennines is the common name which is given to the long chain of mountains, which begins on the coasts of Genoa, and, bending to the South, runs through the whole of Italy till it reaches the straits which separate Sicily from the mainland. The Apennine is called by Virgil, *Pater Apenninus,* either because it commands several vast forests, or because many rivers flow from it, or because its mountains are the highest in Italy.

[29] It is the white Chamelian, or Carline thistle; because it is believed that this plant was shown the Emperor Charlemagne by an angel, to cure his army of the plague. Wading, ad aim. 1213.

finished their meal, he gave orders for the construction of a small chapel under a very tall beech tree, and a cell, which Francis had asked him for, and, calling the others aside, he said: "Since your founder has given his consent to the donation I made you two years ago of this mountain, you may consider it as yours, and hence both myself and mine will be always devoted to your service whenever you shall need it. You will not be able to please me more than by addressing yourselves to me, looking upon me as your servant, and even, if you will do me that favor, considering me as one of your brethren." After the departure of the count, the holy Patriarch made them the following discourse, relative to the count's kindness, which they took care to commit to writing:

"My dear children, it is God who thus turns the hearts of the faithful towards His little and useless servants, in which He does us a very great favor. On what we have hitherto received let us place our hopes for what is to come; if that seems but little, the Lord, who is infinitely liberal,[30] will add to it by His goodness still greater benefits, provided we are faithful to Him. Let us, then, leave to Him the care of all that relates to you,[31] and He Himself will feed you, as He fed Elias, Paul, and Anthony in the desert. The birds of the air neither sow, nor reap, nor gather into barns, yet your heavenly Father nourishes them,[32] how much more will He do this for His servants? If He tries you, it will be only for a time, for it is written, that He will not suffer the just to waver forever; the eyes of the Lord are on them that fear Him, and on them that hope in His mercy to deliver their souls from death and feed them in famine. Trust not to the princes of the earth,[33] nor to the charitable offers made you by our benefactor, Count Orlando, for cursed is the man that trusteth in man, and makes flesh his arm.[34] This lord has acted nobly by us, and according to His piety; let us do on our parts what depends on us, and fail not therein; that is to say, let us not have recourse to his generosity, as to a treasure of which we are the masters, and in that respect let us have the greatest reserve that we may not in any respect trench upon holy poverty. Be sure, my dear children, that our best resource for providing for our wants, is to have none to provide for. If we are truly evangelical poor, the world will have compassion upon us, and will generously give us all that is necessary for our subsistence; but if we swerve from holy poverty, the world will shun us; the illicit means which we might take for avoiding indigence, would only make us feel it the more." Is not such a discourse sufficient to show us, that St. Francis had great talents and judgment, joined to great knowledge of the practice of virtue?

Count Orlando had a church built on Mount Alvernia, according to the plan which the Saint had given him, which, it was confidently said, had been

---

[30] 2 Reg. 12: 3.

[31] Ps. 54 (55):25.

[32] Matt. 6: 26.

[33] Ps. 32: 8.

[34] Jer. 17: 5.

given to him by the Blessed Virgin, who appeared accompanied by St. John Baptist, and St. John the Evangelist.

While they were at work at his building and at the cells for the brethren, Francis explored the mountain on all its sides, to discover the sites best adapted for contemplation. He found one, where there were some large openings in the rock, great masses overhanging them, deep caverns, and frightful pits; and what seemed to him to be most curious, there was a rock so split that the interior formed a room with a smooth flooring, and a sort of ceiling which had a small opening which admitted the light. He was anxious to know whether this was the natural formation of the rock, or whether it was not the effect of an earthquake; and, after having recited the seven penitential Psalms, he begged God to grant him information on this head. An angel acquainted him, in an apparition, that this had happened at the death of Jesus Christ, when the earth shook and the rocks were rent asunder. This circumstance gave Mount Alvernia additional value in the eyes of the servant of Jesus Christ crucified. He never afterwards saw these openings without thinking of the sufferings his Divine Master endured on the cross,[35] and without wishing that his feelings of compassion might break his heart. In the opinion of the holy Fathers, the rocks which were rent when Jesus Christ expired were reproaches to the Jews for the hardness of their hearts, and this reproach falls equally on Christians who are insensible to His sufferings.[36]

We can have no difficulty in thinking, with Cardinal Baronius, that the rocks on Mount Alvernia were split at the death of our Savior, since the earthquake was universal, according to the opinions of Eusebius, St. Jerome, and many others, and even according to the testimony of pagan authors.

It is also very credible that the Son of God has manifested to His special servants, some of the effects of this motion of the earth, in order to impress more vividly on their minds the remembrance of His passion: and may we not think that the Lord, who is the beholder of all ages,[37] as the wise man says, and who had selected Mount Alvernia as the place in which He would do His servant Francis the favor of imprinting the stigmata on him, as we shall see further on, was pleased to give this mountain some resemblance to that of Calvary, where St. Cyril of Jerusalem assures us, that in his time the rents caused by the earthquake were seen?

Among the masses of rock on Mount Alvernia, there is one much more elevated and much larger than the rest, and which is separated from them by precipices, to which there is no access but by throwing a bridge across. There, as in an insulated citadel, a celebrated brigand had his stronghold, who was called the Wolf, on account of the plunder and murders he committed in the surrounding country, either by himself, or by the gang of which he was the

---

[35] Matt. 27: 51.

[36] S Hieron. *in Amos.* cap. 3.

[37] Ecclus. 36: 19.

chief. He often, also, by means of a flying bridge, confined travelers in this place, whom he had surprised on the highroads, and whom he detained till their ransom was paid. The establishment of Francis and his brethren displeased him greatly: people of that sort do not like having neighbors. He gave them several times notice to begone, and he threatened them should they not obey. Their great poverty gave them nothing to fear from thieves, but there was just cause for apprehending that the murderer might massacre them all. Divine Providence, however, saved them by a change which might well be called the word of the Most High. The villain came one day determined upon expelling them, and used the most atrocious language to them. Francis received him with so much mildness, listened to him with so much patience, and induced him by degrees to hear reason, so that his anger entirely fell, and he not only consented to their remaining, but he begged that they would admit him into their poor dwelling. He witnessed during several days their angelic mode of life, and he became so changed, that he determined upon adopting a similar plan. The Saint perceiving that from a ravenous wolf he was become a gentle lamb, gave him the habit of the Order, and the name of Brother Agnello, under which he expiated his crimes by religious penance, of which he rigidly fulfilled all the duties. This fact was of such notoriety, that the rock to which he used to retire has always been called since, and is still known, by the name of Brother Wolf's prison.

CHAPTER IV
COUNCIL OF THE LATERAN—APPROVAL OF THE RULE

Leaves for Rome—Discovers some relics by revelation—Makes predictions, and performs miracles and conversions—Arrives at Rome whilst the Council of Lateran is sitting—The Pope declares to the Council that he has approved the Rule—He appoints a general chapter at St. Mary of the Angels, whither he returns—He holds the chapter, and sends his friars to various countries—He thinks of going to Paris—Reunites an illustrious family that had been divided—Rejoices in his poverty, and asks of God a greater love of holy poverty—SS. Peter and Paul appear to him at Rome—His alliance with St. Dominic—He goes to Florence, where Cardinal Hugolin dissuades him from going to Paris—He returns to the Valley of Spoleto, and sends three of his disciples to France—A celestial vision induces him to ask of the Pope a cardinal protector for his Order—What he says on this subject—He preaches before the Pope—What happened to him in the pulpit—The Pope gives him Cardinal Hugolin, as protector of the Order—He preaches in the Valley of Rieti—Delivers the country from two plagues, and makes some conversions there—He appoints a general chapter at St. Mary of the Angels, for the year 1219—What he did during the year 1218—Efficacy of his prayers—He wishes to pull down a new house which he found at St. Mary of the Angels.

LL THINGS BEING put in order at Mount Alvernia, he left it to go to Rome. He passed through Monte Casale, Fabriano, Osimo, Ancona, Macerata, Ascoli, Camerino, and many other places, preaching in all the truths of salvation, gaining disciples, founding houses for his Order, prophesying and working miracles; we shall only put on record here the most remarkable, and those that are most edifying.

God favored him, as He had done St. Ambrose, with power of discovering relics which were hidden. He knew by revelation that there were some in a certain church in which he had prayed, and some business calling him away from thence, he communicated the circumstance to his brethren, desiring them to take them from thence and place them in a more suitable situation; but they either through forgetfulness or neglect did not do so. One day as they were preparing the altar for mass, they found under the altar-cloth some beautiful bones, from which a sweet perfumed smell issued, and they immediately recollected that these were the relics of which their father had spoken. At his return he inquired whether they had been disinterred, and the religious, having told him exactly what had occurred, he said: "Blessed be the Lord, my God, who, of His goodness, has done what you ought to have done out of obedience." But he imposed a penance upon them in expiation of their fault.

At the monastery of Monte Maggiore, a joy and interior consolation which he felt on entering the church, made him sensible that the high altar contained something which had been used by the Blessed Virgin.. He spoke of it to the religious, who searched narrowly, and found that it was true. In ecclesiastical history we find that God had often caused the relics of His saints to be discovered, in order to do them honor, and the holy Fathers have taught the faithful to venerate them. There are only heretics who have been capable of treating them with contempt and profaning them; they are for the children of the Church a tender object of devotion, and a pledge of the Divine protection.

While he was preaching at Fabriano in the middle of the marketplace, some workmen who were employed at a palace made so much noise, that it prevented his being heard. Having entreated them to be quiet for a short time, to which they paid no attention, he said that the work of those who were building the house would be of no use, because the Lord did not build it, but that it would soon fall; however, that neither man nor beast would be injured by it; and this happened but a few days after it had been finished, as he had foretold. He assured the people at the same town, that at a place called the Poor Valley, his brethren, who were poor, would some day have a habitation. And, in fact, in the year 1292, the town of Fabriano placed Friars Minor there.

Among the most considerable establishments which he placed on his route, was that of St. Mary of the Stony Valley, so called from its being situated in a very rocky valley, between two mountains, four miles distant from Fabriano. It was a church dedicated to the Blessed Virgin, with a monastery, which the religious of St. Benedict had abandoned in order to take refuge in the town, on account of the wars, and it is one of the most beautiful solitudes of all Italy. Devotion to the Mother of God, and the love of retreat, had induced Francis to ask for this place; and it was given him by those who were its proprietors. The first time he went there, he lost his way, with his companion, and asked a plowman to take him to the valley. "What," says the man, "shall I leave my plough and lose my time, to serve you?" However, he took him to the place, mollified by Francis' mildness, and by his promising him that he should be no loser by so doing: on returning, after receiving the Father's blessing, he found his field quite plowed.

Some workmen who were employed repairing a house which had been given him, at a place called Trabe Bonata, being very tired, asked him to give them some wine. He sent two of his brethren to procure some in a neighboring village, from some charitable benefactor; but the workmen being very urgent, out of compassion for them he went to a spring, made the sign of the cross over it, and in an instant, instead of water, wine issued from it, which flowed for a whole hour. Those who drank of it published in all places the miraculous effect of the Saint's charity.

In a parish called La Cittá, he was very well received by the Curate, whose name was Raniero, with whom he became very intimate, so that he was in the habit of visiting him, and going to confession to him. One day after confession he gave him, in a very humble manner, notice, that he, the Curate, would become one of his brethren, because they had become too closely united to live different kinds of lives: "But," he said, "this will not happen till after my death." The event verified the prediction: as soon as the Curate learnt that his friend Francis shone by an infinity of miracles, and was just canonized, he entered the Order of Friars Minor, and adhered to the rules with great regularity.

The holy man coming to Osimo, he was met, notwithstanding his great humility, and brought into the town, with great honors. The next day he preached on the vanity of the world, in so persuasive a strain, that all his hearers, penetrated with compunction, turned their thoughts seriously to their reformation, and thirty young men entered his Institute.

In the same journey, he and his companion lodged at the house of a gentleman, the greatness of whose soul equaled the antiquity of his nobility, and whose politeness was joined to piety. The welcome he received there was followed by this open-hearted proffer: "Man of God," he said, "I place my person at your disposal, and all that I possess, all is yours, do as you please with it; if you want clothing, or a cloak, or books, or whatever it may be, take it, and I will pay for it. Be assured that I am wholly at your service. God has given me wealth; I have wherewithal to assist the poor, and it is but just that I do not fail in so doing."

Francis merely at the time contented himself with making those grateful acknowledgments which so handsome and obliging an offer required; but when he left him, he could not refrain from admiring the generosity of this gentleman, and he said to his companion: "Indeed, brother, he would be an excellent subject for our Order; he is humbly thankful for what he has received from God; he loves his neighbor very sincerely; he gives willingly to the poor; and he exercises hospitality from his heart; he is extremely affable and polite; and politeness is sister to charity; it puts down contention and promotes concord; he is naturally benevolent; and this feeling is highly pleasing to our Father who is in heaven, who causes the sun to rise on the good and on the wicked.[38] So many excellent qualities which I see in this young man, make me wish to have him to be one of us, and I should admit him with pleasure. We must pay him another visit, and exhort him to devote himself to the service of God; perhaps the Holy Spirit may incline him to do so; meanwhile let us implore the Lord to grant our wish, if He judges it right." In fact, they did pray for this purpose.

Some days afterwards they returned to this person's house, who had the curiosity to watch what Francis did in the night; he saw him in prayer, and in an ecstasy raised from the ground, and surrounded by a splendid light, and he felt interiorly a certain celestial fire, which inspired him with an ardent desire

---

[38] Matt. 5: 45.

to imitate his mode of life. In the morning, he communicated his feelings to the Saint, who was already made aware of them by revelation, and who thanked the Giver of all good gifts for them. The postulant gave all he had to the poor, took the habit of a Friar Minor, and lived holily, preserving always the same affable and polite manners, with which he received the guests of the convents in which he resided, which endeared him still more to the Patriarch, who was very zealous in the exercise of hospitality. The duties of hospitality, lauded by the pagans, taught by the Gospel, enforced by the Apostles, and all the holy Fathers, are exercised in the Order of St. Francis with so much the more care as, being totally dependent on charity, they consider themselves bound to give all in the same manner, and they apply to themselves these words of the Son of God to the Apostles, on the gift of miracles: "Freely you have received, freely give."[39] This is what draws down the blessing of God, and which makes so many houses subsist, without any revenue, by the charity of the faithful.

The holy patriarch of the Friars Minor arrived at Rome when everything was preparing for the opening of the Twelfth Ecumenical Council, the 4th of Lateran, one of the most numerous ever held in the Church.[40] Innocent III had convoked it for the extinction of heresies, for the reformation of morals, for regulating the discipline of the Church, and for the recovery of the Holy Land by the union of the Christian princes.

Francis came to Rome to induce the sovereign pontiff to give a public approval to the Rule of his Order, which was of the highest importance in order that the prelates might have it in their power to distinguish the poor of Jesus Christ, true children of the Church, from certain sectaries of those times who affected, as has been already said, to bear the marks of apostolic poverty.

What the servant of God required was put in force; the pope declared before all the Fathers of the Council,[41] that he approved the Order and the Rule of St. Francis, although he had hitherto issued no Bull. This is a fact which is related by the companions of the Saint who wrote his life, and by two authors of the Order a St. Dominic, Jordan of Saxony, a disciple of that blessed Patriarch, and St. Antoninus.[42] Moreover, in order to avoid too great a variety of religious orders, the council prohibited the formation of any new ones, and directed that the existing ones should be considered sufficient, and it is clear that the pope could not, in this instance, avoid making known the approbation

---

[39] Matt. 10: 8.

[40] Ursperg ad ann. 1215.

[41] Preachers and Minors, because of the services the Church receives from them, it sufficiently shows that it approves of them; it means merely to imply that those two orders were only solemnly sanctioned by Bulls, subsequent to the Lateran Council. For, as to the verbal approbation, it is certain that Innocent III gave it in 1210 to the Minors, and St. Bonaventure expressly says so, and we shall see that Honorius III also says so in the Bull which he issued in 1223, when he confirmed the rule. As to the Order of Preachers, it was approved by Innocent III, at the Lateran Council in 1215, and confirmed at Rome, in 1226, by the Bull of Honorius III.

[42] Jord. de Sax. *de vit. Frat.* lib. 1, cap. 24. S. Anton, chron.

he had given to an Order so new and peculiar as was that of the Friars Minor, who, in the last five years, had spread over Italy, and were established in Rome.

The holy friendship which was subsequently formed between St. Dominic and St. Francis, renders it proper that we should here record that St. Dominic came also to this Lateran Council, together with Fulke, bishop of Toulouse, in order to propose to the pope an intention he had of instituting an order of preachers, and[43] that the pope had seen in a dream St. Dominic supporting the Lateran church, which was falling, in the same way as he had seen Francis supporting it five years before. He praised his undertaking, but told him, according to the decree of the council, to return with his brethren, and prepare a rule for the guidance of the order, and then come back to have the order confirmed, which the holy patriarch complied with.

The Council of Lateran having terminated its labors,[44] Francis left Rome at the beginning of December to return to St. Mary of the Angels, after having sent circular letters to the houses of the Order, convoking the general chapter, which was to meet in that convent at Whitsuntide of the following year.

When he had reached his convent, Clare, who, being very humble, had accepted only through obedience the quality of abbess of St. Damian, wished to throw it up into his hands, to which he would by no means assent, because he knew that by the disposition of Divine Providence, she was to form the disciples who were to establish his Order in various places, from whence it was to spread throughout the Church.

Clare had admitted many virgins during the three years she had presided over St. Damian, among whom were some of her own relatives. Beatrice, the youngest of her sisters, came a short time afterwards; and Hortolana, her mother, as soon as she became a widow, decided upon consecrating herself to God, with her three daughters, in the same monastery, where miracles testified to the holiness of her life. Finally, the virtues of Clare were so resplendent, and the miracles which it pleased the Almighty to work by her means, threw so much splendor around her, that, according to the remark of Pope Alexander IV, in the Bull of her canonization,[45] the truth of the prediction which was made to her mother, was clearly seen: "That she would give to the world a light which would even enlighten the world." The sequel of the life of the Father will afford further opportunity for speaking of the daughter.

The Benedictines of Mount Soubazo, in this year, gave the holy Patriarch a convent on this very mountain, two miles from Assisi. It has been called the prison of St. Francis, because he often shut himself up there in contemplation after his apostolical labors. His oratory is still seen there: his cell, the stone and the wood which served him for bed and pillow, and a copious spring which, by

---

[43] Jord. de Sax. *MS.* cap. 20, 21, and 22. Theod. ad Appold. *vit. S. Domin.*

[44] The Council sat twenty days; from the feast of S. Martin to that of S. Andrew.

[45] *Bollar. Rom.* tom. 1.

his intercession, he obtained from God.

From the beginning of the following year, 1216, to the 30th of May, the festival of Whitsuntide, the day on which the general chapter was held, which was the first[46] of the Order, he had as much leisure as he could desire for conversing with God, for giving instruction to his brethren at St. Mary of the Angels, and to the town of Assisi and its environs. In the assembly, provincial ministers were appointed, to whom power was given for admitting postulants into the Order, which the founder had previously reserved to himself. One whose name does not appear, was sent into Apulia, but John de Strachia was sent into Lombardy; Benedict of Arezzo, into the Marches of Ancona; Daniel the Tuscan, into Calabria; Augustin of Assisi, into the Terra di Lavoro; Elias of Cortona, into Tuscany. Evangelical laborers were chosen for different nations. Bernard de Quintavalle, for Spain; John Bonella, a Florentine, with thirty companions, for Provence; John de Penna, and sixty of his brethren, for Upper and Lower Germany; Francis took for his share Paris and what is properly called France and the Low Countries.

Those who were destined for distant countries were not dissatisfied; each one went to the department allotted to him with pleasure, as if it had been that of his own choice. This was a proof of their virtue, and a favorable omen for the combats they were about to have with the devils, because obedience alone carries off the palm,[47] according to the words of the Scripture; and that, in the opinion of the holy Fathers, those who, for the love of God, submit their will to the will of others, are conquerors to whom it is given to exercise great authority over the fallen angels, whose degradation was brought about by disobedience and rebellion.[48]

The apostolic laborers being all assembled at the feet of their Father, to receive his orders, he addressed them with paternal tenderness, in the following discourse:

"In the Name of the Lord, go forth modestly, two and two, observing strict silence from the morning till after the hour of Terce, praying to God from your hearts. Let no idle or useless words be heard among you; although you are traveling, your deportment should be as humble and as decorous as if you were in a hermitage, or in your cells. For wherever we are, and whithersoever we may be going, we have always our vocation with us; our brother, the body, is our cell, and the soul is the hermit, who dwells in it to think of God and to pray to Him. If a religious soul does not dwell quietly in the cell of the body, the external cells will be of little use to him. Behave, then, in such manner in the world, that whosoever may see or hear you, may be moved to devotion, and praise our Heavenly Father to whom alone all glory belongs. Proclaim

---

[46] This is what Wading proves against those who assert that the general chapter of 1219, called the Chapter of the heads, was the first. Ad ann. n. 1.

[47] Prov. 21: 28.

[48] S. August, *in Ps. LXX*, serm. 2, a.

peace to all men, but have it in your hearts, as well as in your mouths. Give to no one cause for anger, nor for scandal; on the contrary, by your own mildness, induce every one to feel benignly, and draw them to union and to concord. We are called to heal the wounded, console the afflicted, and to bring back those who err; many may seem to you to be members of the devil, who will one day be disciples of Jesus Christ."

What Francis said of the inutility of exterior cells, where the soul is not at ease in the cell of the body, is in conformity to these words of St. Bernard:[49] "You may be alone when you are in the midst of the world, as it may so happen that you may be in the midst of the world when you are alone."[50]

The children of the holy Patriarch received his blessing; and having recommended themselves to the prayers of their companions, they set out for those places to which obedience sent them. The success of the several labors will be adverted to further on. The missionaries for Provence remained some days after the breaking up of the chapter, to receive further instructions relative to their mission. The day of their departure, there were only three loaves of bread in the convent, two of which had been sent there by Clare; these were found sufficient for more than thirty who were there, and there was a great deal to spare, a circumstance which was considered to be a good omen.

Francis, having animated all the others by his zeal, prepared himself for setting out for Paris. Besides the natural affection he had for France, of which he liked the language, as it was familiar to him, he chose this city preferably to many others, because he knew that their devotion was great towards the blessed sacrament, and this was a great attraction for his piety.

May the Parisians ever entertain and transmit to their posterity this fervent devotion of their ancestors, which Pope Urban IV,[51] who was a native of France, stirred up in the hearts of the faithful forty-six years afterwards, by the institution of the Feast of the Most Holy Sacrament, which is celebrated throughout the Church, with so much solemnity. The bull which he issued on this occasion, enters into the strongest and most moving arguments calculated to inspire veneration, love, and the zeal which the precious memorial of the goodness of the Son of God calls for, and to invite to a frequent and worthy participation in the divine mystery, which the Council of Trent has since expressed its anxiety to see reestablished.[52]

Before his departure, Francis undertook to reconcile the members of the

---

[49] Many beautiful things on this head may be seen in the Letter to the Carthusians of Mont Dieu, attributed to St. Bernard, but which Mabillon thinks was written by William, Abbot of St. Thierry, near Rheims. This sentence is found in it "Cum quo Deus est, nunquam minus solus est, quam cum solus est." *Oper. S. Bernardi*, tom. 5, *Epis. ad Frat. de Monte Dei*, cap. 1

[50] Serm. 40, *in Cant.* n. 5.

[51] Bullar Rom. tom. I, An. 1262.

[52] Sess. 13, cap. 3, and Sess. 22, cap. 6,

illustrious family of the Baselennesi, a long time disunited by unhappy family dissensions, and he succeeded to the satisfaction of all parties. Out of gratitude they had built for him, on one of their estates on a spot near the Tiber, surrounded with very beautiful trees, a convent called St. Angel of Pantanellis.

He chose to go once more to Rome to recommend to the Holy Apostles his journey to France. On the road, having seated himself close to a spring to take his meal, he put some pieces of bread, which had been given to him on his quest, and which were very hard and moldy, on a stone near him; he expressed much satisfaction, and he pressed his companion Massé to give thanks to God for so great a treasure; and he repeated several times the same thing, elevating his voice more and more. "But of what treasure are you talking," said Massé, "at a time when we are in want of many things?" "The great treasure is," replied Francis, "that, being in want of so much, God has had the goodness to furnish us by His providence with that bread and this spring, and to find us this stone to serve as a table."

He went shortly after into a church, where he prayed to God to give him and his children the love of holy poverty; and his prayer was so fervent that fire seemed to issue from his countenance. Full of this celestial ardor, he went towards Massé with open arms, calling him by name with a loud voice; Massé, in great astonishment, going to throw himself into the arms of his Father, was raised into the air several cubits high, and felt such sweetness in his soul, that he frequently afterwards declared that he had never experienced anything like it. After this ecstasy, Francis spoke to him on the subject of poverty in an admirable strain, which we shall relate hereafter.

When at Rome, in a chapel of the church of St. Peter, while he was praying with tears that the holy Apostles would give him instructions on the subject of holy poverty and of an apostolic life, they appeared to him surrounded by lights, and, after tenderly embracing him, said: "Brother Francis, our Lord Jesus Christ has sent us to tell you that He has favorably heard your prayers and tears on the subject of holy poverty, which He Himself had followed, as well as His Blessed Mother, and we, who are His Apostles, after his example. This treasure is granted to you for yourself and for your children; those who shall carefully adhere to it, will have the kingdom of heaven for their reward." The servant of God, filled with consolation, went to his companion Massé, to whom he communicated what had passed, and they went together to give thanks at the place which is called the Confession of St. Peter, which is his tomb.

While Francis was at Rome, Pope Innocent III died at Perugia.[53] He was of the illustrious house of the Counts of Segni, which has given five popes to the Church, the last of whom was Innocent XIII, of blessed memory. It was at the University of Paris that his merit was first noticed; he shone there above the many who were its honor and its ornament. It was his rare and transcendent

---

[53] He died on the 16th of July, after having held the keys sixteen years six months and nine days.

qualities which induced the cardinals unanimously to elect him to the pontificate; and these qualities shone with additional splendor when his humility urged his resistance to the election, from which he prayed with unaffected tears to be released. His government and the works he has left to posterity, show that he had great genius, great science, prudence, and probity, with solid piety, and ardent zeal. "He was," says a French contemporary writer, "a man of great courage and great wisdom, who had no equal in his day, and who did marvelous things."[54] He was indeed one of the most eminent men who have filled the chair of St. Peter. The affection he bore to Francis, and the favors he conferred on his Order, have compelled us to do this justice here to his memory, which no good author has refused him.[55]

On the 18th of July, they elected for his successor Cardinal Savelli, who took the name of Honorius III. He was a learned and worthy man. He generally followed the designs of his predecessor, and had a similar affection for the religious orders, of which he gave substantial proofs in the favors he bestowed on that of St. Francis.

Some months after his election, he gave his approval of the Order of St Dominic. This holy patriarch having returned to his companions to fix upon a rule, as had been recommended to him by Pope Innocent at the Lateran Council, and having adopted the rule of St. Augustine, to which he had added some more austere regulations, came back to Rome to procure the approval of the Holy See. While he solicited it from Honorius, who had arrived from Perugia, he made acquaintance and contracted an intimacy with Francis, in consequence of a miraculous vision which he had in the church of St. Peter, where he prayed unceasingly with great fervor for the success of his enterprise.

He saw the Son of God seated on the right hand of His Father, who rose up greatly irritated against sinners, holding three darts in His hand, for the extirpation of the proud, the avaricious, and the voluptuous. His holy Mother threw herself at His feet, and prayed for mercy, saying that she had persons who would remedy the evil; and she at the same time introduced to Him Dominic and Francis, as being proper persons for reforming the world, and reestablishing piety; this pacified Jesus Christ.[56]

Dominic, who had never seen Francis, met him next day, recognized him,

---

[54] Rigord. tom. 5, Hist. Franc. Script. Page 66.

[55] There is only Math. Paris who has ventured to calumniate this great Pope. But he is a writer whose credit is very low with equitable men, in consequence of the malignant and inveterate hostility he evinces against all the Popes, which renders him on this head unworthy of belief. The work of this calumniator has only been quoted by Protestants in order to give support to their invectives against the Holy See. See Baronius ad Ann. 1216, n. 62. One is disgusted at finding in an Ecclesiastical History, written in the vulgar tongue, the atrocious and false accusations of Math. Paris against the memory of the great and holy Pope Innocent III, and this is not the only part of the history alluded to that excites indignation.

[56] Theodor, ab Appold. in vit. S. Dominic, lib. 2, cap. I.

ran to him and embraced him, saying: "You are my companion; we will work in concert with each other; let us be strictly united, and no one will be able to master us." Francis himself communicated this favor of Heaven to the children of Dominic: and St. Vincent Ferrer, and some other authors quoted by Wading, say that Francis had received a similar favor from Heaven.[57] The event proved the truth of the vision. Dominic alone, without any human aid, having nothing to command success but poverty, humility, and prayer, obtained the approbation of his order, which was an affair of great difficulty, particularly at the commencement of a pontificate, when the pope is occupied by most important affairs.

We may here notice the groundwork of the ardent zeal of the Friars Preachers and the Friars Minor for the glory of the Mother of God. Persuaded that their orders were established under her protection, and that she is especially the mother of their holy patriarchs, they strive by every means in their power to restore the devout veneration due to her. It is the common interest of all the faithful who see that she is, according to the expression of the holy Fathers, their advocate and their mediatrix; that she prays and solicits for them; that she interposes between them and the wrath of her Son, and appeases Him: this affords great room for confidence in her, and should induce them to invoke her for their conversion and met sanctification.

Dominic and Francis, confident of the protection of the Blessed Virgin, entered into a strict friendship and resolved to spare no pains in their exertions for the glory of God, and concerted together as to the best means for attaining their object.[58] Upon which an author quoted by Wading, makes a most appropriate reflection:[59] "It was," he says, "something admirable to see two men, who were poor, badly clad, without power or interest, despicable in the eyes of the world, divide between them the world itself, and undertake to

---

[57] S. Anthon. chron. part 3, lib. 23. cap. 3, Wad. ad ann. 1216, n. 6, Bzov. supra, *Bullar. Rom.* tom. 1, Honor. 3. S. Iren. lib. 3.

[58] In the circular letter which Humbert, General of the Friars Preachers, and John of Parma, General of the Friars Minor, addressed to the two orders in 1255, and which was adopted in the following year by St. Bonaventure, in which the two patriarchs are praised by beautiful comparisons taken from Scripture, we read these affecting words: "Consider, dear brethren, with what sincerity you Are bound to love each other; you, whom our holy mother the Church brought forth at the same time; you, whom similar engagements constitute real brothers; you, whom the goodness of God has equally destined from sill eternity to under Lake the same work, which is the salvation of souls. O what charity, what concord do not our sainted Fathers Dominic and Francis, and the first religious of our orders, require from us, they who loved each other so tenderly, and gave each other such proofs of it; who looked upon each other as angels; loaded each other with civilities; aided each other, as Jesus Christ has aided us all; shared in the common progress of the orders; praised and assisted each other, and took the greatest care to avoid the smelliest thing likely to give the slightest scandal or annoyance to either order." All the letter is in a similar style and loses nothing of its beauty after five centuries, and is calculated to make as much impression now on the religious as when first sent. Chron. Praedic. Wading, Annal. Min. ad an. 1216.

[59] Ferdinand. Castilio. apud. Wad, ad ann. 1126 n. 16.

conquer it. Who would not have turned into ridicule hearing them seriously consult together on such an undertaking, which they seemed to have so little means of carrying into execution? Nevertheless, they succeeded; because what is weak and powerless in the eyes of the world, God selected by their means to confound what is strong."[60] It is a resemblance of St. Peter and St. Paul, proposing to themselves, in the same city of Rome, to convert the universe by the preaching of the Gospel; and this shows that God made use of similar means for reanimating the faith, to those which He had employed to establish it.

It is reported, that while Dominic and Francis were still at Rome,[61] Angelus, of the order of the Carmelites, who was afterwards martyred in Sicily, was also there; that, preaching in the church of St. John Lateran, where the two others were among the hearers, he foretold that they would become two great pillars of the Church; that when the sermon was finished, they foretold to one another what would happen to each of them, and even that Francis would receive the stigmata; that the three together cured a man afflicted with leprosy, and passed a day and a night together in prayer and conversing on holy subjects.

Francis left Rome at the end of the year, intending to continue his journey into France. He passed through Sienna and by Mount Alvernia and arrived at Florence in the month of January, 1217, to pay his dutiful respects to Cardinal Ugolino, who was Papal Legate there. This cardinal, who had declared himself his protector and his friend, when he went to request the approbation of his rule from Pope Innocent III, in 1210, received him with great kindness, detained him some days, inquired into the affairs of his Order, and said to him on the subject of his journey: "Francis, your Order is still in its infancy. You know the opposition it met with in Rome, and you have still there some secret enemies; if there is not some one there to watch over your interests, it will be an easy matter to cause all you have obtained to be revoked. Your presence will go a great way in upholding your work, and those who are attached to you will have a greater stimulus for giving you their support. As to myself, I am from this moment wholly yours."

The holy man, after having thanked the cardinal, replied: "I have sent many of my brethren into far distant countries. If I remain quietly in our convent, without taking any share in their labors, it will be a great shame for me; and these poor religious, who are suffering hunger and thirst, will have great reason to murmur and complain; but instead of that, if they find that I work as much as they do, they will bear their fatigues more willingly, and I shall more easily persuade them to undertake similar missions."

---

[60] 1 Cor. 1:27.

[61] The continuators of Bollandus find some chronological difficulties in the meeting of these holy personages, to which no satisfactory answer has been found, and which throw doubts upon it, so that it is not here given for certain.

The Cardinal, feeling for the sufferings of these missionaries, said: "But why, brother, have you the harshness to expose your disciples to such arduous journeying and to so much suffering?" "My Lord," replied Francis, who was urged by a prophetic spirit, "you think that God has sanctioned the Institute for this country only; but I tell you that He has formed it for the good of the universe, and for the salvation of all men, without excluding the Infidels: for religious of this Order will go into their territories, and provided they live in conformity to the Gospel, God will provide amply for all their wants, even among the enemies of His name."

These words made a great impression on the Cardinal, who was a very holy man, and increased his affection for Francis, whom he again exhorted in stronger language than before, to remain in Italy to consolidate an Institute which was to have such beneficial results. The saint having yielded to the reasoning of the Cardinal, entreated him to be the protector of the Friars Minor, according to his promise, and to be so good as to be present at the next general chapter; after which he took the road to the valley of Spoleto.

There he learnt that some of his brethren had been seriously ill- treated by several prelates, and that at the court of Rome there were persons who spoke against his Order. This news confirmed him in the resolution he had taken to remain in Italy; and he named three of his disciples for the French mission, to wit: Pacificus of the Marches of Ancona, the celebrated poet, whose conversion we have related; Angelus, and Albert, both of Pisa.

He likewise intended to request the Pope to nominate a Cardinal of the Holy Roman Church, to protect his Order against all who should attack it. Three of his companions, the writers of his life, say that he was induced to this by a celestial vision in his sleep. He saw a hen endeavoring to gather all her chickens under her wings, to protect them from a hawk; she could not cover them all, and many were about to become its prey; but another large bird appeared, spread its wings over them, and preserved them from the danger. On awaking, Francis prayed our Lord to explain to him the meaning of this, and he learned that the hen represented himself; and the chickens were disciples, that the bird with the large wings represented the cardinal, whom they were to solicit for their protector. He told all this to his brethren, and addressed them as follows:

"The Roman Church is the mother of all the churches, and the sovereign of all religious orders. It is to her that I shall address myself to recommend to her my brethren, in order that her authority may silence those who are hostile to them, and that she may procure for the children of God full and perfect liberty to advance quietly in the way of eternal salvation;[62] for when they shall be under her protection, there will be no more enemies to oppose them, nor disturb them; there will not be seen among them any son of Belial to ravage with impunity the vineyard of the Lord. The holy Church will be zealous for

---

[62] 3 Reg. 5: 4; Nahum, 1: 15.

the glory of our poverty; she will not suffer that the humility which is so honorable to her, shall be obscured by the clouds of pride. It is she who will render indissoluble among us, the bonds of charity and peace, rigorously punishing the authors of dissensions. Under her eyes, the holy evangelical observance will ever flourish in its pristine purity; she will never permit these holy practices to flag even momentarily, those practices which shed around them a vivifying odor. May the children, then, of that holy Church be very grateful for the great favors which they receive from their mother; let them kiss her feet with profound veneration, and remain forever inviolably attached to her."

The first words of this discourse show that St. Francis was perfectly cognizant of the prerogatives of the Church of Rome, and of the extent of the authority of the Holy See. It was not in vain that he sought her protection, since his Order was established, extended, supported, and sometimes even renovated under this powerful authority; and the attachment to the Holy See, which he so strongly recommended to his brethren, has been so visibly manifested during five centuries, that it has procured for them the esteem and love of all Catholics, as well as the hatred of the heretics, so that they have the honor of having some share in the eulogiums which St. Jerome passed on to St. Augustine: "The Catholics esteem and respect you, and, what enhances your glory, all the heretics detest you. They hold me in equal hatred; and if they dared not put both the one and the other of us to death, they have at least the wish to do so."[63] This wish of the heretics has not been without effect as regards the children of St. Francis, for of a thousand martyrs which they reckon in his Order, a very great number of them were put to death with greater cruelty in this and latter times by the sectarians than by idolatrous tyrants. Heresy will be ever so, the daughter of a parent, who, according to the words of Jesus Christ, was a murderer from the beginning.[64]

The holy Patriarch went then to Rome, where he found Cardinal Ugolino, who was returned from Tuscany, to whom he communicated the intention he had of soliciting the pope for a protector. The cardinal at the same time expressed his wish to hear him preach before the pope and the sacred college. Francis excused himself from this as much as he could, assigning for reasons, his ignorance, his simplicity, and his uncultivated mind, which unfitted him for speaking in the most August assembly in the world. But he was obliged to yield to the pressing instances of the cardinal, who entreated him as a friend to comply, and even ordered him to prepare himself for the task, recommending him to compose carefully a sermon wherein there should be as much erudition and reasoning as such an audience required.

---

[63] Macte virtute, in orbe celebraris. Catholici te conditorem antiquae cursum fidei venerantur atque suspiciunt; et quod signum majoris gloriae est, omnes haeretici detestantur; et me pari persequuntur odio, ut quos gladiis nequeunt voto interficiant. Hier, ad August.

[64] Joan. VIII: 44.

Up to that time, the servant of God had never prepared himself for preaching; he only spoke from the pulpit what the Holy Spirit inspired. Nevertheless, he, in this instance, obeyed the cardinal; he prepared a sermon as carefully as he could, and learned it by heart. When he came into the presence of the Pope, he forgot every part of the discourse, and could not utter a syllable of it. But after having humbly explained the circumstance, and implored the aid of the Holy Spirit, words flowed copiously from his mouth, and he spoke with so much eloquence and animation, that the Pope and cardinal were deeply affected, in order, says St. Bonaventure, that it might be evident that it was not he who spoke, but the Spirit of God that spoke in him.[65]

Having been admitted to an audience of the Pope in presence of Cardinal Ugolino, he said: "Most holy Father, I am distressed at becoming importunate for the interests of your lowly servants, the Friars Minor, while you are occupied with so many important affairs which regard the whole Church. I entreat you to give us this Cardinal, to whom we may have recourse in our wants, always under your sanction, since it is from you, the Head of the mystical Body, that all power emanates." The Pope granted his request with alacrity, and recommended the Cardinal to take great care of the Order. From that time, the Order of Friars Minor have always had a Cardinal Protector, whose powers are extended as the Pope shall see fit; the terms of the Rule, which oblige the Order by obedience to apply for one, show that it was the intention of Francis, that his powers should be most ample.

Cardinal Ugolino was one of the most accomplished men of the city of Rome;[66] his person well made, his countenance mild and majestic, his genius quick, with great memory and eloquence, possessing in perfection all human sciences, civil and canon law, and particularly the Holy Scriptures; he was very expert in all public business; a lover of virtue and order, and of a pure and exemplary life.

His first care in undertaking the office of Protector, which he did willingly, was to defend the Friars against all those who attacked them, to conciliate the Prelates in their favor, and to spread them into all parts for the salvation of souls; his great authority silenced their enemies. As often as his affairs admitted of it, he assisted at their general chapters; when he officiated pontifically. Francis acted as his Deacon, and preached. He conformed to the rule of the Institute as much as was in his power, and was, when with them, as one of themselves, and even endeavored to appear as the lowest among them.

A contemporary author, who was an ocular witness, expresses himself thus: "O how often has he been seen humbly to divest himself of the marks of his high dignity, put on the poor habit, and, with bare feet, join the religious in the regular exercises, in order to imitate their evangelical life!"[67] A lively and

---

[65] Matt. 10: 20.

[66] Cod. Vat. apud. Rayn. ad ann. 1217.

[67] Tho. Celano, apud. Wad. ad ann. 1217, n. 8.

enlightened faith, a solid and fervent piety, and a superior mind, convinced him that since the time of the abasement of the Son of God, humiliation is honorable, and adds to the splendor of the highest dignities; a truth which is not understood by persons of little faith, by the proud, the indevout, and those of little mind.

This great Cardinal respected Francis as much as he loved him, looking upon him as a man sent down from heaven. His presence was a source of pleasure to him, and he often admitted, as the above-quoted author states, that from the time he had made acquaintance with this holy man, as soon as he saw him and heard him speak, all that caused in him uneasiness of mind, or grief at heart, was dispelled; his countenance became serene, and his soul was filled with fervor.

Francis, on his side, had great veneration for the Cardinal, whom he insisted on his brethren considering as the Pastor of the Flock, and, with an attachment as tender as that of an infant for the mother's breast, he gave him in all things marks of the profoundest deference. One day, hearing that he was about to receive a visit from him, he ran away and hid himself in the thickest part of the wood. The Cardinal had him sought for, and went himself in search of him, and, having found him, asked him as his friend to tell him why he avoided him. "My Lord and my Father," answered the humble Francis, "as soon as I knew that your Grandeur[68] intended to honor me with your presence, me who am the poorest and the most despicable of men, I was covered with confusion, and I blushed at the thought of my baseness, finding myself wholly unworthy to receive so distinguished an honor, for I truly revere you as my Lord and my Father." These feelings were partly owing to a vision he had had, which revealed to him that this Cardinal would be Pope; he foretold it to him, which is recorded by St. Bonaventure; and in the private letters which he wrote to him, he put on the heading: "To my Reverend Father and Lord Ugolino, who is one day to be the Bishop of the whole world, and the Father of all nations."[69]

The respectful gratitude of the Friars Minor required that we should insert all these anecdotes in memory of Cardinal Ugolino, who honored the Holy Patriarch of his Order, as well as that of St. Clare, with his affection, his protection, and his liberality, and who surpassed all his former favors ten years afterwards, when he was Pope under the name of Gregory IX.

When Francis had obtained from the Pope so powerful a Protector, and had put his various affairs in order, he set out on his return to St. Mary of the

---

[68] The title of Eminence was only given to cardinals in 1630.

[69] S. Bernard had said a century before that the Pope was the Prince of Bishops; the Bishop of the world; the Pastor of pastors; that, by a singular prerogative of the Apostolic See, he has a plenitude of power over all the churches; and, to discover what is not confided to his care, one must leave the world. Epist. 132, 139, and 210.

Angels, but he spent the remainder of the year in the valley of Rieti,[70] where he performed many wonderful things, of which one of his companions has given a very ample account.[71]

At Grecio, or Grecchia, a very dissolute town in which he first preached, no one frequented the Sacraments; no one listened to the Word of God, and marriages within the prohibited degrees were of ordinary occurrence. What he said to them to urge them to repentance made such impressions on them, that they entreated him to make some stay among them. He willingly agreed to do so, in the hope of their conversion, which took place in a short time; meanwhile he retired to a mountain, from whence he came to Grecio and other places to preach.

On returning one day from Cotanello, a neighboring town, and not being able to find the way to the mountain, he asked a farmer to be his guide. This man excusing himself, saying that there were wolves in that direction that committed great havoc, Francis promised him and pledged himself as his surety, that he should not be attacked by any wolf either in going or coming back; he found that the saint was correct, for, in returning, two wolves which were in the way, played with him as dogs do, and followed him to his house without doing him any harm. The farmer reported this over all his neighborhood, and said that, assuredly, the man to whom he had served as guide, must be a great favorite with God, who gave him such absolute command over the wolves. Upon this they assembled in great numbers, and came to the Man of God, entreating him to deliver them from their calamities.

"Two sorts of calamities bore hard upon them," says St. Bonaventure, "wolves and hail." The wolves were so ravenous in the environs of Grecio, that they devoured both cattle and men; and the hail fell every year in such quantity and of such large size, that their crops of corn were destroyed, and their vineyards sorely damaged. Francis preached on this subject, and pointed out to them that scourges of this nature were the punishment of sin; and he ended by saying: "For the honor and for the glory of God, I pledge my word to you, that if you choose to give credit to what I say, and have pity on your own souls, by making a good confession, and showing worthy fruits of repentance, God will look upon you with a favorable eye, will deliver you from your calamities, and render your country abundant in all sorts of good things.[72] But I also declare to you that if you are ungrateful for these benefits, if, like the dog, you return to the vomit, God will be still more irritated against you, and you will feel the effects thereof twofold by the fresh afflictions He will send you." They believed the preacher, and did penance; from that moment the scourges

---

[70] Many think that it is the place called by Pliny, Umbilicus Italiae, the description of which is in the seventh Book of the Æneid. *Est locus Italice in medio sub montibus altis.*

[71] Chron. M. St. Angeli, *Reatini de rebus gestis a Sancto Francisco, in Valle Reatina* Ap. Wading, ad ann. 1210, n. 3.

[72] Prov. 26: 11.

ceased; nothing more was heard of wolves, and there was no more hail; and, what was most remarkable, continues St. Bonaventure, was that when it hailed in the vicinity, the cloud, on nearing their lands, either stopped or went off in another direction, to fall elsewhere. This lasted as long as they remained faithful to God.

Four authors, in different centuries, who have written the history of the Valley of Rieti, assure us, that when dissoluteness recommenced in that country, the wolves returned and made great havoc.[73] Wading, who wrote in Italy in the last century, says that the inhabitants of the valley admitted this to be the case. It is certain by the testimony of the Holy Scriptures, that the sins of the people call down not infrequently the scourges of the wrath of God, which may be averted by repentance, or be rendered useful to salvation. But how many afflicted sinners are there, of whom it may be said with the prophet, "O Lord, You struck them, and they have not grieved; You bruised them, and they have refused to receive correction; they have made their faces harder than the rock, and they have refused to return."[74]

A knight, whose name was John Velita, who was converted by the preaching of Francis, became his intimate friend, and used often to go to see him on the mountain in his hut, which was made of the branches of two large hornbeams intertwined. As he was an elderly man, and very corpulent, whom the steepness of the road greatly fatigued, he begged Francis to come nearer to the town, which would be agreeable to all, and he offered to build him a convent on any spot he should select. The servant of God assented to the proposal, and, smiling, promised the knight not to settle farther from the town than the distance to which a child could throw a lighted brand. Upon this they went together down the mountain, and when they reached the gates of Grecio, the knight sent the first child he met to fetch a lighted brand, and desired him to throw it as far as he could, not thinking he could throw it very far. But the child, with a strength surpassing that of men, threw the brand to a distance of more than a mile, and it fell on a hill belonging to the knight, and set fire to the wood which covered it, and lit at length on a very stony spot. This prodigy made it clear that God desired that a convent should be built there, and it was cut out of the rock. The oratory, the dormitory, and the refectory, which are still extant, on the ground floor, are only thirty feet long by six broad; precious remains, which show us the love of poverty which planned them.

The Saint founded three other establishments in the valley of Rieti, at St. Mary of the Woods, at Monte Raniero, or Monte Columba, and at Pui Buscone. These four houses, which are situated in eminences on the four sides of the valley, formed together a cross. In each of them, as in the town of Rieti, and all

---

[73] Ad Ann. 1217, n. 13.

[74] Jerem. 5: 3.

around the lake which surrounds it,[75] traces are shown of several miracles which were performed by the man of God.

He returned to St. Mary of the Angels in the month of January, 1218, and he determined upon convoking a general chapter, which he notified by circular letters, to be held at Whitsuntide of the year 1219, in order that he might be made acquainted with the state of the missions entrusted to his disciples, and that he might send missionaries into parts where there had hitherto been none; this was an inspiration of the Holy Spirit, who pointed out to him the progress his Order had already made, and the great good which would accrue to the Church by its universal extension.

While he was thus occupied by his important projects for the salvation of souls, God, in order to prevent any emotions of pride stealing into his heart, and to maintain therein a profound humility, was pleased to permit that he should be attacked by a violent temptation; it was an extraordinary depression of spirits, which lasted several days.[76] He made every effort to surmount it by his prayers and his tears; and one day when he was praying with more than ordinary fervor, a celestial voice said to him, "Francis, if you had the faith of a grain of mustard-seed, and you were to say to this mountain, go there from here, it would go."[77] Not understanding the meaning of these words, he asked what mountain it was; and he was answered: "The mountain is the temptation." He immediately replied, weeping and humbling himself, "Lord, Thy will be done." And from that moment the temptation ceased, and his mind became perfectly at ease.

The year 1218 was divided between the stay he made at St. Mary of the Angels, for the instruction of his brethren, and some excursions he made to Mount Alvernia and to some other places, where new dwellings were made over to him. His route was always marked by the fruits of his preaching, and by the splendor of his miracles. Passing by Montaigu, above the Valley of Caprese, before a church of St. Paul, which was being repaired, and seeing that two of the masons could not succeed in lifting a stone, which was to be placed as a jamb for the door, his compassion and zeal induced him to lift it and place it as required, which he did alone, and with a strength which was not that of a

---

[75] It is a small lake which empties itself into the great Lake of Velino, where the river of the same name passes, which is now called, *"Il lago di pie di luco."*

[76] Mark of Lisbon, bishop of Oporto, in Portugal, author of the *Chronicles of the Order of the Friars Minor*, says, in the first book, cap. 72, that it was a deep melancholy which caused him to be disgusted with everything, even prayer, and that it lasted two years. St. Francis de Sales, in his *Introduction to a Devout Life*, part 4, chap. 55, and other spiritual writers, only say that it was a painful affection of the mind, which lasted several days. It may be that Mark of Lisbon, being in Italy, where he compiled his work, may have seen some manuscript which put two years instead of two months. However, the Holy Spirit usually caused the Saint to feel in his soul a joy which was manifest in his face, and communicated itself to his companions, as we shall see further on. And, finally, it is not possible to make a deep melancholy of two years agree with his actions. It could not have taken place during his whole life.

[77] Matt. 17: 19.

mortal. The abbot of the monastery of St. Justin, in the diocese of Perugia, met him, and alighted from his horse to compliment him, and to speak to him on some matters of conscience. After a conversation replete with unction, the abbot, recommending himself humbly to his prayers, Francis replied: "I will pray with all my heart;" and they parted. At a little distance from thence, the Saint said to his companion: "Wait a little, brother, I will here perform my promise." He knelt to pray; and while he was so doing, the abbot, who was riding on, felt his mind inflamed with a suavity of devotion such as he had never before experienced. He stopped, and the vivid impressions with which God favored him, threw him into an ecstasy. When he was come to himself again, he became aware that it was entirely owing to the prayers of Francis, and he became the friend of the Order, and he mentioned what had occurred to him to several persons as a thing which was quite miraculous.

On his return from his last journey in 1218, which was much longer than any of the others had been, Francis found that a new building, large and commodious, had been erected in his absence, close to the Portiuncula convent. Displeased at seeing this infringement of the rules of holy poverty, he took some of his brethren with him, and went on the roof, to begin to break it down, which he certainly would have carried through, had not some of the people from Assisi, who were there, informed him that the building belonged to the town; that it had been built by them for the foreign religious, who daily arrived there, it being dishonorable to the town to see them compelled, in consequence of the want of room in the convent, to sleep outside, and even in the fields; that the town had destined this building for their accommodation, and that they would be received there in its name. On this he came down, and said to them: "If that, then, is your house, I leave it, and shall not meddle with it; we shall have nothing to do with it, neither myself nor my brethren; take care of it yourselves." It was decided in consequence by a deliberation of the municipality, that the magistrates should provide for the repairs.

St. Francis exorcises Arezzo through Brother Sylvester. —Giotto

St. Clare. Crypt of the Basilica of St. Francis, Assisi, Italy.

The meeting of St. Francis and St. Dominic. —Fra Angelico

St. Francis preaches before the Pope. —Giotto

THE LIFE OF ST. FRANCIS OF ASSISI

BOOK III

CHAPTER I
THE GENERAL CHAPTER

He goes to Perugia, to consult the cardinal protector—His opinion on the promotion of his friars to ecclesiastical dignities—He returns to St. Mary of the Angels—More than five thousand Friars Minors are present at the chapter he had appointed—He addresses the assembly, and forbids them troubling themselves about their food—He receives more than five hundred novices during this chapter—He forbids indiscreet mortifications—The devils are incensed against him and his Order—He humbles his friars to preserve them from vainglory—He confounds those who wish the Rule mitigated—He wishes not for privileges which can engender disputes—He gives his friars instructions about their conduct to ecclesiastics—He obtains from the Pope letters apostolical, confirming the approval of the Order—What he decrees in the chapter.

HE TIME OF THE GENERAL CHAPTER drew near, of that chapter which became so celebrated by the number of religious which attended it, and by many other marvelous circumstances. Before its assembling, the holy Patriarch proposed to go to Perugia, to confer with the cardinal protector, who was legate there, on the affairs of the Order. Wading states, on good authority, that St. Dominic was there at the same time,[1] and that they had several deliberations together with the legate, who had a similar esteem for both.

One day when they were in serious conversation on the affairs of the Church, the cardinal asked them whether they should consider it advisable for some of their members to be raised to ecclesiastical dignities; "for," said he, "I am persuaded that they would have no less zeal for the glory of God and the salvation of souls, than those bishops of the early ages of the Church, who, although in great poverty, animated by ardent charity, fed their flocks with

---

[1] Father Echard, author of the Dissertations which are at the head of the work entitled, *"Scriptores Ordinis Praedicatorum,"* is by no means satisfied with Wading, with the continuators of Bollandus, and with Fleury, who say that St. Dominic was at Perugia with St. Francis at Cardinal Ugolino's, in 1219. He has no doubt that the learned Jesuits of Antwerp will look into this with great accuracy, when they come to speak of St. Dominic and St. Francis, and then admit having taken chimeras for solid and indisputable things. At any rate, the sons of St. Francis will not except against the learned Jesuits, whom a son of St. Dominic has chosen as the judges; and they will be sure of three things; 1st, that these learned and religious critics will admit that they were in error, and avow it sincerely, and will adduce proofs of it; 2nd, that they will weigh the reasons adduced by Father Echard, and those of Wading; 3nd, that as respects the two orders, their decision will be perfectly impartial. *Script. Ord. Praedict. recens,* tom. 1. Wad. *ad ann, 1219,* Dissert. 3.

salutary instructions and the example of a good life." After a contest of humility between the two patriarchs, as to who should speak first, Dominic, urged by Francis to take the lead, said to him: "You excel me in humility, and I will excel you in obedience." He then gave the cardinal this answer: "My lord, my brethren may well consider themselves as holding a very elevated rank. What is there more honorable than teaching others from the evangelical pulpit? What should well-thinking minds desire more than to be employed in defense of the faith, and to combat the enemies of the Church? For this reason I strenuously desire that my brethren may remain as they are, and I will keep them so as long as I can." Francis made the following reply: "My lord, my brethren have received the appellation of Minors, in order that they might never have the presumption to become great. If it be your intention that they shall bear fruit in the Church, leave them in their vocation, and never permit them to be raised to prelatures."

The cardinal was greatly edified by their answers, and highly commended the humility of their opinions, but he did not therefore change his views. He thought, on the contrary, that such ministers would be most useful in the Church, considering the corruption of the times.

The Church has since followed the opinion of this eminent dignitary, having made many bishops and cardinals from the two orders, and several have been even elevated to the sovereign pontificate, as we see in this day our holy father Benedict XIII being of the order of St. Dominic.[2]

But the Friars Preachers and the Friars Minor, who have preserved the spirit of their vocation, have never had any other feelings than those of their holy patriarchs on the subject of ecclesiastical dignities. They have refused them[3] as long as they could, and those who have accepted them, have been compelled to do so by superior authority, which they could not be dispensed from obeying.[4]

St. Bonaventure expresses himself so strongly on this head, that we have thought it desirable to give his own words, not to weaken them. "What must we say of those Friars Minor, who have been raised to the episcopate? I answer, that if the Church compels them to take upon themselves the care of souls in this station, so that they cannot absolutely refuse to do so, they must

---

[2] Benedict XIII, who was elected Pope on the 29th of May, 1724, after the Conclave had sat two months and nine days.

[3] Pope Innocent XIII, of happy memory, has placed before the Christian community an example of this kind, in beatifying Andrew Conti, of the family of the Counts of Segni, which was that also of this Pontiff, religious of the Order of St. Francis, nephew of Pope Alexander IV, who refused to receive the Roman purple which his uncle sent him, and who liked better to practice, as a Friar Minor, poverty, humility, and all other virtues, which God honored in his person by many splendid miracles. S. Anton, chron. part 3, tit. 24, cap. 9, § 41. Wading, ann. tom. 2, ad an. 1298.

[4] It is well known that our holy Father Pope Benedict XIII only consented to his election after considerable resistance, and then not to be opposed to the will of God, which he was obliged to admit that it was.

not be considered as having left the Order, provided they aim at a continuance in it as much as in their power, as in the bosom of their mother. But if, on the contrary, they aspire to the episcopate without being called thereto, and even without being compelled to accept it, merely to be disembarrassed from the austerities of their Order and the inconveniences of a poor state of life, I believe they will have the same lot as he had who said: 'I will ascend and sit in the mountain of the covenant, in the sides of the North'."[5]

The holy doctor followed these principles; he refused the archbishopric of York, in England,[6] one of the richest churches in Europe, of which Pope Clement XIV sent him the bulls. It was solely on receiving the positive order of Gregory X that he could be induced to be made Cardinal and Bishop of Albano. It was with regret and lamentation that he received the insignia of the Cardinalate in the midst of the most debasing acts of religious humility; he made no alteration in his manner of life, well knowing that episcopal consecration cannot make void the obligation of vows, as is declared by the Church in Papal ordinances and general councils,[7] which St. Thomas has learnedly explained in the following terms: "Those religious who are raised to the episcopate, are obliged to observe all that their rule directs, which is not incompatible with the functions of their episcopal character."[8] Such is the doctrine of this worthy child of St. Dominic, which another of his children, our most Holy Father Benedict XIII, put in practice when Bishop and Cardinal, and still continues to practice on the apostolic throne, to the edification of the whole Christian Church.

Brother Leo, the companion and confessor of St. Francis, who was at Perugia, and who assisted at all the conferences, says that they spoke much on the propagation of the faith and the salvation of souls; that, having made reciprocal inquiries into the peculiarities of their respective orders, Dominic proposed to Francis to unite them, and make but one order, in order that the difference of the Institute should not divide those whom the intimate friendship of their fathers had closely united. To this proposition Francis replied: "My dear brother, it has been God's will that our orders should be different, the one more austere than the other, in order to their being by this variety better adapted to human infirmity, and to give an opportunity to such as could not bear a life of very great austerity to embrace one which was somewhat milder." Leo adds, that they took steps for maintaining permanent agreement between the two orders; and, after having mutually praised their

---

[5] Isaiah 14: 13.

[6] Vit. St. Bonav. cap. 14. Sixt. 4, const. 76, in Bullar. Rom. tom. 2. S. Anton, chronic, part 3, tit. 24, cap. 8. Wading, ad an. 1265 and 1274.

[7] Innoc. I. Epist. 2, ad Victrie, epist. Rothomag. Nicol. I. Epist. 55, ad Egilon. Archiep. Senon. in Council, antiq. Galliae, tom. 3, p. 274, concil general 8, can. 27, concil general 12. Lateran 4, can. 6. See P. Thomassin in the discipline of the Church, part 3, liv. I. chap. 32, n. 19.

[8] 12. 2. quest. 185, Art. 8.

congregations, they recommended to their companions who were present, reciprocal respect and friendship for each other; that Dominic requested Francis to give him his girdle, which was a cord with large knots; and, having obtained it after many entreaties, he wore it during the remainder of his life under his habit, as a tie and perpetual symbol of the charity which so intimately united them.[9]

Francis having discussed with the Cardinal Protector all the affairs of his Order, left Perugia to return to St. Mary of the Angels. As he discoursed on the road with his companion Leo, on the virtue of humility and entire abnegation of self, he said in a moment of fervor:

"My dear brother, I do not believe myself to be a Friar Minor, and, in truth, I am not one, unless I can bear humbly and with entire tranquillity of mind, all that could happen to me under circumstances which I can figure to myself. I suppose, then, that my brethren came to seek me, with great respect and confidence, to assist at the General Chapter which is about to be holden, and solicit me to preach at it. If, after having exhorted them in such terms as God shall have inspired me, they were to rise up against me, and manifest openly that they hold me in aversion, saying: 'We will no longer have you to govern us; we are ashamed of having such a man as you at our head, who has neither learning nor eloquence, who is simple and ignorant, with very little prudence and experience; therefore, in future, do not have the arrogance to call yourself our superior.' If they were to put other affronts upon me, and to drive me ignominiously from the assembly, I should not consider myself to be a true religious, unless I were to receive all this as patiently and with equal serenity of countenance as I should receive those who would load me with praise and honor."

To this he added: "Assuredly, places of honor are very dangerous to salvation, not only from the vainglory which is to be feared, but likewise from the government, which is very difficult; whereas, in opprobrium, there is nothing but merit to be acquired. If I am removed from the headship, I shall be exempt from being accountable to God for a great number of souls. Prelature is a station of danger, and praise brings one to the very edge of the precipice. In a humble, lowly station, there is much to be gained. Why, then, do we look to and prefer what is dangerous to what has so much more spiritual advantage, since it is for this that time is given to us?" These are sentiments which should be well pondered by persons in every station of life, whether they aspire to employments, or fear the losing of them. The profound humility of St. Francis does not admit of a doubt of his having gone through the trial which he here supposes; and even in putting it thus hypothetically, he strengthened in his mind the virtue requisite for supporting it in reality. These sorts of

---

[9] But besides Brother Leo, Bernard de Besse, secretary to St. Bonaventure, who had lived with Leo, relates the same anecdote, as does likewise Colvenerius, professor of Louvain, and many others. Wading, ad an. 1219.

suppositions, which might be stumbling-blocks to the weak, are very useful to those who aspire to perfect humility.

The Friars Minor assembled for the General Chapter of their Order at the convent of St. Mary of the Angels, or Portiuncula, near Assisi, at the Feast of Pentecost, and their number exceeded five thousand. The circumstance is truly amazing, particularly when it is recollected that some remained in their respective convents; that the Order had only existed ten years since its institution; and that the novices had always been admitted by the founder himself, except since the Chapter of the year 1216, when he had given the provincial ministers power to receive them. It is nevertheless certain, that more than five thousand Friars Minor assisted at this celebrated Chapter: the fact is attested by four of St. Francis' companions, who were present at it; by St. Bonaventure, who lived with them[10] and by many others. There is no modern author who does not consider it as proved.[11]

What can be said on this subject, except that it pleased God to recall in some measure, by the rapid establishment of this Order, the wonderful spread of the Gospel by the preaching of the Apostles? St. Augustine says that the Apostles were as dark clouds from whence lightning and thunder emanated;[12] that, by their poverty and their simplicity, they shone in the eyes of the universe; that by the powerful virtue and splendor of their admirable actions, they overthrew everything which was opposed to the empire of Jesus Christ, and in a short time, christianized the world. May we not also say, that Francis and his companions, men poor and simple, were a representation of the Apostles; that Jesus Christ rendered them powerful and eminent in words and works, to bring back sinners to His empire, and that by them, in an inconceivably short period of time, an immense number of Apostolic men was collected and formed who embraced the same institute, in order to exercise the same ministry? What assists us in comprehending that in ten years it had been possible to build a sufficient number of houses, to contain so many thousand men is, that they were poor and without any income.

The religious of this Chapter were lodged in huts made of matting, erected all round the Portiuncula convent, from which this Chapter has been called the

---

[10] Fr. Echard doubts there having been five thousand Friars Minor at this chapter, and he grounds this doubt on St. Bonaventure not having recorded it; from whence he concludes, either that this fact was unknown to the holy doctor, or was considered by him to be inaccurate. But he would have had no reason for this doubt if he had read his Legend, of which the following are the precise words: "Multiplicatis jam fratribus, coepit eos ... in loco Sancto Mariæ de Portiuncula ad generale Capitulum convocare ... ubi licet omnium necessariorum esset penuria, fratrum que multitudo ultra quinque millia conveniret aliquando; divina tamen opitulante clementiâ et victus sufficentia suberat, et salus comitabatur corporea et spiritualis jucunditas affluebat." A mistake of this nature will, doubtless, attract the attention of the learned Jesuits of Antwerp, whose criticism the erudite Dominican calls for. *Script. Ord. Praedic. Recensiti*, tom. 1, Dissert. 3.

[11] Raynald., Spond., Bzov., Fleury, the Abbé de Choisi, Baillet.

[12] S. Augus. In Psal. 96, n. 7 and 8.

"Chapter of Mats." They were there separated from the world, but perfectly united among themselves, all lovers of watching and fasting after the example of their Father; zealous in prayer and in the recital of Psalms, in spiritual reading, and in readiness to execute all works of mercy, and having no other hope than that of the happiness of a future life.

Cardinal Ugolino, as Protector of the Order, came to preside over the Chapter, and all the religious went in procession before him. He opened the Assembly on Whitsunday the 26th of May.[13] He officiated pontifically, and preached; and he deemed it right to inspect all the ranks of this holy army of the Lord, in which he found everything in good order. These soldiers of Jesus Christ were not seen wandering about; but all were collected in groups, a hundred in one spot, sixty in another, more or less, and conversing on holy subjects, on their own salvation, or on that of their neighbors, and on the means of reforming the morals of a corrupt world. The Cardinal, delighted with so interesting and unusual a scene, said to those who followed him, as Jacob had when he met the angels on his way: "Truly, this is the Camp of God."[14] We might also apply to it what Balaam could not prevent himself from saying, when he saw the Israelites encamped: How beautiful are your tabernacles, O Jacob, and your tents, O Israel![15]

Francis, as a general in his camp, went through all the tents; he encouraged his troops to fight valiantly the battles of the Lord, assuring them of receiving assistance from on high, animating some, and fulfilling in every place the duties of a vigilant chief.

He assembled all his brethren, and addressed them in an excellent discourse, of which the following embraces the subject: "We have promised great things; and we have been promised greater. Let us keep the first, and let us sigh after the others. Pleasure is of short duration; the penalty is eternal. Sufferings are light; glory is infinite. Many are called; but few are chosen. Each one will receive according to his deserts."

On this beautiful text he exhorted them, in the most forcible and moving terms, to the practice of virtue and to the duties of a religious life, urging them, above all things, to implicit obedience to our Holy Mother the Church, to a contempt of the world, to purity of mind and body, to a love of holy poverty and humility, to charity, to concord and mildness, to continued watchfulness, and to an ardent zeal for the salvation of souls. He recommended to them to pray for all the faithful, and particularly for the exaltation of the Holy Roman Church, and for the benefactors of the Order. After which he positively forbade them to have any anxiety whatever for anything concerning the body, and he quoted to them these words of the Psalmist: Cast your care upon the

---

[13] The continuators of Bollandus remark, that Whitsunday fell this year on the 25th of May; nevertheless, it appears that it was on the 26th. Act. SS. tom. 2, Maii. Vit. S. Angel, carmel. pg. 828.

[14] Genes. 32: 2.

[15] Num. 24: 5.

Lord and He shall sustain you.[16] He had conformed strictly to the rule he laid down, for he had made no provision for the Chapter.

St. Dominic, who, out of friendship for St. Francis, had come with six of his companions to this assembly[17] and who heard this discourse, was fearful lest what he had forbidden was perhaps an exaggeration, and that it might seem to be tempting the Lord, if some steps were not taken for procuring food for so great a multitude. But he was of a very different way of thinking shortly after when he saw arrive from Assisi, Perugia, Spello, Foligno, Spoleto, and many more distant towns, ecclesiastics, laity, nobles, burgesses, and persons of every state of life, who brought with them not only what was necessary for the subsistence of such vast numbers, but pressed forward to serve the religious themselves with an emulation of humility and charity.

So marked an interposition of Providence in behalf of these evangelical poor struck the Patriarch of the Friars Preachers with astonishment; and it is believed that it suggested to him the intention which he carried into execution the year after, when he assembled the first general Chapter of his Order at Bologna,[18] in which it was resolved that the Friars Preachers should adopt the system of entire poverty, and consider it as the fundamental rule of their Order, renouncing forever all property in land, or revenue arising therefrom, even what they had at Toulouse, which the Pope had confirmed to them by his first Bull. In dying, he recommended to them this evangelical poverty as the foundation of their institute; and lest this foundation should be undermined by the prudence of the flesh, he forbade in the strongest terms, on pain of the curse of the Almighty, and of his also,[19] the introduction into the Order of any temporal possessions.

May what made so strong an impression on the mind of St. Dominic teach the faithful never to be mistrustful of the care of Divine Providence! However, we are not to look for, or expect miraculous assistance; they are not in the

---

[16] Psalm 54: 23.

[17] Father Echard maintains strenuously that the chronology of the Life of St. Dominic, does not tally with his having assisted at the chapter of the Friars Minor held at St. Mary of the Angels in 1219. It is one of the points to which he calls the attention of the Jesuits of Antwerp, who have said positively that the holy Patriarch was there, and Fleury has followed them; until these learned critics shall have decided, we relate the fact as we have found it, and of which Wading brings credible evidence. *Script. Ord. Praedic.,* tom. I, Dissert. 3. Act. *SS. supra Hist. Eccles,* de Fleury, lib. 78, n.20 Wading, ad ann. 1219.

[18] These are Fleury's own words, which are merely translations from the authors of the Order of St. Dominic.

[19] S. Antoninus observes that the Holy See, which has the plenitude of power, has, for good reasons, dispensed with this point in the Order of St. Dominic; and the Council of Trent has since given permission to all monasteries and to all houses, whether of men or women, to possess property and funds even to the mendicant orders, and to those who, by their constitutions, were forbidden from having any. The only exception from this is the Order of St. Francis, who profess to keep the rule of their founder with the greatest strictness. St. Anton, chron. part 3, chap. 4,153. Counc. Trent, sess. 25, de regul. cap. 3.

ordinary course of God's dispensations; but after doing all that depends on ourselves, provided there be no irregularity on our part, and that our desires are within the bounds of moderation, without any impatience as to the event, we may assure ourselves that, according to the words of the wise man: "No one hath hoped in the Lord and bath been confounded."[20]

Several prelates, and other persons of quality, who had been invited by Cardinal Ugolino to the Chapter, as to a grand and admirable sight, had the curiosity to examine everything minutely. They saw the religious in their miserable huts, coarsely dressed, taking but a slender proportion of nourishment, sleeping on mats spread on the earth with a log of wood for a pillow. They noticed at the same time that they were quite calm, that joy and concord were universal amongst them, and that they were entirely submissive to their saintly founder. Admiring all these things, they said to each other: "This shows that the way to heaven is narrow, and that it is very difficult for the rich to enter into the kingdom of God.[21] We flatter ourselves that we shall eke out our salvation in the enjoyment of all the comforts of life, having our ease in all things, while these people, to save their souls, deprive themselves of everything, mortify their bodies, and are notwithstanding not without great apprehension. We should like to die as they will, but we do not choose to live as they live." Similar reflections converted a great number of persons, and more than five hundred took the habit of the Friars Minor during the Chapter.

The Holy Patriarch found that many of his religious submitted themselves to extraordinary mortifications, which either shortened their days or rendered them useless to the Order by the illnesses which were the consequence. He therefore publicly forbade them, by the virtue of holy obedience, to make use of any such, and he ordered all who had coats of mail, iron girdles, or other instruments of mortification, to leave them off and deliver them up to him. This was done, and some most extraordinary modes of inflicting self-punishment were discovered. The number of coats of mail and iron girdles which were delivered up were more than five hundred; they were put into a heap, and the Patriarch thought proper to show them to the Cardinal and his company for their edification. They were astonished on witnessing so great a love of such penitential austerities, in men of such pure and holy lives. In their presence he forbade his brethren all sorts of indiscreet mortifications, which are injurious to the body, representing to them that they either hasten death, or throw the body into such a state of languor and weakness, as makes it unfit for spiritual exercises, or an impediment to the practice of good works, to labor for the glory of God, and to giving good example to their neighbors. Oh, fortunate and happy times, when it was necessary to check such failings!

God made known to Francis, in a revelation he had during the sitting of the chapter, that the prince of darkness, alarmed at the fervor of the new Order,

---

[20] Eccles. 2: 11.

[21] Matt. 7: 14; Luke 18: 24.

had collected thousands of demons, to concert together on the means of bringing it to ruin; and that one of them, more astute than the rest, had put forth an opinion which it had been decided should be acted upon. It was, not to attack the Friars Minor openly, but to have recourse to artifice; to induce them to receive into their society nobles, learned men, and youths. Nobles, in order by their means to introduce effeminacy in which they had been brought up; learned men, who, proud of their learning, should have a contempt for humility; and youths, who, being weak and delicate, would greatly relax in the regular discipline.

Religion teaches us that there are demons, and that they are subordinate one to the other; that God, when it pleases Him, permits them to tempt mankind, and even torment them corporally; and St. Paul speaks of "the Prince of the powers of this air."[22] We know what Satan did to holy Job; and what our Lord said to St. Peter: "Satan hath desired to have you, that he might sift you as wheat;"[23] and what He noticed elsewhere: "When an unclean spirit is gone out of a man, he takes with him seven spirits more wicked than himself, and they enter in and dwell there."[24] Thus we need have no difficulty in believing that the prince of darkness had collected such a number of demons against St. Francis and his institute. St. Gregory[25] says, that they attack with greater violence those in whom they find a greater disposition to holiness, and that the principal demons are employed in the attacks on the bravest soldiers of Jesus Christ. What must be the wrath of these malignant spirits against the apostolical men, whose lives are wholly employed in effecting the salvation of souls!

Francis had already been made aware by the means of a young female who was possessed, as St. Bonaventure relates,[26] that the devils, irritated by the injury he did them, had assembled against him, and then he merely said, as St. Paul did, I am the strongest. But he was alarmed when he learnt from God Himself the increase of their rage. He retired for two days to an oratory to pray for grace to be able to escape from their snares, and that he might be protected by good angels. His prayer gave him fresh courage; he returned to the chapter, and addressed his brethren with energy on the watchfulness with

---

[22] Ephes. 2: 2.

[23] Matt. 12: 43 and 45.

[24] Wading mentions a revelation made to St. Bridget, relative to the efforts and artifices employed by the devils against the Order of St. Francis, and the words of a heretic possessed by a devil, who was exorcized by St. Dominic at Carcassonne. Very wholesome instructions are to be derived the reform; but, as to what was said to St. Dominic, Bzovius might have been more just to the Order of St. Francis. He has been equally unjust on other occasions in his *Ecclesiastical Annals;* Wading has corrected him mildly and with caution in the *Annals of the Friars Minor,* and Dermicius Thadcus, in a book entitled, *Nitela Franciscanae Religionis,* (The dormouse of Franciscan Religious —Editor's note) printed at Lyons, in 1627, with approbation, by Claude Landry, in 4.

[25] Sanct. Gregor. *Moral,* lib. 29, cap. 22, n. 44, Edit. Bened.

[26] Sanct. Bonav. *in Hexam.* Serm. 18. post med. 1 Cor.

which it was incumbent on them to work out their salvation, without placing too much reliance on the holiness of their state of life, from which they must be apprehensive lest they should fall off by the machinations of their enemy. "You know," he said, "the examples we have; Satan fell from Heaven, and drew with him a number of the angels; he caused Adam and Eve to be driven from Paradise; he prayed to be allowed to sift the Apostles as wheat is sifted; and he did so with such effect, that one of them betrayed his Master, another denied Him, and all fled when He was captured."

The Saint then explained to them what God had made known to him of the designs of the devil; and in order that the enemy's malignity might fall on himself, he warned them to pay more attention in the reception of novices to the sentiments of the mind than to the advantages of birth; to be very careful that the learned whom they should admit, should be devoid of pride, and were fit to edify others by their humility, and to be careful that such as joined them in the flower of youth, should be informed of all which they would have to put in practice in future.

For the holy man did not think it requisite, in consequence of Satan's malice, to prohibit noblemen from joining his Order, since their example has great influence, and the elevated sentiments which are found in that class, render them more fit to do great things for the service of God. He did not wish to drive away the learned, since learning is necessary for the exercise of the functions of religion, and since those men who join the knowledge of sound doctrine to an evangelical life, are most instructive teachers in the Church, for the dissipation of error and the establishment of virtue. He also desired that they should receive such young men as should present themselves in the tenderest age, "because it is good for man to bear the yoke from his youth:"[27] to leave the world, before having any knowledge of it, except through the lights of the Church, and to offer themselves as pure victims, rather than to bring to Him the remains of a heart stained by the passions; and, moreover, our Savior said to His disciples, who turned away the children who came to Him: "Suffer them, and forbid them not to come to me."[28]

We know that there are in the world censorious people who condemn the custom of permitting young persons to enter into a religious state: it would be easy to show, if it were not for fear of rendering this work too voluminous, that their arguments are based on a superficial foundation, and are contrary to the maxims of Christianity; we therefore content ourselves with saying that at the Council of Trent,[29] which was guided by the Spirit of truth in its discipline, as well as in its dogmas and morality, permission was given to persons of either sex, to make profession of a religious at the full age of sixteen; that rule

---

[27] Jerem. Thren. III: 27.

[28] Matt. 19: 13 and 14.

[29] Sess. 25, de regul. cap. 15.

is authorized by the ordinances[30] of all Christian princes, and it therefore seems very extraordinary that any individuals[31] should be rash enough to oppose their private opinions to so respectable an authority.

Francis, who was desirous of encouraging the fervor of his disciples, apprised them of what they had to fear, and anticipated the smallest inclinations to pride in them, by salutary humiliations. The Cardinal Protector having one day preached before all the religious of the chapter, and having concluded his sermon by bestowing on them considerable praise, the holy Patriarch asked his permission to address the audience. He foretold to them, and represented in lively colors, all that was to happen to the Order; the temptations to which they were to be exposed; the tribulations they were to suffer; the changes that would be brought in, and their decline. He reproached them with their laxity, and with their want of fervor in cooperating with the peculiar graces they had received from God; he spoke so energetically, that, in censuring their foolish obsequiousness, if such a fault they had, he covered them with confusion. The cardinal was somewhat mortified, and said: "Pray, why, brother, did you gainsay me, setting the imperfections of your brethren in opposition to the praises I had given them?" "My lord and my father," answered Francis, "I did so, in order to preserve the substance of your praise. I was apprehensive that such praise being given by a person of your exalted rank, might inspire vanity into the minds of those in whom humility has not as yet thrown out deep roots." This affords great matter for reflection for those virtuous persons who voluntarily receive praise, at least when it is artfully administered; and for indiscreet flatterers, who expose virtue to a dangerous trial.

What occurred on the following day, showed that the holy man had received from God the perfect means of appreciating men's minds. Brother Elias, who was the provincial for Tuscany, brother John of Strachia, who was provincial for Bologna, and several others came to the Cardinal Protector and entreated him to tell Francis, as from himself, that he ought to listen to the advice of his brethren, among whom there were many learned men, fully

---

[30] All that was done on this subject in France is brought together in 4th tome of the *Memories du Clerge* 1710, tit.l, cap. 1.

[31] The author of the *Lois Ecclesiastiques,* chap. 12, maxim 7, page 555, gives the words of the Council of Trent, and the Ordinance of Blois for such as make their profession at the full age of sixteen; and in the maxim he says, "The Ordinance of Orleans did not permit males to make their profession till the age of twenty-five, and the females till the age of twenty. If this was still adhered to, fewer persons would be seen who repented of having embraced a state of life which they had entered with maturer reflection. Was it right in the author to repeat approvingly the *Article of the Ordinance of Orleans,* which that of Blois had corrected by another, which a general Council, the Ordinance of our kings, and the decrees of our superior courts authorized, and which is a law in the Canonical and Civil Jurisprudence? Ought he not to have known that if some religious persons repent of the choice they have made, this may occur as often from their neglecting the duties of their vocation, as from their having wanted a vocation? He ought to correct this sentence in his book, in which other faults have been pointed out to him.

capable of governing; particularly as he himself was a simple and unread man, whose ill health did not permit him to bring their affairs into good order. They added, that respect ought to be paid to the ancient rules of St. Basil, of St. Augustine, and of St. Benedict, and that we should not differ so widely from them by a new rule and excessive severity, as if we wished to be better than our fathers.

The cardinal took his time, and then proposed all these things to Francis, as maxims which he deemed good for the government of the Order. The saint being immediately made aware by the Spirit of God, that these things had been suggested to him, rose up from the place in which he had been seated with the cardinal, took him respectfully by the hand, and led him to the brethren who were assembled in chapter, and said:

"My brethren, my brethren, God has called me by the way of simplicity and humility, in order that I might follow the folly of the cross: it is for His glory and my confusion, and for the security of your consciences I am about to tell you what He said to me: 'Francis,' He said, 'I desire that you may be in the world a new little idiot, who shall preach by your actions and by your discourses the folly of the cross. You and your own must follow me only, and not any other manner of life.' Speak not to me therefore of any other rule," he added, "for I shall not follow, nor prescribe any other than what God has in His mercy given me; those who swerve from it, I fear, will feel the Divine vengeance, and will be covered with confusion, when at length they shall be obliged once more to enter into this path."

Then addressing himself to the cardinal, he said: "My lord, these wise people, whom your lordship praises so much, would wish by their worldly prudence to deceive both God and you; but they deceive themselves, endeavoring to destroy what God has ordained for their salvation, through me, his unworthy servant. I attribute nothing to myself of what I do, or of what I say; I rely not on my own lights in the government of the Order; I arrange everything by long prayers with our Heavenly Father, who governs it sovereignly, and who has made His will known to us by so many manifest signs, in order to bring to perfection the work He has commenced by so miserable a man as I am, for the salvation of souls, and the edification of our holy mother the Church. Those who prefer the wisdom of the world to the will of the Lord, expose themselves manifestly to be lost." Having spoken thus, Francis retired.

The cardinal, who admired the energy of his words, and the light which disclosed to him at once the most secret thoughts, said to the superiors who were abashed: "My dear brethren, you have seen how the Holy Spirit has himself spoken by the mouth of this apostolical man; his words came forth as a two-edged sword, which has penetrated to the bottom of the heart.[32] Take care that you do not grieve the Spirit of God; be not ungrateful for the favors He

---

[32] Hebr. 4: 12; Eph. 4: 30.

has done you. He is truly in this poor man, and manifests to you, through him, the marvels of His power; in listening to him, it is Jesus Christ that you hear; in despising him, it is Jesus Christ whom you despise.[33] Humble yourselves, therefore, and obey him, if it is your desire to please God, and not lose the fruit of your vocation; for I know by experience, that everything which either the devils or men are about to attempt against his Order, is revealed to him. Whatsoever may be said to him with good or bad intention, it is difficult to find him off his guard; neither my advice, nor that of any other person, will turn him from his purpose." The provincials who had given rise to this scene were moved, and submitted themselves to the will of the Patriarch.

Among the religious who had congregated at the chapter, there were many who came to seek a remedy for the ill-treatment they had received in many places out of Italy, which had its rise in two causes; the first was, that they had no authenticated letters to show that their institute had been approved by the Church; the second was, that the pastors would not allow them to preach. They begged therefore that the Pope might be solicited to give them written testimonials to certify that they had his approbation of their institution; and, moreover, that they should obtain from the Holy Father a privilege, in virtue of which they might preach wherever they thought proper, even without leave from the bishops.

The holy founder could not hear this second article without indignation. "What! my brethren," said he, "are you still devoid of understanding;[34] and do you not know the will of God? It is His pleasure that we should gain the good-will of our superiors by our respect for them, and by humility; and then by word and good example, those who are under them. When the bishops see that you live holily, and that you do not encroach on their authority, they will themselves apply to you to work for the salvation of the souls which are committed to their care; they themselves will collect their flocks to listen to you, and to imitate you. Let it be our sole privilege[35] to have no privilege

---

[33] Luke 10: 6.

[34] Matt. 15: 16

[35] When Cardinal Baronius says that St. Francis did not approve of privileges obtained in order to withdraw themselves from Episcopal authority, and that those enjoyed by his Order had been obtained by Brother Elias, a man who was guided by the prudence of the flesh, he could not mean this as applicable to the immediate dependence on the Holy See, in which the Order of Friars Minor is; for it was St. Francis himself who, in 1210, solicited from the Pope the approval of his rule, where this dependence is specially noticed; and it was only in 1211 that Elias entered the Order. Father Thomassin, who quotes this passage from Baronius in the same sense, should have noticed the mistake. Baron, ad ann. 676, n. 7. Thomassin, Discipline de l'Eglise, part 4, lib. I, cap. 52, n. 13. It must further be remarked, that it was two bishops, those of Assisi and Sabina, who seconded Francis's application, and strenuously solicited Innocent III to approve his rule, which rendered his Order immediately dependent on the Holy See. The holy Patriarch then chose to have this sort of privilege, with sill its consequences, without which his Order, as he intended it to be, could neither be established nor exist; but he did not choose that any other should be applied for; and if his Order had any other subsequently, the Sovereign Pontiffs gave them by their own accord, and for reasons

calculated to swell our pride, to give ourselves a confidence which shall be to the prejudice of others, and be the cause of contentions. Let us ask nothing of the Holy See but what is calculated to aid us in serving God, in extending the faith, and in gaining souls under the good pleasure of the prelates, without causing any disturbance among the people."

Some represented that they had found many of the heads of the parochial clergy so harsh, that they had been unable to mollify them, either by entreaties, or by labor, by submissiveness or good example, so as to obtain leave to preach to their parishioners, or to receive from them any corporal assistance; to which Francis replied.

"My brethren, we are sent to the aid of priests, to make good that in which they may be deficient. Each one will receive his reward,[36] not according to the degree of his authority, but in proportion to his labors. Know, then, that what is most agreeable to God is, to work for the salvation of souls, and that we shall best succeed in this by living in concord with the priests than by living separately from them; if they throw obstacles in the way, God, to whom all vengeance belongs,[37] will give them in His good time what is their due. Be therefore submissive to ecclesiastical superiors, in order to avert as much as may be in your power any jealousies.[38] If you are children of peace, you will soon ingratiate yourselves with the clergy and the people, and this will be more acceptable to God than if you gained over the people, and thereby gave scandal to the clergy. Hide the faults of the priests, make good what they are deficient in, and be only in consequence the more humble."

The religious of St. Francis must not be surprised if they, even in these days, meet with opposition in the exercise of their holy ministries. It is an occurrence which the similarity of men may at all times bring about;[39] and which St. Paul experienced more than any other in the course of his ministry. But let them be careful to put in practice the advice of their Father, in order that they may be able to say in truth with the apostle: "We have injured no

---

known to themselves.

[36] 1 Cor. 3: 8.

[37] Deuter. 32: 35.

[38] Father Thomassin, in his *Discipline de l'Eglise*, points out the close alliance there is between the secular and regular clergy, and after having adduced many striking proofs of this, he concludes: "That these two states, having been so united originally, they could not in after times but preserve these mutual relations and communications so essential for their glory and mutual preservation." To which is added, that these ties should be still stronger between the ecclesiastics and the mendicant Orders, such as the Friars Minor, since these latter, having no titles, no benefices, no revenues, are destined by their rules, by the Popes, and by the bishops, to exercise the apostolical ministries solely as auxiliaries; and that, as the harvest is abundant, and as the numbers of workmen are sometimes small, the pastors should see, without envy, ministers of good-will will who come to share in their labors. *Discipline de l'Eglise*. Part I, lit I., cap. 47. Part 2, lib 1, cap. 36. Part 3, lib. I, cap. 32 and 33, and lib. 4, cap. 2. Part 4, lib. I, cap. 50.

[39] 2 Cor. 10:11.

man."[40] And, finally, the advice which he gave them must induce us to notice his moderation and his discretion, in an age when the Church had reason to renew the laments of one of the prophets against the pastors of Israel.[41]

He judged it proper, by the advice of the Cardinal Protector, to procure apostolic letters to make known the approbation his institute had received; and he obtained them from the Pope, who was then at Viterbo. These were the first which were given to the Order of Friars Minor: their contents are as follows:

"Honorius, Bishop, servant of the servants of God, to the Archbishops, Bishops, Abbots, Deacons, Archdeacons, and other superior ecclesiastics.

"As our dear son, brother Francis and his companions, have renounced the vanities of the world, and embraced a state of life which the Roman Church has justly approved; and, following the example of the apostles, are about to go into different parts to announce the word of God; we beg and exhort you in our Lord, and we command you by these apostolical letters, to receive as catholic and faithful, the brothers of this Order, the bearers of these letters, who may apply to you, to be favorable to them, and to treat them with kindness, for the honor of God, and out of consideration for us. Given this 3rd of the Ides of June, the third year of our pontificate."

Many cardinals and other illustrious persons added their letters of recommendation to those of the Pope, particularly Cardinal Ugolino, the protector of the Order, who testified by a document addressed to all prelates, which certified the intimate knowledge he had of the virtues of the Founder and of his religious, and the great fruit that was to be expected from them for the propagation of the faith, and the benefit of the whole Church. They made a great number of authenticated copies of these letters, in order to give to those whom Francis had resolved to send in all directions, even into the most distant lands.

Three things were decreed at this general chapter. The first was, that on every Saturday a solemn mass should be celebrated in honor of the immaculate Blessed Virgin Mary. This glorious title of Immaculate, which the general councils of the seventh and eighth centuries, and the ancient fathers of the Church, have given to Mary, has been used by the Council of Trent,[42] which has declared in its decree on the subject of original sin, "that it is not its intention to include therein the blessed and immaculate Virgin Mary, Mother of God." The use which the Friars Minor made of it in 1219, shows clearly that they adopted, as did their sainted Patriarch, the common opinion of the Greek church, which was already spread in various parts of the Latin Church, in honor of the Conception of the Blessed Virgin, because they thought it wholly pure and exempt from the stain of original sin. Their successors have always, with admirable zeal, maintained this opinion, which God in so far blessed, that

---

[40] 2 Cor. 7: 2.

[41] Ezech. 36: 1, et seq.

[42] Sess. 5, de Peccato Origin.

they have had the advantage and consolation of seeing the Institution of the Feast of the Conception in the whole Church, by an Apostolic Constitution,[43] which the Council of Trent has renewed; and many Sovereign Pontiffs[44] have declared to all the faithful that the object of the festival is to honor the Blessed Virgin under this opinion, that she was conceived without the stain of Original Sin, forbidding under severe penalties the writing or speaking to the contrary.

It is proper to notice here, that at the head of the Friars Minor, who supported the proposition of the Immaculate Conception, was the celebrated John Duns Scotus, so respected in the Church for his penetrating genius, for the solidity of his doctrine, and for his singular piety. He silenced his opponents, and his success was so manifest that it was considered that he had the special protection of the Blessed Virgin,[45] and his reasonings were so convincing that the University of Paris admitted them, and declared in favor of the doctrine of the Immaculate Conception, which it has maintained ever since. In the fifteenth century, the faculty of Theology passed a solemn decree on this point, in which it declared that in consonance with the opinions of its predecessors, and in order to oppose the enemies of the Blessed Virgin, it bound itself by oath to maintain the proposition that the Mother of God was preserved from Original Sin; framing a law, not to receive any doctor who should not take this oath; which is continued to the present day.

In this is the pious triumph of the Sons of St. Francis, who, in gratitude for so singular a privilege, honor the Blessed Virgin as the Patroness and Protectress of their Order, under the title of her Immaculate Conception, and by celebrating the festival thereof with every possible solemnity.

The second statute directed, that express mention should be made of the names of St. Peter and St. Paul, in the prayer, "Protégé nos Domine, etc.," and in another which begins with these words: "Exaudi nos Deus," etc., in memory of what had been revealed to St. Francis, that these apostles interceded powerfully with God for his institute. This was practiced by the whole Church

---

[43] Declarat haec ipsa sancta Synodus, non esse suae intentionis comprehendere in hoc decreto, ubi de peccato originali agitur, beatam et Immaculatam Virginem Mariam, Dei Genitricem; sed observandas esse constitutiones felicis recordationis Sixti Papae IV sub poenis in eis constitutionibus contentis, quas innovat. Concil. Trident. Sess. 5, de Peccato Originali.

[44] Alexander VII has collected in his Constitution, *Solicitudo omnium Ecclesiarum* of the 3rd of December, 1661, all that had been done by his predecessors on the subject of the Immaculate Conception of the Blessed Virgin. We see clearly therein, what the Roman Church thinks upon it. There are on this subject several excellent Latin treatises; the most complete one in French is that of M. Trevet, the Cure of Gonnecour in Normandy, printed at Rome in 1709. It is a refutation of the prescriptions published in 1676, by M. de Launoi, who is a furious opponent of the Mystery of the Conception, not withstanding the prohibition of the Holy See.

[45] Wading relates, on the testimony of many authors, and on the tradition of the city of Paris, that Scotus, about to discourse in support of the Immaculate Conception of the Blessed Virgin, prayed first before one of her pictures, and that the picture bowed its head to confirm his reasoning. From the same tradition we learn that the picture in question is the one which is seen with its head bowed down at the door of the lower chapel of the palace at Paris. Wading, ad ann. 1209.

when Innocent IV revised and reformed the Roman Breviary, through Aymon, an Englishman,[46] who was the fifth general of the Order of Friars Minor.

In the third statute it was said that poverty should be apparent in everything, in the convents which they should build; that the churches should be small and low, and that the walls of the rest of the buildings should be of wood or mud. Some difficulties were started to this; many represented that in their provinces wood was dearer than stone, and that walls of masonry, if they were not too high, would better denote poverty, because they would be solid and not compel frequent repair. The holy Founder would not argue this matter with them; for it is remarked that not to give rise to any dispute, and not to give scandal to the weak, he often condescended to the opinions of others in similar matters. Nevertheless he recommended to them all, not to receive either churches or houses which were not in conformity to holy poverty which was their rule.

It was not possible always to follow out his intentions. The prelates and princes who were greatly attached to his Order had beautiful convents built, which his religious could not avoid receiving; and St. Bonaventure even says that a numerous community which has different exercises to perform, requires large houses, although care should be taken that holy poverty should be apparent throughout, and that superfluity should not preponderate over what is reasonably necessary.

---

[46] Wading ad ann. 1244, n. 2.

CHAPTER II

THE FRIARS MINOR GO THROUGHOUT THE WORLD

He sends his friars through the whole world—He writes to all the ecclesiastics in the world—And to all the temporal magistrates in the world—And to all the superiors of his Order—The travels of his Friars in various parts of the world—In Greece—In Africa—In Spain and Portugal—In France—In the Low Countries—He himself prepares to go to the Levant—His opinions on the government of the monastery of St. Damian, and other houses of the same Order.

HE CHAPTER being ended, Francis, following the example of the apostles, divided the world among his brethren, in order to bring it all in subjection to the Empire of Jesus Christ. After long prayer according to his custom, he made known to them that he took for himself and twelve of his companions Syria and Egypt. He named Benedict of Arezzo for Greece; Giles and Electe for Africa, with others whom he associated to them. As the greater part of Spain groaned under the domination of the Saracens, he added to those whom he had before sent there, John Parent, and more than a hundred new missionaries, in order that they might spread themselves into all parts. Into Provence, into France, and into the Low Countries he sent the same as before. For Gascony, in particular, he selected Christopher, a religious who had the simplicity of a dove, and who died at Cahors, and whose miracles have rendered his memory celebrated.

Angelo of Pisa was appointed Provincial in England, whither he was to take many more apostolic workmen. The Patent which was furnished him was very short; the following is the tenor of it, such as it is found at Mount Alvernia: "I, Brother Francis of Assisi, Minister General, command you, Brother Angelo of Pisa, to go to England, there to take upon yourself the office of Provincial: Adieu! Brother Francis, of Assisi."

The first mission to Germany had not been successful. Those who had been sent thither by the preceding Chapter, not knowing the language, and answering badly the questions put to them, were suspected from their poor and unusual habit to belong to those heretics who were prosecuted in Italy, in consequence of which they were cruelly ill-treated and driven away. The recital which they gave on their return made Germany so unpopular among the brethren that they said that none ought to go there but such as aspired to martyrdom, and that many prayed to heaven to be preserved from the ferocity of the Germans. Francis did not think proper to send any more there till such time as he should have received some novices from thence who might go there with others; but he sent some into Hungary.

He selected for the distant missions the most talented of his brethren, and the most perfect in virtue, and he gave them excellent instructions as to the exercise of their missions. He likewise added to the authentic copies of the Papal Bull and of the recommendations of the Cardinals, three other letters which he addressed to the ecclesiastics, to the magistrates, and to the Superiors of the Order. They are so edifying that we deem it useful to insert them here. This is the first:

"To my Reverend lords in Jesus Christ, all the Ecclesiastics who are over the whole world, and who live in the Catholic faith, Brother Francis, their lowly servant, sends greeting, and kisses their feet.

"Being indebted to all the world, and my infirmities not permitting me to discharge in your regard what I owe, I beg you to receive with great charity what I lay before you in these few words. Let us reflect, all of us who are in the condition of clergymen, on the great sin which some commit, through ignorance, against the very holy Body and the very holy Blood of our Lord Jesus Christ, and against the very holy words with which they are consecrated; for we know that His Body and His Blood can only be present after the pronunciation of the words which consecrate them. We have and we see nothing of this most High Lord, which is real and sensible in this world but His Body and His Blood, and His words which have served to redeem us, and to make us pass from death to life, as it is by His word that we were created.

"Nevertheless, let all those who celebrate these sacred mysteries, and in particular those who do so without due discernment, consider what is in many places the meanness of the chalices in which they consecrate, and of the corporals and other linen which are used in the holy Sacrifice; with what irreverence the Body of our Lord Jesus Christ is placed, deserted, carried, and received by some and administered by others. Sometimes, even His name and His written word are cast under foot and trodden on; so true it is that the sensual man does not perceive the things which are of the spirit of God.[1]

"Does religion not awaken us to the outrages offered to this Lord, full of goodness, who places Himself in our hands, whom we touch, and whom we receive daily in the holy communion? Are we ignorant that we shall one day fall into His hands? Let us, therefore, correct these defects, together with all others, never again to fall into them.

"Wherever we find the Body of our Lord Jesus Christ inconveniently deposited, let it be removed and enclosed with great reverence and care. So, also, if His name or words are found scattered about, let them be collected and placed in some decent place. We know that we ought to attend to all these things, according to the order that the Lord has given us on these points, and according to the decrees issued by our holy mother the Church. Whosoever

---

[1] 1 Cor. 2: 14.

shall fail in this, let him know that on the day of judgment he will be made responsible for it to our Lord Jesus Christ.

"Those who shall cause this writing to be copied in order to spread it quickly, and to cause it to be practically attended to, let them be assured that God will bless them. May our Lord Jesus Christ fill you, and fortify you by His grace, all you ecclesiastics who are my Lords."

We must perceive from this that St. Francis, with all his evangelical simplicity, had considerable acquired knowledge. He speaks as a correct theologian of the consecration which can only be performed by the words of Jesus Christ.[2] He exacts, as did Origen and St. Augustine, that equal respect shall be paid to His words, as to His Body.[3] The authority which he points out to prove how much the name of God is to be respected, as is His word and all that serves for His worship, show that he was well versed in the Holy Scriptures,[4] and that he was instructed in the Ordinances of the Canon Law.[5] We may also conjecture with Wading, that, being very zealous in promoting cleanliness and decency in everything about the altar, and for the suitable administration of the Eucharist, and being, moreover, highly esteemed by the Pope, it was he who induced Honorius III to make the rule on this head, which is found in the decretals.[6]

The mere title of his letter deserves attention. He addresses it to the ecclesiastics who live in the Catholic faith; and as he expresses it in his will, according to the form of the Roman Church; from which it may be concluded that he did not desire to write to such as were heretics, or in schism, following in that the doctrine of St. Paul,[7] who warns his disciple, Titus, to hold no communication with them, and that of St. John who forbids receiving them into our houses, or even to greet them.[8] The light and the purity of his faith were sufficient to inspire him with these sentiments, but the acquaintance he had of the apostolical constitutions give us room to think that he was guided

---

[2] This is what theologians generally teach, grounded on the sacred Scriptures, on tradition, the liturgies, on the authority of the holy Fathers, Greek and Latin, on the doctrine of the Councils, and the greatest reasoning which the Greeks at the Council of Florence acknowledge they could not but admit. It would be useless to endeavor to renew and support the peculiar opinion that the form of the Eucharistic consecration does not consist alone in the sole words of Jesus Christ, and that the prayer or invocation is an essential part thereof. The proofs of this opinion are too weak and the consequences may be dangerous. *Council of Florence*, page 1163 and 1164, tom. 13, *Collect. Concil.* See *Refutation de la Dissertation*, etc., by the R. P. Bougeant, of the Society of Jesus, at d'Houry's, 1727.

[3] Orig. Horn. 53 in Exod. Hom. August, vel Cesar, Arel. Serm. Caesar, n. 2; Sermonnd. tom. 5 Oper. S. Aug. Vad. annot. in Epist. 15 S. Francisci.

[4] Levit. 4: 12; 21: 6; 20: 1, et seq. Deuter. 6: 6 et seq.; Isaiah. 52: 11; Ezech. 23:26 et alibi. 1 Cor. 11: 27 and 28.

[5] *De Consecr.* Dist. I cap. *Nemo.* cap. *Altaris*, cap. *Vestiment.* cap. *Vasa* cap. *Ut calix*, et alibi.

[6] Decret. Greg. Noni, cap. *sane de celebr. Miss.*

[7] Tit. 3: 10.

[8] 2 John 1: 10.

also by the two celebrated canons[9] which our holy Father Benedict XII, when Archbishop of Benevento quoted in his second letter to the Cardinal de Bissy, against those who did not pay due obedience to the Holy Roman Church, and prevented others to submit to it.[10] The letter which Francis addressed to the magistrates was couched in these terms:

"To all the powers, governors, consuls, judges, magistrates, who are in the whole earth, and to all others who may receive these letters; Brother Francis, your lowly and despicable servant in our Lord, sends greeting, and wishes you peace.

"Consider attentively that the day of death is at hand; for which reason I entreat you with all the respect in my power, not to forget God, in the midst of the embarrassments caused by the affairs of the world, nor to violate His Commandments; for all those who shall withdraw from the Lord, are accursed, and He will forget them.[11] On the day of their death, all that they appeared to have will be taken from them; the more they shall have been learned and powerful in this world, the more will they be tormented in hell. I advise you, therefore, my lords, above all things, to enter on a sincere course of penance,[12] to receive humbly and with love, the most sacred Body, and the most holy Blood of our Lord Jesus Christ, in memory of His Passion; to refer to God the honor He has done you, in confiding to you the guidance of His people, and to cause every night some signal to be made to give notice to all, to honor the Lord Almighty, and to return Him thanks. If you fail in this, take notice that you will be called to account for it at the day of judgment. Those who shall keep this writing at their homes, and act up to what it contains, will receive God's blessing."

There are many things in this letter worthy of notice, and which are not less salutary for the instruction of the faithful, than honorable to St. Francis.

1. The man of God has no condescension for the false delicacy of worldlings who cannot bear to hear death spoken of; he begins by telling them that death is at hand, in order to bring them more efficaciously to repentance. So it is that preachers should announce, without any human respect, the salutary truths which displease their hearers; thus they should speak of purity where licentiousness is common; of restitution, where fraud and usury are found; of charity, in opposition to the harshness of the rich; of submission to the Church, where there is the spirit of resistance to its decisions, and so of the rest.

2. He exhorts to frequent communion those persons who are engaged in worldly affairs, because in the midst of the difficulties and embarrassments

---

[9] Canon. *Si Romanorum*. Dist. xix, I. Canon. *Nulli fas est*, Dist. xix, 5.

[10] *Recueil de Lettres dans l'instruction pastorale de M. le Cardinal de Bissy*. 1722, pg. 132.

[11] Psalm 107: 21; Hosea 2: 6; Matt. 25: 19; Sap. 6: 7

[12] Wading quotes the manuscript from which he has taken these words which are not found in others, but which must have been in the original. —Note 5, in Epist. 15, S. Francisci.

which are inseparable from them, they may live in such manner as to be in a state to participate frequently in the divine mysteries, which is in conformity to the intention of Jesus Christ and the spirit of the Church. It is upon this principle that the children of St. Francis have labored and greatly contributed to reestablish among the faithful the frequent use of communion.

Wading thinks that the Saint,[13] in exhorting to the frequentation of communion, names the Body and the Blood of Jesus Christ separately, because he had in mind communion under the two species,[14] which in his time was still given in some churches, and even in the time of St. Thomas of Aquino. But it may be said, that it was from a pure and tender devotion for the precious Blood, the effusion of which has redeemed us, and that it is an article of faith, that we receive it with the Body when we communicate under the sole species of bread.

It is to the zeal of St. Francis that we are indebted in some measure for the pious custom of ringing a bell at night to collect the faithful in the churches for the purpose of prayer; since his days it has been practiced in Italy. St. Charles Borromeo[15] in the fourth council of Milan, considers it as an ancient custom.

Many other countries of Europe have followed it, and we see with edification that it is observed with tolerable regularity in France, both in the towns and in the country. Those who cannot attend this public prayer ought, in the opinion of St. Charles,[16] to collect their families in the evening to pray together; our fathers used to do so, and why should their children fail in so doing?

The advice which the Saint gives to the magistrates, to refer the honor they have received to God, and to take care to cause Him to be honored, comprises all the extent of that maxim of Christianity, which lays down that religion is the principal object of government and policy; that[17] temporal authority which emanates from God should have nothing more at heart than to cause Him to be served, to protect the Church, to support her decisions, to preserve her discipline, and to put a stop, by the severity of laws, to all novelties which are contrary to the purity of faith and to everything which tends to the corruption of morals.

---

[13] Annot. 6, in Epist. S. Francisci.

[14] The communion under one sole species of bread for the laity was the practice of the Church from the earliest ages on many occasions, and was generally adopted with similar wisdom by the Council of Constance, as Bossuet, the learned bishop of Meaux, demonstrates, with the same precision and solidity as is found in his other works against the Protestants. *Traité de la Communion sousles deux especes,*1682.

[15] Conc. Mediol. 3. Part quaest. 80, art. 12.

[16] Conc. Mediol. 4, part I, chap. 24, de Orat.

[17] Three excellent works have been written on this subject, in which this truth has been clearly proved. The first is *Traité dogmatique et historique des Edit. &c.,* by Father Thomassin, priest of the Oratory, printed at the royal press, in 1705. *Traité de la police,* by M. de la Mare, in 1705. *Politique tiree de l'Ecri Lure Sainte,* a posthumous work of Bossuet, bishop of Meaux, printed in 1709.

The holy Patriarch wrote as follows to the superiors of his Order: "To all the Wardens of the Friars Minor,[18] who shall see these letters. Brother Francis, the lowest of the servants of God, greets them, and wishes them peace in our Lord.

"Know that there are high and sublime things before God, which man considers sometimes as mean and despicable;[19] and that there are others, on the contrary, which men highly esteem, and which are very contemptible in the eyes of God. I entreat you, as forcibly as I am able, before the Lord our God, to deliver to the bishops and other ecclesiastics the letters which treat of the most holy Body and of the most holy Blood of our Lord Jesus Christ, and to bear well in mind what we have recommended to you relative to this mystery. Be careful, also, to have the other letters copied, and to have them distributed as soon as possible to the governors, consuls, and magistrates, in which they are warned to take care that the praises of God be publicly celebrated. I greet you in our Lord."

He explains in the first place in this letter,[20] two principles which were taught by Jesus Christ and by St. Paul, as to the different way in which God and man judge of things, and without making any particular application of what he had adverted to, he immediately goes on to say: "I entreat you to deliver my letters to the ecclesiastics and magistrates." It was as much as to say to those with equal discernment and humility: "Although my letters are written in a very simple style, and in that view of them they may appear to you not calculated to make much impression on those to whom they are addressed, and to procure for you their protection; nevertheless, do not fail to deliver them, for God may use them to touch their hearts more efficaciously than more eloquent discourses." And, in effect, they did touch the hearts of those who read them, who entreated the Friars Minor to accept houses which they offered them without waiting to be asked for them.

As soon as the several missions had been fixed upon, and authenticated copies of all the letters had been delivered to each of the parties, the missionaries prepared to set out. Before we give an account of St. Francis' voyage to the Levant, we think it desirable to give an abridgment of what his children did in various parts of the world, because the principal glory is due to him, and these proceedings naturally belong to the history of his life.

Benedict of Arezzo embarked with his companions for Greece, where their preaching, backed by the holiness of their lives, and confirmed by miracles, produced abundance of fruit for the salvation of souls, and procured so many houses for the Order that in a very short time it was formed into an entire province, and was called Romania.

Giles and Electe, who anxiously aspired to martyrdom, and who were only

---

[18] That is to say, provincial ministers, as will be seen by what follows.

[19] 2 Cor. 1: 25; Luke 16: 55.

[20] Wading, note 2, in Epist. 14, S Francisi.

lay-brothers, had appeared to St. Francis to be more fit to be sent to the Saracens than even those of the clergy, and they hastened to go into Africa, with several others. What chiefly animated the zeal of brother Giles, as the author of his Life remarks, was his having heard that the Saracens treated with great cruelty those Christians who spoke ill of the law of Mahomet.[21] When he reached Tunis with a party of missionaries, he generously preached the faith in public, and this continued for some time. A person who was looked up to among the Saracens for his great wisdom, having come forth from his retreat, told the people that they ought to put to the sword all those infidels who spoke against the law of their prophet. Giles and his companions were delighted at the prospect of an early martyrdom; but the Christians with whom they had their domicile, fearing lest they might be included in the massacre, took away these preachers and compelled them to go on board a vessel in the harbor, and did not permit them again to land. As they did not cease addressing the Muslims who crowded to the sea-shore, with a view to induce them to embrace the faith of Jesus Christ, their desire to sacrifice their lives for His glory being so ardent, the Christian residents hastened to have them removed to Europe. Thus seeing that even their fellow-believers were opposed to their views, they returned to Italy.

Electe was more fortunate; during some years he performed the functions of an apostle in another town in Africa, where he received the crown of martyrdom. A body of Saracens rushed upon him while he was preaching, upon which he fell on his knees, grasped the Rule with both his hands, asked pardon for his faults from God and from his companions, and then presented his neck to the infidels who took away his life. This did not happen till after the death of St. Francis. He had entered the Order when very young, and had lived in it with great austerity, always wearing a coat of mail on his bare body, so that he prepared himself for the martyrdom of blood by the martyrdom of penance, as was recommended to the Christians in time of persecution.[22]

Those who went into Spain with John Parent proceeded with so much speed that ten of them arrived at Saragossa by the feast of the Assumption; a very short time after their departure, Bernard de Quintavalle, who was sent into this kingdom after the Chapter of 1216, had established two convents, the one at Toledo, the other at Carrion de los Condes, a town in the kingdom of Leon. Some of his companions had been admitted at Lerida, and at Balaguer, in Catalonia, under very extraordinary circumstances, which are omitted not to be too prolix. Zachary and Gautier, who had been sent into Portugal, had had much to suffer in the beginning; but Queen Urraqua, the wife of Alphonso II, who then reigned, was a most pious princess, and, having caused their institute to be examined by very learned men, and having had full assurance of the holiness of their lives, she obtained leave from the king for their being

---

[21] Act. SS. 23 April.

[22] Tertul. *ad Mart.* cap. 3, et *de cult, femin.* cap. 13, S. Cyprian *de Laps.* cap. 3, et seq.

received into his states, and permission for their building convents. A house was given them, with a chapel attached to it, of St. Anthony, near Coimbra, where the court then was, and subsequently one on a larger scale at Lisbon. Princess Sancia, the daughter of Sancho I, and sister of Alphonso II, highly praised by historians for her piety and chastity, protected Zachary, and gave him a third house, called of St. Catharine, at some distance from the town of Alenquer, which was her own; but in consequence of the distance and the insalubrity of the air, she some years after converted her own palace into a convent, which she gave to the Friars Minor. Gautier, one of Bernard's companions, who had made many great conversions by his virtues and his miracles, near Guimaraens, had built a convent not very far from that town.

While they were in that of St. Catharine, a singular thing occurred, which we have not thought right to omit here on account of the instruction it contains. One of the ladies, in waiting on the princess whose name was Maria Garcia, often came to have some pious conversation with one of the holy religious, who was very averse to receiving her, because he feared the company of females. One day when he was at prayer, she came to the church, and expressed a wish to see him, but he refused to go to her. The historian says that in order to obtain what she wished for, she did what women generally do under such circumstances, she became more importunate, and cried bitterly, and protested that it would give her great pain if she might not speak to the holy man. He therefore came, to get rid of her importunities; but he brought some straw in one hand, and some fire in the other; he set the straw on fire in her presence, and then said to her: "Although, madam, all your conversations are pious, I refuse to hold them with you in private, because what you see has happened to the straw, is what religious persons have to fear may occur to them if they have private and familiar discourse with women; and at least they lose the fruits of their holy communications with God in prayer." The lady blushed, retired, and troubled him no more. St. Jerome, who so strongly recommended to ecclesiastics and religious to avoid conversations with the female sex would certainly have approved of this action.[23]

What we have just related was the fruit of Bernard de Quintavalle's mission, and that of his companions, in Spain and Portugal, from the year 1261.

John Parent arrived at Saragossa in the month of August, 1219, with nine of his brethren who were followed by many others soon after; he addressed himself to the Bishop and to the magistrates who assembled to hear him. He explained to them who Francis of Assisi was, his vocation, his mission, his mode of life, his Institute, the approbation given to his Rule by Pope Innocent III and Honorius III, and the testimonials given to him by several Cardinals. He remarked to them that the new Order had been exceedingly multiplied in a very few years, and that they had seen more than five thousand religious at the general Chapter which had been lately assembled in the neighborhood of

---

[23] S. Hieron. Epist. ad Nepot. 34, alias 2, et ad Rustic 95 alias 4.

Assisi, which was considered to be miraculous; that their Father had sent a great number of his children into all parts of the world to combat vice and encourage virtue, which circumstance should be considered as a bountiful effect of Divine Providence towards His Church, in such calamitous times. He concluded by saying: "If our Institute is agreeable to you, we earnestly entreat you to give us some small place in which we may recite the Divine Office, and fulfill the other ministries which our Founder has recommended to us. Have no anxiety as to our subsistence, for we solicit no part of your goods; we content ourselves with very little; we are poorly clad; work and questing furnish us with all that we require."

All the assembly admired the spirit of humility which prevailed through this discourse, and the reading of the Papal Bull, with the testimonials of the Cardinals, were proofs that nothing had been set forth but what was true. But when they had read the letters which Francis had addressed to the Bishops and Magistrates, they conceived such a liking to the Order, that they took immediate measures for giving to John Parent and his companions a dwelling of which they took possession on the 28th of August.

The Order of St. Francis, as well as that of St. Dominic, began from that time to spread through all Spain.[24] On all sides preachers of the two orders were found, and new convents were erected, as Luke, Bishop of Tuy, a contemporary author, mentions in his Chronicle when he speaks of the marvels of the reign of St. Ferdinand, king of Castile and Leon. It would clearly appear that both the one and the other were in the city of Leon about that time, since the same author, in his excellent work against the Albigenses, says that they exerted themselves with great zeal and energy against the heretics, who, to seduce the faithful, published pretended miracles which they asserted to have been performed by the bones of one Arnold,[25] a man of their sect who had been dead sixteen years, and accused the ecclesiastics and religious who exposed their impostures of heresy. Such is the mode adopted by certain sectarians; they endeavored to establish their false doctrine by fictitious miracles;[26] while they insolently refused credence to those which the Catholic

---

[24] Luc. Tud. chron. pag. 123. Hisp. illustr. tom. 4. Id. de altera vita, etc., lib. 3, cap. 9 and 14. Biblioth. Patr. tom. 25, Edit. Lugd. 1577.

[25] There is another Arnold, a native of Brescia, who was a disciple of Abelard, who was the chief of the Arnoldists; against whom St. Bernard wrote to pope Innocent II, and to bishops, and who was hanged and burnt at Rome in the year 1135. There was also an Arnold of Villeneuve, a celebrated physician, a thorough fanatic, whose errors were condemned by the Inquisition and by the Faculty of Theology at Paris, in the year 1300, etc. St. Bernard, *Epist. 189, 193* and *196.* Mariana, *Hist. Hispan.* lib. 14, cap. 9. *Hist. Univer. Paris,* tom. 4 pag. 120 and 121.

[26] God, who is truth itself, and the sole Author of true miracles, can never perform any to authorize error. But He sometimes performs some among the heretics and by their hands, to confirm Catholic truths. As He did one in favor of baptism in the church of Paul, a Novatian bishop, as related by the historian Socrates, lib. 7, cap.
17. See on this head the Pas Loral Instruction of the bishop of Soissons, p. 14 and seq. And the Abbé of Tournely *Praelect. Theol. de Incarnation,* in which they quote several passages from the Fathers,

Church admitted as certain; and all have sufficient audacity to treat as heretics the orthodox who prove them to be heretics themselves.

The mission to France was equally successful with that of Spain.[27] Pacifico and his companions who began it in 1216, were exposed to hunger, cold, and all other kinds of inconveniences, which men are exposed to suffer when out of their own country, unknown, and destitute of everything, and moreover living an unusual and extraordinary sort of life. They went to that office of the night which is called matins in those churches in which it is said at midnight, as is still the custom at Notre Dame, in Paris. If there was no service in the places where they were, they then prayed by themselves at that hour, and they passed the whole night at the foot of the altar; after which, if no one offered them a meal, they went questing from door to door. The remainder of the day was spent in the hospitals, making the beds of the lepers and other sick, dressing their wounds, and rendering them such other services of humility and charity as they had learned from the example and instruction of their Father Francis. So saintly a life attracted the attention of all, gained their esteem, caused many to embrace the Institution, and procured for them many establishments.

The most considerable was that of Paris, which was situated some years after in the very place where the great convent of the Observantines is now The abbot and the community of St. Germain-des-Pres gave this locality to the Friars Minor, to remain there as their guests,[28] from which we see that the children of St. Benedict, who favored those of St. Francis in France, entered into the spirit of the Rule which prohibited their possessing anything as property. The charity of the religious of this abbey went still further; they bought with their own money from the canons of St. Merry, a piece of ground attached to the enclosure of the house in order to accommodate their guests. The cession was confirmed by the famous Bishop of Auvergne, William of Paris, in 1230.

Wading says[29] that in 1234 the king, St. Louis, purchased this property from

---

and the following one from St. Thomas. A malis qui falsam doctrinam enuntiant, nunquam fiunt vera miracula ad confirmationem suae doctrinae; quamvis quandoque fieri possunt ad commendationem nominis Christi quem invocanl et virtute Sacramentorum quae exhibent. 2, 2, quaest. 178, art. 2, ad 3.

[27] Wading, ad aim. 126. n. 9, et ad aim. 1219, n. 41. *Hist. Eccles. Parsien.* lib. 15, cap. 3, n. 20

[28] *History of the city of Paris,* tom. I, page 284. *Hist, of the Abbey of S. Germain-des-Pres,* page 119, art. 49. Ut ibi maneant tanquam hospites. The author of the History of the City of Paris printed in 1725, tom. I, lib. 6, p. 235, makes an observation contrary to the Decretal of Pope Nicholas III., Exiit qui seminat, in which all are excommunicated who alter the sense.

[29] Ad ann. 1234, n. 16. He says, moreover, that the act of acquisition, which is dated in the month of April 1234, and sealed with the seal of St. Lewis, is in the Abbey of S. Germain-des-Pres. Father du Bois, priest of the oratory, in his *History of the Church of Paris,* lib. 15, ch. 3, n. 2, says, that it was another house in the same locality which was ceded to the religious of St. Francis, by the religious of the Abbey, and that St. Louis in exchange remitted to the Abbey a quit rent of a hundred sous of Paris, which they had to pay the king for a right of fishing, which he had granted to them. De Breuil

the Benedictines, and gave it, free from all ground-rent to the Friars Minor, and that he caused some considerable building to be erected upon it, and particularly a large and beautifully decorated church, which was dedicated by the title of St. Mary Magdalen. We know by history and by incontestable documents, that this pious king, and Queen Blanche, his mother, had the greatest esteem for the religious of the Order of St. Francis and loaded them with favors. In 1240, the abbot and community of St. Germain-des-Pres, in compliance with a Brief of Pope Gregory IX, agreed to sell two pieces of land to enlarge the enclosure of the Friars Minor, which were purchased by certain pious individuals at a valuation which was placed upon them by Adam, Bishop of Senlis. King Philip-le-Bel added another piece of land in 1298[30] and in the year 1561, the Magistrates of the Hotel-de-Ville added to these, in consideration of the good services of these religious against the Huguenots, and for the defense of the faith.

The splendid church, the precious memorial of the piety of St. Louis,[31] and of his esteem for the Order of St. Francis, was by accident entirely reduced to ashes, on the 19th November, 1580, to the great regret of the Catholics, while the Huguenots who were in the habit of defiling the altars, and setting the sanctuaries on fire, irritated to the highest pitch at the success of the Friars Minor against their heresy, in their sermons, and in their controversial works, rejoiced at the conflagration and exulted over it, as the Idumeans at the taking of Jerusalem,[32] who would have wished that its very foundations should be rooted out.

This misfortune had scarcely happened, than King Henry III, the princes, magistrates, and the municipality, deliberated upon rebuilding the church, and contributed to that effect.[33] They began to work at it the following year, by the zeal and assiduity of the illustrious Christopher de Thou, first President of the Parliament, whose science, equity, piety, blameless life, and great talents had secured to him the esteem of his Sovereigns, the love of the people, and the respect of the whole world; and whose memory has been transmitted to posterity in the writings of the most learned men in Europe whom he loved and protected.

The Order of St. Francis chose, in 1600, for their temporal Father and

relates the same thing in the second book of the *Antiquities of Paris*, which is quoted by the Abbé Dubois; and it is again found in the Hist, of Paris, tome I, p. 285. Nevertheless, nothing of all this is noticed in the *History of the Abbey of S. Germain-des-Pres*, printed in 1724, wherein we find noticed things relative to the convent of the Observance, which might as well have been omitted.

[30] Wading remarks that some citizens of Paris had likewise purchased some pieces of land to add to those which Philip le Bel had added to the Order.

[31] Wading, ad ann. 1234, n. 21. It was three hundred and twenty feet long, by ninety broad. It was magnificently ornamented, and there were some splendid mausoleums of princes and princesses, and other persons of the highest rank. De Breuil, *Antiquites de Paris*, 1234, n. 23.

[32] Psalm 135 (136): 1, 9, and 10.

[33] Wading, ad ann. 1234, n. 22.

protector in the whole kingdom, John Augustus de Thou,[34] President *"au mortier"* and son of the above, so celebrated for his integrity, his wisdom and learning, and who joined to the functions of his office, and to the political affairs which were confided to him by Henry III and Henry IV, an arduous labor, the fruits of which were the magnificent history of his own times, a work quite on a par with anything written by the ancients. This excellent magistrate, whose piety and family propensity attached him greatly to the Friars Minor, caused the sacred edifice which his father had begun to be continued, and brought to perfection.

Angelo of Pisa, one of the missioners sent by St. Francis, was the first warden of the Parisian convent. This convent soon became a college, where young men, from all parts of the world came to study, and, subsequently, to take out degrees in the university. Several great men[35] have, in the last five hundred years, rendered this college illustrious, and its renown is still kept up by doctors whose inviolable attachment to the Holy See and to the Episcopate, at a time when the Church has been greatly agitated, must render them dear to all who are zealous for the faith. No one will find fault with our having spoken at some length of the establishment which was made in the capital of France, while recording the acts of the first missions sent into that country by the holy Founder of the Order of the Friars Minor, nor that we have noticed the gratitude due to their benefactors, and done justice to their learned and orthodox doctors; on this last head, De Breuil,[36] in the antiquities of Paris,[37] expresses himself energetically, and very honorably as to the great convent of the Observantines.

Pacifico, whom St. Francis had appointed provincial of the French missions, sent some of the religious into different parts of the kingdom, where they were well received. He went with some companions into Hainault, and other provinces of the Low Countries, where, by the liberality and under the protection of the Countess of Flanders, Joanna of Constantinople, he caused many houses to be built. Those of Sens, in Artois, of St. Tron, in the province of Liege, of Valenciennes, Arms, Ghent, Bruges, and Oudenarde, were among his first. We may read in the history of the modern heresies what the Friars Minor have done and suffered in the Low Countries for the support of the faith.

Thomas de Chantpre,[38] a Canon Regular of St. Augustine, and subsequently

---

[34] *Memoire hist. Diction,* n. hist.

[35] Alexander de Hales (d'Hals), John de la Rochelle, St. Bonaventure, Richard de Middleton, in Latin, Media Villa, William Warren, John Scot, Nicolas de Lyra, Francis Mayronis, Peter Aureole, and numbers of others, in the preceding centuries, and in the present century.

[36] Since the work of De Breuil enlarged by Malingre is the groundwork of the History of Paris, printed in the year 1724, he should not have omitted in the five volumes what he had thought himself obliged to say in a single one in favor of a celebrated house.

[37] 2d book, page 240, of Malingre's edition of 1640.

[38] Cantiprat lib. 2, de Apibus cap. 28, Meyerus ad ann. 1220, Molan, ad 11, Julii.

a religious of the Order of St. Dominic, states, as an eyewitness, a very marvelous thing which deserves to be recorded in the life of St. Francis, since it occurred during his lifetime, relative to his Order. At Ihorouth, a town in Flanders, a child of five years of age, whose name was Achaz, of a good family, having seen, in 1219, the habit of the Friars Minor,[39] begged his parents to give him a similar one. His entreaties and tears induced them to gratify him. He was therefore habited as a Friar Minor, with a coarse cord and bare feet, not choosing to have any money, not even to touch it, and he practiced as much as was in his power the exercises of the religious. Among his companions he was seen to act the preacher, cautioning them against evil, exciting them to virtue by the fear of the pains of hell, and by the hopes of the glories of heaven; teaching them to say the Lord's Prayer, and the Angelic Salutation, and to honor God by genuflections. He reproved such as did anything wrong in his presence, even his own father, if he heard him swear, or saw him in a state of inebriety. "My father," he would say, with tears in his eyes, "does not our cure tell us that those who do such things will not possess the kingdom of God?"[40] Being one day at church with his mother, who was dressed in a handsome gown of a flame color, he pointed out to her a crucifix, as a censure on her vanity, and warned her to be careful that the color she wore did not cause her to fall into the flames of hell, which warning had so great an effect that his mother never after wore anything but the plainest dress. Such a precocious mind, with so much matured wisdom and piety, was universally admired, and everyone took pleasure in seeing and listening to this amiable child.

God took him from this world before he had attained his seventh year. In his last illness, he confessed, and solicited most earnestly to be allowed to receive the holy communion. The curé not venturing to comply with his request, on account of his tender age, although his reason was so mature and his holiness so manifest, he raised his hands to heaven, and said, in moving accents: "My Lord Jesus Christ, You know that all that I wish for in this world is to receive You. I begged for You, and have done what I could; I hope with entire confidence that You will not deprive me of the happiness of possessing You." He then consoled and exhorted his parents and others who surrounded him, after which he gave up his pure soul to God, praising Him, and pouring forth prayers to Him.

The ocular witness adds two circumstances which are very remarkable; the first is, that the religious habit which this holy child wore disappeared, and could never afterwards be found. The second, that the Friars Minor who, as well as himself, went to pray at his grave, could not go through the *De profundis* which they had commenced, notwithstanding all the efforts that they made to do so; by which they understood, that so pure a soul stood in no need of prayer; and, no doubt, they only endeavored to offer up some under

---

[39] Wading, ad ann. 1220, n. 66.

[40] Gal. 5: 21.

the impression that a mind so early in other respects matured, might have been capable of contracting some stain.

While the mission to France and the Low Countries made great progress under the direction of Pacificus, Christopher and his companion labored successfully in Gascony, which they began by the establishment of the convent of Mirepoix, which the lords of the ancient and illustrious house of Levi gave them with great marks of esteem. The religious whom the holy Patriarch had sent into Hungary, had at that time no success. They were so ill-treated, and so often stripped of their miserable clothing, that, seeing no prospect of becoming useful, they returned into Italy. But they were indemnified for this in the year 1235, by Belus IV, King of Hungary, who settled the Friars Minor in his country, and employed them in his important affairs. Those who were destined for England, not having arrived there till the year 1220, because they stopped on their way at Paris, we shall only speak of them in that year.

Francis, having despatched his disciples to several missions allotted to them, as has been said, prepared to go himself to the Levant, with a zeal equal to that with which he had inspired his brethren, when Cardinal Ugolino, the protector of the Order, entered into discussion with him on the subject of the government of the establishment of St. Damian's, in which Clare presided, and of the other monasteries of females which had been commenced on that model, which were becoming numerous, as besides those in Italy there was already one at Burgos, in Spain.

The holy Patriarch replied in these terms to the cardinal: "I neither established, nor procured the establishment of any other monastery of females except the one in which I placed Clare to keep enclosure; and I have not taken upon myself the care of any other, either to attend to its regular discipline, or for its subsistence, which I and my companions will provide for by questing, as the state of poverty requires. Nothing has displeased me more than the eagerness some of my brethren have had to establish in other places houses for religious females, and to govern them; I am also much dissatisfied that they should have given them the name of Minors. I entreat you, therefore, my lord, to remove my brethren, as much as possible, from the care of, and familiar discourse with religious females, if you desire to preserve their good repute, and to see them increase in virtue; and to take measures to have these called either Poor Ladies, or Poor Recluses, until such time as a more appropriate name shall be devised."

Yielding to those reasons, and several others which Francis adduced, the cardinal, who was a man of great prudence, undertook to arrange this affair with the Pope, recommending him only most earnestly to take care of Clare and her companions. Francis did not fail in this; he bound himself to do so both verbally and by the following letter, which Clare takes notice of in her will.

"To my dear sister Clare, and to the other sisters of St Damian, Francis greets them in Jesus Christ.

"Since, by divine inspiration, you have become daughters and servants of the Most High, the Sovereign King, and Celestial Father, and have chosen the Holy Spirit for your spouse, in order to live up to the perfection of the gospel, I will take upon myself and promise you to have always care of you, either personally or through my brethren, with as much solicitude and vigilance as for themselves. I greet you in our Lord."

The attention which the holy Patriarch paid to the monastery of St. Damian, led his religious to think that they might assist the other monasteries which followed the same rule, without reflecting, that Clare and her companions, who first had embraced the high perfection of holy poverty, of which there were no precedents in previous ages, were deserving of peculiar distinction, and that the guidance of a single monastery could have no ill consequences.

They were, moreover, urged to it by the advice of the bishops, and by the entreaties addressed to them, and were not adverse to it, from motives of charity towards virgins consecrated to Jesus Christ in a very austere state of life. But the Saint who foresaw the embarrassment which this would cause to his Order, and other inconveniences which might arise from it, dissuaded his brethren as much as he could from these dangerous services, and often said, energetically: "I much fear that when God took wives from us, the devil gave us sisters." This short sentence comprises a profound meaning, which may serve for the instruction of all those who, in the performance of the sacred ministry, are under the necessity of having communications with persons of the other sex.

Cardinal Ugolino, by the advice and authority of the Pope, leaving to Francis the guidance of the monastery of St. Damian of Assisi, took upon himself the direction of all the others who had adopted that rule, and nominated as visitor-general under his orders, a prudent religious of the order of Citeaux, called Ambrose. He gave them the rule of St. Benedict, with constitutions which Wading gives at length. We do not transcribe them here, because, in the year 1224, St. Francis gave them another rule, which will be spoken of lower down, and which is the only one which ought to be called the rule of St. Clare or of the second Order.

Ambrose, having shortly after died, the same commission was given by the Pope, at the solicitation of the Cardinal Protector, to brother Philip the Long, one of Francis's companions, with power to nominate religious of his Order, to regulate the monasteries in conformity with that of St. Damian. Philip had contrived to procure this appointment for himself without having consulted the saint, and it was from a zealous motive for the perfection of the religious females, who did not, in those times, find many men capable of directing them in the kind of life which they had taken upon themselves. He thought that men who had undertaken a similar mode of life would be better calculated to instruct and govern them than such as only know the life theoretically. It must be admitted that this is usually true; but there are found worthy ecclesiastics of whom it may be said, as of St. Francis of Sales, that, without being in the religious state, they have its spirit, to say nothing of the grace of the ministry, which flows peculiarly on all directors who join to purity of faith, purity of morals, the exercise of prayer, the study of the Scriptures, and perfect disinterestedness, having no predilection for any one of the religious whom they direct.

However good Philip's intention may have been, Francis disapproved of his zeal, and said to him: "Brother Philip, you have done wrong. Up to this time, the fistula has only been in the flesh, and there were hopes of its being cured; but now that it is in the bone, it is incurable."

He expressed his sentiments on this subject in a very energetic manner, by the penance he imposed on another of his companions, Stephen. As they were walking together on the banks of a river, this religious told him that he had been to one of these monasteries of females by order of the visitor, but that he admitted having done so contrary to his intention and begged his pardon. The Father reprehended him severely for it, and ordered him, in expiation of his faults, to plunge into the water with his habits on: it was in the month of December. Stephen having instantly obeyed, "Extinguish," said Francis, "in this water those sparks of a dangerous but pleasing and insinuating fire; wash in it, and cleanse yourself in it from those secret stains which you have perhaps contracted without perceiving it." After, he continued his route which was still two miles before it was to end, going first, without turning to look at his companion who was dripping wet. When he reached the convent, he relaxed the rigor of his penance, speaking to him in soothing and charitable terms, and assisting him in drying his clothes. This action will only surprise those who know not to what lengths the saints carried the delicacy of their sentiments on the subject of the purity of the heart, and how easy it is to sully it.

However, what St. Francis said to Philip, when he told him that he had rendered the wound incurable by imposing the guidance of the female monasteries on the Order, became prophetic. For the services they subsequently exacted from the Order, which they pretended were their due in consequence of the care which St. Francis had taken of the monastery of St. Damian, became so burdensome, that a decree was passed at the general Chapter held at Pisa, in 1263, at which St. Bonaventure presided, to give them entirely up. Some powerful interest used at the Roman Court prevented this decree from being acted upon, and the holy general who saw the inconveniences which St. Francis had foreseen and wished to have obviated, could not remedy them.

All the precaution he took was to have it authentically made known and to have it declared by the Pope that whatever the Friars Minor did for the good of the religious of St. Clare, was done out of pure charity, and nowise from duty; and in order that length of time might not give a claim of prescription, the nuns were obliged to sign a document, the form of which was sent to them. Thus we must not imagine that the Order has any great predilection for their government; it will be at any time glad to shake it off if the Pope will but consent to its doing so. While this care is committed to the zeal of the Order, it will be necessary, on the one hand, for the nuns to behave themselves respectfully to those who exercise this charity in their regard; and, on the other, the religious must bear in mind that they have the guidance of a sex in which even in its devotions the characteristics of our first mother are to be feared.

CHAPTER III

St. Francis and the Sultan

He sends six of his friars to Morocco—He starts on his voyage to Syria, with twelve companions—He rejects a postulant too much attached to his parents—A house at Ancona is given to him—He appoints, by means of a child inspired by God, those who are to accompany him to Syria—He embarks at Ancona, and anchors at the isle of Cyprus—Arrives at Acre—Distributes his companions in different parts of Syria, and comes to the army before Damietta, and predicts the ill-success of the battle the Crusaders are about to give—His prediction is accomplished—He finds out the Sultan of Egypt—Announces to him the truths of the faith, and offers to throw himself into the fire to prove them—He refuses the Sultan's presents—Is esteemed and respected—The good dispositions with which he inspires the Sultan—He obtains permission to preach in his States—He confounds an immodest woman by throwing himself on burning charcoal—He receives some disciples from the army of the Crusaders—Visits the holy places—Some whole monasteries of religious embrace his Institute.

T HE HOLY PATRIARCH being now about to set out in order to preach the Gospel to the Muslims of the Levant, resolved to send to those who were in the west, some of his brethren. He chose six for Morocco: Vidal, a very prudent and pious religious, whom he nominated Superior; Berard de Carbio, from the vicinity of Nami, who was well versed in the Arabian language; Peter, of St. Geminien, and Otho, who were in priests' orders; and Ajut, and Accurse, who were lay-brethren.[1] Having sent for them in the presence of all the others, he spoke to them as follows:

"My dear children, it is God who has commanded me to send you amongst the Saracens, to make known His faith, and refute the law of Mahomet. I shall go in a different direction to work for the conversion of the same infidels, and thus I shall send preachers over the whole earth. Prepare yourselves, therefore, to fulfill the will of the Lord. To render yourselves worthy of it, take great care to preserve peace and concord among yourselves, as the ever-subsisting ties of

---

[1] Bollandus, in the second tome of the *Acts of the Saints* for the month of January, page 62. n. 2, makes Wading say, ann. 1219, n. 48, eum (Berardum) Arabicae linguae ut cumque peritum concionatorem vere egregium fuisse. Nevertheless, the following is what we find in the same place in the annals of Wading, in the Lyons edition of 1625, and in that of 1644, which we have before us in writing this: Frater Berardus perite callebat linguam Arabicam. We do not know whether it is a mistake which Fleury has followed in his *Ecclesiastical History*, book 78, n. 25, or whether there be some change in the other editions of Wading, which we have not seen.

charity. Avoid envy which was the first cause of the loss of mankind.[2] Be patient in tribulations, and humble in success, which is the means of coming off victorious in all encounters. Imitate our Lord Jesus Christ in his poverty, chastity, and obedience; He was born poor, He lived poor, and it was in the bosom of poverty that He died. To manifest how highly He loved chastity, He chose to be born of a virgin, He took virgins for His first soldiers, He kept, and counseled virginity, and He died in presence of two virgins.[3] As to obedience, He never ceased from practicing it from His birth to His death on the cross. Place your hopes in the Lord, He will guide and assist you. Take our rule with you, and a breviary, in order that you may be punctual in saying the Divine Office, and be always submissive to Brother Vidal, your Superior. My children, although I am greatly pleased to see the goodwill with which you embrace this undertaking, yet our separation is painful to my heart from the sincere affection I bear you; but the commands of our Lord are to be preferred to my own feelings; I entreat you to have the Passion of our Lord Jesus Christ always present to your mind; it will strengthen you and powerfully animate you to suffer for His glory."

These apostolic men, encouraged by this address of that Father, replied that they were ready to go into any country and expose themselves to the severest labors for the interests of the faith; that he need not hold out an example for them, by going himself among the infidels, as if his word was not sufficient; that they did not think his orders too strict, and that they expected assistance from above for carrying them into execution; but that they required his prayers and blessing in order to gather some fruit in unknown lands, among barbarous people, enemies of the Christian name. "He," rejoined the saint, with great animation, "who sends you, it is He who will take care of you; you are under His protection, under the protection of God; you belong no more to me from this moment; I tear you from my bosom to send you as His laborers." They threw themselves on their knees, kissed his hands and prayed for his last blessing which he gave them weeping, in the following terms: "May the blessing of God the Father be upon you, as it descended on the apostles; may it strengthen you, guide you, and console you in your sufferings. Fear not; the Lord is with you, as an invincible warrior; go, in the name of God who sends you."

We shall speak of their voyage when we come to relate the martyrdom they suffered in Morocco, on the 16th of January, 1220.

At length, Francis, anxious for the crown of martyrdom of which he had been twice disappointed, confided the government of his Order during his absence to Brother Elias, the Provincial of Tuscany, and set out on his voyage to Syria with twelve companions, the principal of whom were Peter of Catania, Barbaro Sabbatino, Leonard of Assisi, and Illuminus of Rieti.

---

[2] Wisdom 2: 24.

[3] His Blessed Mother and St. John the Evangelist.

In the Marches of Ancona through which they passed, in order to embark at the last-named place, a young man came to solicit to be received into the society of Friars Minor, and the saint said to him: "If you are in the intention of joining the Poor of Jesus Christ, go and bestow on other poor all that you have." The postulant went away and gave all he had to his parents whom he loved very much, without giving any to the poor. He then returned and said how he had disposed of his property. Francis censured his conduct in the strongest terms, considering him as a man who would be totally useless, and nowise fit for evangelical perfection. "Tender brother," he said to him, (for so he called all those whom he considered good for nothing) "Tender brother, go your ways, you have neither left your country nor your kindred; you have given what you had to your parents, and disappointed the poor; you do not deserve to be received into the company of those who make profession of holy poverty. You commenced by the flesh, which is an unstable foundation for a spiritual edifice." This carnal and animal man returned to his parents, resumed his property, and rather than give it to the poor, he gave up the good purpose he had entertained.

The love of his relations did as much disservice to this young man as the love of riches did to him whom our Savior desired to sell all he had and give unto the poor.[4] Perhaps also he had an intention of finding a resource in what he gave to his relations, which is contrary to the entire renouncing of everything which Jesus Christ requires. For which reason, when St. Bonaventure relates this circumstance, he says, that St. Francis only admitted those into his Order who gave up all they had, and did not in any manner keep anything back.

The man of God received many novices on his way. Many of his brethren in the vicinity accompanied him as far as Ancona, to witness his embarkation; sorrowful, as had been the faithful of Miletus and Ephesus, who accompanied St. Paul embarking for Jerusalem,[5] although he had not told them, as the apostle did, that they would see him no more. The arrival of this holy band was so agreeable to the magistrates at Ancona, that they immediately allotted a spot for the erection of a convent, and had it commenced at their own expense. It was so large that when Francis returned from Palestine he caused it to be reduced out of love for holy poverty, and gave the model of a church which is still extant with a larger one, which was added to it.

The captain of a vessel who was about to take succors to the Christian forces before Damietta, was so good as to receive him, one of twelve, on board his ship. All the religious who were there were desirous of going to sea with him, and each one vied for the preference, not only that they might accompany the Patriarch, but that they might obtain the crown of martyrdom, which they ardently wished for; but not to mortify any of them, and to show

---

[4] Matt. 19: 21.

[5] Acts 20: 25 and 28.

no preferences, he prudently and with the mildness of a common father, addressed them as follows:

"My very dear children, there is not one of you, from whom I should wish to be separated; I wish you would all accompany me in the voyage I am about to make; but it would have been unreasonable in me to ask the captain of the vessel to take you all. On which account, and that none should have reason to complain, nor to be jealous of the others, I will not make the selection; it must be made by God." And thereupon calling a child who happened to be on board, he said: "The Lord has often made His will known by the mouth of children, and I have no doubt he will do the same now; let us ask this child, and let us credit what he shall say; God will speak through him." Then asking the child, whether it was God's will that all the religious who were with him should put to sea and make the voyage with him, the child replied with a firm voice: "No, it is not God's will." He then again asked which of them among those who were there present he should take? The child, inspired by the Almighty, selected eleven, pointing them out with his finger, and going up to them as he named them.

The religious, full of astonishment, were all satisfied: those who were destined to remain behind as well as those who were selected to accompany him. They fell on their knees, received the blessing of their common Father, and separated after having given to each other the kiss of peace.

Francis embarked with his eleven companions; they weighed anchor, and shortly after they reached the island of Cyprus, where they remained a couple of days. In this interval, one of the religious committed a fault which was soon atoned for. In a gust of passion he made use of some harsh expression to one of his brethren before the others, and before another person who might have been scandalized at the scene. Reflecting on what he had done, and being immediately sorry for it, he took up some dung, and, returning to the spot, he put it into his mouth, and began chewing it, saying, "It is but just that he who has offended his brother by his speech, should have his mouth filled with filth." This act of penance was fully satisfactory to him who had been offended, and made such impression on the gentleman who had witnessed the scene, that he offered himself and all he possessed to the service of the Order.

From Cyprus, Francis proceeded to Acre,[6] from whence he sent his companions, two and two, into such parts of Syria in which missionaries were most wanted. He himself preached for some days in the vicinity of the town, where he did some good, and then embarked again with Illuminus to join the army of the crusaders who were besieging Damietta. We shall now speak of the crusade, and of this siege.

---

[6] A town of Phoenicia in Syria, on the confines of Palestine, called by the Hebrews Acon, and Ptolemaide by Ptolemy, king of Egypt. It is called St. John d'Acre, because of the long stay there of the knights of St. John of Jerusalem.

At the council of Lateran,[7] which was held in 1215, Pope Innocent III represented so energetically the miserable state to which the Christians in the Holy Land were reduced under the domination of the Saracens, that in order to deliver them from so cruel a slavery, the council ordered the assembly of a similar crusade to that which had been ordered two centuries before, for the same object. The bishops proclaimed it everywhere with great ardor, and the Pope, to give it greater weight, went himself into Tuscany to preach it after having published it at Rome. This great Pope dying on the 16th of July, 1216,[8] Honorius III, who succeeded him, imitated his zeal, and wrote to the princes and prelates of all Europe, and sent legates everywhere, to urge the execution of what had been decreed in the council of Lateran. The success was as prompt as it was fortunate, so that at the time fixed, that is, on the 1st of June, 1217, an infinity of crusaders, principally from the North of Europe, were in readiness to set out for Palestine, by land and by sea.[9]

After some expeditions, the crusaders thought that, instead of operations in Palestine, to which they had hitherto confined themselves, it would be advisable to carry the war into Egypt, because it was thence that the Sultans sent large armies into the Holy Land against the Christians; and this had been the opinion of Pope Innocent at the Lateran Council.[10] It was therefore decided to lay siege to Damietta, the strongest town in Egypt, and from its situation the key of that kingdom. The first of those who sailed arrived before the place on the 30th of May; they disembarked, and intrenched themselves without meeting with any resistance, and when the remainder of the army arrived, the attack commenced.

The siege lasted nearly eighteen months, with ultimate success, and some astonishing acts of bravery were witnessed. Coradin, (or Moaddam) the Sultan of Damascus, came with an army much more numerous than that of the Crusaders, and besieged them in their entrenchments; and Meledin, (or Melic Camel) his brother, Sultan of Egypt or of Babylon,[11] having brought an equally numerous army, they drew up their troops in order of battle, on the last day of July, 1219, in the early morning, and appeared before the Crusaders' lines, which they attacked on several points. The battle was obstinately contested; it lasted till night, and the Saracens seemed to have the victory, but it was torn from them, chiefly by the indomitable bravery of the French, supported by the Grand Master of the Temple, and the Teutonic knights, who drove the infidels far from their lines with great slaughter. Dissensions then arose between the

---

[7] Conc.. Lat. 4, Serm, I, Inn. Pop,

[8] Ep. Honor. III. Lib. 1, epist. 1, et seq.

[9] Raynald, ad ann. 126, n. 28.

[10] Jac. Vitry. *Hist. Orient,* lib. 3, ad ann. 1218.

[11] He was called Sultan of Babylon, from his capital city called Babylon of Egypt, or the new Babylon, to distinguish it from the Babylon of Asia on the Euphrates, built by Nimrod, the capital of Chaldea. It was opposing Memphis, near the Nile, and on its ruins Grand Cairo is built.

cavalry and infantry of the Crusaders.[12] They accused each other of cowardice, a reproach very grating to military men; the consequence was, that a turbulent rivalry ensued, in order to prove which had the greatest courage, and they compelled John de Brienne, king of Jerusalem, who commanded the army, to lead them to the enemy and offer him battle.

It was at this moment that Francis arrived at the camp, having no other arms than those of faith.[13] He said to his companion, with deep sighs: "The Lord has revealed to me, that if they come to blows, the Christians will be worsted. If I tell them this, I shall be considered as an idiot; and if I do not tell it, my conscience will reproach me. What do you think of it?" His companion, whose name was Illuminatus, and who indeed was filled with light, replied: "My brother, do not let the opinions of men guide you; it is not the first time that you have been looked upon as one bereaved of sense. Clear your conscience, and fear God more than the world." Francis immediately went and warned the Christians not to fight, and foretold them that if they did, they would be beaten.

Minds were, however, too much excited to listen to sound reason; the words of the saint were taken for ravings. On the 29th of August, when the heat was overpowering, the whole of the Christian army left their lines and offered battle. The enemy at first retired, in order to draw the Crusaders to an extensive plain, where there was no water, and when he saw that thirst and fatigue had caused their ranks to be broken, he turned suddenly and fell upon the cavalry of the right wing which he took in flank; it was soon broken and dispersed; its rout caused the infantry which was supported by it, to fly, and the whole army would have been cut to pieces had not the king, followed by the knights of the three orders of French, Flemish and English, and other troops, posted themselves in front and stopped the Saracens who were pursuing the fugitives, and effected a beautiful retreat. The Christians lost on this occasion near six thousand men, besides prisoners, among whom were many of considerable note. This loss[14] was the accomplishment of what Francis

---

[12] Jac. Vitry, *ibid,* ad ann. 1219.

[13] The author of the History of the Crusades, 2 tom. lib. 9, speaks thus: "It was then that St. Francis, contrary to his custom interfered in matters which were not wholly religious, and did all in his power to oppose this resolution (to give battle). As the Spirit of God agrees with common-sense he foretold, with great reason, that so ill- concerted an undertaking would be fatal." Are we to be told that a saint interferes in matters which are not wholly religious, when he foretells, by inspiration from God, the loss of a battle? Was anything of this kind said of the prophets who predicted fatal events? Moreover, why is the prediction of St. Francis to be attributed partly to the knowledge he had of the ill-concerted measures? He spoke from the very day he arrived in the camp; he knew nothing of the country, nor of war, nor of the measures about to be taken. Was it not intended to diminish what was supernatural and marvelous in the prediction?

[14] It did not put a stop to the siege. The town of Damietta was taken by the Crusaders, on the 5th of November of the same year.

had foretold;[15] and it showed, adds St. Bonaventure, "that his valuable advice ought not to have been disregarded, since, according to the words of the Holy Scriptures, the soul of a holy man sometimes discovers true things, more than seven watchmen that sit in a high place to watch.'"[16]

The faults of the Crusaders, and the ill-successes which often attended their measures, have given room to minds disposed to censure to condemn all wars undertaken against infidels, or heretics. Nevertheless, the Crusades, during two centuries, were suggested by the Sovereign Pontiffs, and by the councils of the Church, proclaimed by most holy personages, and authorized by their miracles; led by Christian princes of all Europe, by many of our kings, by a Saint Louis, by men full of religious zeal, such as Godfrey of Bouillon, and Simon, Count of Montfort. Is there not somewhat of rashness in including such men as these in one sweeping condemnation? If all the Crusaders had not equally pure intentions; if debauchery insinuated itself into their armies, if prudence did not always regulate their proceedings; if sometimes even success did not crown their best-concerted measures, are these sufficient grounds for blaming the enterprise, or, are we only to judge of measures by the event?

Saint Bernard preached the crusade which was decided on in the year 1144, of which Louis VII, King of France, had first formed the plan, and of which Pope Eugenius III, and the bishops of France approved. The preaching of the holy abbot was publicly supported by a prodigious number of miracles,[17] which even his humility could not dissemble. Two powerful armies, the one commanded by the Emperor Conrad. III, the other by the King of France, with the princes and nobility of the states, were calculated to inspire the infidels with terror. Nevertheless, from various causes, nothing could have been more unfortunate than the issue of this war; and, as the loss of these two armies was felt through the whole of France and through the whole of Germany, where St. Bernard had preached, and promised glorious success, public indignation fell upon him, and he was treated as a false prophet. What he wrote to Pope Eugenius in his justification, must be considered as an answer to all those who, even in these days, condemn the Crusades, the result of which was disastrous.[18] He says, "that Moses, in God's name, had solemnly promised the

---

[15] This prophecy is related by the three companions of St. Francis, by St. Bonaventure, by Marin Sanut, and by many other writers, both ancient and modern. Raynald ad ann. 1219. Wading, ad ann. 1219, n. 7.

[16] Ecclus. 37: 18.

[17] The author of *The History of the Crusades* leaves to every one the choice of believing as he thinks proper of the miracles performed by St. Bernard while preaching the Crusade. He gives two reasons which he affects to draw from two passages: the one from the *Life* of the saint, written by his secretary, Geoffry, book 3, ch. 4, the other from the second book *De Consideratione*, ch. 1. But we have only to read the second passages to be convinced that these miracles were numerous and very public. See the notes of Father Mabillon, in cap. 1, lib. 2, *de Consideratione,* and in Epist. 4, ad Tolosanos. *Histoire des Croisein* 4, tom., lib. 3, pg. 209, and liv. 4, pg. 280.

[18] S. Bernard *de Considerat,* lib. 2, cap. 1.

people of Israel to lead them into a very fertile land, and that God had even confirmed that promise by splendid miracles; that, nevertheless, all those who went out of Egypt perished in the desert without entering into the land of promise, in punishment of the sins of the people during the journey; that it cannot be said that this punishment was a contradiction of the promise, because the promises which God, in His goodness, makes to man, never prejudice the rights of His justice;" and this reasoning the saint applies to the crimes committed in the armies of the Crusades.

The Crusades, they say, were the devotion of those times, and had become fashionable. Yes, the devotion of those times: the devotion of the Popes, of the kings, of the princes, and of all the faithful of those days was to drive the infidels from the Holy Land, of which they had unjustly become the possessors; to reestablish the holy places consecrated by the actions and sufferings of the Son of God; to prevent the Muslims from extending their dominion, so that the Christians should not groan under their tyranny; and sometimes to reduce, by force of arms, certain heretics who were in open rebellion, such as the Albigenses, when there was no other means of arresting the progress of their sect. Let it now be shown what is the devotion of our times, and in what it is preferable to that of our forefathers which they condemn. Truly, it is only requisite to have some share of good-sense, to be prepared to admit that there was true piety in the minds and in the conduct of those who lived in those days, as well as in the age and in the country in which we live.

This digression may, perhaps, appear long, but we could not dispense with it for the honor of the religious and of the preceding ages; and, besides, it is connected with the life of St. Francis, who certainly approved of the Crusades, although, by a supernatural inspiration, he blamed a particular enterprise of the Crusaders which had the unfortunate issue which he had foretold.

The ardor of his charity which urged him to labor for the conversion of the Saracens, and to expose himself to martyrdom, induced him to take the resolution to present himself to the Sultan of Egypt. "We saw," says James de Vitry, "brother Francis, the founder of the Order of the Friars Minor, a simple and unlearned man, though very amiable and beloved by God and man, who was respected universally. He came to the Christian army, which was lying before Damietta, and an excess of fervor had such an effect upon him, that, protected solely by the shield of faith, he had the daring to go to the Sultan's camp to preach to him and to his subjects the faith of Jesus Christ."[19]

The two armies were in sight of each other, and there was great danger in

---

[19] There is a detailed account of what passed there, taken in part from J. de Vitry, bishop of Acre, and subsequently Cardinal and bishop of Frascati, who was present at the siege of Damietta, and who saw St. Francis there; partly from St. Bonaventure, on the testimony of the three companions of the holy patriarch, and of M. Sanut, a writer well informed on the affairs of the Levant. J. Vitr. *Hist. Occid.* cap. 37, et *Epist. ad Lotharing,* ad calc. *Hist. Orient,* lib. 3. St. Bonav. *Legend S. Francis,* cap. 9 and II. Mar. Sanut, *secret, fidel. cruc.* lib. 3, part II, cap. 7 and 8, tom. 2. *Gesta Dei Franc.*

going from one to the other, particularly as the Sultan had promised a handsome reward in gold to any one who should bring him a Christian's head. But this would not deter such a soldier of Jesus Christ as was Francis, who, far from fearing death, eagerly sought it. He betook himself to prayer, from which he arose full of strength and confidence, saying with the prophet: "Since You are with me, O Lord, I will fear no evil, though I should walk in the midst of the shadow of death;"[20] and he set out for the infidel camp.

Two sheep which he met on setting out, gave him much joy. He said to his companion: "My brother, have confidence in the Lord, the word of the Gospel is being fulfilled in us, which says: Behold I send you forth as sheep in the midst of wolves."[21] In fact, only a very little farther on, some Saracens rushed upon them, as wolves upon sheep, insulted and beat them, and bound them. Francis said: "I am a Christian, lead me to your master;" and God permitted that he should be so led to comply with the desire of His servant.

The Sultan Meledin asked him who sent them, and for what purpose they came? Francis answered with courageous firmness: "We are not sent by men, but it is the Most High who sends me, in order that I may teach you and your people the way of salvation, by pointing out to you the truths of the Gospel." He immediately preached to him, with great fervor, the dogma of One God in Three Persons, and the Lord Jesus Christ, the Savior of mankind.

Then was seen verified what our Savior said to His apostles: "For I will give you a mouth and wisdom which all your adversaries shall not be able to resist or gainsay."[22] Meledin became so mild and tractable, that, admiring the courage of Francis, he listened quietly to him for some days, and invited him to stay with him. The man of God said: "If you and your people will be converted, I will remain for the love of Jesus Christ. And if you hesitate between His law and that of Mahomet, let a great fire be lit up, and I will go into it with your priests, in order that you may see thereby which is the faith to follow." "I do not believe," replied the Sultan, "that any of our priests would go into the fire, or suffer any torments for his religion."[23] He answered thus because he perceived that as soon as the fire was proposed, one of the eldest of the priests, one who was of the most considerable of them, got quickly away. "If you will promise me," added Francis, "that yourself and your people will embrace the Christian faith, in case I come forth from the fire safe and sound, I will enter it alone; if I am burnt let it be imputed to my sins; but if God preserve me, you will then acknowledge that Jesus Christ is the true God and Savior of

---

[20] Psalm 22 (23): 4.

[21] Matt. 10: 6.

[22] Luke 21: 15.

[23] S. Francis called those priests whom the Muslims call Imams, who are the ministers of their religion, who have the care of their mosques, and perform the public prayers there under the authority of the chief Imam. We have retained the term priest, because it is in the Legend of St. Bonaventure. See the *Biblioth. Orientate* of D'Herbelot, under the word Imams.

mankind."

Meledin acknowledged that he dared not accept this challenge, lest it should be the cause of a sedition; but he offered him rich presents which the servant of God despised from his heart as so much dirt. Such entire disengagement from the good things of this world inspired the Prince with such veneration and confidence that he entreated the Saint to receive his presents, and to distribute them among the poor Christians or to the churches for the salvation of his soul. Francis who had a loathing of money, and who did not find in the Sultan any groundwork of religion, persisted in his refusal of these offers. He, moreover, thought it was time to leave the infidels when he saw no prospect of effecting any good, and where he had no further chance of gaining the crown of martyrdom; and he learnt by a revelation that what he intended was conformable to the will of God. The Sultan, on his part, fearing that some of his people might be moved by the discourse of Francis, and, being converted, might join the Christian army, caused him to be escorted with marks of consideration to the Christian camp before Damietta, after having said to him in private: "Pray for me, that God may make known to me what religion is most agreeable to Him, in order that I may embrace it."

Was it not a sight worthy of God, of angels, and of men, to see on one side Francis, clothed in sackcloth, pale, emaciated, disfigured by his penitential austerities, pass through an army of infidels, and present himself boldly before their Sovereign, speak to him against the law of their prophet, and exhort him to acknowledge the divinity of Jesus Christ? and, on the other side, the Sultan of Egypt, the mortal enemy of the Christians, elated by the victory he had just gained over them, and anxious to shed more of their blood, suddenly lose all his ferocity, become mild and tractable, listen attentively to the poor one of Jesus Christ, endeavor to retain him, offer him large presents, admire his poverty, his disinterestedness, his courage, ask the aid of his prayers, that he might know and embrace the true religion, and send him back to the Christian camp with honor? How certain it is that the religion of Jesus Christ will never be made more respectable and amiable to the infidels than by the practice of the exalted virtues which it teaches, and by which it became established in the world.

Another scene which is not less striking in the eyes of piety, is the heart of Francis, burning with anxiety to shed his blood for the glory of his Master, and not being able to satisfy that ardor. Already, in the hope of attaining it, he had embarked for Syria, and contrary winds had driven him back to the Christian shores. He had gone into Spain in order to pass into Africa, when a violent illness compelled him to desist from the undertaking. He thinks he already grasps the palm, when he finds himself in Egypt; in order to hasten the accomplishment of his desires, he places himself in the hands of the infidels, and attacks the tyrant on his throne; when, instead of the opprobrium and tortures which he sought, he finds nothing but mildness and curiosity, attentions and honor. He seeks for martyrdom, and martyrdom flies from him. "It was," St. Bonaventure remarks, "by an admirable disposition of Divine Providence, who chose that the ardent desire of his faithful servant should give him the merit of martyrdom, and that his life should be preserved to receive the glorious stigmata which were to be impressed on his body by a singular prerogative, in reward of his great love for Jesus crucified, who inflamed his heart."

Wading relates,[24] upon the authority of a religious of the Order, who was a contemporary of St. Francis, whose name was Ugolino of St. Mary of the Mount, corroborated by some other writers of the Order, that the sultan was converted and baptized. Some later authors deny this,[25] and remark that they have mistaken the Sultan of Egypt for the Sultan of Iconium, who never saw St. Francis, and of whom James of Vitry says,[26] that he was believed to have received baptism at his death which happened in the year when Damietta was besieged. It is admitted that Wading was mistaken[27] in quoting this passage to prove the conversion of the Sultan of Egypt, but that does not weaken the evidence of Ugolino. He says that Francis went a second time to the sultan before his return to Italy; that he urged him to be converted, and that, not being able to induce him to overcome the human obstacles which stood in the way, he prayed fervently for him for several successive days, and that his prayers were heard; which he communicated to Meledin, who imbibed great affection for him, and wished to detain him, but he departed according to the command that he had received from heaven; that some years after, this prince being dangerously ill, the Saint appeared to two of his religious who were in Syria and ordered them to go to him, instruct him, baptize him, and remain with him till he should expire; all which was complied with. There is nothing in all this which is not very probable, and which is not consistent with circumstances that cannot be called into question.

1. We have seen, in the narratives of James of Vitry, and of St. Bonaventure, that Meledin said to Francis, "Pray for me, that God may make known to me which religion is most agreeable to Him;" and that he wished to induce him to receive his presents, in order to distribute them to the poor Christians, or to the churches, for the salvation of his soul.

2. After he had seen the holy man, he treated the Christians with great

---

[24] In the work entitled, *Scriptores Ordinis Minorum,* at the word Hugolinus de Sancta Maria in Monte, it is said: "I have in my hands the manuscript beautifully written, of the history in which Ugolino relates the life and actions of St. Francis and his companions."

[25] Spond. ad ann. 1219, n. 3. *Histoire des Croisades,* tom. 2, lib. 9. p. 263.

[26] J. Vitr. *Hist. Orient,* lib. 3, ad ann. 1219, page 1142.

[27] Wading has apparently thought that the Sultan of Egypt had died at Iconium, although this town, which is in Asia Minor, is very far from it, and he did not know that there was a Sultan of Iconium. Moreover, he did not reflect that Meledin having lived many years afterwards, could not be the person whose death Le Vitry recorded in 1219, at the siege of Damieta.

humanity,[28] and shortly after their discomfiture, he sent some of his prisoners to their camp, to offer terms of peace. In the year 1221, their army which was coming to offer him battle, entangled itself between two branches of the Nile, where it must have inevitably perished. "He behaved to his enemies," says one of our authors,[29] "in such a manner as could not reasonably have been expected from a Saracen, and which in these days would do honor to a Christian prince were he to do it."

3. An author, whose testimony on such a point is beyond suspicion,[30] says, "that this sultan, being on his death-bed, caused a large sum of money to be distributed among the poor Christians who were sick in the hospitals, and that he left a considerable revenue for the same purpose; that he enfranchised many slaves, and that he had operated various other acts of mercy, and that his death was greatly lamented by the Christians, whom he spared to the utmost of his power; that the Emperor Frederic was long inconsolable, having had strong hopes that he would have received baptism according to a promise[31] he had given him to that effect, and that he would strenuously contribute to the propagation of Christianity in the Levant."

4. It may have happened that St. Francis, who was then in heaven, appeared to two of the religious of his Order, and that he sent them to Meledin; that these religious instructed and baptized him; and that the thing was done secretly from the circumstances of the times; that the authors of those times were not informed of it, and that Ugolino learned it from the religious themselves. In short, it is not improbable that the conversion of this soul should have been granted to the zeal, labors, prayers and tears of such a friend of God as St. Francis. Thus, the baptism of the sultan is not so very uncertain, and those who have recorded it[32] have not given the Saint praise which may be called false, as Wading has been acrimoniously taxed with. After all, if Meledin was not converted, it is a judgment of God, which those must be fearful of who recommend themselves to the prayers of the pious, forming projects of conversion, and even doing some good works, and yet positively resist the grace vouchsafed them, which requires an effectual change of heart. If he was converted, which is probable, it was a great effect of divine mercy, which sinners must not abuse by deferring their repentance; these graces are very rarely given, and those who wait for them run great risk of their salvation.

There is good reason for thinking that he gave Francis and his companions leave to preach in his dominions, since it is well known that the Friars Minor

---

[28] Sanut supr. Cap. 9.

[29] *Hist, des Crois.* as above, liv. 10, page 291

[30] Math. Paris, p. 318, Edit. Paris, 1644.

[31] It was no doubt in 1229, when this Emperor, who was Frederick II entered into a treaty with him. Rayn. 1229.

[32] *Hist, des Crois.*, as above, liv. 9, p. 263 and 264.

began from that time to spread themselves amongst the Saracens, as James de Vitry says: "Even the Saracens, blinded as they are, admire the humility and perfection of the Friars Minor, receive them well, and provide them cheerfully with all the necessaries of life, when they go boldly amongst them to preach the gospel; they listen to them willingly, speaking of Jesus Christ and His doctrine; but they beat them and drive them away if they attack Mahomet, and hold him as a bar and infidel."[33]

An anecdote, related by St. Bonaventure, may have easily happened in those times. A Saracen seeing some Friars Minor, was moved by their poverty and offered them some money, which they refused to accept, and this astonished him. Having understood that it was for the love of God that they refused money, he conceived such a liking for them, that he undertook to provide them with everything necessary for them as long as he was able. The holy doctor exclaims on this: "O inestimable excellence of poverty, which is so powerful to inspire a barbarian with such tender and generous compassion!" It would be a shameful and very criminal thing, were Christians to despise and trample under foot this precious evangelical pearl, for which a Mohammedan showed such esteem and respect.

While Francis remained in Egypt, he did not gather much fruit from among the infidels; but his words were a fertile seed which his disciples reaped the abundant harvest of, when afterwards sent thither by Gregory IX and Innocent IV.

Ugolino of St. Mary, who has been before quoted, and some others say that he himself had the first fruits, after a signal victory which he gained over the devil, who tempted him to sin through a female of considerable beauty. The Saint, they say, having then received the gift of counsel, replied that he would consent, provided he might choose the place. It was a room in which he spread burning coals, on which he laid himself down, after having taken off his miserable tunic; he then said to the Egyptian:

"This is the place which suits me, I choose this fire in order to escape from other fires; if those inflame you, then no water so well adapted to quench them as this." God, by a miracle, prevented his being burnt, and the wanton female, touched by grace, fell on her knees and asked pardon, and then retired penetrated with contrition. Francis instructed her in the truths of religion; she became a Christian and chaste, and was so fervent, that, like another Samaritan, she brought over many others. This is one of the extraordinary actions sometimes found in the lives of the saints, in which the sanctity of those who are the actors in them, and the good which results from them manifest that they are the fruits of a divine inspiration.

The Saracens were not the only objects of the zeal of Francis. He labored also for the salvation of the Christians in the army of the Crusaders, and some

---

[33] *Hist. Occid.* cap. 32

of them became his disciples. James de Vitry, Bishop of Acre,[34] writing to his friends in Lorraine informed them that Renier, the Prior of St. Michael,[35] had joined the Order of the Friars Minor; and that three of the most eminent of his clergy had followed his example, and that it was with difficulty he prevented the chorister and several others from taking the same course, to which he adds that this religious Order spreads fast in the world because it is an exact imitation of the form of the primitive Church,[36] and of the life of the Apostles.

The most ancient records of the Order assure us that after some months' residence in Egypt, the holy Patriarch went to Palestine, and visited the holy places, but they enter into no particulars. What we may safely conjecture is, that God, who led him into the Holy Land, seemed to say to him, as He had said to Abraham: "Arise and walk through the land in the length and in the breadth thereof, for I will give it to you;"[37] and repeat what He said of Caleb: "I will bring him into this land which he hath gone round, and his seed shall possess it."

Rather more than a hundred years after his death, the Sultan of Egypt permitted the Friars Minor to take charge of the Holy Sepulcher of our Lord, and they still have the care of it in the midst of the infidels, under the protection of the eldest son of the Church.[38] This privilege, which is so honorable for the Order of St. Francis, and justly considered by them as the fruit of the fervent devotion of the blessed Patriarch to Jesus Christ crucified, will be more particularly spoken of when we come to notice the history of the stigmata.

From Palestine Francis went to Antioch, the capital of Syria, and passed by the black mountain, where there was a celebrated monastery of the order of St. Benedict. The abbot who had died only a short time before, had foretold that there would soon come to their house a saintly man, who was much beloved by God, the Patriarch of a great Order, who would be poorly attired and of mean appearance, but very much to be revered; in consequence of which the religious, hearing of his coming, went in procession to meet him, and received him with all the honors due to a man of God. He remained some days with them, and the holiness which they observed in him made such an impression upon them, that they embraced his institute,[39] placing all their effects at the disposition of the patriarch of Antioch. Some other monasteries followed their example; and in a few years, there was a flourishing province in that country, which continued until such time as the Saracens ravaged the whole of Syria.

---

[34] J. Vitr. Epist. ad Lotharing, ad col. Hist. Orient, lib. 3.

[35] It is perhaps a town in Lorraine, vulgarly called St. Mirtrul.

[36] He makes a more ample eulogium in another place, which will be noticed hereafter.

[37] Genesis 13: 57. Numb. 14: 24.

[38] Spond. ad ann. 1236, n. 11; Wading, ad ann. 1233, n. 59, et ad ann. 1224, n. 20.

[39] Wading replies to the difficulties which seem to throw doubts on this event, ad ann. 1219, n. 66, et seq.

CHAPTER IV
The First Franciscan Martyrs

He returns to Italy—Establishes his Order in various places—Preaches at Bologna with great success—What he says and does on seeing a house of his Order too much ornamented—Returns to St. Mary of the Angels—Confounds the vanity of Brother Elias and abolishes the novelties which he introduced into the Order—In a vision the fortunes of his Order are made known to him—He holds the chapter, in which he deposes Brother Elias, and in his place substitutes Peter of Catania—He renounces the generalship—Will not receive anything from novices entering his Order—He learns the news of the martyrdom of the friars he had sent to Morocco—The martyrdom of these friars is the cause of the vocation of Anthony of Padua.

HILE FRANCIS was thus employed in extending his Order in the East, Brother Elias, who was his vicar-general in the West, was destroying it there. He said to the religious, in their conferences, that the life of their Founder was worthy of the highest praise, but that it was not given to all to imitate it; that among the things which he had prescribed for them, some appeared in the eyes of prudence very difficult of observance, others absolutely impracticable and beyond the strength of man; that, in the opinion of the most prudent, some modification was requisite and some change required, some practices tolerated, which were not so strictly regular, from regard to human weakness in a time of infirmity and of decay. By specious insinuations of this nature, he brought over many to his opinions, and even some of the provincials who ventured to represent the simplicity of their Father as imprudent. The vicar-general, nevertheless, in conjunction with the ministers, made some regulations for the government of the provinces which were very useful; but, by a strange inconsistency, at the time when they were talking of modifications, they prescribed total abstinence from meat, and forbade its use either in or out of the cloisters, which was a direct contradiction of the rule, which permits the Friars Minor, except in times of fasting, to eat, according to the terms of the Gospel,[1] whatsoever is put before them.

All those who had the true spirit of God were greatly grieved to see that human prudence was preferred to the divine will, and that the vineyard of the Lord was rendered desolate by Brother Elias. They put up fervent prayers to

---

[1] Luke 10. 8.

God for the speedy return of their pastor, so necessary for the flock; and, after having secretly concerted together, they sent Brother Stephen into Syria, to communicate to their Founder what was going on. Stephen went and gave him a full detail of all things. Francis was not cast down by this deplorable intelligence, but he had recourse to God, and recommended to His protection the family he had received from him. As to the regulation which prescribed entire abstinence from meat, he, with great humility, asked the advice of Peter of Catana, who replied: "It is not for me to judge; it is for the legislator to decide thereon, as on all the rest." Francis deferred the decision till his return, and embarked immediately for Italy.

His voyage was not a long one; they soon anchored at the Isle of Candia, from whence they came to Venice where they landed. He sent circular letters to convene the chapter which he proposed holding at the ensuing Michaelmas, to remedy the evil which had been brought about by Brother Elias. He built a small chapel near the Venetian lakes, (Lagunes),[2] in which two of his religious were to say the Divine Office, in memory of an extraordinary thing which happened to him at this place, which will be related with other similar ones. This first establishment was enlarged some years after, and was followed by the building of a convent in Venice itself, which the magnificence of a patriarch of the house of Grimani has rendered very considerable.

The Saint then went to Padua, Bergamo, Brescia, the island of the lake of Garda, to Cremona and Mantua; at all these places there were convents of his Order. We are assured that St. Dominic joined him on his way; that they conferred together and with John of Navarra de Torniella, Bishop of Bergamo, on the salvation of souls; that they made some pious visits to the solitaries of the valley of Astino, and that the patriarch of the Friars Preachers celebrated mass there, that of the Minors being the deacon at the service. When they were in spiritual conference at Cremona, the religious came to request them to bless the well, and to solicit the Almighty to purify the water which was thick and muddy. Dominic, at the entreaty of Francis, blessed a vessel full of the water, and caused it to be thrown back into the well, and all which was subsequently drawn from it was clear and wholesome to drink.

The two saints separated, but, shortly after, met again at Bologna. Francis, going to Bologna, met a woman whose son was epileptic, and who came to beg the aid of his prayers. He wrote on a slip of paper some short but very devout ejaculatory prayers which he desired might be taken to the sick youth; they had no sooner been given to him, than he was entirely cured; in gratitude whereof, he placed himself at the service of the Friars Minor in the convent of Parma.

The reputation of the holy man was so great, that, according to Sigonius,[3] the streets were choked with the number of students who wished to see and

---

[2] This is the name given to the sinuosities of the Adriatic Sea around Venice as far as the Lido.

[3] Sigonius de Episc. Bonon. lib. 2, ad ann. 1220,

hear him. It was with difficulty that way was made for him to reach the principal square, where he preached in so sublime a manner that they thought they heard an angel and not a man. The greater part of the audience was converted; and many solicited the habit of the Order, among whom were Nicholas of Pepulis, Bonizio, Pelerino, Falleroni, and Riger or Ricer of Modena. Nicholas was that learned jurisconsult who had been so kind to Bernard de Quintavalle in 1211, when every one had treated him with contempt at Bologna. Bonizio exceeded in the love of holy poverty, and was very useful to the Saint in affairs of importance, by the talent he had of managing with prudence. Pelerino and Riger were young gentlemen from the Marches of Ancona, who were students at Bologna, and to whom Francis foretold all they would do in the course of their lives. The first would only be a lay-brother, although he was well versed in canon law; it was said of him that when he was in company with men of the world, either from necessity or from charitable motives, he left them as soon as he could; and when he was censured for so doing as being guilty of rudeness, he replied: "When we have sought Jesus Christ our Master,[4] we have never found Him either amongst relatives or amongst our acquaintances. The second attached himself to his holy Patriarch, and strove to imitate him in all things. Although he was eminently favored with the gift of chastity, he nevertheless avoided with great care the conversation of females, and he said to those with whom he was intimate, who were surprised at it: "I should perhaps lose the gift with which I have been favored by a just judgment of God, if I took fewer precautions: he who loves danger will perish in it."[5]

Here is an authentic testimonial as to one of the sermons which Francis preached at Bologna in the year 1220; it is taken from the Archives of the church of Spalatro, and it is found in the history of the bishops of Bologna, written by Sigonius:

"I, Thomas, citizen of Spalatro, and Archdeacon of the cathedral of the same town, saw, in the year 1220, on the day of the Assumption of the Mother of God, St. Francis preach in the square in front of the little palace where almost the whole city was collected. He began his sermon thus: 'The angels, the men, and the demons.' He spoke of these intelligent beings so well and with such precision, that many learned men who heard him, were astonished to hear such a discourse from the mouth of so simple a man. He did not diverge to draw a moral from different subjects, as preachers usually do, but as those who dilate upon one point, he brought everything to bear upon the sole object of restoring peace, concord, and union which had been totally destroyed by cruel dissensions. He was very poorly clad, his countenance was pale and wan, and his whole appearance was uninviting; but God gave such force and efficiency to his words, that they led to the reconciliation of a great number of

---

[4] Luke 2: 44.

[5] Ecclus, 3: 27.

gentlemen who were greatly exasperated against each other, and whose irritation had caused the shedding of no small quantity of blood. The love and veneration for the Saint were so universal, and went so far, that men and women ran to him in crowds, and those esteemed themselves fortunate, who could only touch the hem of his garments."

The author who records this testimonial adds that he performed miracles also in Bologna. A child of quality was taken to him, who had what is called a pearl on his eye, which rendered him quite blind of it, and no remedy had been found for it. Francis made the sign of the cross over him from the head to the feet, and he was perfectly cured. Having subsequently entered the Institute of his miraculous physician, he saw much better with the eye on which the pearl had been than with the other. This miracle, which was known throughout the city, increased so much the zeal and respect which the Bolognese had for the servant of God, that they could not tear themselves from him, and they gave him a second house for his institute, situated in a wood about a mile from the town.

After these apostolical functions, he went to see Cardinal Ugolino, who was then legate in Lombardy, by whom he was received with marks of the most sincere affection. He proposed next to visit the convent of his Order which was close to one of the gates of Bologna, but as soon as he saw it, finding it much more spacious and handsome than was requisite for strict poverty, he turned away his eyes from it, and said indignantly: "Is this the dwelling of the poor evangelical laborers? Such grand and superb palaces, are they for Friars Minor? I do not acknowledge this house as one of ours, and I do not look upon those who dwell in it as my brethren. I, therefore, order and enjoin all those who wish to continue to bear the name of Friars Minor, to leave this house forthwith, and to give up to the rich of the world buildings which are only fit for them."

He was so implicitly obeyed, that even the sick, among whom was Brother Leo, one of his first companions, who is the relator of this circumstance, were carried out on the shoulders of their brethren and exposed to the air. There they all remained till the arrival of the legate, who, having been informed of what was going on, had come and appeased the holy man. He represented to him that it was necessary to allow the convents to be more spacious, in order that the infirm might have more air for restoring their health, and that such as were well should have more room for relaxing their minds. "But as to the property," he added, "I can assure you that your brethren have no part in it, as it remains entirely in the founders. Moreover, if you have any further scruples on the subject, I declare to you that I take the whole upon myself in the name of the holy Roman Church."

Francis could not resist the powerful reasoning of the prudent and pious legate, the protector of his Order. He, therefore, consented that his brethren should remain in the convent; he even ordered them to return to it, but he would not go into it himself, and he chose to take the repose which nature required, in the house of the Friars Preachers, where he passed some days with his friend Saint Dominic.

It would appear that St. Bonaventure had this circumstance in view, when he said: "that if it happened that St. Francis found in the houses which his brethren occupied, anything which looked like property or that was too elegant, he wished the houses to be pulled down, or that the religious should quit them, because he maintained that the Order was grounded on evangelical poverty as its principal foundation, so that if this poverty was adhered to in it, it would flourish, but that it would perish if it was set aside."

While the Saint was with the Friars Preachers, one of them, from feelings of compassion, begged him to return to his children, and to pardon the fault they had committed, but he replied: "Indulgence which gives rise to an easy relapse into sin, is not to be commended. I will not sanction by my presence what has been committed against holy poverty." This charitable religious endeavored to induce him at least to see them, in order that they might be made aware of their fault, and be corrected. "We will come back here together," he said, "if you do not choose to remain there, after having performed this duty of superior." Francis yielded to this prudent advice; he went to his children, and seeing them grieved and repentant, and ready to receive the penance he might inflict, he pardoned them.

His indulgence did not extend to the provincial, whose name was John de Strachia, one of those who wished to have the rule mitigated in 1219. He censured him severely for having had so beautiful a house built, or, at least, for having permitted it to be built. He upbraided him in strong terms for having, without consulting him, opened a school for the studies of the Friars Minor, and for having made regulations for its conduct more favorable to science than to piety. He did away with this school, because he chose that his religious should pray rather than study, and that the other provincials might learn to be more humble and more religious in all that had relation to studies.

And here we must advert to what happened at a later period; the provincial had the rashness to reestablish the school after the departure of the Founder, who, having been informed of it, and knowing from interior revelation the obduracy of this man, cursed him publicly, and deposed him at the ensuing chapter. The Saint was entreated to withdraw this curse, and to give his blessing to brother John, who was a noble and learned man, but he answered: "I cannot bless him whom the Lord has cursed." A dreadful reply which was soon after verified. This unfortunate man died, exclaiming, "I am damned and cursed for all eternity." Some frightful circumstances which followed after, his death confirmed his awful prognostic. Such a malediction which pride and disobedience brought upon this learned man, ought to strike terror into those vain men who forsake piety for science, and in whom great talents have no other effect than to produce in them great attachment to their own conceits, and proud indocility, which induces, at length, even a revolt against the Church.

St. Francis was not averse to studies, as will be seen, when, two years after, he caused theology to be taught. But he chose that they should so study as not to extinguish the spirit of prayer. He approved of science, but of that only, which the Holy Spirit calls religious,[6] which is sanctified by the fear of the Lord, of which St. Augustine says: "that it is the companion of charity, and teaches humility."

Cardinal Ugolino proposed to the servant of God that they should make a retreat of some days together, at Camaldoli,[7] in order to give his body some rest, which was borne down by fatigue, and relax his mind from the various cares which oppressed it. He willingly assented to this, because he liked the life of a recluse. They, therefore, went to this holy solitude, and they remained there nearly a month, solely employed in meditation on heavenly things.[8] The cardinal took a cell at the entry of the desert where it is still to be seen; and Francis took one near it, which had been inhabited by St. Romuald. It has since taken the name of St. Francis' cell, and is only occupied by the prior, or major of Camaldoli. The writers of the country add, that the festival of St. Francis is celebrated solemnly there, and that it is decreed by the statutes that the anthem which the Friars Minor chant shall be sung on that day: Salve, Sancte Pater, etc.

The two pious solitaries went from thence to Mount Alvernia, where they only stayed a few days. The cardinal returned to Bologna, and Francis took the route for Assisi, in order to open the chapter at St. Mary of the Angels, as he had given notice.

On the way, St. Bonaventure acquaints us what occurred to him. His infirmities and fatigue having compelled him to mount on an ass, his companion, Leonard of Assisi, who followed him on foot, and was also very much fatigued, gave way to human feelings, and said to himself: "His parents were not the equals of mine; yet, there he rides, and I am forced to trudge on foot and lead him." As he was thus giving way to these thoughts, Francis, to

---

[6] Ecclus. 1: 17 and 26; S. August, in Psalm 142, n. 5.

[7] This is the celebrated monastery which gave its name to the Order of Camaldulites, founded in the tenth century by St. Romuald, on the rule of St. Benedict, with peculiar constitutions and the white habit. This place is in Romagna, in the states of Florence, on the further side of the river Arno, near a small town of the same name.

[8] This is what led Father Tornamira, a Sicilian Benedictine, in the last century, to imagine and put in writing, that St. Francis had entered the Order of St. Benedict; that the religious of that order had instructed him and assisted him in the composition of the Rules of the Friars Minor, that this Rule is in perfect accordance with that of St. Benedict, and many other things destitute of any probability, so that, if his book had not been condemned at Rome, as it was by the sacred Congregation in 1682, it would not by its circulation have made much impression. Father Dominic de Gubernatis, chronologist of the Order of Friars Minor, has not omitted to point out the incorrectness of the fancies of the Sicilian, in his work entitled Orbis Seraphicus, tom. I, lib. 4, ch.8. 13 et seq. P. Tornamira in S. Bened., Patriarch, lib. 1.

whom God had made known what was passing in Leonard's mind, dismounted, and said: "No, brother, it is not fitting that I should ride while you walk on foot, because you are better born than I am, and are of greater consideration in the world." Leonard, greatly surprised, and blushing for shame, threw himself at his Father's feet, acknowledged his fault, and with tears solicited his pardon.

As soon as the holy Patriarch entered the valley of Spoleto, his children came in crowds from various parts to meet him, and to congratulate him on his return. He was greatly gratified on seeing them, and communicated freely with them, encouraging the weak, consoling those who where in affliction, censuring such as were in fault, and exhorting them all to adhere strictly to the rules. It was there that he received a confirmation of the complaints which had been made to him in the Levant, against the government of Elias, his Vicar General, and he had himself the proof of it.

Elias ventured to present himself to him, in a cleaner habit, and one made of finer cloth than those of the other brethren, the cowl of which was longer and the sleeves wider, and he assumed an air little suitable to his profession. Francis, dissembling what was passing in his mind, said to him before the assistants: "I beg you to lend me that habit." Elias did not dare refuse: he went aside and took it off and brought it to him. Francis put it on over his own, smoothed it down, plaited it nicely under the girdle, threw the cowl over his head, and then, strutting fiercely with his head erect, he paced three or four times round the company, saying, in a loud voice: "God preserve you, good people." Then taking the habit off indignantly, he threw it from him with contempt, and, turning to Elias, "That is the way," he said, "that the bastard brethren of our Order will strut." After this he resumed his usual demeanor and walked humbly with his old and tattered habit, saying: "Such is the deportment of the true Friars Minor." Then, seating himself amongst them, he addressed them in the mildest manner, and spoke on poverty and humility, of which he so forcibly pointed out the perfection, that it seemed to them that those whom they had previously considered the poorest and most humble, had made but small advance in the practice of those two virtues. In fine, he annulled all the novelties which the vicar general had introduced into the Order during his absence, except the prohibition of eating meat, which he thought it necessary to retain some time longer, lest he might be thought to encourage gluttony.

The means he had taken to curb the foolish vanity of brother Elias, showed both his prudence and his authority, and made such an impression on his disciples, that there was not one of them who ventured to say a word in favor of the vicar-general, although he had his partisans amongst them.

Some time afterwards, the Patriarch had an opportunity of taking off the prohibition of eating meat, in consequence of a wonderful event which is worthy of being recorded.

A young man in the dress of a traveler, came in haste to the door of the convent of St. Mary of the Angels, and said to Brother Massé, who was the porter: "I wish to speak to Brother Francis, but I know he is meditating in the woods; call Brother Elias to me, who is said to be learned and prudent, in order that he may satisfy a doubt which presses upon me." The porter was turned away by Brother Elias, and was puzzled what reply to give the stranger, not to scandalize him, and not to say what was untrue. The young man anticipated him, saying, "Brother Elias does not choose to come; I must therefore beg you to go to Brother Francis, in order that he may desire him to come to speak to me." Massé went, and did as he was requested, and Francis, having his eyes fixed on Heaven, said, without changing his position: "Go and tell Brother Elias that I order him to speak to the young man."

This order vexed Elias, and he came to the door in great irritation, asking what he was wanted for? "Do not be angry," said the young man, "I ask you, if those who profess to follow the Gospel may not eat whatever is given to them, as Jesus Christ has observed; and if any one may rightfully direct the contrary?" Elias, seizing hastily the door to shut it: "I know all that," he said, "and have no answer to give you but go your ways." The young man replied: "I cannot tell what you would answer, but I know very well that you ought to give an answer."

When Elias got calm in his cell, he reflected on what had passed, and on what would be proper to say in answer to the questions which had been put to him; and, finding it difficult, and being sorry that he had given the young man so ungracious a reception in whom he thought he had remarked something extraordinary, he returned to speak to him, but he was gone and could not be found. Francis learned from God that it was an angel, and, on his return to the convent, he said to brother Elias: "You do what is not right; you turn contemptuously away angels who come from God to visit and instruct us; I greatly fear that your pride will render you unworthy of the humble institution of Friars Minor, and that you will die out of that state." It was then that he revoked the statute which forbade eating meat.[9]

---

[9] The author of the *Hist, de la Ville de Paris*, printed in 1725 by Desprez and Desessarts, tom. x, lib: 6, pp. 284 and 285, admits that there is no founder of a religious order who has carried evangelical poverty, humility, penance, contempt of the world, and the general privation of everything worldly farther than St. Francis has, but he adds: "We are bound, however, to remark that he is the first of the religious in the West, who has allowed the use of meat to those of his Order who are in health." He who has called on his readers to make this remark, would have done well to tell us what relation it has to the history of the city of Paris, and why he has inserted it, with many other things relative to the first Convent of the Friars Minor in that city, without which his work, with some greater correctness, would still be too extensive? It will not be objected to him that St. Benedict did not prohibit his religious from eating poultry and other birds when in health, because on this head they are satisfied to abide by the decision of Don Mege, and the celebrated Abbot of La Trappe. But we will tell him that if he wished to make a remark as to the use of meat, which St. Francis allowed to those of his Order, he should have added that the holy Founder, wholly devoted to the Gospel teaching, was compelled to let men devoted to an apostolic life have as the apostles did; and that he

Bernard of Quintavalle returning from Spain, and being on the border of a river which he could not cross, the same angel appeared to him in the same form, and greeted him in the Italian language. Bernard, surprised at hearing the language of his country, and taken with the good looks of the young man who addressed him, asked him from whence he came. The angel then told him what had just occurred between him and brother Elias. He took him by the hand, carried him across the river, and disappeared, leaving him so full of consolation, that he had no fatigue during the remainder of his journey. When he arrived in Italy, and had related the circumstance, with the day and hour, he found that it was in fact the same angel.

Before the opening of the chapter, Francis, reflecting mournfully on the relaxation which had been introduced into his Order by those who ought to have been most zealous in promoting the purity of its observance, had a vision, which was very extraordinary. A great statue appeared before him, and he saw it with his bodily eyes; it greatly resembled that which Nabuchodonosor had seen in a dream, the interpretation of which had been given him by the prophet Daniel.[10] God chose to employ this mode to acquaint the holy Patriarch with the various revolutions which would take place in his Order, and he signified them to him by the statue itself, by the different metals of which it was composed, either thus to modify by these humiliating foreshowings the honor which he derived from being the Founder of so wonderful a work as that of the establishment of his Order, or to inspire him with the intention of sending up fervent prayers to heaven, which should draw down graces on his flock at all times; which, in fact, he did with a profusion of tears; or, in fine, it was a foresight given him of the relaxations which would be introduced, to enable him to advise his religious to be more vigilant, as St. Paul had predicted the errors and irregularities which were to occur in the Church, in order to excite the vigilance of the bishops.[11]

In Nabuchodonosor's vision, a stone was separated from the mountain, which, striking the feet of the statue, shivered it to pieces; the statue was wholly broken, and disappeared.[12] This did not occur in the vision which Francis had; for the great body of religion which it represented, which has had its vicissitudes, as all others, and with more luster than any, because of its more extensive and greater exposure to the eyes of the public, has nevertheless continued to have existence, to maintain itself, to serve the Church at all times, and to furnish it with saints; it has even often renewed itself with features which bring to mind its primitive beauty; by which it may be said to be a type of the mystical body of Jesus Christ, which notwithstanding the decay of ages,

---

was well aware that, having no revenues, and subsisting on charity, they could not keep perpetual abstinence, and that, nevertheless, they kept it at different times for more than half the year.

[10] Dan. 2: 31 and 37.

[11] Acts 20: 19; Tim. 4: 1; 2 Tim. 3: 1.

[12] Dan. 2: 34 and 35.

does not cease to have vigorous and healthy members, by faith, hope, and charity, who are as fervent as those of the earliest periods.

The holy Founder having listened to all that was said against the government of Brother Elias, and to what he had alleged in his justification, held his chapter on the festival of St. Michael, in the convent of Portiuncula. He substituted Brother Gratian, in the room of Brother John of Strachia, as provincial of Bologna, of which we have spoken before; and Brother Peter of Catania, in place of Brother Elias; Peter had been the second of his disciples, and into his hands he committed the whole guidance of his Order, not only because he did not think himself able to look to it in person, on account of the multitude of religious now belonging to it, and of his infirmity, but in order to improve himself in the virtue of humility, to which he was so much attached.

He then assembled them all and said: "I am now dead to you all; there is Peter of Catania, who is your superior, whom henceforward we must all obey, you and I," and prostrating himself at the feet of Peter, he promised to obey him in all things as minister general of the Order. This title of minister general was displeasing to the religious, who did not wish it should be given to any one during the lifetime of their Father, and they agreed that he who took his place should only have the title of vicar general.

Francis being on his knees, with his hands clasped, and his eyes lifted up to heaven, said, with affecting emotion, "My Lord Jesus Christ, I recommend to You this family, which is Your own, and which up to this moment You have confided to me. You know that my infirmities incapacitate me from having any longer the care of it; I leave it in the hands of the ministers; if it should so happen that on their part, negligence, scandal, or too great severity, should be the cause of any one of the brethren perishing, they will render to You, O Lord, an account of it at the day of judgment."

From that time till his death he continued as much as it was in his power in the humble state of an inferior, although he did not fail to communicate to the superiors the lights which God gave him for the good government of the Order, and on several occasions he could not avoid acting as its Founder and General.

St. Dominic, his friend, had similar feelings as to the employments of office. In this year he held the first chapter of his Order at Bologna, and wished to resign the station of superior, of which his humility made him consider himself incapable and unworthy; but his religious would not permit it. These have been the feelings of all the saints, because they knew that, for the purpose of salvation, it was safer to obey than to command.

Eight days before the chapter, Pope Honorius issued a Bull addressed to Francis, and to the superiors of the Friars Minor,[13] by which he forbade them to

---

[13] The original of this Bull, sealed with lead, is preserved at Rome, in the Archives of the Convent of Ara Coeli, n. 38, and it is this which St. Francis quotes in the second chapter of his Rule, when he says, speaking of those who are professed according to the Ordinance of our Holy Father the

receive any one to profession, unless after a twelve-month's probation,[14] and directing that, after profession, no one whosoever, should leave the order; forbidding, also, any persons from receiving such as should quit it. What gave rise to this measure was that, at the commencement of the Order of Friars Minor, and of that of the Preachers, there were some who made their profession without a novitiate, for an unfixed term, according as the superiors thought proper under different circumstances, and this sort of precipitate engagement was found to have its inconveniences.

Peter of Catania, acting as vicar general, and finding that he could not provide for the multitude of religious who came to the convent of St. Mary of the Angels, as to the chief monastery of the Order, thought that, in order to provide for this, some portion of the property of the novices might be retained; on which he consulted Francis to know whether he thought the suggestion proper, and if he would permit it. Francis said: "My brother, God preserve us from this sort of charity, which would render us impious in respect of our rule, in order to acquire consideration in the sight of men." The vicar then asking what he should do for the relief of the guests; "Strip the altar of the Blessed Virgin," replied Francis, "take away all the ornaments which are there; the Lord will send you what is requisite to restore to his Mother what we shall employ in charity. Believe firmly that the Virgin will be pleased to see her altar stripped, rather than that there should be any contravention of the Gospel of her Son;" and he took occasion again strenuously to recommend holy poverty.

He also said many things relative to books, to science, and to preaching, which will be recorded in another part of his life. Brother Caesar of Spires, who had been professor of theology before becoming a Friar Minor, and who was a man of great piety, having heard all that the Father said on the subject of science, and the learned, had a long conversation with him on the state of his soul, and on the observance of the rule, which he concluded thus: "My Father, I have made a firm resolution, with God's grace, to observe the Gospel and the rule, according to the instruction of Jesus Christ, until my death; and now, I have a favor to ask you, which is that, if it may happen in my lifetime that some should swerve from it, as you have foretold, you give me your blessing from this moment, and your leave to separate myself from such transgressors, in order that I may adhere to the rule alone with those who have a like zeal with myself." Rejoicing at this proposition, Francis embraced him and blessed him, saying: "Know, my son, that what you solicit is granted

---

Pope, they will not be permitted to leave the Order.

[14] The Pope says in his Bull, which Wading relates in extenso, that there is hardly any religious Order in which a certain time of trial is not allowed before profession is made. Pope Alexander II, at a subsequent period, directed that the professions, made in the Orders of the Friars Preachers and Minors, without having been preceded by a year of novitiate, should be null; and the Council of Trent makes it a law for all Orders of any kind, whether of males or females. Cap. Non solum, de regular. et transeunt, ad religion., in Concil. Trid., sess. 25, de Regul. cap. 18. The Ordinance of Blois conformed thereto, in the 28th Article.

to you by Jesus Christ, and by me;" and placing his hands on his head, he added: "You are a priest forever according to the order of Melchisedech;" the holy man desiring to have it understood thereby that all the promises he had received from Jesus Christ, would have their accomplishment to the end, in those who adhere to the rule to the letter, without comment and with holy joy.

It was at this time that he addressed a letter to the religious of his Order,[15] and particularly to the priests, upon the profound veneration which we ought to have for that August mystery of the Eucharist. As it is very long, we have reserved it also for the last book, where we shall point out the misuse which heretics and some modern critics have made of a passage in this letter.

In the course of the year 1220, Francis received the news of the martyrdom of the five religious whom he had sent to Morocco. We must relate the circumstances,[16] since they belong to the life of the holy Patriarch, who gave this mission to these valorous soldiers of Jesus Christ, and that they were the first martyrs of the Order in his lifetime.

Berardus, Peter, Otho, Ajut, Accursus, and Vital, their superior, having left Italy for Morocco, after having received their Father's blessing, as has already been noticed, arrived shortly after in the kingdom of Arragon, where Vital was detained some time by a lingering illness, which induced him to think that it was not God's will that he should continue his journey. He therefore let the other five proceed, who soon reached Coimbra, and were favorably received by Urraca Queen of Portugal, the wife of King Alphonso II. This princess conceived so high an opinion of their virtue and placed such confidence in them, that she entreated them to pray to God to reveal to them the time at which she should die. They promised to do so, although they considered themselves unworthy of making such a request; but they were so favorably heard, that they foretold to the queen that they were to suffer martyrdom with all the circumstances thereof, that their relics would be brought to Coimbra, and that she would receive them honorably, after which she would be called from this world; predictions which were fully verified. They went from thence to Alanquer, where the Princess Sancia, sister to the king of Portugal, approving their plans, induced them to put secular clothing over their religious habits, without which precaution they would not have been able to pass into the territories of Morocco.

Having reached Seville, which was then occupied by the Moors, they remained a week concealed in the house of a Christian, where they threw off their secular clothing. Their zeal induced them to go forth, and they got as far as the principal mosque, which they attempted to enter in order to preach to

---

[15] Wading thinks this letter was written by St. Francis in the year 1226, during his last illness; but he gives no proofs of this in his notes on the letters of the Saint, of which this is the twelfth. Father Anthony Melissan de Macro, in his *Supplement des Annales de l'Ordre*, printed at Turin, in 1710, is convinced that it was written in 1220, and we have adopted his view for the reasons he gives. Wading, *ad ann.* 1226, n. 10, and in *argum. in Epist.* 12, S. Francisci, *Suppl. Annal. Ord. Min.*, pag. 26.

[16] Bollandus has given their Acts on the 16th January. Ad SS. Januar. Tomus 3.

the infidels, but they were driven back with loud cries and severely beaten. From thence they went to the gate of the palace, saying that they were ambassadors sent to the king from Jesus Christ, the King of kings. They were introduced, and said many things relative to the Christian religion, to induce the king to be converted and receive baptism; but they afterwards added much against Mahomet and against his law, which irritated him to such a degree, that he ordered them to be beheaded; but being mollified by the entreaties of his son, he was satisfied with having them confined at the top of a tower, from whence he had them removed to the ground-floor, because, from above, they continued to speak of Jesus Christ, and against the prophet, to those who entered the palace. Having caused them to be again brought before him, he engaged to pardon them, if they would change their religion: "Prince," they replied, "would to God that you would have mercy on yourself! Treat us as you think proper. It is in your power to take away our lives, but we are sure that death will lead us to a glorious immortality." The king, seeing their unshakeable firmness, sent them, by the advice of his council, to Morocco, with Don Pedro Fernandes de Castro, a gentleman of Castile, and some other Christians.

They found there the Infant Don Pedro of Portugal, who had retired to that country in consequence of some misunderstanding which he had with his brother, King Alphonso, and who now commanded the troops of the king of Morocco. This prince received them with great respect and charity as apostolical men, and had them provided with every thing necessary for their subsistence. Knowing what had occurred to them at Seville, in consequence of their preaching, and seeing that, consequently, they were still in a state of great weakness, he endeavored to dissuade them from doing the same thing in Morocco; but the generous missionaries, solely intent upon their pious object, ceased not to preach without any fear, wherever they met with any Saracens.

One day, when Berardus was giving instruction to the people and was declaiming against Mahomet from a wagon, the king passed by, going to visit the tombs of his predecessors, and seeing that he continued his talking notwithstanding his presence, he thought the declaimer must be out of his mind, and instantly directed that all the five should be driven out of the town, and sent back to the country of the Christians. The Infant Don Juan gave them an escort to convey them to Ceuta, whence they were to embark. On the road, they got stealthily away from their escort, and returned to Morocco, where they recommenced preaching in the great square. The king, being informed of this became greatly irritated, and had them imprisoned, in order to starve them to death. They were there twenty days with out meat or drink.

During this time the heat became so excessive and caused so much sickness, that it was thought that the hand of God fell heavily upon them to avenge his servants. The king became alarmed, and by the advice of a Saracen named Abaturino, who loved the Christians, he liberated the prisoners. They were extremely surprised to find that, after twenty days' confinement, without any nourishment whatsoever, they came out in full health and strength.

As soon as they had left the prison, they were anxious to recommence their preaching; but the other Christians, who were apprehensive of the wrath of the king, opposed themselves to it, and had them taken to the place of embarkation; but they again made their escape, and returned to Morocco. Then the Infant Don Pedro was induced to keep them in his palace, and to place guards over them to prevent their appearing in public.

This prince being obliged to set out, some short time after, to take the command of the army which the king sent against some rebels, he took the Friars Minor with him, as well as several other Christians, fearing lest, during his absence, they should escape from those who had charge of them. As he returned victorious, his army was three days without water, and was reduced to the greatest distress. Brother Berardus resorted to prayer, and having made a hole in the ground with a pickaxe, he caused a spring to flow from it, which sufficed for the whole army, and enabled them to fill their goat-skins, after which it dried up. So palpable a miracle procured for them from all parts the greatest veneration. Many even went so far as to kiss their feet.

When they returned to Morocco, the Infant continued to take the same precautions as before, to prevent their appearing in public; nevertheless, they found means to get out secretly one Friday, and to present themselves before the king, as he was passing, according to his custom, to visit the tombs of his predecessors. Berardus again got upon a wagon, and spoke in his presence with astonishing intrepidity. The king, irritated beyond control, gave orders to one of the princes of his court to have them put to death. This prince only had them put in prison, because he had witnessed the miracle which we have recorded above.

They were very ill-treated in this confinement, but continued to preach even there, when there were either Christians or Saracens to listen to them. All this occurred towards the end of the year 1219.

At the beginning of the year 1220, the Saracen prince who had received the order to put them to death, having sent for them from the prison, found them very firm in their faith, and that they spoke with the same boldness against their prophet Mahomet. He was so enraged at this, that, forgetful of the miracle he had witnessed on the return of the army, he directed them to be kept separated and tortured in various ways. They tied their hands and feet, and dragged them along the ground by a cord fastened round their necks, and they were so cruelly scourged that their bowels nearly protruded. Thirty men who were employed on this cruel service did not leave them till they had poured boiling vinegar and oil into their wounds, and rolled them upon broken pieces of earthenware covered with straw.

Some of those who guarded them, saw a great light which came from Heaven, and which seemed to raise these religious up, with an innumerable number of other persons; they thought that they had left the prison and entered it in great haste, where they found them in fervent prayer.

The king of Morocco, informed of what had been done, desired that they might be brought into his presence. They brought them to him naked, their hands tied, and they were driven in with blows and cuffs. A Saracen prince who met them endeavored to induce them to embrace the law of Mahomet. Brother Otho rejected the proposition with horror and spat on the ground, to mark his contempt of such a religion; this brought upon him a severe box on the ear, upon which he turned the other side, according to the direction of the Gospel, and said to the prince: "May God forgive you, for you do not know what you are doing."[17]

When they had reached the palace, the king said to them: "Are you then those impious persons who despise the true faith, those foolish persons who blaspheme the prophet sent from God?" "O king," they answered, "we have no contempt for the true faith; on the contrary, we are ready to suffer and die in its defense; but we detest your faith, and the wicked man who was its author." The king, imagining that he might perhaps gain them over by the love of pleasure, of riches or of honors, said to them, in pointing out to them some beautiful women whom he had brought there on purpose: "I will give you those women for wives, together with large sums of money, and you shall be highly esteemed in my kingdom, if you will embrace the law of Mahomet; if not, you shall die by the sword." The confessors of the faith answered without hesitating: "We want neither your women nor your money: keep those for yourself, and let Jesus Christ be for us. Subject us to what tortures you please, and take away our lives. All suffering is light to us, when we think of the glories of heaven." Then the king, having lost all hopes of overcoming them, took his scimitar, and with his own hand split their skulls in two; and thus was completed the martyrdom of the five Friars Minor, on the 16th of January, 1220.

Their bodies, having been dragged out of the town and cut to pieces by the infidels, were collected by the Christians; and the Infant Don Pedro took them into Spain, from whence he sent them into Portugal to King Alphonso, not daring as yet to revisit his own country. This king, accompanied by Queen Urraca and some of the grandees of the kingdom, came with the clergy to meet them, and had them placed with great pomp in the monastery of Regular Canons of the Holy Cross, at Coimbra, where they still are. The celebrated miracles which were achieved there in great numbers, as well as those which were performed in Morocco and on the way to Europe, are recorded by contemporary authors, who have written their acts.[18] Pope Sixtus IV recognized them solemnly as martyrs, in the year 1461, and gave permission to the religious to say their office.

---

[17] Matt. 5: 39.

[18] Act. SS Jan.

At the time of their death, the Princess Sancia of Portugal, was in the act of prayer; they appeared to her with a bloody scimitar in their hands and told her that by their martyrdom they were on their way to heaven, where they would pray to God continually for her, who would thus reward the good she had done them.

What they had foretold Queen Urraca, as to the time of her death, came to pass, and her confessor, a canon regular of Santa Cruz, a most exemplary man, of great piety, was made acquainted with it by a very marvelous vision. A short time after the bodies of these glorious martyrs had been placed in the church of this monastery, he saw in the middle of the night the choir filled with religious, who were singing very melodiously, which surprised him exceedingly, neither knowing what brought them there, nor how they got in. He asked one of them, who replied: "We are all Friars Minor. He whom you see at the head, is Brother Francis, whom you have longed so much to see; and the five who are more resplendent than the rest, are the martyrs of Morocco, who are honored in this church. Our Lord has sent us hither in order to pray for Queen Urraca, who is dead, and who had great affection for our Order; and he has willed that you should see all this, because you were her confessor." The vision disappeared, and the confessor's door was immediately knocked at, to communicate to him that the queen was dead.

The severe vengeance with which God visited the king of Morocco and his subjects[19] was also noticed. The right hand with which this prince had struck the holy martyrs, and the whole of his right side, from the head to the feet, was paralyzed and became perfectly dry. During three years, no rain fell in the whole country, and an infinity of people died by pestilence and famine, which scourges lasted five years, God choosing to proportion the duration of the punishment to the number of the martyrs. All these marvels which he operated in their favor, and the title of martyrs, which the Church gives them, must convince every faithful Christian, enlightened by the wisdom which is from above, that it was by a particular impulse from the Holy Spirit that they exposed themselves to death with so much ardor, against the advice of the other Christians. Human prudence is very rash when it takes upon itself to blame what is approved by God and by His Church.

It would be difficult to express the joy which filled the heart of Francis, when he learned that his brethren had suffered martyrdom. He said to those who were with him: "It is now that I can rest assured that I have had five true Friars Minor!" and he called down a thousand blessings on the convent of Alanquer, where they had prepared themselves for martyrdom, which had such effect, that there have been always since a great number of religious there, and at least one who has been distinguished for religious perfection.

Brother Vital, who had been the superior of these generous martyrs, was delighted on hearing of their triumph, and greatly regretted not having shared

---

[19] Act. SS. Jan.

therein. It was not in good-will that he was deficient; he was only arrested by his illness, of which he died at Saragossa some time afterwards.

One of the authors[20] of the life of St. Dominic, tells us that this great patriarch, who held his general chapter at the time, was in ecstasies of joy, when he heard that five Friars Minor had received the crown of martyrdom; that he looked upon it as the first fruits of the plans of his friend Francis, and, at the same time, as a powerful incentive for his brethren to aspire to what is most perfect, which is to suffer for the faith of Jesus Christ. The Friars Preachers have profited by the example, as is evinced by the great number of martyrs of their order, by whom the Church has been enriched.

It was not without a special dispensation of Providence that the relics of the five martyrs were deposited at Coimbra, in the church of the Canons Regular of Santa Cruz, since our Lord made them subserve to the vocation of St. Anthony of Padua, who is one of the most striking ornaments of this renowned order.

He was a native of Portugal, of a very noble family of Lisbon, born in the Year 1195,[21] and had received the name of Ferdinand,[22] in baptism. The first years of his life had been passed in innocence and piety; the fear of being seduced by the world, and the wish to consecrate himself wholly to God, made him take the resolution, at the age of fifteen, to enter the Order of Regular Canons, in the convent of St. Vincent, at Lisbon. Two years afterwards, in order to avoid the frequent visits of his friends, which interfered with habits of retirement, he asked permission of his superior to remove to the convent of Santa Cruz, at Coimbra, which is of the same Order. He had some difficulty in obtaining this leave, because they had great esteem for him personally. He made use of the quiet he now enjoyed to apply himself to the study of sacred literature, and, as if he had foreseen what he was to do at a future period of his life, he not only taught himself what was requisite for his own sanctification, but also what was useful for instructing others in the paths of virtue; he gathered also from the Holy Scriptures, and from the study of the fathers, what could serve to confirm the truths of faith, and to impugn error. The assiduity with which he pursued his studies, together with the excellence of his memory, and his surpassing talents, with the light he received from Heaven, rendered him in a short time very learned.

The relics of the five Friars Minor who had been martyred at Morocco, and

---

[20] Ferd. de Castill. Hist. Praedic, lib. I, cap. 51, apud Wading, ad ann. 1220, n. 51.

[21] Some authors quoted by Bollandus and by Wading, say that the father of St. Anthony of Padua was known by the name of Bouillon and believe that he took it from the Castle of Bouillon, which Godfrey of that name who was king of Jerusalem has rendered so celebrated. He may originally have been from that county, and as he was of high quality, have come from a branch of the House of Ardenne, to which the county of Bouillon, afterwards a duchy, belonged. The Mother of the saint was Tavera, of an illustrious Portuguese family, Act. SS. ut supra, pag. 796. Annot. litt. B. Wading, ad anno 1220, n. 53.

[22] Act. SS. Jan. Dic. 13, tom. 2.

which were taken to Santa Cruz, at Coimbra, at that time, inspired in his heart an anxious desire to die for Jesus Christ as they had done, and made him entertain the thought of becoming a member of that Order, as the school of martyrdom. Some old authors,[23] add that St. Francis,[24] who was then at Assisi, appeared to him, and induced him to embrace his Institute, foretelling him what would happen to him.

The Friars Minor of the convent of St. Anthony of Olivares, near Coimbra, having come to the Canons Regular of Santa Cruz to quest, Ferdinand could not control his zeal, but taking them aside, he opened to them the wish he had to enter their community. They were highly pleased on hearing this, and fixed the day with him for putting his design into execution. In the meantime, he asked leave of the superior of Santa Cruz to effect the change, and with great difficulty obtained it. The Friars Minor returned on the appointed day, and gave him the habit of the Order, in the convent of Santa Cruz itself, and took him back with them to that of St. Anthony. The loss of so estimable a member was very distressing to the canons;[25] one of them who felt it more than the others, said to him with bitterness, as he left the house: "Go, perhaps you shall become a saint." To which Ferdinand answered with humility: "When you hear that it is so, you will doubtless give praise to God." He was not satisfied with having changed his order; he chose likewise to change his name, in order by that means to disappoint those who might endeavor to seek for him; and as St. Anthony was the titular saint of the convent, he begged the superior to call him Anthony, which is the name he was ever after known by, and to which was added of Padua, because his body reposes in that city, and is there honored by the faithful.

The wish to shed his blood for the faith of Jesus Christ, which was the source of his vocation, was constantly increasing in his mind and gave him no rest. He solicited leave from the superiors to go into Africa, which was granted to him, as had been promised him, when he entered the Order. Being come into the land of the Saracens, he was seized with a violent illness, which

---

[23] Act. SS. supra, p. 707. Annot. lit. I, and Wading, ad ann. 1220, n. 54.

[24] Mariana is greatly in error when he says in his History of Spain, book 12, chap. 8, that St. Francis, being in Portugal, St. Anthony of Padua joined him, and embraced his state of life; for it is certain, that St. Francis went into Spain in 1213, and returned in 1214; that St. Anthony, born at Lisbon in 1196, according to Wading, took the habit of regular Canon in 1211, and did not enter the Order of St. Francis, till the year 1220. It is a mistake which ought to be noticed in the French translation of this history, which was printed in 1725, with notes, tom. 2, liv. 12, n. 66.

[25] Paciecus, an author quoted by Bollandus, says that the Canons regular of Santa Cruz, were greatly displeased that their confrere Ferdinand should have left them to become a Friar Minor, and that their indignation was so great, that Pope Gregory IX was forced to address a brief to the Prior, in which he warned him that unless his religious gave over insulting the Friars Minor, he should call upon the Bishop of Visceo to punish them. The Brief is dated in the seventh year of his pontificate, on the 12th of June. This was the year 1227, the next after the death of St. Francis; St. Anthony being then living. This is precisely 550 years ago, and still we are not sure that the wound is completely healed in the Order as yet. Act. SS. supra, p. 707 vol. I. Annot. lit.

confined him the whole winter, and obliged him to return to Spain in the spring for his recovery. He embarked for this purpose, but the Almighty, who had destined him for the martyrdom of the apostolical life, and who intended by his means to convert an infinity of souls in Italy and France, gave him a passage in a contrary direction. The wind drove the vessel he was in to Sicily, where he landed, and from thence, in the following year, we shall meet him in the general chapter at St. Mary of the Angels.

CHAPTER V
ENGLAND AND GERMANY

His friars pass into England—He visits some convents—Writes to the Vicar-General—Receives his resignation, and re-appoints, by the command of God, Brother Elias to his place—He holds a chapter, and sends missionaries to Germany.

T WAS IN THE YEAR 1220, that the Friars Minor, Angelus and Albert, both natives of Pisa, after having staid some time at Paris in order to arrange the first establishment there, crossed the channel to England, whither Francis had sent them at the general chapter of 1219. The religious of St. Dominic had already a convent at Canterbury, where they received the two new comers with great charity. King Henry III, who reigned at that time, settled them with royal magnificence at Oxford, where he held his court, and he conceived so great a liking for them, that he had a lodge built near their convent, to which he occasionally retired in order to converse with them.

The reason which primarily induced him to show them so much consideration, was his having learnt from authentic sources what had occurred to them on their journey from Canterbury to Oxford.[1] The prior, the sacristan, and the cellarer of the abbey of Abingdon, who were at one of their farms, contrary to the usual practice of their Order, where hospitality is always given, as recommended by St. Benedict, refused it to these poor religious, and turned them from their doors, although it was at night-fall.[2] A young religious, who was in their company, seeing that they were about to pass the night in the wood, introduced them secretly into the barn, brought them some food, and recommended himself urgently to their prayers. In the night he had a dreadful vision of the justice with which God visited the prior and the two others, but which did not fall on him, because he had been charitable. In the morning he went to them with a view of telling them what he had seen in his sleep, and found them all three dead in their beds. Struck with astonishment he left the farm, from whence the two Friars Minor had departed before daybreak, and went to relate what had happened to the abbot of Abingdon; they both had serious reflections on this subject, which ended in their entering into the Order of Friars Minor. So extraordinary an occurrence could not be kept secret; many persons heard it; the king was made acquainted with it, and this caused the

---

[1] S. Anton, chron. part 3, lit. 24, cap. 7, s. 2.

[2] Wading, ex chron. ant. MS. ad ann. n. 1220, n.

favorable reception he gave to Angelus and Albert.

His open protection, with the sanctity of their lives, caused the Institute to flourish throughout the kingdom. Several doctors of theology embraced it; and subsequently Robert Maideston, Bishop or Hereford, an enlightened prelate of great distinction at court, obtained leave from Gregory IX to give up his bishopric to take the poor habit of St. Francis, under which he became a model of humility. In some convents, schools were established, the principal one at Oxford, which produced many learned men.[3]

Three hundred years after, King Henry VIII destroyed all these monuments of science and religion, which his predecessor Henry III had raised with so much zeal, and tyrannically treated the successors of those who had been received with so much benevolence. The strange revolution which the incontinence and heresy of this prince brought about in England, reduced the Friars Minor, and all other missionaries, to the necessity of running greater risks in endeavoring to maintain the remnant of faith, than what they have to incur amongst the infidels.

We suppress all comment on so deplorable a subject, and we are satisfied with offering up our prayers to the Almighty,[4] that He would deign to cast the

---

[3] Wading says, on the authority of some English writers, in the year 1220, n. 62, that Robert Grossetete established the school of the Friars Minor at Oxford; and that, being Bishop of Lincoln, he continued to show them much favor, wrote in commendation of the Order, labored with them in the elucidation of the Scriptures, and left them by his will his library. But if they profited by his learning and his good will, they did not imitate him in his bitter invectives against the Sovereign Pontiffs. We do not understand why the author of the *Histoire Ecclesiastique,* who censures these dreadful effusions, has nevertheless copied his scandalous expressions, and says that he died in the odor of sanctity, that it was even said that he had worked miracles at his death. Tom. 17, liv. 83, n. 45. The Ecclesiastical History has no need of such documents, nor of such saints, nor of such miracles, which were never acknowledged by the Church. Moreover, the author of whom we speak, only quotes in support of what he says, Matthew Paris, who has only beatified the Bishop of Lincoln because of the aversion they both had for the Popes, and who, on other occasions, gives a terrific account of this very prelate. To form a correct opinion of Robert Grossetete, Bishop of Lincoln, it is necessary to read the second letter of the Bishop of Newbury, printed in 1719. p. 107.

[4] God forbid that, under the pretext of facilitating the reunion of the English to the Catholic Church, we should adopt the opinions of an author who some years ago strove to prove, against the opinion of the Church, that they have a succession of Bishops validly consecrated; and who, in order to justify them, published some manifest errors as to the sacrifice of the Mass, and the real presence, and the priesthood, and the forms of the Sacraments and the character imprinted by them on the rites and ceremonies of the Church, on the authority and primacy of the Pope, and other important points. The Cardinal de Noailles, Archbishop of Paris, by his mandement of the 18th of August, 1727, condemns the writings of this author, as containing false, erroneous, scandalous doctrines, injurious to the Church and to the Holy See, favoring schism and heresy, and even contrary on many points to the Catholic doctrine; and he forbids, on pain prescribed by the laws, his subjects from reading these works. The cardinals, archbishops, and bishops, assembled in extraordinary meeting at Paris, twenty in number, censured them on 22nd August, 1727, as follows: "Censure of the books of Brother Peter Francis Le Courayer, Canon regular of S. Genevieve, entitled *Dissertation on the Validity of English Ordinations,* &c. —Defense of the Dissertation on the validity of the English Ordinations, &c." They declare all the propositions inserted in the censure respectively false, rash, captious, ill-sounding, scandalous, injurious, to the Church and the Holy See, favoring schism and

eyes of His mercy upon those islands, which formerly gave so many saints to the Church; that by His grace, the talent and learning which are found there, may be employed in searching for the truth and appreciating that truth which the illustrious Pope St. Gregory had taught there in the sixth century; that these talents may be no longer employed in the defense of a variety of sects, equally at variance with the doctrines of antiquity, condemned by the principles of the Christian religion, and by the rules of right reasoning; and that it shall no longer be said that men of learning make use of the lights they have received and cultivated, to countenance every description of falsehood; so that, as St. Leo said of idolatrous Rome,[5] dictating to almost all other nations, she herself was the slave of all their errors.

Some of the French bishops entertained scruples relative to the institution of the Friars Minor; they thought their mode of life was not approved of, and thinking unfavorably of those who followed it, they behaved harshly in their regard; Pope Honorius, being made acquainted with this, addressed a Brief to all the prelates of that kingdom, and in particular,[6] to the archbishop of Sens, and to the bishop of Paris:

"Honorius, Bishop, the servant of the servants of God, to our venerable brethren the archbishops and bishops, and to our dear sons the abbots, priors, and other ecclesiastical superiors of the kingdom of France, health and apostolical benediction.

"We remember to have written to you before in favor of our dear sons, the brethren of the Order of Friars Minor, in order that, for the love of God, you should have consideration for them. Nevertheless, we have heard that some of you will not suffer them in your dioceses, having scruples as to the approbation of the Order; although they have not found anything in them calculated to create suspicion, as we have been assured by persons fully worthy of credit; and that, moreover, our letters of recommendation ought to have sufficed to have prevented any ill opinion to have been formed against them. We desire, therefore, that you may know that we look upon the Order of Friars Minor as one of those which are approved of, and we acknowledge them to be Catholic and pious men. For which reason we have thought proper to warn and exhort you by the present letters, to receive the aforesaid brethren in your dioceses, as being truly faithful and religious persons, and to show them particular attention, out of the respect you have for God and for us, who

---

heresy, erroneous, and already condemned by the Council of Trent, and heretical. At Paris, printed by Wido Mazieres, and J.B. Garnier, printers to the Queen, S. Jacques Street, at the sign of Providence. In consequence of this censure of the bishops, whose opinion had been solicited by the king, his majesty caused the two works to be suppressed, by decree of the Council of State of the 7th Sept., 1727.

[5] S. Leo in *Nat. Apost.*, serm. 1.

[6] Wading says, that these two Briefs, addressed to the Archbishop of Sens, and to the Bishop of Paris, are in the original in the archives of the great Convent of the Observance at Paris. Ad. ann. 1220, n. 56.

recommend them to you. Given at Viterbo, the 4th of the Calends of June, in the fourth year of our Pontificate." This was the 29th of May 1220.

Francis left the convent of Saint Mary of the Angels, in the beginning of the year 1221, in order to visit some of his other convents. Peter of Catania, the vicar-general, found some opposition to his government. Although he was naturally of a mild disposition, he had, nevertheless, sufficient firmness to chide those who were not regular in their conduct, and this was not agreeable to all; those who were in fault declared their opposition to him, and there were even some who resisted his orders, and others who censured him. This is what superiors of all kinds have to expect who do not resemble the high priest Heli,[7] whom the spirit of indifference, the blamable love of ease, and the human wish for popularity, do not render so weak as to suffer those evils which it is their duty to check and put a stop to, and to neglect the good which it behooves them to support.

The vicar-general, grieved and vexed by the obstacles thrown in his way, wrote to Francis on the subject, and received the following reply:

"To my reverend father in Jesus Christ, Brother Peter, minister general, Brother Francis sends greeting:

"May the Lord be your defense, and may He preserve you in His holy charity. My dear brother, I recommend you to have great patience in all your conduct, so that if any one of your brethren, or any one else, whoever he may be, should happen to thwart you, or should even venture to strike you, you should take all this as so much grace bestowed upon you; be always sincerely in this disposition, and never swerve from it. Love those who behave in this manner to you, and do not expect any change on their parts, unless in so far as it shall please God to do you the favor to cause them to mend; this is what you should propose to yourself in loving them. The mark by which I shall know that you love God, and that you have an affection for me, who am His servant and yours, is that no one of our brethren, whatever faults he may have committed, shall leave you without having felt the effects of your mercy; should he not ask it of you, be beforehand with him, and ask him if he wishes for it; and if, after having refused it, he comes constantly before you, show him, in order to bring him back to a proper way of thinking, more affection than you would even show to me. Have always compassion for such as are in this state; and let the guardians[8] know, when you have an opportunity, that it is your decided intention to act up to this. Let all the brethren, who may be cognizant of the fault of one of them, abstain from reproaching him with it, and let them forbear from making it known; but, on the contrary, let them

---

[7] I Reg. 2: 24 and 29, 3: 13.

[8] The Superiors of the houses of the Order of S. Francis, are called Guardians, because the humility of the holy Patriarch did not choose that they should be called Priors. Regul. S. Francis, cap. 6. Guardian means, as does *custos*, a man employed to take care, to preserve, to watch, to look after. It is derived from Guardianus, or Gardianus, Guardium, Guardin, Guardia, terms of low Latin taken from the German, warden, which has the same signification. Dict. Etymologique de Menage.

entertain feelings of compassion for him, and keep the thing secret. It is not such as are in health who need a physician, but they who are ill.[9] If one of the brethren, by the temptation of the evil one, should unhappily fall into a mortal sin, let him be obliged by virtue of obedience to address himself to the guardian, who will also be obliged by obedience to send him to the *custos*,[10] and let the *custos* take care to provide for the conscience of the guilty, as he could wish his own to be taken care of. And let it not be permitted to any of the *custodes* to enjoin him any other penance than this: 'Go and henceforth sin no more.'[11] Do as I direct you."

When St. Francis does not permit the superiors to enjoin any other penance for a mortal sin than this: "Go, and henceforth sin no more," we see clearly that he only speaks of regular and public penances,[12] such as would be given for a secret fault, and in no way of those which are enjoined, *in foro conscientiae,* for the expiation of the sin, or for the prevention of relapse. For just before, he obliges the *custos,* by obedience, to whom one of the brethren guilty of mortal sin shall have been sent, to provide for the conscience of that religious as he would his own to be provided for.

Now, the *custos,* in such a case, could not think it reasonable, if a penance at once satisfactory and preservative were not imposed on him. For public faults the holy Founder no doubt intended that they should be publicly punished, since he gave the example on several occasions, as we shall see. If in this letter he recommends mildness and clemency rather than justice and severity, it is because he adopted the sentiments of our blessed Savior, whose mildness to sinners who were not proud nor obstinate, as the Pharisees, was so great; it was because he knew what St. Paul says, "that advice must be given to our brethren in the spirit of meekness; reprove, entreat, rebuke, with all patience and doctrine;"[13] finally, because writing to the vicar-general, who was grieved by the forwardness of some of the brethren, and fearing lest some human considerations might be mixed up with his zeal, he had the intention

---

[9] Matt. 9: 12.

[10] The *Custos* signifies the Provincial. St. Bonaventure remarks that the name of *custos* was given by St. Francis to the General, the Provincials, and even to the Guardian, to mark the duty of the office, and not the title of the grades; and when he says in the 6th chapter of the rule, and elsewhere, *Ministri et Custodes,* it is as if he said the ministers who are to watch and be careful."*Ministerium dicit humilitatem, Custodia vigilantiam insinuat pastoralem?*Now, as the holy Doctor was well versed in the form of the government of the Order, we must acknowledge that, in the beginning, there were none of these *Custodes,* who have since been established in the provinces which Are extensive, to have charge of a certain number of convents, under the direction of the Provincial. There was also a *Custos* of the *Custodes,* who was elected by the Chapter of the province, to go in the capacity of a Discreet to the General Chapter, with the Provincial; and this election is still observed even in those provinces where there Are no *Custodes* any longer. S Bonav. Expos, in Reg. cap. 4 and 8.

[11] 1 John 8: 11.

[12] Wading did not think of that, when he put in his 15th note upon this letter: "Cum grano salis est intelligendum."

[13] Galat. 6: 1. 2 Timothy 4: 2.

and wish merely to mollify and soften him; and, indeed, every one who is in place is naturally inclined to be harsh to those who counteract his authority, and therefore on this head required rather to be curbed than urged on.

Peter of Catania acted entirely upon the terms of the letter of his Patriarch; but he did not long continue in the post of vicar-general.[14] Wading believes that he died in this year, 1221, on the 10th of March, and he is followed in this opinion by Father Artus du Moutier, a Franciscan, by Bollandus, and by Fleury, who thought the date certain because it was grounded on the epitaph on the tomb of Peter of Catania, in the church of St. Mary of the Angels, but what we have brought forward in the note which is below,[15] clearly shows that Peter died on the 2nd of March, 1224. Now, in the general chapter held in this year, 1221, at Whitsuntide, on the 30th of May, another vicar-general was appointed,

---

[14] Artus a Monast. Mart. Fr. 10 Martii, Act, SS. Bolland. Tom. 2. Mart, die 10 inter Praetermiss. Hist. Ecd. tom. 6, lib. 78 n. 43.

[15] Octavius, Bishop of Assisi, relates and notices the figures on the epitaph, which mark the year and the day of the death of Peter of Catania, and show that Wading has been mistaken in them. It is in his book entitled *Lumi Serafici di Portiuncula*, from which we have already taken quotations. These are his own words: "Non posso di meno di notare un grave fallo di Cronologia nell'annalista Frecescano Luca Vadingo, per altro accuratissimo ed reuditissimo. Egli pone la morte di Fra Pietro Catania nel 1221, alli 10, di Marzo; e poi nel 1223, pone che andò a Roma con S. Francesco. La cagion dello sbaglio si è perché in fatti gli antichi monumenti lo dicono compagno di questa andata; per l'altra parte poi la pietra del monumento suo in Portiuncula, dove anche oggi si vede ha l'inscrizionne equivoca. In quella sta così: MCCXX. VII, d. Martii. L'ha cosi intesa il Vadingo: MCCXXI, e poi VI id come a dire, millesimo ducentesimo vigesimo primo, sexto idus Martii, ma in realtà deve leggersi così, MCCXXIV, poi ii, d. cioè a dire: millesimo ducentesimo vigesimo quarto, secunda die Martii."

Father Megrigny, a Capuchin, and afterwards Bishop of Grasse, whose memory is revered in the Church for his zeal against the reformers, and for his eminent virtues, bears witness to the correctness of the figures taken by Octavius; according to what Father Assermet, of the great convent of the Observatines, Dr. Of the Sorbonne, relates in his critical and anti-critical History of the Indulgence of the Portiuncula, printed at Lyons, in 1719. The Bishop of Grasse, passing by there (the Convent of St. Mary of the Angels near Assisi), on his return from the General Chapter, told me that the epitaph was written as the Bishop of Assisi points out in his *Lumi Seraphici*. Moreover, no one will be rash enough to call into question the truth of a fact publicly attested by a bishop who saw it with his own eyes in his diocese, where every one may see it as he did.

It is clear that the numbers on the epitaph have been ill-placed by the carver, MCCXX. VII d. Martii. Wading has placed them thus: MCCXXI. VI. Id. Martii, and finds them to stand for, millesimo ducentisimo vigesimo primo, sexto idus Martii. The bishop of Assisi arranges them thus: millesimo ducentesimo vigesimo quarto secunda die Martii. We believe that no one will hesitate in agreeing with the bishop. His opinion has been followed by Father Mathias Grouwels, a Franciscan professor of theology at Louvain in his Critical History of the Indulgence of Portiuncula, written in Latin, and printed at Antwerp in 1726 by Verdussen, of which work we shall speak in our remarks on this indulgence. But what must fix the death of Peter of Catania, in the year 1224, and not in 1221, is that there exist authentic records which prove that he was alive in 1223. Wading saw these and quotes them in the year 1223, with the name of Peter of Catania, so that by an extraordinary anachronism, he represents him as alive in the 1223, him whom he had reported as dead in 1221, and whose death he told us was attended with peculiar circumstances. This is one of those faults which are fallen into by those who are neither deficient in extent nor in exactness generally, and which do not show any intention to mislead the reader.

who certainly held that office in the year 1223, as we shall see; and, moreover, it does not seem likely that so holy a man as Peter of Catania should have been deposed by St. Francis, besides which no author has spoken of it. We cannot therefore avoid concluding that he resigned his place out of humility, and to be freed from a burden that saintly persons often find too much for them.

Francis, having received the resignation of his vicar-general, on his return from his visitations, deferred the choice of his successor till the assembly of the chapter which was held on Whitsunday. He consulted God on the election, who made known to him by revelation that Brother Elias should be restored; he communicated this to his companions, and when the chapter met, he named Elias vicar-general.

We may feel assured that after having deposed him for laxness, he would not again have placed him at the head of his Order, had he not been certain that God himself had ordered it. As soon as the saints are made aware of the will of God, they have no thought but of obeying, whether it be that they know His reasons, or that they be hidden from them. Thus, three hundred years before St. Francis, St. Stephen, the third abbot of Citeaux,[16] did not fail sending Arnaud to Morimond to be its first abbot, although he knew by divine inspiration, that this post would be prejudicial to him, and that it would not turn out well: it was enough for him that it was God's will that he should be so sent. Thus we find in Holy Writ that Eliseus, by God's order to Elias, consecrated Hazael king of Syria, whom he foresaw would bring such great evils on the people of God, that the foresight moved him to tears. Human prudence must not censure in the saints what they have only done from supernatural views, against their own impressions, and their own inclinations. In these extraordinary cases we must only adore the counsels of divine wisdom, without endeavoring to penetrate them: acknowledge, as Tobias did,[17] that all His ways are ways of mercy, truth, and justice; and say with one of the prophets: "Thy loss comes from yourself."[18]

At the chapter Francis sat at the feet of Elias and, as his infirmities prevented him from making himself heard, it was through Elias that he proposed all that he wished to communicate to the assembly. Towards the close he pulled him by the tunic and told him in a low tone of voice his intention of sending some of the brethren into parts of Upper Germany, into which they had not yet penetrated. Elias laid the affair before the brethren in the following terms: "My brethren, this is what the Brother says" (for thus they designated Francis, as a mark of great respect). "There is a part of Germany, the inhabitants of which are Christians and devout; they go, as you know, through our country during the heats with long staves and great jack-boots,

---

[16] Manriq. Ann. Cisterc. ad ann. 1215, Cap. 3, n. 3. Essai de l'Histoire de l'Ordre de Citeaux, tom. 1, p. 206. 3 Reg, 19, 55 and 6, 4 Reg, 8, 11, and 22.

[17] Fab, 3, 2.

[18] Hosea, 13: 9.

singing the praises of God and His saints, and thus visit the places of devotion. I sent some of our brethren into their land, who returned often having been sorely ill- treated. For this reason, I compel no one to go thither, but if there are any sufficiently zealous for the glory of God and the salvation of souls to undertake this journey, I promise him the same merit as is attached to obedience, and even more than if he made a voyage over the sea."

About ninety offered themselves for the mission which they considered as an opportunity for suffering martyrdom. The chief was named with the title of provincial minister of Germany, and Brother Caesar, a German, was selected for that office; he was an ecclesiastic of Spire, who had been drawn into the Order by the preaching of Brother Elias,[19] some time before, he himself having the character of a good preacher. He had permission to select those whom he desired to take with him from among those who had volunteered; however, he only chose twenty-seven, twelve of whom were priests, and fifteen lay-brethren, among whom there were some Germans, and some Hungarians, excellent preachers. He remained nearly three months in the valley of Spoleto, with leave from Francis, and sent his companions into Lombardy to prepare themselves for the great work they were about to undertake; then they set forth dividing themselves into small groups of three and four. We shall further on give the details of their journey, and of their labors and success.

In the choice which Cesar made of those whom he thought adapted to the German mission, something occurred which at first was amusing, but which turned out very serious and very useful. Some one having suggested to him to take one of the brethren named Jourdain, he went to him and said: "And you Brother Jourdain, you will come with us?" "Me?" replied he, "I am not one of yours; if I rose up, it was not with any intention of going with you, it was to embrace those who were about to go into Germany, and who, I am certain, will all be martyred." He was so apprehensive that the Germans by their cruelty, and the heretics of Lombardy by their artifices, would be the causes of his losing his faith, that he daily prayed to God for the favor of being kept away from the one and from the other.

Cesar, continuing to urge him to go with him, and Jourdain continuing to refuse, they went to the vicar general, who, after having been informed how the matter stood, said to Jourdain:

"My brother, I command you, on your holy obedience, to decide absolutely upon going into Germany or not to go." This order put his conscience in a dilemma: if he should not go, he feared its reproach for having followed his own will, and did not like to lose a glorious crown; and, on the other hand, he could not determine on going, thinking the Germans so cruel as he had been led to believe. In order to come to a conclusion, he consulted one of the

---

[19] Although he was relaxed and had some vanity, God nevertheless made use of him for the salvation of souls, which proves that His word operates independent of the disposition of those who announce it, in the hearts of such auditors as are prepared to attend to it.

religious who had greatly suffered in the first mission, and had been stripped in Hungary no less than fifteen times, who said to him: "Go to Brother Elias, and tell him that you are neither willing to go into Germany nor to stay here, but that you will do whatsoever he shall desire you to do. You will hardly have addressed him, that your difficulties will be done away." He followed this advice, and Elias ordered him by the obligation of obedience to accompany Brother Caesar into Germany. He went and labored assiduously, and more than any of the others, to extend the order throughout the country. His obedience quieted his mind, which his own choice would have failed to procure him, for a man is never more satisfied with himself than when he obeys. "Experience shows," says St. Bernard, "that the yoke of obedience is light, and that self-will is oppressive.[20]

Anthony had heard in Sicily that the chapter was to assemble at St. Mary of the Angels, and although he was still in a state of weakness, he had come to it with Philippinus, a young lay brother of Castile. When the chapter was over, the brethren were sent back to their convents by the vicar general, but no one asked to have Anthony, because no one knew him, and he appeared so feeble, that he did not seem fit for work. He offered himself therefore to Brother Gratian, who was provincial of Bologna, or of Romagna, whom he begged to take him, to instruct him in the rules of regular discipline, making no mention of his studies, or of any talent he had, and showing no other desire than to know and love the crucified Jesus. Gratian, delighted with these his sentiments, asked to have him, and took him with him into his province, with Philippinus, who was sent to Città di Castello, and from thence to Columbario, in Tuscany, where he died a holy death. Anthony, who only wished for solitude, had leave from the provincial to live at the hermitage of Mount St. Paul, near Bologna, where he wished to have a cell cut in the rock, which was separated from all the others, which the brother who had cut it out for himself ceded to him. There he lived in as much solitude as obedience allowed him, devoting himself to contemplation, fasting on bread and water, and practicing such other austerities, as to be thereby so weakened, that, according to the relation of his brethren, he could hardly stand when he came to them.

Although he was full of zeal, he did not dare attempt to preach; the martyrdom which he had escaped in Africa had rendered him timid; he abandoned himself to Divine Providence, without any other anxiety than that of exciting himself to the more perfect love of God, and strengthening himself in the hope of enjoying the good things of Heaven, and resisting the attacks of the tempter, who strove to dissuade him from the holy exercise of prayer. Living thus in great simplicity among his unpretending brethren, he disguised under a plain exterior the vast lights he received from Heaven; but by that humility he deserved to be brought forward for the accomplishment of the

---

[20] De Precept, et Disp., cap. 10. De dilig. Deo, cap. 13.

designs of Providence, who generally prepares those in secret, whom he destines to splendid ministrations, and who brought forward this His servant, as will be hereafter shown.

St. Francis before the Egyptian Sultan. —Giotto

Trial by fire before the Sultan. —Domenico Ghirlandaio

St. Francis contemplating death.
—Caravaggio

THE LIFE OF ST. FRANCIS OF ASSISI

BOOK IV

CHAPTER I

Third Order—Portiuncula Indulgence

S. Francis begins his third Order of Penance—Draws up the rule for it—What his idea was in founding this Order—He returns to St. Mary of the Angels—Sends Agnes, the sister of Clare, to Florence, to be Abbess there—He obtains from Jesus Christ the Indulgence of St. Mary of the Angels, or of the Portiuncula—Pope Honorius III grants him the same indulgence—Clare and others, hearing him talk of God, are ravished in ecstasy.

FTER THE CHAPTER, Francis, notwithstanding the bad state of his health, actuated by his zeal, undertook to preach repentance in the towns adjacent to Assisi, where he preached at length, in forcible language, on vice and virtue, and the sufferings and happiness of a future life. The inhabitants of Canaria[1] were so moved by his preaching, that they followed him in crowds, forsaking their usual occupations. Many also, from the neighboring villages, joined them, and all together solicited him to teach them how to profit by his instructions.

Many married men were desirous of separating themselves from their wives, in order to embrace the religious state, and many married women were anxious to shut themselves up in cloisters; but the holy Patriarch, not wishing to break up well-assorted marriages, nor to depopulate the country, advised them to serve God in their own houses, and promised to give them a rule by which they might progress in virtue and live as religious, without practicing the austerities of that state of life.

He was under the necessity of repeating the same injunctions in several towns in Tuscany, particularly in Florence, where similar views prevailed, and where they had already commenced building a monastery for females, who were desirous of renouncing the world. While he was yet ruminating on the mode of life he should prescribe for them, he assembled them all, and formed them into two congregations: the one of men, and the other of women. Having

---

[1] Father Helyot, in the History of Religious Orders, tom. 7, chap. 29, page 215, says that Saint Francis having learn I, by a revelation made to Saint Clare and her brother Silvester, that God had called him to labor for the salvation of souls, came with brothers Massé and Angelus of Rieti to the small town of Canaria, where he established the Third Order. This is a great mistake, made in following other authors. The Saint then went to Bevagna and this was in 1212. It was only in 1221, that he went to Canaria, and that the Third Order was instituted at Poggibonsi. All this is clearly laid down in the annals of Wading, and has been followed by the author of "Annales Latines du Tiers Ordre de la Penitence," printed at Paris by Rob. Chevillon in 1686.

given each of them a president, they gave themselves separately up to exercises of piety and practices of mercy, with so much fervor, that a contemporary author compares them to the Christians whom Tertullian so eloquently eulogizes. With the alms which the two congregations collected, they built a hospital for the sick and aged, on the outskirts of the town, where all the virtues of charity were assiduously exercised; an establishment which is extant at this day.[2] St. Antoninus, when archbishop of Florence, removed these pious assemblies to a locality near the Church of St. Martin, for the convenience of the poor. The vicinity of the church and their good works procured for them the name of the "Good Men of St. Martin;" and they were afterwards called the "Penitents of St. Francis," because they followed the rule of the Third Order of Penance, which the Saint instituted.

This zealous preacher, having gone from Florence to Gagiano, near Poggibonsi, in Tuscany, met a shop-keeper of his acquaintance, whose name was Lucchesio, who had been very avaricious, and an enthusiastic partisan of the faction of the Guelphs,[3] but who, having been converted a few months before, now lived a very Christian-like life, gave away great sums in alms, attended the sick in hospitals, received strangers hospitably into his house, and endeavored to instill similar sentiments into Bonadonna, his wife. They had already asked Francis to put them in a way of sanctifying their lives, which should be suitable to their position; and the holy man had given them this answer: "I have been thinking of late of instituting a Third Order, in which married persons might serve God perfectly; and I think you could not do better than to enter it." After having given the subject serious consideration, Lucchesio and his wife entreated him to admit them into this new Order. He made them assume a modest and simple dress, of a grey color, with a cord with several knots in it for a girdle, and he prescribed them verbally certain pious exercises, which they were to follow until such time as he should have composed the rule.

This was the beginning of the Third Order of St. Francis, which many persons in the environs of Poggibonsi embraced, and which was soon established in Florence by the congregation of men and women of which we have just spoken. The following year, at latest, the Founder composed[4] a rule

---

[2] Marian. Flor. Chron. c. 20.; Tert. Apol. cap. 38 et 39.

[3] This shows that the Guelphs and Ghibellines had their partisans in Italy before the year 1228, although they only broke out in that year, according to the writers quoted by Spond, ad ann. 1228, n. 4. He notices all that is most probable as to the origin of the names of those two factions, which, after all, leaves the question in great uncertainty. See also "Histoire de la Decadence de l'Empire," liv. 5, PP. 435 et 494.

[4] Some persons have thought that the Rule of the Third Order was composed by Pope Nicholas IV; but Wading proves clearly that Saint Francis is the author of it, and St. Bonaventure notices it also in the 4th chapter of his Legend. Nicholas IV, who confirmed it in 1289, made such alterations in it as he thought proper, as has been said, and as he himself declares in his Bull "Unigenitus" as given by Ant. de Sillis, Lib. de Orig. et Progress Tert. Ord., tom. 2, p. 7. Wading, in "Regul. Tertiar. Argum."

for this Order, which he called the Order of the Brethren of Penance, in which the sisters were comprised, which was also called the Third Order, or the Order of Tertiaries, as relative to the two older Orders: the Order of Friars Minors, which is the first, and that of the Poor Clares, which is the second. This rule was subsequently confirmed by Pope Nicholas IV, with some changes, which he considered advisable as well in regard to the times as to the Order itself.

The holy Patriarch manifests therein not only the zeal which animated him in all that concerned the purity of the faith, but also the prudence which guided all his actions. He requires that all those who apply for admission into the Order shall be carefully examined in the Catholic faith, and their submission to the authority of the Church, and he directs that they shall only be received after having made profession of all the orthodox truths; and that great care shall be taken not to admit any heretic, nor any one suspected of heresy; and should any such be detected after having been admitted, he insists on their being immediately informed against. He, likewise, directs that their previous conduct may be inquired into, to ascertain whether any notorious crimes are imputed to them, or whether their morals are irreproachable, and he desires that they be warned to restore what they have which belongs to any other person; and he forbids receiving any married female[5] into the Order without the consent of her husband.

The profession consists in a promise to keep all God's commandments, and to perform such penances as the visitor shall enjoin for faults committed in breach of the practices required by the rule. The habit is similar to what was given to Lucchesio and his wife; but so that this may be dispensed with, according to the state of life of the persons, and the customs of the country in which they may be. The spiritual exercises laid down in the rule, have nothing in them which can interfere with the different stations of persons living in the world. Days of fasting and abstinence are prescribed, but modified prudently for the infirm, for pregnant women, for travelers, and for laboring people; and it is clearly explained that these observances are not obligatory under pain of

---

[5] We cannot understand why Father Helyot, in making the analysis of the Third Order, in the "History of Religious Orders," tom. 7, eh. 29, p. 217, says that it is necessary to inquire whether the person who wishes to enter it is not engaged in the bonds of matrimony, which is an obstacle to his reception, unless he has his wife's consent, and, reciprocally, the wife that of her husband. These two articles are not in the Rule of the Third Order. 1. St. Francis was careful not to say that the bonds of matrimony were an obstacle to the reception, since it was to married persons that he first proposed entering the Order; and since St. Bonaventure says that he instituted it for clerics, laymen, for virgins, and for married persons of either sex. 2. He forbids receiving married women without the consent of their husbands, but he does not require the consent of the wives; for he knew very well that, in the Old Law, if a wife had made a vow, she was not obliged to keep it, if her husband disapproved of it; upon which St. Augustine says that his quality of chief gives him an authority which the wife has not, over exercises of piety and other things. It is not true, therefore, that a husband requires the consent of his wife for making profession of the Third Order instituted by St. Francis. "Num. XXX., 12,13." "S. August. Ep. ad Ecdic. 272, Edit. Bened."

sin, and that they only bind the transgressor to perform the penance imposed on him, unless the transgression has at the same time contravened any law of God, or commandment of the Church.

St. Francis, moreover, strenuously recommends to the brethren and sisters, to avoid all words tending to swearing or imprecation, the theater, dancing, and all profane meetings; to undertake no law-suits, and to live in fraternal union; to take great care of the sick of the Order, to bury the dead, and to pray for them.

He adds to this, an article which is deserving of peculiar notice; it is, that all persons who enter the Order and have property over which they have the disposal, shall make their wills[6] within three months after their profession, lest they should die intestate. We see that his intention was to make them think on death, and to have their minds free for meditating on the important affair of their salvation, and to prevent those dissensions which frequently occur after the death of such as have not regulated their temporal affairs, before being called away. Wills which are made during a last illness are frequently exposed to deceit and fraud. They are never better made than when executed while the testator is in good health,[7] in possession of all his faculties.

By the institution of the Third Order, Francis proposes to himself[8] to reanimate the fervor of the faithful, to induce all the world, those in orders, laity, married persons of either sex, and such as were living in a state of celibacy, to a stricter observance of God's commandments, to live a more Christian and Catholic life, and to add the practice of virtues to the duties of civil life. His views met with astonishing success; the Order was established,

---

[6] He does not speak of wills written entirely in the testator's own hand, because he was in a country of written law, where they are not valid. But in France they Are so, as being less likely to have been suggested, and more likely to mark plainly the testator's wish.

[7] In order to make one's will properly, it is desirable to consider the state in which we shall be at the time of death; to set aside all prejudices, all anger, to dispose conscientiously of one's effects, with equity, with charity, after having consulted God and one of His ministers, and even a man conversant with the law and customs of the country, to avoid those errors which give rise to the annulling of wills. It is very unusual to see a well-made will.

[8] The Rule of the Third Order, with explanations which mark its spirit and its object, has been given to the public by several of the children of St. Francis; amongst whom it is right to distinguish Father Claudius Frassen, of the great convent of the Observantines of Paris, Doctor of the Sorbonne, whose learned and pious works and rare virtues have rendered his memory precious to the Order of Friars Minors, and to the whole Church. The best editions of the Rule of the Third Order which he has explained, are those which have been printed by Ed. Couterot, at the "Bon Pasteur;" there are some things in the later editions which are not to my taste. Denys the Carthusian has explained this Rule also, with much light and piety, such as are found in all his other works. Father Thomassin, Priest of the Oratory, says that the Third Order of St. Dominic, the Rule of which was confirmed by Pope Innocent VII, in the year 1405, that of the Servites, and that of the Third Order of St. Francis de Paul, are all similar to that of St. Francis. "Discipline de l'Eglise." Part 4, liv. 1, eh. 62, n. 13. Ed. Frangaise, 1679.

and spread with the greatest rapidity through all conditions of life.[9] Cardinals, bishops, emperors, empresses, kings, queens, considered themselves honored in being admitted into it, and it has given to the Church an infinite number of saints and blessed of either sex, who are publicly revered with her sanction. Wading says, that in his day, (that is in 1623,) there were at the court of Madrid more than sixty lords who belonged to the Third Order; and Cardinal Trejo, who had joined it, wrote to him in these terms on the subject of the works of St. Francis, which that author was about to give to the public with learned notes.

"You praise me with some surprise, that wearing the purple of Cardinal, I should have taken the habit and made solemn profession to adhere to the rules of the Third Order of St. Francis. Could I do less than devote myself wholly to his Order, I, who owe to him all that I have, and all that I am? Does not the cord of St. Francis deserve to gird even royal purple? St. Louis king of France, St. Elizabeth queen of Hungary, wore it, as well as many other sovereigns and princesses. In our own day, Philip III king of Spain, died in the habit of the blessed father; Queen Elizabeth, wife of Philip IV, the reigning monarch of Spain, and the Princess Mary, his sister, have made their profession in the Third Order. Why, then, should it be a subject of astonishment to you, that a cardinal should cover his purple with a garment of ash color, and gird himself with a cord? If this dress seems vulgar and vile, I require it the more, because, finding myself raised to a high degree of honor, I must humble myself the more in order to avoid pride. But is not the garb of St. Francis, which is of ash color, a real, purple which may adorn the dignity of kings and cardinals? Yes, it is a true purple, dyed in the blood of Jesus Christ, and in the blood which issued from the stigmates of His servant. It gives, therefore, a royal dignity to those who wear it. What have I done, therefore, in clothing myself with this garment? I have added purple to purple, the purple of royalty, to the purple of the cardinalate; thus, far from being humiliated by it, I have reason to fear that I have done myself too much honor, and that I derive from it too much glory."

These sentiments of this learned and pious Cardinal, are well calculated to silence the proud and irreligious spirits who turn into ridicule practices which the Church approves, and which her most illustrious children embrace with fervor. We have seen Queen Ann of Austria receive, at Paris, the holy habit of

---

[9] The Third Order spread so rapidly, that twenty years after its institution Peter des Vignes, Chancellor and favorite of the Emperor Frederic II, wrote to the Prince to say that the Friars Minors had established two societies, one of each sex, and that there was hardly any one who had not his or her name in it. This was to justify the irritation of his master who was incensed against the Friars Minors, because according to the intention of their Holy Patriarch, they supported the interests of the Holy See, whose bitter enemy he was. This Prince excited a violent persecution against the Third Order, which lasted till his death, in 1250, as st. Rose of Viterbo had foretold, who was herself of that Order, and whom the officers of the emperor sent with her whole family into exile, for having converted several heretics, and reconciled many schismatics to the obedience of the Holy See, by her reasoning. Petr. a Vineis, Epist., lib. 1 Epis. 37. Wading, ad ann. 1252, n. 8.

a penitent, and make profession[10] of the rule of the Third Order of St. Francis; Queen Maria Teresa of Austria, wife of the renowned king, Louis XIV, follow this example, and even permit herself to be chosen superior of the sisters of the congregation, established in the church[11] of the great convent of the Observance, under the protection of St. Elizabeth of Hungary, and assist at the various pious exercises with great edification.

The Holy See has loaded the brethren and sisters of the Third Order with many spiritual favors, and has granted them many privileges and indulgences, and has given to them a participation in all the merits which are gained in the other two Orders. What is singular is, that shortly after its institution, congregations of Tertiaries were formed,[12] in which they lived in community of property, making the three vows of poverty, chastity, and obedience, and practicing the works of mercy; and that the Sovereign Pontiff raised them to a religious body.[13] Thus, besides the secular Third Order, there is now a religious one, of both sexes, which Pope Leo X confirmed and extended by his Bull, dated 28th of January, 1521, in which he abridged the rule and adapted it to the observances of the religious state. St. Elizabeth of Hungary, being a widow, joined the three vows of religion to the profession of the Third Order of St. Francis, three years after the death of the blessed Patriarch, which makes her to be justly considered as the mother of the religious of both sexes of the Third Order, since she was the first Tertiary who took these solemn vows.[14]

---

[10] Father Helyot inserts the document of her profession, which bears her own signature, the original of which is preserved in the Nazareth Convent at Paris, to which that princess sent it. "Hist, des Ord. Relig.," tom. 7, c. 29, p. 224.

[11] Father Frassen notices in his "Explication de la Régle," p. 297 et seq., and p. 31 of the edition of 1684, that Queen Maria Teresa made her profession of the Third Order in the great convent of the Observance at Paris; that she contributed by her royal munificence to the building of the beautiful chapel where the assemblies of the Order are held; that she laid the first stone, and that, at the earnest entreaties of this pious queen, Pope Clement IX granted by his Bull, dated July 1st, 1669, a plenary indulgence in perpetuity in this chapel for the feast of St. Elizabeth, who is the Patron.

[12] Many religious companies, as Father Helyot observes, have had for their founders persons who belonged to the Third Order of St. Francis. Cardinal, de Berulle, who founded the Congregation of the Priests of the Oratory, and M. Olier, who founded the Seminaries of St. Sulpice, were both of the Third Order. Father Frassen says that Olier, who was a man of most exemplary life, entered it with such fervor, that his example drew many others into it; that he induced the ecclesiastics of his seminary and the parishioners of St. Sulpice to become children of St. Francis, becoming, as he himself was, brothers of Penance; and that they caused a revival of the congregation of the Third Order in the convent of the Observantines.

[13] With respect to the time of this establishment, we have nothing more correct than what Helyot says, ch. 30.

[14] Some have called in question St. Elizabeth's having been of the Third Order, and really a religious; but as to the former, we must believe St. Bonaventure, who speaks positively on the subject, and assures us that he had it from the saint's confessor. —Serm. de S, Eliz. tom, 5, Oper. And, as to the latter, Pope Gregory IX, who had been in communication with this Princess, notices in the Bull of her canonization, that she took the religious habit, and submitted herself to the yoke of obedience; which proves that he considered her vows as solemn ones, made under the authority of the Holy

Lucchesio and his wife, who were the first Tertiaries whom St. Francis received, acquired by the exercise of prayer and good works, a holiness which God honored by many miracles during their life and after their death; but the wife was sanctified by the husband. Although she had embraced, after his example, the state of piety, she continued to disapprove the great donations of alms which he made, and to prevent them as much as was in her power, in consequence of that spirit of avarice and self-interest, which constantly induces such tempers to fear that they shall come to want.

One day, Lucchesio having given all the bread that was in his house to the poor, he begged his wife to give something to others who followed. She flew into a passion, like the wife of Tobias;[15] and having reproached him with the care he took of strangers to the prejudice of those of his own household, she said that it was quite plain that his fasts and watchings had disordered his brain. The husband, as patient as he was charitable, was not irritated by these reproaches, but quietly requested his wife to look into the place where the bread was kept, thinking of Him, who by His power had satiated several thousand persons with a few loaves and fishes.[16] She did so, and found a large quantity of fresh bread, sufficient to supply the wants of all the poor. This miracle had such an effect upon her, that from that time forward, he had no occasion to exhort her to the performance of works of mercy; both husband and wife gave themselves up to them with emulation, and devoted themselves to them until their deaths. The husband's charity shows us that almsgiving does not impoverish; but that, on the contrary, God increases, even sometimes by miracles, the property of such as give liberally; and the conversion of Lucchesio's wife shows that the spirit of interest and avarice, covered by pretense of economy, renders piety false and deceitful.

After having established his Third Order, Francis preached in several parts of Tuscany, and received an establishment at Columbario, in a very solitary situation, which was the more agreeable to him from the great attraction he had for contemplation. He had it erected under the title of the Annunciation of the Blessed Virgin, in honor of her divine maternity; he then returned to St. Mary of the Angels.

An abbess was requested from the monastery of St. Damian for that of Moncel, of the same institute, which was forming at Florence; he consulted thereon the cardinal protector, and by his advice he selected Agnes, the sister of Clare. Agnes, out of obedience, set out willingly; she found a very fervent, very united, and very submissive community, and the Sovereign Pontiff granted all that she required for their spiritual wants. But Agnes was seriously

---

See, although she had not made the vow of enclosure, and that she went out for the practice of good works. There are many writers who speak of her as a religious. See "Hist, des Ordres Religieux", tom. 7, eh. 38, p. 294.

[15] Tob. 2: 22.

[16] Math. 14: 15; Mark 8: 6

grieved to have to part from Clare, and to satisfy her heart, she wrote to her a most affectionate letter, full of the most tender sentiments, in which we see that the feelings of nature are elevated and sanctified by virtue, instead of being weakened.

At that time, about the month of October, Francis obtained the famous indulgence of St. Mary of the Angels, or of Portiuncula, of which we shall here relate the circumstances.

The great lights and inspirations which this holy man received in prayer, discovered to him the wretched state of sinners; he deplored their blindness, and was moved to compassion, and he often prayed for them. One night, when he was soliciting their conversion from God with great fervor, he was directed by an angel to go to the church, where he would find Jesus Christ and his Blessed Mother, accompanied by a host of celestial spirits. Greatly rejoiced, he went and prostrated himself to render due homage to the Majesty of the Son of God. Our Savior said to him, "Francis, the zeal which you and your followers have for the salvation of souls is such, that it entitles you to solicit something in their favor, for the glory of my name." In the midst of the marvels which enraptured him, he made the following prayer: "Our most holy Father! I entreat You, although I am but a miserable sinner, to have the goodness to grant to men, that all those who shall visit this church may receive a plenary indulgence of all their sins, after having confessed them to a priest; and I beg the Blessed Virgin, Your Mother, the general advocate of humankind, to intercede that I may obtain this my request." The Blessed Virgin did intercede, and Jesus Christ spoke the following words: "Francis, what you ask is great, but you will receive still greater favors; I grant you this one; I desire you, nevertheless, to go to my vicar, to whom I have given power to bind and to loose, and to solicit him for the same indulgence." The companions of the Saint who were in their respective cells, heard all these things; they saw a great light which filled the church, and the multitude of angels; but a respectful fear prevented them from approaching.

In the early morning, Francis assembled them, and forbade their speaking of this miraculous event, and then set out with Massé of Marignan for Perugia, where Pope Honorius then was.

When he came into his presence, he said to him: "Most Holy Father, some years ago I repaired a small church[17] in your dominions; I beg you to grant to it a free indulgence, without any obligation of making an offering." The Pope replied, that the request could not reasonably be granted, because it was but just that he who wished to gain an indulgence should render himself deserving

---

[17] He expresses himself to this effect, because the church of St. Mary of the Angels was near Assisi, and that the Duchy of Spoleto, of which Assisi is a part, was, as it still is, in the Ecclesiastical States.

of it by some means, particularly by some work of charity.[18] "But," added he, "for how many years do you ask me for this indulgence?" "Most Holy Father," replied Francis, "may it please your Holiness, not to give me so many years but so many souls." "And in what way do you desire to have souls?" rejoined the Pope. "I wish," added Francis, "that it may be the good pleasure of Your Holiness, that those persons who enter the church of St. Mary of the Angels, are contrite, shall have confessed their sins, and have properly received absolution, may receive an entire remission of their sins,[19] as well in this world as in the next, from their baptism, to the time of their so entering the church." The Pope then said to him, "Francis, what you solicit is a thing of great importance. The Roman court has not been accustomed to grant any similar indulgence." "Most Holy Father," returned Francis, "I ask not this for myself, it is Jesus Christ who sent me; I come from Him." Upon which, the Pope said publicly three times: "It is my desire that it be granted to you."

The Cardinals who were present, represented to him, that in granting so important an indulgence, he was subverting the throne of the holy law, and that of the sepulcher of the holy apostles. "The concession is made," replied the Pope, "nor is it right it should be revoked; but let us modify it." And recalling Francis, he said to him; "We grant you this indulgence which you have solicited. It is for all years in perpetuity[20]; but only during one natural day, from one evening including the night, to the evening of the following day." At these words Francis humbly bowed down his head. As he went away, the Pope asked him: "Whither are you going, simple man? What certitude do you have of what you have just been granted?" "Holy Father," he replied, "your word is sufficient for me. If this indulgence is the work of God, He will make it manifest. Let Jesus Christ and His Blessed Mother, and the angels, be the notary, on this occasion, the paper, and the witnesses. I require no other authenticated document." This was the effect of the great confidence he had in the truth of the apparition.

He left Perugia to return to St. Mary of the Angels, and midway he stopped at a village named Colle, at a leper hospital, where he rested awhile. On awaking, he had recourse to prayer; then he called Massé, and said to him with great exultation: "I can assure you that the indulgence which has been granted

---

[18] Michael de Medina, an excellent theologian, who assisted at the Council of Trent, says that, in those times, no indulgence was granted without an obligation of giving alms towards gaining it; that these alms were employed to defray the expenses of the wars in the Holy Land, in repairs of churches, most of which were in a ruinous state, particularly in Italy: and that, as to these last, they were called manus adjutrices. De Indulg. cap. ult; Edit. Venet. 1563.

[19] That is, of the punishment due to their sins; for the guilt of sin is remitted by the sacrament, and not by the indulgence. St. Francis expresses himself here as the Popes do in their Bulls: "We grant a plenary indulgence and full remission of all their sins to sill the faithful who," etc.

[20] In 1967 Pope Paul VI revised the indulgences and removed many long standing concessions unless they were re-applied for. The Franciscans, however, applied again for the Portiuncula indulgence and it was granted by the same Pope in 1974. —Editor's note.

to me by the Sovereign Pontiff is confirmed in heaven." The day had not been fixed; it was not so, until the beginning of the year 1223, with other marvelous circumstances which will be hereafter related.

Clare wished to see once more the Church of St. Mary of the Angels in which she had renounced the world, and to take another meal with Francis, her spiritual Father. He refused her his leave for some time; but his companions having represented to him that he treated a virgin whom he himself had consecrated to Jesus Christ, with too much harshness, he consented to what she wished.[21] An appropriate day was fixed on, and she came to the convent of Portiuncula, accompanied by some of her nuns, and some Friars Minor who went on purpose to the convent of St. Damian.

After having prayed fervently in the church, and visited[22] the convent, the Friars and the nuns seated themselves round the refection which Francis had had laid out on the ground, in pursuance of his usual practice of humility, which was his daily observance, whenever it was in his power. The first nourishment they took was for the soul. The holy Patriarch spoke of God, but in so moving a manner, and with so much unction and animation, that all who heard him were thrown into ecstasy, as he was himself. At the same time, the convent, the church, and the woods seemed to the inhabitants of Assisi and environs, to be on fire. Many ran thither to afford their aid; but finding everything in good order, they entered the convent, where they saw, with still greater surprise, the whole assembly in a state of ecstasy. By that they were made aware that what had seemed to them to be a fire, was the type of the fire which inflamed these holy bosoms, and they returned greatly edified.

By this marvel, the Lord clearly showed that He approved the request, which Clare had made, to be allowed to come to the Portiuncula; as by another marvel He approved of the prayer which St. Scholastica made to detain her brother, St. Benedict, whom she wished to hear speak of the happiness of the future life, in the place in which they had just dined together.[23] Such was the condescension of His goodness for the consolation of these two saints, and it is thus that, according to the words of the prophet, "He fulfills the wishes of those who fear Him."[24]

---

[21] The first positive law which there is in the Church, obliging nuns to enclosure, is grounded on the Constitution of Pope Boniface VIII, cap. Periculor, de Stat. Regul. in 6, which was renewed by the Council of Trent, Sess. 25, de Regul. cap. 5. Thus Clare and her companions might legally go out of the monastery; besides which, they had the leave of their superior. The Council even permits nuns to leave their convent for any legitimate cause approved by the bishop.

[22] Although it has been strictly ruled not to permit females to enter into convents of religious men, yet the Holy See has nevertheless not hesitated to give such leave in special cases; these leaves have been recalled by Pope St. Pius V, and by Pope Gregory XIII, Const. 28, forbidding their entry under the severest penalties. It is not to be doubted that St. Francis, the Founder and General of his Order, was empowered by Pope Honorius III to allow the entry into his convents at his discretion.

[23] St. Gregor. Dialog. Lib. 2, cap. 33.

[24] Psalm 144: 19

The repast finished without any one having chosen to eat anything, so much were they filled with celestial nourishment, and Clare returned to the monastery of St. Damian. There, her sisterhood received her with so much the more satisfaction, as they had been fearful that they would have given her the direction of some new establishment, seeing that they had, a short time before, sent her sister Agnes to Florence as abbess. They knew that Francis had said to her on other occasions: "Be prepared to go wherever it may be necessary;" and that she had obediently answered, "My father, I am ready to go whithersoever you may send me." Her having gone out seemed to them a preparation for some longer journey, and their grief for having lost Agnes, their dear companion, increased the fears they had, lest they should lose Clare also, who was in their regard a most excellent mistress of spiritual life. But they had not, thereafter, any similar alarms; this was the only time in forty-two years that their holy mother left the enclosure.

CHAPTER II

THE DEVIL CONFOUNDED WITHIN AND WITHOUT

He cannot bear the distinction of persons which Brother Elias made—Makes a terrible prediction—He gives his blessings to seven of his brethren, to go and preach the faith to the Moors, and they are martyred—He makes a journey, which is attended with remarkable circumstances—Cures a cripple—Mixes with the poor, and eats with them—Foretells of an infant, that he would one day be Pope—He changes the bed of thorns into which St. Benedict had thrown himself, into a rose-bush, and performs other great miracles—Goes to honor the relics of St. Andrew, and those of St. Nicholas—He stands upon red-hot coals to confound a bad woman—Discovers a trick of the devil—He visits Mount Garganus—His presence silences a demoniac—He learns at St. Mary of the Angels the success of the German mission.

LIAS, THE VICAR GENERAL, gave Francis great uneasiness, by his erroneous views. Many of the Friars Minor came to see their Patriarch, who received them with every mark of kindness. The vicar made great distinction between them. He was very particular in honoring those whom science and dignities rendered considerable in the Order; he never failed giving them the first places, and he took care to satisfy all they needed; while he left the others in the lowest places, and often without attending to their necessary wants. In his station he did what the apostle St. James forbids all Christians to do, whether to rich, or to poor; he made a distinction of persons.[1]

Their common Father, who could not endure that so great a difference should be made, particularly amongst persons of the same Institute, affected, one day, at table, after grace had been said, to call two of the most simple of the brethren, and to place one on each side of him, without showing any attention to the merits of others. He did this, not because he disapproved of peculiar consideration being shown to those to whom it is due, according to the maxim of St. Paul,[2] in consequence of their character, their dignity, or their personal qualifications, but because he did not choose that these considerations should be to the disadvantage of those who had not similar circumstances to recommend them, and to whom, according to the same apostle, besides the feelings of charity to which they and all others are entitled,

---

[1] James 2: 1.
[2] Rom. 12: 10, and 13: 7.

a certain degree of honor should be shown.

The vicar general, who was not impressed with a similar way of thinking, was highly indignant at this act of the Saint, and murmuring to himself, he said, "Ah! Brother Francis, it is quite certain that your extreme simplicity will be the ruin of the Order. You place alongside of you, men who have neither learning nor talents, and you affront those who are the support of the Order by their science." Francis, who by a supernatural revelation, was made aware of what his vicar had passing in his mind, replied immediately to his thought. "And you, brother Elias, you do much greater injury to the Order by your vanity, and by the prudence of the flesh, with which you are filled. The judgments of God are impenetrable; He knows you as you are, and, nevertheless. He chose that you should be superior of the Order; and it is His desire that I leave it in your hands. Alas I fear that the people, and he who governs them, resemble each other, and that God has only given a pastor, such as He foresees the flock will be." The holy Patriarch well knew that the whole of the flock would not be corrupted by Brother Elias, and that the majority of the members would resist him, as it came to pass. And thus the fear which he experienced in general terms, was a warning to keep them all to their duty. But what he added was a true prophecy: "Unhappy man, as you are, you will not die in this Order; God has so decreed. You have been weighed in the balances, and have been wanting,[3] because you are puffed up with the science of the world."

The following is the way in which this matter is related in the ancient legend which is followed by St. Antoninus.[4] Francis, knowing by a revelation that Brother Elias would die out of the Order, and would be damned, avoided conversing with him, and even seeing him. Elias noticed this, and did not rest till he discovered the reason. Terrified and dismayed at such a prophecy, he threw himself at the feet of his kind master, and entreated him to intercede with God to prevent one of the flock committed to his care, from perishing eternally. "Let not the sentence which has been revealed to you, discourage you; for the Lord[5] may change His decree, if the sinner corrects his sin. I have such confidence in your prayers, my very dear Father, that I should think they would mitigate[6] my sufferings even if I were in hell, as you have been told I

---

[3] Dan. 5: 27

[4] St. Anton. Chron. part. 3, tit. 24, c. 9, § 3, Wading, ad ann. 1253.

[5] "Novit Deus mutare sententiam, si tu noveris emendare delictum." St. Ambros. in Luc. lib. 2, n. 33, De Poenit. Dist. 1, Cap. Novit Dominus.

[6] The common opinion of Catholics is, that the sufferings of the damned are never mitigated, although some of the most illustrious of the holy Fathers, who admit that they are eternal, sis faith teaches, have nevertheless thought that prayers, alms deeds, and the Sacrifice of the Mass might afford them some mitigation. Father Petau, who quotes these with precision, remarks that the Church never prays for the damned, and that she would do so, if she thought it could procure them any relief. Theol. Dog. tom. 5, De Angel.

shall be. Pray for me, my Father; pray, and I have no doubt but that God will modify His decree, and that I shall be converted." Francis prayed, and obtained from God that Brother Elias should not be damned, but he could not obtain the reversal of the decree which said that he should not die in the Order. It was, in fact, out of the Order that he died; but, previous to his death, he gave great signs of contrition, as will be seen further on.

Wading makes on this a judicious remark, worthy of a sound theologian. He says that Brother Elias, who was universally admitted to be a learned man, was not ignorant that the decrees of God which are absolute, are immutable, because He himself is incapable of change; but he also knew that the Lord sometimes expressed Himself in absolute words against sinners, which decrees are merely threats, which may be changed by their repentance, without His changing, according to what He has said by the prophet Jeremiah: "I will suddenly speak against a nation, and against a kingdom, to root out, and to pull down, and to destroy it.[7] If that nation against which I have spoken shall repent of their evil, I also will repent of the evil that I thought to do them." Jonas sent from God, had positively announced that in forty days Nineveh should be destroyed, and nevertheless the penitence of the Ninevites hindered the destruction of their city.[8] St. Gregory[9] says, that in this sense God changed His decrees, but did not change His design; and St. Thomas says,[10] that God proposes the change of certain things, but that in His will no change takes place. Sinners, however, must not abuse this doctrine, and imagine that God only threatens them, and that He will not damn them, for He has an absolute will to damn eternally those who die in mortal sin, as well as to crown with immortal glory such as die in a state of grace. In truth, it is His wish that sinners should be converted, and He places the means in their power by His mercy; "But," says St. Augustine, "He has not promised a tomorrow to your delay; "and as the apostle has it: "According to your hardness and impenitent heart you treasure up to yourself wrath against the day of wrath, and revelation of the just judgment of God, who will render to every man according to his works."[11]

The example of the holy Patriarch, who had sought three times the crown of martyrdom, and the triumph of the five brethren martyred at Morocco, had inspired many with an ardent desire to die for Jesus Christ. Shortly after Elias had been restored as vicar general, Daniel, minister in the province of Calabria, asked leave to go and preach the faith to the Moors, with six other brethren, whose names were Samuel, Donule or Daniel, Leo, Hugolin, Nicholas, and

---

[7] Jerem. 18: 7 et 8.

[8] Jonah, 3: 4, 9 & 10.

[9] St. Greg. Moral, lib. XVI.

[10] Id. Part quaest. 19, art. 7.

[11] St. Aug. in Psalm cxliv, n. 11; Rom. ii, 5, and 6.

Angelus. Having received the permission of the vicar general, and the blessing of Francis, they embarked in a port of Tuscany, from whence they sailed to Tarragona. Their first intention was to have gone to Morocco, to mingle their blood with that of their martyred brethren, but some reasons, probably favorable to their intention, induced them to go to Ceuta.

Daniel arrived first with three of his companions, the master of the vessel not having thought proper to take on board more. They lived out of the town, in a village inhabited by traders from Pisa, Genoa, and Marseilles, because Christians might not enter the town without a particular permission. Their occupation here was to preach to these traders, until they should be joined by their companions, who arrived there on the 29th of September.

The following Friday, which was the first of October, they consulted together as to their future plans, and the aids they should require in the formidable combat they were about to sustain. On the Saturday, they confessed and received the Holy Communion, without which, when it is possible to receive it, St. Cyprian[12] would not suffer confessors to be exposed to martyrdom for the faith, because it is the Body and the Blood of Jesus Christ which gives the strength to endure it. St. Chrysostom and St. Bernard,[13] also, say that it is the firmest defense which can be opposed to the temptations of the devil, and to the allurements of sin, which are powerful motives for having recourse to frequent communion.

The seven brothers went forth from the holy table, according to the expression of St. Chrysostom,[14] "as roaring lions, breathing fire and flames," and they could not restrain the zeal which animated them. On the evening of the same day, they washed each other's feet, in order to follow the example of the Son of God, who washed His disciples' feet before His Passion; and very early on the Sunday morning, before there were any persons in the streets, they entered the town, having their heads strewed with ashes, and commenced crying out with a loud voice, "There is no salvation but through Jesus Christ."[15]

The Moors soon collected, abused and beat them, and led them to the king. The missionaries then repeated, in presence of the learned in the law, what they had previously said to the people, "That it was requisite to believe in Jesus Christ; that there was no salvation in any other name than His," which they proved by the most forcible arguments. The king, who fully understood that in thus upholding the name of Jesus Christ they rejected that of Mahomet, looked upon them as idiots, and thought that their shaven heads, with a crown of hair round them, was a proof of their folly. However, to prove their constancy, he had them confined in a loathsome jail, where he kept them eight

---

[12] St. Cyprian. Epist. 54.

[13] St. Chrysost., Hom. 45 in Joan, and 24 in 1, ad Cor; St. Bernard, in Cena Dei.

[14] Ibid.

[15] Acts, 4: 12.

days in irons, and where they were cruelly treated.

Their confinement did not prevent their finding means to write to the Christians who were in the vicinity of Ceuta. Their letter was addressed to Hugh, Cure of the Genoese, and to two religious, one of their own Order, and the other of the Order of Friars Preachers, who had just returned from the farthest part of Mauritania. They blessed, in the first instance, the Father of Mercies, who consoled them in their tribulation; and, after having quoted several passages from the Scriptures to justify their mission and to animate themselves to suffering, they assured their brethren that they had borne witness, and strongly argued in presence of the king, "that there is no salvation but in the name of Jesus Christ;" and they concluded by referring to God the glory of all that they had done.

The judge, whose name was Arbold, wishing to see what they did in prison, saw that they were no longer chained, that their faces shone with a splendid light, and that they sang the praises of God with extraordinary joy. The king, having been apprised of this, caused them to be brought before him on Sunday, the tenth of October, and offered them great wealth if they would become Muslims. They boldly replied, that they utterly despised all the things of this world and of the present life, in consequence of the happiness of the future life. They were then separated, and each was separately tempted, by promises and threats, but they were all found steadfast in their resolution. Daniel, speaking with great energy, one of the Moors cut him across the head with his scimitar, from which he did not even wince, and another exhorted him to embrace the law of Mahomet, to save his life with honor. "Wretch!" exclaimed Daniel, "your Mahomet and all his followers are but ministers of Satan, and your Koran is but a series of lies; be no longer misled, but embrace the Christian faith."

As soon as the seven brothers were collected together, six of them threw themselves at Daniel's feet, who had procured this mission for them, and who was their leader, and said to him with tears of joy: "We give thanks to God and to you, our father, for having procured for us the crown of martyrdom; our souls will follow yours; bless us and die; the struggle will be soon over, and we shall enjoy eternal peace."

Daniel tenderly embraced them, gave them his blessing, and encouraged them by these words: "Let us rejoice in the Lord; this is for us a festival day; angels surround us, the heavens are opened to receive us; this day we shall receive the crown of martyrdom, which will last forever."

In fact, the king, seeing that they were resolute, and not to be shaken, condemned them to be beheaded. They were stripped, had their hands tied behind them, and were taken to the place of execution, whither they went as to a banquet, preceded by a herald, who proclaimed the cause of their death, and where, after having recommended their souls to God, they were decapitated, on the tenth of October,[16] in the year 1221.[17]

Children, and other infidels broke their skulls to pieces, and mutilated the remains of the holy martyrs; but these precious relics were gathered up by the Christians, and removed into the storehouse of the Marseillese, and were afterwards buried in their dwellings beyond the walls of Ceuta. It is asserted that some years afterwards they were transferred to the church of St. Mary, near Morocco, and that God manifested them by miracles, and particularly by a splendid light, which even the Moors saw during the night; and that some time afterwards an Infant of Portugal, having obtained them from a king of Morocco, had them removed into Spain, where fresh miracles rendered them celebrated. Whatever truth there may be in the account of these translations, it is not known now where the relics of these seven martyrs are. What is certain is, that the faithful had their memory in great veneration, and that in 1516, the Friars Minor solicited leave from Pope Leo X, to recite an office in their honor, which leave he most willingly granted to them, placing them in the number of martyrs recognized by the Church, as they are commemorated in the Roman Martyrology on the 13th of October.[18]

We may imagine the satisfaction their triumph gave to Francis, from the ardent desire he always evinced for the crown of martyrdom, and the tender love he bore for his children. He had, moreover, in this year another great consolation on this subject. Pope Honorius sent to almost all the bishops of Europe, desiring them to send him four men from each province, or at least two, noted for their science and the integrity of their lives, whom it was his intention to commission to preach to the idolaters, and to the Saracens, for

---

[16] It was, according to some, on the 9th, and according to others, on the 8th of October. See Wading, ad ann. 1221, and the Franciscan Martyrology, 13 October.

[17] Wading maintains, upon good grounds, that they were martyred in 1221, in the lifetime of St. Francis. He proves this from an ancient manuscript, entitled "Vinea Sancti Francisci," from which Surius has taken their acts; by the ancient Breviary of the church of Braga, in Portugal; by the ancient Breviary of the Order of Friars Minor; by Maland, in his additions to the Martyrology of Usuard, and by Cardinal Baronius in his notes on the Roman Martyrology. Saint Antoninus is the first who has said that Brother Elias gave them leave to go and preach to the infidels the year after the death of St. Francis, which was in the year 1227. He has been followed by some, but his testimony is not supported by any proof, and must not be preferred to the authority of a manuscript and two breviaries to which it is posterior. Thus it should not have been put in the Breviary of the Order of St. Francis, printed at Paris, at the first Lesson of the second Nocturn of the feast of these holy martyrs, "anno ducentesimo vigesimo septimo," and more particularly because the terms of the ancient breviary have been preserved in it. "Fratre Elia generali minisitro, Patrisque Francisci tunc agente vices," which shows that Elias was Francis' vicar, and, consequently, that the Patriarch was still alive; if Elias is called general minister, it is because he performed the functions of that office, and that the holy man gave him that title. The breviary then must be corrected in this particular, and "anno ducentesimo vigesimo primo" placed in lieu of the former date. We have since seen a breviary, printed at Rome, in which the same date is mentioned as in the Paris edition. It should be seen whether the editors have stronger arguments for it than those of Wading.

[18] Their feast has been Iransfcrred to 13th October, on account of the Octave of St. Francis. Martyrol. of the Franciscans. Nota, ad diem 13th October.

whose conversion he was most anxious, and amongst the number thus selected there were many Friars Minors, and Friars Preachers who generously exposed themselves to every sort of peril for the salvation of souls.

The intimate union which the love of God had formed between St. Dominic and St. Francis, induces us to notice here, that the Blessed Patriarch[19] of the Dominicans died this year, on the sixth day of August, at the age of fifty-one years.[20] The eminent sanctity of his life, the great miracles he performed, particularly in raising three dead persons to life, and principally Napoleon, the nephew of Cardinal Stephen de Fossanuova, which was so extraordinary; the ardor and splendor of his zeal for the destruction of heresy, his inviolable attachment to the holy See, his tender piety to the Blessed Virgin, whom he causes to be generally and daily honored in the devotion of the Rosary, and the establishment of his Order, so useful by its science, by its piety, and by the great services it had rendered to the Church, which must make it revered by all the faithful, cause him to be illustrious through the entire Church; and among the Friars Minor, there is not one who, if animated by the spirit of St. Francis, must not have a special devotion for St. Dominic, and a respectful affection for those of his Order.[21]

Charity, which inflamed the breast of Francis, soon drew him from his retreat. He set out on the beginning of the year 1222, for the Terra di Lavoro, Apulia and Calabria, and, in the course of this journey, God worked many splendid miracles by his hand.

Passing, first, through the town of Toscanella, on the road to Rome, he received hospitality from a knight, whose only son was lame in both legs, and was in a state of suffering through his whole body. The afflicted father asked him to procure the cure of his son from God; he abstained from doing this for some time out of humility, esteeming himself unworthy of being heard for

---

[19] Wading found his portrait drawn in the following terms in the "Legend of St. Francis," composed by order of Pope Gregory IX, and in another of the same date: "He was of a middle size, slender and well proportioned. His face was handsome, and countenance pleasing; his voice was sonorous, and his hands long; his hair, which adorned his whole head, was of a light color, rather reddish, as was his beard. From his countenance and from his eyes, there were flashes which were imposing, and called forth respect. A religious joy was observable in his looks, unless the compassion he felt for the miserable made him appear sorrowful." The same author adds, that the holiness of St. Dominic, his astonishing eloquence, and something majestic in his countenance, added to a virginal modesty, gained him the affection of the Spaniards, his countrymen, of the French, and Italians, and of persons of every other nation, so that he acquired an ascendency over their minds, and turned them as he pleased. —Wading, ad ann. 1221, n. 48.

[20] His feast was fixed by Pope Paul IV, for the 4th of August because the 5th and 6th ware already filled by other festivals.

[21] There must be no exception on this head; unless it was grounded on a letter of the Rev. Father A. Cloche, general of the Order, dated Rome, Feb. 26th, 1717, on the deliberation of the Provincial Chapter of Lower Germany, held at Louvain, May 3d, 1719, and on the approbation given to a book printed at Paris, in 1727, entitled "La Solide Devotion du Rosaire." See the "Memoires du Trevoux," Sept. 1727. Nouvelles Litteraires, article d'Espagne.

others, but being prevailed upon by reiterated entreaties, he placed his hands upon him, and made the sign of the cross upon the boy, who, at the same moment, stood upright and firm on his legs, and was entirely cured, to the great astonishment of his whole family.

At Rome, he made acquaintance, and became intimate with a nobleman, named Mathew de Rubeis, of the illustrious family of the Orsini. One day, on which he had been invited to dinner there, and having got there at the appointed hour, not finding his host yet returned from town, he joined, unperceived, the poor to whom they were giving a meal, and he received the alms with them. The nobleman arrived shortly after, and inquired where Brother Francis was, and as they did not find him, he declared he would not eat his dinner, if he did not come. While they were looking for him, he saw him seated in the yard with a group of poor. He went to him, and said: "Brother Francis, since you won't dine with me, I am come to dine with you;" which he did, placing himself on the ground near him, and in the group, where he found himself very comfortable in that company. When he heard that the holy man had established a Third Order for secular persons of all ranks, he prayed for admission into it, and had himself instructed in the practices to be observed. The consideration which his rank in life gave him in the world, threw great splendor on the new institution, and drew many persons to it.

There was a little child called John whom he requested Francis to bless; the servant of God gave him his blessing; he took him in his arms and foretold his father that he would bring great glory to his house, for that he would be Sovereign Pontiff. Then, fixing his eyes upon the child, he spoke to him as if he had had the use of reason; he entreated him seriously, and in most affectionate terms, to be favorable to his Order; after which the prophet continued as follows: "He will not be a Religious of our Order, but he will be its protector; he will not be reckoned among its children, but he will be acknowledged as its father; and our brethren will be delighted at seeing themselves under his shadow. I consider the immense benefits we shall receive from this child, I see them already in his little hands." Such a prediction caused as much pleasure as surprise to the lord of the family of the Orsini, but he never spoke of it till he saw its fulfillment, which happened fifty-five years afterwards. His son, cardinal, under the title of St. Nicholas, was chosen Pope in the year 1277, and took the name of Nicholas III. His singular benevolence for the Order of the Friars Minor showed that its holy Founder had not spoken in vain to him in his infancy.

From Rome Francis went to visit the grotto of St. Benedict. He considered with great attention the bush covered with thorns, into which the great Patriarch of the monastic life had the courage to throw himself, in order to overcome a temptation of the flesh.[22] In admiration of such extraordinary

---

[22] St. Greg. Dial. lib. ii., cap. 2.

fervor, he touched this bush as a sacred relic; he kissed it, and made on it the sign of the cross. God, in order to honor his two servants,[23] changed it immediately into a beautiful rose-tree, the flowers of which have served in many cases for the cure of the sick; the place has since been held in greater respect. In a chapel which is near it, and which was consecrated by Gregory IX, we see that Pope, with Francis on his left hand, who holds a scroll of paper, on which these words, taken from the Gospel of St. Luke, are written, "Peace be to this house,"[24] words which he constantly used as a salutation.

The remainder of his journey was remarkable for many other wonders which were worked through his means, in announcing the word of God. While preaching at Gaeta,[25] on the border of the sea, seeing that a crowd of people were anxious, from a devotional feeling, to touch him, he threw himself into a boat to avoid these demonstrations of respect, which were disagreeable to him. The boat, which had no sailors in it, floated to a certain distance out to sea, and then became stationary; from thence he gave instruction to those who were on the shore, and the crowd dispersing after having received his blessing, the boat returned of itself to its former place. St. Bonaventure exclaims on this: "Who, after this, will have a heart so hardened and so irreligious as to despise the preaching of Francis, to which inanimate things lent their aid, as if they had reasoning faculties?"

The inhabitants of Gaeta, admiring the power which God gave to His servant, entreated him to stay some time in their town, and to permit them to build there a convent for his Order. He assented to this, and the work was commenced forthwith. While the church was in progress, a carpenter was crushed by the falling of a beam. As the other workmen were carrying him home, Francis, who was returning from the country, met them, and directed them to lay the dead man on the ground; he then made the sign of the cross on him, took him by the hand, called him by his name, and commanded him to arise. The dead man rose immediately and went back to his work. This is well-known in the country by successive tradition, and a small chapel has been erected, under due authority, on the spot where the miracle was performed, in

---

[23] This is what a poet has expressed in the following verses:
"Virgineum sepit florem Benedictus acutis
Vepribus, et proprii rore cruoris alit.
Hinc dumeta novas tanto fcecunda liquore,
Franciscique manu culta tulere rosas.
Falsa quidem roseo cecinere e germine Vates
Sed latuit falso carmine vera fides.
Scire cupis rosei flos exeat unde pudoris?
Sola rosas potuit gignere puncta Venus."
See Wading, ad ann. 1222, n. 5.

[24] Luke 10: 5.

[25] Or Gaiete, a town in the Terra di Lavoro, in the kingdom of Naples, so called, according to Virgil, from the nurse of Æneas., who died there. -Æneid VII.

order to perpetuate the memory thereof.

The earliest authors of the life of our Saint record a very singular miracle which he performed on his route, in the house of a gentleman. All the inhabitants of the place were gone to the great square to hear him preach. A female servant who had been left in a house to take care of a child, wishing to hear the sermon, left the child alone. On her return, she found the child dead, and half-boiled in a copper of hot water, into which it had fallen. She took it out, and in order to hide the disaster from the father and mother, she shut it up in a trunk; the parents, however, learnt their misfortune, which was the more afflicting as this was their only child. The husband entreated his wife not to let her distress appear, out of respect for the servant of God, who was to dine with them. During dinner, Francis endeavored to inspire them with a holy joy, knowing what the Almighty had in store for their consolation, and at the end of the dinner he feigned to wish to eat some apples. They expressed their regret that they had none to offer him; but pointing to the trunk in which the child was shut up, he said: "Let them look there, and some will be found." It was in vain that they assured him that there were none there; he insisted on having the trunk opened. The gentleman, to oblige him, and with a view of hiding the object of their grief, opened the trunk, when, judge of his astonishment on finding his child alive and well, and, with a smiling countenance, holding an apple in each hand. Transported with joy, he carried the child and placed it in the arms of the holy man.

The people of Capua were so moved by his preaching, and by the miracles he performed, particularly on his having saved from the waters a woman whom the river Volturnus had carried off, that the town made him the offer of a convent. St. Anastasius, Bishop of Civitá di Penna, gave him another, with great marks of regard, after having gone out to meet him, on an inspiration he had in his sleep that Francis would come the next day to his town, a circumstance which is recorded by a painting in the church, and is explained in two Latin verses.[26]

The servant of God having preached during the entire day at Montella, went to pass the night in a wood in the vicinity of that town, where he seated himself with his companion under an evergreen oak.[27] Some persons who passed by, in the morning, perceived that there was no snow where the two Religious sat, although there had been a heavy fall in the night, and they related the circumstance to the lord of Montella, who sent for Francis, and

---

[26] Cœlitus admonitus, Praesul Permensis it ultro:
Complexusque Patrem, dat quoque sponte locum.

[27] Marianus of Florence, quoted by Wading, ad ann. 1222, n. 14, says that, in his time, two hundred years after St. Francis, this ever-green oak was still alive, and that a Religious having cut it, because it impeded the view of the town, he fell immediately ill, and died in a few days, in great suffering. This shows that it is God's will that even the smallest memorials of the marvels He works in honor of His saints, shall be respected.

entreated him to remain in that country, or, to leave some of his companions amongst them, for the instruction of the people. He left two, for whom they built a house on the very spot where heaven had been so favorable to him, and the wood was sanctified hereby, which had previously been the resort of robbers.

The force which God gave to his discourses, and the miracles of which He made him the instrument, converted sinners, and animated the piety of the good. Both the one and the other were anxious to retain him amongst them, or, at least, to have some of his religious. In this journey alone, he founded more than twenty houses, among which was one at Amalfi,[28] whither his devotion had led him to honor the relics of the apostle St. Andrew.[29] The inhabitants of Acropoli, who at first had been deaf to his instruction, were penetrated with contrition, and gave him a convent, after having been reproached with the hardness of their hearts by a multitude of fish, that God caused to collect round a rock from which Francis preached those truths which this people had refused to listen to.

The Emperor Frederic II was, at that time, with his court at Bari.[30] The servant of God went there, no doubt, to venerate the relics of the great bishop St. Nicholas;[31] he preached in the town, and, as his discourses were always made suitable to the wants of his auditors, he spoke energetically on the dangers of the court, and particularly against impurity. Some courtiers who heard him, reported the circumstance to the emperor, who remarked that it often happened that those who did these things in private, were the most violent in exclaiming against others in public; that it was not known whether this preacher was one of that sort, but, in order to ascertain it, he should be invited to supper, and a female should be secretly introduced into his bedroom; this was accordingly done, and the Saint resorted to similar means to what he had used in the case of the Saracen female who had solicited him to sin in

---

[28] A town in the kingdom of Naples, the seat of an archbishop.

[29] These sacred relics had been brought to Naples, with those of St. Luke, in the year 357, on the 3rd of March, by the care of the Emperor Constantius, and had been deposited in the Church of the Apostles. Chron. Hier. ann. 357. Idat. Fast. ann. 356, 357. St. Hieron. in Vigilant. The French and Venetians having taken the city of Constantinople, in the year 1204, carried away a great number of relics, and Cardinal Peter of Capua, Legate of the Holy See, had the body of St. Andrew, which he gave to the church of Amalfi, his native place. From that time, St. Andrew has been the titular of that church, and the patron saint of Amalfi. The account of this translation is found in the 7th tome of "Italia Sacra," page 272. It is taken from the original which is preserved in the cathedral church. See the notes of Baronius on the Roman Martyrology of the 9th of May.

[30] The Emperor was, in fact, in Italy, in the year 1222. Raynald. ad ann. 1222, n. 31 & 32, et ad ann. 1223, n. 1.

[31] The relics of this holy bishop were brought to Bari, a maritime town of Apulia, on the Adriatic Sea, in 1087, by some merchants of that town, who had taken them from the town of Myra. God has honored them by an infinite number of miracles, and one of the most celebrated pilgrimages is made to that place. Ourson, Archbishop of Bari, had the history of the translation and miracles written by John, Archdeacon of that church, in the year 1088. Surius places it on the 9th of May.

Egypt. He placed himself on red-hot coals, and invited the wanton to imitate him; she was so terrified at this, that she betook herself to flight.

The emperor, who had had the curiosity to spy into what was going on, with some of his courtiers, through a chink[32] which was purposely prepared, went into the room, and said to Francis: "I see that God is with you, since the fire has not burnt you; you must be thankful to Him, and we will beg His pardon for having put you through such an ordeal." Then having dismissed those who were with him, he willingly listened to what the Saint said to him on the subject of his salvation. But the evils which this irreligious and debauched prince did to the Church, in which the Friars Minor had a considerable share, and which their zeal for their mother brought upon them, are too clear proofs that what the Saint said to him bore no profitable fruit.

On leaving Bari, he found on the road a purse,[33] which appeared to be full of money. His companion, who was aware of his great charity, said that he ought to take it for the poor. Francis refused to do so, saying that it was only a snare of the devil, and that, if it was really money which had been lost, it would not be right to take what belonged to others to give away in alms; so they continued their route. His companion was not satisfied; he thought that an opportunity was lost of doing a good action, and he tired Francis with his remonstrances. The holy man, who was very mild and very obliging, returned to the spot where the purse was, not intending to do what his companion wished, but to expose to him the artifice of the evil spirit. A young man was passing at the time, in whose presence he told his companion to take up the purse; he, trembling from a secret misgiving of what was about to happen, would have been glad not to have anything to do with it; but, obliged to obey, he put his hand to it, which he had no sooner done than he saw a large snake slide out, which disappeared with the purse. On which, Francis said to his companion, "Brother, money is, as regards the servants of God, but as a venomous serpent, and even the devil himself." We may here add, that it is the same thing for those who are too fond of it, and who avariciously keep it, or make it serve for the gratification of their passions. A chapel, which has been built in that place, is a memorial of the teaching of the Patriarch to the poor of Jesus Christ.

His devotion induced him also to visit the grotto consecrated by the

---

[32] Wading says that in order to preserve the memory of this event, the tower in which it occurred was called, and is still called, the Tower of St. Francis.

[33] St. Bonaventure, Legend, cap. 7, says that it was a sort of deep purse, called in the language of the country, Funda. It is thought that Macrobius uses this word in the same sense. 2 Saturn, cap. 4. See "Ducange's Glossary" at the word Funda, where he quotes St. Bonaventure.

apparition[34] of the Archangel Michael, on Mount Gargano.[35] They wished, out of respect, to take him to the very spot where the blessed spirit was manifested, and where mass is offered up, a privilege which is not allowed to all. But through humility he stopped at the door, and, as he was urged to enter, he said: "Dare not go farther; this place is awful; it is the dwelling of angels, whom men should respect in all ways." The place where he stopped to pray is shown to this day. These sentiments of humility should abash those Christians who crowd round our altars in unbecoming postures, and particularly those worldly women who, in immodest postures and an air of vanity, approach contemptuously the sanctuary in which the sacred Body of Jesus reposes.

Francis placed some of his religious near Mount Gargano and in some other parts, after which he came to Gubbio, where he cured a woman, the sinews of whose hands were contracted.

Near Gubbio, a soldier called Benvenuto, asked to be admitted into the Order; he was admitted as a lay-brother, with directions to wait upon the lepers. Profound humility, implicit obedience, an ardent charity, the love of poverty and of silence, assiduity in prayer, perfect patience in sickness, and a tender devotion to the Blessed Sacrament, rendered this soldier an excellent religious. God honored him with so many miracles during his lifetime and after his death, which happened in the year 1232, that Pope Gregory IX had information taken on the subject, in 1236, through the bishops of Malfi, Molfetta, and Venosa, and permitted these three dioceses to allot to him an office, which is now said by the whole Order of Friars Minor, on the 27th of June.[36]

There lived, between Gubbio and Massa, an old advocate of the Roman court, called Bartholomew Baro, who had retired thither to avoid the tumults and dangers of the world, and lived in great reputation of sanctity. Francis, delighted at what he had heard of him, wished to see him. They discoursed on spiritual things, and Bartholomew, hearing that there was a Third Order, willingly entered into it. The holy Founder, who saw that great prudence was associated with his consummate piety, placed confidence in him for the affairs of his Order, and left some of his religious with him.[37]

---

[34] The learned Mabillon is far from thinking as M. Baillet does; he has admitted the truth of this apparition which is authorized by the traditions of the country, and by the Roman Martyrology of the 8th of May. See "Acta, SS. Ord. S. Bened.," Sec. 3, pars 1, p. 85, nat. A.

[35] Mount Gargano, now called St. Angelo's Mount, is in the kingdom of Naples, in the province of Capitanate, near Manefredonia, a town built form the ruins of Siponte.

[36] Raynald, ad ann. 1256, n. 28. Martyr. Franc. 27 June.

[37] Although St. Francis had no law-suits, and certainly would not have any, yet he knew very well that in the government of a religious body, it was often necessary to seek information in canonical jurisprudence, and sometimes even in the civil. Thus, the confidence he placed in this talented advocate for the affairs of his Order, shows the excellence of his judgment.

St. Antoninus relates,[38] that Bartholomew had in his hermitage a man possessed by the devil, who was incessantly talking, but who did not speak a word during the three days that Francis was there. After his departure he recommenced talking, and Bartholomew having asked him why, during the stay of Francis, he had kept silence: "It was," he said, "because God had so tied his tongue that it was out of his power to speak a single word." "How is it, then," replied Bartholomew: "is Francis so great a man, that his presence has such an effect?" "Truly," rejoined the demoniac, "his virtue is so great, that all the world will see in him most wonderful things. It is not long since our prince called us all together, and told us that God, who in all times had sent men for the conversion of sinners, has similar designs in regard to this man, and that Jesus Christ proposes to renew His passion in a pure man such as Francis is, in order to imprint it in the hearts from whence it is obliterated."

As this was said two years before Francis received the stigmata, it would seem that the prince of darkness had some knowledge of the favors[39] which Jesus Christ intended to confer on Francis. St. Augustine says,[40] that the Son of God made Himself known to the demons on earth, making certain signs to them of His presence; but that it was only as much as He thought proper, and that He made use of it, when necessary to inspire them with terror; and that, at other times. He left them in doubt as to His divinity. According to this doctrine, it might be said that God, to confound the demons, had made known to their chief His intention to renew the passion of Jesus Christ in the person of Francis, without informing him in what manner this was to happen, for it is certain that this spirit of darkness, neither by his natural lights, nor by conjectures, had the means of discovering a favor which solely depended on the Divine will.

At length, having labored for the salvation of souls with great fatigue, nearly the whole year, the holy Patriarch returned to his dear home, St. Mary of the Angels, to attend more immediately to his own sanctification. He there received Brother Caesar of Spire, who had returned from Germany, and the subject of whose mission we must now resume, having lost sight of it since the year 1221.

This zealous missionary left Italy with twenty-seven companions, divided into small parties, and before the feast of St. Michael, they arrived successfully at Trent, where they remained fifteen days, during which the bishop provided liberally for all their wants. On the day of the festival, Caesar preached to the clergy, and Barnabas to the people. An inhabitant of the town, named Pellegrino, was so moved by Barnabas's discourse, that he had all the brethren

---

[38] Chronic, part iii, tit. 24. cap. 7, § 3.

[39] Matt. 4: 3, and 8: 29; Luke, 4: 34 and 41.

[40] St. Aug. de Civ. Dei, lib. ix, cap. 31. St. Thom. I part, quaest. 64, art. 1; et in 2, sent. dist. 17, quaest. 2, art. 2.

newly clothed, and shortly afterwards he sold all his property, gave it to the poor, and took the same habit himself.

Caesar left some of the brethren at Trent, exhorting them to the practice of patience and humility, and then set out with the remainder. In their way they attended with greater interest to spiritual than temporal wants, although they had commissioned some of their companions to provide what was necessary for them. The bishop of Trent, whom they found at Posen, detained them for some days, and gave them leave to preach in the whole of his diocese. From thence they went to Brixen, where the bishop received them very charitably; but from thence they had much to suffer in the mountains, where they could procure nothing to eat, after long and fatiguing marches, and were reduced to feed upon wild fruits, and even then they had a scruple of tasting these on Friday morning, because it was, by their rule, a fast, although they had slept in the open air, and had had scarcely anything to eat the preceding day. But God supported them, and they reached Augsburg, where the bishop embraced them all, and gave them special marks of his benevolence. They were equally well received by the vidame, his nephew, who was so kind as to give up to them his dwelling. The whole of the clergy showed them great consideration. And among the people there were none who did not show them respect and affection, and their teaching did much good.

In 1221, near the feast of St. Gall, which is on the sixteenth of October, Caesar assembled the first chapter of the Order which had been held in Germany; there were about thirty of his brethren, whom he distributed in several provinces of this vast country. Some were sent to Wurtzburg, Mentz, Worms, Spire, and Cologne, where they exerted themselves with much success for the salvation of souls, and built convents. Giordano was sent with two companions to Saltzburg, and the archbishop of that city received them with great benevolence. Three others went to Ratisbon, where they founded one excellent establishment. The provincial followed them, animating them by word and example. While at Wurtzburg, he gave the habit of the Friars Minor to a young man of good family, named Hartmod, who had had a good education, and he called him Andrew, because the day of his reception was that of the holy apostle. And having taken holy orders some time after, he became a celebrated preacher, and was the first warden in Saxony. Rodinger was also admitted into the Order, who was afterwards warden of the convent of Halberstad, and director of St. Elizabeth of Hungary, before Dr. Conrad of Marburg.

In 1222, Caesar, having received a great number of novices, some of whom were made priests, assembled a chapter at Worms, and finding that the Order was taking solid root in Germany, he instituted as vice-provincial, Thomas de Celano, and returned into Italy with Simon de Collazon, who had preferred the humble state of Friar Minor to the nobility of his birth. The reason of Caesar's return was the anxious desire he had to see once more his holy Patriarch, and his companions in the valley of Spoleto, with whom he was intimately united through virtue. He was a man greatly attached to contemplation, very zealous for holy poverty, and highly esteemed by his brethren, who, after their holy Father, looked up to him above any other.

The religious whom he had left in Germany pursued their mission with great success. Even in this year, or shortly after, they penetrated, with the Friars Preachers, into the kingdom of Sweden, and into some other countries of the north, according to the testimony of John the Great, Archbishop of Upsal, and Legate of the Holy See,[41] who notices this circumstance in the history of his church.

This prelate remarks that one of the first who entered the institute of the Friars Minor, was Laurence Octavius, an illustrious man, whose conversion made so much sensation, that it drew into the order many persons of high rank. The poor habit which he wore, and which he honored by his splendid virtues, and particularly the love of suffering, did not render it less venerable than his learning, his eloquence, his prudence, and his great talent for preaching, which caused him to shine in the eyes of the world, and which had the effect of being of the greatest service to religion throughout the country, as the historian remarks.[42]

Octavius could not avoid giving his consent, in the year 1244 or 1245, to the election which was unanimously made of his person, by the clergy and people, for the archbishopric of Upsal, which was confirmed by Innocent IV. In this dignity, he continued to live the life of a true Friar Minor, and did so much for the salvation of his flock, as well as for the benefit of the whole kingdom, during the interregnum which followed the death of King Eiricbalde, and for the election of his successor, that, if heresy had not destroyed in Sweden all sentiments of piety with the light of faith, his memory would still be honored there as one of their greatest as well as holiest persons. He died a saintly death, in the year 1267, and chose to be buried among the Friars Minor, with whom he would have wished to have spent his life.

---

[41] Hist. Ups., lib. ii, sub fin.

[42] The Swedes received the faith in the ninth century, but it did not spread through the whole country at the same time. Hist. Joan. Magn. lib. v. cap. 17. Baron, ad. ann. 826, n. 42.

CHAPTER III
TREASURE IN ITALY

Bids Anthony preach—Gives Anthony permission to teach theology to the brethren—Alexander Hales enters the Order—Jesus Christ appoints the day for the Indulgence of the Portiuncula—He obtains from the Pope a confirmation of the same day—Promulgates it, with seven bishops—He has a revelation about his Rule—God makes known to him that he must abridge it—The Holy Spirit dictates it to him—Some entreat him to moderate it—Jesus Christ tells him it must be kept to the very letter—His brethren receive it—What it contains—He declares it comes from Jesus Christ, and speaks in praise of it—He obtains a Bull from the Pope, in confirmation of the Rule—Is attacked by devils.

HILE THE INSTITUTE OF ST. FRANCIS thus flourished in Germany and in the North, a treasure was discovered in Italy, which had been up to this time overlooked. It was the great St. Anthony of Padua, who was leading a hidden life in the hermitage of St. Paul near Bologna.

His superior sent him, with some others, to Forli, in Romagna, to take orders. There were also some Friars Preachers there. Being assembled together at the hour of conference, the superior[1] of the place requested the Friars Preachers to give them an exhortation. As they excused themselves because they were not prepared, he turned to Anthony, and without being aware of the depth of his learning, he ordered him to say whatever the Holy Spirit should suggest to him. Anthony replied with great humility that he was ill fitted for such a task, and that he was much more qualified for cleaning the plates than for preaching. However, yielding to the superior's reiterated order, he began to discourse with simplicity and timidity; but God, proposing to place conspicuously the lamp which was hidden under the bushel,[2] he continued his discourse with so much eloquence, and showed himself to possess so profoundly learned a doctrine, that the audience was most agreeably surprised, and admitted that they had never heard anything to equal it; and they did not know which most to admire, his learning or his humility.

It was, indeed, requisite to be possessed of rare and extraordinary humility, to hide with so much care such sublime learning, and talents so varied; for Anthony had earnestly requested the guardian of the convent in which he was,

---

[1] An author says that it was the Bishop of Forli, whose name was Albert. Act. SS. Vit. Sanct. Anton., 13 June, p. 708, in Annot., littl B.

[2] Matt. 5: 15.

to employ him in cleaning the plates and dishes, and in sweeping the house. This man, who, according to the saying of the apostle, was "A vessel of honor, sanctified and profitable to the Lord, prepared unto every good work,"[3] treated himself, and wished to be considered by his companions, as one of the vilest amongst men. He was deserving of the highest place, and took the very lowest. He was so deeply versed in the Holy Scriptures, that his memory served him as a book, and he penetrated so well into the most obscure passages that he was the admiration of the most profound theologians; but he was more anxious to be confounded with the unlearned, and to be unknown, than to let his learning be discovered, and to appear capable of instructing others.

We may here notice a reflection of St. Bernard[4] on a somewhat similar case: "Let this passage be remarked by those who undertake to teach what they have not learnt themselves; seeking for scholars, without having had masters, they are the blind leading the blind.[5] But justice is done them; although it is admitted that they have some talent, it is soon found that they have nothing solid, and they are treated with contempt."

The fortunate discovery that was thus made of the talents of Anthony, soon reached the ears of Francis, who ordered him to apply himself to the pulpit. He desired, however, that the preacher, in order to exercise his ministry with the greatest effect, should study theology at Vercelli, under the abbot of St. Andrew, who gave lessons with great reputation, and who is supposed to have been the celebrated Doctor Thomas, a canon regular of the abbey of St. Victor of Paris, who was sent to be the first abbot of the abbey of St. Andrew of Vercelli, which was founded about the year 1220. Anthony had for a fellow student another Friar Minor, named Adam de Marisco, an Englishman, who was afterwards a doctor of the university of Oxford, the holiness of whose life, whose learning, and whose writings rendered him famous throughout the whole realm of England, and who was subsequently elected bishop of Ely.[6]

The application which Anthony gave to the study of theology did not prevent his preaching during the Lent at Milan, and as other times in some parts of the duchy.[7] But his preaching was no hindrance to his studies, because the lights he had previously acquired, and those he received from above, together with his splendid talents, gave him an insight into the most sublime truths. His progress was so quick and so great, that his master often declared, that he learnt many things from his scholar. Speaking of the book of the celestial hierarchy which he was explaining, he said that his scholar ran over

---

[3] 2 Tim. 2: 25.

[4] Vit. St. Malach. c. ii, n. 4.

[5] Matt. 15: 14.

[6] Hist. Chron. Pedemont. cap. 36. Franc. Aug. a Basil. St. Petr., apud Act. SS. supra, p. 729, in Annot. let. B.

[7] Litt. A. Wading. Scr. Ord. Min. Act. SS. ib. p. 730, litt. C.

the several orders of blessed spirits with so much precision, and a penetration so surprising, that it might have been thought that the whole heavenly host passed before him. This exalted wisdom, joined to his eminent virtues, induced his illustrious preceptor to give him the name of Saint, and to apply our Blessed Lord's eulogy of St. John Baptist to him: "He was a burning and a shining light."[8]

Anthony was applied to by his fellow-students to communicate to them the learning in which he abounded, and to give lessons in the convent, but he would not take upon himself to exercise the functions of master, without having first consulted the holy Founder of the Order. He wrote to him on the subject, and received the following answer:

"To my dear Brother Anthony, Brother Francis sends greeting in Jesus Christ.

"I entirely approve of your teaching the brethren sacred theology; in such a manner, however, that the spirit of prayer be not extinguished in you or in them, according to the rule which we profess. Adieu."[9]

This is a proof that Francis was not hostile to study, but that he only wished it to be conducted in a religious manner, without prejudice to piety. Anthony, having obtained leave, taught first at Montpellier, and then at Bologna, where studies were again set on foot, to which disobedience had put a stop, as has been said; then he taught at Padua, at Toulouse, and in other places where he was stationed: always joining to this holy exercise, that of preaching with wonderful success.

At the time when he began taking lessons from the Abbot of Vercelli, the most celebrated doctor of the university of Paris took the habit of the Friars Minor. This was Alexander d'Hales or d'Hels, or Hales, thus named from the place of his birth, in the county of Gloucester, where, from the year 1246, Richard, Earl of Cornwall, had founded a convent of the Order of Citeaux.[10] Having gone through his course of humanities in England, he came to Paris, where he studied philosophy and theology, took a doctor's degree, taught, and was universally admired.[11]

St. Antoninus[12] believes that what led to his vocation was that, having made a vow to grant, if he possibly could, whatever should be asked of him for the love of the Blessed Virgin, for whom he had a singular devotion, a person who was questing for the Friars Minor, came and said to him: "It is quite long

---

[8] Joan, 5: 35.

[9] Act. SS. supra, p. 728 et 730, in Annot. litt F. Reg. Frat. Min. c. 5.

[10] Others write his name D'Ales. In the "Monasticon Anglicanum," on the subject of the foundation of this monastery, Dugdale writes "In manerio de Hayles," and names it, "Haylesense monasterium." Monast. Anglic., tom. I, p. 928, edit. 1682. In Latin, he is called Alensis.

[11] According to the custom of those times, which was to give titles of honor to men of learning, he was called the Irrefragable Doctor; Doctor of Doctors; Fountain of Life. Wading ad ann. 1245, n. 19.

[12] Chron. part, iii, tit. 24, ch. 8, § 1.

enough that you have been laboring for the world, and you have acquired celebrity in it. I entreat you, for the love of God, and of the Blessed Virgin, to enter into our Order, which you will honor, and you will sanctify yourself." The doctor was surprised at this request, but God touched his heart, and he replied to the brother: "I shall follow you very soon, and shall do as you wish," and shortly after, he took the habit of a Friar Minor. Others, however, are of opinion, that he was induced to quit the world by the example of his fellow countryman, John of St. Gilles, an illustrious doctor, who, preaching one day to the clergy, with great energy, on voluntary poverty, in the convent of the Friars Preachers, descended from the pulpit in the middle of his sermon, and in order to give force to his words by his example, he took the habit of St. Dominic, and returned to the pulpit to finish his discourse.[13]

However this may be, the holy life and happy death of Alexander Hales in the Order of St. Francis, bore testimony to his having been called by God. It is said that, at first, the practices were difficult to him, and that some interior suffering made him think of leaving the Order,[14] but that, in this agitation, he saw in spirit Francis bearing a heavy wooden cross, and endeavoring to carry it up a very steep hill; that he offered to assist him, but that the holy Patriarch spurned his aid indignantly, saying, "Begone, you feeble man; you have not the courage to bear your own light cross, and you would attempt to bear this heavy one!" And this vision having enlightened the doctor who was a novice, he was delivered entirely from the temptation under which he labored.

He continued to teach with the same repute; and the faculty of theology, to do honor to his merits, gave him the privilege of presenting for a doctor's degree one of his brethren and disciples; which he did the first time, by an interior revelation, in favor of Brother John de la Rochelle, who afterwards became very celebrated.[15] Alexander had many other disciples distinguished both for their learning and their piety, but there are none who have done more honor to his instructions than St. Bonaventure, and, according to the opinion of many authors, St. Thomas Aquinas.[16] Among his writings, which are very

---

[13] Hist. Angel. Harpsfield, Saec. 13, cap. 11. Chron. Nic. Triv.: in Scilip Dacher., tom. viii, p. 573.

[14] St. Anton, supra.

[15] Id. ibid.

[16] Both the Popes Sixtus IV and Sixtus V, notice in their Bulls that St. Bonaventure and St. Thomas Aquinas were fellow-students. Cardinal Bellarmine, Possevin, and Labbe, of the Society of Jesus; Nicholas Harpsfield, Archdeacon of Canterbury, and John Pits, an English Doctor, Spond, and many others say that these two saints were disciples of Alexander Hales. Bzovius, a Polish Dominican, speaks in precise terms on that head in his "Annales Ecclésiastiques," tom. 13, ad ann. 1250, n. 11. "Discipulos ille (Alexander Halensis) habuit duos, Divos Bonaventuram et Thomam Aquinatem." This circumstance in which there are many chronological difficulties. Some maintain it, others deny it. —The continuators of Bollandus, 14 July, Comment. Praev. In Vit. St. Bonav. § 3, are puzzled by the contradictory evidence produced by Wading and by Echard, and they do not decide the difficulty. On this, as on the opinions of the Schools, people may dispute, but it should be with good temper. In consequence of not having adhered to this principle, Father Noel Alexander was blamed

numerous, and on all sorts of subjects, his Summa is much esteemed, in which, by order of Pope Innocent IV,[17] he arranged methodically the theological subjects.[18] This is the first Summa which was compiled, and it has served as a model for all others. Pope Alexander IV[19] spoke in the highest terms, both of the author and of his work.

Gerson, chancellor of the university of Paris, in speaking of Alexander's doctrine, expresses himself as follows:[20] "It is not to be told how many excellent things it contains. I declare to have read in a treatise, that some one having asked St. Thomas what was the best mode of studying theology, he replied, 'To study the works of a single theologian;' and being asked what theologian it was desirable to fix on, he named Alexander Hales. Thus," continues Gerson, "the writings of St. Thomas, and principally[21] the Secunda Secundae, show how familiar the works and doctrine of Alexander were to him."

So that learned men entered the Order of Friars Minor, as St. Francis had foretold; and this is the reason why he recommended that prayer should be joined to study, lest learning should obliterate piety.

The indulgence granted to St. Mary of the Angels, or the Portiuncula, two years previous to this time, had not yet had the day fixed on which the faithful

---

by his own friends in 1680, and Echard by the authors of "Mémoires de Trevoux," in 1722. —See Supplem. De Script. Eccles. P. Casim. Oudin, p. 510. Mém. De Trevoux, 1722. Jan. Art. 3.

[17] Trithemius, Bellarmine, Possevin, Labbe, and many others say this: and it is the more probable, as certainly Pope Alexander, or his successor, ordered the superiors of the Friars Minor to complete the Summa which Alexander Hales had in dying left incomplete.

[18] Assermet. Theol. tom. ii. Quaest. Fromm.

[19] Echard gives us the Brief of Alexander IV, Script. Ord. Praedic. tom. I, p. 321, col. 1. In it the Pope directs the Superiors of the Friars Minor, in virtue of holy obedience, to complete the Summa of Alexander Hales; he says that this Summa is a river, having its sources in Paradise, a treasure of science and wisdom, full of irrefragable sentences, which crush falsehood by the force of truth, that it is highly useful to those who seek to make progress in the knowledge of the divine law: that it is the work of God, and can only be attributed to celestial wisdom; that the author could not have composed it, without having been full of God, and inspired with the Holy Spirit. Popes Sixtus IV and Sixtus V have not given less praise to the doctrine of St. Bonaventure; and other Sovereign Pontiffs have given similar praise to that of St Thomas. They had in view the doctrine of the Church, explained, cleared up, and methodically propounded by those illustrious Doctors for the instruction of the faithful, and for confuting heretics, and in no ways private opinions, upon which they frequently differ, and which the Church thinks proper to leave open to the Schools as long as they have nothing in them which disagrees with orthodox dogmas. See the 9th letter of the author of "Reflexions sur le Bref de notre Saint Pére le Pape Benoit XIII, aux Dominicains" addressed to the author of "Thomisme Triumphant," p. 40, 1727. This letter and the preceding ones were printed at Ypres, with approbation, by P. I. Rave.

[20] Gerson, in Epist. de Laudibus Bonav. tom. I, p. 554. Edit. Paris. 1606, et Edit. nov. tom. I, p. 117.

[21] This passage is of itself sufficient to prove that A. Hales composed a Summa of the virtues, and that Gerson had read it Many authors reckon it among his works, and T. de la Caille, in his "History of the Press," says that it was printed at Paris, by J. le Petit, in 1509. If it is not now to be found, it is only the fate of many other works besides that one.

could gain it. Francis waited till Jesus Christ, who first conceded so precious a boon, should Himself mark the day, nor was he disappointed. It occurred as follows:

One night, when he was praying in his cell, at St. Mary of the Angels, in the beginning of the year 1223, the tempter suggested to him not to watch and pray so much, but rather to adopt other modes of penance, because, from his age, more sleep and rest was absolutely necessary for him, and these watchings would be his death. Being aware of the malice of his infernal enemy, he retired to the woods, and threw himself naked into a bush of briars and thorns, till he was covered with blood. "For," said he to himself, "it is much better that I should suffer these pains with Jesus Christ, than that I should follow the advice of an enemy who flatters me."

A brilliant light which surrounded him, discovered to him a great number of white and red roses, although it was the month of January, and the winter was very severe. This was an effect of the power of God, who had changed the briars into rose-trees, which have ever since been evergreen and without thorns.

Angels, who appeared in great numbers, said to him: "Francis, hasten to return to the Church, Jesus Christ is there, together with His blessed Mother." At the same time, he perceived himself miraculously clothed with a new habit of pure white; he gathered twelve roses of each color, and went to the Church. After a profound adoration he addressed the following prayer to Jesus Christ, under the protection of the most Blessed Virgin: "Most holy Father, Lord of heaven and earth. Savior of man, deign, through Your great mercy, to fix the day of the indulgence which You have been pleased to grant to this sacred place."

Our Lord answered him, that it was His desire that it should be from the evening of the vigil of the day when St. Peter the apostle was delivered from his chains, to the evening of the following day. Francis, again asking in what manner this should be publicly made known, and whether his own assertion would be given credit to, he was directed to present himself before the vicar of Jesus Christ, to take with him some white and red roses as testimonials of the truth of the fact, to take with him some of his brethren, who would testify to what they had heard; for, from their cells which were near the church, they had, indeed, heard all that had been said. Then the angels sang the hymn "Te Deum laudamus." Francis took three roses of each color in honor of the most Blessed Trinity, and the vision disappeared.

This wonderful vision was attested to by his companions; but it is only necessary here to remark, that the critics, who are hostile to all that is marvelous, cannot say that there is anything in this which is incredible. At the marriage of Cana our Lord changed water into wine.[22] At his transfiguration,

---

[22] John, 2: 9.

"his garments became white as snow,"[23] that is to say, brilliant as the shining fight which emanated from his whole body. At His birth a multitude of the heavenly army appeared to the shepherds, "praising God, and saying, Glory to God in the highest," etc.[24] Could He not, then, in honor of His servant, change the briars into rose-trees, and clothe him with celestial fight, to manifest the purity of his soul, and cause the angels to sing a hymn of the Church in thanksgiving for the favor He had just granted to man?

In the revelation of the relics of St. Stephen, the first martyr, which was made to Lucian, a priest of the Church of Jerusalem, which is one of the most celebrated events of the fifth century, and which has ever been considered so true and credible a narrative, that the universal Church has assigned a special festival in its commemoration, on the third day of August, when the relics of the holy martyr are seen as shown to Lucian by the blessed Gamaliel, under the figure of a golden basket filled with red roses, in order to point out the bodies of other saints which were in the same place, other golden baskets were shown to him filled with white roses. Now, if it pleased God to represent the martyrdom of St. Stephen[25] by red roses, and his charity, which was the cause of it, by a basket of gold, could He not also choose that the appearance of white and red roses, in the middle of winter, should be a miraculous proof of the indulgence which He granted to Francis, and the whole together a sensible representation of the effect it produces, which is, to purify souls by the application of the merits of Jesus Christ, according to the words of the Apocalypse? "They washed their robes and have made them white in the blood of the Lamb."[26]

Francis, accompanied by Brothers Bernard de Quintavalle, Peter of Catania, and Angelus of Rieti, set out for Rome, where he related to the Pope all that had happened at St. Mary of the Angels, in proof whereof, he presented to him the roses he had brought, and his companions testified to what they had heard. The Pope, astonished to see such beautiful and sweet-smelling roses in the depth of winter, said: "As to myself, I believe the truth of what you tell me, but it is a matter which must he submitted to the cardinals for their opinions." In the meantime, he directed his attendants to see that they should not want for anything.

The next day, they came before the Consistory, where Francis, by the Pope's desire, said, in presence of the cardinals: "The will of God is that whosoever shall, with a contrite and humble heart, after having confessed his sins, and received absolution by a priest, enter the Church of St. Mary of the Angels, in the diocese of Assisi, between the first vespers of the first day of

---

[23] Matt. 17: 2.

[24] Luke, 3: 13,14.

[25] Epist. Lucian. De Revel. Corp. Steph. Mart. n. 4, ad Calc. tom. Oper. St Aug.

[26] Apoc. 7: 14.

August and the vespers of the second day, shall obtain an entire remission of all the sins he may have committed from his baptism until that moment." The Sovereign Pontiff, seeing that the words of Francis were not thought to have any deceit in them, having conferred with the cardinals thereon for some time, confirmed the indulgence. And he subsequently sent to the bishops of Assisi, Perugia, Todi, Spoleto, Foligno, Nocera, and Gubbio, to meet at the Church of St. Mary of the Angels, on the first of August of that year, and there solemnly to publish this indulgence.

All these prelates met on the day specified, and having mounted a large platform,[27] which had been prepared outside of the church, they made Francis mount there also, to explain to the assembly, which was very numerous and gathered from all parts of the country, the cause of their meeting. He spoke with so much fervor that it seemed to be rather an angel who addressed the meeting than a man, and he ended his discourse by announcing the plenary and perpetual indulgence which God and the Sovereign Pontiff granted to this church every year on that day. The bishops were not satisfied with his publishing it to be in perpetuity. "Brother Francis," they said, "although the Pope desires us to do on this occasion whatever you wish, it is not, however, his intention that we should do things which are not suitable; therefore you must give notice that the indulgence is only to last for ten years." The Bishop of Assisi was the first to restrict it to this time, but he could not help saying, as St. Francis had, "in perpetuity." The other bishops endeavored successively to announce this restriction, but God permitted that, without intending it, they should all say, "in perpetuity." By this, they were made sensible of the will of God, and willingly proclaimed the indulgence to be perpetual.

Many of those who were at the sermon preached by Francis, have left testimony in writing to the effect, that he had in his hand a small scroll on which was written these words: "I wish you all to go to Paradise. I announce to you a plenary indulgence which I have obtained from the goodness of our heavenly Father, and from the mouth of the Sovereign Pontiff. All you who are assembled here today, and with a contrite and humble heart have confessed with sincerity, and have received absolution from a priest, will have remission of all your sins; and in like manner, those who come every year with similar dispositions, will obtain the same. I wish it had lasted eight days, but I could not obtain it."

Such is the way in which the famous indulgence of St. Mary of the Angels, or of Portiuncula, was published on the second day of August; an indulgence which the Sovereign Pontiffs have since extended to all the churches of the Order of St. Francis.

---

[27] Wading says that they still preserve, respectfully, pieces of the wood which supported this platform, and they are shown through a grating under the altar in a beautiful chapel, which has been built on the spot, near which is a garden of rose-trees, ever-green, and without thorns. Ad ann. 1223, n. 8.

The seven prelates consecrated the Church of St. Mary of the Angels, and performed a similar ceremony for the Church of St. Damian, at the request of Francis and Clare, and the remembrance of this is commemorated yearly at Assisi, on the ninth of August.

The benevolent feeling which Honorius III expressed to the holy Patriarch, when he was at Rome, for the indulgence of the Portiuncula, induced him to wish that this Pontiff would authorize solemnly the Rule of the Order, which Innocent III had only verbally approved, and he had in the night the following revelation, which is thus recorded by St. Bonaventure.

It seemed to him that he had taken up from the ground some very small crumbs of bread, in order to distribute them to the half-starved brethren who surrounded him, and how, fearful lest such small crumbs should fall out of his hands, a heavenly voice said to him: "Francis, collect all these crumbs and make a host of them, and give of it to such as wish to eat of it." He did so, and all those who did not partake of it devoutly, or treated it contemptuously, after having received it, seemed to be infected with leprosy. In the morning, he related all this to his companions, and was distressed at not comprehending the mystery. The following day, while he was at prayer, a voice from heaven said to him: "Francis, the crumbs of last night are the words of the Gospel, the host is the Rule, and the leprosy is iniquity."

The term of Host, to designate the Rule, is worthy of particular consideration. Its import is that, as bread without leaven, which is called the Host, is made of the finest flour, so the Rule is composed of what is most perfect in the Gospel; and as this bread, by the words of consecration, is changed into the body of Jesus Christ, the true host immolated on the altar, so those who make profession of the Rule, must be transformed into hosts, or victims, and immolate themselves to God. It is thus that St. Paul warns Christians, "To become as a new paste without leaven,"[28] and to pass the whole time of their lives as a continual festival, "presenting their bodies a living sacrifice, holy and pleasing unto God."[29] St. Peter also says to these, that they are a "Spiritual house, a holy priesthood,[30] to offer up spiritual sacrifices

---

[28] 1 Cor. 5: 7, 8.

[29] Rom. 12: 1.

[30] Luther concluded from this that all Christians are by their baptism truly priests, and have power to administer the Sacraments, even to consecrate the Body of Jesus Christ. Other innovators have since endeavored to persuade the Laity, and particularly females, that all the faithful who assist at Mass consecrate with the priest, and they have purposely given them the Ordinary of the Mass in Latin and the Vulgar tongue, in order that each might pronounce the words of consecration; so that there have been women who really believe that they consecrated. The Catholic Church teaches that this power is only given to priests by virtue of their character; that they alone are the successors of the Apostles, in the priesthood, and that to them alone, in the persons of the Apostles, Jesus Christ said: "Do this in memory of me." When St. Peter said to the Christians that they were a holy assembly of priests, he speaks of a purely spiritual priesthood, taken in a very extended sense, which consists in a self-offering as a victim, by prayer and good works; which the Apostle calls spiritual

acceptable to God by Jesus Christ."[31]

The Oracle of heaven communicated to Francis that the Rule which he sought to have approved, and which was composed of sentences from the Gospel, required abridgment, and putting into order with greater precision. In order to effect this, he was inspired, after the publication of the indulgence, to go to Mount Columbo, near Rieti, where he retired into an opening in the rock, with Brothers Leo and Bonzio, fasting on bread and water, and this fast, according to the statement of Marianus, lasted forty days. There he wrote the Rule, according to the dictation of the Holy Spirit to him, in prayer. On his return to St. Mary of the Angels, he put it into the hands of his vicar, Brother Elias, to read it, and keep it. Elias thought it too severe, and some days afterwards, in order to suppress it, he feigned to have lost it by negligence. The holy men returned to the same place, and wrote it out a second time, as if God had dictated it to him with His own mouth.

The vicar-general communicated to some of the provincial ministers what had happened, and told them that the Founder was desirous of imposing upon them a stricter mode of life than that to which they had hitherto adhered. They concerted together what they should do to avert this, and it was agreed that Elias, as vicar-general, should go and represent to him the inconvenience of such increased austerity, and the objections of his brethren. Elias, who was aware of the firmness of Francis in these matters, and had been severely rebuked by him on other occasions, acknowledged that he did not dare execute this commission alone, but he offered to accompany them for the common cause, and they consented to this arrangement.

While they were drawing near to the mountain, Francis had a revelation of what was passing. When they had reached the top, he left the opening of the rock quickly, and demanded of Elias what he and all these ministers who were with him wanted. Elias, with downcast eyes, and trembling, said, in a low tone of voice: "These ministers, having learnt that you were about to give them a new Rule above the strength of man to endure, have engaged me to come here, in my capacity of vicar-general, to entreat you to modify it, because they will not receive it, if it is too austere."

At these words, the Saint, in great emotion and shuddering, raised his eyes to heaven and exclaimed: "Lord, did I not say that these people would not believe me? As to myself, I will keep this Rule to the day of my death, with those of my companions who love poverty; but I shall not have it in my power to compel those who do not choose it, and who make so much resistance."

Jesus Christ appeared in a luminous cloud above Francis, and said, so that

---

victims. Such is the general and common priesthood which is proper for all the faithful, and not the priesthood, which is peculiar to, and appertains, solely, to priests. Luther, De Miss, privat., De captiv. Babylon., De institut. minist. Eccles. Concil. Nic. can. 14. Concil. Trident, sess. 22. cap. 1. Bellarmin. de Sacram, in gen. cap. 24, 25.

[31] 1 Petr. 2: 5.

all heard him: "Little man, why are you discontented, as if this was your work? It is I who have dictated the Rule; no part of it is yours. I insist on its being literally observed to the very letter, without gloss or comment. I know what frail man can endure, and what support I can and will give him. Let those who will not keep the Rule leave the Order; I will raise up others in their place; and if it be requisite, I will bring them forth from these stones."[32]

Then Francis, from the top of the rock on which he had knelt down, addressed these words to the vicar-general and to the others, who were greatly alarmed, "You now know that your conspiracy has been solely an opposition to the will of God, and that instead of taking into consideration what He can do for us, you have only consulted the feeble light of your human prudence. Have you heard, have you, yourself, heard the voice which came forth from the cloud, and which spoke so audibly? If it did not resound in your ears, I will take steps to cause you to hear it once more." Upon this, Elias and his companions, astounded and beside themselves, retired without saying a single word.

The holy Patriarch having returned to join his faithful children in the small fissure of the rock, in which they lay prostrate at the voice of the Lord, said to them: "Rise up now, and fear nothing, but as true soldiers of Jesus Christ put on the armor of God, in order to be on your guard against the snares which the devil will not fail to throw in the way of your following Him."[33] He left the mountain and went to the nearest convent to show the Rule to his brethren, intending to communicate it afterwards to the others, in order to know what each one thought of it. His countenance, animated and shining, was a manifestation that God himself had dictated to him the rule of life which he proposed to them. It was a striking representation of Moses coming down from Mount Sinai, his face shining brightly.[34] The resemblance cannot be too much admired in its several relations. Moses, after a fast of forty days, received, on a mountain, the Law which God gave him. Jesus Christ having fasted forty days, was on a mountain when He taught that doctrine which embraces, as St. Augustine observes, all the perfection of the Christian life.[35] And it was on a mountain that it was His pleasure to give His servant Francis, who fasted rigorously, a Rule in which the perfection of the evangelical life is contained, as if it was intended to show, as the Holy Fathers think, by the elevation of the place, the sublimity of the sort of life. These fortunate resemblances are undoubtedly most honorable to the Patriarch and his children, but the glory is to God alone.

Some having read the Rule, said to Francis, that it was necessary that his

---

[32] Matt. 3:9.

[33] Eph. 6: 13.

[34] Exod. 34: 29, 30.

[35] Math. 4: 2. et 5:1 et seq.; St. Aug. de Serm. Dom. in monte, cap. 1, n. 1.

Order should have something in common, as the other religious Orders had; seeing that the number of the brethren was already very great, and that, according to all appearance, the Order would be so extended, that it would not be possible to exist in so restricted a state of poverty. The Saint returned to the place he had left, and having had recourse to prayer, he consulted Jesus Christ, the true Legislator, who gave the following reply: "It is I who am their portion and their inheritance; I do not choose that they should be encumbered with the things of this world.[36] Provided they adhere strictly to the Rule, and that they place their confidence in me, I will take care of them; I will not suffer them to stand in need of anything necessary to life; the more their numbers increase, the more will I manifest my providence to them."[37]

We must here render to that adorable and loving Providence the justice due to it. It has never been wanting to the Order of St. Francis, and they have never had greater proofs of His care than when they have chosen to live most poorly. We see verified to the letter, in these poor evangelical brethren, the imitators of Jesus Christ crucified, what is said in the twenty-first psalm, in which the Son of God has clearly foretold His Passion: "The poor shall eat and shall be filled, and they shall praise the Lord that seek Him, their hearts shall live forever and ever."[38] Were He now to ask the religious of St. Francis, as He asked the apostles "When I sent you without purse, or scrip, and shoes, did you want for anything?"[39] There is not one who would not answer as they did: "No, we have not wanted for anything." For a poor evangelical brother is bound to consider himself as not wanting anything while he lives, and to look upon having nothing but what is necessary as the treasure of his state of life.

A religious Order which, without any revenue, maintains many thousand men, was a subject of admiration for an infidel prince, and the Founder was considered by him as a very great man. He was not aware of the cause of this wonderful effect, but religion teaches us that it is God himself who provides for the wants of His servants, by the charity with which He inspires the faithful.

Francis communicated to the ministers what our Lord had said to him. They submitted to everything, and returned with him to St. Mary of the Angels, where the Rule was approved by the brethren who were there, and was sent into the provinces to be examined before it was submitted for confirmation. It contains twelve chapters, of which the following is the substance.

The first chapter is expressed in these terms: "The Rule and the Life of the Friars Minor consist in the observance of the Gospel of our Blessed Lord Jesus

---

[36] Psalm. 15: 5.

[37] Psalm. 54 (55): 25.

[38] Psalm 21 (22): 27.

[39] Luke 22: 35,36.

Christ, living in obedience, without property, and chastely. Brother Francis promises obedience and reverence to our most Holy Father Pope Honorius, and to his successors canonically elected, and to the Roman Church. Let the other brethren be bound to obey Brother Francis and successors."

We have before noticed the Catholicity of the holy man; it is here seen, and it will everywhere be seen with similar zeal. The words, "Let the other brethren," etc., were not in the first Rule, although Francis being the founder of the Order, and Pope Innocent having appointed him general thereof, the brethren were bound to obey him. But there is reason to think that he inserted them here, in consequence of the resistance of the vicar-general, and some provincial ministers, who made some difficulty in accepting the Rule; besides which, it was necessary to notice the obedience due to the General of the Order and his successors.

In the second chapter he speaks of the reception of novices, which he leaves solely to the provincials, who are to examine them strictly as to the Catholic faith and the sacraments of the Church. He desires the postulants may be told to sell all they have, and to distribute it to the poor, if possible, but that they are not to interfere in this distribution. Noticing in particular the habits of the novices, and of those who are professed, he recommends that in general all shall be poorly clad, and shall be able to patch their own habits; he permits shoes to be worn in cases of necessity, which shows, says St. Bonaventure,[40] that the Friars Minor, except in cases of extreme necessity, should be barefooted, as Jesus Christ had prescribed to the apostles.[41] He warns the brethren not to look with contempt on, and not to judge those who are delicately clad, and who are daintily fed: "Let no one judge or despise any one but himself."

The third chapter embraces three things; 1st. That the clerks shall recite the Divine Office, according to the practice of the Roman Church; that the laity shall recite, for each part of the Divine Office, a certain number of times the Lord's Prayer,[42] and pray for the dead. 2nd. That besides the periods directed by the Church, they shall all fast from the feast of All Saints till

---

[40] St. Bonav. Exp. in Reg. c. 2, et Tr. de Sand. Apost.

[41] It is thus that the holy Doctor understood the passage of St. Matthew, X: 10 and that of St. Mark, VI: 9, as St. Jerome and St. Augustine had, followed by many learned expositors. St. Hier, in cap. x, Math. et in Epist. ad Agerach et in Epist. ad Eustoch. de Custod. Virgin. St. August, de Consens. Evangel, lib. ii, cap. 30. Tostat. in cap. x, Math. Quaest. 60, et alii.

[42] St. Francis does not add here the Angelical Salutation to the Lord's Prayer, because, at that time, it was not in the Divine Office. It was not prescribed to the lay brothers in the Statutes of Guigues, General of the Carthusians, nor in the Rules of the Templars or of the Carmelites. Mabillion remarks after Cardinal Bona, that it is only found in the Breviary of Cardinal Santa Croce, before that of Pope Pius V, and Cardinal Bona thinks that it was not in the Long Office, because it was in the Little Office of the Blessed Virgin, which was said from the 10th century. Bona, de Divina Psalmodia, cap. 16, § 2. Act. SS. Ord. S. Bened. sec. 5, Praefat. n. 157, et seq. The Lay Brothers of the Order of St. Francis do not, however, omit to add the Angelical Salutation to the Lord's Prayer in their office.

Christmas,[43] and all the Fridays throughout the year, which he prescribed in memory of Christ crucified, the great object of his devotion. He also proposes to his brethren a fast of forty days, beginning with the Epiphany, and he invites them to this, promising them the blessing of God for it; but he leaves them at liberty on this head, and says that, in cases of evident necessity, they are not obliged to corporal fasting, by which he shows that a spiritual fast must be kept at all times, according to the doctrine of the Holy Scriptures,[44] and that of the Fathers of the Church. 3rd. He exhorts them to have no discussions or disputes, and not to judge others when they go into the world, but to be meek, peaceable, modest, tractable, and humble, and to speak civilly to all persons, according to the rules of politeness. He forbids their riding on horseback, unless illness or an evident necessity compel them to it. He directs that in whatsoever house they may enter, they shall say: "Peace to this house;"[45] and he permits them to eat, according to the Gospel, whatever may be offered to them.

What he had most seriously at heart is developed in the fourth chapter: That the brethren shall not receive money on any pretext whatsoever. He forbids this expressly, in conformity to what our Savior said to His apostles: "Do not possess gold, silver, nor money in your purses."[46] Nevertheless, he orders superiors to provide carefully, by means of spiritual friends, for clothing of their brethren, for their wants in sickness, as they shall deem it requisite, according to the seasons, the places, and the cold climates; always having regard to what has already been said, that they are not to receive money.

By the expression, "spiritual friends,"[47] the holy Founder means those persons to whom the Friars Minor address themselves in confidence as to friends in God, and whom they request to pay for what they cannot get without money. Now, notwithstanding the aversion and sort of horror which he had of money, he desires to have his spiritual friends induced to give it, or cause it to be given, for clothing his brethren, and for assisting them in sickness, when these things cannot be obtained in any other way, in order to show the better by that, how far the obligation of the superiors extend on this head. If, then, a superior of the Order of St. Francis neglects to provide for his brethren the clothing they might reasonably require; if in their illness he does not give them that succor which fraternal charity dictates; if he does not procure for them all the solace and comfort which are desirable; if he were to have recourse to spiritual friends, and make use of their charity for less

---

[43] It was formerly a common custom amongst the faithful to fast at those times. See "Thomassin, Traite des Jeunes."

[44] Isaiah 57: 3, et seq. St. Basil. Homil. 1 et 2, de Jejun. St. August. Serm. 205, n. 3, et alibi.

[45] Math. 10:12; Luke 10: 5 et 8.

[46] Math. 10: 9.

[47] Pet. Marchant. Expos, litt. in Regul. St Franc, cap. 4.

essential and less needful objects, he could not act in a manner more in opposition to the views of the holy Patriarch, and in greater contravention of the Rule; he would violate the two great precepts, of the love of God and of his neighbor, even the laws of humanity; he would subject the brethren to severe and dangerous trials, which might affect their salvation, and he would not avoid the dreadful sentence which Jesus Christ will pronounce against those who shall have neglected Him, naked and sick, in the persons of the poor.[48]

Labor is recommended in the fifth chapter, but with this remark: "That they are to occupy themselves in it in such manner as, by avoiding idleness, which is hurtful to the soul, the spirit of prayer and devotion be not extinguished, to which all temporal objects are to be made subservient."

On this head, the Order of the Friars Minor and the other mendicant orders, were attacked in the days of St. Bonaventure and St. Thomas Aquinas, by some learned men, who pretended that these Religious ought to labor with their hands rather than to exercise the sacred ministries. But these two renowned theologians replied with arguments so strong and so solid to the reasoning of these critics, that it is surprising that it has been since attempted to repeat them.[49]

St. Bonaventure,[50] in particular, pointed out to them that personal labor is not a precept of the Rule of the Friars Minor, but that it was recommended by St. Francis to avoid idleness, and that he himself had worked so little, that nothing was ever found of his personal labor, during his whole life, that was of the value of a sixpence; these are the precise words of the holy doctor, to which he added, that the lay brethren were sufficiently occupied in the convent and out of the convent, for the service of the community, and that, as to the priests, it was much better that they should apply themselves to study and to other spiritual exercises which are proper to their state, than to the labor of their hands. In fact, it would be ridiculous to say that doctors, preachers, confessors, and priests, who spend their lives in singing the praises of God, and lending their spiritual aid to their neighbors, and clerks, who study in order to qualify themselves to serve the Church, should be obliged to learn a trade in order to labor at it.

It was in vain that the Book of St. Augustine on the Labor of Monks was referred to in reply,[51] since he only speaks of monks, that is, of solitaries by profession, who were not employed in the sacred ministries, and because in his Retractationes, he says positively that he only wrote against those monks who did not choose to do anything at all, and who asserted that, in their state of

---

[48] Matt. 25: 41-45.

[49] St. Thom. Opus. 34. alias 19, contr. Imp. Relig. c. 5.

[50] St. Bonav. de Tribus Quaest. ad Magist. in nom. Expos, in Reg. cap. 5. Determ. Quaest. circ. Regul. St. Franc. Quaest. 11.

[51] St. Aug. Lib. ii, Retract, c. 21.

life, they were not required to labor, misapplying some passages of the Holy Scriptures to authorize their idleness. Moreover, he admits that those who preach the Gospel may live by the Gospel, and are not obliged to perform manual labor.[52]

If St. Paul[53] who served the altar, nevertheless worked for his maintenance, it was because he did not choose to assert his right, for particular reasons which related to the good of his mission.[54] In similar cases his example should be followed, as it has been, by many holy bishops and priests, according to the testimony of St. Epiphanius.[55] But the apostle did not lay it down as a law; he proves that the preachers of the Gospel should be supported by the faithful. As to his having added manual labor to his ministry, St. John Chrysostom makes no other remark than the following:

"We who often forego the ministry of preaching should blush at the idleness of our lives."[56] This great preacher humbly made the reproach to inactive ministers, a defect of which he, certainly, was guiltless.

The Friars Minor are forbidden in the sixth chapter to possess any property whatsoever,[57] neither house, nor place, nor any other thing. It is desired that

---

[52] Id. de Oper. Monach. c. xx, n. 23 et 24.

[53] Act. 18: 3; et 20: 34.

[54] 1 Cor. 4: 12. et 9: 12, et alibi.

[55] St. Epiph. Haer. lxxx, 5, 6.

[56] I Cor. 9: 7, at seq. St. Chrysos. Homil. 39, in Act. Apost.

[57] The author of the History of the City of Paris, who has been before quoted, in speaking of St. Francis and his first disciples, says: "That the spirit of their institute was to have no property whatever, either in common or individually, not even the houses in which they dwelt. For which reason, he adds, they only received them as borrowed, and considered the property as that of the founders. For the subtle reason had not been urged, as it was in the following century, by severed Doctors who wished to make either the Pope or the Roman Church proprietors of the convents of the begging Orders, so that neither the one nor the other would have been either richer or poorer." Tom. I, lib. 6, p. 285. This writer ought to have known that the Religious of St. Francis profess to this day not to have any property, either in common or individually, neither house, nor anything else whatsoever. He ought not to have been ignorant that the Sovereign Pontiffs Nicholas III and Clement V have made known in conformity with what had been done by their predecessors Gregory IX, Innocent IV, and Gregory X, that they took to themselves, and for the Holy Roman Church all property given to the Friars Minor, and particularly the Churches and Graveyards. How then could he attribute to the subtlety of Doctors an arrangement expressly notified in the Constitutions received by the universal Church, inserted in the code of Laws, and renewed, in 1625, by Pope Urban VIII, with order to conform to it, without noticing any others? That the property in things of which the Friars may have the use, belongs to the Pope, or to the Sovereign of each state, or to those who give them, and who wish to preserve the right over them; that as long as these exist, they may be taken back, and the Friars have no legal means of preventing it; and they are even deprived of the power of going to law about it. It must be admitted that, in reality, this poverty in community is greater than where the right is retained of defending the property belonging to the community. The Proprietors of the houses of the Order of the Minors are richer from it, since they may always resume what belongs to them; besides that, as Pope Nicholas III says their charity merits an eternal reward, and the Minors are *the poorer*, since they are always exposed to give back what does not

they should consider themselves as strangers in this world, that they may serve the Lord in poverty and humility, and that they solicit alms with confidence, without feeling any shame in the act, since Jesus Christ became poor in this world for the love of us. "My dear brethren," says St. Francis, "such is the excellence of this sublime poverty, that it makes you heirs to the kingdom of heaven; it has stripped you of the goods of this world in order to make you great in virtue. Let this be your practice; this is what leads you to the regions of the living; bind yourselves, therefore, entirely to it, and for the name of Jesus Christ never wish for anything but the kingdom of heaven." He then adverts to the sincere and tender friendship which the brethren should feel towards each other, disclosing to each other with confidence their wants, wherever they may meet. "For," says he, "if a mother nourishes her son according to the flesh, with how much more affection should each one love and nourish his brother according to the spirit? And if any of these fall sick, the others must attend to him as they would wish to be attended in similar circumstances." This is what Jesus Christ taught: "All things whatsoever you would that men should do to you, do you also to them."[58]

The reasoning which St. Francis enters into, to demonstrate with what affection his brethren must love each other and lend their aid to each other, is very solid and very pathetic. From the love a mother has for a son according to the flesh, and from the care she takes of him, he draws this consequence; that they must love their brethren still more according to the spirit, and take much more care of them. The consequence is correct, says St. Bonaventure.[59] Love which has charity for its basis, is stronger than that which proceeds from flesh and blood, because charity, having an infinite object for its basis, all that is finite cannot withstand it; it overcomes even the natural fear of death. In fact, charity inspires greater tenderness, renders more careful and more active, gives more fortitude and more constancy than any other love. May the children of the blessed Patriarch have it always in their hearts, and manifest the proofs of it to their brethren! They are all obliged by their Rule to render mutual services to each other in their illnesses, as much as it may be in their power, and permitted by obedience. The obligation is particularly binding on those to whom the care of the sick is confided by the superiors; but it is principally imposed on the superiors themselves, who are the servants of the others by their position, and who are bound to see, by continual vigilance, that the sick are properly taken care of. It is a most important duty which St. Bonaventure[60] considers to be included in these words of the Son of God: "By this shall all men know that you are my disciples, if you have love one for

---

belong to them.

[58] Matt. 7: 12.

[59] St. Bonav. Expos, in Reg. cap. 6.

[60] St. Bonav. Expos, in Reg. cap. vi.

another;"[61] and the fulfillment of this duty increases the charity which prescribes it, according to the words of Wisdom: "Be not slow to visit the sick, for by these things you shall be confirmed in love."[62]

The seventh chapter only relates to those penances which are to be imposed for grave faults; on which subject the superiors are admonished not to be discomposed, and not to be moved to anger by the sins of others, since that destroys charity, both in themselves and in the brethren.

The eighth chapter treats of the election of the minister general, and of the assembling the general and provincial chapters.

The ninth directs that the preachers shall not preach in a diocese, if the bishop is opposed to it; nor before having been examined and approved by the minister general; that their discourses shall be examined and corrected; that they must study for the instruction and edification of the people, preaching upon virtues and vices, on eternal punishment and glory, and all this in a few words. St. Bonaventure[63] says that, by this last circumstance, St. Francis means that everything that is useless to the subject should be expunged from their sermons, and he adds that this should be literally understood and acted upon, for sermons which are too long are fatiguing, and disgust the audience.[64] The one agrees with the other; for sermons are not too long when nothing is said but what relates to the subject, and when too many heads are not introduced. He also remarks: 1st. That the Friars Minor are to study preaching as part of their state in life, since their rule dictates to them the manner in which they are to preach. 2nd. That it was the intention of their Father that they should study, since he desires that their discourses should be accurate and corrected, which they cannot be without study.

The superiors and inferiors are instructed in the tenth chapter; the former, as to the mode of governing, the latter, as to obedience, and the holy Patriarch exhorts all to the practice of the most sublime virtues. He desires that those who are illiterate shall not give themselves the trouble of studying, which St. Bonaventure says is to be understood of the lay-brethren, to whom study is unnecessary.[65]

In the eleventh chapter there are some prudent precautions in regard to women, and particularly as to religious women, in order that no suspicion may attach to the Friars Minor.

The twelfth chapter is written under the impression that the Friars Minor will be sent to preach to the infidels, which has been the case, since the very

---

[61] Matt. 7: 12.

[62] Ecclus. 7: 39.

[63] St. Bonav. in cap. ix, Regul.

[64] A writer has observed that St. Augustine, when he was advanced in years, preached shorter sermons than when he was young, not to fatigue his audio by too much instruction. Tillemont's Memoirs, tom. xiii, pp. 248, 249.

[65] St. Bonav. in cap. xii, Regul.

beginning of the Order until the present day; but it is recommended to the superiors only to permit those to go whom they shall deem best qualified. The sainted Legislator, in directing, out of obedience, to the ministers to solicit from the Pope, a cardinal of the holy Roman Church, as protector of the Order, says: "In order that being always submissive to this holy Church, and prostrate at its feet, always firm and steady in the Catholic faith, we may practice poverty and humility, and practice the law of the holy Gospel of our Lord Jesus Christ, as we have faithfully promised."

Such is the Rule of the Friars Minor, reduced to twelve chapters from twenty three, which formed the number of the first Rule. It is short, but replete with evangelical perfection. If it be wished to have a good and ample commentary on it, it will only be requisite to study the actions and works of the holy Founder.

Speaking of the Rule, he said to his children, "I have not put anything into it of my own; I caused it all to be written as God revealed it to me;" and he adduced this motive to excite them the better to keep it. He confirmed the revelation in his will, in the following terms: "When the Lord confided to me the guidance of the brethren, no one communicated to me how I was to behave towards them, but the Almighty himself revealed to me that I ought to live according to the form prescribed by the Gospel; I caused it to be written out in few and simple words," etc.

This is the eulogium he passed on it: "My brethren and my dear children, a very great favor was done to us in giving us this Rule; for it is the book of life, the hope of salvation, the pledge of glory, the marrow of the Gospel, the way of the cross, a state of perfection, the key of Paradise, and the bond of our eternal alliance. None of you is ignorant how greatly advantageous to us holy religion is. As the enemy who fights against us is extremely clever in inventing and executing everything which is malicious, and strews in our way all sorts of snares to effect our perdition, there are many whose salvation he would have brought into great peril, if religion had not been their shield. Study, therefore, your Rule, all of you, not only for alleviating your pains, but in order that it may remind you of the oath you have taken to keep it. It is necessary that you should employ yourselves in meditating on it, that it may sink into your hearts, and be always before your eyes, so that you may observe it with exactness, and hold it fast at your deaths."

St. Bridget being in prayer at Jerusalem, where she was interceding for a Friar Minor who had some conscientious scruples on the subject of the Rule, our Savior caused her to hear the following words: "The Rule of St. Francis was not the composition of the human mind; it is I who made it; it does not contain a single word which was not inspired by My spirit; and thus he gave it to the others."[66]

---

[66] Revel. Sanct. Bridgit. lib. vii, cap. 20.

Pope Nicholas III says, that it bears on the face of it, the evidence of the Trinity; that it is descended from the Father of Light, that it was taught to the apostles by the example, and by the doctrine of His Son, and that the Holy Spirit inspired it to the blessed Francis and to those who had followed him.[67] He declares, as Gregory IX had done before, that it is established on the word of the Gospel, authorized by the life of Jesus Christ, and supported by the actions and words of the apostles, who founded the Church militant.

It consists, according to the remark of St. Bonaventure,[68] in observing the Holy Gospel of our Lord Jesus Christ, because all its substance is taken from the pure source of the Gospel. It is, therefore, no new rule; it is only a renewed rule, literally the same as what the Son of God laid down for the apostles, when He sent them forth to preach; and this is what must give great spiritual consolation to those who keep it. This holy doctor[69] considers the impressions of the wounds of Jesus Christ, which Francis received from the hand of the living God, some time after the revelation of the Rule, as a bull of Jesus Christ, by which that High Pontiff confirmed it; and Pope Nicholas III was of the same opinion, in his Decretal.

Finally, the Rule of the Friars Minor, given by St. Francis, is wholly evangelical,[70] and wholly apostolical; there never was one which was so universally and so promptly followed. Men illustrious by their birth, by their knowledge, by their talents, by their virtue, embraced it and have followed it, during more than five centuries, in all parts of the Christian world; it has given to the Church a new family, in numbers most extensive, whose fecundity does not become exhausted, and it has produced a great number of saints.[71]

The children of the Patriarch, having most willingly received it, he left

---

[67] In Sexto de Verb, signif. Exiit qui seminat.

[68] St. Bonav. Expos, in Reg. Fr. Min. cap. I

[69] Id. Leg. St. Franc. cap. iv.

[70] Upon this principle, some have asserted that the Rule of the Friars Minor is a divine law, and cannot be done away. This requires explanation. If it is looked on as extracted from the Gospels, it cannot be denied that it is divine law, and independent of any human authority, since the Gospel is the word of the Son of God. It is for this reason that Cardinal John of St. Paul said to the other cardinals, in presence of Pope Innocent III, as we have related: "If we reject the request of this poor man, under the pretext of his rule being a novelty, and too hard to be kept, let us be careful that we do not repudiate the Gospel itself, because the rule of which he solicits your approval, is in conformity with what the Gospel teaches." But if this rule is considered a form of life prescribed for a particular order, and applied by the Pope, it is clear that it is not a divine law, and that for adequate reasons a Pope may suppress it, as in other cases. Alvar. Pelag. de Plancl. Eccles. lib. ii, cap. 61. Emman. Roder. Quaest. Regul. tom. I, Quaest. 4, art. I. Wading, ad ann. 1223, n. 14. Joan. Perrin. Doct. Paris. Supra Dispens. Fr. Min. Petr. Marchant. Expos. Litt. in Reg. FF. Min. Quaest. 3. proem. et fundam, duod. part 1, titul. 4, p. 55 et seq.

[71] Our Holy Father, Pope Benedict XIII, has canonized two others, the 10th and 28th of December, 1726; the blessed James de la Marche, and the Blessed Francis Solano. On the 9th of the same, he created Father Lourmer Cogga, General of the Order of St. Francis, a cardinal, and the following day he canonized a saint of the same Order.

them in the month of October, in order to solicit the approval of the Sovereign Pontiff. When at Rome, he was invited to dine with Cardinal Ugolino, the protector of the Order, who had a sincere affection for him; but he did not come to the invitation, until he had begged some pieces of bread, as he was accustomed to do, when he was to dine with persons of rank. Being at table, he drew this bread from his sleeve and began to eat of it, and he gave some to the other guests, who partook of it from devotion. After dinner, the cardinal embraced him, and said, smiling: "My good man, why, as you were to dine with me, did you put the affront on me, to go and beg bread first and bring it to my table?" "My Lord," replied Francis, "far from doing anything to affront you, I did you honor, in honoring, at your board, a much greater Lord than you are, to whom poverty is very agreeable, especially that which goes as far as voluntary mendicancy, for the love of Jesus Christ. I have resolved not to give up in favor of false and passing riches, this virtue which is of royal dignity, since our Lord Jesus Christ became poor for us,[72] in order that, by His poverty, we might become rich, and heirs to the kingdom of heaven, in our quality of poor in spirit."[73]

An admirable reply, which is quite in unison with what was said by St. Gregory Nazianzen. "If I am reproached for my poverty, I am sure that it is my treasure;"[74] and with these words of St. Ambrose, on the birth of Christ: "His poverty is my patrimony; He chose to want for everything, in order that all others might be in abundance."[75]

The cardinal presented Francis to the Pope, that he might solicit the confirmation of his Rule. The Holy Father read it, and, finding it too severe, he desired some changes might be made in it; but, the man of God protesting by everything that was most sacred, that he had not put a single word into it, and that Jesus Christ had dictated it, as it there stood, the Pontiff, later discussing it with the cardinals, confirmed it.[76]

His Bull commences thus:

"Honorius, bishop, the servant of the servants of God. To our dearly beloved sons. Brother Francis, and other brethren of the Order of Friars Minor, health and apostolical benediction. The Apostolic See is accustomed to assent to pious intentions and to favor the laudable wishes of those who solicit her favors. For which reason, our dear children in Jesus Christ, we confirm by apostolical authority, and we strengthen by this present writing, the Rule of your Order, which was approved by Pope Innocent, of glorious memory, our

---

[72] 2 Cor. 8: 9.

[73] Math. 5: 3.

[74] St. Greg. Naz. Orat. 28, n. 33.

[75] St. Ambr. in Luc. lib. 2, n.

[76] Wading says that a part of the hall in which the Rule was confirmed, is now the chapel of the Friars Minor Penitentiaries of St. John Lateran. Ad ann. 1223, n. 16.

predecessor, expressed in these terms."[77]

After having gone through it all, he concludes as follows: "Let no person, therefore, have the temerity to violate the contents of our present confirmation, or to contravene it. Should any one dare to do so, let him know that he will incur the indignation of Almighty God, and that of His blessed apostles, St. Peter and St. Paul. Given in the Lateran palace, the twenty-ninth day of November, 1223, the eighth of our pontificate."

The original of this Bull, with its leaden seal, is preserved at Assisi, in the convent of St. Francis, where Wading saw it, in 1619, with a copy of the Rule written by St. Francis' own hand.[78]

The Pope, at the same time, issued another Bull, addressed to the prelates of the Church, in which, having noticed that, according to the Rule of the Friars Minor, no one may be admitted to profession till after a year's probation, and that no one, once professed, may leave the Order, he makes known that he has given the superiors power to excommunicate such as shall leave it, and he enjoins all bishops to consider them as such, and to denounce them, if requisite, in order to compel them, by this means, to return to the Order. There are always tares among the wheat,[79] wicked with saints in religious congregations, as indeed in the whole Church; God permits this for good reasons, and this should not diminish the esteem and respect which are due to the body. The same Pope had granted, in 1222, at the request which Francis had made to him in the name of the whole Order, that they might be allowed to say the divine Offices in a low tone of voice, and with the doors of their churches closed, in times of general interdicts. This concession is dated from Anagni, the 29th day of March, in the sixth year of his pontificate. On the same day he sent a commission to the superiors of the Friars Preachers and Friars Minor of the diocese of Lisbon, where they were already in great repute, to reform, with some others, certain abuses which had been adopted by the clergy in the administration of the sacraments. The favor which Francis had solicited for the times of interdicts makes it clear that he was not averse from having some privileges, and that his children do not act in opposition to his spirit, when they solicit them for legitimate causes.

We must not delay recording here that, in 1224, Honorius granted permission to the Friars Minor to use portable altars for the celebration of mass; that in 1225, some bishops in France having set themselves up in opposition to this, the Holy Father wrote from Rieti to the archbishop of Rheims to remove these obstacles; and some other prelates having been still more averse from their having this privilege, so as even to have pronounced

---

[77] This must not be understood literally, but according to the sense, for the whole substance of the first Rule which Pope Innocent III had approved verbally, is found in the second Rule, which was approved by the Bull of pope Honorius III.

[78] Wading, in 2 Regul. Sanct. Franc. Argum.

[79] Matt. 8: 27.

sentence of excommunication against the Religious of the Order, and against those who should receive them, he wrote to the bishops of Paris and Tournai, to put a stop to the excesses which he did not hesitate to qualify as rash.

CHAPTER IV
THE FIRST NATIVITY—THE STIGMATA

Celebrates the feast of Christmas with much fervor—Our Lord appears to him as an infant—His sentiments on the celebration of feasts—Discovers a stratagem of the devil—His prophecy to Bologna—He commands one of his dead brethren to cease working miracles—Draws up a rule for Clare and her daughters—Summary of this rule—He sends his cloak to St. Elizabeth—Appears with his arms stretched out in the form of a cross, while St. Anthony was preaching—Foretells a conversion, which immediately came about—He goes into retreat on Mount Alvernus—His contemplation and raptures—Jesus Christ promises him special favors—He fasts rigorously—A piece of his writing delivers his companion from a temptation—What he had to suffer from the devil—He prepares for martyrdom—He receives extraordinary favors in prayer—His perfect conformity to the will of God—Jesus Christ crucified appears to him under the figure of a Seraphim Receives the impression of the wounds of Jesus Christ—He composes canticles full of the love of God—Tells his brethren of the Stigmata.

HILE FRANCIS was still at Rome, he proposed to himself to celebrate the festival of the nativity of our Lord Jesus Christ at Grecio, with all the solemnity possible, in order to awaken the devotion of all in that vicinity. He wrote a letter on the subject to his friend, John Velita, begging him to prepare all things; and in order that there should be no room for censuring what he was about to do, he spoke to the Pope about it, who approved highly of this pious ceremony, and granted indulgences to those who should assist at it.

St. Bonaventure informs us that, before his departure from Rome, he went to pay his respects to Cardinal Leo Brancaleone, titular of Santa Croce, with whom his friendship began in 1210, when he first came to have his Rule approved. This cardinal invited him to stay some days in his palace, because the severity of the weather and the floods might impede his journey; it was the month of December. He retained, to remain with him, with Francis' leave, Brother Angelo Tancredi, whose miraculous conversion we have related; at that time, there were but few of the cardinals who did not wish to have some of the Friars Minor in their company; such was the veneration they had for their virtue at the Roman court. Francis, however, found excuses for not spending more than two or three days in the palace of Brancaleone, saying that it was not fitting for the poor to dwell in the palaces of princes. The cardinal told him that he would receive him as a pauper, and give him a bed, not in his palace, but in an adjacent tower near the city walls quite out of the way of any noise, where he might repose from his fatigue for some time. Tancredi entreated him not to refuse this satisfaction to a prince of the Church, who was a person of great piety, and a generous benefactor to the Order; therefore, out of respect, and from gratitude, he consented to stay, and with his companion took up his abode in the tower.

The following night, when he was about to take some repose, the devils came and beat him so long, and so violently, that they left him half-dead. He called his companion, and told him what had happened, and he added: "Brother, I believe that the devils, who can do nothing without the leave of the Almighty, have ill-used me to this degree, because of my having remained with great people, here; if so, it augurs no good. My brethren who dwell in very poor houses, knowing that I am the guest of cardinals, might suspect that I enter willingly into the concerns of the world, that I glory in honors, and that I am living daintily I therefore think that a man who is to be an example to others, should leave the court, and dwell humbly with the humble, in places adapted to the profession of humility, in order that he may inspire those with fortitude, who suffer the inconveniences of a life of poverty, by suffering with them." In the morning, he took leave of the cardinal, and set out for Grecio.

It is necessary here to remark that St. Francis, who permitted some of his brethren to remain with the cardinals, did not think that he himself, who was the Superior, ought to spend a single night in their palaces, lest others should be disedified thereby, and that it was his duty to give good example to all. This shows how much persons in power should strive not to do anything calculated to give bad examples, and to abstain from certain things which, though irreprehensible in themselves, and which would not be animadverted on in an individual, might be a cause of scandal in one in high station, who ought to be a model of virtue. On this principle, St. Paul said to the Christians: "All things are lawful for me, but all things are not expedient. All things are lawful for me, but all things do not edify. I do all for your edification."[1] He recommended his disciples, Timothy and Titus, whom he had ordained bishops, to be "an example to the faithful, in word, in conversation, in charity, in faith, in chastity, in the practice of good works."[2] St. Gregory, St. Bernard, and all the Holy Fathers have always required of prelates, as a primary qualification, that they should greatly edify; which is the more necessary in the superiors of religious communities, as their example is under more immediate observation.[3]

The bad health of Francis, the beating which he had received from the devils, and a constant fall of rain, compelled him to ride on an ass. During his

---

[1] 1 Cor. 10: 22, 23; 2 Cor. 12: 19.

[2] 1 Tim. 4: 12; Tit. 2: 7.

[3] St. Greg, in Job. lib. ii, cap. 3. et Reg. Past. lib. ii, cap. 6. n. 27. Edit. Bened. St. Bernard, in Cant serm. 76, n. 9. De Div. serm. 35. et 100 et alii, passim.

journey he dismounted to say the Divine Office, standing; he remained on the same spot without paying attention to the rain, and did not mount till he had quite finished. We shall speak on a future occasion of his respect, piety, and great attention in the performance of this holy exercise.

Having reached Grecio, he found all things prepared for the celebration of the festival by his friend Velita. They had prepared a crib in the wood, in which was represented the nativity of our Savior; they had placed straw there, and, during Christmas-night, they took there an ox and an ass. Many Friars Minor had been collected there from the neighboring convents, and the people of the environs came in crowds to the ceremony. The wood was lit up by numerous torches, and resounded melodiously from the sound of a thousand voices which sang the praises of God with untiring zeal. Francis, full of devotion, and with his eyes bathed in tears of holy joy, knelt before the manger, above which an altar had been placed, where mass was celebrated at midnight; he acted as deacon, and after having sung the Gospel, he preached on the birth of the new-born King, become poor, and to whom, from a sentiment of great affection, he gave no other name, when he alluded to Him, than that of the Child of Bethlehem.

Velita, who had prepared the ceremonial, assured them that he had seen a most beautiful child in the manger, who was asleep, and whom Francis tenderly embraced in order to awaken it. There is so much the more reason for giving credit to this marvel, says St. Bonaventure, that he who relates it, as having been an eye-witness of it, was a very holy man, and that it was confirmed by many miracles; for the straw on which the child appeared to be sleeping, had the virtue of curing various maladies amongst cattle; and, what is still more wonderful, those who came to visit the spot, however tepid and indevout they may have been, were inflamed with the love of God. After the death of the Saint, a chapel was erected on the spot, and the altar was placed on the manger, in order that the flesh of the man-God immolated on the cross, might be eaten on the spot on which He had chosen to appear as a sleeping infant.

After the ceremony, Francis retired to the convent of Grecio, where some of the provincial ministers had collected, who had come thither to communicate to him the affairs of their respective provinces. The refectory had been set out in a better style than usual, with napkins and glasses, not only on account of the solemnity of the day, but to show respect to the guests. Francis was displeased at this, and, during dinner, he went to the door of the convent, and took the hat and staff of a pilgrim who was soliciting alms, and then, in this garb, came to the refectory to beg as a poor pilgrim. The superior, who knew him by his voice, said to him, smiling: "Brother pilgrim, there are here very many Religious, who stand in great need of what has been bestowed upon them out of charity; however, come in, and they will give you what they can." Francis came in and sat himself on the ground, where he ate very contentedly some scraps of bread and other things which they gave him on a platter, without choosing to have anything else.

After dinner, he made them a beautiful discourse upon the poverty of Jesus Christ and His Blessed Mother, in which he took occasion to say that savory dishes were ill-suited to the table of poor Religious, particularly on Christmas-day, when the Blessed Virgin had hardly a meal to eat, and when the Infant Jesus had no place in which He could be laid but a stable, where animals were sheltered. He concluded by telling them that the feasts of our Lord and those of the saints, were better kept in the poverty which they had taken so much pains to practice, than by partaking of superfluities and dainties which they had held in abhorrence.

Saint Bonaventure relates his having given a similar instruction on an Easter Sunday. Not having been able to beg out of doors, because he was in a very retired situation, he asked alms of his brethren, as being poor and a stranger, in memory of our Savior, who appeared on the day of His resurrection, under the figure of a stranger, to the disciples who were going to Emmaus;[4] and he afterwards said to them, that going through this world as strangers and pilgrims, as true Israelites, they were bound to celebrate the Passover in a spirit of poverty, which is His passage from this world to His Father.[5]

These instructions are particularly valuable to the Religious, and especially for those who make profession of strict poverty; but there is no faithful Christian who should not know, that in abstaining from servile work, he nevertheless profanes the holiness of festival days, when he employs them in worldly diversions. St. Augustine says,[6] that those Christians who, in celebrating the solemn festivals of martyrs, take occasion to make them an excuse for debauchery and insult, in some degree, torture them, as their executioners did; and that those who trench upon temperance, when the feast of Easter is celebrated, are carnal persons, who expose themselves to being excluded from celebrating it eternally with the angels. In order to sanctify the Lord's Day and other festivals, they should be employed in exercises of piety, in entering into the spirit of the mysteries which the Church celebrates, and in proposing to themselves the example of the saints whom we intend to honor.

Francis remained some time at Grecio, where, one night, when he intended to lay himself down to sleep, he felt a severe headache, and a shivering over his whole body, which quite impeded his resting. Thinking that this might be caused by a feather pillow which his friend Velita had compelled him to accept, in consequence of his infirmities, he called his companion, who was near his cell, and said: "Take away this pillow: I believe the devil is in it." His

---

[4] Luke, 24: 15,16.

[5] John, 13: 1.

[6] St. Aug. in Psalm lix, n. 15; in Psal. lxix, n. 2; et Serm. 252, n. 2.

companion, who took it away, found it extremely heavy, and he had hardly left the cell, that he found himself motionless and dumb. The Father, not doubting of the malignity of the devil, ordered the brother, under obedience, to come back directly; the wicked spirit having immediately left him, he came back and related the state in which he had found himself. The Saint, confirmed by this in the idea with which he had been impressed, that what he had suffered had been brought on by his enemy, he said: "It is true that yesterday, when reciting Compline, I perceived that the devil was approaching, and I prepared to resist him. He is full of malice and artfulness; as he could not sully a soul which God protects by His grace, he endeavored to injure the body, and to prevent the necessary aid being afforded to it, in order to induce it to commit some fault, at least of impatience, and prevent his having recourse to prayer." The holy man was delivered from his sufferings, and got the rest he could not obtain, when his head was laid upon a feather pillow. To what a height of perfection did not God propose to raise this His faithful servant? He did not even allow him to have a small relief from his sufferings. He is a holy God, jealous of the sanctity of souls,[7] who desires to have them purified by all sorts of sacrifices; but, then. His rewards are great.

In this year, 1223, Francis had convened the usual chapter at Whitsuntide, when Brother Albert of Pisa, who had returned from England, was made provincial of Germany, instead of Brother Cesar of Spire. Of Albert we shall have occasion to speak further on. Francis had also sent some of his brethren to establish a convent in an excellent situation near the town of Urbino, which convent was built at the joint expense of the inhabitants of Montebarocchio, and Montegiano.

The historians of the city of Bologna[8] mention his having gone thither in the course of this year, when he preached in the great square, and that, knowing their great immorality, he exclaimed very often, in a loud voice: "City of Bologna, great calamities would, ere this, have befallen you, and you would have been very miserable, if you did not have a powerful protector in my very dear brother, Dominic, who intercedes unceasingly for you." He did not leave the city before she had put a stop to numerous irregularities; and it is believed that there occurred a circumstance, at that time, which is related by one of its historians.[9] While Francis was preaching in the great square, an earthquake was felt, which caused great alarm among the people, because there had been several others in the course of the year, which had thrown down many houses; but the Saint, without manifesting any emotion, continued his discourse, showing to his auditors, that by these direful events, God warns men to quit their evil ways, and that the fruits of so doing would be their speedy

---

[7] Deut. 5: 9, 10.

[8] Sigon. et Leand. apud Wading ad ann. 1223, n. 25.

[9] Sigon. de Epist. Bonon. lib. ii.

conversion.

Whilst Francis was at Grecio and in its environs, Peter of Catania, his first vicar-general, died in the convent of St. Mary of the Angels, on the 2nd day of March, 1224.[10] As soon as he was in the tomb, God bore witness to his merit by many miracles. The people crowded to his grave, and left valuable offerings, which greatly disturbed the quiet of the Religious, and caused them much uneasiness on account of their strict poverty. Francis, having been informed of it, went to the tomb, and, moved by holy zeal, he addressed the dead man in a commanding tone, which God alone could have inspired him with: "Brother Peter, whilst you were living, you always obeyed me punctually: I command you to obey me similarly now. Those who come to your grave are very troublesome to us. Our poverty is offended, and our quiet infringed on, so that our discipline becomes relaxed; thus, I command you, by your vow of obedience, to refrain from performing any more miracles." His order was obeyed. From that moment, no more miracles were performed on the tomb of Brother Peter.

An ancient manuscript chronicle which is preserved in the Vatican, mentions that Francis, having directed the body of Brother Peter to be removed sometime afterwards, it was found that it was turned and kneeling, the head bowed down, and in the posture of one who obeys a command given him. To mark the value of obedience and the respect due to it, God was pleased to permit a dead person to obey the orders of a superior, as if he had been living.

A similar prohibition from performing miracles after death, is recorded in the Life of St. Bernard.[11] Gosvin, abbot of Citeaux, who was at his funeral with many other abbots of his Order, seeing the commotion caused by the numerous miracles which were worked there, and fearing this would become prejudicial to regular discipline, approached respectfully to the coffin, and forbade the saint from performing any more miracles, in virtue of his obedience. And, in fact, from that time, there were no more performed at that shrine publicly, although God performed others privately by his invocation. The author adds, that St. Benedict[12] requires in his Rule, an obedience without reserve, according to the example of Jesus Christ, who was obedient unto death,[13] and that the soul of St. Bernard rendered itself obedient even after death to a mortal man.

Clare, and her daughters of the monastery of St. Damian, entreated Francis to give them a written rule, and a form of life similar to that of the Friars

---

[10] See the long note on Peter of Catania in the beginning of the year 1221, in p. 223, Book III of this Life.

[11] Vita St. Bern. lib. vii, cap. 28; tom. 2. Apoc. edit. Mabill.

[12] Reg. St. Bened. cap. vii.

[13] Phil. 2: 8.

Minor, in order that, in his absence and after his death, they and those who should succeed them might live up to it. These Religious of St. Damian, did not wish to receive the Rule of St. Benedict, nor the constitutions prepared by Cardinal Ugolino, which the other monasteries, established on the plan of St. Damian, had willingly accepted, and which were of great severity: these nuns desired to have a rule which should be of greater rigor.

The holy Patriarch consulted the same cardinal on this subject, he being the protector of both Orders; and they jointly composed a Rule in twelve chapters, which was similar in all respects to that of the Friars Minor, with modifications and usages proper for females. If anything made Francis hesitate, the cardinal gave his opinion either to modify certain parts, or to take precautions on others, and he inserted some articles from the constitutions which had before been drawn up. While he was writing, he could not help shedding tears, in reflecting that young females were willing to practice austerities so much above their strength.

We shall only give a summary of this Rule, in order to show the prudence of the Founder. Ever attentive to the purity of the faith, he desires that Clare,[14] in the name of the sisterhood, as he had done in the name of all his brethren, shall promise obedience and respect to Pope Honorius, and to his successors canonically elected, and to the Roman Church; that those who present themselves to be received, shall be carefully examined on the Catholic faith, and on the sacraments of the Church; and that the sisters shall always have for their protector the cardinal who shall be appointed to that situation for the Friars Minor, by the Pope, in order that, being always submissive to the holy Church and prostrate at its feet, they may ever remain firm in the Catholic faith.

We might not think perhaps that this precaution was requisite for persons of the female sex, whose lot, in every state, is submission and silence; but St. Francis knew that, being naturally curious, they do not let this propensity prevail, less in matters of religion than in other things; and, to take from them all opportunity of letting this injure their faith, he thought it prudent to bind them to the Roman Church, and to the Holy See, by a vow of entire obedience and inviolable attachment. In fact, it is the most efficacious method for restraining an indiscreet curiosity, and for preserving the faith pure and unspotted. Moreover, St. Jerome, who was extremely delicate on this point, wishing to prevent the illustrious Demetrias, who had consecrated herself to Jesus Christ by a vow of virginity, from adopting the errors of Origen, which the priest Rufinus, and Melania, the Elder, had brought from the East, and which then began to spread, gave her this excellent advice in a letter written on the subject of her consecration:

"Follow the faith of the holy Pope Innocent, the disciple and successor of

---

[14] Reg. St. Clar. cap. I, et xii.

Anastasius, and do not receive any strange doctrine, although perhaps you may flatter yourself to be sufficiently clever and sufficiently enlightened to detect its illusions."[15]

Besides, the holy Patriarch was aware that the heretics in all ages took great care to seduce women into their views; whether they were devout or worldly, they were equally useful to them. Ecclesiastical History furnishes sufficient proofs of this, and our age is not deficient in examples. It is well known to whom these words of St. Jerome to Jovinian and Pelagius are applicable: "You have Amazons in your camp. In order to obtain their good graces, you give them liberally knowledge of the law, and you assert in your writings that women ought to possess this knowledge, although the apostle teaches the contrary, that they ought to be silent and submissive."[16] St. Francis, therefore, acted very prudently, in binding, by the strongest and the most sacred ties to the Roman Church and to the Holy See, these religious females, as well as the brethren.

He desired that no female too aged, or infirm, or of weak intellect, should be received; as experience, he said, teaches that these defects are a great obstacle to the regularity of observance.[17]

All the monasteries did not follow his Rule as to young persons, whom he did not permit to be admitted as Religious, till they had attained the proper age, directing that their heads should be shaved, that they should put off their secular dress, and be attired in the coarse stuff used by the community. If persons belonging to the world, and if some Religious, have their reasons why these regulations should not be complied with, it is nevertheless true, on the evidence of the Religious themselves, that pensioners dressed as those who lived in the world, without any vocation for the cloister, and often with dispositions quite opposed to such vocation, particularly when they have attained a certain age, are always the cause of irregularity in a regular community. The bishops who are well aware of this, have often made wise and prudent regulations on the subject of these pensioners, but they have had great difficulty in compelling their observance. It is true, there are institutions of females which are established for the instruction of girls, and in other orders, they are sometimes, as it were, compelled to take pensioners; but in all these establishments it must be a subject requiring great watchfulness, and be one of great anxiety; and we cannot but congratulate the Religious of St. Clare who adhere strictly to their Rule on this head, which is far more important than it may be thought.

In that part in which St. Francis speaks of the confession of the sisters,[18] he

---

[15] St. Hier. Ep. ad Demet.. 97, alias 8.

[16] St. Hier. adv. Jovin. lib ii. sub. fin. Id. Dial. adv. Pelag. lib. I; I Cor, XIV, 34 et 35.

[17] Reg. S. Clar. cap. ii.

[18] Reg. S. Clar. cap, iii.

makes a very useful remark, which may be of service to all persons of the sex; that is, not to say a single word in the confessional but what relates to the confession, and which has not a direct relation to the salvation of the soul. If the Religious would follow this advice literally, they would not be so long at their confessions, and would derive more fruit from it; besides which, they would find it more easy to be provided with confessors.

The instructions which he gives to the abbess,[19] are equally good for all superiors. "As soon as she is elected," says this Holy Man, "let her reflect on the burden which she takes upon her, and of which she is to render an account to God. Let her conform herself to the community in all things, in her clothing, in her food, at church, in the dormitory, in the infirmary; let her preside less by her rank, than by the holiness of her conduct, in order that her sisters, seeing her example, may obey her more from affection than from fear; let her be on her guard against particular friendships, lest, being more attached to some, she may give scandal to others; let her be a source of consolation to the afflicted, so that she may be their last refuge, lest, if she does not assuage their grief, their weakness may cause them to fall into despair." He recommends her to be of easy access to her sisters, to consider herself as their servant; not to put herself in a passion at their faults, to correct them with humility and charity. Entering upon the care of temporal things, he desires the abbess to consult the sisters on the affairs of the house, because it often happens that God discovers to the least, what is most for their advantage. He forbids her to contract any considerable debt, unless with the consent of the community, and from evident necessity, and, above all, not to receive any trust, which is always a subject of inconvenience and scandal.

It is on these important principles of the religious state that he directs all the sisterhood to work together[20] and for the community, and to have nothing of their own; to go seldom to the grille, and to keep entirely away from it in Advent and Lent; never to go alone, and to converse, when there, without seeing or being seen; never to speak at the gate of the monastery; not to write, or to receive letters without leave of the abbess, and to be careful to keep enclosure carefully.

His attention extends even to the lay-sisters[21] who serve the community out of the enclosure. "Let them," he says, "be guarded in their conduct with persons of the world, speaking as little as possible, in order to edify them. When they are under the necessity of going out, let them stop only where it is requisite; above all, let them be very circumspect in regard to men, that they may not give the smallest scope for evil suspicions or evil talk. Let them not be so rash as to bring back to the monastery anything they may have heard out of

---

[19] Ib., cap. iv.

[20] Reg. S. Clar. cap. vii, 5, 1, 1 et seq.

[21] Reg. S. Clar. cap. ix.

it; and let them understand that they are strictly forbidden to communicate out of doors anything which may pass within the walls of the convent, and with which the world might not be edified." No more suitable instructions could be prepared for lay-sisters of all convents of nuns.

Finally, the holy Founder points out[22] the qualifications which the visitors, confessors, and other Religious ought to have, who are employed in giving spiritual or temporal aid to the sisters, "in order that all things," as St. Paul says, "may be done decently and according to order."[23]

For the rest, the strength of mind, discretion, and tender charity of St. Francis, is strikingly apparent in all he dictates, as to the imposition of penances, the dress of the sisters, and the care of the sick.[24]

St. Clare says in her will, addressing herself to the sisters "Our blessed Father, St. Francis, has written for us a form of life, principally that we may ever persevere in the practice of holy poverty, to which he has exhorted us, not only by his word and example, but by many writings which he has left us."[25] Pope Innocent IV expressly declares in the Bull[26] which he issued at the earnest entreaty of St. Clare, three days before her death, that the Rule which he confirms was given them by St. Francis. All is his, except some very trifling things, in no way essential, which seem to have been added to it by Cardinal Ugolino, by St. Clare, and by the Pope. There are a number of monasteries in which it is observed in its full vigor, and it is called the First Rule of St. Clare, because none of the modifications are found in it, which were subsequently added to it by Cardinal Ugolino (when Pope, by the name of Gregory IX), by Innocent IV, in 1246, and by Urban IV, in 1264.

The sanctity of Elizabeth, the daughter of Andrew the Second,[27] king of Hungary, the wife of Louis, Landgrave of Thuringia and Hesse,[28] shone at this time with great splendor. Francis often testified to the cardinal protector, the great esteem in which he held her. What he principally admired in this princess was her humility, charity, mortification, and the love of poverty, in the midst of the grandeur of the world. One day, whilst they were conversing, the cardinal said that such virtue deserved that he should send her his cloak,

---

[22] Ibid., cap. xii.

[23] 1 Cor. 14: 40.

[24] Reg. S. Clar. cap. viii, et ix

[25] Wading ad ann. 1253. n. 1, 5, et 6.

[26] Id. in Reg. St. Clar. argum.

[27] He is surnamed Jerusalimitanus, because he took the Cross for the Holy Wars. His wife, the mother of St. Elizabeth, was Queen Gertrude, daughter of Berthold, Duke of Carinthia.

[28] He was eminently endowed with all the qualifications of a great prince and a perfect Christian. He took the Cross for the Holy War, and died on the voyage, at Oiranto, in Calabria, in the odor of sanctity, in 1227. The author of the History of the Crusades, says that he was equal in piety to his wife Elizabeth, and, on the testimony of the historian of the Landgraves of Thuringia, says that it pleased God to give splendid proofs thereof, by miracles which were performed at his tomb.

that it was a present which was fitting, and that gratitude for all the favors which the princess had bestowed on his Order, did not admit of his refusing it. Francis humbly declined doing this; but the cardinal took the cloak from his back, and ordered him to send it to Elizabeth,[29] which he did. Elizabeth received it with great veneration, she kept it as a precious pledge of ecclesiastical poverty, which she tenderly loved, and which she embraced three years afterwards, when she heard of the death of the Landgrave, her husband. Being herself on the point of death, she gave it, as a mark of friendship, to one of her females, who at that sad moment asked her for a mark of her affection, and she said to her: "I leave you my cloak: don't regard the poorness of the texture, but reflect seriously on the value of such poverty. I declare solemnly, that my dearly beloved Jesus Christ was favorable to my wishes, and loaded me with comfort, every time[30] that, wearing this cloak, I sought to seek His adorable countenance."

It was in this year, 1224, that the marvelous apparition recorded by Wading was seen, which is noticed as follows in the legend of St. Bonaventure:

"Although Francis could not attend the provincial chapters, the order which he had laid down for these assemblies, the fervent prayers which he put up for their success, and the influence of the blessing which he gave them, were as if he were present at them. Sometimes even, God, by His almighty power, caused him to appear among them in a sensible manner, as it happened at the chapter at Arles. While that excellent preacher Anthony was discoursing to the brethren on the Passion of the Son of God, and on the inscription on His cross, 'JESUS OF NAZARETH, KING OF THE JEWS,' one of the Religious, named Monald, a man of exemplary virtue, moved by the Spirit of God to look towards the door of the chapter-house, saw the Blessed Francis, raised into the air with his arms extended in a cross, give his blessing to the assembly. They then became filled with great spiritual consolation, which was an interior testimonial assuring them of the presence of their Father, and confirming what Monald had seen. This became more certain, afterwards, by the avowal which

---

[29] The Rev. Father Archangel, a Religious penitent of the Third Order of St. Francis, who wrote the life of St. Elizabeth, says: "That the Saint accompanied this present with an admirable letter, written with that spirit of zeal, holiness, and love, by which his soul was penetrated, and that in the course of the letter he congratulated St. Elizabeth on all the graces she had received from God, and which the Divine mercy had enabled her to turn to such profit." The writer quotes Wading, and the life of St. Elizabeth, which is in manuscript at Louvain. Nevertheless, Wading does not mention any letter, ad ann. 1226, n. 61, although he gives the very words of the Louvain manuscripts. We may reasonably believe that a letter was sent with the cloak, but it must be admitted that it is not forthcoming, for if Wading had seen it in manuscript, we cannot doubt that he would either have copied the whole of it, or at least have given extracts from it.

[30] In the Manuscript life of St. Elizabeth, which is at Louvain, we find, on the testimony of a celebrated preacher, whose name is brother Berthold, that he had seen and had this cloak in his hands, in a house of the Hospittallers of the Teutonic Order, in a place in the diocese of Spire, which he calls Album Castrum.

Francis made respecting it."

"We should have no difficulty in believing this," continues St. Bonaventure, "for God, by His almighty power, rendered the holy Bishop St. Ambrose,[31] during a mysterious sleep, present at the funeral obsequies of St. Martin; in a similar manner it was His pleasure that the truths announced by His preacher Anthony, on the subject of the cross of Jesus Christ, should receive greater weight by the presence of His servant Francis, who carried the cross with such exemplary courage, and preached it with such zeal."

Having given a Rule to the sisters of St. Damian, and transacted all that related to the three Orders, he recommended strongly to the vicar, Brother Elias, to attend carefully, and to see that everything was carried into effect, and then thought it necessary to take some time to attend to his own interior. For it was his custom to go from one good work to another, in which he imitated, St. Bonaventure says, the angels[32] whom Jacob saw in his dream, going up and down the mysterious ladder, the feet of which rested on the earth, but its summit reached the heavens. This angelic man so employed the time which was given him, in which to amass treasures of merit, that he was constantly occupied either in descending to his neighbor by the laborious ministries of charity, or in elevating himself to God in the quiet exercise of contemplation. When circumstances had compelled him to give more time to the service of souls, he afterwards retired to some lonely and noiseless place, to remove from his own, by giving his thoughts solely to God, all the filth which might have attached itself to it, in his discourse with men. Our Lord often gave His apostles examples of retreats, and they cannot be too often recommended to those who labor for the salvation of their neighbors.

Francis, therefore, went with some of his brethren to meditate in the convent of Celles, near Cortona. He met on the road a lady of good family, who was very pious and in great affliction, having a husband who used her cruelly, and prevented her from serving God. She told him that she was come to pray to God for the conversion of her husband, and he made her this answer: "Go in peace; and rest assured that your husband will soon afford you consolation; only tell him from God and from me, that now is the time of mercy, and that afterwards will be the time of justice." The lady received the Father's blessing, and said what she had been desired to her husband. The Holy Spirit descended at the same moment on this man, and he became so

---

[31] This marvelous event is recorded by St. Gregory of Tours and the tradition has been uniform and unfailing in the churches of Tours and Milan. Cardinal Frederic Borromeo, Archbishop of Milan, cousin and successor to St. Charles, maintained its correctness with pertinacity, against some critics of his age. Cardinal Baronius takes a different view, because he asserts that St. Martin did not die till after St. Ambrose; but the continuators of Bollandus proved clearly that St. Ambrose survived St. Martin by several months, at least; all these proofs are collected with accuracy in a dissertation on the time of the death of St. Martin, which is at the end of his life, written by the Abbé Gervase, and printed at Tours in 699. St. Gregor. Turon. De Mirae. S. Martin, lib. I. cap. v.

[32] Genes. 28: 12.

changed, that he said to his wife in a mild tone of voice, "Madam, let us serve God and work out our salvation." He passed thus many years with her in continence, with which she had inspired him, and they died most holily on the same day.

We saw in the first two Tertiaries, a wife sanctified by her husband. This is precisely what St. Paul says:[33] "The one may contribute to the sanctification of the other." In fact, St. Chrysostom[34] thinks that a virtuous woman who is mild and prudent, is more likely to bring back a profligate husband to the service of God, than any other person; and that the solid piety of a husband, with good manners and discreet firmness, may soften the asperity of an ill-tempered woman, or at least render her less fractious.

All that Francis did at Celles, was to give himself up to contemplation; and, in order that the place itself should be favorable to meditation, he resolved, after having been there a short time, to retire to the desert of Mount Alvernia; it was the Holy Spirit who inspired him with the desire to go thither, where he was to receive the glorious privilege of the stigmata. As he passed through the country of Arezzo, his great infirmities compelled him to ask for an ass to continue his journey. There was not one in the village, but a person offered him a horse, which he was under the necessity of accepting: it was the only time that he had been on horseback since his conversion; for, whenever he had been forced to ride, he took the most despicable animal, in order to set an example to his brethren. In the village to which the horse was sent back, there was a woman who, for several days, was suffering cruelly from labor-pains, without being able to be delivered, so that no human hope remained of saving her life. The people of the place, seeing the horse brought back which had carried the Saint, took the bridle and placed it on the woman's bed, in full confidence that he who had had the use of it, would come to her aid; and, in fact, she was immediately, most fortunately, delivered. This fact is one of those related by St. Bonaventure.

On Mount Alvernia Francis reaped extraordinary consolations in meditation; he was filled with ardent desires of heaven, and, at the same time, he felt that the celestial gifts were communicated to him in greater abundance. These interior feelings which threw his soul into ecstasies, raised his body into the air to greater or less height, in proportion to their degree, as if an extreme disgust for every thing that was connected with the earth, gave him a stimulus to raise himself to his celestial home.

Brother Leo, his secretary and his confessor, attests to have seen him raised sometimes to the height of a man, so that they could touch his feet, sometimes, above the tallest beech-trees, and sometimes so high, that he was elevated out of sight. When he was not raised higher than the height of a man, Leo kissed

---

[33] 1 Cor. 7: 14.

[34] St. Chrysos. Homil 19, in cap. vii, 1 Cor.

his feet and watered them with his tears, with tender devotion, saying the following prayer: "My God, be merciful to me, a sinner such as I am, by the merits of this Holy Man, and deign to communicate to me some small portion of Your grace." When he lost sight of him, he prostrated himself and prayed, on the spot on which he had seen him elevate himself.

St. Thomas[35] and many others believed that St. Paul in his rapture may have been elevated in body and soul into the third heaven, that is, into the Empyrean, into Paradise, into the place where the angels and the blessed are; and we must not call this in question, since the apostle himself says, that he does not know whether he was raised up in the body or out of the body. St. Teresa,[36] whose works are published by authority, says that she had sometimes raptures in which she was raised from the ground by a supernatural power, whatever resistance she might make; that others saw her in this state, and she saw herself in it. We may therefore believe that God raised the body of His servant Francis, while his soul was in raptures by interior operations; more particularly, as the thing is attested by so trustworthy a witness as Leo, who certifies having seen it with his own eyes. "God," says St. Teresa, "grants extraordinary favors to a soul, to detach it entirely from everything that is earthly, by the body itself, so that life becomes burdensome to it, and that it suffers a sort of torment brought on by a violent desire of possessing God, which is a martyrdom both agreeable, and, at the same time, painful; but we must be under the impression, that with ordinary grace, which God increases in proportion to faithfulness, we may attain to an entire disengagement from worldly affairs, and to that longing for heaven which, as Christians, we are obliged to feel."

One day, when Francis was restored from one of the ecstasies which had raised him from the ground, Jesus Christ appeared seated at a low stone table, where the Saint was in the habit of taking his meals, and speaking to him with the familiarity of a friend, as to the protection which He proposed to give to the Order after his death, He made known to him the following points: first, that the Order would last to the end of the world; secondly, that those who should persecute the Order, would not be long-lived, unless they became converted; the third and fourth points, related to favors which our Savior promised not only to the Friars Minor, but to those who were sincerely attached to them.

These favors are very great, but there is nothing incredible in them. As to the first, although it be true that the Order of Friars Minor may be abolished by the Pope, as may every other order, yet there is every reason to believe that it will exist continually in the Church, out of respect for the Gospel on which it is wholly based; and it is not impossible that this may be God's will. As to the

---

[35] 1a, 2ae, Quaest 175, art. 5, et 6; et in 2 Cor 12, lect. 1, 2 Cor XII: 2.

[36] Life of St. Teresa, ch. 20.

second, it would be by no means surprising that the Divine Justice should punish, by a premature death, those who should be so irreligious, and have so much malignity, as obstinately to persecute an Order which was instituted to do good to all mankind, and to be of service to the entire Church. The prophet says, that the Lord sometimes gives sensible marks of His protection to the just, by cutting off from sanguinary and disingenuous men a portion of their days.[37] As to the graces which Jesus Christ promises to the Friars Minor and to the friends of their Order, we may easily understand that there are some peculiar to the Religious who have the fortitude to embrace a line of life wholly evangelical and apostolical; and that God grants also special graces to those Christians, who, from a principle of religion, become friendly to this Institution; but it must be borne in mind that these graces require, under all circumstances, a free and faithful cooperation, without which there is nothing to hope for, as to the next world, in whatever state of life the party may be. It would be a gross and most deplorable illusion, to flatter one's self that, not living as we ought to live, we might be saved merely because of being a Religious of the Order of St. Francis, or because we have a friendly feeling for the Order.

When our Lord had disappeared from the table,[38] Brother Leo, not knowing what had happened, was about to prepare it, as usual, for their meal, but Francis stopped him, saying: "It must be washed with water, with wine, with milk, with oil, and with balm, for Jesus Christ has condescended to sit on it, and to make known to me from thence what will be communicated to you hereafter."

As Brother Leo had not the articles he required, he only took oil, as Jacob had done, to consecrate this table to the Lord, and, having poured it upon it, he pronounced these words: "This is the altar of God."[39] He then told his companion the four favors which had been promised and added that there was a fifth which he should not repeat; it was thought that it was out of humility; for, after his death, it was revealed to Brother Leo, that it consisted in that God, in consequence of the merits of the Saint, had deferred punishing the country by famine, to give sinners time to be converted; and, as they did not avail themselves of it, after his death, this scourge fell on the land, and was followed by a great mortality.

Towards the feast of the Assumption of the Blessed Virgin, he retired into the most secret part of the mountains, where his companions built for him a

---

[37] Ps. 54 (55): 24.

[38] Alvernia; but as pieces were constantly broken off to carry away from motives of devotion, for the last three hundred years, it has been placed in a chapel of the same church, where, surrounded by an iron grating, it is seen with the following inscription: "Table of St. Francis, on which he had extraordinary apparitions, and which he consecrated by pouring oil on it, saying, 'This is the altar of God.'"

[39] Genes. 28: 18, and 35: 14.

small and unpretending cell. He remained there with Leo, having forbidden the others to return to him till the feast of St Michael, and on no account to permit any persons whomsoever to have access to him. It was then the time of the fast which he prescribed for himself, in honor of the Archangel, one of the nine periods of fasting he observed during the year, which will be noticed elsewhere. Proposing to fast this year more rigorously than in the preceding years, he directed Brother Leo to bring him nothing but bread and water once a day, and that, towards evening, and place it at the threshold of his cell. "And when you come to me for Matins," he added, "don't come into the cell, but only say in a loud voice, 'Domine, labia mea aperies;' and if I answer, 'Et os meum annuntiabit laudem tuam',[40] you will come in, otherwise you will go back." His pious companion, who had nothing more at heart than to obey him, and be useful to him, complied minutely with all he said; but he was often obliged to return in the night, because the Holy Man was in ecstasy, and did not hear him.

The reward of his solicitude was to be freed from a mental agitation, which he had found very troublesome; although it was not a temptation of the flesh, he nevertheless was ashamed of it, and did not dare make his Father acquainted with it; he only wished to have something written by him, which he thought would enable him to overcome the temptation, or at least enable him to bear it with less difficulty. The Father, knowing by revelation the state of his mind and his wish, desired him to bring him paper and ink, and he put on the top of the paper, in large characters, the letter "Tau," after which he wrote some praises of God, with this blessing: "May the Lord bless you and take you into His keeping; may He show you His countenance, and take pity on you may He turn His eyes towards you, and give you His peace. May God bless Brother Leo."[41] "Take this paper," he said, "and keep it carefully all your life." Leo had no sooner received it than his temptation left him; he preserved it carefully till his death, knowing the virtue that was attached to it. This writing is still extant at Assisi, in the sanctuary of the Church of St. Francis, and God has permitted it to be frequently used for the cure of diseases. St. Bonaventure says that, in his days, it had been the means by which several miracles had been effected.

Francis experienced on Mount Alvernia, what had occurred to St. Anthony[42] in the desert of Thebais: after having been the means of freeing others from the attacks of the devil, he was exposed to them himself. The subtle spirit often suggested evil thoughts to him. He placed horrid specters before him, and he even visibly struck him severe blows. Once in a very

---

[40] These verses are from Psalm 50 (51) and are the first verse of Matins in the Roman Breviary: "O Lord you will open my lips." R: "And my mouth will announce your praise." —Editor's note.

[41] Num. 6: 24, 25, 26; Ps. 66 (67): 1.

[42] Vit. S. Anton, n. 48 et 51, tom. I, Oper. S. Athan.

narrow path, and on the edge of a deep precipice, he appeared to him in a hideous figure, and threw himself upon him to cast him down; as there was nothing by which he could support himself, Francis placed his two hands on the rock,[43] which was very hard and slippery, and they sank into it, as if it had been soft wax, and this preserved him from falling. An angel appeared to him to put away his fright, and to console him, causing him to hear celestial music, the sweetness of which in so far suspended the powers of his soul, that it seemed to him that it would have been separated from his body, had it lasted much longer.

He resumed his prayer in which he returned thanks for having escaped the danger, and for the consolation he had received; then he set about considering what might be the will of God. He was not, as St Bonaventure remarks, like to those inquisitive minds, who rashly endeavor to scrutinize the ways of God,[44] and who are overwhelmed with His glory; but as a faithful and prudent servant, he endeavored to discover the intention of his Master, only from the anxiety he felt to conform himself to it in all things. A divine impression induced him to think that, if he opened the Book of the Gospel, he would learn from Jesus Christ what in him and for him would be most agreeable to God. Having, therefore, again prayed with great fervor, he told Brother Leo to take the New Testament from the altar, and open it; Leo opened it three times in honor of the most Holy Trinity, and, each time, he opened it at the Passion of our Blessed Lord. Francis, who was filled with the Spirit of God, understood from that, that, as he had imitated Jesus Christ in the actions of His life, he must now conform himself to His sufferings, and in the pains of His Passion.

Although his body was greatly weakened by the austerities he practiced, by which he incessantly carried the cross of the Son of God, he was not alarmed at the idea of having new sufferings to endure; on the contrary, he put on fresh courage for martyrdom, in which, he thought, consisted that conformity to the Passion of Jesus Christ, according to the wish he had three times entertained of exposing himself to it. For the love he had for the good Jesus, remarks St. Bonaventure, was so lively, that the following words of the Canticles, seemed to be applied to him: "His lamps are lamps of fire and flame."[45] The charity which inflamed his heart was so ardent and forcible, that all the waters of tribulation, and all the fury of persecution would have been unable to extinguish it. It is in this sense that St. Paul said: "Who shall separate us from the love of Christ? shall tribulation? or distress? or famine? or nakedness? or danger? or persecution? or the sword?"[46] Such is the exalted

---

[43] Wading quotes a writer who died in the fifteenth century, who says that the impressions of the Saint's hands were still seen on the rock. Ad ann. 1224, n. 8.

[44] Prov. 25: 27.

[45] Cant. 8: 6, 7.

[46] Rom. 8: 35.

love,[47] which Christians should have for God, if they desire to love Him eternally; their hearts must be ready and willing to make every sacrifice, and to suffer everything in order to preserve this divine love.

Some days after the opening of the book of the Gospel, Leo had come at midnight to say aloud, at the door of Francis' cell, "Domine labia mea aperies" according to the order he had received; and receiving no reply, he had the curiosity to advance a step further, and to look through the chinks of the door, to see what was going on. He saw the cell entirely illuminated, and a bright ray of light come from heaven, and rest upon the head of the Saint; he heard voices which made questions and answers; and he remarked that Francis, who was prostrate, often repeated these words: "Who are You, O my God, and my dear Lord? and who am I? a worm, and Your unworthy servant." He also saw him put his hand three times into his bosom, and each time stretch it out to the flame.

The light disappeared, the conversation ceased, and Leo wished to retire quickly; but the Father heard him, and rebuked him severely for having watched him, and thus seen what ought to have been secret. Leo asked pardon, and having obtained it, he humbly entreated his master to explain to him, for the greater glory of God, the things he had seen, which Francis did in these terms:

"God manifested himself to me in the flame which you saw; He explained many mysteries to me, by His infinite goodness, and He communicated to me an immense knowledge of himself, and I was so overpowered with admiration, that I exclaimed: 'Who are You, Lord, and who am I?' For nothing has tended more to my knowledge of what I am, than the contemplation of the infinite and incomprehensible abyss of the perfections of God, although from afar, and under obscure veils.

"The Lord then having condescended to discover to me, as much as I am capable of knowing of His infinite greatness, I could not avoid making this reflection; that it is certain that every treasure is a mere nonentity before God. While I was thus meditating, it was His pleasure to direct that, for all the good He had done me, I should make Him some offering; I replied that my poverty was so great, that except the poor habit which I wore, I had nothing in the world but my body and my soul, which I had long since dedicated to Him. The Lord then urged me to offer Him what was in my bosom, and I was surprised to find there a beautiful piece of gold, which I immediately offered to Him; I found three pieces successively, which I presented to Him in the same manner; it was when you saw me extend my hand in the flame. I gave thanks to God for His many benefits, and for the means He put in my power to make Him some acknowledgment. He gave me to understand that the three pieces of gold, which were highly agreeable to Him, represented the three modes of life

---

[47] See Bourdaloue's beautiful Sermon on the Love of God; it is one of the most useful instructions that can be given to Christians.

which it had been His will that I should institute, and also the three vows of poverty, obedience, and chastity, when they are kept as they ought to be by religious persons." After this recital he sent Leo away, and forbade his prying in future into what he should be doing in private.

When he said that nothing had tended so much to the knowledge of what he was, as the contemplation of the infinite perfections of God, he well knew that the best mode to attain the knowledge of God is to know one's self, as St. Augustine and St. Bernard teach us;[48] that is to say, that in order to our obtaining peculiar lights which open to us the grandeur of God, it is necessary to be thoroughly impressed with our own vileness, be sensible of our misery, and annihilate ourselves, because the Divine Majesty only communicates itself to the humble. But St. Francis proposed to himself to explain that, when it pleases God to manifest himself in some manner to a soul which is duly sensible of its nothingness, it is better impressed with its own nothingness, by the disproportion it sees between the Sovereign Being and His creature, which discovers to it a thousand imperfections which it was not previously aware of, as a ray of the sun, penetrating into a room, discovers a multitude of atoms of which we were previously unaware.

We may also form to ourselves an idea of it by our knowledge of human ignorance; a half-learned man is less sensible of his ignorance, and sometimes he is not at all aware of it; he thinks he knows everything; but a very learned man knows that he is ignorant of an infinity of things, and finds his mind very confined. So also souls which are interiorly enlightened as to the greatness of the Divinity, are more perfectly aware of their own nothingness, and are more humble than those who have not similar views. The mode adopted by the former is to dive into its own nothingness by the light of faith, to humble itself continually, in order to attain to a more exalted idea of the greatness of God and to repeat frequently this prayer of St. Augustine: "O God, who are always the same! may I know myself, may I know You."[49]

The self-knowledge which St. Francis possessed in such perfection, prepared him sufficiently for the signal favor which God proposed to confer upon him, according to the principle of St. Augustine,[50] that deep foundations are requisite for a building of great height.

About the festival of the Exaltation of the Cross, which is on the fourteenth of September (it is believed that it was on the eve), an angel appeared to him and gave him notice, as he afterwards communicated to some of his companions, to prepare himself for all that God would do for him. "I am prepared for everything," he replied, "and I shall not in any way oppose His holy will, provided he condescends to assist me with His grace. Although I am

---

[48] S. Aug. Tract, xviii, in Joan. n. 10; S. Bernard de Div. Term. ii, n. 1, in Cant. Serm. xxxvi, n. 6.

[49] S. Aug. Soliloq. lib. ii, n. 1, tom. I, Opera Omnia.

[50] Id. Serm. lxix n. 2. Edit. Bened.

a useless man, and unworthy that God should cast a thought on me, nevertheless, as I am His servant, I beg He may act by me, according to His good pleasure."

This generous concurrence, which had martyrdom in its view, was the last disposition which the Almighty required previous to giving to Francis the peculiar and signal prerogative of the stigmata, that is to say, previous to imprinting on his body the five wounds of our Savior Jesus Christ. We are about to put on record this marvelous event as nearly as possible in the very words of St. Bonaventure, which we have extracted from his two legends.[51] He does not name the precise day, but Wading assigns good reasons for thinking it occurred on the festival of the Exaltation of the Cross.

"Francis, the servant and truly faithful minister of Jesus Christ, being one morning in prayer on one side of the mountain of Alvernia, elevating himself to God by the seraphic fervor of his desires, and by the motives of tender and affectionate compassion, transforming himself into Him who, by the excess of His charity, chose to be crucified for us; he saw, as it were, a seraph, having six brilliant wings, and all on fire, descending towards him from the height of heaven. This seraph came with a most rapid flight to a spot in the air, near to where the Saint was, and then was seen between his wings the figure of a crucified Man, who had his hands and feet extended and fastened to a cross. His wings were so arranged that he had two of them on his head, two were stretched out to fly with, and he covered his whole body with the two others.

"At the sight of such an object, Francis was extraordinarily surprised; joy, mingled with grief and sorrow, spread over his soul; the presence of Jesus Christ, who manifested himself to him under the figure of a seraph in so marvelous a manner, and with such familiarity, and by whom he found himself considered so favorably, caused in him an excess of pleasure; but the sorrowful spectacle of His crucifixion filled him with compassion, and his soul felt as if it was pierced through with a sword. Above all, he admired with deep concern that the infirmity of His sufferings should appear under the figure of a seraph, well knowing that this does not agree with His state of immortality; and he could not comprehend the intention of the vision, when our Lord, who appeared outwardly, communicated to him interiorly, as to His friend, that He had been placed before him in order to let him know that it was not by the martyrdom of the flesh, but by the inflammation of the soul, that he was to be wholly transformed into a perfect resemblance to Jesus Christ crucified.

"The vision vanished, after having had a secret and familiar conference with him, leaving his soul filled with seraphic ardor, and imprinting on his body a figure similar to that of the crucifix, as if his flesh, like softened wax,

---

[51] They call his second Legend, the abridgment which he made of the first, in order that it might be read in the Divine Office. All that is said of the stigmata in either of them, is narrated with great exactness. Those who have only read the small Legend of the Office, must not be surprised to find some trifling circumstances in it, which are not in the more extended one.

had received the impression of the letters of a seal. For the marks of the nails immediately began to show themselves on his hands and feet, such as he had seen them on the figure of the crucified man. His feet and hands were seen to be perforated by nails in their middle; the heads of the nails, round and black, were on the inside of the hands, and on the upper parts of the feet; the points, which were rather long, and which came out on the opposite sides, were turned and raised above the flesh, from which they came out. There was, likewise, on his right side[52] a red wound, as if it had been pierced with a lance, and from this wound there often oozed a sacred blood, which soaked his tunic, and anything he wore round his middle."

This is the new prodigy which Jesus Christ chose to exhibit in favor of Francis, in order to render him more like to himself. He marked him and ornamented him with His own wounds, by a singular and glorious prerogative which had never, previously, been conceded to any one, and which justly excites the admiration of the Christian world. St. Bonaventure is of opinion that all human encomium falls short of what it deserves. In fact, in the midst of all the marvels which we find in the life of St. Francis, we are compelled to admit that this is the one which, without any exaggeration, may be termed incomparable. What can there be so beautiful as to be visibly clothed with Jesus Christ, to bear on his body the lively resemblance of those wounds which are the price of our redemption, the source of life, and the pledge of salvation? What interior conformity must the Servant have had with his Master, to have deserved to have so marked a one exteriorly, for, no doubt, the one was in proportion to the other! This faithful Servant having embraced the cross from the very commencement of his conversion, he carried it in his heart, in his mind, in his body, and in all his senses; all his love or his desires were centered in the cross, it was the standard of his militia. Therefore did Jesus Christ, whose goodness appears with magnificence towards those who love Him, after having honored the zeal of Francis by various apparitions in His crucified state, choose, as a crowning of all His favors, that he should be himself crucified, in order that, as the love of the cross constituted his merit before God, the glory of being so miraculously fastened to it, should render him admirable in the sight of mankind.

Such was the sort of torment which God reserved for him in order to satisfy the extreme desire he had to suffer martyrdom, on which St. Bonaventure exclaims: "O truly fortunate man, whose flesh not having been tortured by the racks of a tyrant, has, nevertheless, borne the impress of the Lamb that was slain. O fortunate soul, who have not lost the palm of martyrdom, although it was not separated from the body by the sword of the

---

[52] Saint Bonaventure says in the 13th chapter of his Legend, "Dextrum quoque latus, quasi lancea transfixum, rubra cicatrice abductum erat;" and in the 14th chapter he says: "Vulnus laterisplaga lateris;" which makes it clear that by the word "Cicatrice" he meant a wound, and an open wound. Could he have had any other meaning, he who adds that blood often issued from it?

persecutor!"

Must we not also admit that the impression of the five wounds of our Savior Jesus Christ on his body was a true martyrdom, a precious martyrdom; rigorous in one sense, and the more so, as it was not the consequence of the cruelty of executioners, but was owing to darts of divine love, and to the very influence of the Son of God, the operation of which is most powerful; sweet and delicious in another sense, and the more so, as it was the effect of a most affectionate communication, and brought about more intimate relations? Our Savior, thus, in some degree, represented in His creature the situation in which He had been on the cross, enjoying sovereign beatitude, while He suffered all the pains and violence of the execution.

It was in all probability after this favor of the stigmata, that Francis composed the two Italian canticles which are found amongst his works. In the first,[53] the burden of which is, *"In foco l'amor mi mise, in foco l'amor mi mise,"*[54] he describes very practically, with figurative and very lively expressions, the struggle he had with divine love, and the attacks he had himself made on that love, the wounds which he received, the flames by which his heart was kindled, and the state of languor and faintness to which he found himself reduced, and, finally, the strength which Jesus Christ had imparted to him, with a tranquillity of feeling exceedingly refreshing. In the second,[55] which is much longer than the first, he describes the strength, elevation, and tenderness, the vehemence of the divine love in his heart; he enters into conversation with Jesus Christ, who answers him; and this love constantly increasing, he declares that he can resist no longer, that he consents to everything, and that he wishes no other relief than to die of love.

St. Teresa, speaking of her situation at prayer, in which she often found herself, as it were, intoxicated with the love of God, and quite beside herself, said:[56] "I know a person who, without being a poet, sometimes made very good extempore verses in spiritual canticles,[57] which expressed beautifully her

---

[53] It was translated into Latin by H. Chifellius of Antwerp, he who has written the war of Grenada in heroic verse; the translation is amongst the works of St. Francis, which were published by Wading in 1623.

[54] "Into love's furnace I am cast, into love's furnace I am cast" —Editor.

[55] Father James Lampugnano, an Italian, of the Society of Jesus, translated this into several sorts of Latin verse, and it is thought that it could not be better done. The translation of this is found with that of the first canticle.

[56] It is in the sixteenth chapter of her Life, written by herself, translated by the Abbé Chanut, one of the three Visitors-General of the French Carmelites, printed in 1691, which is in every respect much superior to that of M. Arnauld d'Andilly of 1670.

[57] They are the sort of Spanish verses called Gloses, in which one verse is repeated at the end of each strophe. The repetition in the glose of St. Teresa is, "Que muero porque non muero:" "I die of grief for not dying." They were printed at Antwerp in the year 1649, in Spanish, with her other works. M. de la Mannoye, of the French Academy, has made an excellent translation of them in French; it would be very desirable that the two Canticles composed by St. Francis were also

sufferings. It was not from her mind that they originated; but, in order to the glory so delicious a suffering caused her, she laid her complaint in this manner before God. She would have wished to tear herself to pieces to show the pleasure she experienced in this delightful pain." These spiritual and divine emotions are neither known nor relished by profane minds and hearts, who only learn from their own corruption, and from the pestiferous books which encourage it, the extravagances and transports of criminal love; but pure minds, who know what it is to love God, and to be loved by Him, are not astonished at the effects which this holy reciprocated love produced in a St. Francis, in a St. Teresa, and in many others. Neither is it surprising that the saints who are full of the thoughts of God, should have had recourse to poetry to express the feelings of their hearts, since the sacred writers, inspired by the Spirit of God, have composed many of the sacred books in poetry,[58] and that the doctors[59] of the Church have addressed to the Almighty in verse prayers full of the tenderest sentiments of piety; it is also what is practiced by the universal Church in her Divine Office.

The precious wounds which Francis had received, were a subject of great embarrassment to him; for, in the first place, he wished to conceal them wholly, well knowing that it is "proper to conceal the secrets of the king," as the angel said to Tobit;[60] and, in the second place, he saw that the wounds were too conspicuous to remain long hidden from those of his companions who had familiar intercourse with him. His hesitation was, whether he should tell them what had occurred, in confidence, or whether he should be silent on the subject, for fear of making known the secrets of the Lord. He called some of them to him and laid before them his difficulty in general terms, and solicited their advice. Brother Illuminatus, he from whom he had received such excellent advice in the camp before Damietta, opining, from the look of astonishment which he remarked in him, that he had seen something wonderful, said: "Brother, you ought to know that it is not only for your own edification, but for that of others also, that God sometimes discovers his secrets to you, for which reason you should be fearful of being reprimanded for having hidden the talent, unless you make known what is to be of service

---

translated by as clever a poet. See the Memoirs of Trevaux, 17, v. 2, Sept. art. 8.

[58] See Dom. Calmet's Dissertation on the Poetry of the Ancient Hebrews, at the beginning of his Commentary on Exodus and on the Psalms, tome ii.

[59] St. Gregory of Nazianzen, St. Ambrose, St. Paulin, and others. Calmet complains, with reason, that wits who are good poets attach themselves to trifles, or to subjects which excite or flatter the passions. He says that the advantages they have received from God in their poetic talents, ought to be employed in rendering the truths and maxims of region agreeable. However, he admits that Christian poetry up to this time had not been successful, which he attributes to the corruption of the age, and to the licentiousness of the upper classes. And indeed this is the principal cause; but it has this further effect, that the truths of the orthodox faith and the maxims of Christian morality are not relished either in verse or prose. Dissert, sur la Poesie des Hebreux.

[60] Tob. 12: 7.

to many."[61]

Francis was struck with this advice, and although on other occasions he was in the habit of saying with Isaiah, "My secret is to myself,"[62] he communicated to them all that had passed in the apparition, but always with great fear; adding, that He who had appeared to him, had communicated things to him which, while he lived, he never would disclose to any one. We must believe, as St. Bonaventure remarks, that the seraph whom he saw attached to the cross in so wonderful a manner, or rather, Jesus Christ Himself in the appearance of a seraph, had said to him, as he had to St. Paul, "Secret words, which it is not granted to man to utter;"[63] either because there are no words in which they can be expressed, or, as a respected author thinks,[64] because there are no souls sufficiently disengaged from sensible objects, and sufficiently pure, to understand them.

[61] Matt. 26: 26.

[62] Isa. 24: 16.

[63] 2 Cor. 12: 4.

[64] Reflexions Morales sur le Nouveau Testament. A Paris chez Montalan 1714 et 1716.

CHAPTER V
SISTER DEATH

They are seen and touched—He leaves Mount Alvernus, to return to St. Mary of the Angels—Cures a child of dropsy—Other miracles which he performed on the way—His prayer in suffering—Canticle of Brother Sun—Makes peace between the bishop and magistrates of Assisi—He learns the time of his death, and rejoices at it—Gives himself a severe penance—He has various illnesses, and suffers extreme pain—He multiplies the grapes in a vineyard—He weeps incessantly, and says he does so to expiate for his sins—He prefers the danger of losing his sight to restraining his tears—A miracle is worked by some of his hair, in favor of this physician—He miraculously heals a canon— His sufferings diminish—Goes to preach—Drives away a devil—Foretells a sudden death, and it comes about—Cures St. Bonaventura in his infancy—Causes to be found for the love of God what could not be found for money—He answers difficult questions, and foretells several things—He causes the blessing which he gave to his brethren to be written out—A letter, which he addressed to the whole Order—They take him to Celles, and thence to Assisi—The bishop has him taken to his palace—The state of his Order at the time of his last illness.

HE CONFIDENCE which Francis had reposed in his companions, did not prevent his taking every precaution possible to hide, as much as it was in his power, the sacred marks with which the King of kings had secretly favored him. From that time forward, he kept his hands covered, so that the nails should not be seen, and he wore slippers, which covered those of his feet. Wading[1] saw in the monastery of the Poor Clares of Assisi, the sort of slippers which St. Clare made for her spiritual Father, so neatly contrived that the upper part covered the heads of the nails, and, the underneath being somewhat raised, the points did not prevent his walking; for these miraculous nails did not take from him the use of his hands and feet, although it was painful to him to use them.

But all the precautions which his humility had suggested, became useless, as it is God's province to reveal, for His greater glory, the wonderful things which He does. The Lord Himself, who had secretly marked on Francis the impressions of His Passion, by their means worked miracles, which manifestly disclosed their hidden and marvelous virtue. Moreover, the saintly man could not prevent his wounds from being seen and touched by persons whose veracity cannot be called in question, and who rendered public testimony thereto; besides which, after his death, all the inhabitants of Assisi saw,

---

[1] Wading, ad ann. 1224. n. 23.

touched, and kissed them. The Sovereign Pontiffs of those days were so convinced of this admirable event, that they issued Bulls to exalt it by their praise, and to repress by their authority those who refused credence to the fact, because they had not seen it with their own eyes. Pope Alexander IV certified it, as having been an eye-witness to it, in a sermon and in a Bull; and St. Bonaventure says that the proofs then collected made it so certain, that they were sufficient to dispel every shade of doubt. This decree of certainty is still further enhanced and rendered more respectable, since Popes Benedict XI, Sixtus IV, and Sixtus V have consecrated and canonized the impression of the stigmata on the body of St. Francis, by having instituted a particular festival in their honor, which is found in the Roman Martyrology,[2] on the 17th of September, and which is kept in the universal Church.

There is so much to be said on this interesting subject, that we have thought it useful to give a particular history of it at the end of this work, in which we shall invincibly demonstrate the truth of the stigmata of St. Francis, against the impiety of heretics and libertines, against hard believers, against the malignity of certain critics, who are even in some sense worse than the former; in which we shall show that these holy wounds are calculated to enkindle the love of Jesus Christ crucified in the hearts of the faithful.

The forty days which Francis had resolved to pass in solitude and fasting having terminated on Michaelmas Day, this new man, whom perfect love had transformed by a lively resemblance into Him whom he loved, descended from the mountain, carrying with him the image of Jesus Christ crucified, not modeled by the hand of a workman on wood or stone, but stamped on his very flesh by the finger of the living God Himself, as St. Bonaventure expresses it. He became more partial than ever to Mount Alverno, where he had received this sacred image, and recommended to his brethren to cherish great respect for this holy place.

As he descended the mountain, he met a number of the country people who had already heard of the marvelous occurrence; it is probable that God had informed the people of it by some extraordinary manifestation. At the time when it occurred, they saw at break of day the mountain illuminated by a most brilliant light, and what they heard, informed them of the reason. They wished to kiss his hands; but they were tied round with bandages, and he only offered them the tips of his fingers.

In a village near Arezzo, they brought him a child of about eight years of age, who had been dropsical for four years, whom he cured instantaneously by touching him. He went afterwards to Montaigne, where Count Albert, the lord of that place, who was his good friend, and at whose house he often took his bed, received him with great pleasure. But the Count was distressed to hear him say that his infirmities would not allow him to return there any more, and

---

[2] Baronius, nota in Martyrol. Rom. 17 Sept.

that the time of his death was hastening on. To mitigate the grief of such melancholy tidings, he entreated the saint to leave him some memorial of their friendship; to which Francis replied, that he had nothing to give but the miserable habit he had on, but that he would willingly leave it him, provided he could get another. The change was soon effected; and it is not to be told how much Albert prized the habit in which Francis had received the impression of the precious pledges of our redemption. After the death of St. Francis he enfolded this poor habit in rich stuffs of silk and gold, and he placed it with great veneration on the altar of the church. The Lords of Montaigne, from father to son, had it long in their possession; and it, at length, came, in the manner related by Wading, into the possession of the Grand Dukes of Tuscany, who preserve it as a precious relic, which is only shown after respectful ceremonies.

The great infirmities which the man of God suffered, obliged him to take an ass to carry him from Montaigne to Mount Casal, through the borough of Saint Sepulcher. When he reached the latter place, which is very populous, the crowd surrounded him, touched him, and pressed upon him, but he was insensible of it; he was as a dead person, not aware what was doing to him, insomuch that, having proceeded a good way from thence, and coming to himself, as one returned from the other world, he inquired of some lepers at the door of the hospital,[3] whether they should soon get to Saint Sepulcher. His mind, contemplating, says St. Bonaventure, with deep attention the brilliant lights of heaven, had not noticed the difference of time, place, or persons; so penetrated was he with divine communications, that he was not aware of what passed around him.

On reaching Mount Casal, he learned that one of his religious was suffering under an extraordinary disorder, which some considered to be epilepsy, and others thought it a true case of possession by the devil, for he had all the violent contortions of those possessed. The Father, who was full of tender compassion for the suffering, was greatly afflicted at seeing one of his children in this deplorable state, and he sent him a mouthful of the bread he was eating, the virtue of which was so great that, as soon as the sick man had swallowed it, he was cured, and thenceforward had no relapse of the disorder.

From Mount Casal Francis went to Castello, and at the house where he went to lodge, he was required to lend his aid to a female whom the devil possessed, and compelled to talk without ceasing. The servant of God with great prudence first sent one of his companions to see and hear her, to examine into the case, to see whether it was really one of possession, or whether the woman was not counterfeiting. She gnashed her teeth; she imitated the cry of an elephant with a dreadful countenance; she affected to laugh when she saw the religious, and ordered him to go away, saying that she

---

[3] These hospitals are called in French "Maladéries", or "Leproséries".

did not care about him, but she was afraid of him who hid himself. The saint, who was in prayer, having heard this, came into the room, where this woman was speaking, without any reserve, before many who were there. As soon as she saw him, she fell on the ground, trembling. He reproached the demon with his cruelty in thus torturing one of God's creatures, and ordered him to leave her, which he did instantly, but with so much noise as manifested his wrath. In the same town he cured a child who had an ulcer, by making the sign of the cross on the dressing which covered it. When the parents of the child took off the dressing, they saw with surprise, in lieu of the ulcer, a fleshy excrescence, like a red rose, which remained during the whole of the child's life, as a sensible proof and memorial of the miracle which had been performed on her.

After an abode of a month at Castello, the man of God set out on his return to Saint Mary of the Angels. Brother Leo, who accompanied him, assures us, that during the whole way, and until his arrival in the convent, he saw a beautiful golden cross, shining with various colors, preceding him, which stopped where he stopped, and advanced as he went on. This pious companion understood from this, that God had chosen to give to His servant the consolation of seeing with the eyes of his body that cross which he had always in his heart, and which he likewise bore in his flesh by the wounds of Jesus Christ.

Nothing is more affecting than what St. Bonaventure says of the feelings of St Francis after having received the impression of these sacred wounds. These are the words of the holy doctor:

"Francis, being crucified with Jesus Christ in mind and body, not only burned with the ardent love of a seraph, but he likewise participated in the thirst[4] for the salvation of souls which the Son of God felt on the Cross.[5] As he could not go, as he usually had done, into the towns and villages, on account of the large nails he had on his feet, he had himself carried thither, to animate every one, although he was in a deplorable state of languor and half dead with his infirmities, to carry the cross of our Savior. He used to say to his brethren: 'Let us now begin to serve the Lord our God, for up to this time we have made but little progress.'

"He was also ardently desirous of returning to his first practices of

---

[4] The thirst of Jesus Christ on the cross was a true and natural thirst, caused, as St. Cyril observes, by extreme exhaustion; and He expressed it to show that He was really man, and that He suffered real pains. It was also to expose Himself to an additional suffering for the plenitude of our redemption, according to what had been foretold by David: "In my thirst they gave me vinegar to drink." But St. Bonaventure sees likewise in it a mystical sense, the burning thirst which Jesus Christ had for the salvation of men, according to the saying of St. Gregory Nazianzcn, that the thirst of God is that we should thirst for Him, "Deus sitiens sitiri;" and St. Augustine, that Jesus Christ, asking the Samaritan woman for water to drink, thirsted for the faith which it was His wish she should have. "Ille autem qui quaerebat bibere, fidem ipsius mulieris sitiebat." Ps. LXVIII: 26. St. Cyril Alex, lib. xii. in Joan., cap. xix. v. 28 et 29; St. Gregory Nazian. Tetrast. n. 87; St. Augustine, Tract. 15 in Joan.

[5] John 19: 28.

humility, to attend the lepers, and to bring his body into subjection, as he had done in the first days of his conversion. Although his limbs were enfeebled by his exertions and sufferings, that did not prevent his hoping that, as his mind was yet vigorous and active, he should still combat and be victorious over his enemy. Under the guidance of Jesus Christ, he proposed to perform some extraordinary things; for when love is the spur, which admits of no neglect nor slackness, it urges to the undertaking of things of greater importance. His body was in such unison with his mind, so submissive, so wholly obedient, that, far from resisting, it was forward in some measure, and went as it were of itself towards the attainment of the great elevation of sanctity to which he aspired."

It being God's will that he should acquire the summit of merit, which is only attained by great patience. He tried him by many sorts of maladies, so grievous, that there was scarcely any part of his body in which he did not suffer excruciating pains. These reduced him to such a state, that he was scarcely more than skin and bone, almost all his flesh was wasted away; but these sufferings he did not consider as such, he denominated them his sisters, to show how much he cherished them.

These words of Saint Francis to his brethren, "Let us begin to serve the Lord our God, for until now we have made little progress," contain one of the most important lessons of the spiritual life. The Wise Man says of the knowledge of the works of God: "When a man hath done, then he shall begin."[6] St. Augustine applies this sentence to the obscurity of the sacred writings, when he says that, the deeper they are searched, the more hidden mysteries are found in them;[7] and it is equally applicable to Christian and religious perfection. It is an error condemned by the Church[8] to believe that a man is capable of attaining in this life such a degree of perfection, as not to be able to increase it; but it would be a deplorable illusion to make use of the language condemned by Saint Bernard:[9] "I have done enough, I will remain as I am: neither become worse, nor better." The just man never says, "It is enough;" he has always hunger and thirst after justice; as the apostles, "He forgets the things that are behind, and stretches himself to those that are before, to press towards the mark."[10]

To believe that we have made progress is not to do so; not to strive to advance is to go back, and to lose one's self. What instruction is here for the most perfect, in the example of a saint who deems himself to have made little progress in the service of God, and who wishes to begin all afresh, at a time when he is found deserving to bear on his body the wounds of Jesus Christ!

---

[6] Ecclus. 18: 6.

[7] St. Aug. Epis. ad Valus. 137.

[8] Clem. cap. Ad nost. De Haeres.

[9] St. Bernard, Epist. 244.

[10] Phil. 3: 13 et 14.

His disorders were only afflicting to Francis inasmuch as they related to the vast projects he unceasingly formed for the good of souls. He was most grieved at the state of his eyes, which made his sight begin to fail. Notwithstanding his other infirmities, whenever he could, he mounted on an ass, and went about, preaching penance, announcing the kingdom of God, and addressing these words to all his hearers: "Jesus Christ, my Love, was crucified." He spoke with so much fervor, and with such assiduity, visiting sometimes five or six towns[11] in the course of a single day, that it might be said that God gave him, as to the prophet, the agility of a deer.[12] However, although in the person of St. Francis the interior man was renewed from day to day, yet it necessarily fell out that the exterior man, borne down by so much austerity and fatigue, began rapidly to decay. The acute pains in his eyes, and the tears he constantly shed, brought on blindness, and it became impossible for him to preach any longer, however desirous he was to do so. Moreover, he would not have recourse to remedies, although his brethren urged him to avail himself of them, because, being already in heaven in mind and heart, he wished, as the apostle had done, "to have his conversation in heaven."[13]

Brother Elias, vicar-general, who felt the loss which the death of its holy founder would be to the Order, was most anxious to procure him relief. His feelings also induced him to wish it; for, with all his faults, he was tenderly attached to his father, and was as a mother to him by the care he took of him: of this all the first writers of the life of Saint Francis bear testimony. He used entreaties and argument to induce him to have recourse to medicine for his disorders, and quoted the following Scriptural texts: "The Most High hath created medicines out of the earth, and a wise man, will not abhor them."[14] He also on this occasion made use of the power he had received from the Saint: he commanded him, on his obedience, not to resist his cure. Cardinal Ugolino, protector of the Order, urged him also to the same effect, and warned him to be careful, lest there should be sin instead of merit in neglecting to take proper care of himself.

The sick man yielded to the advice of his friends. He was removed to a small and poor cell, very near the convent of Saint Damian, that he might be nearer to Clare and her sisterhood, who loved him as their father, and who prepared the medicines for him. He remained there forty days with the Brothers Massé, Ruffin, Leo, and Angelo of Rieti; but the disorder of his eyes became so painful, that he could get no rest night or day; when he endeavored to procure a little sleep, he was prevented by a number of rats, which infested the hut, and ran over his table and bed so daringly, that it was thought to be a

---

[11] They Are very near to each other in the vale of Spoleto, whither he usually went.

[12] Ps. 17: 36; 2 Cor. 4: 6.

[13] Phil. 3: 20, et I: 23.

[14] Eccl. 38: 4.

stratagem of the evil one.

Seeing himself overwhelmed by an accumulation of disorders, he made the following prayer humbly to God: "My Lord and God, cast Thine eyes upon me, and lend me Thine aid; grant me grace to bear with patience all these ills and infirmities." A voice forthwith made him this answer: "Francis, what price should be set upon that which shall obtain a kingdom which is above all price? Know that the pains you suffer are of greater value than all the riches of the world, and that you ought not to be rid of them for all that is in the world, even though all the mountains should be changed into pure gold, all its stones into jewels, and all the waters of the sea into balsam."[15] "Yes, Lord," exclaimed Francis, "it is thus that I prize the sufferings You send me; for I know that it is Your will that they should be in this world the chastisements of my sins, in order to show me mercy in eternity." "Rejoice, then," added the voice, "it is through the way in which you are, that heaven is reached." At these words he rose up full of fervor; and wishing that Clare, who was almost always ill, should benefit by what he had just heard, he sent for her, and conversed with her until the dinner-hour of the tender goodness of God to man, even in the dispositions of His Providence, which have the appearance of being the most severe.

Men who are enlightened by the light of faith, must they not be convinced of these Christian truths? That the most perfect have some sins to expiate; that the saints can only attain to heaven by suffering; that the kingdom of heaven, which is invaluable, cannot be purchased at too great a price; and that God never manifests His paternal regard in our favor more evidently than when He afflicts us in this world in order to show us His mercy in the next? What fruit might not be gathered from sicknesses and other sufferings; what alleviations, what consolations, and even what joy, might not be found, if these holy truths were but reduced to practice, which unfortunately are only viewed theoretically, and with little or no application!

Francis being at dinner, and beginning to eat, stopped suddenly, and, with his eyes raised to heaven, exclaimed in a loud voice: "May God be blessed, glorified, and exalted above all!" Then leaving the room in an unusual manner, he threw himself on the ground, where he remained motionless in ecstasy during a whole hour.

When he came to himself, one of the brethren whose name was Leonard, who had witnessed what had passed, and had heard what he had exclaimed, spoke to him of it, as if what he had done had been very unbecoming. "My dear brother," said Francis, "I had great cause for what I did, which I will communicate to you confidentially, upon condition that you will tell no one of it during my lifetime. If a king promised to give a kingdom to one of his

---

[15] Balsam is a very precious plant. Josephus says that the Queen of Saba presented some plants to Solomon, and that from that time balsam became common in Judea, where it is now very scarce; it was the most esteemed of any in the world. —Josephus, Antiq, lib. viii. cap. 2.

subjects, would not that person have great reason to rejoice? What, then, did I do that was unseemly, I whom the Almighty assured of His kingdom? I was so overpowered with joy, that I could not control the motions of my heart; you must excuse the excess in the expressions of my satisfaction, whatever it may have been, and however it may have seemed to transgress the rules of decorum. But what I did is not enough, I will praise God still more; I will unceasingly praise His holy name. I will sing hymns to His glory during the remainder of my days."[16]

After which he sat down, and after having reflected a little, he got one of his companions to write an Italian canticle, which begins thus: "Altissimo, Omnipotente, bon Signore; tue son le laude, la gloria, l'onore, ed ogni benedizione, etc." "O God, most high, most powerful, most good! to You belong praise, honor, glory, and every blessing: these are solely to be referred to You; neither is any man worthy to pronounce Your holy name. Praise be to You, O Lord, my God! by all your creatures." He speaks of the sun as the most brilliant of all, of the moon, the stars, the air, the wind, the clouds, the seasons, the water, the fire, the earth and all that it contains, giving praise to God for each of His creatures, whose beauties and properties he recites.

This canticle resembles that which was sung at Babylon,[17] in the fiery furnace, by the three young men who were thrown into it, for not having adored the statue of Nabuchodonosor. They called upon all creatures, inanimate and irrational, to praise God, as David had done before;[18] and St. Francis calls upon all to praise Him, because of His creatures. It comes to the same thing; for inanimate creatures, as St. Jerome observes, only praise God by making Him known to men, and by placing before them His magnificence. When they are considered as His work, says St. Augustine, we find in them numberless reasons for singing hymns to His glory; and if His greatness is manifested in His glorious works, He is not less great in those which are less so. Whatsoever God has made, praises God; there is only sin, of which He is not the author, which does not praise Him. It was Francis's desire that all his brethren should learn his canticle, and recite it daily, and that Brother Pacificus, the famous poet, of whom we have before spoken, and who was then in France or in the Low Countries, should put it into well-sounding verse. He called it the Canticle of the Sun, because of the preeminence of that beautiful planet, in which, David says, God seemed to have taken up His abode, in order to show himself to us.[19]

Some days after he had composed this, great strife arose between the

---

[16] Eccl, 51: 15; Ps. 63 (64): 35, and 103 (104): 34.

[17] Dan. 3: 37, et seq.

[18] Ps. 148. S. Hier. in cap. iii. Dan. III. S. Aug. in Ps. LXVIII. n. 5 cont. Faust, lib. xxi. cap. 5, et in Epist. Tract, iii n. 9.

[19] Ps. 13: 5.

Bishop of Assisi and the magistrates of that place. The prelate placed them under an interdict, and they, in their manner, took a similar course with him, forbidding anyone to have intercourse with him, to sell anything to him, or to his people, and to purchase nothing from them. The holy man, deeply grieved at this dissension, and to see that no one interfered to bring about a reconciliation, added the following words to his canticle: "*Laudato sia mio Signore, per quelli que perdonano per lo tuo amore etc.*": "Be You praised, O Lord for those who, for Your love, pardon offenses, and bear patiently tribulation and sickness. Blessed are they that endure all that occurs in peace, because You who are the Most High, will crown them." He then said to his companions: "Go confidently from me to the magistrates, and tell them that I beg them to go to the bishop. When they come into his presence, be not bashful, but sing alternately this canticle, with the last couplet, as being God's choristers."

His companions complied strictly with all he had ordered. The bishop and the magistrates, out of respect for the interference of the saint, consented to see each other; and they had no sooner heard his canticle sung, than, the grace of God moving their hearts by the artlessness of the words, they embraced each other, and made each other mutual apologies.

As his malady did not show symptoms of amelioration, Elias had him removed from the convent of St. Mary of the Angels to Foligno, in hopes that change of air might be of service to him. And he was in fact somewhat relieved by it; but God made known, by an extraordinary revelation, that he would continue to suffer until death. Elias found himself overpowered with sleep, and in his slumber he saw a venerable old man, clothed in white, with pontifical ornaments, who told him that Francis must prepare himself to suffer patiently for two years more, after which, death would deliver him, and would cause him to pass into perfect repose, free from all pain. He communicated this to Francis, who said that the same thing had been communicated to him; and then, filled with joy, not only on account of the eternal felicity again promised him, but because the time was fixed when his soul was to be released from the prison of his body, he added this further couplet to his canticle: "Be praised, my Lord, for death our sister, from which no living man can escape," etc. "Blessed are they who, at the hour of death, are found conformed to Your holy will, for they will not be overtaken by the second death.[20] Woe to those who die in mortal sin! May all creatures praise and bless God, obey Him and serve Him with great humility!" If we are surprised to find St. Francis call death our sister, we must bear in mind that the holy man, Job, said to rottenness: "You

---

[20] That which St. John calls in the Apocalypse "the second death," is eternal damnation; and the first death is not the death of the body, but that of the soul by sin, which strips it of the grace of God, its true life. The death of the body is only death, properly speaking, when it occurs in a state of mortal sin, because it places the criminal soul under the empire of the second death, which is damnation. When it occurs and the soul is in a state of grace, it is called, in Christian phraseology, a pleasing sleep, a happy passage. Apoc. 2: 11, and 20: 6.

are my father; and to the worms, you are my mother and sister."[21]

His sufferings being somewhat relieved, he was taken back to St. Mary of the Angels, where he wished to have a spiritual conference with Brother Bernard, of Quintavalle, the first of his children; but he was then in the adjoining wood, whither, according to his custom, he had retired for contemplation. He got himself taken there, and called his disciple three times by these affecting words: "Brother Bernard, come and talk to this poor blind man." Bernard, who was wholly absorbed in God, not making any answer, he was somewhat excited and grieved, and before returning, he made the religious, who had accompanied him, retire, to endeavor to discover by means of prayer what could have induced Bernard to have neglected him in this manner. A voice from heaven addressed these words to him: "Little man, why are you so disturbed? Must the Creator be given up for the creature? Brother Bernard was conversing with me when you called him; I retained him, not for his consolation only, but in order to teach you that God does not always leave spiritual men masters of themselves, and able to obey other men; that there are many things which ought not to be condemned in them, and that their actions are not to be judged of by ordinary rules."

Francis, trembling, recalled his guide, and holding him by the hand, he went to several parts of the wood to seek for Brother Bernard, and when he had found him, he prostrated himself at his feet with great humility, and asked pardon for the fault he had committed; and laying himself on his back, "I order you," he said, "to trample on me three times, and to place your foot on my mouth." Bernard, with tears in his eyes, resisted as much as he could; but not daring to disobey such a master, he felt compelled to do as he was ordered. The saints see things in a very different light from what we do, and consider with quite other feelings the errors they fall into. Who would have thought that so trifling an inadvertence was to be expiated by so humiliating and so severe a punishment? Respecting what was said to St. Francis, that God does not always leave spiritual men masters of themselves, and capable of obeying others, etc., there are some observations to be made, that it may not be misinterpreted. What was said to him was in allusion to a supernatural state when in prayer, wherein God suspends all the powers of the soul, in such a manner that it can neither see, nor hear, nor act, and of certain spiritual actions out of the line of ordinary rules, which God sometimes requires of His servants, as is seen in the prophets, and in a great number of saints who have been canonized by the Church. It would be rash to expect that a person under such circumstances should do all that others would have him do, and to censure his conduct as being out of the ordinary course. This is the sense of what was said to Francis respecting the ecstasy of Bernard, and he knew it by experience, having been often in a state of ecstasy.

---

[21] Job, 17: 14.

But it must not be concluded that any operation of God on a soul ever dispenses it from obeying legitimate authority, since it is His will, as St. Paul says, "that every one shall be submissive to the powers that be,"[22] and He cannot contradict Himself. One of the rules which theologians[23] lay down for distinguishing true ecstasies and revelations from false ones, is to examine whether the persons to whom such things occur are regular in their duties, very humble and very obedient. St. Teresa, who was very discerning in these matters,[24] said to her daughters that, if they attempted to unite themselves to God by any other means than by obedience, they would only unite themselves to their own self-love. By that, this excellent saint clearly proved the truth of the extraordinary favors she received from Jesus Christ in prayer, for she obeyed her confessors implicitly, so far as to act directly contrary to the particular inspirations which our Lord imparted to her, on which he said to her: "You do right in obeying, and I will make known the truth."

If St. Francis had found Brother Bernard in an ecstasy, and as his superior he had commanded him to come to him, Bernard would have come: God would have permitted it; but as he did not call him in that capacity, but as a friend, God kept him back, and did not restore him to his senses. In the year 1237,[25] a follower of St. Francis, the blessed Brother Giles, of whom we have spoken, was one day motionless in an ecstasy, without any sensation, in the presence of, and in the palace of Gregory IX, at Viterbo; and the Holy Father being desirous of testing the effect of obedience on this ecstatical man, said to Brother Giles: "I order you, in virtue of obedience, to resume your usual appearance." At the very moment Giles came to himself, and threw himself at the Pope's feet.

Two things result from what has just been said: 1st. That souls whom it pleases God to honor with peculiar communications have only to answer to their immediate superiors, who are in His place, and that no others are to interfere with them, or to judge their actions, or to endeavor to make them swerve from their purpose. 2nd. That such souls as are devoted to prayer, are to be greatly respected when God favors them with His supernatural gifts; but that their humility, their fidelity, and their obedience are to be much more esteemed than their ecstasies, and that it is in those virtues that they are to be imitated.

The whole of the year 1225, Francis passed in various illnesses and in great sufferings. Towards autumn, Cardinal Ugolino and Brother Elias induced him to be removed to Rieti, where there were able physicians and surgeons who

---

[22] Rom. 13: 1.

[23] See Card, a Turrecremata Prol. in Revel. S. Brigitt. cap. ii. Gers. de Dist. ver. Revel, a fals. tom. I. fol. 585.

[24] See S. Teresa on the foundation of the monastery of the Carmeltes of Medina del Campo, ch. v. In her Life, written by herself, chap. xxix. and xxxiii. and in several parts of her works.

[25] Wading ad ann. 1237, n. 7. Act. 88, 23 April. Vit. B. Ægid, cap. Ill n. 13, et in annot. Lit. H.

could attend to the state of his eyes. As soon as it was known in the town, all the inhabitants met, and went to meet him; but, in order to avoid all the honors preparing for him, he had himself taken to St. Fabian, a village two miles from Rieti, where he lodged at the cure's.

The Pope was at Rieti, with all his court, at that time: many of the principal persons of the court, and even cardinals, came to St. Fabian to visit the holy man. While they were in conversation with him, the persons of their suite went into the cure's vineyard to eat grapes, and they gathered so many that the vineyard was nearly stripped. The cure was much displeased at this, and complained to St. Francis, who asked him, how much he thought he had lost? "I usually," replied the cure, "have made fourteen measures of wine, which were sufficient for the consumption of my house." "I am sorry," said Francis, "that they should have done you so much damage, but we must hope that God will find a remedy for it, and I firmly believe He will, and that, from the grapes which remain in your vineyard, He will give you fourteen measures of wine and more." The cure saw this prophecy fulfilled, for he made twenty measures from the few grapes which had been left. The magistrates of Rieti caused, at a subsequent period, a convent to be built for the Friars Minors on this spot; and the same Pope, Gregory IX, out of respect for the saint, chose to consecrate the church himself; in which are still seen representations of the miracle.

After some days Francis could no longer avoid going to Rieti, where the persons of the court received him with honors, which he gladly would have dispensed with; and he lodged there with a pious citizen, named Theobald, a Saracen, who had settled in the town.

The dejection of spirits which his sufferings had brought upon him, made him desirous of having some instrumental music to cheer him; but, says St. Bonaventure, decorum did not allow him to ask for it, and it was God's pleasure that he should receive this agreeable consolation by means of an angel. One night, when he was at prayer, he heard some one walk round his bed playing on the guitar, without his being able to see any one. The sound, which was marvelously harmonious, raised his mind so entirely to God, and filled his soul with so much delight, that he thought himself in the enjoyment of the joys of the other world. His intimate companions perceived it, and they frequently observed that God gave him extraordinary consolations, for the effects they produced on him were so manifest, that it was impossible for him to disguise them, and then he admitted to them from whence they arose.

This shows that, if the saintly sufferer wished to hear some instrumental music, it was in order to listen to it for the glory of God, as St. Augustine observes was the case with David,[26] and not for any purely human gratification, nor to take any ordinary pleasure therein, nor even for the assuagement of his violent sufferings.

---

[26] S. Aug. de Civit. Dei, lib. xvii. cap. 14.

It is true that harmonious sound will procure this relief; and without referring to what ancient writers say[27] on this head, without noticing Saul, we know that there are feelings of the body and mind, in which we experience what the wise man supposes to be a common occurrence, "that music rejoices the heart:"[28] man being born with a taste for proportion, and finding himself full of concert and harmony, it is no way surprising that the harmony and proportion of sounds should cause strong and vivid impressions on him.

St. Francis, who may have been naturally more affected by music than others, may also have reasonably wished for its solace, more from a desire to prevent the depression of his spirits from the violence of his sufferings, than from being deprived of the consolation by a principle of mortification. But he was too spiritual a man not to have us convinced that his wish proceeded from a purer and more noble motive. He desired to prevent his mind from being too greatly depressed, in order to render himself more equal to interior operations, and to unite himself more easily and more intimately to God. As the prophet Eliseus,[29] who, having been greatly excited against the king of Israel, caused a Canticle of the temple to be sung to him, with a harp accompaniment, in order to calm his irritated mind, and to prepare him for the lights of the Lord, as to the knowledge of future events. St. Augustine also observes,[30] that, after his baptism, the chant of the hymns and psalms sung in the church excited in his heart tender sentiments of piety, and drew from his eyes floods of tears.

The marvelous effect which the celestial music which God caused him to have produced in his mind, shows that, on this subject, he entertained similar sentiments to those of the holy doctor,[31] that it is a science given to man by the liberality of the Creator, to represent to them the admirable harmony by which He governs the world, in order to guide them by the channel of the senses, and the melody of sounds, to the knowledge and love of immutable truth. This is also the true use of music, and it is only with this view that the Church permits it in the divine service. That which is soft and effeminate, which is calculated to excite the passions, the channel of ambiguous expressions, not the less dangerous for being so cloaked, should be considered by Christians as an abuse the more deplorable, as it has even been censured and condemned by the pagans.[32]

---

[27] Athenae, lib. xiv. cap. 5. Plutarch, lib. de Musica, n. 12 et 20. Plin. Hist. lib. xxviii. cap. 2. St. Clem. Alex. lib. ii. Paedagog. cap. iv. et Strom, iib. vi. cap. 7. St. Basil. De leg. lib. Gentil n. 7.

[28] 1 Reg. 16, 17 et 23.; Eccli. 11: 20.

[29] 4 Reg. 3: 15. St. Greg, in Ezech. lib. I. Hom. I. n. 15.

[30] St. Aug. Confess, lib. ix. cap. 6.

[31] Id. de Orig. Anim. Epist. 166 alias 28, n. 53. De Musica, lib. vi. n. 1. De Civit. Dei, supra.

[32] Horace says that the Romans, having gained great victories, gave themselves up with impunity to spending their festival days in drinking and diverting themselves; that licentiousness then seized upon verse and music, and that the flute-player added the lasciviousness of his gestures to the tones of his art, which were previously chaste and solemn:

All the skill of the physicians and surgeons of Rieti not having had any effect towards the cure of their patient, he had himself taken to his convent of Fonte Colombo, where they were to continue their remedies; and it was their opinion that a hot iron should be applied above his ear, from which it was expected he would obtain relief. For this reason his brethren urged him to give his consent, which he willingly did, in hopes to recover his sight thereby, and then to continue his exertions for the salvation of souls; and also because, the operation being very painful, he would have an opportunity of voluntary suffering.

When they were about to apply the red-hot iron, he could not avoid feeling a natural sense of fear; in order to overcome it, he addressed the fire as we should speak to a friend: "My brother," said he, "the Most High has given you great beauty, and has made you most useful; be favorable to me on this occasion. I entreat the great God who created you, to temper your heat, so that I may be able to bear it." He then made the sign of the cross on the instrument, and without any fear presented himself to receive the impression. His companions, not having courage to witness the operation, left the room. The physician and surgeon remained alone with him, and the hot iron was pressed from over his ear to his eyebrow, into his flesh, which was very tender.

After the operation, the brothers having returned, he said to them: "Praise the Lord, for I assure you I neither felt the heat of the fire, nor any pain." Then he reproached them mildly in these words: "Why did you fly, you pusillanimous men, and of little faith? He who preserved the three young men in the furnace of Babylon, could He not temper in my favor the heat of my brother, the fire?" We shall see further what an exalted principle it was which induced him to qualify all creatures by the names of his brothers and sisters. He said to the physician: "If the flesh is not sufficiently burnt, replace the hot iron." The physician, struck with so much fortitude in so feeble a body, saw that it was miraculous, and said to the religious: "I see truly today a most wonderful occurrence."

St. Bonaventure, who relates this, makes the following observation: That Francis having attained so high a degree of perfection, his body was subject to his mind, and his mind to God; with admirable harmony it followed from thence, by a peculiar disposition of Divine Providence, that inanimate creatures which obey God, obeyed His servant also, and forebore from hurting

---

Postquam coepit agros extendere victor, et urbem
Latior amplecti murus, vinoque diurno
Placari Genius, festis impune diebus,
Accessit numerisque modisque licentia major....
Sic priscae motumque et luxuriam addidit arti Tibicen. -DeArtePoet.
Socrates, Plato, Cicero. Pliny, in their days, contrasted the simplicity, gravity, and solemnity of the ancient music with the license and lasciviousness of the new.

him, according to this "O Lord!"[33] the creature being subject to You, as to its Creator, renovates its strength to torment the wicked, and softens it to contribute to the good of those who trust in You."

It is, moreover, remarkable that St. Francis feared when he saw the red-hot iron, he who had consented to have the remedy applied, because it was severe, and who had offered, when in Egypt, to cast himself into the fire to prove the truth of the Christian religion. It is thus that God permits His saints to become sensible of their natural weakness in trifling things,[34] in order that they may be sensible that in greater things all their strength depends upon His grace.

In sickness and in health Francis unceasingly shed abundance of tears: it was an effect of the gift he had received, and of his tender devotion; but he told his brethren that he wept for the expiation of his sins, although he had attained to an extraordinary purity of mind and body. He laid it down to them as a maxim, that those who strive to attain perfection, ought daily to purify themselves by tears of repentance. The reason he gave for this was, that man, being clothed with frail flesh, could not so perfectly imitate the Lamb without spot, who was crucified, as not to commit some faults occasionally. St. Augustine[35] was of a similar way of thinking, and maintained that either the laity or the clergy, of the most exemplary lives, must be careful not to leave this world without having made a true penance proportioned to their respective wants. He himself, when on the bed of death, recited the Penitential Psalms with great compunction, shedding at the same time abundance of tears.

The disorder in the eyes of St. Francis was caused by the tears he continually shed. His physician told him he ought to restrain them, unless he wished to lose his entire sight; and this is the reply he gave him: "My dear Brother Doctor, for the love of corporal sight, which we enjoy in common with flies, we must not set aside for a single instant the Divine illustrations; for the mind has not received the favor on account of the body, it has been granted to the body on account of the mind." He liked better, says St Bonaventure, to lose corporal sight than to check for a single moment that tender and affectionate

---

[33] In the Book of Wisdom, the manna is spoken of, which melted when it was exposed to the sun, but that fire, instead of melting it, baked it, and rendered it fit for being eaten by the Hebrews, which was wonderful; for the manna was a sort of dew, similar to the small particles of ice which are seen on the grass in hoar-frosts; and the fire sent from heaven against the Egyptians with an extraordinary quantity of rain, instead of being extinguished by the vast proportion of water, was only more violent, and burnt everything. —Exod. 16: 14; 9: 23, et seq. Ps. 104 (105): 31. Sap. 16: 17 et 19.

[34] The illustrious martyr, Saint Felicitas, the companion of St. Perpetua, being in labor in the prison into which she had been thrown for the faith of Jesus Christ, and screaming from the violence of the pain she suffered, one of the guards asked her what she would do when she should be exposed to the wild beasts in the amphitheater, and she made this beautiful reply: "It is I who suffer at the present moment; but there will be another who will suffer in me and for me, because I shall there suffer for Him." —S. Augustine, serm. 281, cap. 3, Act. Sinc. Mart., page 93, n. 15.

[35] Possid. Vit. S. August, cap. xxxi.

devotion which calls forth tears, by which the interior sight is purified and rendered competent to see an infinitely pure God.

What he said to his physician on the fear of losing his sight, is in accordance with the views of St. Anthony, the patriarch[36] of cenobitical life, which he communicated to the celebrated Didymus, on the grief of having lost it. Conversing one day with this learned man, who was blind, and sensible of the pain this loss caused him, "I am surprised," he said, "that, being so wise and learned as you are, you should be grieved at being deprived of what ants and flies have, and that you do not on the contrary rejoice in possessing what the saints and apostles have alone desired to have."[37] Such is the way in which the saints estimated the good and evil of the things of the world, and, as all Christians ought to estimate them, by the light of faith.

In order to show some gratitude to the physician for the trouble he took in his regard, Francis one day desired the brethren, in his presence, to take him to dine with them. They represented to him that their poverty was such that they had nothing which was fit to place before a person of his consideration, for this physician was in great estimation, and very rich. "Men of little faith," replied the saint, "why have you these doubts? Why have you not considered more favorably the merit of obedience? Go and take to the refectory our honorable brother, the doctor." They took him, seeing that he would consent to partake of their poor fare out of devotion, but, just as they were sitting down to table, there was a ring at the bell: it was a woman, who brought, in a basket, several dishes exceedingly well dressed, which a lady, who lived at a country house, six miles off, sent to the servant of God. He desired that these might be offered to the physician, and that he might be told that the Lord took care of His own. The doctor admired the hand of Providence, and said to the religious: "My brethren, we do not sufficiently understand the holiness of this man; and even you who live with him, have no conception of the secret virtue with which his mind is replenished."

This physician was not less charitable than learned; he had great pleasure in prescribing for this sick man, he frequently visited him, and paid the expense of the medicines he required. God, who considered as done to Himself what was done to His servant, who could not repay him, rewarded him in this world by a miracle worked in his favor.

He had laid out all his ready money in building a house which was only just finished, when one of the principal walls was found to have a large crack in it from the top to the bottom, which no human art could make good. Full of faith and confidence in the merits of Francis, he begged his companions to give him something which the holy man had touched. After many entreaties they gave him some of his hair, which he placed at night in the fissure in the wall.

---

[36] Vit. S. Ant. n. 68 et 69, tom. 1. Op. S. Athan, 389

[37] S. Hier. Epist. 100, alias 33, ad Castruc.

He came back in the morning, and found the whole so completely closed, that not only he could not get back the hair, but it was no longer perceivable that there had been any rent in the wall. The good offices which he had manifested to a worn-out body prevented, says St. Bonaventure, the ruin of the house he had just built.

Some days after, Francis was taken to Rieti, where the bishop lodged him in his palace; they brought to the foot of his bed, upon a tressel, one of the canons, who was dangerously ill; he had been a very worldly man, who had lived a dissipated life, but who, struck with the fear of approaching death, entreated the saint to make the sign of the cross upon him. "How," said Francis, "shall I make the sign of the cross on you, who, without any fear of the judgments of God, have given yourself up to the lusts of the flesh? I will do it, however, because of the pious persons who have interceded in your favor. But, bear in mind that you will suffer much greater ills, if, after your cure, you should return to the vomit; for the sin of ingratitude makes the last state of the man worse than the former."[38] He then made the sign of the cross upon the sick man, who immediately arose, praised God, and exclaimed, "I am healed." All the bystanders heard his bones crack, as when dry sticks are broken. That unhappy man, however, did not remain long without plunging again into vice; and one night, as he was in bed at the house of a canon where he had supped, the roof of the house fell in and crushed him, without hurting any one else.

"It was," says the same holy doctor, "by a just judgment of God; for the sin of ingratitude is a contempt of the graces of God, for which we ought to be most thankful; and the sins into which we again fall after repentance, displease Him more than any others. Will it never be understood that, in the diseases of the soul, as in those of the body, there is nothing so dangerous as a relapse?"

The pains felt by Francis were in some degree assuaged, his sight was restored, and he made use of this interval to have himself taken into several parts of Umbria, of the kingdom of Naples, and of the adjacent provinces, in order to work for the salvation of souls. At Penna, a young religious who was naturally good, and of great promise, came to ask his pardon for having left the Order; which he had only done at the instigation of the evil spirit, who persuaded him that, by living privately, he could better sanctify himself. As soon as the saint saw him, he fled to the cell, and shut the door; when he came out again, his companions expressed their surprise at what he had done: "Do not be astonished," he said, "at my having fled; I saw on this young man a frightful demon, who was endeavoring to throw him down the precipice, and I acknowledge to you that I could not bear his presence. I have prayed as earnestly as I could for the deliverance of this poor brother from such a seducer, and God has heard my prayer." Then, having sent for him, and telling him what he had seen, he exhorted him to be on his guard against the snares

---

[38] Matt 12: 14; John 15: 14.

of the devil, and not to separate himself again from his brethren: "For, if you do otherwise," he added, "you will not fail to fall into the precipice from which the mercy of God has preserved you." The docile and faithful religious passed the remainder of his days in great piety, and in the exercises of a regular life.

At Calano, a town of the duchy of Marsi, in the farther Abruzzo, where Francis was come to preach, a common soldier pressed him so earnestly to come and dine with him, that he could make no excuse. He therefore went, with one companion, who was a priest, a circumstance which was very serviceable. The poor family of the soldier having received them with great joy, the saint began to pray, as was his custom, and he had his eyes constantly raised to heaven. He then said to the soldier, privately, "My brother and my host, you see I have acceded to your request in coming to dine with you. Now, follow my advice, and make haste; for it is not here, but elsewhere, that you will dine. Confess your sins with as much exactness and sorrow as you can; the Lord will reward you for having received His poor ones with such good religious intentions." The soldier, placing confidence in what the servant of God said to him, made his confession to Francis' companion, regulated his temporal affairs, and prepared himself, as well as he could, for death. When that was done, he sat down with the others to table, and a minute afterwards he expired suddenly. Then were the words of the Gospel fulfilled,[39] that he who should receive a prophet as a prophet, that is to say, not seeing in him any other qualification, receives also the reward of the prophet; inasmuch as the prediction of Francis enabled him to fortify himself by penance against death, which he did not think to be so near at hand; and that his merits brought him nearer to the enjoyment of eternal happiness.

It was probably in this apostolic tour that the servant of God performed a miracle on the person of St. Bonaventure, who, under the dispositions of Divine Providence, was to become one of the most illustrious of his children. He was born at Bagnarea in Tuscany, a town belonging to the Ecclesiastical States, in the year 1221, and he was baptized by the name of John. His father, John Fidenza, and Ritella, his mother, joined to the nobility of their birth a large fund of piety. In his infancy he was seized with a mortal illness, of which he was cured by St. Francis, which was one of the reasons why he determined to write his Life. "I should fear," he says in his preface to his Legend, "that I should be accused of criminal ingratitude if I neglected to publish the praises of him to whom I acknowledge that I owe the life of my body and my soul."

It is reported, with the circumstances which he himself may have told, and the memory of which may have been preserved by tradition, that his mother, having no further hopes of saving him by means of medicaments,[40] came and presented him to St. Francis, who was renowned in Italy, at that time, for the

---

[39] Matt. 10: 41.

[40] Petr. Galasin. in Vit. S. Bonav. cap. iv.

splendor of his sanctity and his miracles; she implored[41] the aid of his prayers, and made a vow that, if the child was saved, she would give him to his Order. The holy man consoled the afflicted mother, and obtained from God the cure of her son, to the astonishment of the physicians, who had deemed his disorder incurable. At the sight of this miraculous cure, he said, in the Italian language: "O buona venturer[42] "How fortunate!" from whence came the name[43] of Bonaventure; and finally, he foretold that the child would become a great light in the Church of God, and that through him his Order would receive great increase of sanctity.[44]

In the year 1243, being then twenty-two years old, he proposed to fulfill his mother's vow, and take the habit of a Friar Minor. This is not the place to narrate his illustrious actions, but we must notice two remarkable circumstances which are connected with St. Francis.

The first is, that, as this blessed patriarch bears the name of Seraphic, because of the divine love with which he was inflamed, when Jesus Christ, under the figure of a seraph, imprinted on him the sacred stigmata, so St. Bonaventure has been called the Seraphic Doctor, "because his whole doctrine, as well as his whole life, breathes the fire of charity." It is a torch which burns and illuminates;[45] it influences while instructing; whatever truths he expounds, he brings back all to God by love, and, to define him properly, he should be styled the Seraphic and Cherubic Doctor.[46] 'Tis thus that Gerson, the Chancellor of the University of Paris, expresses himself.

"If I am asked," he continues, "which amongst the doctors seems to me the best calculated to instruct, I answer, without detracting from any other, it is

---

[41] Octavian. de S. Bonav. Orat. § 4.

[42] *Wading, ad ann. 1221, n. 45.*

[43] He added to it the name of John, Frater Joannes Bonaventure; others before him had borne the name of Bonaventure, as Wading and the continuators of Bollandus observe. Wading, ad ann. 1221, n. 45. Act. SS. Vit. S. Bonav. 54, Jul. Comment. § 3. The Greeks called him, in their language, Ευτυχης; (Eutuches), which means happy, and is similar to Bonaventure. Some have called him Eustathius and Eustachius, but erroneously or only to notice, according to their signification, that he maintained the truths of religion with immovable firmness, and that he was in the Church as soil abounding in good graces.

[44] The continuators of Bollandus consider the circumstances doubtful, by the very expressions of St. Bonaventure in the preface to his Legend, which give room to suppose that St. Francis was already in Heaven when his mother prayed for his cure. We cannot avoid admitting that their remark is judicious, and worthy of examination; nevertheless, since they do not bring it forward as a positive proof; as, in fact, it may be controverted, we adhere to the common opinion. Whatever may be as to the circumstances, the fact is beyond dispute, that Bonaventure was snatched from the jaws of death by the merits of Saint Francis. Neither can it be denied that he was a great man in the Church, nor that the Order of Friars Minors received a great increase of sanctity through him. The only thing in question, therefore, is, as to one prediction more or less in the Life of the blessed patriarch, where so many are incontestable. -Act. SS Supra Comment. § 3.

[45] Joan. 5: 35.

[46] Gers. de Exam. Doct. et Epist. de Laud. Bon. p. 553, et seq tom. I Edit. Par. 606.

Bonaventure, because he is sure, solid, exact, and devout, at one and the same time; and separating from his theology all questions foreign from the purpose, all superfluous dialectic, and that obscurity of terms with which so many others load their works, he turns into piety all the beautiful lights he gives to the mind. In a word, there is not a doctrine more mild, more salutary, more sublime, than his; and indevotion alone can neglect it. As to me," he adds, "having recommenced studying it since I am grown old, the more I advance the more I am confounded, and I say to myself: 'What is the use of so much talking, and so much writing? Here is a doctrine which is quite sufficient of itself, and it is only necessary to transcribe and to spread it into facts.'" Such is the opinion of the celebrated Gerson as to St. Bonaventure, before he was canonized, declared a Doctor of the Church, and honored by the title of Seraphic, which he shares with his blessed father. The Abbot Trithemius, of the Order of St. Benedict, passes a similar eulogium on him, to which the Sovereign Pontiffs, Sixtus IV and Sixtus V, have added the crowning point in their Bulls, the one for his canonization, the other for his doctorship.

The second particularity of his life, which had relation to St. Francis, is that he gloriously verified his prediction as to the fruits of sanctity which he was to bring to the Order. Having been elected general when he was five and thirty years of age, in consequence of his great talents and eminent virtues, he governed his brethren for eighteen years with so much zeal, light, mildness, and wisdom, that he perfectly made amends for the evil which the relaxation of some and the perplexity of others had occasioned. He prepared such judicious regulations for the form of government, for the recital of the Divine Office, for the regularity of discipline, that they have served as a basis and foundation for all the statutes which have since been introduced into the Order.

He decided on the difficulties which occurred as to the observation of the Rules, and this with so much precision, that, in order to follow them exactly and conscientiously, without scruple it is only necessary to practice what he has clearly laid down. He composed spiritual treatises, so elevated, so instructive, and so affecting, that they are alone sufficient to guide the Friars Minors, or all other persons of piety, to the sublimest perfection. He answered the philosophers of his day with so much strength and judgment, who attacked the Mendicant Orders, despite of the sovereign Pontiffs, by whom they were approved, that his works, with those of the Angelic Doctor, St. Thomas of Aquino, will ever cover with confusion whosoever may attempt to renew the former disputes on this head.

The exertions which St. Francis made, during a short interval from pain, for the salvation of souls, in an unfavorable season of the year, increased all his maladies. His legs became inflamed, and he was obliged to lie up in a small hamlet near Nocera. When this was known at Assisi, the fear they had lest he should die on the way, and lest his country should be deprived of his precious remains, induced the authorities to send means to bring him into town.

This deputation, returning with the patient, arrived at the dinner-hour in the village of Sarthiano, where they found nothing to be purchased for their meal, although they offered a double price for every thing they wanted. Upon their complaining of this, Francis said: "You have not found anything, because you have had greater confidence in your flies than in your Lord" (he called their money flies); "but return to the houses where you have been, and ask them humbly for alms, offering to pray to God for them in payment. Don't think, under false impressions, that there is anything mean or shameful in this, for, since sin came into the world, all the good which God so liberally bestows on man, on the just, and on sinners, on the worthy and unworthy, is done by means of alms, and He is the chief almsgiver." These men overcame their bashfulness, and went cheerfully to beg for the love of God, and got whatever they wanted, although they had not been able to obtain it for money; God having so touched the hearts of the inhabitants, that, in giving what they had, they offered spontaneously every other service.

In this destitution where money was of no use, the rich poverty of Francis was a fortunate supplement, observes St. Bonaventure; and the instruction he gave in denominating all the bounties of God as so many alms from the time man had fallen into sin, is a lesson for those worldlings who despise the state of voluntary dependence on the charity of the faithful. It is an article of faith, that sin has reduced us all to a state of extreme poverty, which can only be relieved by the gratuitous liberality of the Lord, which is a pure alms. Although we may, with the grace which He infuses into us, justly merit an increase of that grace, and win eternal life, "yet," says St. Augustine,[47] "our merits are the gifts of God, and must be considered as charitable gifts, not only because they are based upon the merits of Jesus Christ, and are his gratuitous promises, but because the commencement of all merit is a grace bestowed out of pure mercy to a sinner who is unworthy of it."

And for this reason St. Augustine represents to himself all men before God, as beggars before the doors of Him who is infinitely rich, who beg for bread, for grace, and for His kingdom.[48] Thus men of the world ought not to feel such contempt for mendicity; they are all obliged to beg, and they do so not only to God, but also to other men, those in the highest conditions of life as well as those of the lowest. What are courtiers, as respects their sovereign, more than professional beggars? This sort of mendicity is not considered disgraceful, because it has for its object splendid advantages, but, in the eyes of faith, and even in just reasoning, it is still more disgraceful, inasmuch as it has its origin in immoderate cupidity.

All these reflections were contained in the short instruction of St. Francis,

---

[47] S. Aug. serm. 333, n. 5, in Psal. xxxviii. n. 8, lib. de Grat. et lib. arb, n. 15, Epist. 194. no. 19, edit. Bened.

[48] Ibid, in Psalm CXLII, n. 17, serm. 56, n. 9. Serm. 63, n. 2.

and they show us that the spirit of God, which is manifested to us by the mouths of the saints, as in the Holy Scriptures, says great things in few and concise words.

The Bishop of Assisi had the man of God brought to his palace, and kept him there till the spring of the year 1226, providing him with everything he required, with great affection. One day, when his stomach loathed everything, he expressed a wish for a particular sort of fish, which the severity of the winter made it difficult to procure, but, at the very moment, a messenger sent by Brother Gerald, the guardian of the convent of Rieti, brought three large fishes of this species, with certain sauces which were calculated to sharpen the appetite and strengthen the patient. Thus it is that it sometimes pleases the Lord to give sensible relief to His friends who have neglected their health and crucified their flesh for His sake.

The children of the holy patriarch, and particularly Elias, his vicar-general, who saw that there was no amelioration in the state of his health, but that, on the contrary, his disorders increased with the renewal of the year, entreated him to allow himself to be removed to Sienna, where the mild climate and the excellence of the physicians might afford him some relief, if there were no hopes of a cure. And they urged this so energetically, that, as he was mild and obliging, he consented to be taken thither at the beginning of April. But all his ills continued, and the disorder of his eyes was greatly increased. A red-hot iron was again applied to both sides of his head, from the ears to the eyebrows, but this had no good effect, though he suffered no pain from it, God having renewed the miracle He had before performed in his favor.

He received many visits while at Sienna, particularly from the Friars Preachers, who knew the strict friendship which bound him to St. Dominic. At the end of the volume we propose placing on record the learned answers he made them on difficult questions which they put to him. One of them, a doctor in theology, having learnt that Francis had foretold to one of his friends in the town what would happen to him at his death, had some doubts on the subject, and came to Francis and asked him if it was true.

The saint assured him it was, and foretold at the same time to the doctor his own death, which he had made no inquiries about; and, in order to impress the certitude of it more strongly on him, he spoke to him of a certain scruple which lay on his conscience, and which he had not communicated to any one; and he explained the subject so clearly to him, that he quite removed his perplexity. The doctor was made fully aware, by this miraculous cognition, that the servant of God had the spirit of prophecy, and he was the more convinced of it at his own death, which happened in conformity with the prediction.

The mild air of Sienna, and the attentive care of the physicians, did not prevent the sufferings of Francis from continuing and increasing. During one night he vomited so much blood, and he was to such a degree weakened from it, that it was thought he was about to expire. His children, cast down and in tears, came to him, like the disciples of St. Martin,[49] when he was on the point of death, and said to him, sobbing:

"Dear father and master, we are greatly distressed to see you suffer so intensely, but we are likewise afflicted for ourselves. After all your labors you are about to go to the enjoyment of eternal repose, but we shall remain without our father and pastor; you have begotten us in Jesus Christ by the doctrine of the Gospel, and we are scarcely born before we lose you. Who will instruct us? Who will console us? You have been everything to us, your presence has been our happiness. To whom do you consign us, in the desolate state in which we are? Alas we foresee that after your departure ravenous wolves will invade your flock. Leave us, at least, something of yours to remind us of your instructions, in order that we may follow them when you are no more; and give us your blessing, which may be our shield against our enemies."

The holy patriarch, casting his eyes affectionately on his children, called to him Brother Benedict of Piratro, who was his infirmarian, and who, during his illness, said Mass in his room: "Priest of God," said he, "commit to writing the blessing I give to all my brethren, as well to those who are now in the Order, as to those who shall embrace it to the end of the world. As my great sufferings and extreme weakness prevent me from speaking, here are in few words my intentions and last wishes: 'May all the brethren love each other as I have loved them, and as I now love them. May they always cherish and adhere to poverty, which is my lady and my mistress; and never let them cease from being submissive and faithfully attached to the prelates and all the clergy. May the Father, Son, and Holy Spirit bless and protect them! Amen.'"

His sufferings being in some degree modified, and his weakness no longer so intense, his zeal induced him to think of instructing and exhorting the absent, for, by the example of the Son of God, he loved his own even to the last.[50] As he could no longer make use of his speech for their sanctification, he caused his companions to write a letter, which he addressed to the minister-general of the whole Order, in which, after very salutary instructions, he confessed his sins with great humility. We reserve this for the last book, because it is very long, and the reflections which arise from its consideration would carry us at this time too far.

As soon as Brother Elias, the vicar-general, learnt the extreme danger in which the father was, he came in great haste to Sienna, and proposed to him to be removed to the convent of Celles, near Cortona. Francis was very glad to see him, and was quite willing to be removed to Celles, where he was attended with great care by the relations and friends of Elias, who were of that country.

---

[49] Sulp. Sev. Epist. Ad Bassul.

[50] Joan. 13: 1.

But, as he became swollen, and the sufferings of his stomach and liver were greatly increased, he requested to be taken to Assisi, which the vicar-general had done with all the care and precaution possible. His return was a source of extraordinary gratification to the inhabitants, who had been fearful of being deprived of so great a treasure had he died elsewhere. They went in crowds to meet him, with great expressions of pleasure, and the bishop received him again into his palace.

Before we put on record the last acts and precious death of St. Francis, it will be proper to notice the state in which his Order was at that time. There were some of his brethren in all parts of the known world. In Europe, they filled all Italy. Greece furnished them a province. The esteem of the great, and the love of the people, procured for them, daily, new houses in Spain, Portugal, France, the Low Countries, and England. They had spread into Scotland, and began to be received in Ireland. Brother Albert, of Pisa, had sent missioners into Upper and Lower Germany, with great success. They had penetrated into Poland, and into the countries of the North. In Asia, those whom the holy patriarch had left, with others who followed, multiplied the missions among the Saracens. In Africa they continued to preach Jesus Christ to the Muslims, and we see by letters dated from Rieti, the 7th October, 1225, which Pope Honorius addressed to the Friars Preachers and Minors, destined by the Apostolic See for the mission into the kingdom of the Miramolin, and to whom he gave very extensive powers, saying of them, "that they renounced themselves, and desired to sacrifice their lives for Jesus Christ, in order to gain souls for Him."

The Second Order instituted by Francis, and called that of the Poor Dames, spread itself also throughout Europe, and the Third Order of Penance likewise made great progress.

The children of this holy patriarch, being thus spread in all parts, preached the Gospel to the infidels, repressed heresies, attacked vice, inspired virtue, and gave admirable examples of poverty, humility, penance, and all perfection.

Anthony, of Padua, preached in Italy and France with so much luster, that he has ever been considered as one of the most marvelous preachers whom Italy ever saw. The strength and the unction of his discourses, the eminent sanctity of his life, the evidence of his miracles,[51] changed the face of the towns in which he announced the word of God. His auditors, penetrated with compunction, and bursting into tears, excited each other to works of penance; the revengeful, the lascivious, the avaricious, the usurers became converted, and resorted to the tribunals of penance, and the number of priests were insufficient to hear the confessions.

---

[51] It is not from Baillet that the miracles of St. Anthony, of Padua, are to be judged; he rejects them all in his usual manner; but the judicious critics, such as the continuators of Bollandus, admit the truth of them, and produce the proofs. —Act. SS. 13. Jem.

In the year 1225 he came to Toulouse,[52] and visited other towns of France, where his principal object was to confront the heretics. Animated with the same spirit which inspired his father, Francis, with so perfect an attachment to the Roman Church and the Holy See, he was the declared enemy of all errors, and he labored with all his strength to root them out. By quotations from the Holy Scriptures, with which he was intimately conversant, and the sense of which he perfectly understood, and by the solidity of his reasoning, he confounded the sectarians, and created a great horror of the false doctrines they taught. With admirable tact he discovered their artifices and frauds, which he laid before the people, to preserve them from their seduction; and, in fine, he pursued them with so much vigor and perseverance, that the faithful gave him the name of the indefatigable mallet of the heretics; none of them ventured to enter the lists with him, nor even to open a mouth in his presence.

God favored him by converting a very great number of their supporters,[53] and, what is very singular, many of the heads of their party. At Bourges a man whose name was Guiald, and whom the historian calls a heresiarch, was so convinced by the power of his words, and by a marked miracle of the real presence of Jesus Christ in the Eucharist, that he persevered till death in the Catholic faith, and in submission to the Church. Another named Bonneville, or Banal, who is also stated to have been a heresiarch, who had been thirty years buried in the darkness of errors, was converted in a similar manner at Rimini by the sermons of St. Anthony, and had a like perseverance. It must be admitted that the favor is very rare. It has been remarked that, among all the authors of heresies, and the chiefs of the sects, there are scarcely any who have been sincerely restored to the Church; they have obstinately persisted in their errors until death, although they had seen them condemned, and some of them were long-lived. It would be easy to adduce examples less remote from our days than that of Theodore Beza, who, at the age of seventy, resisted the pressing solicitations of St. Francis de Sales,[54] and died some years afterwards in the errors of Calvin, whose successor he was. It is a just judgment of God against these proud men, who have rebelled against their mother the Church, who lose an infinity of souls by the ill use they make of their talents, authority, and all other means by which they seduce them.

---

[52] Sur. et Act. SS. vit. S. Anton. 13 Jem.

[53] Ib. Sur. Cap. 9 and 17. Act. SS. Pp. 708, 725.

[54] He went by order of Pope Clement VIII to Geneva to confer with Theodore Beza, to induce him to return into the Catholic Church, and he returned there three times to the great peril of his life. Beza was so much moved, so taken up by the reasoning and the mildness of St. Francis de Sales, that, pressing his hand, and raising his eyes to Heaven, he said with a sigh: "If I am not in the right way, I daily pray to God, in His infinite mercy, to lead me into it." He felt more than any other the weakness of his party; his conscience filled him with poignant remorse, he was agitated, and his agitation was visible in his countenance; nevertheless, he did not surrender; human respect, long habit, the shame of unsaying, and certain secret engagements, prevented his embracing the truth of which he was convinced. —Life of St. Francis de Sales by Marsallier, lib. III.

The state in which, as we have just shown, St. Francis left his Order when on the point of death, must be looked upon as one of the principal marvels of his life. God had predestined him for this great work; he labored at it for eighteen years without ceasing, with all possible assiduity, and, on the eve of quitting this world, he might say, in conforming himself to Jesus Christ, after having profited by His grace, "I have glorified You on earth; I have finished the work You gave me to do, I now go to You."[55] Happy the Christian whose conscience bears him thus out on the bed of death, who can say that he has endeavored to do what God required of him, and fulfilled the duties of his profession.

---

[55] Joan. 17: 4, 13.

St. Francis celebrates the Nativity at Grecio. —Giotto

St. Francis appears while St. Anthony preaches on the Titulum Crucis. —Giotto

Francis receives the stigmata from Christ in the form of a Seraph. —Giotto

The Stigmatization of St. Francis. —Peter Paul Rubens

The soldier dines at the eternal banquet. —Giotto

The death of St. Francis. —Giotto

The Stigmata of St. Francis is verified by the knight Girolamo. —Giotto

St. Clare mourns the death of her spiritual father. —Giotto

The Last Communion of St. Francis. —Peter Paul Rubens

Right: *The Death of St. Francis.* —Fra Angelico

Vision of the Angelic Throne which St. Francis will take up. —Giotto

St. Francis preaching to the birds.—Giotto

THE LIFE OF ST. FRANCIS OF ASSISI

BOOK V

CHAPTER I
THE DEATH OF ST. FRANCIS

The violence of his illness does not prevent him from exhorting his brethren—He is touched at the fatigue which his illness caused them—Thanks God for the pains he suffered—Dictates a letter to Clare and her daughters—Rejoices and thanks God for his approaching death—Blesses his children—Has himself carried to St. Mary of the Angels—Gives a special blessing to Bernard, the eldest of his children—What we may presume were his dispositions in receiving the last sacraments—He stretches himself naked on the bare ground—Desires to be buried in the Place of Execution—Exhorts his brethren, and makes his will—He has the praises of God sung when at the point of death—He speaks to his children, and blesses them for the last time—Has the passion of Jesus Christ read to him—He recites the 141st psalm, and dies after the last verse—Miraculous proofs of his beatitude—State of his body after death—The Stigmata are seen and touched publicly—Clare and her daughters see and kiss the Stigmata—He is buried at Assisi, in the church of St. George—The circular written after his death.

HE CRUEL and continued pain under which the holy patriarch suffered, did not prevent his giving instruction to his children, his providing for their spiritual wants, and giving answers, with admirable presence of mind, to various questions which were put to him relative to the observance of the Rule, and the government of the Order. He spoke as freely, and with as much composure, as if he felt no inconvenience. As his body became weaker, his mind seemed to acquire fresh vigor. We do not insert here the admirable things he then said, because they would occupy too much space, but they will be found at the end of this work.

One day, when his sufferings were greatly aggravated, he remarked that they were taking great pains in endeavoring to afford him relief, and fearing that fatigue would cause some of those who were about him to become impatient, or that they might complain that their attendance on him prevented them from applying to their spiritual exercises, he addressed them affectionately, saying: "My dear children, don't tire of the trouble you take for me, for our Lord will reward you, both in this life and in the next, for all you do for His little servant; and if my illness takes up your time, be assured that you will gain more from it than if you were to labor for yourselves, because the aid you give me is given to the entire religious, and to the lives of the brethren. I also assure you that God will be your debtor for all that you will spend for me."

It is very true that those who assisted the saint in his illness labored for the entire religious, and for the spiritual life of his brethren, because they aided in the preservation of him who was so necessary to his Order; and they put it in his power to give further instructions to his brethren who were now in it, and to those who were to enter it in future.

On another occasion, when his sufferings were apparently bringing him to extremity, one of his infirmarians said to him: "Brother, pray that God may treat you with less severity, for it seems that His hand presses too severely upon you." At these words Francis exclaimed in a loud voice: "If," said he, "I was not aware of the simplicity and uprightness of your heart, I should not dare to remain in the same house with you from this instant, who have had the rashness to criticize the judgments of God in my regard;" and immediately, notwithstanding the weak state in which he was, he threw himself on the ground with such violence that his worn-out bones were all bruised; he kissed the ground and exclaimed: "My God, I return to You thanks for the pains I endure, and I pray You to add to them a hundred-fold, if such should be Your good pleasure. It will be pleasing to me to know that, in afflicting me, You do not spare me, for the greatest consolation I can enjoy is, that Your holy will shall be fulfilled." He had in his sufferings similar feelings to those of holy Job,[1] and he expressed himself in a similar manner. Ought not all Christians to have such feelings in their illnesses and other afflictions? Are the saints not to be imitated in this? May we not, by the grace of God, which assuredly will not be wanting, practice those virtues by which they became saints?

Clare and her daughters, hearing that their father was so dangerously ill, sent to express to him the grief which it caused them, and they entreated him to mitigate their sorrow by sending them at least his blessing. The holy patriarch, full of tenderness for these pious virgins, and sympathizing in their grief, and in that which they would feel on his death, sent them some verses he had composed in the praise of the Lord, and added to them a letter of exhortation, in which doubtless he gave them his blessing most amply, but this is not found in his works. We find in them only the following fragment, which may belong to the letter he had written to them at that time:

"I, Brother Francis, little man, choose to follow the example of the life and poverty of Jesus Christ, our most high Lord, and that of His holy Mother, and to persevere in it to the end. I beg you also, all you whom I consider as my Ladies, and I recommend you to conform yourselves at all times to this life and to this poverty, the sanctity of which is so great. Be careful not to swerve from it in the least, nor to listen to any advice, nor to anything which may be said to contravene it."

The oldest historians of the Oder say that, in the letter he sent them shortly before his death, he entreated them, that, as the Lord had brought them together from many places, in order that they might apply themselves to the practice of the sacred virtues of charity, humility, poverty, and obedience, they should use every effort to pass their lives accordingly, and to die in their

---

[1] Job, 6: 9 and 10.

perseverance. He exhorts those of his sisters who were suffering from sickness, to have patience under their ills. And because he knew how austere they were, he recommended them to use with discretion, and with joy and thankfulness, the alms which Divine Providence sent them. In fine, he promised Clare that she should see him, and, in fact, after his death she and her daughters did see him, as shall hereafter be related.

The same writers add, that he had always entertained peculiar affection and regard for these holy religious females, thinking that the holiness of their life, which had been from the beginning one of great poverty and mortification, reflected glory on the religious state, and was a source of great edification to the whole Church. He wrote to them several other times, to encourage them in virtue, and particularly in the love of poverty, as we find by the will of St. Clare,[2] but the letters are not extant.

Even at this day we are sensible of the truth of what he said; nothing is more glorious for the regular state, and nothing more edifying for the whole Church, than to see the nuns of St. Clare, who kept the rule of their Order without the slightest mitigation, who renounce the possession of any property whatsoever, whether private or in common, who live wholly on alms, and in such a state of rigorous austerity, that the stronger sex would find to be quite appalling. In no other monasteries, notwithstanding, are more harmony, more content, more liberty of mind, or more of that joy found, of which our Savior has said, that "It is in the heart that their joy shall be full, and that no man shall take it from them."[3]

As soon as it was known in Assisi that the holy man was at the point of death, the magistrates placed guards round the episcopal palace, with orders to keep strict watch, lest his body should be taken away the moment he should have expired, and thus the city should be deprived of so precious a treasure.

The physician, whose name was John Lebon, a native of Arezzo, communicated to him that death was approaching; his brethren told him the same thing. Full of joy, he began to praise God, and having caused some of the choir-singers to be called in he sang with them in a loud voice the last verses which he had added to the Canticle of the Sun: "Be praised, O Lord! for death our sister, which no man living on earth can escape."

Elias, whose thoughts were always governed by human prudence, was fearful lest his singing should be considered a weakness of mind arising from the fear of death, and entreated him to stop. "Brother," replied Francis, with extraordinary fervor, "permit me to rejoice in the Lord, and to thank Him for the great tranquillity of my conscience. I am, through His mercy and His grace, so united to my God, that I have just reason to manifest the joy that He gives me, who is the high and most liberal Giver of all good gifts; and do not

---

[2] Wading, ad ann. 1253, No. 5.

[3] John 16: 22 and 24.

imagine that I am so wanting in courage as to tremble at the approach of death."

He had his children brought to him, and he blessed each one of them as the Patriarch Jacob had done,[4] giving to each an appropriate blessing. Then, after the example of Moses,[5] who blessed all the faithful Israelites, he gave a general and ample blessing to the whole Order.

As he had stretched his arms one over the other in the form of a cross, as Jacob[6] had done in blessing the children of Joseph, his right hand came upon the head of Elias, who was kneeling on his left. He asked who it was, for his sight was quite gone, and being answered that it was Brother Elias, "Tis well," he said, "my right hand is properly placed on him. My son, I bless you in all and above all. Inasmuch as under your hand the Most High has increased the number of my brethren and children, thus I bless them all in you. May God, the Sovereign Lord of all things, bless you in heaven and on earth. As for me, I bless you as far as is in my power, and even more than that; but may He who can do all, do in you what I cannot! I pray that God may bear in mind your labors and your works, and that He may give you a share in the rewards of the just, that you may obtain the blessings you wish for; and may what you solicit worthily be fulfilled!"

The reader may perhaps be surprised that Francis, who knew Brother Elias, and who had learnt by revelation that he was to die out of the Order, should have given him so ample and so detailed a blessing; but we must recollect that He who enlightens the saints, inspires them with views similar to His own. He loves and favors those who are in a state of grace, although He foresees the great sins they will commit hereafter. What affection had He not for David, and what favors did He not heap upon him before he became guilty of the adultery and homicide which rendered him so criminal! Thus, in a manner, the holy patriarch, in blessing Elias, only had in consideration the good dispositions in which he believed him to be at that time, independent of the future, which God had revealed to him, and which was not to guide him in this instance. Moreover, Elias was his vicar-general, and was so by an order from on high; he had labored usefully in the works of the Lord; the talents he possessed put it in his power to do still more good service; we cannot deny that he was sincerely and tenderly attached to his father, and that he had an ardent zeal: all these circumstances united might have induced the saint to give him an ample blessing, nor was it without good effect, since he died in sentiments of sincere repentance.

The man of God finding the day of his death, which Jesus Christ had revealed to him, draw near, said to his brethren in the words of the Prince of

---

[4] Genesis 49, 28.

[5] Deuteron, 20: 2.

[6] Genesis 48: 14.

the Apostles, "The laying away of this my tabernacle is at hand;"[7] and he begged them to have himself taken to the convent of St. Mary of the Angels, wishing, as St. Bonaventure remarks, to render up the spirit which had given life to him, in the place where he had received the Spirit of grace. He was, therefore, removed, according to his desire; and when he was come to the place between the town and the convent, he asked if they had reached the hospital of the lepers, and, as those who were carrying him replied in the affirmative, he said: "Turn me now towards the town, and set me down on the ground." Then raising himself upon the litter, he prayed for Assisi, and for all its inhabitants. He likewise shed tears, in considering the ills which would come upon the city, during the wars which he foresaw, and he then gave it this blessing: "Be blest by the Lord, O city, faithful to God! because many souls will be saved in you and by you. A great number of the servants of the Most High will dwell within your walls, and among the number of your artisans not a few will be chosen for eternal life."

Some time after his arrival at St. Mary of the Angels, he called for paper and ink, that he might acquaint Lady Jacqueline de Septisal of the proximity of his death: she was the illustrious Roman widow who was so much attached to him. "It is right," he said, "that, dying, I should give that consolation to a person who afforded me so many during my life." This is what he dictated for her; what follows shows that it was on a Sunday, the twenty-eighth of September:

"To the Lady Jacqueline, the servant of the most High, Brother Francis, the poor little servant of Jesus Christ, sends greetings, and communication with the Holy Spirit, in Jesus Christ.

"Know, my very dear lady, that Jesus Christ, blessed for ever, has done me the favor to reveal to me the end of my life: it is very near. For which reason, if you wish to see me alive, set out as soon as you shall have received this letter, and hasten to St. Mary of the Angels, for, if you arrive later than Saturday, you will find me dead. Bring with you some stuff, or rather, a sackcloth, to cover my body, and some wax-lights for my funeral. Pray, bring also some of those comfits which you made me take when I was sick at Rome."

At these words he stopped, having his eyes raised to heaven, and said it was not necessary to go on with the letter, nor to send a messenger, because the lady had set out, and was bringing with her all that was required; and, in fact, she arrived shortly after with her two sons and a considerable suite, bringing with her the stuff, a quantity of wax-lights, and certain electuaries which were comforting for the stomach.

The religious asked her how she could have come so opportunely, without having had notice given her, and how she came to bring all that was requisite for the time. She told them that during the night she had received an order

---

[7] 2 Peter 1:14.

from heaven, and that an angel had desired her not to leave out any of the things which had been ordered.

There are three things to be noticed in the letter of St. Francis to this lady:

1st. He begins by these words, "Know, my very dear lady," This marks a spiritual and very holy friendship, which was grounded on, and had for its object, the love of God alone. St. Paul, writing to Philemon, expresses himself in a similar manner:[8] "To our very dear Sister Appia;" and St. John, after having assured Electa, a lady of distinction, that he loved her in truth, both herself and her children, adds: "Now, madam, the prayer which I address to you is, that we should love each other."[9] We see in the letters of St. Chrysostom, of St. Jerome, and St. Francis de Sales, the affection with which charity inspired them for Christian virgins, women, and widows. We must not, however, take their example as our authority for making use in general of these expressions, which charity suggested; for all the ministers of Jesus Christ have not the perfection and authority of the apostles, the fathers of the Church, certain holy bishops, and apostolical men; and all their spiritual daughters are not like the great souls, whom these excellent masters led into the paths of holiness.

2nd. St. Francis gave this lady a last mark of his confidence, and encouraged her pious feelings in applying to her for sackcloth and wax-lights; but at the same time he put in practice, to the last, those maxims of poverty which were so dear to him, since he did not choose that his body should be covered, nor his obsequies illuminated, but by what he received as alms.

3rd. We do not perhaps understand why this holy man, who was so entirely dead to all the feelings of sense, should have requested the same lady to bring him some of those preparations which he had taken, in former illnesses, to strengthen him; but the reason is this: he was aware of the precise day on which he was to die; it was his wish to give instructions to his brethren to the very last moment; he had still much to say to them, and a will to make, which was of no small length; his sufferings often brought on fainting and weakness, which prevented his speaking, and they naturally hastened the approaches of death. All this induced him to adopt all human means which should enable him to fulfill what he knew to be in the order of Providence, not venturing to solicit a miracle for himself. Could he have acted more prudently or from purer motives?

The porter came to announce the arrival of the lady, and to inquire whether she should be admitted into the convent, for it had been expressly forbidden by the Rule to permit the entry of any female into any of the houses

---

[8] Philemon 1:2.

[9] 2 John 1 and 5.

of his Order;[10] and he had this very strictly enforced at St. Mary of the Angels. But he answered that this lady was not to be included in the law, since her dwelling was always open to the Friars Minors, and it was no more than right to permit her to enter into their convent. She was, therefore, received with her two sons; and she came to throw herself at his feet, as Mary Magdalen is represented at the foot of the cross; she kissed and bathed with tears the precious wounds, and she also performed the functions of Martha, rendering to the servant of Jesus Christ all the service in her power. On the Wednesday morning, she proposed to send away her suite, because she thought he would not die so soon; but he prevented her, assuring her that he had only four more days to live; after which, he said, "You will pay me the last respect, and then you may return with your people."

On Friday, the third of October, he collected all his brethren together, blessed them a second time, and having blessed a loaf of bread with the sign of the cross, he gave to each a piece as a symbol of union and fraternal charity. They all partook of it with great devotion, representing to themselves, in this repast of love, the last supper which Jesus Christ ate with His disciples.

Brother Elias, who wept bitterly, was the only one who did not eat his portion, which was perhaps a mournful foreboding of the division he was to introduce into the Order. In truth, he kept the piece he had received from their father respectfully in his hand; but, as if he had cast aside the peace which was offered him to take possession of his heart, instead of at least keeping the morsel of bread, he gave it to Brother Leo, who asked him for it: great care was taken for its preservation, and God permitted that it should be subsequently used for the cure of many maladies.

All the brothers had melted into tears, and the holy patriarch inquired where Bernard, his eldest son, was. And Bernard having drawn near, "Come, my son," he said, "that I may bless you before I die." Feeling that he was kneeling on his left, while Brother Giles was on his right,[11] he put his hands

---

[10] Although at that time no positive regulation forbade women to enter the convents, as has been observed, it was, nevertheless prohibited by separate regulations, which were only dispensed with for valid reason. The positive law, subsequently made, does not include Sovereigns, Princesses of the Blood Royal, and the Foundresses of convents. —Suarez, De Relig. tom. iv. lib. I. cap. 7. Pelizzar. Manual. Regul. tom. I. lib. iii. cap 6.

[11] Others say that Bernard, being called to receive the blessing, proposed to Brother Elias, out of respect for his dignity as vicar-general, to place himself on the father's right hand, and that he went to the left, and that both were kneeling; that then the saint, who had entirely lost his sight, placing his right hand on the head of Elias, said, "This is not the head of Bernard, my eldest son;" and then crossing his hands, his right hand came on the head of Bernard, whom he blessed. This would have been a very natural representation of what the Patriarch Jacob did in regard to Ephraim and Manasses (Genesis XLVIII: 4). Wading relates the circumstance in this manner in his edition of the works of St. Francis, published anterior to his Annals of the Order; but he altered this, because he found other narratives more in conformity to the originals which he had afterwards seen; and he takes notice of the change: which shows how correct he endeavored to be. —Wading, Opusc. S. Francis, tom. iii. Bened. 6, et ad ann. 1226, n. 29.

again crosswise, so that his right hand came on the head of Bernard, to whom he gave this blessing:

"May the Father of our Lord Jesus Christ bless you with all the spiritual blessings which He has shed from on high on His Son. As you were chosen the first to give good example of the evangelical law in this Order, and to imitate the poverty of Jesus Christ, to whom you generously offered your goods and your person in the odor of sweetness, so may you be blessed by our Lord Jesus Christ, and by His poor servant; and may you be so blessed in your going out and coming in, waking or sleeping, living and dying. May he who blesses you, be filled with blessings; and may he who curses you, not remain unpunished. Be the lord of your brethren, and let them be all subject to you. Let all those whom you shall approve, be admitted into the Order, and all whom you shall reject, be rejected. Let no one have authority over you, so that you may be at liberty to go and dwell where you think proper."

Bernard having retired, with his eyes bathed in tears, Francis said to the others: "My intention is, and I direct that whoever may be appointed Minister-General, he may love and honor Brother Bernard as myself, and that all the Provincial Ministers, as well as all the brethren of this Order, may look upon him as they have done on me; in fact, I leave him to you as the half of my soul. There are few who are able to appreciate his virtue: it is so great, that Satan never ceases from tempting him, molesting him, and laying snares for him. But, by God's help, he will get the better of all, to the great profit of his soul, and he will find himself in an extraordinary manner in perfect tranquillity." Those who were present, and who afterwards lived with Bernard, witnessed the fulfillment of these predictions. His eminent sanctity, well known to Francis, and of which he foresaw the perseverance, was the reason why he ordered the others to respect him as their master, and why he rendered him independent, in order that he might have full leisure to give himself up to contemplation, which had such charms for him. For a similar reason, he gave him power to admit or reject novices, as his prudence should dictate; a privilege which was the more appropriate, as Bernard had been the first to enter into the Order.

St. Bonaventure is silent as to the manner and fervor with which the servant of God received the last sacraments,[12] following in that the method of

---

[12] Saint Athanasius, in the life of Saint Anthony, does not mention his received the sacraments at his death; nor Saint Possidius in his Life of Saint Augustine, nor Sulpicius Severus in the Life of Saint Martin. There can be no doubt that these great saints did receive them, not only because of their great piety, but because it was the custom of the Church. We see this in the life of St. Ambrose, in which Paulinus, his secretary, states, n. 47, that the Body of our Blessed Savior was given him by Honoratus, Bishop of Vercelli, and that he died with this excellent Viaticum. A writer of the Life of St. Bernard does not say that he received the Viaticum and Extreme Unction, but another writer of the same Life expressly notices that he did receive them; and both these authors were his contemporaries. The author of the Life of Saint Bernard, published in 1704 by J. De Nully, ought to have mentioned this circumstance, with many others which he has omitted, and not have finished

many old authors, who, in the lives of saints only notice those things which are peculiar and marvelous, without speaking of the common and ordinary actions of all Christians. But we have only to bear in mind the great respect St. Francis had for all the practices of the Church; the spirit of penance by which he was animated; the vivid and tender affections of his heart towards the Passion of the Son of God, and the mystery of the Holy Eucharist; the ardor of his zeal to cause Jesus Christ to be adored in the August sacrament, and revered in all that related to it; his eagerness in recommending the frequent approach to the holy communion, and the constant recourse he himself had to this balm for the soul, so as, for fear of being deprived of it, choosing to have Mass said in his own room during his illnesses: all these recollections, being united, are demonstrations of what must have been the dispositions of the saint when the last sacraments were administered to him.

He particularly desired all his brethren to have a peculiar veneration for the church of St. Mary of the Angels, because it had been revealed that the Blessed Virgin had a singular affection for this church among all those which were dedicated to her name, and upon this subject he spoke as follows, with great animation:

"It is my desire that this place shall be always under the direction of the person who shall be Minister-General and servitor of the Order; and that the minister shall be careful to select for its service only good and holy brethren; and that the clerks who shall be appointed to it shall be taken from those of the Order who are the best and the holiest, and are the best instructed for the celebration of the divine offices, so that their brethren and the seculars may be edified in seeing and hearing them. Let them also be particular in choosing the lay brethren to be placed there; let them be discreet, mild, and humble men, whose lives are holy, who shall serve the others without entering into idle discourse, not talk of the news, or what is passing in the world, nor of any thing which does not relate to the salvation of souls.

"It is also my desire that none of the brethren shall come here except the Minister-General and his companions, and that no secular shall be admitted, in order that those belonging to the place may the better preserve themselves in purity and holiness, and that the place itself may remain pure and holy, being solely devoted to singing the praises of the Lord. When God shall be pleased to call any one of them to Himself, I desire that the Minister-General may send another whose life shall be equally holy. My intention is that, if the brethren shall swerve from the path of perfection, this place shall be ever blest, and shall remain as the example and model for the whole Order; as a sort of

---

drily by saying, "God decided his fate, and he expired." Thus the silence of some authors must not prevent us from believing that the saints put in practice at their deaths what was the uniform custom of the faithful.

candlestick before the throne of God,[13] and before the altar of the Blessed Virgin, where lamps shall be ever burning, to obtain from the goodness of God that He may grant His pardon to the brethren for all their faults, and preserve and protect this Order which He has planted with His own hand.

"My children," he continued, "be careful never to abandon this spot, and if you are driven out on one side, return by the opposite one; for it is holy, it is the dwelling-place of Jesus Christ, and of the Blessed Virgin, His mother. It is here that the Lord, the Most High, has multiplied our numbers, from being very few; here, by the light of His wisdom, He enlightened the minds of His poor ones; here, by the ardor of His love, he inflamed our hearts; here, whoever shall pray devoutly, will obtain[14] whatever he may ask; and whoever shall sin here, will be punished with greater rigor. Wherefore, my children, have a great veneration for this place, which is truly the dwelling of the Almighty, peculiarly beloved by Jesus Christ and His blessed Mother. Employ yourselves here joyfully, and with your whole hearts, in praising and blessing God and His Son, our Lord Jesus Christ, in unity with the Holy Spirit. Amen."

The day at length arrived which had been fixed by Divine Providence for terminating and rewarding the labors of this faithful servant of God: it was a Saturday, the fourth of October. St. Bonaventure, who considers him on his death-bed as a work well finished by the chisel of suffering, as a precious jewel cut and polished, to be placed in the sacred edifice of the celestial Jerusalem, remarks that, finding himself near his end, and animating himself with fresh fervor, he stretched himself naked on the ground. "It was," says the holy doctor, "sensibly to manifest that he had nothing in common with the world, in these last moments of his life, in which the devil might still attack him;" which is what St. Gregory recommends when he says, that "it is necessary to be naked to wrestle with adversaries who are naked, because they have no property in the world."[15] Thus Francis, stretched on the ground without even the penitential sackcloth, his eyes, as usual, raised to heaven, and thinking solely on the glory which awaited him, covered with his left hand the wound which was on his right side, to prevent its being seen, and he then said to his

---

[13] We see clearly that he had here in view the golden Candlestick with seven branches, which Moses placed in the Tabernacle, in the spot called The Sanctuary; and that which the prophet Zacharias saw, as well as those which were seen by Saint John, as stated in the Apocalypse. He made the application in a moral sense to his brethren, who, as ardent luminaries, were to offer to God, in the church of Saint Mary of the Angels, fervent prayers which would be favorably received. He had a right to make this application, since, in the Apocalypse, a whole society, an entire Church, is designated under the figure of a Candlestick. —Exod. 25: 14; Zachar. 4: 2; Apoc. 1: 12.

[14] He seems to allude here to the entire remission of sins by the indulgence of the Portiuncula for those who, being well disposed, shall pray in the Church of St. Mary of the Angels, according to the concession made by Jesus Christ and by His Vicar.

[15] Greg. Hom. 32, in Evang.

brethren: "I have done all that relates to myself; I entreat Jesus Christ to instruct you as to what you are to do."

All the brethren were penetrated with grief and shed tears. One of them, whom the holy man called his guardian, knowing by inspiration what he wished for, went quickly to fetch a tunic, a cord, and the other parts of the dress of a Friar Minor, and brought them to him, saying: "Here is what we lend you, as to a poor man; take them out of obedience." He accepted this alms, and was rejoiced that he was faithful to the last to poverty, which he called his lady and his mistress; then raising his hands to heaven, he gave glory to our Lord Jesus Christ, that, being disengaged and free from everything, he was about to go to Him.

At the beginning of his conversion he stripped himself before the Bishop of Assisi, in imitation of the poor life of our Savior and to resemble Him more completely in His state of poverty, of nudity, and of suffering on the cross, he stripped himself before his brethren at his death, and chose to leave this world naked as he came into it, or, at least, only in a habit which he had received as an alms: such was his love of poverty. His zeal went even further; he ordered his brethren, by the obedience of charity, to stretch him naked on the ground as soon as he should be dead, and to leave him in that state during the space of time that it would take to walk a mile slowly. This was a further imitation of the Savior, who, after His death, remained some time on the cross before He was taken down to be buried. "Oh!" exclaims St. Bonaventure, "with what truth may it be said that this was verily a Christian man, who has rendered himself perfectly conformable to Jesus Christ while living, or dying, or dead, and who has merited the honor of such a conformity, by the impression of the five wounds!"

What is further remarkable is, that they asked him where the desired to be buried, to which he answered: "In the vilest of places, on the Infernal Hill, on that side where criminals are executed."[16]

This place was out of the town of Assisi, near the walls, vulgarly called the Infernal Hill, perhaps on account of its being the place of execution. The servant of God wished to be buried there, in order to be in strict conformity with his Divine Master, "who chose," says St. Jerome, "to be crucified in the usual place of execution,[17] as a criminal among criminals, for the salvation of men, and to be placed in a tomb which was close by." His wish became a prophecy, for, two years after his death, as will be explained hereafter, a church was built in his honor on the Infernal Hill, when the name was changed into that of the Hill of Paradise, and the site of the church was so contrived that his body was placed precisely on the spot where the gallows

---

[16] Wading, ad ann. 1228, n. 79.

[17] S. Hieron. in cap. 27, Matt. 5: 33.

had been formerly erected.[18]

Seeing his last hour drawing nigh, he summoned all his brethren who were in the convent, and after having addressed some words of consolation to them, to mitigate the grief they felt for his death, he exhorted them to love God as a tender Father. Then he spoke to them for a long time on the care they should take to persevere in the faith of the Church of Rome, in poverty and in patience, under the tribulations which awaited them, as well as in adherence to their holy undertaking. He made use of the most moving expressions in recommending to them to make progress towards eternal goods, to be armed with vigilance against the dangers of the world, and to walk exactly in the paths of Jesus Christ; remarking to them that the observance of His Gospel was the basis and essence of their institution, and that all their practices had that in view.

Up to this time we had to admire the presence of mind and he strength which the saint manifested in the midst of his sufferings, and of the weaknesses which were hastening on his last moments. But there is much more room for astonishment when we find that, after all the exertion we have witnessed, he was still able to dictate a tolerably long will, full of luminousness, of feeling, and of vigor. We must think that the man-God, who spoke to the last moment so distinctly from the cross, with a tranquillity and grandeur which marked His divinity, had communicated some portion of His strength to His creature, Francis, to have rendered him capable of an effort almost supernatural. We deem it desirable to give in this place his last will, such as he dictated it to Brother Angelo, one of his companions. It is wholly spiritual, because the sainted patriarch left to his children only spiritual goods: these were, as St. Bonaventure observes, poverty and peace.

THE LAST WILL OF SAINT FRANCIS

"The Lord has given me grace, to me, Brother Francis, thus to begin to do penance. When I was in the state of sin,[19] it seemed to be very bitter to see lepers, but the Lord having Himself taken me amongst them, I was merciful in their regard, and, in leaving them, I felt that what had appeared to me so bitter, had been changed into deliciousness for my soul and body.

"After that I tarried little in the world, I left it, and our Lord gave me so much faith in the Church, where He is, that I adored Him in it, in saying simply: 'We adore You, O most holy Lord Jesus Christ! here and in all Your churches which are on earth, and we bless You for having redeemed the world

---

[18] Wading, ad ann. 1235, n 19.

[19] Although he had never lived a disorderly life, he, nevertheless, called the first years of his life a state of sin, because he then loved vanity surd pleasure, and because this love is a sin which leads to the commission of others. "Love not the world, nor the things hat are of the world," says the Apostle St. John (1 John, II: 15), and in Baptism we renounce the pomps of Satan, that is, the maxims and vanities of the world.

by Your holy Cross.'

"He likewise gave me, and He still gives me, so much faith in priests, who live according to the forms of the Holy Roman Church, because of their character, that, if they were to persecute me, it would be still to them that I should have recourse; and had I as much wisdom as Solomon had, were I to find priests poor according to the world, I would not, contrary to their wish, preach in the churches in which they dwell. I mean to fear them, to love them, to honor them, and all others as my masters. What induces me to do this is, that I see nothing in this world so discerning of this same Son of God, the Most High, as His very sacred body and His most holy blood, which they receive, and which they alone administer to others.

"Now, it is my desire that these most holy mysteries may be honored and revered above all other things, and that they may be put in places where they may be carefully preserved. Wherever I shall find the very holy names and the very holy words of the Son of God in improper places,[20] I wish that they should be removed, and I beg that they may be taken away, and placed in some more proper locality. We must also respect all theologians, and all those who dispense to us the very holy word of God, as ministers who communicate to us spirit and life.

"When the Lord had committed to me the guidance of the brethren, no one taught me what I ought to do; but the Most High Himself revealed to me that I was to live according to the formula of the Gospel.[21] I caused it to be written out in few and plain words, and our Holy Father, the Pope, confirmed it.

"Those who came to me, to engage in this mode of life, gave to the poor all that they had. They were satisfied with our tunic,[22] covered with pieces inside and outside, if they chose,[23] with a cord for a girdle, and a pair of drawers: and we desired nothing more. We, who are clerks, said the office as other clerks do; the lay brothers said the Pater Noster. We willingly took up our abode in poor and abandoned churches, we were simple-minded persons, and were submissive to all the world.

"I worked with my own hands, and I will still work,[24] and it is my fixed

---

[20] He spoke as if he was not on the point of death, in order to make the greater impression on his brethren respecting the veneration to be shown to holy things.

[21] His testimony leaves no doubt, but that the Rule of the Friars Minor was revealed by God.

[22] With the tunic must be included the cowl. The Rule permitted them to have a second tunic without a cowl; but many went without it, out of mortification.

[23] They added patches to the tunic, from a spirit of poverty, and to make them last the longer, and have fewer new ones. It was also in opposition to the foolish vanity of the age, and to become more agreeable to God, by rendering themselves more vile and contemptible in the eyes of the world, according to this view of Saint Bonaventure: "Ut seculi stultitia in fratrum habitu ostendatur. Qui se stultum et despicabilem exhibet huic mundo, ipsi Deo efficitur pretiosus." —Expos. in Reg. Frat. Min. cap. 2.

[24] By this he showed his love for labor, although he knew that the time for his death was approaching, in order that he might thereby induce his brethren to fly idleness.

desire[25] that all the other brethren shall apply themselves to some useful labor; let those who know not how to work, learn to do so, not from any wish to gain by what they may do, but for good example, and to fly idleness. If we are not rewarded for our work, let us have recourse to the table[26] of the Lord, seeking alms from door to door. He revealed to me that we should make use of this mode of salutation: 'May the Lord give you His peace.'

"Let the brethren be very careful not to receive, on any account, either churches or houses, or anything which may be built for them, if it be not conformity with holy poverty, which we have promised to abide by in the Rule; and let them always live there as strangers and travelers. I strictly forbid, under obedience, all the brethren, whoever they may be, to have the daring to solicit[27] any letter from the court of Rome, by themselves, or through the

---

[25] Pope Gregory IX, who had been the intimate friend of Saint Francis, and who was perfectly acquainted with his intention declared in the year 1230, four years after the saint's death, that his will did not impose any new obligations on his brethren, which was confirmed by Pope Nicholas III, in 1279. The article, therefore, relative to manual labor must be referred to the fifth chapter of the Rule, on which Nicholas III has said: "We declare that, on a due consideration of the words of Saint Francis, it does not appear to have been his intention to subject to manual labor those who are employed in study, or in the service and on the Divine ministries; since we see in the example of Jesus Christ, and of many of the holy fathers, that the labor of the

mind is to be preferred to that of the body; and the more so as what concerns the soul is of greater importance than corporal affairs. But this part of the Rule must be understood to relate to those who are not employed in such spiritual exercises, in order that they may not live in idleness; unless when they are legitimately employed in the service of the other brethren, or elevated in so high a degree of prayer and contemplation, that it would not be right to take them from it to employ them on manual labor." —Decree, Exiit qui seminat in 6, de verb, signif. This declaration of Gregory IX, given by Wading, is taken from the Registry of the Vatican, n. 73.

[26] He calls the goods of the rich the table of the Lord, because they have received them from Him in order to assist the poor therewith, and because Jesus Christ receives, in the person of the poor, what is given by the rich. These Are two truths of religion, taken from the Gospel, and often dwelt upon by the fathers, and which cannot be too much meditated on by those who Are possessed of this world's goods.

[27] He did not by this forbid praying for the Apostolical letters requisite for the support and government of his Order, which is immediately dependent on the Holy See, since he himself had frequently solicited such. He only speaks of such as might be prayed for from views contrary to the spirit of holy poverty, humility, and the patience with which he required his brethren to love and labor for the salvation of souls. The body of the Order has never solicited favors of this nature. See Pet. Marchant. Fundam, duod in Coron tot. Oper. pag. 183 et seq.

Some Friars Minors with some Friars Preachers, who had been selected by Pope Honorius to go on a mission into the kingdom of Miramolin, they represented to His Holiness that, to succeed among these infidels, to penetrate into the prisons where the Christians were confined, and administer the sacraments to them, it would be sometimes necessary for them to wear secular dresses, to let their beards and hair grow, and even sometimes to receive money to have wherewithal to live. The Pope granted them these permissions, deeming it a case which required these dispensations, this is very like what is practiced at the present moment in England, without which the Catholics there would be deprived of all spiritual aid. M. Fleury, who notices this, should have added that in this the Friars Minors do nothing which is contrary to the spirit of their Rule, because the evident necessity of the case and the salvation of souls must be preferred to a clause in the Rule. The Bull of Pope Honorius medium of any other person, either for a church or any other place, on pretense of preaching, or even for the safety of their persons in case of persecution. But, should they not be received in one place, let them fly to another, there to do penance with the blessing of God.

"I will implicitly obey the Minister-General[28] of this Confraternity, and the Guardian, whom it may please him to give me; and I consent to be so bound in his hands that it will not be in my power to go, nor to do anything against his will, because he is my master. Although I am simple and infirm, it is my desire[29] always to have a clerk to say the Office to me, as the Rule directs. If there should be some who do not say the Office, according to the Rule, or who should wish to make any alteration in it, or should not be Catholics, let all the brethren, wherever they may be (and should such an one be there), be compelled by obedience to take him to the custos, the nearest to the place at which they may be; and let the custos be obliged by obedience to guard him night and day, as a prisoner, so that no one may be able to rescue him, until he delivers him up to his minister;[30] and let this minister be strictly bound by obedience to have him taken by brethren who are able to keep him safe, day and night[31] as prisoner, until he is delivered up to the Cardinal of Ostia, who is the protector and censor of this confraternity.

"Let not the brethren say that this is another Rule; it is a memorial, a warning, an exhortation, and my last will, which I, Brother Francis, your very little servant, address to you, my brethren, who are blest by God, in order that we may the better observe in a more Catholic[32] manner, the Rule which we

---

is dated 17th March, 1226, —Raynald. ad. ann. 1226, n. 60. The permission which these Friars Minors requested from the Pope to be allowed to let their beards grow, shows clearly that they did not wear them in the beginning of the Order. Wading gives other proofs of his; and the continuators of Bollandus, Act. SS. Vit. S. Anthon. 13. Jun. p. 714, and p. 741, confirm it, by giving the ancient portraits of the Blessed Benedict of Arezzo, and of St. Anthony of Padua, neither of which has a beard. They say that the Friars Minors who were priests, did not wear their beards to conform to the custom of the clergy of the 13th century; and that it appears that Saint Francis, who was only in Deacon's orders, did not shave out of humility; but we shall see, in the description of his person, taken from his historians, that he had very little beard.

[28] He had lived and he died with a sincere desire to obey, although he was the founder of the Order, and that two Popes, had appointed him its Minister-General.

[29] He speaks thus to inspire his brethren with zeal for saying the Divine Office, even in their illness.

[30] Wading supposes this to be the Minister-General, but it is more probable that it is the Provincial Minister.

[31] We here remark the zeal of Saint Francis for the preservation of the purity of faith in his Order. He infuses similar dispositions by this spirit. The Friars Minors would not suffer any one of their Order to swerve with impunity from the orthodox doctrine. They are ardent Catholics, born and open enemies to all novelties.

[32] He makes use of the term, *Catholice* to show that, as unity of mind is the reason why the faithful are called Cathohcs all over the world, so also the Friars Minors must observe their Rule in a Catholic manner, that is to say in a similar spirit, and in a similar manner, without any peculiar opinion which should occasion schism or division.

have promised the Lord to obey. Let the Minister-General, and all other ministers and custodes[33] be bound by obedience not to add anything to these words, nor to suppress anything which is in it.[34] Let them always have with them this writing, joined to the Rule, and in all the chapters which they may convene, when they read the Rule, let them also read these words.

"I likewise strictly forbid, under the law of obedience, all my brethren, whether clerks or laity, from making any comments[35] on the Rule, and on this writing, saying: 'It is thus that it should be understood.' But, as the Lord has done me the favor to dictate it to me, purely and simply, let it be similarly understood, purely, simply and without comment, and put the same in practice to the end, by holy actions.

"Whosoever shall observe these things, may he be filled in heaven with the blessing of the celestial Father, the Most High, and on earth with the blessing of His well-beloved Son, and of the Holy Spirit, the Comforter, with the assistance of all the celestial virtues, and of all the saints: and I, Brother Francis, your very little servant in our Lord, I confirm to you, as much as in my power, this very holy blessing, within and without. Amen."[36]

Such were the last dispositions of St. Francis, which he called his last will.

---

[33] *Ministers and Custodes;* that is to say, according to Saint Bonaventure as has been observed, the Ministers who are Custodes, so appointed to have a care, to guard. One might say that Custodes in this place signifies guardians.

[34] He forbade making any alteration in his will because he made it only in order that they should follow up the Rule with greater precision, that Rule of which God was the Author, who would that it should be literally observed. In the Book of Deuteronomy, Moses forbids them to add or take from any of his words. In the Apocalypse, Saint John makes use of severe threats against those who should add to, or take from, the prophecies of that book. -Deuter. 4 et 12; Apocalyp. 22.

[35] We must not be surprised that Saint Francis forbade making any comments (glosses) on his Rule, since Jesus Christ had declared that it was to be literally kept without comment. Pope Nicholas III, in his decretal, Exiit qui seminat, being a declaration as to the Rule of the Friars Minors, forbids, under pain of excommunication, latae sententiae, to make comments even on this decretal, unless to make the explanation clearer, or more grammatical; or for the more clear understanding the text, or the construction of certain words, without altering the sense in any manner, nor twist it to give it any other than what it literally bears. If the decretal, which is declaratory of the Rule, is not to be commented on, this must apply more forcibly to the Rule itself. It is therefore only permitted to explain it, simply literally, in the proper and express sense of the words, according to the intention of the holy founder, as Saint Bonaventure and others have done. For the same reason those parts of the will which relate to the Rule, are not to have any comments made on them; and as to the other parts, there is no Friar Minor who must not conform to them as much as possible, in order to comply with the views of his blessed father. Moreover, it is the old practice of the Order to read in all the communities on every Friday of the year the Rule and the Will, not only to obey the holy founder who recommended the reading of these two documents, but to impress frequently upon the members the duties of their profession.

[36] He had been empowered by God to confirm this solemn blessing. This is wonderful; but is it not still more so that Jesus Christ should have said to Saint Peter in establishing him His Vicar and visible Head of His Church: "I will give to you the keys of the kingdom of Heaven. And whatsoever you shall bind upon earth, it shall be bound also in Heaven: and whatsoever you shall loose upon earth, it shall be loosed also in Heaven"? —Matt. XVI. 19. See St. Gregory Dial. fib. ii. cap. xxiii.

A similar name is given in ecclesiastical history,[37] to the instructions which were given by St. Ephraim on his death-bed; and this name may be properly given to the exhortations addressed by the saints to their disciples in parting from them. They followed the examples of the patriarchs,[38] of Tobias, and of Mattathias but principally that of the Son of God, who, before His Passion, addressed to His apostles a discourse full of the tenderest sentiments, His testament of charity, which he finished on the cross, in favor of His blessed mother, and of the disciple whom He loved. As all Christians are bound faithfully to fulfill what Jesus Christ has pointed out to them before quitting the world, it is also requisite that the children of the founders of Orders, who were animated by His Spirit, should be faithful in practicing what their fathers have said to them when dying. This is what an ancient author has beautifully expressed in relation to the last will of St. Francis: "O testament of peace! O testament never to be forgotten! which must be in every way respected, in opposition to which no innovation must be admitted; will most valid, not by the death of the testator, but by the immortal glory he has received. Happy those who do not despise this incorruptible testament of charity, this fertile basis of humility, this inestimable treasure of poverty, which has been bequeathed by so great and so illustrious a father."[39]

After the holy man had made known his last wishes, he sent for Brother Leo, his confessor, and for Brother Angelo, whom he directed to sing in his presence the Canticle of the Sun, because death was very near: this is the canticle of which we have spoken, in which he gives glory to God for all His creatures, and also for death. As he was assured by revelation that death would remove him to eternal life, its proximity filled him with joy, which he evidenced by causing the praises of God to be sung.

When the canticle was finished, he placed his arms one over the other in the form of a cross, a saving sign, to which he had been always devoted, as St. Bonaventure remarks, and stretching them over his brethren who stood around him, he gave his blessing for the last time, as well to those who were present, as to those who were absent, in the name and by virtue of Jesus crucified. He then pronounced the following words with great mildness and suavity: "Adieu, my children, I bid you all adieu; I leave you in the fear of the Lord, abide ever in that. The time of trial and tribulation approaches; happy those who preserve in the good they have begun.[40] As to me, I go to God with great eagerness, and I recommend you all to His favor."

He then called for the book of the Gospels, and requested them to read to him the Gospel of St. John, at that part where the history of the Passion of our

---

[37] Int. Oper. S. Ephrem.

[38] Genes. 9: 27, 48 and 49; Tob. 4 and 14; 1 Mach. 2; John 13, 14 and 19.

[39] Ad Calc. Test, inter Oper. S. Franc.

[40] Act. 20: 32.

Blessed Savior begins by these words: "Ante diem festum Paschae" before the feast of the Passover. After this had been read, he began himself to recite, as well as he could, the hundred and forty-first psalm, "Voce mea ad Dominum clamavi:" "I have cried to You, O Lord, with my voice;" and he continued it to the last verse, "Me expectant justi, donec retribuas mihi:" "The just wait for me, until You shalt reward me." In fine, all the mysteries of grace having been fulfilled in this man, so beloved by God, his very soul, absorbed in divine love, was released from the shackles of his body, and went to repose in the Lord. It was on a Saturday, in the evening, on the fourth day of October, in the forty-fifth year of his age, the twentieth of his conversion, the eighteenth of the institution of his Order, and the beginning of the third since he had received the Stigmata.

Such a death makes good what the holy fathers of the Church say,[41] that the perfect Christian dies with joy, and with pleasure. There is no one who would not wish for such a death. The most worldly would desire with Balaam, that their life should end as that of the just; but the perfection of the just must be imitated to afford any hope of the end being similar: death is only mild and consoling in proportion to the fervor of a Christian life.

St. Bonaventure places on record many proofs which they had of the glory of St. Francis at the moment of his death. One of his disciples[42] saw his blessed soul, under the figure of a brilliant star, rise upon a white cloud, above all the others, and go straight to heaven. This marked, says the holy doctor, the splendor of his sublime sanctity, with the plenitude of grace and wisdom, which had rendered him worthy of entering into the regions of light and peace, where, with Jesus Christ, he enjoys a repose which will be eternal.

Brother Augustine of Assisi, Provincial of the Terra di Lavoro, a just and saintly man, who was in the last stage of a severe illness, and had ceased to speak, suddenly exclaimed: "Wait for me, my father, wait for me; I will go with you." The brethren, quite astonished, asked him who he was speaking to. "What," said he, "don't you see our father, Francis, going up to heaven?"

At that very moment his soul separated itself from his body, and followed that of his father. Thomas of Celano, and Bernard of Bessa, companions of St. Bonaventure, also mentioned that a holy man of their day had a revelation to the effect, that the souls of several Friars Minors were delivered from the sufferings of purgatory, and were joined with that of the holy patriarch, to enter heaven with him.

The Bishop of Assisi being then on a devotional tour to Mount Gargano, to visit the church of the Archangel Michael, Francis appeared to him on the

---

[41] S. Aug. in Epist. Joan, tract. 9, n. 2. S. Greg. Homil. 15, in Evang, n. 3. S. Bernard, serm. ii in Fest. Sanct. Apost. n. 6. Num. XXIII: 10.

[42] Saint Bonaventure does not name him; but others assure us that it was Brother James of Lodi, who is buried at Saint Mary of the Angels, and whom God has honored by many miracles. —Wading, ad ann. 1226, n. 38.

night of his death, and said: "I leave the world, and am going up to heaven." The prelate, in the morning, mentioned to those who accompanied him what he had seen; and on his return, having made exact inquiry, he found that the apparition had appeared to him at the very time of the saint's death. His body was placed naked on the ground, and was left there some time, as he had desired. It was afterwards washed,[43] and covered with the tunic which Lady Jacqueline of Septisal had brought from Rome. This illustrious and pious widow had then the consolation to view at leisure and to kiss the wounds which had been imprinted on the holy man, and which she so greatly revered. She was animated with such fervor, that, after having defrayed the expense of a magnificent funeral for him, she went back to Rome, put her affairs in order, renounced the world entirely, and then returned to Assisi, where she passed[44] the remainder of her life, in watching and prayer, at the tomb of her spiritual father.

The body of St. Francis, after his death, was an object worthy of admiration, according to this description of it, given by St. Bonaventure on the testimony of those who had seen it, and reported verbally to him all the circumstances, conformably to what had been taken down in writing. On his hands and on his feet black nails were seen as of iron, wonderfully formed of his flesh by divine power, and so attached to his flesh, that, when they were pressed on one side, they protruded farther on the other, as hard excrescences, and all of one piece. Nothing now prevented the wound on his side from being seen, which he hid with so much care during his lifetime, this wound, and which had not beep made by the hand of man, which resembled the opening in the side of our blessed Savior, from which the sacrament of our redemption issued,[45] and that of our regeneration. Its color was red, and the edges, rounded

---

[43] Two authors say that he was opened, and that his heart and bowels were deposited in the church of Saint Mary of the Angels, in order to have at least a portion of his relics there: and they ground this on the saint having said that his heart would remain in the convent of Saint Mary of the Angels, when he designated the Infernal Hill as the place for his grave, the spot where criminals were executed. This is what is asserted by the religious of this convent at the present time. Wading is not convinced of the accuracy of this, and many others reject it altogether, believing that respect prevented them from opening his body: which seems to be probable, and is corroborated in Assisi by a tradition gathered from the testimony of some persons who were so fortunate as to have seen and touched the body. If he said that his heart would continue at Saint Mary of the Angels, it may be understood of the peculiar affection he always entertained for that place. Wading ad ann. 1226, n. 40.

[44] She died in the year 1239, and was buried at Assisi in the church which had been built in honor of St. Francis. Her two sons, who were Roman Senators, were likewise buried there. Wading ad ann. 1235, n. 24, and, ad ann. 1239, n. 14.

[45] The holy fathers say that the water which issued from the side of Jesus Christ represented Baptism, which is the sacrament of our spiritual regeneration; and that the blood represented the Eucharist, the sacrament which contains the price of our redemption,—the body and blood of our Savior which nourishes us spiritually for the support of the life which we received in Baptism. Now, as Baptism is the first of the sacraments, and the Eucharist is the greatest of them all, the same saints

off, gave it the appearance of beautiful rose. The flesh of the saint, which was naturally of a brownish color, and which his diseases had rendered tawny, became extraordinarily white. It called to mind the robes whitened in the blood of the Lamb,[46] with which the saints are clothed His limbs were flexible and pliable as those of an infant: evident signs of the innocence and candor of his soul. The whiteness of his skin contrasted with the black nails of his hands and feet, and with the wound in his side, which resembled a fresh-blossomed rose, exhibited a variety of color which was beautiful and pleasing, and was the admiration of those who saw it. His body, in fine, was the representation of the Passion of Jesus Christ by the wounds imprinted on it, and of the glorious resurrection, by the qualifications it had received.

This marvelous and novel sight mitigated the affliction of his children; it strengthened their faith, inflamed their love, and quite enraptured them; and, although the death of so amiable a father caused them to shed torrents of tears, they, nevertheless, had their hearts filled with joy when they kissed the impressions of the wounds of the great King imprinted on his flesh.

As soon as the news of his death was spread, and the circumstances of the Stigmata came to be spoken of, the people came in crowds to see them: each person wished to see them with his own eyes, and assure himself of the truth of an event which was the cause of so much joy to the public. A great number of the citizens of Assisi were permitted to approach, to see and to kiss the sacred Stigmata. One of them named Jerome, belonging to the army, a learned and prudent man, whose reputation was very extensive, finding it difficult to give credit to so wonderful a circumstance, examined the wounds more particularly and more minutely than the rest, in presence of the brethren, and of many persons of the town. He felt the feet, the hands, and the wound in the side of the saint's body; he moved the nails, and convinced himself so perfectly of the truth of the fact, that he was afterwards a most zealous advocate and witness to it, and made oath to its truth on the holy Evangelists. "It was," St. Bonaventure remarks, "a case similar to that of the Apostle St. Thomas,[47] who, from being incredulous, became, a faithful witness after having put his hands into the wounds of the Savior, in order that his faith, preceded by incredulity, should strengthen our faith, and prevent us from becoming incredulous."

The brethren, who had been present at the death of the blessed patriarch, passed the remainder of the night in singing the praises of God around the

---

teach us that the Sacraments of the Church came forth from the side of Jesus Christ, and from that came forth the Church, His Spouse, after His death, as Eve was taken from the side of Adam during his sleep. On which St. Augustine exclaims: "O death, which revives the dead! What is there which is more pure than this Blood? What is there more salutary than this wound?" —St. August. In Joan. tract. 120. And St. Chrysostom says: "Every time you draw near to receive this Divine beverage, figure to yourselves that it flows from the side of Jesus Christ to your mouth."

[46] Apoc. 7: 13 and 14.

[47] John 20: 27.

body, with a number of other persons, who had collected there for the purpose, insomuch that it was more resembling a feast of celestial spirits than the funeral service of a mortal.

The next morning, which was Sunday, the holy corpse was carried to Assisi on the shoulders of the principal persons of that city, and those of the highest rank among the Friars Minors; hymns and canticles being sung the whole way, while the concourse followed, carrying in their hands lighted torches, or branches of laurel.

The procession passed on to the church of St. Damian, where Clare and her nuns awaited it, and where it halted for a short time, to afford them the consolation of seeing and kissing the Stigmata. In admiring this extraordinary prodigy, and lamenting the death of such a father, they called to mind the promise he had made them during his last illness, that they should again see him before their death. Clare endeavored to draw the nail from one of his hands, which, as the head of it was raised above the palm of the hand, she thought she would be able to effect; but she found it impossible. She, therefore, only dipped a piece of linen in the blood which exuded; and she took the measure of the body, by which she had a niche made of similar size, on the side of the tribune which the religious occupied, in which the image of the saint was afterwards placed. These pious virgins would have been glad to have detained the body longer, but it was necessary to resume the route to Assisi, where he was buried in the church of St. George, with every possible veneration and respect. It was there he had received the first rudiments of education, it was there he had preached for the first time, and there was his first place of repose.

Brother Elias, in his quality of vicar-general, wrote a circular letter on his death, which he sent into all the provinces of the order. The copy[48] which the provincial of France received, was thus directed: "To my well-beloved brother in Jesus Christ, Brother Gregory, minister of the brethren who are in France, and to all his brethren, and to ours. Brother Elias sends greeting."

He first expresses his grief in very affecting terms, and in alluding to the loss the Order had sustained, he passes a high eulogium on the sanctity of their common father, with many citations from the Sacred Scriptures, very aptly applied. Then, he says, that what must console the children of the blessed

---

[48] This letter was in the original in the archives of the convent of Friars (Recollets) at Valenciennes in the last century; and a copy of it was sent to Wading, which he inserted in the Annals of the Order. Father William Spoelbereh, a Friar Minor of the province of Lower Germany, author of the new edition of a book entitled, "Speculum B. Francisci et sociorum ejus," printed at Antwerp in 1620 by Gerard Wolschatius, has said in pari ii. p. 102, that the same letter was preserved in the same place, as an ancient and precious document. But it is no longer there; perhaps it was removed when the town passed under a new domination after the war, and the religious of the country removed to some other place; but there remains in the convent of Valenciennes a copy similar to the one which Wading published; and from the copy smother was sent to the Recollets at Paris, which has been collated on the spot by Gildard du Flos, Apostolic Notary.

patriarch is, that his death opened to him eternal life, and that previously he had pardoned all the offenses which he might have sustained from any of them. This article only regarded Brother Elias and his adherents, for they were the only ones who had caused him any displeasure, and, according to all probability, Elias only adverted to it to soften the feelings of many who were irritated with him in consequence of his relaxation. After this preliminary he communicates to them a great cause for rejoicing in the miracle of the Stigmata, which he treats as follows:

"We had seen our brother and our father, Francis, some time before his death as one crucified, having on his body five wounds similar to those of Jesus Christ, nails of the color of nails of iron, which perforated his hands and feet, his side being laid open as by the wound of a lance, from whence blood often percolated. Immediately after his death his face, which was not handsome during his life, became extraordinarily beautiful, white and brilliant, and pleasing to behold; his limbs, which the contraction of the muscles, caused by his great sufferings, had stiffened like to those of a corpse, became pliant and flexible as those of a child: they could be handled and placed in any position which might be wished."

He then exhorts them to give glory to God for so great a miracle, and adds: "He who used to console us in our afflictions is no more, he has been taken from us; we are now orphans, and have no longer a father. But, since it is written, that 'to the Lord is the poor man left: He will be a helper to the orphan,'[49] let us address our prayers to Him, my dear brethren, and let us entreat Him to give us another chief, who, as a true Machabee, shall guide us and lead us to battle." The sequel showed that Elias wished to be himself the Machabee, the head of his brethren. At the close of the letter he ordered prayers for the deceased, saying: "It is not useless to pray for the dead; pray for him, as he requested we should: but at the same time pray that we may obtain from God a participation in His grace. Amen." It was signed, "Brother Elias, a sinner."

Although he had no doubt but that the holy man was in glory, he, nevertheless, did not omit praying for him, not only to comply with the wish of the deceased, and not to forestall the decision of the Holy See, but, also, because he bore in mind what St. Augustine had said,[50] that the sacrifices and prayers offered for the dead whose life has been irreproachable, are acts of thanksgiving.

---

[49] Psalm 9: 14

[50] S. August. Enchirid. cap. cix. n. 29.

CHAPTER II
THE SPIRITUALITY OF ST. FRANCIS

Devotion of St. Francis towards Jesus Christ crucified—To what a degree he loved poverty—How great was the austerity of his life—His watchfulness in the custody of his senses to resist temptations—His humility.

EFORE GIVING AN ACCOUNT of the canonization of St. Francis[1], and of the celebrated translation of his body to the church which was built in his honor and in his name at Assisi, we must call attention to several instances of his heroic virtue and his holy doctrine, which we have reserved for this last book, not to interrupt the course of the history; and we shall add some particulars as to the marvelous gifts which heaven had so liberally dispensed to him.

The eminent perfection of St. Francis was grounded on a tender and fervent devotion to Jesus Christ crucified. This adorable object had a powerful attraction for his heart, was the source of all the graces he received, and the model of all the virtues he practiced. From the sufferings of our Savior he made for himself, as St. Bernard[2] had done, a nosegay of myrrh, which he always carried in his bosom; he considered attentively the sufferings of his Beloved, he suffered them himself, and they called forth his sighs and his tears; it was his wish that the fire of this love might transform him entirely into Him who had borne them. And, by a return of love, he received that signal and precious favor, which he communicated in confidence to his companions, which always made him feel that he was in the presence of his Savior, as if he saw Him with his own eyes. In the colloquies, in the letters, and in the prayers which are found in his works, we see the admirable feelings he entertained for the crucified Jesus, and how much it was his wish that the whole world should know, love, and imitate Him; but there is nothing more to this purport than the two canticles which he composed shortly after he had received the impression of the Stigmata: he there, in the most vivid terms, expresses the tender affection with which these wonderful wounds had inflamed him. All this is collected together at the end of the particular history we give of the

---

[1] A discussion of the Canonization of St. Francis was in Challipe's French original, but it was not provided in the Oratorian edition, which this version is taken from. —Editor.

[2] S. Bernard, in cant. serm. xliii. n. 3.

Stigmata.

The poverty of the Son of God, in His birth, during His life, and at His death, made such impression on the heart of Francis, that he embraced this virtue with inexpressible ardor.

Seeing that it was rejected by the world, and looking upon it as the pearl of the Gospel, to acquire it, he abandoned father, mother, and all that he had. No person ever sought after riches with so much avidity, and no one ever guarded his treasure with so much care. He never wore, until his death, anything but a worthless tunic, and he refused himself everything but what was absolutely necessary. He would yield to no one in poverty, although he considered himself the most abject of all. If he saw any one worse dressed than he was, he considered it as a reproach to himself. One day, meeting a poor man who was almost naked, he said to his companion with a sigh: "There is a poor man who shames us. We have chosen poverty for our greatest riches, and in him you see it shine far more than in us."

For his nourishment, he greatly preferred what he solicited for the love of God from door to door, to what was offered to him. He frequently considered within himself, and it brought tears into his eyes, how poor our Savior and His Blessed Mother had been in this world, and the reflection induced him to live in greater poverty.

As to the cells, he always chose the smallest. One of his secular friends having had one built, which was only made of wood, though pretty neat, in the hermitage of Sarthiano, he found it too fine, and said he would not enter it a second time unless it was put into a state of poverty; so that, in order to induce him to return, it was necessary to cover it roughly with branches of trees, both without and within. He left it afterwards because one of his companions had said to him, "Father, I am come to look for you in your cell." "I will not occupy it any longer," he replied, "because you consider it mine in calling it my cell: another may live in it, to whom it will not be appropriated."

This is what his companions tell us on the subject: "We have often heard him say, we, who have lived with him: I will not have as mine either dwelling—place, or any other thing; for our Master has said: 'The foxes have holes, and the birds of the air, nests; but the Son of man hath not where to lay His head.'"[3]

He was also accustomed to say: "When our Lord went to fast in the desert, where He remained forty days and forty nights, He had no cell prepared for Him, nor any other covering; it was only in some crevice of that mountain that He took repose." The same authors add, that, in order to imitate Jesus Christ perfectly, Francis desired to have neither convent nor cell which could be called his. And, moreover, if sometimes, on arriving, he pointed out to his brethren the cell which he proposed to occupy, he checked himself

---

[3] Luke 9: 58.

immediately, as having shown too much solicitude, and went into another, which had not been prepared for him. Shall, then, the children of the Patriarch of the poor be censured when they imitate this tenderness of conscience; and when, to show their aversion to the possession of property, they call even the things which are most essential for them to have the use of, by terms which show that they hold them in common, and that they have nothing which is their own?

Although the servant of God possessed every virtue in a very high degree, yet it was remarked that the virtue of poverty was the one which was above all the others; and this it pleased the Almighty to make known by an admirable vision. When the saint was going to Sienna, three very poor women, who resembled each other both in size and countenance, and appeared to be of the same age, presented themselves before him, and greeted him in these words: "May the Lady Poverty be welcome!" This salutation filled him with joy, because nothing was more grateful to him in greeting him than to speak of poverty, which was so dear to him. The vision immediately vanished, and his companions, who had seen it, had no doubt that there was something mysterious in it; that God meant thereby to discover to them something which related to their father. And in fact, says St. Bonaventure, these three women, who were so like to each other, were not bad representations of chastity, obedience, and poverty, which constitute the beauty of evangelical perfection, and were the very eminent characteristics of the saintly man; and the expressions which these women made use of in greeting him, showed that he had chosen poverty as his special prerogative, and the principal object of his glory; and, indeed, he was in the habit of calling it sometimes his lady, sometimes his mother, and sometimes his wife.

He constantly recommended it to his disciples; and if he perceived anything in them which did not coincide with his views of strict poverty, he was shocked at it. Many times he explained to them that his intention was, that a Friar Minor should have no other clothing than what was laid down by the Rule. On this principle he would not give a Provincial leave to have any books for his own use which he might have collected; and when a Provincial asked him what he should do with the books which had cost so much money, "Brother," he replied, "I will not, because of your books, corrupt the Gospel, according to which we have promised not to have anything of our own in this world: do what you please with your books, but my permission shall not be a snare for you, nor a stumbling-block."

One of his solicitudes was, that his brethren should not build any other than small and poor convents. "So do," he said to them, "that poverty shall be apparent among you in all things, principally in your houses; and do not live in them as if they were your own, but as belonging to some one else, as strangers and travelers."

A Siennese gentleman, who wished to have an establishment of Friars

Minors in that city, and whose name was Bonaventure, came to him, to know how he would have the convent built. "My most honored brother," Francis replied, "the place which you intend for us seems to me very appropriate, and we return you a thousand thanks for it. This is how it should be built upon. The brethren must first examine the ground, and see how many acres will suffice them, paying great attention to holy poverty, which they have promised God to adhere to, and to the good example which it behooves them to give on this head. After that let them address themselves to the bishop, and say to him: 'My lord, a gentleman of great influence here has given us, for the love of God, and the salvation of his own soul, a piece of ground fit to build a convent on. As you are the pastor of the whole flock which is confided to you, and of the whole of the Friars Minors who are at present in your diocese, as well as of those who will dwell therein hereafter, you are their protector and father, full of kindness; it is to you we come first, to be permitted to erect on that spot a poor and unostentatious dwelling, with the blessing of God, and with yours.'

"Having received the bishop's permission and his blessing, let them make a deep ditch, and, instead of walls, let them plant a thick hedge, as a mark of poverty and humility; let the house be of wood and of earth, with cells in it, in which they may pray and walk, as much for avoiding idleness as for adhering to the seemliness of their station. The church must be small; for they must not, on pretense of preaching, nor under any other pretext whatever, build large and handsome churches. They will give better example to the people in preaching in other churches,[4] and will manifest thereby that they are truly humble; moreover, when prelates, and other members of the clergy, or religious of other orders, or seculars, come to see them, a poor house and small cells will be a more edifying sermon in their regard, than well labored discourses."

The holy founder was desirous that all the houses of his Order should be built upon this plan; but the princes and other benefactors had very beautiful edifices constructed according to their views of magnificence, and to their piety. Brother Leo, having been informed of this by his brethren, and others, who arrived from the further side of the Alps, spoke to Francis on the subject, to know what his opinion was on this head. "My brethren," he replied, addressing himself to all who were present, "there are even now some of our own people who build spacious convents; and others will come after us, who will build some so magnificent that the lords of the earth might dwell in them, and they will wear costly habits; but it will be well in those days if they avoid committing mortal sins."

---

[4] This is followed up sufficiently, since the Religious of St. Francis fill so many pulpits in cathedrals and in the parishes. If they preach sometimes in their own churches, it is in consequence of the multitude of the faithful, and other reasons relative to the salvation of souls, in the different circumstances of time and place.

He believed that these great convents might be built without sinning mortally against the vow of poverty, but he saw also that much would be found in them contrary to the perfection of that virtue; and therefore he said that then it would be enough if mortal sin was avoided. The same may be thought of their tunics, which may be good and substantial, particularly in cold climates, provided the brethren, in accordance with the Rule, wear habits that are worthless. St. Bonaventure[5] notices the legitimate reasons for building spacious and commodious houses, and calls attention to five points,[6] in which those would sin grievously who should exceed on this head; and he says that the worthlessness of the habit must be judged of by the price and by the color.

However, religious persons know this important maxim of Christian morality, that, in order to avoid mortal sin in the observation of the law, it is necessary to endeavor to abstain from those transgressions which may be only venial. Any contrary disposition is dangerous, either because it is extremely difficult to distinguish mortal from venial sin, as St. Augustine remarks;[7] or on account of the weakness of human nature, which urges one on beyond what is intended, and which becomes undeserving of the special graces which God gives to avoid falling into mortal sin, when he chooses to permit himself all that appears to him to be only venial. On this principle the saints whom God has raised up in the Order of the Friars Minors, in order to keep up the primitive fervor of the institution, have been very particular in following, with the greatest nicety, the regulations as to their buildings and dress, in order to attain the highest perfection of poverty.

It is not possible to record in this place all the praise which the holy founder gave to this evangelical virtue. He called it the Queen, not only because it shone with splendor in JESUS CHRIST, the King of kings, and in His Blessed Mother, but because it is elevated above all earthly things, which it tramples under foot. "Know," he used to say to his brethren, "that poverty is the hidden treasure of the Gospel, the basis on which an order rests, the special path to salvation, the support of humility, the mother of self-renunciation, the principle of obedience, the death of self-love, the destruction of vanity and cupidity, the rod of perfection, the fruits of which are abundant, though hidden. It is a virtue descended from heaven which acts within us, and enables us to despise everything which is despicable; it subverts all the obstacles which prevent the soul from perfectly uniting itself to God by humility and charity; it causes those by whom it is beloved to become active as pure spirits, and enables them to take their flight towards heaven, to converse with angels, though still living on earth. It is so excellent and so divine a

---

[5] S. Bonavent. determ, circa regul. S. Franc, quaest. 6.

[6] Those who are bent upon building and ornamenting religious edifices should read what the holy Doctor says on this subject. He approves only of what is reasonably necessary, considering the times, places, and persons.

[7] S. August. Enchir. n. 2. In Psalm LXXXVIII, serm. n. 3. et alibi.

virtue, that vile and abject vases such as we are, are not worthy of containing it."

In order to obtain the grace of poverty, he often put up the following prayer to Jesus Christ: "O Lord Jesus point out to me the ways of poverty, which are so dear to You. Have pity on me, for I love it with such intensity that I can find no repose without it, and You know that it is You who gave me this ardent love. It is rejected, despised, and hated by the world, although it is a lady and a queen, and You have had the goodness to come down from heaven to make poverty Your spouse, and to have from her, by her, and in her, perfect children. O Jesus, who chose to be extremely poor! The favor which I ask of You is to give me the privilege of poverty; I ardently desire to be enriched by this treasure; I entreat You that it may be mine, and of those who belong to me, and that we may never possess anything of our own under heaven for the glory of Your name, and that we may exist, during this miserable life, on those things only which are given to us, and be very sparing in the use we shall make even of these. Amen."

This friend of poverty did not confine it to the repudiation of all external things: he carried its perfection to the most elevated spiritual point. "He who aspires to its attainment," he said, "must renounce not only all worldly prudence, but in some degree all learning and science, so that, being stripped of all sorts of goods, he may place himself under cover of the protection of the Most High, think only of His justice, and cast himself into the arms of the Crucifix.[8] For it is not to renounce the world entirely, if any attachment to its lights, and to one's own feelings, remains in the secret recesses of the heart." He did not assert that, in order to arrive at the perfection of poverty, it was necessary to be without learning, but he required that learning should not be considered by the possessor as an interior property, from which self-love should be fed; that there should not be that secret attachment to mental illumination, which is the primary source of error, and the basis of the obstinacy of heretics; that all our knowledge should be referred to God, and that we should in some sense strip ourselves of it to acquire the perception of God alone, and of His holy law. St. Hilary said, speaking in the same sense, that we must always bear in mind that we are men, that we have nothing of our own, not even the use of our senses and faculties; that these come from God, and that we must only use them as things which are in a continual dependence on His will.[9] This is an important instruction for the consideration of the learned.

The lively affection which St. Francis bore for the crucified Jesus, from the moment of his conversion, rendered him very austere towards himself. Not

---

[8] He makes use of the following words of the Prophet in the sense usually given them: "Quoniam non cognovi litteraturam, introibo in potentias Domine, memorabor justitiae tuae solius." Psalm 70 (71): 17.

[9] S. Hilar., cap. iv., in Matt.

only could he not suffer that the tunic which he wore should have anything soft in it, but he chose that it should be rough and harsh; when he found that it had become too soft, he put, inside, knotted cord to counteract it.

It was usually on the bare ground that he laid his body down, that body which was worn out by fatigue; sometimes he slept, sitting with his head resting on a stone or piece of wood. As to food, he scarcely took what was absolutely necessary for his nourishment, and to keep life together. When in health, he seldom permitted anything to be put before him which was cooked, and then he either strewed ashes upon, or added water to it, to take away the taste. Pure water was his only beverage, and then he drank so little that it was insufficient for quenching his great thirst.

Besides the Lent kept by all Christians, he kept eight others in the course of the year. The first, of forty days, from the day after the Epiphany, in memory[10] of our Lord's fast in the desert, after He had been baptized by John, which took place on the sixth day of January, according to the old tradition of the Church.[11] The second was from the Wednesday in Easter week, to Whit Sunday, to prepare himself for receiving the Holy Spirit. The third, from the day after the festivals of Pentecost to the feasts of Peter and Paul, in honor of these blessed apostles. The fourth from the day after their festivals to the Assumption, in honor of the Blessed Virgin. The fifth in honor of St. Michael, from the Assumption to the feast of that angel. The sixth, from that feast to the first of November, in honor of all the saints. The seventh, from All-Souls to Christmas, to prepare himself to celebrate the birth of Christ. The eighth, from the feast of St. Stephen to the Epiphany, in honor of the three kings. Thus was his life a perpetual fast.

When he went abroad he ate whatsoever was[12] put before him, not only to observe the direction of the Gospel, but in order to gain worldlings to Jesus Christ, by conforming to their ways; but when in the convent, he resumed his habits of abstinence, and this mode of life was very edifying to laymen. The more he advanced towards perfection, the more he mortified his flesh, as if he only then began, and he hit upon new plans. We cannot form a more correct opinion of the evangelical hatred he bore his body, than by noticing the terms he made use of to express it. After having finished Compline, and spent a considerable time in prayer, in a deserted church, in which he passed the night, he wished to take some rest. As the evil spirits prevented him from so doing, by suggestions which frightened him, and made him tremble, he mustered courage, rose, made the sign of the cross, and said in a loud voice: "Devils, I declare to you from Almighty God, that you may use against me all

---

[10] The Lent, which is common to sill the faithful, was likewise instituted in honor of the fast of Jesus Christ. It has been fixed before Easter, as a preparation for the solemn memorial of His death and resurrection; it is an Apostolical tradition.

[11] Baron, ad ann. 31, n. 18. —Pagi. crit. ad ann. 25, 3, et ad ann. 29, 3.

[12] Luke 10: 8.

the power given to you by my Lord Jesus Christ, and do all the harm you can to my body. I am ready to suffer everything, and assuredly you will oblige me greatly, for this body is a great burden to me; it is the greatest enemy I have, the most wicked, and the most crafty; and you will revenge me by so doing."

Brother Giles said of St. Francis: "He only wanted one thing: bodily strength. If his body had been as robust as mine, no man would have been able to imitate his macerations."[13] This is what is most wonderful in what he did, with so weak and delicate a constitution. There can be no doubt but that the grace of Jesus Christ gave him powerful support, but it required his fortitude to respond proportionally to that grace. If we were courageous in the service of God, we should mortify our bodies more than we usually do, particularly by abstinence, which is not less in accordance with reason and medicine, than it is to Christian morality.

He exhorted his religious to austerity in their food, in their clothing, and in everything else. For he was convinced, as was St. Augustine,[14] that it is difficult to satisfy the demands of the body, without in some degree sacrificing to sensuality; and he used to say, "Our Savior praised St. John Baptist for his having clothed himself coarsely. According to His word. 'Behold they that are clothed in soft garments, are in the houses of kings,'[15] it must not be in the huts of the poor. I have found by experience that the devils fly from those who lead an austere life; and St. Paul teaches us, that they that are Christ's have crucified their flesh with the vices and concupiscences."[16] It will be seen in the sequel how he knew how to temper what seemed excess in the mortifications of his brethren.

The austerity of his life did not render him less attentive in watching over his senses. He applied himself assiduously to their mortification, in order to preserve constantly the purity of his body and mind. The perfection he had acquired did not make him relax in any degree of his vigilance. He turned away his eyes from every object that might wound the soul; he never looked a woman in the face, nor did he know any one by sight. His maxim was, that we must be very much on our guard in speaking to Christian virgins, and that the best way to strengthen them in chastity is, to exhort them with chaste and pure eyes.

"My brethren," he said, "we must avoid with great care having any conversations or familiarity with women, and even looking at them; and so much the more must this be attended to, that in this we see the weak lose themselves, and the strong become weak. Unless our virtue is well tried, I am convinced that it is difficult to converse with them without contagion, as it is

---

[13] Act. SS. 23 April, Vit. B. Ægid. part 3, cap. v., n. 70.

[14] S. August. Confess, lib. x., cap, 31.

[15] Math. 11: 8.

[16] Galat. 5: 24.

'to walk on coals of fire without burning the soles of the feet,' as the Scripture says. 'It is dangerous to bear in one's mind images which are capable of rekindling flames which have been extinguished, and to soil the purity of a chaste mind.' All conversation with woman is frivolous and vain, unless in the confessional, and to give them good advice as to their salvation, or for reasonable decorum; and then it should be in few words. What other objects can a religious have in conversing with them? Too great security puts one less on his guard against the enemy; and, if the devil has the smallest hold on a man, he will soon increase that till it becomes formidable."

The servant of God taught his brethren to fly idleness, on account of the bad thoughts of which it is the source, and it is by useful occupation and frequent discipline that rebellious and idle flesh must be subdued. "I desire," he said, "that my brethren may work and be occupied, lest, being idle, forbidden things may become spread over their hearts and their tongues. He who desires to live by the labor of others, without doing anything, deserves to be nicknamed Brother Fly; because, doing nothing that is worth anything, and spoiling what is good, he becomes odious and despicable to all the world." If he came upon any one wandering about, and without occupation, he applied to him these words of the Apocalypse: "Because you are lukewarm, I will begin to vomit you out of my mouth."[17] His example was an excellent lesson for not losing time, and fostering the idleness of the flesh; he employed himself always holily, and he called his body brother ass, which required to be well worked, to be severely beaten, and to be badly fed.

Silence was not considered by him to be a small virtue; he considered it as a guard to the purity of the heart, according to the maxim of wisdom: "Life and death are in the power of the tongue;"[18] by which he understood the intemperance of speech, as well as that of taste. But he principally wished his brethren to become exact in keeping evangelical silence, which consists in abstaining from all idle conversation, of which an account must be rendered at the day of judgment,[19] and he severely reprimanded those who were in the habit of saying useless things. In fine, his instruction was, that they should endeavor to destroy all vice, and to mortify the passions; and that, in order to succeed in this endeavor, every thing should be cut off which could serve as an attraction, and, therefore, that the exterior senses by which death enters into the soul, should be continually mortified.

As soon as he felt the smallest temptation, or if he only foresaw it he took every precaution for resisting it. At the beginning of his conversion he frequently threw himself, in the depth of winter, into freezing water in order to subdue his domestic enemy, and to preserve his robe of innocence without

---

[17] Apoc. 3: 16.

[18] Prov. 18: 21.

[19] Matt. 12: 36.

stain, asserting that it is far less painful to a spiritual man to suffer the rigor of the severest cold, than to feel interiorly the slightest attack upon his purity.

We have seen, in his Life, that he threw himself into the midst of thorns, to drive away the tempter who wanted to induce him to moderate his watchings and his prayers. One of his actions, the circumstances of which are thus related by St. Bonaventure, shows what was the purity of his heart, and with what force he resisted the impure spirit.

One night, while he was at prayer in his cell, at the hermitage of Sarthiano, he heard himself called three times by his name. After he had answered, a voice said to him: "There is no sinner in the world whom God does not pardon if he be converted; but whoever kills himself by too rigorous a penance, will never find mercy." Francis was made aware by a revelation that these deceitful words emanated from the old enemy, who wished to induce him to relax in his austerities, and he soon had sensible proof of it, for, "he who by his breath sets fire to coals," as holy Job says, "tempted him strongly to sin against purity."[20] As soon as he became aware of it, he inflicted a severe discipline on himself, saying to his body: "O brother ass! this is what suits you, this is the way in which you should be chastised. The tunic you wear is that of religion, and is a mark of its holiness. It is not permitted to one who is impure to wear it: that would be a theft." As the devil represented to him probably that he might marry and have children, and have servants to wait upon him, he responded to that by turning his own body into derision, and treating it cruelly. With admirable fervor he burst from his cell, and threw himself naked upon a large mound of snow; he made seven balls of it with his hands, and then said to himself: "The largest of these snowballs is your wife, four others are your two sons and two daughters, and the two last are your man and your maid-servants. I must think of clothing them, for they are perishing with cold, and if this solicitude is overpowering, think of nothing else than serving God fervently."

At this the tempter fled, and the saint returned victorious to his cell, and he never after had a similar temptation. One of his brethren, who was at prayer in the garden, saw by the light of the moon what was going on, and Francis, being aware of it, could not avoid explaining to him the whole temptation: "But," said he, "I forbid you strictly from saying a word on the subject during my lifetime." It was only known after his death.

Those who know how far the scrupulousness of chaste souls will carry them, will not feel surprised that, after the example of many other saints, he had put in practice such severe mortification, to shield himself from the slightest taint on his purity.[21] His lively and agreeable turn of mind are

---

[20] Job 41: 12.

[21] Heretics, who are as blind to the practice of virtue as they are to belief in the truth, have dared to censure this action of St. Francis as an extravagance, which, in fact, is a heroic act of purity, and Bayle has dared to say that Francis of Assisi had lost his senses through very false ideas of devotion.

apparent in the way in which he taunted his body when suffering from extreme cold; this also shows how much self-possession he had under the severest trials, and by what sentiment he was actuated in his penances.

St. Bonaventure says that, as a skillful architect, he laid down humility for the foundation-stone of his spiritual edifice, and that it was from Jesus Christ that he had acquired this wisdom. The foundation was so solid that humility became natural to him, as well as poverty, and that it is justly that he is called the humble St. Francis. He was in the eyes of all a mirror of holiness, but in his own eyes he was but a sinner; on all occasions he sought to vilify himself, not only in his own mind, but in that of others.

Upon one occasion Brother Pacificus, while praying with him in a church, was raised in an ecstasy, and saw several thrones in the heavens, among which there was one more splendid than the rest, ornamented with precious stones. As he was pondering for whom this magnificent seat could be destined, a voice said to him: "This was the seat of an angel, and now it is reserved for the humble Francis." Some short time after, when conversing with the saint, he led to the topic of the knowledge of one's self, and he asked him what idea he had of himself, upon which St. Francis answered quickly: "I consider myself the greatest of sinners." Pacificus maintained that he could not conscientiously either say so or think so. "I am convinced," replied Francis, "that, if the most criminal of men had experienced the great mercies I have received from Jesus Christ, he would be much more grateful for them than I am." This beautiful effusion confirmed Pacificus in the opinion he had entertained, that the vision he had seen was a true vision; and it is quite in accordance with the maxim of the Gospel that, "whosoever shall exalt himself, shall be humbled; and that he that shall humble himself, shall be exalted."[22] It is humility that raises men to those places from whence pride cast down the fallen angels.

We have seen the extraordinary things which Francis did in order to humble himself; for the same motive he felt no difficulty in making public the defects he thought he discovered in himself. If he found himself attacked by any temptation to pride, vainglory, or any other vice, he never failed communicating it to those who were present, whether they were religious or seculars. One day when he was followed by a great concourse of people, he gave his cloak to a poor woman who had asked him for an alms, and some minutes after he turned round to the crowd and told them in a loud voice that he had sinned from vainglory in so doing. We may imagine that his humility was at that moment very great, which prevented him from distinguishing

---

What idea could such a man as Bayle form of devotion, whose religion is still a problem, and whose scandalous dictionary contains not fewer obscenities and infamies, than blasphemies and impieties? This infernal publication should not be searched on pretense of its learning, and of the agreeableness and variety of its style. Should this trifling literary pleasure be preferred to the care a Christian should take to avoid everything which is contrary to the truths of faith and the purity of morals?

[22] Matt. 23: 12.

between voluntary consent and the feeling over which we have no control.

He took great care not to do anything in private which he should have had any hesitation in doing in public, and which was not in conformity with the opinion people had of his sanctity. His illness rendered it necessary he should eat meat in the Lent he kept before Christmas, but this relaxation consisted only in the use of lard; but he, nevertheless, accused himself of it in public, as an act of gluttony. His companions have recorded what he said: "I wish to live in hermitages and in other solitary places, as if I was seen by all the world; for, if people have a great opinion of me, and I were not to live as they think I do, I should be guilty of scandalous hypocrisy." The vicar of his convent suggested that he should permit his tunic to be lined with fox-skins, to keep his chest warm, which his disorder had greatly weakened. "I consent to this," he replied, "provided you put a similar set of skins outside, that the world may know the relief which is inside also." This condition put a stop to the proposition.

Praise mortified him, and he liked that people should blame him, and he rejoiced in being despised. When he heard people express by acclamation the merits of his sanctity, he made some of the brethren say to him, "You are a vulgar man, ignorant and useless in the world, a nobody;" and when he answered, with pleasure depicted on his countenance, "May the Lord bless you, my dear child, what you say is quite true, and is exactly what the son of Peter Bernardo deserves to hear." To those who called him a saint he used to say, "Don't praise me, I may still sin; I have no assurance that I shall not: a person must never be praised whose end cannot be known." And he addressed the following words to himself: "Francis, if the Most High had bestowed so many favors on a thief as He has on you, he would be much more grateful than you are."

The great honors which were paid him as a saint were very distressing to his humility, and he avoided them as much as possible; but when he could not escape from them, he received them with a humble tranquillity, referring all to God, and meditating on the Passion of Jesus Christ.

One day when great honors were paid him, his companion remarking that he received them without showing any reluctance, said: "Father, don't you see what they are doing in your honor? and far from refusing to receive the applause manifested in your regard, as Christian humility requires, you seem to receive them with complacency. Is there anything which a servant of the Lord should more sedulously avoid?" This is the reply which the holy man made him: "Brother, although it may appear to you that they are paying me great honors, nevertheless, know that I consider them as little or nothing in comparison with those which ought to be paid me." His companion was not only surprised, but almost scandalized, on hearing him utter such sentiments; but, not to expose his weakness, Francis added: "Now, be attentive to this, and understand it properly. I refer to God all the honor which is paid me, I attribute nothing to myself; on the contrary, I look upon myself as dirt by my baseness, and I stick in this mire more and more. It is as those figures of wood or stone for which respect is had. They neither fail nor retain anything of it, it comes back to what they represent; but they remain always the same material, either wood or stone. Now, when men know and honor God in His creatures, as they do in me, who am the vilest of all, it is no small profit to their souls."

This is the magnanimous humility of which St. Thomas speaks,[23] by which a man honors in himself the great gifts of God, permits them to be there honored, and practices the great virtues to render him more worthy to receive new ones, while he shrinks from the contemplation of his own misery. Such was the humble Francis, in permitting, for the glory of God, and the salvation of his neighbor, that the supernatural gifts which had been imparted to him, should be honored in his person, while he himself only considered his own nothingness; and afterwards he retired into solitary places, where he passed whole nights in meditating upon this nothingness, and on the infinite mercy of God, which had loaded him with graces.

Being one day with Brother Leo in one of these solitudes, and being without the books necessary for saying the Divine Office,[24] he invented a sort of humiliating psalmody for glorifying God during the night. "My dear brother," he said to Leo, "we must not let this time, which is consecrated to God, pass without praising His holy name, and confessing our own misery. This is the verse which I will say: 'O Brother Francis! you have committed so many sins in this world, that you have deserved to be plunged into hell.' And you, Brother Leo, your response will be, 'It is true; you deserve to be in the bottom of hell.'" Leo promised, however repugnant he felt, to answer as his father desired; but, instead of that, he said: "Brother Francis, God will do so much good through your means, that you will be called into Paradise." The father said to him, with warmth: "You don't answer as you ought. Here is another verse: 'Brother Francis, you have offended God by so many bad deeds, that you deserve all his maledictions.' Answer to that: 'You deserve to be among the number of the cursed.'" Leo promised again; but when the saint had said his verse, striking his breast, and shedding abundance of tears, Leo pronounced these words:

"Brother Francis, God will render you such, that among those who are blessed, you will receive a peculiar blessing." "Why don't you answer as I desire you?" said Francis, surprised. "I command you, under obedience, to repeat the words which I am going to give you. I shall say: O Brother Francis, miserable man! After so many crimes committed against the Father of mercies, and the God of all consolation, do you think he will have any pity on me? In truth you are undeserving of pardon.' Brother Leo, answer immediately: 'You

---

[23] 2ae. 2ae. Quaest. 29, Art. iii., ad quartum.

[24] The Divine Office was then very long, and there were only manuscript books, which were very expensive; for this reason, when the Order was in its beginning, they had none in many of the houses, particularly in solitary places.

deserve no mercy'." Leo, however, said: "God, our Father, whose mercy infinitely surpasses our sins, will pardon you all yours, and will load you with His favors."

Then Francis said somewhat angrily: "Why have you dared to transgress the rule of obedience, and to answer so often so differently to what I desired?" Leo excused himself most respectfully, saying: "My very dear father. God is my witness that I had each time intended to repeat the words which you had directed me, but He put into my mouth the words I uttered, and caused me to speak, notwithstanding my resolution, according to His good pleasure." The humble servant of Jesus Christ admired this disposition of the Lord; but persisting, nevertheless, in his intention of humbling himself, he entreated Brother Leo to repeat, at least once, the following words, which he pronounced with many sighs: "O Brother Francis, miserable little man! Do you think that God will have mercy on you, after so many crimes which you have committed?" "Yes, my father," replied Leo, "God, your Savior, will have mercy on you, and will grant you great favors. He will exalt you, and glorify you eternally, because he who shall humble himself shall be exalted.[25] Nevertheless, pardon me for not having said what you desired. It is not I who speak, it is God who speaks in me." Finally, Francis bowed to what Leo communicated to him, who only disobeyed him by an impulse of the Holy Spirit; and they conversed during the remainder of the night on the great mercy of God to sinners, with great consolation. Such persons as have the spirit of God, and the love of perfect humility, will find nothing but what is noble and great in the simplicity of this colloquy; and it is for such that it has appeared to us useful to record it.

It has been already remarked, with St. Bonaventure, that St. Francis had given to his brethren the name of Minors, and to their Superiors that of Ministers, in order that their very name should cause them to be humble. These are the maxims by which he used to impress this upon them:

"The Son of God debased Himself in coming from the bosom of His Father to us, to teach us humility by His example and by His word, as our Lord and Master." "What is exalted in the eyes of man is an abomination before God."[26]

---

[25] Matt. 23: 12.

[26] "This is what our Lord said on the subject of the Pharisees, who drew upon themselves the esteem of men by exterior acts of piety, but which God had in abhorrence, in consequence of the views with which they were filled. This may also be applied to innovators who impose on the multitude by the regularity of their exterior, and the severity of their morals, by an ah of great piety and by large alms; but God detests their pride, which renders them rebels to the Church, and makes them lose their faith. The virtues which are noticed in them are not true Christian virtues, worthy of eternal life; for these virtues, Saint Augustine says, must be grounded on faith: 'Without faith,' as pure and holy as what was required by Saint Paul, 'it is impossible to please God.' Moreover, the loss of faith, which often proceeds from the corruption of morals, very often is the cause of their corruption. There is scarcely any sect, of which it may not be said, what Saint John said of Babylon, that its name is Mysterium: Mystery of iniquity." —S. Augustin, contr Julian, lib. iv., n. 24 and 25; Hebr. 11: 6; Tit. 1: 13, et alibi; Apoc. 17: 5.

Man is nothing but what he is before God, and is nothing more. It is folly to feel glorified by the applause of man; it is better to be blamed than praised, for blame induced the person to correct himself, while praise leads to his fall. No man should pride himself for doing those things which a sinner may do as well as he. A sinner may fast, pray, weep, macerate his body, but what he cannot do, as long he is a sinner, is to be faithful to his God. Now, this is what we may glory in, to render to God the glory which is due to Him, to serve Him faithfully, and to return with like fidelity all that He has given.

Happy the servant who finds himself as humble amidst his brethren, inferiors like himself, as in presence of his superiors! Happy the servant who does not believe himself better when men load him with praises, than when he appears in their eyes simple, vile, abject and despicable! Happy the servant who bears reprimanding with meekness, who acknowledges his fault with humility, and voluntarily punishes it; who is sufficiently humble to receive a reprimand without offering an excuse, and the shame of a fault, of which he has not been guilty! Happy the religious who has not been desirous of the elevation he has attained, and who always wishes to be at the feet of the others! Woe to the religious who has been raised by the rest to an honorable post, and who has not the inclination to descend from it!

The example of Jesus Christ, who "was obedient unto death, even to the death of the Cross,"[27] inspired St. Francis with great love for obedience. Although he was appointed superior by order of God and of the Pope, he was always desirous of obeying rather than commanding. In his travels, he promised obedience to him who accompanied him, and he rigidly kept that promise. One day he communicated the following in confidence to his companions: "Among all the graces which I have received from the bounty of God, this is one: that, if they were to appoint a novice of an hour's standing to be my guardian, I would obey him as implicitly as if he was the oldest and the most serious of our brethren." He was not satisfied with having renounced being General of the Order, to obey the Vicar-General; he asked Brother Elias, who filled that situation, to give him a guardian, in whose will he should depend in all things. Brother Angelo, of Rieti, was given to him, and he obeyed him with entire submission.

The instructions he gave his brethren on the subject of obedience contained all the perfection which could be given them: 1st. To renounce their own will, and to look upon it as the forbidden fruit, which our first parents could not eat of without being guilty. 2nd. To abandon themselves wholly to their superior, so that they should neither do nor say anything which they know he would not approve of; and that they should do what he wishes the moment he has spoken, without waiting for his speaking a second time. 3rd. Not to examine whether what is ordered is difficult or impossible, for, said St.

---

[27] Phil. 2: 8.

Francis, "When I order anything which is above your strength, holy obedience will enable you to effect it." 4th. To submit their lights to those of the superior, not with a view of obeying him in anything manifestly contrary to salvation, but to act upon his views, although they may think their own better and more useful. 5th. Not to consider the man, nor his qualifications, in the obedience they bow to, but the authority he has, the place he fills, and the greatness of Him for whose love they are subject to man.

This last point is the greatest sacrifice of a religious life; but a necessary sacrifice, one which is just, and worthy of God, and the most certain proof that our obedience is grounded on our love for Him. It is not difficult to follow the dictates of a superior of acknowledged talent and merit; the hardship is to submit with humility, without remonstrance or murmur, to one who has not these qualifications. This also it is which enhances in the eyes of God the value of religious obedience; it may then be considered as a sort of martyrdom of the mind, which will receive its crown in heaven, as well as that of the body. Nevertheless, it is requisite to be cautious, lest antipathy or some other motive, and the natural revolt of the human heart against authority, should cause a superior to appear contemptible, who really is not so. Finally, the religious are highly interested in practicing holy obedience, whoever may be the superior; it is, as St. Francis remarks, so abundant in fruits, that such as bend to the yoke pass not a moment of their lives without some spiritual profit: it increases virtue, and procures peace to the soul.

He was asked one day, who was to be considered to be truly obedient, and he instanced a dead body. "Take," said he, "a dead body, and place it where you please; you will see that it shows no repugnance at its removal, it utters no complaint at its situation, nor of dissatisfaction at being left where it is. If you put it in an honorable place, its eyes will remain closed, it will not raise them. If you clothe it in purple, it will only be paler than before. That is true obedience; it asks no reason as to why it is put in motion, it is indifferent as to where it is placed, and does not require to be moved. If such a one is raised to the dignity of superior, he remains equally humble; the more he is honored, the more does he think himself unworthy of it.

"I have often," he continued, "seen a blind man led by a little dog, and who went wherever his guide took him, in good roads and in bad. This is another resemblance of one who is perfectly obedient: he should shut his eyes, and be blind to the commands of his superior, think of nothing but submitting immediately to him, without stopping to examine whether the thing be difficult or not, only keeping in view the authority of him who gives the order, and the merit of obedience."

Disobedience is insupportable; he considered it as the unfortunate offspring of pride, which is the source of all evils, and of which he had great horror. One day while praying in his cell, and meditating between God and his brethren, he saw in spirit one of them who refused to perform the penance imposed on him in chapter by the Vicar-General, and excusing himself as to the fault of which he had been accused. He called his companion, and said: "I saw on the shoulders of this insubordinate brother the devil, who was wringing his neck, and leading him as by a bridle. I prayed for him, and the devil, abashed, loosed his hold immediately. Go to him, and tell him to bend immediately to the yoke of obedience." In fact, the brother did submit as soon as he was told this, and threw himself humbly at the feet of his superior.

Another, who had erred in some way against obedience, was brought to Francis, that he might correct him; but he appeared so penitent, that the saint, who liked the humility of repentance, felt himself inclined to pardon the fault. Nevertheless, lest the facility of pardon should be abused, and to show what chastisement disobedience deserved, he ordered his cowl to be taken from him, and thrown into the fire. Some minutes after, he desired it to be taken out of the fire, and to be returned to him, when it was found that the fire had not injured it in the least; "God having shown by this miracle," St. Bonaventure observes, "the power He gave to his servant, and how agreeable to Him humble repentance is."

The conduct of the holy founder was more severe to one of his brethren, who was obstinately disobedient. After having caused him to be stripped, he desired the others to put him into a pit, and to fill it up with earth, in order to bury him alive; when they had filled it up to his chin, "Brother," he said, "are you dead?" The religious, absorbed in grief, replied: "Yes, father, and I ought to die in reality for my sin." Francis, moved by compassion, had him dug out, saying: "Come forth from thence, if you are truly dead, as a good religious ought to be, to the world and its concupiscences. Obey the smallest sign of the will of your superiors, and make no more resistance to their orders than a dead body could do. I wish for followers, not living, but those who are dead."

It was only a feint to frighten him; but it served to show that disobedience in religion, particularly when it is accompanied by obstinacy, must be severely punished. In fact, obedience is the basis of the religious state; and if this virtue be shaken, the fabric must tremble and be destroyed. For this reason St. Benedict directed that a religious who persevered in disobedience, should he excommunicated, and receive corporal punishment.[28] Nor must we be surprised at this, since in the Old Law,[29] God commanded that an incorrigible son should be stoned on the complaint of the father or mother,[30] in order that

---

[28] Reg. S. Bened., cap. 23.

[29] Deut. 21: 18, et seq.

[30] On this passage, M. de Sacy says, that "it was a figure of the inflexible justice which God will exert against all the sons of the Church, whom neither the prudent remonstrances of this affectionate mother, nor the warnings of him (the Pope) whom He desires that we should consider as our father, have been able to convert. These two formidable witnesses will combine against them at the judgment-seat, and they will be eternally punished for their revolt." Why do they not submit to the Pope and to the Church, not to expose themselves to this rigor?

all Israel, after such an example, should be awed with fear. We find, in the life of St. Francis, many examples of severe penances inflicted by him for disobedience; such as sending Brother Rufinus to preach without a cowl, for having excused himself from going on account of his want of genius for that employment.

He once called Brother Juniper to employ him on something, and this brother not having immediately obeyed, because he was busy in planting a juniper tree, he cursed the tree that it should never grow, and it remained always in a dwarf state. The Fathers of the Desert were similarly exact in their attention to obedience, insomuch as to leave a letter unfinished when they had to attend to the orders of a superior.[31]

---

[31] Cassian, de Instit. Renunt., cap. xii.

CHAPTER III
LOVE FOR CHRIST AND HIS MOTHER

His obedience—His gift of prayer and contemplation—His love of God—His sentiments of filial love on the mystery of the Incarnation—On the fast of Jesus Christ in the desert—On the mystery of the Eucharist—S. Francis, in his humility, would not be made priest—The vision he had on this subject—His devotion towards the Mother of God.

HE VIRTUES OF ST. FRANCIS, which we have recorded, and those which we have yet to narrate, were cultivated by the exercise of prayer. He had the gift as soon as he was called to the service of God, and he followed it up so faithfully, that he consecrated to it his heart, his body, all his actions, and all his time. In-doors, or out of doors, walking or seated, working or resting, his mind was always raised to heaven; he seemed to live with the angels. As he was always diffident of himself, he had recourse to prayer, and consulted the Almighty, with perfect confidence in His goodness, in all that He had to do. Although he could pray in any place he might happen to be in, nevertheless, he found solitary spots best adapted for recollection; he sought them out, and often retired to them. This shows us why he made so many houses of his Order, where there had previously been hermitages only.

Careful in attending to the interior calls of the Holy Spirit, if he perceived one coming on, he let his companions go forward, and stopped, not to receive it in vain, and to enjoy it to its full extent. When he prayed in community, he avoided all exterior signs, which might discover the secret dispositions of his mind, because he loved secrecy. He did not find the precaution difficult, because he was wholly absorbed in his interior, and united himself so intimately to God, that he was almost without exterior motion. If it happened that he was surprised by a visit from heaven in the presence of his brethren, he had always something ready to propose to them, to take off their attention. When he returned from prayer, in which he had been marvelously transformed, he strove to conform himself to his brethren, lest what they might perceive might draw from them applause, which would deprive him of his reward by inspiring him with vanity.

But in the solitudes he was under no restraint, and gave his heart entire liberty. The woods resounded with his sacred sighs and laments, the earth was moistened with his tears, and he struck his breast with violence. Sometimes he addressed himself to God as to his sovereign Lord; sometimes he spoke to Him as to his judge; sometimes he prayed to Him as to his father; and at other times, he conversed with Him as a friend converses with his friend. He solicited the pardon of sinners with loud and energetic exclamations; and he expressed his horror at the Passion of Jesus Christ in loud laments, as if he had been present at it. All this was seen and heard by some one or other of his companions, who had the pardonable curiosity to watch his proceedings. The devils tormented him severely during his prayers, and that in a very sensible manner, as St. Bonaventure informs us; but, protected by celestial aid, he continued his prayers with additional fervor, in proportion to the efforts they made to distract him.

God favored him with the gift of contemplation in a sublime degree. His companions bear witness that they have often seen him in a state of ecstasy, in which he had lost all the use of his senses, and in which all the powers of his soul were suspended. Once they saw him, during the night, raised from the ground, and his arms extended in the shape of across, surrounded by a luminous cloud, as if to betoken the divine light which filled his mind. St. Bonaventure says that they had efficient proof that God at such times revealed to him some of the great secrets of His wisdom; but His faithful servant only made such part of them known as were for the glory of his Master, or the utility of his neighbor.

One of his brethren, not finding him one evening in his cell, went to look for him in the wood. Having penetrated a short distance into it, he heard him praying, with loud cries, for the salvation of men, and addressing the Blessed Virgin with moving sighs, humbly imploring her to show him her Son. He then saw the blessed Mother of God descend from heaven, with great splendor, and place her Son into the arms of Francis, who received Him as Simeon had received Him in the temple of Jerusalem,[1] with the profoundest respect; he caressed the Infant most tenderly, entreating Him for the conversion of sinners, and the salvation of the world. At this sight the religious fell on the ground, half dead, and remained on the spot where he fell. Here the saint found him, as he was returning to the convent for Matins; he brought him to himself from this fainting, but strictly forbade him from telling any one what had occurred; but he, thinking it for the glory of God not to be obliged to obey in this instance, communicated the marvel to all the others.

A novice whom the holy patriarch had received, and whom he was taking to the convent of the novitiate, wished to know what he did during the night. In order to succeed, he tied his cord to that of the father, whom he saw asleep in the fields, in which they had been obliged to remain, and laid himself down near him, in order that he might be roused as soon as he should stir. A few

---

[1] Luke 2: 28.

hours afterwards, Francis wished to get up, but finding himself fastened by the cord, he untied the knot, and went to pray under some neighboring trees. The novice, not finding him when he awoke, went to seek him under the trees. A celestial light caused him to draw near a spot, where he stopped, and from whence he saw Jesus Christ, surrounded by angels, His Blessed Mother, and St. John the Baptist, who were in conversation with him. His astonishment made him fall on the ground, where he remained till Francis, to whom God had imparted the circumstance, came and raised him up, and restored him to his senses, forbidding him to speak of the vision. The young man, who continued to live very holily, kept the secret; but, after Francis's death, he published what he had seen.

God chose that his servant should be respected in the secret retirements to which he went to pray, and that he should not be disturbed at those times. The Bishop of Assisi knew this by his own experience. One day, when he had come to the convent of Portiuncula, as he frequently did, he wished to go at once into the cell where the saint was at prayer; but scarcely had he seen him in that attitude, when he was pushed back by an invisible hand, his body became stiff, and he was unable to speak. Much astonished at this accident, he made his way back, as well as he could, to the other brethren; God restored his voice, and he made use of it, to acknowledge that he had committed a fault The Celestial Spouse, in the Canticles, conjures the daughters of Jerusalem, "not to awaken her whom he loves, and not to disturb her repose until she awakes of her own accord."[2] St. Bernard, on this, says that such as are given to prayer should not be troubled about useless affairs, and that those who disturb them when they are conversing with God, become enemies of heaven.[3]

In consequence of the knowledge which Francis had of the sweets and fruits of mental prayer, he constantly urged his brethren to practice it, and they profited so fully by his instructions, that most of them became spiritual and contemplative men. "A religious," he said, "must principally desire to acquire the spirit of prayer. I believe that, without that, peculiar favors cannot be obtained from God, nor any great progress made in His service. When one is sorrowful and uneasy, he should have immediate recourse to prayer, and remain before his heavenly Father, until such time as the joy of salvation is restored to him. If one remains in this state of depression and disturbance, this disposition, which comes from Babylon, will increase, and produce rust, unless it be purified by tears."

He taught them to shun the tumult of the world, and to seek for solitary places in which to pray, because he knew that the Holy Spirit communicates Himself more intimately to souls in such places; but he recommended them to be perfectly secret as to the favors they might receive; his maxim being, that a

---

[2] Cant. 2: 7, and 3: 5.

[3] S. Bern., in Cant., serm. lii. n.6

slender human communication often causes the loss of that which is of inestimable value, and has the effect of preventing the Lord from again communicating what He had previously given; that when one is visited by God, he should say: "It is You, O Lord! who sent me this consolation from heaven, to me who am a sinner, wholly unworthy of Your bounty. I commit it back to Your keeping; for I feel myself capable of stealing Your treasure from You;" and when he returns from prayer, he should show as much humility and self-contempt as if he had received no peculiar favor.

All the masters of spiritual life have had similar opinions of the value of mental prayer as this contemplative saint, and they have pointed out the necessity of it for advancing in the ways of virtue. St. Teresa wrote so sublimely on this practice, that the Church prays to God that "her heavenly doctrine may be our nourishment." She declares that she was near being lost, from having given it up, but that our Lord had done her the signal favor to urge her to resume it; she exhorts all to apply themselves to it, even should they make but small progress in it, because it is always useful, and, if persevered in, will be attended with great benefit. This is what directors might represent to those who seriously wish to attend to their salvation, and to say to them, with the same saint, that "mental prayer is nothing else but holding friendly intercourse with God, often remaining alone in conversation with Him, who we know loves us."

The practice of mental prayer no way diminished the zeal of St. Francis for vocal prayer,[4] which every Christian ought to resort to as he did. Vocal prayer was practiced and taught by Jesus Christ;[5] the Church employs it in her public worship. "We require it," says St Augustine,[6] "to assist our memory and understanding, and to animate our fervor"; finally, God desires that we should offer to Him "a sacrifice of praise," and that it shall be "the fruits of our lips and hearts, giving glory to His name,"[7] because our body and soul belong to Him. Piety had inspired the holy man to compose vocal prayers on various subjects, which he often repeated, and some of which he recited daily. He said the Lord's Prayer with particular devotion, weighing all the words, and meditating on the sense they contain, as is seen by the paraphrase of it he composed, and which we think it useful to insert at length.

'Our Father,' most happy and most holy, our Creator, our Redeemer, and our Consoler. 'Who art in heaven;' in the angels, in the saints, in the illuminated, in order that they may know You, who inflames them by Your

---

[4] J. Alvarez de Paz, of the Society of Jesus, speaks highly of vocal prayer before his treatise on mental prayer. —De Studio Orationis, tom. iii. Oper.

[5] Our Lord addressed vocal prayer to God, His Father, after the Supper, John, 7: 1. And he taught vocal prayer to His apostles, when He said to them: "You shall therefore pray in this manner: Our Father who art in Heaven," etc. —Matt. 6: 9.

[6] S. Aug. epist. ad Probam, xiii., alias cxxi., cap. ix., et de Serm. Dom. in monte, lib. ii., cap. 3.

[7] Hebr. 13: 15.

love; for, O Lord! You are the light and the love who dwells in them, and who are their beatitude by satiating them: You are the sovereign and eternal good, from whom all good proceeds, and without You there is no other good. 'Hallowed be Thy name:' so as to make Yourself known to us by vivid lights, so that we may see the full extent of Your bounty, the duration of Your promises, the sublimity of Your majesty, and the depth of Your judgment. 'Thy kingdom come:' in order that You may reign in us by grace, and that You may bring us to Your kingdom, where You are clearly and perfectly loved, where we become happy in Your society, and where You are eternally enjoyed. 'Thy will be done on earth as it is in heaven:' in order that we may love You 'with our whole hearts', thinking always of You 'with our whole soul', ever longing for You, 'with all our mind', referring to You all our views, seeking Your glory in all things; 'with all our strength', employing in Your service, for Your love, all the strength of our bodies and souls, without making any other use of them; that we may love our neighbor as ourselves, using all our efforts to draw them to Your love; rejoicing in all the good that happens to them, as if it was our own; being grieved at any ills which may befall them, and giving offense to none. 'Give us this day our daily bread:' it is Your beloved Son, Jesus Christ; we ask You for Him, in order to remind us of the love He has shown us, and of what He has said, done, and endured for us; we ask You to make us fully comprehend these things, and cause us to revere them. 'Forgive us our trespasses,' by Your infinite mercy, by the passion of Your beloved Son, our Lord Jesus Christ, by the merits and intercession of the Blessed Mary, and of all the elect.

"'As we forgive them that trespass against us': what may be not altogether remitted on our part, grant us the favor, O Lord! to remit entirely, in order that, for love of You, we may sincerely love our enemies, and may intercede for them fervently at Your throne; that we may not render to any one evil for evil, and that in You we may endeavor to do good to all. 'And lead us not into temptation',[8] hidden, manifest, sudden, grievous. 'But deliver us from evil:' past, present, and to come. Amen: willingly and gratuitously." These two words show that he ardently desired what he prayed for; and that it was purely for the glory of God, without any temporal interest.

He recited the Divine Offices with a devotion full of respect, and with great fervor. St. Bonaventure says that, although he suffered greatly from pains in his head, from his stomach, and from his liver, he never leant while reciting it;

---

[8] That is to say, permit us not to be led into temptation, and inclined to sin, for, as Saint James says, "God is not capable of tempting to evil." And when He allows the devil so to tempt us, it is not with a view of our yielding, as Zuinglius, Calvin, and Beza have dared to say; on the contrary, it is to give us the opportunity of conquering and meriting by His grace. Now, although it be true that God, by an effect of His wisdom and goodness, permits temptations for the benefit of mankind, He, nevertheless, teaches them to mistrust their own weakness, to solicit His favor not to be exposed to temptations, and, should they arise, His grace to get the better of them. S. August epist. 130, cap. xi., et de Dono Persever., cap. 5.

that he stood during the whole time, with his head uncovered, his eyes looking down. In traveling, he always stopped to say it; however much it might rain, he never omitted this pious practice, and he gave this reason for it: If the body rests, in order to take its food, which will, as well as himself, soon become the food of worms, with how much tranquillity ought the soul to take its spiritual nourishment, which is to cause it to live eternally!

The verse, *Gloria Patri*, etc., made a lively impression on his heart; once he repeated it in thankfulness to God for His bounty after each verse of the Magnificat, which Brother Leo was reciting, and he exhorts all to say it frequently. A lay brother, who was strongly tempted to apply himself to study, having come to ask his permission, "My dear Brother," said he, "learn the Gloria Patri, etc., and you will know the whole of the Holy Scriptures." The brother obeyed, and had no further temptation on that head.

The distractions which his lively imagination caused him during the holy exercises, appeared to him to be great faults, and he never failed to confess them, and to expiate them by penance, asserting that we ought to be ashamed of being distracted by trifles when speaking to the great King. Once during Tierce, the thought of a little vase which he had made came into his head, and called on his attention; he immediately went and took it, and threw it into the fire, saying: "I will sacrifice it to the Lord, whose sacrifice it has hindered." But he acquired the habit of reciting the Office so attentively, that this sort of distractions seldom importuned him.

His application was equally strong and respectful in reciting the Psalms, as if God had been present in a sensible manner; and he found so much sweetness in the name of God, that he seemed to have the taste of sweetness on his lips, after having pronounced it. Thus the prophet said to the Lord: "How sweet are your words to my palate! More than honey to my mouth."[9] Francis had also interior joy in pronouncing the holy name of Jesus, which communicated itself to his exterior, and produced on his senses a similar effect as if he had tasted something agreeable to his palate, or heard some harmonious sounds.

He desired that these sacred names should be peculiarly reverenced, not only when people thought of them, or pronounced them, but whenever they saw them written. This is the reason why, in his last will, he recommends his brethren to pick them up should they find them scattered about in unseemly places, and put them in a better locality, lest they should be disrespectfully trampled upon. This must be considered not as a mere nicety of feeling, but as a sentiment inspired by faith, which teaches us to venerate the word of God. If a great bishop[10] has thought it proper to compare the abuse of the sacred word, when it is announced, to the profanation of the body itself of Jesus Christ, may we not, in the same spirit, say that he who permits that word to be trampled

---

[9] Psalm 118: 103.

[10] Serm. ccc., n. 2, in Append, tom. v., Oper. 2, Aug. edit. Ben. Tribuitur. S. Caes. Aul. episc.

upon when it is written, becomes in some measure as guilty as if he had allowed the sacred body of our Savior to be treated with similar indignity?

It was the love of God which gave St. Francis so much zeal for mental prayer, as well as for that which is vocal. He sought his Beloved, from whom he was only separated by the wall of his flesh. To be present to Him in spirit, and to contemplate Him, were his sole consolations, and his anxiety to gain these was intense. But then the frequent exercise of prayer increased his love, and inflamed it to that degree, that St. Bonaventure does not think it possible to find words to express it. This divine charity penetrated his whole interior, as fire penetrates a burning coal. Only by hearing the term of the love of God pronounced, he was moved and inflamed, and this movement made the affections of his soul thrill, as the strings of a musical instrument sound on being touched.

To excite himself more and more to the love of God, he made use of all creatures, as of so many mirrors, in which he viewed the supreme reason, the sovereign beauty, and the principle of being and of life. They were for him as so many steps by which he raised and united himself to the object of his love, as so many streamlets in which he tasted, with inconceivable unction, the infinite purity of the source from whence all that is good is derived; so many delightful strains whose harmony resounded on his ears, and which, as David in his Psalms,[11] he invited to praise and glorify Him who had given them their tones. Wholly inflamed with love, he prayed to be enabled to love still more, and he addressed the following prayer to God, which is found among his works: "Grant, O Lord! that the mild vehemence of Your ardent love may separate me from everything which is under heaven, and may consume me entirely, in order that I may die for the love of Your love, since it was for the love of my love that You deigned to die. I solicit this through Yourself, O Son of God! who lives and reigns with the Father and the Holy Spirit for ever and ever. Amen."

And here is another, which he used to say every day: "My God and my all, who are You, O sweet Lord! and who am I, Your servant, a miserable worm? I wish to love You, most holy Lord, I wish to love You. O God! I have consecrated to You my heart and my body. If I had the means of doing more for You, I would do it, and I ardently wish I had the means."

This poor evangelical could not give more to God than his body and soul. He continually offered the sacrifice of his body, by the rigor of his fasts, and that of his soul, by the vehemence of his desires; "by which," says St. Bonaventure, "he conformed in a spiritual manner to the practice of the Old Law, which was to offer holocausts out of the tabernacle, and to burn incense within it."[12]

---

[11] Psalm 141 (142).

[12] Exod. 30: 5; and 40: 27.

The sacrifice of his desires went to a great extent. For the love of God he had renounced all the things of this earth; he had stripped himself of everything, so that he was literally naked; he had embraced the severest poverty, and practiced the most austere penitential life; he had devoted himself to the ministry of preaching, and to the establishment of his Order; his life was but a course of labors and fatigue, but he reckoned all that as nothing; he wished to do much more, to mortify himself more rigorously, to forward thereby the glory of God, because, according to the words of our Savior, this is the greatest mark of love which a friend can give to his friend.[13] This was the motive of the ardent desire he had to endure martyrdom, and of the three voyages he undertook in search of it: seeing that he could not succeed, he lowered his views to wishing for and soliciting grace to know what he could do, to testify his love for God. The Lord granted his desire, favoring him with the impression of His five wounds, which rendered him a living and, at the same time, an expiring martyr; but it inflamed his heart to such a degree, that then he wished to die for love, and to be absorbed in the love of Him whom he loved, saying in a holy transport, in one of his canticles: *"Per amor si clamo. Amor che tanto bramo, fa mi morir d'amore. Amor, amor, fa mi in te transire."*[14]

Inflamed with divine love, he endeavored to spread the fire on all sides. He often made it the subject of his discourses, and it was usually the motive he employed to animate his brethren to the practice of virtue. When he proposed anything that was difficult to them, such as to go about soliciting alms, "Go," he would say, "and ask it for the love of God." He found a noble prodigality in asking it for that motive, and he thought those demented who preferred money to the love of God, the price of which is incalculable, and sufficient to purchase the kingdom of heaven, and which the love of Him who has so loved us must make infinitely dear to us. They were surprised one day to find that he could bear the severity of winter in so miserable a habit as that which he wore, and, full of fervor, he gave this reason, which contains a very useful lesson: "If we were inwardly inflamed with a longing for our celestial country, we should easily bear exterior cold."

It was his wish that a Friar Minor should love God with an effective, liberal, and generous love, which should enable him to suffer calmly and joyfully pain and opprobrium for the object of his love. This is what he said one day to Brother Leo, on the subject, in a conversation which Leo himself has recorded at full length: "If a Friar Minor had a clear and distinct knowledge of the course of the stars, and of all other things in the universe; if he possessed all the sciences, all the languages, and a perfect knowledge of the Holy Scriptures; and if he spoke with the tongues of angels, cast out devils, performed all sorts of miracles, even that of raising one from the dead who had

---

[13] John 15: 13.

[14] I cry out for love itself. The love which I so crave, makes me die of love. Love, love, make me cross over into you. —Editor.

been four days in the tomb; if he had the gift of prophecy, and that of discerning the affections of the heart; if he preached to the infidels with such success as to convert them all, and if he should edify the world by his sanctity, all that would not be to him the subject of perfect and true joy."

Afterwards, to show in what this true joy consisted, he proposed a supposition, similar to one he had made on another subject, and very like to this hypothesis of St. Paul: "Who shall separate us from the love of Jesus Christ? Shall tribulation, or distress, or famine, or nakedness, or persecution, or the sword?"[15] From which he concluded, that all that there is in heaven or on earth could not separate him from the love of God, which is grounded on Jesus Christ our Lord.

"I suppose," said St. Francis, "that we were to arrive at the convent of St. Mary of the Angels very wet, covered with mud, perishing with cold, dying of hunger, and that the porter, instead of letting us in, were to leave us at the gate in this pitiable state saying angrily, 'You are a couple of idle vagabonds, who stroll about the world, and receive the alms which the real poor ought to get.' If we bear this treatment with patience, without being discomposed, and without murmuring; if even we think humbly and charitably that the porter knows us well for what we are, and that it is by God's leave that he behaves thus to us, mark this down as perfect joy.

"I suppose, moreover, that we continue to knock at the door, and that the porter, considering us importunate, should come out and give us some severe boxes on the ears, and say, 'Get along, scoundrels, go to the hospital, there is nothing for you to eat here.' If we bear all these things patiently, and we pardon him from our hearts, and with charity, note, this would be a subject for perfect joy.

"Let us, in fine, suppose, that in this extremity the cold, hunger, and the night, compel us to entreat, with tears and cries, to be allowed to enter the convent, and that the porter, in great irritation, darts out with a stick full of knobs, takes us by the cowl, throws us down in the snow, and beats us till we are quite covered with bruises: if we bear all this ill usage with joy, with the thought that we ought to participate in the sufferings of our blessed Savior, Jesus Christ, note this and note it carefully, that this is for a Friar Minor, the subject of a true and perfect joy.

"Now hear the conclusion of all this. Amongst all the gifts of the Holy Spirit, which Jesus Christ has granted and will grant to His servants, the most considerable is, that of conquering one's self, and of suffering pain and opprobrium for the love of God, in order to respond to the love He has for us. In all the miraculous gifts which I have noticed, there is not one from which we may derive so much glory; we have no share in it, it is all from God; we only receive what He gives us, and, as St. Paul says, 'If you have received, why

---

[15] I Cor. 4: 7.

do you boast, as if you have not received it?'[16] But we have our share in the tribulations which we suffer for the love of God, and we may make it a subject of glory, as the same apostle has said: 'God forbid that I should boast save in the cross of our Lord Jesus Christ.'"[17]

St. Francis was far from thinking that we may glory in our sufferings, as of a favor which we have not received, since he acknowledges that it is the greatest gift of the Holy Spirit, conformably to what St. Paul said to the Philippians: "To you is given not only to believe in Jesus Christ, but also to suffer for His sake;"[18] and to what is written of the apostles: "And they, indeed, went from the presence of the council, rejoicing that they were accounted to suffer reproach for the name of Jesus."[19] He only proposed to say that our sole cause of glory is, that God permits us to be associated to the cross of Jesus Christ, in which alone we are glorified. Thus it is to God that he refers all the glory of our sufferings, which indeed is His, since, without the aid of His grace, we should not suffer as we ought, and without the cross of Jesus Christ we should have no merit. But he correctly says, and he speaks the true orthodox faith, when he adds, that we have a share in the merit of what we suffer, and when he draws the distinction between that and miraculous gifts. St. Chrysostom has spoken in the same manner, and says that our virtues are in so far the gifts of God, that they are also merits of our will, for which God has been pleased to render Himself indebted to us, by the promise He has made to reward them.[20]

May the tender and generous love of St. Francis, which we have endeavored to portray, excite all those who shall read his life to love God, and to manifest their love, not only by their actions, but by their patience in adversities. May they love Him, so as to be enabled to say, with the same saint: "May the mild violence, O Lord! of Your ardent love, separate me from all that is beneath the heavens, and wholly absorb me!" And with St. Augustine: "O my God! I love You with an ardent love. If I do not as yet love You enough, compel me to love You still more. O love, which ever burns without ever being extinguished! My God, who are nothing but charity, inflame me!"[21] Jesus Christ, in speaking of His love,[22] said: "I am come to send fire on the earth,[23]

---

[16] Gal. 4: 14.

[17] Rom. 8: 35, 38, 39.

[18] Phil. 1: 29.

[19] Acts 5: 41.

[20] S. Chrys. Homil. 4, in cap. I., epist. ad Philip., ver. 29.

[21] S. Aug. Confess, lib. 13. cap. viii., and lib. 10, cap. xxix.

[22] Although these words are usually understood as of the fire of divine love, some interpreters think that they signify the fire of the persecutions which were to be enkindled at the publication of the Gospel. If that be so, it may be said that one fire communicated itself to the other; for it was requisite to have an ardent love of God, to be able to endure the persecution.

[23] Luke 12: 49.

and what will I but that it be kindled?" The holy Catholic Church, our mother, uses all her efforts to kindle it in the hearts of her children; she never ceases repeating to them that the greatest commandment of the Christian religion is the first, and this is it:[24] "You shall love the Lord your God with your whole heart, with your whole soul, with all your strength, and with all your mind." She sets before them every argument which may induce them to its perfect observance; and when she represents to them the severity of God's judgments, the rigor of the pains of hell, it is to lead them to this love, through fear, as God Himself does, which St. Augustine declares in the following terms: "Lord, You command me to love You, and, if I fail to do so, Your wrath is enkindled against me, and You threaten me with frightful misery, as if it were not one sufficiently great not to love You."[25]

After this, who will not feel the greatest indignation against those who, by the blackest of all calumnies, have dared to say, and to put in writing, that the head of the Church and the body of bishops had abolished the grand precept of the love of God, and have given to their own sect the glory of maintaining it? The Lord said to the sinner by His prophet: "Why do you declare my justices, and take my covenant in your mouth?"[26] A similar reproach may be made to this sort of sinner, who, according to the oracle[27] of the Son of God, is already condemned, because he does not believe: "Why do you speak of the love of God, who do not have it, and cannot have it, because your rebellion against the legitimate authority established by Jesus Christ, has caused you to lose your faith, without which that divine love cannot be entertained, that supernatural and divine charity, 'which is spread over our hearts by the Holy Spirit.'"[28] Listen to the Church, submit with humble docility to her decisions, and you will learn from herself what your conscience has already made known to you, that she teaches her children to have a pure faith, a wholesome faith, which has nothing false in it, which is firm and immovable, and is at the same time a faith acting and perfected by charity. This is the reason she so often lays before them the example of the saints, who had an inviolable attachment to that faith, and who were inflamed with the love of God, as St. Francis was.

The mystery of the Incarnate Word, "that great mystery of piety, which has been manifested in the flesh,"[29] produced in his heart sentiments so pious and so tender, that they were observable exteriorly, by actions of extraordinary fervor, as we saw in the grand solemnity which he celebrated at Grecio on Christmas night. "Consider," he says, in his letters, "that the most high Father

---

[24] Matt. 22: 38; Deut 6: 5; Luke 10: 27.

[25] S. Aug. Confess, lib. 1, cap v.

[26] Psalm 49 (50): 17.

[27] John 3: 18.

[28] Rom. 5: 5; Tit. 1: 13; 1 Tim. 1: 5; Coloss. 1: 23; Gal. 5: 6.

[29] 2 Tim. 3: 16.

has sent from heaven His archangel, St. Gabriel, to announce that His most worthy, holy, and glorious Word should descend into tho womb of the most Blessed Virgin Mary. And, in truth, He did so descend, and took from her true human flesh, passible and mortal, such as ours is: 'Being rich, He became of His own accord poor.'[30] He chose, by preference, poverty in this world for Himself and for His Blessed Mother. He gave Himself thus to us, in conformity to the will of His Father, to wipe away our sins on the cross, by the sacrifice of His Blood, and to leave an example of us to follow in His tracks,[31] for it is His wish[32] that we should all be saved through Him; but there are few who desire the salvation He proffers them, although His yoke is sweet, and His burden light."[33]

When he spoke of the incarnation and birth of the Son of God, it was with affectionate devotion; he could not hear the words, "the Word made flesh," without manifesting great joy. The religious of a monastery where he was one day, remarked this emotion, and took occasion to ask him if it was right to eat meat on Christmas day, when it fell on a Friday, or if it was not better to abstain from it. "Not only do I think," he replied, "that men may eat meat on this day, in which the Word was made flesh, but I wish that princes and rich persons would throw meat and corn in the highways, in order that the birds and beasts of the field should rejoice, in their way, in the joys of so great a festival; I wish, even, that some was placed on the walls, if they could derive sweetness from it."

We see plainly that these are hyperbolical expressions, flowing from his heart, by the emotions of his spiritual joy, by which he was actuated; but, in saying that men might eat meat on Christmas day, although it fall on a Friday, he speaks in conformity with the usage of the Church, which, however, is a

---

[30] 2 Cor. 8: 9.

[31] 1 Pet. 2: 21.

[32] Saint Francis, who was truly Catholic, expresses himself on dogmatical points with all the precision of the language of the Church. He says that Jesus Christ desires that we should all be saved through Him; Saint Paul also declares that "He will have all men to be saved, and to come to the knowledge of the truth." —1 Tim. II: 4. This is what is noticed in many other parts of the New Testament, and what all the holy fathers, whether Greek or Latin, have constantly taught. "God," says St. Augustine, "desires that all men shall be saved; not so, however, that they shall be deprived of free-will: it is on the good or ill use they make of this that God most justly punishes or rewards them." —Lib. de Spir. et litt. cap. xxxiii. Finally, every Catholic is bound to believe the three following truths which are defined by the Church: 1st. That God desires that he should be saved, and that Jesus Christ has shed all His blood for this object. 2ndly That as this, His desire, is sincere, He consequently gives him the graces necessary for his salvation 3rdly. That He is not the first to abandon those who have been once justified by His grace. This is a powerful motive to induce us to labor with confidence for our salvation; and altogether, with fear and trembling, to have recourse to prayer, because we may be the first to abandon God, in which case He may cast us off, and damn us eternally. —Concil. Arausic. secundum cap. xxv., Const. Innocentii 10, adv. Lib. Jansenii, Concil. Trid., sess. 6, cap. xxi.

[33] Matt. 11: 30.

permission, and not a law. Pope Honorius III[34] pointed it out clearly to the Bishop of Prague, in Bohemia, in the following rescript of the year 1222: "We answer that, when the feast of the Nativity of our Blessed Lord falls on a Friday, those who are not under the obligation of abstinence by a vow, or by a regular observance,[35] may eat meat on that day, because of the excellence of the festival, according to the custom of the universal Church. Those, however, who abstain on that day, from devotion, are not to be censured."

St. Francis was, moreover, much affected by the goodness of our Savior, who, after His baptism, went into the desert, and there fasted forty days and forty nights, without eating anything during that time, for the expiation of our sensuality, and to set us an example of fasting.[36] He honored this holy retreat by a fast of forty days, which he commenced on the seventh day of January, and which he passed in some solitary place, confined to his cell, keeping strict abstinence in fasting and drinking, and employing himself solely in praising God and in prayer. It was also during this Lent that he received the most signal favors from Jesus Christ.

His soul was penetrated with ardor for the mystery of the sacred body and blood of our Lord. The work of so tender a love, and of such condescending goodness, threw him into an excess of admiration, and put him quite beside himself. He communicated frequently, and with so much devotion, that it inspired others with similar feelings; they saw him almost always, after having communicated, as if in a spiritual intoxication, and raised into ecstasy by the sweetness he tasted in partaking of the body and blood of the Lamb without spot. At Mass, when at the elevation, he said this prayer: "Celestial Father, my Lord and my God, cast Thine eyes on the glorious countenance of Your Christ, and have pity on me and on other sinners, for whom Your beloved Son, our Lord, has condescended to die, and who has chosen to remain with us in the sacrament of the altar, for our salvation and consolation: who with You, eternal Father, and the Holy Spirit, sole God, lives and reigns to everlasting ages."

The profound veneration which is due to the August mystery of the Eucharist, the solicitude which we ought to have to hear Mass, approach to the sacred altar, and to prepare ourselves, in order worthily to communicate, were points on which he used to dilate in his conversations, in his instructions, and in his letters.

As faith in the Real Presence is the principle of the worship which is due to Jesus Christ, under the sacred symbols, he supported it, arguing with the heretics, who sought to controvert it: "'O ye sons of men, how long will ye be

---

[34] Decret. lib. iii., tit. 46, cap. Explicari.

[35] On this principle, the Friars Minors, who, by their Rule, are obliged to fast on all the Fridays of the year, are not exempted from it in those years in which Christmas day falls on a Friday.

[36] Matt. 4: 1 and 2; Luke 4: 2.

dull of heart? Why do you love vanity, and seek after lying?'[37] Why do you not admit the truth, and why do you not believe the Son of God? He Himself assures us, He the Most High, that what is consecrated at the altar by the hands of the priest, is His most holy body and His is most holy blood, since He says: 'This is my body, this is my blood of the New Testament. He who eats my flesh, and drinks my blood, has eternal life.'[38] What He has said, that He does. Every day, from the height of His throne, he comes to us under mean species, as He debased Himself in descending into the womb of the Blessed Virgin. Every day[39] He descends from the bosom of His Father, on the altar, into the hands of the priest. As He showed Himself to the holy apostles in true flesh, so He shows himself to us in the consecrated bread. In seeing Him with the eyes of their body, they considered Him with the eyes of faith, and believed that He was their Lord and their God. We also, in sensibly seeing the species of bread and of wine, must firmly believe that it is His most holy body and His most holy blood, living and true. In this way He is always with the faithful,[40] according to what He said: 'Behold, I am with you all days, even to the consummation of ages.'[41]

"Those who saw our blessed Lord in His human nature, and did not believe Him to be the Son of God, are condemned;[42] and those who see the bread and

---

[37] Psalm 4: 3.

[38] Matt. 26: 26, 28.

[39] Mass then was said every day in Saint Francis's time, which it is necessary to notice, in consequence of the abuse which the heretics have made of this letter, which we will give farther on.

[40] This is one of the meanings in which this passage may be read, for Jesus Christ is at all times with the faithful, by His real presence in the mystery of the Eucharist, this sacrament being preserved in the Tabernacles, and that our Lord is there as long as the elements continue; as the Council of Trent has defined, anathematizing all such as shall assert the contrary. —Sess. 13, can. 4. But the literal sense of these words, "Behold, I am with you all days, even to the consummation of the world," is the promise which Jesus Christ makes, to give to the apostles and their successors all the aid they may require for the fulfillment of their ministry, and to be always the invisible Head of the Church: which proves its perpetuity. He will continue to the end of the world, and it will see all the heretical sects extinguished, one after the other. The continual assistance of Jesus Christ renders the Church also infallible, in what she proposes to our belief, and in what she rejects. Finally, the Church, dispersed over sill the earth, has the same infallibility as the Church assembled in council, since, without that, it would not be true that Jesus Christ, according to His word, would be with her at sill times, sill days, omnibus diebus. These are orthodox truths, to which can only be opposed heresies and those crafty evasions which emanate from the spirit of error.

[41] Matt. 28: 20.

[42] Those who have died in their incredulity, because it was voluntary and criminal. Saint Augustine says that Jesus Christ, by His actions and by His words, has always intended to impress upon mankind that He was God and man; and it is to this passage in St. John, that he refers, "Non poterant credere" "They could not believe," he replies: "Quare non poterant, si a me quaeratur, cito respondeo, Quia nolebant; malam quippe arum voluntatem praevidit Deus:" "If I was asked why they could not believe, I reply immediately: Because they did not choose to believe, and God had foreseen their evil inclinations." The same holy doctor says, in speaking of heretics in another place: "Multum errant, quoniam superbi sunt, et non possunt discere, quia nolunt credere." "They fall into grievous

wine, consecrated by a priest, and do not believe it to be truly the body and blood of our Lord Jesus Christ, are likewise condemned."[43]

We see from this argument that St. Francis knew how to oppose heretics, and defend the orthodox truths; for, what stronger proof can there be of the dogma of the Real Presence, than the very words which the Son of God made use of at the institution of the mystery of the Eucharist? Words which are clear and precise, recorded by the Evangelists and by St. Paul, which were susceptible of no figurative sense in the circumstances under which they were spoken, and which the Church, which is guided by His Spirit, has always understood in their proper and natural sense. It is the unanswerable argument, which all the controversialists have employed against the sacramentarians, and which is the stronger from the futile answers by which it has been met.

The life of the holy man has furnished many examples of the ardent and respectful zeal which animated him in all that regarded churches or altars, or all the things which were used for the sacrifice of the Mass, and for the divine service. As he could not bear anything dirty or slovenly, in the country churches, he took the trouble of cleaning everything himself; and lest they should want altar breads for Masses, he made them himself in iron forms, which were made in a very workmanlike manner, which he took into the poor parishes: some of these molds are carefully preserved in the convent of Grecio.

The peculiar respect that he had for priests is seen in the expressions he made use of to manifest it on all occasions, and which we have already noticed. We shall only add what he one day said: "We have been called by the Lord to aid the prelates and clergy of the holy Church in the work of faith. For which reason we are obliged to love them, and to treat them with every possible honor. Moreover, the Friars Minors only bear the name of Minors, that they may be such in fact, and the most humble of men. Besides, from the commencement of my conversion, God having inspired the Bishop of Assisi to give me some very sage advice, and to encourage me in the service of Jesus Christ, I, for that reason, and many others, grounded on the excellence of the Episcopal dignity, am determined to love and revere the bishops, and to look upon them as my lords; and not only them, but even the poorest of the priests."

And here is the place to put on record the celebrated letter he addressed to the religious of his Order, and particularly to the priests. It will show, better than anything else, the profound veneration he had for the mysteries of the

---

errors, because they are proud, and they cannot learn because they won't believe." The heretics of our days Are quite like those of old times. John XII: 39; S. Aug. Tract. 28, n. 1, and Tract. 53, n, 6, in Joan. De Agon. Christ., cap. xv.

[43] Jesus Christ says: "He who believes not is already condemned." What is the condemnation of those of whom St. Paul speaks, who have received the faith and professed it, have swerved from it and fallen off, and have been wrecked, as regards faith, from the love of novelty, by an obstinate resistance to the authority of the Church? —Tim. 6: 10, 21, and 1.19; John 3: 18.

Eucharist.

"TO ALL THE REVEREND AND VERY AMIABLE BRETHREN, TO THE MINISTER-GENERAL OF THE ORDER OF MINORS, HIS LORD AND HIS MASTER; TO ALL THE MINISTERS-GENERAL WHO WILL, AS SUCH, SUCCEED HIM; TO ALL THE PROVINCIALS AND CUSTODES; TO ALL THE PRIESTS OF THIS FRATERNAL CONGREGATION, WHO IMITATE THE HUMILITY OF JESUS CHRIST; AND TO ALL THOSE WHO LIVE IN SIMPLICITY AND OBEDIENCE, THE FIRST AND THE LAST: BROTHER FRANCIS, A VILE AND INFIRM MAN, THEIR LITTLE SERVANT, SALUTES THEM, IN HIM WHO HAS REDEEMED US, AND HAS WASHED AWAY OUR SINS IN HIS BLOOD: JESUS CHRIST, OUR LORD, WHOSE NAME IS THE MOST HIGH, SON OF GOD, BLESSED FOREVER. AMEN.

"Now listen to me, all you who are my masters, my children, and my brethren. What I have to say to you is to open the ears of your hearts to the voice of the Son of God, and to obey Him. Keep, with all your heart, His commandments, and practice His counsels in a spirit of perfection. 'Praise Him because He good, and glorify Him by your works.'[44] The Lord our God presents Himself to us, as His children; for which reason, my brethren, I conjure you all, with all the charity I am master of, and kissing your feet, to treat, with all manner of respect and honor, the Body and the Blood of our Lord Jesus Christ, by which we have been reconciled to God the Father Almighty,[45] and peace has been established both on earth and in heaven."[46] I also entreat, by our Lord, all my brethren who are priests, as well as those who aspire to the priesthood, and who will be admitted into it, that every time they propose to celebrate Mass, they may do so with purity of conscience, and in a pure manner, that they may offer the true sacrifice[47] of the most sacred Body and Blood of our Lord Jesus Christ with veneration, with holy intentions, without any interested views, without being led to it by any fear of displeasing, or wish to please, any one; but may all your will be solely directed, according to the grace which Almighty God will grant you, to that same great God to whom alone you must

---

[44] Psalm 135 (136): 1; Tob. 13: 6.

[45] Rom. 5: 2.

[46] Coloss. 1: 20.

[47] These words of Saint Francis, written more than five hundred years ago, were an anticipated condemnation of the following error: "That the Mass is only a commemorative and representative sacrifice, a representation only of that of the Cross, and a memorial of the immolation of Jesus Christ; that Jesus Christ offers Himself merely in figure; that it is not on the Real Presence that idea of the Eucharistic Sacrifice is founded; that the Anglicans might admit the same sacrifice that we do in the celebration of the Eucharist, even in rejecting the dogma of the Real Presence," etc.

desire to be pleasing, because it is He alone who[48] operates in this sacrifice as He pleases, according to what He has said: 'Do this in memory of me.'[49] Were any one to act otherwise, he becomes a traitor and a Judas.

"My brethren, who are priests, remember that it is written in the law of Moses, that, by command of the Lord, the transgressors were put to death, although they had only been wanting in exterior ceremonies. What much more rigorous punishments do you not think he deserves who shall have treated as an unclean thing the blood of the Alliance, by which he has been sanctified, and shall have thus outraged the spirit of grace?'[50] For, a man who is defiled treats with contempt, and tramples under foot, the law of God since, as the Apostle says, he eats unworthily, without discerning this holy bread, which is Jesus Christ, from other meats, and mingles it with unearthly actions.[51] Nevertheless, the Lord declares by the mouth of a prophet, 'that he who does the work of God negligently or deceitfully,[52] is accursed.'[53] And it is on account of the priests, who do not choose to consider these truths seriously, that He lets fall on us all the judgments recorded elsewhere: 'I will curse your blessings.'[54]

"Listen attentively to what I say, my brethren. If we venerate, as in right we should, the Blessed Virgin Mary, because she bore in her holy womb the Son of God; if St. John Baptist trembled in approaching Jesus Christ, and did not dare to touch the crown of His head[55] to baptize Him; if the sepulcher, in which He was laid for some time, inspires so much respect: what justice, that sanctity, what merit, ought he not to have who touches Him with his hands,

---

[48] Although the priests consecrate at Mass, it is nevertheless true that Jesus Christ solely operates, because it is only the Almighty power which can effect the miracle of the Transubstantiation at the words of the priest, as He pledged Himself to do, when He said: "Do this in memory of me." It is one of the proofs of the opinion of the school of Scotus, who maintained that the sacraments are the causes, not, not physical, but moral and instrumental, of the grace which they confer, which does not prevent their being the true, certain, and infallible cause thereof. This opinion is much adopted by Theologians. See Du Hamel, Theol. tom. 6, De Effect. Sacram;.; Toornely De Sacram genere, quaest. 3.

[49] Luke 22: 19.

[50] Exod. 12: 15 and 19; Lev. 17: 14; Num. 9: 10; Heb. 10: 29.

[51] 1 Cor. 11: 29.

[52] The expression of the Vulgate is fraudulenter, that of the Septuagint is negligenter. Saint Francis notices them both, which shows that he read the Scriptures very attentively, and took notice of the different versions. He means to say that whoever communicates unworthily is a deceiver and a cheat, who insults Jesus Christ while affection to love Him, as Judas who betrayed Him with a kiss: "Osculo filium hominis tradis?" Luke 22: 48.

[53] Jerem. 48: 10.

[54] Malach. 2: 2.

[55] Saint Bernard says likewise of St. John Baptist, who baptized our Savior, plunged in the water, holding his hand on his: "Fremit ille: quid mirum si fremit homo, nec audet attingere sanctum Dei verticem, caput adorandum Angelis reverendum Potestatibus, tremendum Principalibus?" Serm. 1, in Epiphan., n. 6.

no longer in a mortal state, but immortal and glorious, in such state as the angels desire more and more to see Him in.[56]

"My brethren, who are priests, consider what is your high dignity, and be ye holy, because the Lord is holy.[57] Because, in confiding this mystery to you. He has honored you above all the others, love Him also, respect Him, honor Him in the same mystery.[58] When you have Jesus Christ present in so marvelous a manner, if there be anything else in the world that occupies your thoughts, it must be admitted that it is a great misery, and a deplorable weakness. All the world should be in astonishment, every one should tremble, and the heavens should rejoice, when Christ, the Son of the living God, is on the altar in the hands of the priest. O admirable grandeur! O surprising goodness! O humble excellence! that the Sovereign of the universe, God, and the Son of God, should debase Himself to such a degree, as to hide Himself, for our salvation, under the humble species of bread. Reflect seriously, my brethren, on the debasement of a God; open your hearts in His presence, humble yourselves before Him, in order that he may raise you up; retain nothing within you of yourselves, in order that He may give Himself wholly to you, and receive from you all that you are.[59]

"I also warn my brethren, and I exhort them in our Lord, that, in the places in which they dwell, only one Mass be celebrated each day, and that it be celebrated according to the Ritual of the Roman Church. If there should be many priests then, let this be observed, notwithstanding. By a love of charity, let one priest be satisfied with hearing the Mass of another, because our Savior Jesus Christ fills with His grace those present and absent, who are worthy of it. Although He is in many places, He is ever the same, indivisible and impassible; and He associates, according to His good pleasure, the only true God and Lord, together with the Father and the Holy Spirit, for ever and ever. Amen."

Melanchthon[60] availed himself of the last article of this letter,[61] in support

---

[56] 1 Peter 1: 12.

[57] Levit. 11: 44.

[58] We find similar thoughts in the books on the Priesthood, and in many of St. Chrysostom's homilies. He may have read these works, and he was animated with the same views as that holy Doctor.

[59] In this sense Saint Augustine says, that "he who approaches to the Holy Table, where he receives the Body and Blood of Jesus Christ, who died for us, should be ready to give his, also, either for the faith or for his brethren." Tract. 47 in Joan., n. 2.

[60] Melanct. Apol. Conf. Aug., art. de Mis.; Bellarm. de Missa, lib. 2, capp, 9 et 10. Bona, de. Reb. liturg., lib. I., cap., 14.

[61] Eckius has denied that Saint Francis was its author. Cardinals Bellarmine and Possevin had doubts on the subject, but the whole Order has recognized it as his, and Wading has given solid proofs of it. Others have thought that he only spoke of the common Mass, called Conventual, or of the Mass of Maundy Thursday; and some have been of the opinion that he had thought that, according to the usage of the Roman Church, only one Mass ought to be said where there were many priests; all that is erroneous, and without any foundation. Eckius, in Enchirid.; Bellarmine, supra., Possev., in Appar.

of his error on private Masses, which he pretended were contrary to the institution of Jesus Christ. Cardinals Bellarmine and Bona have clearly demonstrated that the use of these Masses has been found to be established from the beginning of the Church; and the very expressions of this letter show that St. Francis was far from finding them to be wrong. He says, "I warn and exhort my brethren to celebrate only one Mass." If he had thought that to celebrate many was acting contrary to the intention which Jesus Christ had in instituting the mystery, he should have said: "I order that only one Mass shall be celebrated, and I forbid the celebration of many;" and undoubtedly he would have said so, he who was so careful to conform in everything to the Gospel, and who, in his capacity of founder and general of his Order, had a right to command and to forbid. Moreover, he knew that his brethren, who were priests, had a right, as all others, to say Mass when they pleased, since he says in the same letter: "Whenever they say Mass, let them say it with purity of conscience."

It was only, then, an advice which he gave them, not to make use of this liberty, for reasons which we shall presently explain. In fine, we have seen in his life that he had Mass said in his room when he was sick: a proof that he did not think this custom very contrary to the intention of Jesus Christ, and he assuredly did not believe it to be so, since, by the admission of the heretics and critics, it was a common practice in his time. His faith was too pure and too firm for him to have thought that the Holy Roman Church would either do or approve of anything contrary to the intention of our Savior. Thus it is calumniously that the sectarians have quoted him; his letter alone convicts them of what is false.[62]

A recent author has mentioned it as a remains of the ancient discipline of the Church,[63] according to which, he assumes that private Masses were not said in the first ages of the Church. But, in the first place, there is not a single word in the letter of St. Francis, which can even lead one to suspect that he meant to revive the primitive discipline. Secondly, the Catholic doctors have proved, in answer to the heretics of the latter ages, that the custom of saying private Masses is of the remotest antiquity, and that the Church never made any law to prevent their being celebrated. Thirdly, that, whether these Masses

---

sac.; Wad., in Epist. 12 S. Franc.; Bona, De Reb. Liturg., supra.

[62] The Spanish Inquisitors should not have attached this note to it—Caute lege—in the Catalogue of books which are to be read with precaution, which was published in 1612; and Wading should not have approved of that note, nor of the use which has been made of it in some editions of the "Bibliothècque des Pères." All that ought to have been noticed is, that the heretics had made a bad use of it, without any good reason. Wading, supra.

[63] It is in a small work of an anonymous, but well-known, author, entitled: "Lettre sur l'Ancienne Discipline de l'Eglise, touchant la celebration de la Messe, qui peut servir de supplément au nouveau Traite des dispositions pour les saints mysteres." The author of this treatise is also the author of the treatise, "De la Priere Publique," and has made himself but too well known. The letter was printed at Paris in 1708, by Ammonneville.

were celebrated more or less frequently in the first ages, in different places, it is certain, and the author admits it, that the practice is very praiseworthy and very holy, that it is approved by the Church, and that the priests may celebrate it daily, provided their intentions are pure, and their dispositions holy. After this, of what use can his book be?[64]

We must now examine what the holy patriarch's motive was, for exhorting his brethren to have only one Mass said daily in the houses of his Order.

Some persons think that, as he had a great leaning towards a life of solitude, the greatest number of his houses were then in solitary places; it was his wish that strangers should not come to them frequently; and that, not to attract them by a number of Masses, he advised his brethren to have but one said daily. Formerly, they were so cautious not to disturb the quiet of the servants of God in their monasteries, that Pope St Gregory,[65] in accordance with his predecessor, Pelagius, forbade the bishops from celebrating solemn Mass in them; and in the Council of Lateran, under Calixtus II, it was forbidden to the abbots and monks to celebrate Mass publicly; that is, to admit seculars into their churches when they celebrated. St. Francis may have intended to have kept his brethren in a state of recollection by the same means.

Nevertheless, his letter shows that he had another motive. Enlightened by the most vivid rays of that light of faith and intelligence which the Holy Spirit sheds on pure minds, he reflected on the mystery of the Holy Eucharist. Jesus Christ, the Son of the living God, who comes to place Himself on the altar, in the hands of the priest, under the humble species, struck him with such astonishment, that it was not possible for him to express himself but by rapture and exclamations. He represented to himself the sublime dignity of priests, the honor they have, far above that of the angels, the eminent sanctity which their character requires, the enormity of the crime of celebrating in a state of sin, and the horror of the punishment it deserves.

Full of these thoughts, he informed the priests of his Order that they ought to feel annihilated in considering the debasement of the Son of God in the sacrifice of the Mass, open their hearts in His presence, and, in return for His giving Himself wholly to them, give themselves so entirely to Him, that they should keep nothing of themselves back. And he immediately adds: "I also

---

[64] He hypocritically denies the facts asserted by the Catholic Doctors to prove he ancient custom of celebrating private Masses; by this he gives support to he heretics. He favors also the indolence and indevotion of those priests who pass whole years without saying Mass, and without bringing themselves into the frame of mind to be able to say it; and gives room to irreligious persons to censure the present measures of the Church, as if she were not equally prudent in sill ages. The letter, moreover, contains many rash and indiscreet things, adverse to piety, and calculated to scandalize the faithful. When persons choose to write on these subjects, they ought to do so in Latin, with great circumspection, and in a Catholic spirit.

[65] S. Greg. Regist. lib. Epist. 46, et in not. edit. nov. Concil. Later, I, Can. 17. Bona, de Reb. Lit. lib. 1, capp. Xiii, xviiii.

warn my brethren, and exhort them, to celebrate but one Mass daily, in the places in which they dwell; and if there should be many priests there, let them be satisfied in observing this; and for the love of charity let them be contented with hearing this one Mass." It is evident that this warning and this exhortation had their source in the fear he entertained that human frailty might hinder them from being every day in a sufficiently holy state, such as he wished them to be, to say Mass.

We may, moreover, remark that he endeavored to impress them with similar sentiments to his own, which had prevented his taking priest's orders. Mark, of Lisbon, observes,[66] that, being seriously pressed to take Orders, he had recourse to prayer, in order to learn the will of God on the subject; that an angel appeared to him, holding a vase full of very clear liquor, and said to him: "Francis, look at this; he who would administer the most Blessed Sacrament, must be as pure as this liquor." Upon which the humble servant of God resolved to continue for the remainder of his life in deacon's orders. In the same sentiment he exhorted his brethren who were in the priest's orders, to humble themselves in the exercise of their holy ministry, in acknowledgment of their unworthiness, by refraining from saying Mass daily, as they might.

Now, there are four things deserving of especial notice in this letter, in order to have it perfectly understood, and in order not to draw consequences from it not in accordance with his intentions.

1. In consequence of his exhorting his brethren not to celebrate Mass daily, it must not be concluded that he wished them to celebrate infrequently. There were then but few priests in the Order; the number was very limited in each house, and he wished them to say their Masses, daily, alternately; therefore, no one among them could be many days without celebrating. Such, consequently, who say their Masses but seldom, cannot shield themselves under the authority of the doctrine of St. Francis. The Council of Trent is not in their favor; it directs the bishops to take care that the priests who have not the care of souls, shall say Mass, at least, on all Sundays and solemn festival days.[67] The primitive Church will also not justify their conduct, for the priests who did not say their Mass in private, assisted at the bishop's Mass, and received the communion from his hands; those, on the contrary, of whom we are speaking, keep away from the Holy Communion, as well as from the altar. They are, nevertheless, aware that this estrangement has been blamed by the holy fathers, who have always exhorted the faithful to frequent communion; that Jesus Christ has given us His Body to be the usual nourishment of our souls; that the primitive Christians received it daily; that, at the close of the fourth century, it was still the custom at Rome, in Spain, and in Africa, according to

---

[66] In the first book of the Chronicles of the Friars Minors, chapter lii., Wading does not mention this circumstance, either through inadvertence, or from not having found it in the manuscripts he had seen.

[67] Conc. Trid., sess. 23., cap. xiv.

the testimony of St. Jerome and St. Augustine;[68] that the Church, in the Council of Trent, conjures her children, by the bowels of the mercy of God, to have sufficient piety to receive frequently the celestial bread; and that it was her wish that, at every Mass, all those who assisted at it should communicate, not only spiritually, and by an interior sentiment of devotion, but by the sacramental reception of the Holy Eucharist, in order more efficaciously to participate of the fruits of the holy sacrifice. The custom of receiving but seldom arises from an erroneous principle, which tends to abolish the use of the sacraments, or from an extreme attachment to sin, which brings about a contempt of the heavenly nourishment, or a state of tepidity and supineness, ending it disgust.

2. It cannot be doubted but that St. Francis had similar feelings of reverence, fear, and humility, for the Holy Communion, to those with which he endeavored to inspire his brethren, in respect to the sacrifice of the Mass. Nevertheless, the love he bore it was predominant in his heart. St. Bonaventure says that he was a frequent communicant,[69] and we see in his letters that he exhorted all to receive the Body and Blood of our Lord. He would, therefore, have approved of his brethren celebrating frequently, and even daily, by an ardent desire to unite themselves to Jesus Christ. St. Augustine, speaking of two men,[70] one of whom, to honor Jesus Christ, did not dare pass a single day without communicating, and the other, who, from a similar motive, did not dare communicate daily, decided that they both did Him honor: the one like Zaccheus, who ran joyfully to his house to receive Him; and the other, like the centurion, who, from humility, did not deem himself worthy to receive Him into his house. We see clearly in this, that it was not upon the custom of seldom or frequently communicating, but upon the more or less frequent communions, that his approval was given. St. Thomas,[71] who is of the same opinion, does not hesitate to say that the love which induces an approach to the sacrament is preferable to the fear which keeps a person away from it, because all the Holy Scripture excites us to love. This was also the opinion of St Augustine,[72] since he says in the same place that the Body of the Lord is the remedy which we ought daily to have recourse to, when we are not unworthy of it; and, in another place, addressing himself to those who had been recently baptized: "You should know what you have received, what you will receive, and what you ought to receive daily. This bread which you see on the altar, which is consecrated by the word of God, is

---

[68] S. Hier. Epist. ad Pammach. pro libris suis, et Epist. ad Lucin. S. August. Epist 54 alias 118 ad Januar. et lib. 2 de serm. Dom. in monte, cap. vii. Conc. Triden. sess. 13, cap. vi., et sess. 23, cap. vi.

[69] S. Bonav. leg. S. Fran., cap. ix.

[70] S. Aug. supra, Epist. 54.

[71] 3a Part, quaest. 80. art. 10 ad tertium.

[72] S. August, serm. 227, ed. nov.

the Body of Jesus Christ."

On this principle the grandeur of the mystery, and the consideration of our baseness, may sometimes prevent a priest from celebrating, and a layman from communicating; but love ought to give them confidence, and prevail on them to approach the holy table. "The peculiar quality of those who ardently love," says St. Chrysostom,[73] "is to desire to be one with that which they love. Jesus Christ, wishing to testify to us the ardor of the love He has for us, has united His body to us so strictly, that we are altogether one with Him, as the members are one body joined to the head."

"After having received the marks of a love so intense," continues the holy doctor,[74] "let us not remain insensible; let us approach the sacred table with fervor, with greater eagerness than infants do the breast of their nurses; and let the most grievous of our disappointments be the privation of this celestial nourishment. Those who are long deprived of it, and who feel no regret at the privation, and who are not excited to wish for this aliment, do not respond to the love which Jesus Christ bears them: they love Him not, since they do not desire to be united to Him; and, in thus refusing to receive Him, they do not honor Him, for it is to this mystery of love that the words of St. Augustine are appropriately applied: 'Ne colitur nisi amando!'[75] He is only honored by loving Him; He only considers Himself honored by love."

3. When St. Francis advised his brethren to celebrate one Mass a day in the houses of his Order, they were for the greater part situated in remote places, to which people seldom came. Now they are almost in every town; the Friars Minors having been called into them for the service of their neighbor, which requires that many Masses shall be said in them. The Council of Trent desires that priests who have the care of souls, shall celebrate as often as it may be necessary to satisfy their obligations.[76] It is here that the religious, who are devoted to aid the pastors, are under the necessity of celebrating frequently. Their holy patriarch, who had an ardent zeal for the salvation of souls as we have seen, and we shall have other opportunities of noticing, would doubtless have consented that, for the edification of the public, they should have bent to this exigence; he would even have recommended them to conform to the usage in future times, had he foreseen that the heretics would have condemned it, as contrary to the intention of Jesus Christ, and that they would have endeavored to deprive the faithful of the consolation of hearing Mass and communicating. His faith, which was pure and active, would not have permitted that error should avail itself of an advice which he had given upon grounds of piety, in the bosom of the Catholic Church. But, if the spiritual advantage of their

---

[73] S. Chrys. Homil. 45 in Joan.

[74] S. Chrys. Homil. 83 in Matt.

[75] S. Aug. Epist. 140 ad Honor., alias 120, cap. xvii.

[76] Conc., Trid. sess. 23, cap. xiv.

neighbor is a motive which may induce the Friars Minors to say Masses frequently, and even daily, this engagement should cause them to have this letter of St. Francis frequently before them, in order to be brought to live with that purity which he inculcates, so that they may never celebrate but with fervor and love, joined to deep reverence, and that one Mass for them may serve as a preparation for the next. If at times they may find themselves less disposed for this solemn act, it is then that they must literally follow the advice of their father, and abstain from celebrating, purifying themselves by penance, and by this means bring themselves into a frame of mind to return promptly to the altar with an increase of love, of desire, and of faithfulness.

4. St. Francis was desirous that such of his brethren who were priests should be pure and holy, that they should celebrate the sacred mysteries with great purity, and should expand their hearts in presence of the Son of God, giving themselves wholly to Him, without retaining any part for themselves. St. Chrysostom says,[77] that there is no purity and sanctity greater than that which ought to be in the breast of a priest, when he offers the awful and tremendous sacrifice; he ought to have as much as if he was in heaven amidst the celestial powers; and, speaking of the Holy Communion, he exclaims: "Who, then, ought to be more pure than he who is permitted to participate in such a sacrifice? What ray of the sun is not inferior in splendor to his hand, his mouth, his tongue?" St Augustine feared entering the priesthood; he found it difficult to perform its functions well;[78] he wept during his ordination; he said that sanctity was the true characteristic of priests; and this is what he addressed to the faithful, on the subject of communion: "Be careful, my brethren, of what you do; eat this celestial bread spiritually; take innocence to the altar at which you receive it."

In the last century, some disingenuous persons, whose noxious doctrine still exercises the patience of the Church, pretended[79] that these sublime dispositions were absolutely necessary for communicants, and that it was

---

[77] S Chrys. de Sacerd. lib. 3, n. iv., et lib, 6, n. iv. Id. Homil. 83 in Matt.

[78] S. Aug. Epist. 21, alias 148. Id. Tract. 26 in joan.

[79] The celebrated work on Frequent Communion was only written to deter the faithful from communicating, under the specious pretext of not having the perfection which the author pretends to have been required by the holy fathers, as a necessary preliminary disposition. But, besides this opinion, which is false and dangerous, he lays down the following proposition: "Saint Peter and Saint Paul are two heads of the Church, who are but one;" which Pope Innocent X declared to be heretical on the 24th of January, 1647, and prohibited the reading of any books which contained it; and Pope Alexander VIII condemned, on the 7th of December, 1690, several other articles which are in the same book. The faithful must not seek instruction on communion in these poisonous sources, but let them read orthodox works which discuss it, particularly the sermons of two illustrious preachers: those of Bourdaloue, for the first Thursday in Lent, for Palm Sunday, the Sunday within the octave of Corpus Christi, and for the twenty-third Sunday after Pentecost; and those of Father Rue, for Palm Sunday, for Tuesday in Holy Week, and for the Monday in Easter week. There they will learn sound doctrine on worthy and frequent communion.

proper to abstain from celebrating or communicating, till the perfection designated had been acquired. They sheltered themselves under the specious pretexts of striving to attain it by penitential exercises; but it was like those of whom St. Ambrose says,[80] that their penance consisted in abstaining from the divine mysteries; that, in that, they punished themselves too severely, and with a sort of cruelty; that they set themselves as a penance the privation of a remedy requisite for the cure of the evil; that they had no regret in consequence of it, which, nevertheless, they ought to feel, because this privation deprived them of celestial grace.

Everyone knows that the Church teaches[81] that no person, whose conscience upbraids him with any mortal sin, whatever contrition he may seem to himself to have, may approach the holy Eucharist, unless having previously purified himself by sacramental confession: to act otherwise would be, as St. Paul says,[82] to be guilty of crime against the Body and Blood of Jesus Christ; it would be to eat his own condemnation, not discerning the Body of our Lord; we must be in a state of grace to receive worthily. It is also well known that all sinners do not resemble the Prodigal Son; that, at the first signs of repentance, they ought not to be admitted to the holy table; that, after certain crimes, after an habitual attachment to sin, a faithful minister must prudently, and according to the spirit of the Church, have sufficient proof of the sincerity of the penitent before admitting him to the holy communion, and even before giving him absolution. St. Ambrose[83] says of false penitents who solicit absolution to go immediately to communion, that they are not loosed, and that they bind the priest; that their consciences are not cleared, and that they implicate him, because he is forbidden from giving what is holy, to the dogs.[84]

If a person communicates frequently and derives little fruit from it, but is tepid and supine, and does not exert himself to avoid venial sins, particularly those which are most considerable and dangerous, it is certain that a prudent director ought to interrupt the course of his communions, and endeavor to inspire him with greater sentiments of penance and fervor, and with an ardent desire to make at an early period a salutary use of the Bread of Life.

Finally, the teachers of spiritual life approved of persons sometimes abstaining from communion, to punish some small faults, to strengthen their fragility by a more lively sorrow, as has been the practice of many of the saints, provided that they quickly return to the divine nourishment which St.

---

[80] S Ambr. de Poeniten., lib. 2, cap. ix.

[81] Conc. Triden. sess. 13, cap. vii.

[82] Cor. 11: 27, 29.

[83] S. Ambrose, de Poenit., lib. 2. cap. ix.

[84] Matt. 7: 6.

Ambrose and St Augustine[85] have called the remedy for ordinary faults, and which is the most effectual means of attaining perfection.

All these maxims are based on the doctrine of the holy fathers. But that, for receiving the body of Jesus Christ, it is necessary to have acquired perfection, and to abstain from it as long as a person is not perfect, is what they never taught. When it was said, that innocence was to be taken to the altar, and that persons ought to approach the holy table with angelic purity, with a holiness more brilliant than the rays of the sun; they imitated the conduct of God in the commandment he gives us to love Him with our whole heart, with all our strength, and with all our mind.[86] The fund of weakness which is in us, says St Augustine,[87] prevents us from loving in this life with all the perfection which those words imply; we shall only love Him in that manner when we shall see Him face to face. Nevertheless, He even now gives us the command, and it is for the purpose of showing us the term of the career which he opens to us, in which it is His desire that, by means of faith, hope, intention, prayer and good works, we should advance, without halting, until we arrive at the plenitude and at the consummation of Divine love.

In the same manner the holy fathers required the most perfect and most sublime dispositions in those who offered up the divine sacrifice of the Mass, or participated in it, in order that they might form to themselves as exalted an idea of the holy mysteries as they had, and that they might continually strive to purify, improve, and sanctify themselves, in order to approach thereto more worthily on each succeeding occasion. It is not possible to attach any other meaning to their words; for they exhorted all persons to Communicate frequently, even daily, and they were well aware that the frailty of human nature gave no room to hope that these eminent dispositions would at all times be found in the participants, where it would be fortunate if they were at length found, after having frequently communicated during a whole life; besides the consideration that these dispositions must be the fruits of frequent communion. It is also in this way that we must understand what the angel said to St. Francis, in representing to him the purity required from priests, by the symbol of a very clear liquid, and that which the saint said to the priests of his Order: "Keep nothing in you of yourselves, in order that He who gives Himself wholly to you, shall receive from you all that you are."

The great love which he had for Jesus Christ, and for the sacrament which contains His Body, His Blood, His Soul, and His Divinity, inspired him with a zeal and a tenderness of devotion to His Blessed Mother, which cannot be expressed, as St Bonaventure remarks. He placed himself and his Order under the protection of this Blessed Mother of God, whom he chose for his advocate;

---

[85] S. Ambr. de Sacram., lib. 4, cap. vi., et lib. 5, cap. iv. S. August. Epist. 54 supra.

[86] Luke 10: 27.

[87] S. August, de Spirit, et Litt., cap xxxvi. et de Perf. Just., c. 8.

and in her, after Jesus Christ, was his chiefest confidence: for, said He, "it is she who made this God of Majesty our brother; through her we have obtained mercy."[88] He used, as we have noticed, to keep a Lent of six weeks, in honor of her glorious Assumption; and he observed it with great sentiments of piety. These are the prayers and eulogiums he was in the habit of addressing her:

"Hail, Mary! Mother of God, ever a Virgin, most holy Lady and Queen, in whom is all the plenitude of grace[89] and every sort of good.

Amongst women there are none born[90] like unto you, you are the daughter and the handmaid of our celestial Father, the great King; and he has chosen you for the mother of His beloved Son. You are the Spouse of the Holy Spirit the Comforter. Hail to you, who are the palace, the temple, and the Mother of our Lord Jesus Christ! I honor all the virtues with which you are filled. You who are as mild as you are beautiful, implore your very dear Son, conjure Him by His great clemency, by the virtue of His most sacred incarnation and that of His most painful death, to pardon our faults. Amen."

---

[88] Saint Cyril, at the Council of Ephesus, and the other holy fathers, attribute to Mary the work and the fruits of our Redemption in this sense which is well understood by the faithful: that, being the Mother of Jesus Christ, our Lord and our God, she gave to the world Him, by whom we have all been redeemed, and in whom we are justified. —Homil. S. Cyrilli in Nestor. Conc. Ephes., part. 2, pag. 583, edit. Labb.

[89] Saint Thomas says that the Blessed Virgin had the plenitude of grace, inasmuch as she received all the grace which was proportioned to her dignity of Mother of God; and he teaches us that this dignity is in a manner infinite, because it forms an intimate union with Jesus Christ who is God; from whence he concludes that Mary is more replenished with grace than all the angels and men, according to the opinion of Saint Peter Chrysologus: "Singulis oratia se est largita per partes; Marias vero simul se totam dedit gratias plenitudo." Is it not thence legitimately inferred that the Blessed Virgin had also the grace of being preserved from original sin? And it is not only the dictum of Saint Thomas, from which the same consequence is deduced. It follows from what Saint Augustine says: "We know that Mary received as many more graces to enable her to triumph entirely over sin, since it is she who was deserving of conceiving and giving birth to Him, who, faith assures us, was exempt from all sin, and who was wholly incapable of having any contact with sin." And is it not in this sense that we must understand the very strong expression of Saint Anselm: "It behoved that the Blessed Virgin, who was to have the same Son as the Eternal Father, should be pure, with such purity, that any greater could not be imagined below that of God Himself?" St. Thomas, 3a Part, quaest. 27. art. 5, et la Part, quaest. 25, art. 6, ad quartum. St. Petr. Chrysol. Serm. 145, de Annunt. S. August, de nat. et grat., cap. xxxvi. S. Anselm, de Concept. Wading, cap. xviii.

[90] Saint Bernard also says that there is one thing in which the blessed Virgin never had and never will have any one like unto her; it is that she has the gladness of maternity with the honor of virginity. This is the privilege of Mary, which will never be given to any other: it is peculiar to her, and is at the same time ineffable. The same saint adds, that all the virtues she appears to have in common with others, are, nevertheless, peculiar to her, inasmuch as they are incomparably more perfect in her than in others. —Serm. de Assumpt.

CHAPTER IV
PERFECTION

Zeal towards the angels and saints—His charity towards his neighbor—His zeal for the salvation of souls—His affection for the poor—The affection of his heart for all creatures—The pains he took to lead his brethen to perfection.

HE INDISSOLUBLE ties of spiritual love, says the holy doctor whom we have quoted, united Francis to the hierarchy of the angels, caused by the marvelous fire which absorbs them in God, and with which they influence the elect. The ardent zeal he had for the salvation of souls, attached him intimately to the Archangel St. Michael, because his employment is to present them to the throne of the Divine Majesty. It was to honor these blessed spirits, that he kept every year a Lent of forty days, before the feast of St. Michael, adding to it a continual exercise of prayer. He had prescribed to himself another Lent, to prepare for the festival of All Saints, who seemed to him to be, according to the expression of Ezechiel, precious stones, glittering as fire, the memory alone of which[1] excited him to a more fervent love of God. The great love which all the apostles had for Jesus Christ, led him to revere them with peculiar devotion, particularly Saints Peter and Paul, in honor of whom he fasted from Whit-Sunday to their feast.

It is useful to remark here that this great saint, who was raised to a sublime degree of prayer, did not neglect, nevertheless, the usual practices of piety with the rest of the faithful. This may serve as a preservative against an illusion which might lead to the belief that they are useless to the spiritual, and that those who are mystical, may dispense with them, to devote themselves to contemplation. His heart was so full and so penetrated with that true and sincere piety, of which charity is the soul, that it seemed to have entire possession of him. It united him incessantly to God, to the friends of God, and to everything which was holy; but, as the apostle says, that it is profitable to all things,[2] it gave him a fund of all that was good, a spirit of meekness, of condescension, and of zeal, to communicate with his neighbor.

---

[1] Saint Bernard speaks in these terms of the memory of the saints: "I acknowledge, my brethren, that this memory excites these ardent wishes in me: that of their society, that of a similar beatitude, and that of their intercession.1' Such wishes lead to an imitation of their virtues, draw down their protection, render the wisher worthy to be admitted into their company, and to participate in their bliss.

[2] 1 Tim. 4: 8.

All men were dear to him, because he saw in them the same nature, the same grace, the image of the Creator, and the blood of the Redeemer. If he had not taken care of the salvation of souls, which Jesus Christ had redeemed, he would not have considered himself among the number of His friends. "Nothing," he said, "is preferable to the salvation of souls;" and he gave several reasons for this, and principally this one: that, for them, the only Son of God had condescended to be nailed to the cross. It was also for them that he labored and lived; for them, in some measure, he called in question the justice of God in prayer, and powerfully solicited His mercy; for them he frequently forewent the sweets of a contemplative life; he undertook journeys, he preached everywhere, he exposed himself to martyrdom, and their edification was one of his motives in the practice of virtue. Although his innocent flesh, already perfectly under the control of the spirit, did not require to be chastised for any faults, he, nevertheless, mortified it in various ways for the edification of his neighbor. When he was censured for his too great austerities, "I am sent," he replied, "to give this example; if I had not the charity to give it,[3] I should be of little use to others, and of none to myself, although I spoke all the languages known to men and angels."

Seeing that a multitude of persons, stimulated by his example, fervently embraced the cross of Christ, he became animated with fresh courage to put himself at the head of these pious troops, as a valiant captain, in order to gain with them a victory over the devil, by the practice of a perfect and invincible virtue.

The sanctity of his life gave him great freedom in his manner of preaching. He spoke fearlessly, without any apprehension of what critics might say, because he had acted before teaching, and he felt and had experienced all he said. The zealous preacher knew not how to flatter. Far from sparing sinners by complacence, he reproached their vices in forcible language, and attacked their disorderly conduct with great vehemence. The presence of the great of the world did not intimidate him; he spoke to them as plainly and forcibly as he had done to the common people, and, as all souls were equally dear to him, he preached as willingly, and with as much zest, to a few people, as to a crowded auditory. This is an excellent model which teaches preachers to be themselves exemplary, to speak the truth without fear, and no to neglect small auditories.

The tender love which St. Francis bore for souls redeemed by the blood of Jesus Christ, rendered him very sensible to their misfortunes. When he knew of any one stained by the filth of sin, he lamented over it with such deep grief, that he was as a mother who brings forth in pain and suffering, to restore it to Jesus Christ. His charity, fertile in expedients, inspired him sometimes to give to wicked persons temporal assistance, with a view of getting them to return

---

[3] 1 Cor. 13: 6.

to the ways of salvation. One day, when he was at the convent of Mount Casal, Brother Angelo, who was the guardian of it, told him that there were in the neighborhood three notorious thieves, who injured considerably the farmers of the vicinity, and daily came and extorted from them the bread which was destined for the convent, without their being able to prevent it. "Brother," he replied, "if you will do what I will point out to you, my confidence in God tells me that you will reform these men, and gain their souls. Go and seek them out: although they are thieves, they are still our brothers. Take them the best bread you have, and some wine, spread a cloth on the ground, and invite them to eat with you; while they are eating, speak to them of holy things, in an insinuating manner, both yourself and your companion; humbly entreat them to injure no one any more. If they promise you this, return to them the next day, and take them something to eat, with bread and wine as before, and tell them that you bring that, as to brethren and friends, who have granted you what you asked of them. If you do this a third time, do not doubt but God will enlighten them, and touch their hearts, and bring them into the right way."

Brother Angelo followed this advice, and gained over the thieves so completely, that they gave up their lives of plunderers, and began to render service to the convent, supplying them with firewood, which they carried to them on their shoulders. Their conversion was complete: one of them entered the Order, and the other two went elsewhere to embrace a penitential life. The guardian used similar means for converting three other thieves, who retired into the recesses of the mountain, after having induced the saint to pray for them. They became afterwards all three Friars Minors, and lived holy lives.

The affection which our saint had always shown for the poor from his infancy, during the first years of his youth, and at the beginning of his conversion, became stronger and stronger, and was manifested on all occasions. St. Bonaventure says that he spared nothing to come to their assistance. Cloaks, tunics, books, the ornaments of the Church, all that he had he gave to them. Many times he has been seen to take the burdens from the poor he met on the road, and bear them on his own weak shoulders. When he returned from begging, he shared what he had received with any that solicited alms at his hands; and as long as anything remained, he never refused any one.

At Sienna, a small cloak had been given to him, which was very necessary for his infirmities; but, in leaving the town, he met a poor person, whose wretched state excited his pity, and he said to his companion: "Let us restore this cloak to him, for it belongs to him; we have only borrowed it, until such time as we should see some one poorer than ourselves." The companion, knowing that Francis really required it, endeavored to prevent his parting with it, but the father made him this answer: "If I did not give this cloak to a poor man, who had more need of it than I have, I should think I had committed a theft, which I should be convicted of by our Sovereign Lord, who is the universal almoner." It was for this reason that, when anything was given him, he asked leave to give it away, if he should meet with any one poorer than himself.

On the same principle, notwithstanding his infirmities, when he was at the convent at Celles, he gave another cloak, which he had received in charity, to a poor woman, who had two little children who were almost naked. One of the brothers having taken it back, promising to give the woman something else instead, "My brother," the saint said immediately, "kneel down and acknowledge your fault; give the cloak back to the woman: she is poorer than I am." His companions got him another, and he gave it again to a man of Cortona, who came to solicit alms for the love of God, at the same convent at Celles, and who said that his wife was dead, and that he had several little children, and that he had no food for them: "I give you this cloak," said the saint, "on this condition, that, if you are asked to give it back, you do no such thing, unless you receive its full value." The brethren, indeed, did all they could to induce him to give it back: they told him there was no one poorer than the person who had given it to him, or who wanted it more on account of his bad health and the rigor of the season. But the man, referring to what his benefactor had said, answered that the cloak was his, and that he would not part with it, unless he received its full value. In order, therefore, to have it returned, they were under the necessity of taking him to a friend who gave him in money what the cloak was considered to be worth.

A very old woman, the mother of two of the Friars Minors, having come to the convent of St. Mary of the Angels to ask for charity, Francis told the guardian to give her something; and he having said that there was not anything then in the convent which could be given, unless it was a book of the Gospel which the brethren read out of, when they were in the choir, "Give it," said the father, "that the poor woman may sell it to provide for her necessities. I believe that that will be more agreeable to God, than reading out of it. What is it that a mother has not a right to require from us, who has given two of her sons to the religious?" Another time, a poor man, half-naked, came to ask for an old habit, or some pieces of one, to cover himself with. Francis desired them to look out for some habit that was not used. As such a one was not to be found, he stole aside and began to unpick some breadths of his own, in order to give them to the man; the guardian, being informed of this, came down hastily and forbade his taking them out: "I will obey you, because you are my superior, but give this poor man something to cover himself with; otherwise I shall have a scruple, and shall be grieved to be obliged to wear an entire habit which is lined, to keep me warm, while this poor naked man is shivering with cold at the gate." He went to the poor man to console him, and did not leave him until the guardian had given him something wherewith to clothe himself; and this alms was no less comforting to his charitable feelings, than the clothing was to the misery of the poor man. By a similar impulse of charity, and in order to prevent their offending God, he gave his cloak to a servant who complained of the great injury his master had done him, cursing him and blaspheming Providence for allowing the poor to be so ill used, on condition that he would leave off cursing and blaspheming.

The physician who saw the saint in his illness, near Rieti, having one day mentioned the extreme poverty of an old woman who was begging, he sent for the guardian, and said: "Here is a cloak which I have worn until such time as some one should be found who has a greater right to it than I have; I beg you to send it, with some of the bread which has been received on the quest, by one of the brethren, to our sister, who is very poor, and let him say that we only give her what belongs to her. I conceive that what is given to us can only be ours until such time as some one shall come forward, who is more in want of it than we are." Not to vex the holy man, the commission was faithfully executed; but the puzzle was, where to get another cloak to give, and a tunic besides, for he had given his own to another poor person. As the guardian was turning this in his mind, some cloth was brought which the lords, attendant on the Pope, who was at Rieti, sent him; and there was enough to make habits for all the brethren.

Some short time afterwards, Francis, being a little less ill, went to preach at Celano, as we have already noticed. He found in the town a poor woman who was almost naked, who asked for something to cover her. He first threw her his cloak, and upon her representing to him that that was insufficient, he threw her the cloak of his companion, saying to him: "Brother, let us put up for a while with the rigor of the cold, in order to give this woman wherewithal to clothe herself. It is not fitting that the true poor should be doubly clad, to warm them, while they see other poor obliged to go in a state of nudity."

The blessed patriarch wished that such of his children who had not studied, and had no talent for preaching, should be employed in serving their brethren, and should frequent the hospitals, there to render the meanest offices to the lepers, with humility and charity. He took them there himself, and was the first to make their beds, to dress their sores, to cleanse away the matter, and to wash them; sometimes he put his tongue to the wounds, and licked them. When application was made by any one to join the Order, he never failed to warn the postulant that he would have to attend the lepers, and he often made this their trial; he rejected those who could not make up their minds to perform these functions, but he tenderly embraced such as submitted willingly to them, encouraged them, and mode them love the lepers, by calling them "Christian Brothers,"[4] as if they were supereminently such.

Brother James the Simple, who came from Perugia, was greatly distinguished by his zeal in this charitable exercise, insomuch that they gave him the name of the steward and physician of the lepers. Francis

---

[4] He probably called them so, because they were the type of our Lord Jesus Christ, of whom the Prophet Isaiah says: "We have thought Him as it were a leper, and as one struck by God and afflicted." — Isaiah, 53: 4.

recommended one to him, whose body was one mass of sores, from his head to his feet. James took such care of him, that, by degrees, he regained his strength; and, thinking fresh air would contribute to his restoration, he took him with him, although still full of ulcers, to the convent of Saint Mary of the Angels. This appeared to the saint, who met him, to have been very indiscreet, and he said to Brother James: "You should not lead about, in this manner, the Christian Brothers; it is neither proper in you, nor good for them. I wish you to serve them in their hospital, but I do not wish you to take them out of it, for there are many persons who cannot bear the sight of them." The leper was distressed at hearing his benefactor thus reprimanded, and he blushed for shame. Francis, perceiving him to have been mortified, threw himself immediately at his feet, and begged his pardon, and, in order to encourage him, he imposed a penance on himself, for which he desired to have leave from Peter of Catana, the vicar of the convent: this was to eat, at the door of the convent, out of the same plate with the leper. After which he embraced and kissed him, and dismissed him satisfied.

There was in the hospital a leper who was so impatient and so violent, that he abused and struck the Friars Minors who served him, and even went so far as to blaspheme God. They reported this to their father, who offered himself to the sick man, to wait upon him: "What can you do for me more than your companions have done?" replied the invalid. "Ever since I have had this insupportable disorder, God has forgotten me. I am in despair, I can live no longer; no one can mitigate my sufferings; neither you nor any one else." Francis, seeing that he was agitated by the evil spirit, left him for a while, prayed for him, and returned to exhort him to be patient, by the most urgent motives. As he saw that the man became calmer, he asked him what it would be most agreeable to him that he should do for him. He said it would be to wash his whole body, for that he could no longer endure the stench of the infection. The saint quickly got some water warmed, into which he put aromatic herbs, and began to wash him himself, while his companion poured out the water. As he washed, his cure advanced, and, at the same time, the grace of God made such impression on the mind of the patient, that, as the water flowed from his body, the tears flowed from his eyes. The washing having terminated, the leper being perfectly cleansed and converted, publicly confessed his sins, asked for mercy, and went through a rigorous course of penance. He died a few months afterwards, and appeared to the saint, thanking him that, by his means, after a light punishment in purgatory, he was about to enjoy eternal glory.

God performed a different miracle on another occasion, to justify the charity of His servant to the poor. At Alexandria de la Paille, a town of the Milanese, where he was received as a saint, he was invited to dinner by a wealthy and pious man. While he was at table, a man of bad character, who was, however, jealous of Francis's reputation, watched all his actions, in order to decry and criticize them: this man counterfeited a beggar at the door, and solicited an alms for the love of God. As soon as Francis heard the appeal for the love of God, he sent him the wing of a fowl, to which he had been just helped. The sham beggar, to whom it was taken, kept it. The next day he produced it, in a large concourse of people, where the saint was preaching, and, interrupting the discourse, he said in a loud voice: "This is the food on which the preacher feeds: should such a man be honored as a saint?" His malice received a signal check; the wing of the fowl which he exhibited, appeared to the bystanders to be fish, and he was thought to have lost his wits. He himself perceiving that what he held up was nothing but fish, was ashamed of what he had said, was touched with remorse, and himself published what had happened. After which, one miracle succeeded another: it was found that what had appeared to be fish, was in reality flesh. Thus did the Lord vindicate the virtue of His servant, punish envy, and convert the envious. The malignity of envy often finds its punishment in the artifices it employs to injure persons of virtue, but it is very unusual for the envious to be so converted.

St. Bonaventure says that St. Francis felt a most tender compassion for all who suffered from temporal ills; that, indeed, he had naturally a feeling heart, but that the goodness of the heart of Jesus Christ, communicating itself to his, rendered it still more compassionate. He was the more sensible of the afflictions of others, as in all the poor, and in all those who suffered, he represented to himself his Divine Master, poor and suffering; in which, continues the holy doctor, he who was himself poor, showed that he was so as a perfect Christian.

When he had it not in his power to alleviate the sufferings of those in indigence or sickness, he endeavored, at least by soothing words, to assuage their feelings. One day, when he was about to preach, he was entreated by a poor and infirm man to recommend him to the auditors. His compassion was excited, and, with tears in his eyes, he said to his companion that he felt the man's ills as if they were his own. His companion answered the man rather drily, who was importunate in asking for alms, and in order to moderate the feelings of the saint, he said: "If we judged by exteriors, this man is apparently in great misery; but, if we could penetrate the interior, we should, perhaps, find that in the whole province there is not an individual richer in wishes, or more eaten up with pride: such characters are frequently found among beggars." Francis censured him severely for having repulsed the poor man, and then judged him with so much asperity, and pointed out to him that in that he grievously offended God. The religious acknowledged his error, and asked pardon on his knees. "I shall not pardon you," said Francis, "unless you take off your habit, prostrate yourself before the poor man, acknowledge your fault, entreat him to pardon you, and to pray for you." The humble penitent did immediately all that he had been desired to do, after which Francis embraced him, and said, with great mildness: "My son, it is not so much against the poor

man that you have sinned, as against Jesus Christ, for He is in all the poor:
they are so many mirrors, in which He represents to us His own poverty, and
that of His Blessed Mother. Therefore, as often as you see the poor and the
sick, respect them, and humble yourself in their presence; consider, with
sentiments of piety, that the Son of God made Himself poor for our sakes, and
condescended to take upon Himself our infirmities.[5]

"If we cherish these Christian-like views, we should not judge so harshly of
the poor, of whom it is no less faulty to judge, than of the rich; and in their
poverty we should find as powerful motives for loving Jesus Christ, as for
affording the succor they require."

The heart of St. Francis was naturally so kind and so tender that he felt an
affection for creatures, but it was from a profound sentiment of piety that he
called them his brothers and his sisters. Going back to the origin of things, St.
Bonaventure says that he considered all that had being as having emanated
from the bosom of the Divinity, and he acknowledged that they had the same
principle as himself. In fact, the creation established amongst them a sort of
fraternity God being the parent of all nature, it is not to be denied that, in this
sense, everything which composes it is brotherly. And who can censure a man
who is wholly religious, for expressing himself in a manner which is grounded
on the first principles of religion? This trait shows both the elevation of his
mind, and the piety of his heart; heretics alone can blame it.[6]

Among animals, those he preferred were such as reminded him of the
mildness of Jesus Christ, or were the symbol of some particular virtue, or
which gave rise to some edifying reflections; and God has sometimes shown
by miracle, how much the motive of these feelings was pleasing to Him. Lambs
were peculiarly agreeable to the holy man, in memory of the meek Lamb who
permitted Himself to be led to the slaughter, for the redemption of sinners; he

---

[5] 2 Cor. 8: 9; Isaiah 53: 4.

[6] The Calvinist, Jurieu, laid hold of this circumstance in the life of Saint Francis, and treated it with
an asperity of censure, of which even the Protestants themselves have highly disapproved on other
occasions. Ferrand, who was a celebrated controversialist, pointed out, after having refuted the
calumnies of the minister, the injustice of his invectives against him for having given the names of
brother and sister to animals, which the saint gave to all creatures. Bayle, who notices these things,
says that he pities Ferrand, who had undertaken the apology of these interesting fraternities; as if
it were a disgrace for man, whom God created, that He should also have been the Creator of animals
and the Father of every thing in nature. But with whom did this philosopher fraternize when he
took such pains to support the extravagant doctrine of the Manicheans on the two principles? By
fallacious and crafty argument, he encouraged libertines and the impious to assert that revelation
is in direct opposition to reason; for this is what is deducible from his captious difficulties. We may
be assured that heretics, who, like himself, consider themselves dishonored by the fraternity of
creatures, nevertheless bring themselves to fraternize with demons, by the pride which renders them
rebels to God, by their revolt against His Church. Saint Polycarp, according to Saint Irenaeus,
thought this connection still greater. Having met, at Rome, the heresiarch, Marcion, who asked him
if he knew him, "Yes," replied he, "I know you for Satan's eldest son." —S. Iren, contr. Haeres, lib.
3, cap. iii.

frequently purchased them, to prevent their being killed.

While he was staying at the monastery of St. Vereconda, which is in the diocese of Gubbio, he found that on the previous night a sow had killed with its teeth a lamb, which had just been born. The Lamb without spot, whom sinners put to death, flashed immediately upon his recollection, and the pity this excited in him, caused him to lament sorely the death of the little animal, which was a symbol of meekness, to curse the cruel beast which had killed it, and to wish that neither man nor beast might eat of its flesh. The sow was at that moment struck with a disease, of which it died in three days. It was thrown into a ravine, not far distant from the monastery, and no animal ventured to touch it; it became dry and hard as a piece of wood. St. Bonaventure remarks, on this occasion, that if God was pleased to punish with death the cruelty of a beast, how infinitely more severe must not cruel and pitiless men think their punishment will be in the other world.

A lad went to Sienna to sell some turtle-doves, which he had taken alive. Francis met him on his way, and said: "These are innocent birds, which are compared in Scripture to chaste and faithful souls.[7] I beg you earnestly not to put them into the hands of persons who would kill them, but to confide them to me." They were given to him, and he put them immediately into his bosom; he spoke to them as if they were capable of reasoning, not only by that natural impulse which induces us constantly to speak to animals, when we caress them, but also by an impression of the spirit of God; for he foretold a great miracle, promising to prepare a nest for them, where they might increase and multiply, according to the intention of their Creator. Having taken them to his convent of Ravacciano, near the walls of Sienna, he forced his stick into the ground before the gate, and the stick became, by the following day, a large evergreen oak. He let the turtle-doves fly into it, desiring them to make their nests there, which they did for many succeeding years; and they were so familiar with the religious, that they came to feed from their hands. Wading says that the tree is still there.

Nor did the young man go unrewarded. Francis told him that he would become a religious of his Order, and that he would acquire eternal glory: he did, in fact, enter the Order, and lived so holily as to deserve it. The miracle was the cause of his vocation, and at the same time sanctioned the affection the saint showed these birds: he only loved God through the affection he showed to His creatures. So also, St. Gregory Thaumaturgus, according to the testimony of St. Gregory of Nyssa,[8] having planted his stick in a spot where a river was breaking down the dyke and doing damage through the country, the Lord changed it suddenly into a large tree, which checked the flood entirely, and served to honor the faith of his servant, and incite the infidels to believe in

---

[7] Cant. 1: 9, and 2:12.

[8] S. Gregor. Nyssen. in vit. S. Greg. Thaumat., Oper. tom. 2, pp. 99 and 192.

Jesus Christ.

The divine love which inflamed the heart of St. Francis, made everything appear amiable to him which could tend to the love and service of God. For this reason he was fond of birds, whose carol seemed to invite mankind to publish the glory of their Creator, who, according to the words of Jesus Christ, "neither sow, nor do they reap, nor gather into barns: yet your heavenly Father feeds them."[9] It was gratifying to him to remark the gray and ash color of larks, the color he had chosen for his Order, in order that they might often think on death. He also loved to admire the disposition of the plumage of such as were crested, which seemed to him to have some relation to the simplicity of his habit. On the lark rising into the air, and singing as soon as it has taken some grains of corn for its nourishment, he remarked with sensible pleasure that this example ought to teach us to give thanks to our common Father, who gives us wherewithal for our sustenance, only to eat for His glory, to despise the earth, and to raise ourselves up to heaven, where our conversation ought to be.[10] He was more fond of these small birds than of any others, because they induced holy thoughts, and he took as much care of them as he could.

As he had noble and spiritual motives for his simplest and most common actions, God made use of this for the instruction of men by the example of a bird. Near the convent of Mount Ranier, or Mount Colombo, there was a nest of crested larks, the mother of which came every day to feed out of the hand of the servant of God, and took sufficient for herself and her brood: when they began to be strong, she brought the little ones to him. He perceived that the strongest of the brood pecked the others, and prevented them from taking up the grain. This displeased him, and addressing himself to the little bird as if it could understand him, "Cruel and insatiable little animal," he said, "you will die miserably, and the greediest animals will not be willing to eat your flesh." In fact, some days afterwards, it was drowned in a basin, which was placed for them to drink out of. It was given to the cats and dogs, to see if they would eat it; but neither would touch it. It may be thought that so trifling an anecdote was not worth recording, but there is nothing trifling in the moral it contains. It is a natural representation of those greedy and insatiable men who devour the substance of their brethren, and envy them all that they cannot despoil them of; enemies of mankind, unworthy of the name of men, thieves, ruffians, ravaging wolves, as they are designated in Scripture,[11] whose voracity, say the holy fathers,[12] surpasses that of wild beasts; whose life is a public calamity; hated and detested by all, during their lives, they die as they have lived, and

---

[9] Matt. 6: 26.

[10] 1 Cor. 10: 31; Phil. 3: 20.

[11] Isai. 1: 23; Ezech. 22: 27.

[12] S. Chrys. Orat. de Avar.

their memory is held in execration.[13]

The tender-heartedness which Francis evinced for animals has been ridiculed by heretics. Nevertheless, the Holy Spirit tells us, by the mouth of Wisdom, that "the just man regards the lives of his beasts."[14] The patriarch Jacob[15] excused himself from following his brother Esau, because his ewes and cows were heavy, and he was fearful he should kill them if he hurried them. When St. Paul said, "Doth God take care of oxen?"[16] he only wished to insinuate that God is far more interested in what regards men; and what is written in the law of Moses, "You shall not muzzle the ox that treads out your corn on the floor,"[17] must be applied with greater reason to the ministers of Jesus Christ, to prove that they have a right to live by the altar. We see in the Old Law many regulations made for the repose of beasts, and for their preservation; it was, in particular, to avert men from any sort of cruelty to their fellow- men; for, it has always been remarked that, such as are cruel to animals, are generally so to men also.[18] Tenderness must not degenerate into extravagance, which would make an idol of a beast, for which they sometimes feel more than for persons who ought to be dear to them, and of which they take more care than of the poor, who are members of Jesus Christ; but natural mildness and a spirit of piety induce us not to injure animals, but to be kind to them.

In this view St. Chrysostom,[19] commenting on the words of Wisdom, which we have just quoted, says that the saints are tenderhearted; that they love all men, strangers as well as their own countrymen and their own families, and that their good feelings are extended to senseless animals.

Sulpicius Severus[20] relates of St. Martin, that, seeing some hounds pursuing a hare, which they were on the point of catching, he ordered them to stop; he had no sooner spoken, than the hounds became immovable on the spot where they were, and they did not stir till the hare was placed in safety.

An author of the life of St. Bernard,[21] who had been his secretary, says that not only men, but irrational animals, also birds, and other beasts, felt the effects of his tenderness. He adds that the saint, in one of his journeys, coming close to a hare, which the dogs were about to catch, and where a bird was nearly seized in the talons of a hawk, delivered them both miraculously by the

---

[13] S. Aug. serm. 367, alias 25, de verb. Dom.

[14] Prov. 12: 10.

[15] Genes. 33: 13.

[16] 1 Cor. 9: 9.

[17] Deut. 20: 4.

[18] Exod. 23; Levit. 22.; Deut. 22 and 25.

[19] S. Chrys. in Epist. ad Rom., hom. 49 in mor.

[20] Sulp. Sev. Dial. 2, de Virt S. Mart., n. 10.

[21] Vit. S. Bern., auct.. Gaufr., lib. iii, cap. 7, n. 28, apud Mabill.

sign of the cross, and then told the sportsmen that all their efforts would be useless for taking this prey, when he was by.

If it had been thought proper not to omit in his life, and in that of St. Martin also, these anecdotes of the goodness of their hearts, which were enhanced by supernatural evidence, and of which God approved by mere efforts of His power, what right can critics have to censure precisely similar circumstances in the life of St. Francis?

The glorious patriarch, who praised God in the minutest things, procured his glory in the greatest. His principal care was to lead his brethren to perfection; to render them worthy imitators of Jesus crucified, capable of exciting His love in all hearts. It would be difficult to point out the founder of an Order who had spoken more, taught more, or exhorted more, than St. Francis: and it may have been noticed that he instructed his disciples in the most solid and eminent virtues. He recommended them to put the Gospel in practice, as they had promised to do, in making profession of the rule; to adore profoundly and with great devotion the Body of Jesus Christ; to hear Mass most devoutly, to celebrate the Divine Office with attention, carefully to keep all the ordinances of the Church; to have the greatest veneration for all priests, humbly to bow in their presence, and to kiss their hands. He even said that, if it could be done, they ought to kiss the feet of the horses on which they rode, to honor the power which they have of consecrating and administering the divine mysteries.

When abroad, it was his desire that his religious should appear with so much modesty, reserve, and circumspection, that every one might be edified thereby, and glorify God therein. "Do not despise the men of the world," he said, "and judge not ill of them.[22] You are not to judge other persons' servants, who are not yours; whether they stand or fall, it is not your affair, but that of their masters. Have peace in your own mind, make it known to others, inspire it to all; labor for the conversion of sinners, for that is your vocation."

Attentive to the regulation of the interior, he incessantly exhorted them to correct the smallest defects; to exercise themselves in the practice of holy prayer, to meditate on the Passion of our Blessed Savior, and to use all their efforts to preserve union and fraternal love. "Happy," said he, "is the man who loves his brother at a distance, as well as when they are together, and who would not say in his absence what charity would prevent his saying in his presence."

This last article called forth all his vigilance. Hearing that one of his brethren had sinned against charity, by some conversation in which he had traduced the reputation of another, he said to the vicar of the convent: "Go quickly, and inform yourself correctly of what occurred; and if you find the accused innocent, give a severe correction to the accuser, which shall mark

---

[22] Rom. 14: 4.

him in the eyes of his brethren. The Order is in danger, if the system of backbiting is not checked; the good odor will be lost, if the poisoned tongue of slanderers is not stopped. I desire that you will take the greatest care to prevent this pestilential malady from spreading. The religious who has injured the reputation of his brother, should be stripped of his habit; he ought not to be allowed to raise his eyes to heaven, till he has restored what he has taken from him."

St. Bonaventure says that St. Francis had as great a horror of detraction as of the bite of a serpent; it is the comparison made by the Holy Spirit.[23] This is the way in which he spoke of it: "My brethren, the vice of detraction destroys the principle of piety; it dries up the source of grace; it is an abomination in the sight of God, who is infinitely good; because he who detracts nourishes himself with the blood of souls, which he kills with his tongue, as with a sword. Detractors resemble thieves and murderers, and are more cruel than these, because the love of Jesus Christ, which is fulfilled by charity, obliges us to be more zealous for souls than for the preservation of the body. What does a brother do, who murmurs against his brethren and against his superiors? Nothing less than pour gall into the Order, which is his mother. Detractors are of the race of Cham, who, instead of covering what ought to have been hidden of his father, came and told his brothers where he had found him.[24] Thus, also, by detraction, they discover and exaggerate the faults of their brethren and superiors, which draws down the malediction of heaven. Detractors root carefully into the defects of others, as swine into filth; and, more unclean than those animals, they nourish their minds with what they find, or, perhaps, with what they invent. By their continual complaints on all sorts of subjects, they are like dogs, that bark and bite on all sides, and gnaw the entrails of their neighbor."

In the sequel of this discourse, the saint points out that those detractors, who constitute themselves censors of others, are hypocrites, ambitious and cowardly flatterers; they strive to appear virtuous, without endeavoring to be so; they bring accusations against the vicious, but do not correct their own vices; they wish to be considered spiritual persons,[25] competent to give

---

[23] Eccl. 10: 11.

[24] Genes. 9.

[25] Saint Paul says: "The spiritual man judges all things, and himself is judged of no man." 1 Cor. 2: 15. The heretics of the last centuries have made a bad use of this text, in support of their fanaticism, as to the particular inspiration on points of faith; this it is to which all the sects are obliged to recur. But the first opinion which a spiritual man forms who follows the spirit of God, is that he must believe all that the Church proposes to his belief, that Church which the Holy Spirit gives to all the faithful, as their mother and mistress; and this opinion is so certain, that no one can controvert it without falling into error. There are men, also, who affect spirituality, and who, under that pretense, take the liberty of judging others, but who are sensibly offended when others censure them. The words of the apostle cannot justify them, for they do not purport that the spiritual man does not judge any one, but that he judges all things; that is to say, that, if he is truly spiritual, he judges all

opinions on all subjects, and not to be themselves judged by any; and they give pernicious praise to those from whom they hope to receive support, while they refuse just praise to those from whom they have nothing to expect.

This vigilant pastor, being one day at prayer, saw the convent as if besieged by an army of devils, not one of whom could effect an entrance. But it so happened that one of the brethren, being greatly incensed against another, came to a resolution to injure him, by calumniating him, and then Francis saw one of the devils enter, who attacked the calumniator with great fury. Moved by the danger in which he saw the religious, he sent for him immediately, and advised him to reject the poison of hatred which he nourished in his heart against his enemy. This friar, alarmed at having been discovered, acknowledged his fault, asked pardon and penance, and went and reconciled himself to his brother. The man of God saw the demon take to flight, and he told the religious he had seen this, who gave fervent thanks to God and to his father, and made a firm resolution not to give any more hold to so cruel an enemy.

It was the custom of the holy founder, daily, to examine into the state of regularity of his convent. He permitted no relaxation to creep in; whatever he found defective, he corrected. He often affixed rude and humiliating penances for trifling faults, not only to keep up amongst his brethren a spirit of mortification, but to teach them to look upon all faults as great and considerable, as relative to the state of perfection into which they had entered.

In the view of rendering them more perfect, he frequently counteracted the bent of their devotion. Brother Massé was a very spiritual man, who was much attached to prayer. Francis, in order to try him, said to him one day, in presence of the others: "Brother, these have received from God a greater gift of contemplation than you have. For which reason, in order to give them more time to give themselves more freely to it, it seems proper that you, who seem more calculated for exterior duties, should have the care of the door and of the kitchen, and, if there is any time over, you will employ it in questing. Take great care that the strangers who may call, do not interrupt your brethren in their meditations. As soon as they may knock at the door, be there ready to receive them, satisfy them with fair words, and do everything which the others would have done, so that it shall not be necessary for any of them to make their appearance. Go in peace, and fail not in doing all these things, in order to have the merit of obedience."

Massé, bowing his head, submitted to the order of his superior, without hesitation or murmur, and, during several days, he acquitted himself faithfully of what had been directed. His companions, who knew his virtue, and the love he had for prayer, had scruples at seeing him in these employments, and

---

things by the light he receives from the Holy Spirit. Those who are guided by the same Spirit do not blame him, because they act on similar principles; but those who have not the Spirit of God, are not capable of judging him.

begged their father to permit them to share these duties with him. He assented, and, sending for Massé, said to him: "Brother, your companions wish to relieve and assist you, and I also wish that they may have a share in the labors." To which Massé replied, "Father, I consider as coming from God whatever duties you direct, whether in the whole or in part." St. Francis, seeing the charity on the one part, and the humility on the other, gave them an exhortation on these two virtues, and distributed the duties among them, with his blessing,

What he had ardently desired for himself, and what he was rejoiced to see some of his brethren look forward to most anxiously, was the perfection which consists in suffering martyrdom: in shedding one's blood for the faith. As he could not obtain this favor, and as it was only granted to a few of his brethren during his lifetime, he endeavored to make up for it by another species of martyrdom, which, as St. Bernard says,[26] is indeed less cruel than the first, but which its duration renders more bitter. It is the martyrdom of mortification, and principally that of voluntary poverty. In fact, this poverty, as he compelled its observance, not only placed him and his brethren in the most humiliating situation in the eyes of the world, but deprived them, moreover, of all the comforts and conveniences of life, exposed them to hunger, thirst, want of clothing, and various other annoying discomforts. All this however, was not, in his view, the consummation of this description of martyrdom. It was still further requisite to suffer patiently, in time of pain and sickness, the want of assistance, which poverty cannot command, to see the disease increase, and death about to follow, from want of necessary succor.

His charity had taken all possible precaution for procuring assistance to the sick of his Order. He had directed that, if any of the brethren fell sick, the others should attend upon them, as they would wish to be themselves waited upon in like circumstances, and with more affection than a mother has for a beloved son. Notwithstanding the great aversion he had to money, he required that the superiors should make application to their spiritual friends, to induce them to give some, in order to assist the brethren in their sickness. But, as he foresaw that this measure might not always be successful, and that poverty in such case would put it out of the power of the superiors to procure what was absolutely necessary for the sick, he pointed out to them what perfection called upon them to do.

"If one of the brethren, in health or in sickness, finds himself unable, through poverty, to procure what his absolute necessities require, provided he has humbly applied to his superior for them for the love of God, let him bear with the privation, for the love of Jesus Christ, who sought for consolation, but found none.[27] It is a suffering which will be in His sight a substitute for

---

[26] S. Bern, in cant. serm. 30, n. 11.

[27] Psalm. 68 (69): 21; Isai. 63: 5.

martyrdom; if this should even increase his disease, he must not fear being guilty of suicide, for he has done all he ought to have done, by applying humbly to his superiors." The maxim is well grounded. St. Chrysostom[28] maintains, that to suffer generously the loss of his goods, as did holy Job, is a species of martyrdom.

St. Bernard says the same thing of voluntary poverty, and remarks that, in the Beatitudes, a similar reward is promised to the poor and to martyrs.[29] On those principles, is not a Friar Minor to be looked upon as a martyr, who, having embraced the strictest poverty, for the love of Jesus Christ, would, rather than contravene it, endure with patience every evil, and even death, and would generously make to God the sacrifice of his health and of his life, in order to practice this virtue to his last breath? St. Augustine[30] affirms that a Christian suffers martyrdom in his bed, when he declines procuring his cure by forbidden means: thus, a sick Friar Minor, who has not the necessary assistance, brought about by his having embraced poverty, according to the evangelical counsel, is a martyr to poverty. Even supposing that it was less owing to poverty, than to the neglect or harshness of his superior, that he was without assistance, he would equally have gained the crown promised to this description of martyrdom, since it would be as an evangelical pauper that he would suffer and die. But woe to that superior who should procure him such a crown! He would be like to those who have made so many martyrs in the persecution of the Church.

When St. Francis learnt that his brethren, by the sanctity of their lives, and by the efficacy of their preaching, brought back numbers of sinners into the paths of truth, and enkindled in their breasts the love of God, he said that such intelligence was to him as most pleasing odors and precious perfumes, by which he was wholly embalmed; and, in his spiritual joy, he loaded these holy and edifying religious with the most ample benedictions. On the other hand, he fulminated dreadful maledictions against such as dishonored religion by their conduct. "Most holy Lord," would he say, "may those who overthrow and destroy by their bad example what You incessantly raise up by the saintly brethren of the Order, be accursed by You and by the whole celestial choir, and also by me, Your little servant."

Any scandal given to little ones gave him so much affliction and heartsore, that he often might have died of it, if God had not supported him by interior consolations. One day, when he was suffering extreme grief on a subject of this nature, and was praying the Father of Mercies for his children, St. Bonaventure informs us that he received the following answer: "Poor little man, why do you disquiet yourself? Because I have appointed you the pastor

---

[28] S. Chrys. in Epist. 2, ad Cor., homil. 1 in mor.

[29] S. Bern. serm. 2, in Fest. Omn. Sanct, n. 15.

[30] S. August. serm., 206. n. 7.

of this religion which I have established, are you unmindful that I am its principal protector? I gave you the direction of it, to you who are a simple man, in order that what I should do through you might be attributed, not to human industry, but to my favor. It is I who called those who have entered it; I will preserve them, and provide for their wants; I will substitute others for those who will die off; I will cause some to be born, in order to come into it; and whatever may occur to shake this religion, which is founded on strict poverty, I will supply it by grace, so that it shall be always upheld." Up to this day, the world has seen the verification of this prophecy. The Order of Friars Minors has been powerfully attacked, and has still many enemies; nevertheless, it still subsists.

It is with respect to this Order and to others, as it is with the entire Church: there will always be in it some perfect and some defective, some strong and some weak. This is what was communicated to Brother Leo in a vision which he had when he was standing by the bed of St. Francis, who was in his last moments. In an ecstasy he saw many religious of the Order, who were endeavoring to pass a large and deep river, by a ford. Some, who had heavy burdens, were drowned, either on the brink, or farther on or in the middle, according as their burdens were heavier or lighter. This scene grieved him sorely, but he had the consolation of seeing others, who had no burdens, who got across the river quickly, and without danger. When he recovered from his ecstasy, the holy invalid asked him what he had seen; and Brother Leo having related his vision, Francis explained it thus: "The river is the world; the religious who bear burdens are those who, neglecting their profession, and violating the rules of evangelical poverty, have a longing for the things of the earth; and by that they are lost in this world, and will suffer just punishments in hell. Those who have passed through the river without danger, are those religious who, refusing to have any communication with the world, are contented with being poorly clad and fed, follow Jesus Christ naked, and have to carry only the yoke of the Lord, which is sweet, and the burden, which is light."[31]

To animate his brethren to perfection, he employed example, rather than precept. When he imposed punishments, if they appeared to him to be too severe, he took them also on himself. Having sent Brother Rufinus to preach at Assisi without his hood, because he had sought to be excused from preaching, he reflected on the severity of this order, and went himself to the church where Rufinus was preaching. The latter having left the pulpit to give it up to Francis, he began his discourse, and instilled into his audience so much compunction, that it was evident that God had blessed the obedience of the disciple and the example of the master.

This admirable preceptor taught no virtues which he did not himself

---

[31] Matt. 11: 30.

practice in an eminent degree; and as those which are exterior make the greatest impression, he practiced extreme austerity, in order that the others should imitate him. Having noticed, on a certain occasion, that some of his brethren had relaxed from the extreme poverty of their nourishment, he thus slyly reprimanded them: "My brethren may well believe that, with so infirm a body as mine is, I require better nourishment than what I get, but I am obliged to be their model in everything; for which reason I propose to give up every alleviation, and to cast aside, with disgust, everything resembling delicacy; to be satisfied with little in everything; to make use of those things only which are the commonest, vilest, and most conformable to strict poverty."

Being in a hermitage in some mountains, in mid-winter, when the weather was rigorously cold and severe, his companions prepared a habit for him, in which they lined the breast, to make it somewhat warmer for him, but he made them take this out, saying: "I am placed here to give example to others; my life must be their rule. I know that there is no harm in wearing a warmer habit in the state I am in, but I see many of our brethren who require it as much as I do, and who could not get it. I must therefore bear this poverty with them, and not differ from them in anything, lest it should be thought that I take greater care of myself than of the others. They will more willingly bear the privation of these wants, when they shall see that I voluntarily go without them." His three companions, the writers of his life, observed that he refused his body the most lawful indulgence, in order that his children should be ashamed of taking those which were less so; and that his maxim was, always to give instruction more by example than by discourse.

He recommended his brethren, also, to preach by example, and, farther on, we shall see some beautiful sentiments in his maxims, relative to preaching. Rodriguez, of the Society of Jesus, an excellent master of spiritual life, mentions,[32] on this subject, a lesson which our saint gave to one of his religious, which we give here, in the very words of the talented academician,[33] who translated the Practice of Christian Perfection, of the pious author. St. Francis, taking one day one of his religious with him, "Let us go and preach," said he; and thereupon he went out, and after having made a tour round the town, he returned to his convent "But, father," said his companion, "are we not going to preach?" "We have done so already," replied the saint. It was the religious reserve which they had used in walking through the streets, which he

---

[32] This anecdote has not been found among the authors of the Order, but it is very characteristic of St. Francis. Besides Wading, who made an exact inquiry into the actions and sayings of the blessed patriarch, admits that he has not collected all, and expresses his hopes to be able to make fresh discoveries. —Opusc. S. Franc., pp. 523, 524.

[33] This translation is by the Abbé Regnier des Marais, of the French Academy, whose writings on all subjects are very good, but who has excelled in this translation. The Practice of Christian Perfection, 2nd Part, 2d Treatise, on Modesty and on Silence, cap. I, page 120 in quarto; or page 155 of the third vol. of the new edition, with augmentations, in 6 vols. 18mo, which has been printed by Seguin the elder.

considered to be an excellent sermon for the whole town. And, in fact, a mortified and humble exterior leads the people to piety and a contempt of the world, and excites to compunction for sin, and to raising the heart and desires to heavenly objects. It is a mute exhortation, which has often more effect than the most eloquent and sublime sermons.

To example and precept, the holy patriarch added frequent and fervent prayers for the spiritual advancement of his children; well knowing that neither he who plants, nor he who waters, contributes to the fruit which the tree bears, but that the interior virtue which fructifies, comes from God.[34] In fine, in order not to be wanting in anything which might be in his power, when his infirmities absolutely prevented his watching over the conduct of his children, he unceasingly exhorted the superiors to fulfill this duty with exactness, and he enforced it by the following powerful motive: that, if one of the brethren should be lost by their fault, they would be accountable for him to Jesus Christ at the day of judgment. He gave them to understand by that, that, after having been the cause of the loss of souls, they had nothing more to expect from Him who had redeemed them with His blood. The superiors, indeed, should often meditate on what St. Paul says: "They who are established to govern, must watch as being to render an account for souls;"[35] that is to say, that their duty is to watch, that their ministry requires this vigilance; and these words which the Lord addresses to the pastors of Israel, by the mouth of the prophet Ezechiel: "If the just man shall turn away from his justice, and shall commit iniquity, he shall die, because you have not given him warning, but I will require his blood at your hand,"[36] are principally meant for the heads of companies, for those who lord it over others by dignities, by authority, if, by their bad example, by negligence, or by weakness, they introduce or uphold relaxation. What will they say when God shall demand of them, as of the city of Jerusalem, after all Judah had been transported to a foreign land: "Where is the flock that was given you, that beautiful flock? What will you say when He shall visit you? for you taught them to fight against you, and instructed them against your own head?"[37] "Let negligent pastors listen to this," exclaims St. Jerome, "those who, instead of protecting their flock, teach the devils to worry them cruelly."[38]

The ardent zeal which animated St. Francis in procuring the perfection of his brethren, comported in him with the tenderest feelings of charity; he always spoke to them mildly, affectionately, and impressively. If he censured them, it was not as a judge, but as a father, without irritation, without raising

---

[34] 1 Cor. 3: 7.

[35] Hebr. 13: 17.

[36] Ezech. 3: 20.

[37] Jerem. 13: 20, 21.

[38] S. Hier. in cap. xiii. Jerem.

his voice; with that tranquillity of manner, which showed at once the extent of his understanding, and the calmness of his heart. The apostolical authority with which he was invested, and the paternal affection he manifested, conciliated so entirely the veneration and love of his children, that they obeyed him punctually in all things, and they even met his wishes the moment they became aware of them. If any one of them was tempted to quit the Order, he used every effort to retain him; and, when the spirit of repentance brought such a one back, he received him most mercifully. One of these asked his leave to quit; the saint replied that he neither could nor ought to grant such a permission. He explained to him the misery to which he would expose himself, by taking such a step; that it would be to give up heaven for the sake of the world, and for man, Jesus Christ Himself, who had suffered so greatly for the love of us, insomuch that all the labors and sufferings in the religious state are insufficient to mark our gratitude for it. This religious was so violently tempted, that he remained inflexible in his bad purpose. He addressed himself to Cardinal Ugolino, the protector of the Order, and to the Pope: the one and the other having refused his request, he threw off his habit, and went away. He was not far from the convent, when a man whom he met said, in a tone of contempt, "Wretch, whither are you going?" "What business is it of yours whither I am going?" replied the other in a passion, "and why do you meddle in this?" The man showed his feet, his hands, and his side, in which there were wounds fresh and bleeding, and said, at the same time:

"You may judge from these wounds, which I suffered on the cross for love of you, how much I am concerned in what you are doing. After such a mark of love, and such goodness, do you carry your ingratitude so far as to forsake me for a perishable and worthless world?" The affrighted fugitive, penetrated by this scene, and by the words addressed to him, prostrated himself at the feet of Jesus Christ, and humbly asked forgiveness of his fault. He then went to seek for Francis, who received him with kindness, and desired him to keep before his eyes, as long as he lived, the signal favor done him by this marvelous apparition. He profited so effectively from it, that he became quite perfect, and died in the odor of sanctity.

Another, who wished to go into his own country, to see his parents, asked permission of his superiors for this purpose, and set out without having obtained it. He was not long on his way before he found himself overpowered with sleep. He sat down under a tree, and, in sleeping, he saw Francis, who, reprimanding him severely, urged him to return. As he obstinately refused, the saint gave him some sharp blows, which woke him, and he found the marks of them on his body. This correction having brought him to his senses, he returned to the convent, and related what had happened to him, and showed the proofs of it. The severity of the father, which had no other groundwork but kindness to the individual, was very salutary to his disciple.

The tenderness of his heart was most observable towards those who were weak, or suffering from temptations. He pitied their afflictions, as a mother would have done, and procured them all the consolation in his power. One of his disciples, having come to beg his prayers, that he might not succumb to a violent temptation against purity, "My son," he said, "do not lose confidence and be not discouraged, as if you were worse than others, because the devil tempts you; it is, on the contrary, for that very reason that you should believe yourself to be a servant of God. No one becomes perfect in his service, without having suffered these sorts of tribulations. If any one boasts of not having any to endure, he should know that God permits this, to assist his weakness; for God is faithful,[39] and will not suffer us to be tempted[40] above our strength. He seldom exposes to great struggles any but those who are of perfect virtue."

A spiritual and interior temptation of a more malignant character than a temptation of the flesh, had for a long time assailed another of his disciples, who threw himself at his feet, and opened the cause of his suffering to him. The good shepherd raised up his feeble sheep, took him in his arms, and knowing, by a supernatural revelation, the anguish he was in, said, compassionately, to him: "My son, be not afraid; this will only be the means of giving you an increase of grace." And then, raising his voice, and speaking authoritatively, he addressed these words to the demons: "Evil spirits, I forbid you making any further attack upon this brother of mine." The temptation immediately ceased, and the religious felt himself freed. Can it be thought surprising that God gives the power of commanding the vile spirits to such eminent charity?

---

[39] 1 Cor. 10: 13.

[40] This is grounded on a principle laid down by Saint Augustine and by the Council of Trent: "God commands nothing which is impossible; but, in commanding, He warns us to do all we can, and to ask for what we cannot do, and he grants His aid, in order to enable us to fulfill His command." From whence it follows that, since it is His will that we should resist temptations, He furnishes us, when necessary, the requisite aid for overcoming them, commanding us, also, not to presume on our own strength, to address ourselves to Him, and faithfully to respond to His grace. —S. August. De Nat. et Grat., cap. xlviii; Conc. Trid. sess. 6, cap. xi. In consequence of this orthodox doctrine, Pope Innocent X, by his Constitution of the last day of May, 1653, declared the following proposition, which is the first of five taken from the book of Jansenius, to be rash, impious, blasphemous, and heretical, and he anathematizes it: "Some commandments of God are impossible to the just, even when they are willing, and strive to accomplish them, according to the strength they have actually, and the grace by which these commands might be rendered possible to them." On the same principle, the Faculty of Theology, of Paris, in the General Assembly, held at the Sorbonne, on the last day of January, 1656, and confirmed on the first day of February, of the same year, declared the second proposition contained in the second letter written by Arnauld, doctor of Sorbonne, to a Duke and Peer of France, expressed in the following terms, to be rash, impious, blasphemous, heretical, and anathematized it: "Nevertheless, my Lord Duke, this great truth, grounded on the Gospel, and attested by the fathers of the church, who show us a just man, in the person of St. Peter, to whom grace, without which we are not equal to anything, had been wanting, at a time when it cannot be said he did not sin, has become sill at once the Calvinistic heresy, if we are to believe the disciples of Molina." This letter had been published at Paris, in Arnauld's name, in the year 1655.

There was one who had a very timid conscience, and was constantly agitated by scruples: Francis censured him in the first instance, paternally, for not treating with contempt, and with more courage and severity, the artifices which the devil made use of for his annoyance. He then ordered him not to take any notice of those things which caused him such heavy scruples, and not to plague himself by confessing them, and thus get rid of the confusion, which is the consequence of entering into those explanations to several confessors. "And, moreover," he added, "I believe that, unless some consent has been given, it is advantageous for the conscience that these vain suggestions should not be made the subject of confession, which I think in your case, in particular." The religious followed this salutary advice, and he found it of so much utility that, although he continued to have a timid conscience, he was no longer troubled with scruples.

Theologians and the masters of spiritual life have given the same remedy, in cases of scruples. If it was extensively used, there would not be so many persons, devotees and religious, to tire their confessors by useless declarations as to bad thoughts which come across them, and as to sins, which they imagine themselves to have committed, because they do not distinguish between involuntary thoughts and formal assent.

There are also other remedies which are given for the disease of scruples; but the most efficacious, in the opinion of St. Antoninus, Gerson, and other theologians, is for a scrupulous person to go always to the same confessor, and submit implicitly to his view, and practice literally whatever he prescribes, being fully convinced that he cannot sin while so doing. Without this obedience, the evil is incurable, and may have the worst consequences, both for the body and soul. Let such, then, imitate the Friar Minor, who obeyed St. Francis and was cured.

However, the advice the saint gave this Friar Minor must not be abused: that of not confessing vain suggestions, which bring on scruples; because this has relation to souls who are purely scrupulous, who, having a horror of sin, endeavor seriously to be virtuous. But as for those persons who are tepid and indifferent, who form for themselves a conscience favorable to the dispositions of their heart, and treat as scruples the confession of certain thoughts and certain actions, which are, at least, of a very equivocal nature; these persons have reason to fear that, what they consider as nothing, and do not mention in confession, may, perhaps, be what God reckons as sins, which ought to be confessed with great exactness.

St. Francis, being ill at Assisi, cured a spiritual wound of a more serious nature than that of a scruple. One of his children, named Ricer, of Bologna, provincial in the Marches of Ancona, a man of a very saintly life, had taken it into his head, at the suggestion of the devil, that the patriarch hated him, because he knew that he was to be damned, and he came to Assisi, in the hopes that this thought would be dissipated, if the saint should receive him kindly. The saint, who had a revelation as to the state of his mind, and of his arrival at Assisi, said to Brothers Massé and Leo, "Go and meet Brother Ricer, embrace him, and kiss him from me, and tell him that, among all my brethren in the world, I love him the most tenderly." They executed the commission given them, and Ricer found himself strengthened in his faith, and filled with joy, and thanked God for the happy success of his journey. As soon as he appeared, Francis, weak as he was, ran to him, and, embracing him, said, with paternal affection: "Ricer, my dear son, you are, among all our brethren, he whom I love from the bottom of my heart;" and, after having made the sign of the cross upon his forehead, he gave him several kisses, and then added "Ricer, my dear child, this temptation was visited upon you for your greater good. But if you do not choose to be a gainer at this price, you will henceforward suffer no more from this temptation, nor from any other;" and, from that time, he never had another.

The authors who mention this anecdote, say that Ricer was strengthened in his faith at the moment that the companions embraced him from St. Francis, because the temptation which induced him to think he was to be damned, attacked his faith. 1. Faith teaches us[41] that neither reprobation nor predestination can be known, except by revelation: now, there was no solid ground for believing that the saint had received any communication from heaven, relative to Ricer. 2. The Church teaches us[42] that, according to Catholic faith, all those who are baptized, must believe that Jesus Christ gives them such aid as is necessary for the accomplishment of all that is requisite for salvation, if they are willing to labor faithfully for its attainment; consequently, that He died for them,[43] and that God desires that they should be saved. 3. St. Augustine[44] lays it down as certain, that God does not abandon those who are once justified by His grace, if He be not first abandoned; and the Council of Trent[45] has adopted the same truth, using the very words of the holy doctor.

This, then, is sufficient to allay the anxiety of such of the faithful whose minds may be made uneasy on the subject of predestination, in consequence of certain passages of the Holy Scriptures, of some expressions of the holy fathers, and of some theological opinions. In fact, since it is clearly revealed,

---

[41] Eccles. 9: 1.

[42] These words are found in the twenty-fifth chapter of the Second Council of Orange, which has been received by the whole Church.

[43] The Abbé Tournely proves clearly from texts of the Holy Scripture, from the Councils which have condemned the predestinarian heretics, from the doctrine of the Council of Trent, from the Constitutions of Popes Innocent X and Alexander VII, who condemned the fifth proposition of Jansenius as impious and heretical, from the authority of the holy fathers, and particularly from that of Saint Augustine, that every faithful is bound to believe that God desires his salvation, and that Jesus Christ died for him. Praelect. Theol. de Deo, tom. I, quaest. 17, art. 10, concl. 2, pag. 321, et seq.

[44] S. Aug. de Nat. and Grat., cap. xxv., et alibi.

[45] Conc. Trid., sess. 6, cap. ii.

and the Church obliges us to believe, that Jesus Christ died for us; that God desires our salvation; that He gives us the means to work this out, and that He is not the first to abandon us, we must absolutely conclude, in the first place, that whatsoever may be in the Scriptures apparently opposed to these truths, does not counteract them, but may be reconciled to them, because truths cannot be in opposition to each other. In the second place, the holy fathers, on those points on which the Church receives their testimony as the channel of tradition, can have said nothing contravening these truths. In the third place, the Church only allows in the schools diversities of opinion on the subject of the mystery of predestination, inasmuch as they are in accordance with these same truths, to which we must always recur.

Theological systems which should depart from these truths, would no longer be simply systems, but confirmed heresies, which the Church would condemn, as it has already condemned them. If there are some opinions in the Catholic schools which it seems difficult to understand, and the explanations of which are unsatisfactory, it must be attributed to the weakness of the human mind, which must speak very imperfectly of what God has not revealed, and as to which we must exclaim with St. Paul: "O, the depth of the riches of the wisdom and of the knowledge of God!"[46] We must not, however, blame the theologians, for they are in some measure compelled by the blasphemies of the heretics, "to elevate themselves to what is inaccessible, to explain what is ineffable, and to do what is not permitted to be done."[47] These are the words of St. Hilary, writing on the mystery of the Most Holy Trinity, against the Arians.

After all that St. Augustine had written against the Pelagians, and the Semi-Pelagians, he addressed the faithful in these consoling words: "You must daily ask the Father of Light, from whom comes every good and perfect gift,[48] the grace of perseverance in His obedience, and have confidence that, in so doing, you will obtain His predestination; for He directs you to place your hopes in Him."[49]

God has hidden from us the mystery of predestination, in order to humble us, and to compel us to perpetual watchfulness; and this is the reason why the Council of Trent says,[50] that no one can be perfectly sure of persevering to the end, and of being of the number of the predestined; but it adds, in the idea of St. Paul,[51] that all should entertain a firm reliance on the assistance of God, who will complete and make perfect the good work He has begun, giving them

---

[46] Rom. 11: 33.

[47] S. Hilary de Trin., lib. ii., n. 2.

[48] James 1: 17.

[49] S. Augus. de Dono Persev., cap. xxxii., n. 62.

[50] Conc. Trid., sess. 6, cap. xii., xiii.

[51] Phil. 1: 6.

the will and means to put it in force, unless they themselves be wanting to His grace. Now, as we have every reason to fear this being wanting, the same Council cautions us, according to the words of the apostles, and of St. Augustine,[52] to work out our own salvation with fear and trembling; because, not having it in our power either to will or to do good for heaven, unless by the aid of grace, we must be fearful of becoming unworthy of it, by our negligence or by our pride; and, moreover, because God may justly call us out of this world as soon as we may have committed a mortal sin. On the part of God, there is great confidence of our salvation; on our part, great room for fear: the one and the other should induce the practice recommended by St. Peter: "Wherefore, brethren, labor the more, that by good works you may make your calling and election sure, for, doing these things, you shall not sin at any time;"[53] that is to say, you will not fall into any considerable faults, which shall cause you to fall from your vocation, and from your election.

May it please the Divine mercy that the temptation of a disciple of St. Francis, on this head, may serve to instruct and console such pious persons who are suffering under similar temptations and to disabuse those who, misconceiving the sense of the Scriptures, of the fathers, and of theologians, are afraid that God does not sincerely wish to save them, will not afford them the means, and may even abandon them, although they may make every exertion to serve Him: which feelings are not only heretical and impious, but are the source of licentiousness, and the principle of despair.

---

[52] Phil. 2: 12, 13; S. Aug. de Nat. et Grat., cap. xxvii., n. 31, et cap. xxxii., n. 36; De Corrept. et Grat., cap. ix., n 24.

[53] 2 Peter 1: 10.

CHAPTER V
THE SPIRITUAL GIFTS OF ST. FRANCIS

His tender charity towards his brethren.—His discretion and wisdom in the government of the Order—His opinion on the necessary qualities of the general and provincial of the Order— His writing—His supernatural and acquired knowledge—His style—The efficacy of his words—His supernatural and miraculous gifts—He drives away devils—Brings the dead to life—Heals the sick—Has the gift of prophecy and discernment of spirits.

HE HOLY PATRIARCH had so tender a love for his brethren, that he could not bear that a shade of sorrowfulness should pass over their minds, lest they should lose their spiritual joy. "My dear brethren," he said to them, "entertain interiorly and exteriorly the holy joy which God gives. When His servants seek to obtain and preserve this spiritual joy, which has its source in purity of heart, in the fervor of prayer, and in other virtuous practices, the devils can do them no injury; and they say: 'We can do no injury to these servants of God; we have no entry to them; they are always joyful, whether in tribulation or prosperity.' But they are highly gratified when they can deprive them of this happy temper of mind, or, at least, lessen its intensity; because, if they can succeed in instilling any of their own venom into them, they will soon turn what has only the breadth of a hair into a beam, by adding something by little and little, unless we endeavor to destroy their work by the virtue of prayer, of contrition, of confession, and satisfaction. For this reason, my brethren, since spiritual joy comes from purity of conscience and the frequent exercise of fervent prayer, labor principally to acquire these two blessings, in order that you should possess it; I am very anxious to see it in you, and to feel it in myself. It is for the devil and his satellites to be sorrowful; but as to us, we can always rejoice in the Lord."

Although the holy man had occasionally reason to be sorrowful, in consequence of the temptations to which he was exposed, or from the fear of the pains of hell, arising from the remembrance of his sins, yet he was ever joyful. He was one day asked the reason of this, and he gave this answer: "My sins sometimes, indeed, make me very sorrowful,[1] and Satan would wish to imprint this sadness on me, in order to make me fall into slothfulness and weariness; but when that occurs, I look on my companion: the spiritual joy I

---

[1] This, then, must have been before God had revealed to him that his sins had been entirely remitted, and that he would enjoy eternal life. At least, the sorrow which they caused him after these two revelations, could not have been accompanied by any fears of the pains of hell.

see in him, renews mine, and the temptation passes off. My joy is a torment to the devils, for they envy me the favors I receive from God. I know and see that, when they cannot injure me by making me sorrowful, they endeavor to strip their spiritual joy from my companions, and, if they cannot succeed either with them or with me, they retire in confusion."

We must notice, in this answer of the holy father, two sorts of sorrow: the one arising from the anguish caused by sin, of which St. Paul says, that "it is according to God, and works penance unto salvation."[2] This does not do away with spiritual joy; on the contrary, it produces it: nothing is sweeter, or more consoling, than the tears shed from the impulse of sincere contrition.

The other sorrow is a depression of spirits, brought about by the devil, who endeavors to render us tepid and sluggish, to give us a disgust for pious exercises, and to induce us to give them up. A good conscience causes spiritual joy. No one has truly cause to rejoice, but he who is well with God faithful to His law, and submissive to His will. A tranquil mind, free and disengaged from the tyranny of the passions, is, in the opinion of Wisdom, a continual feast.[3] It is true happiness: "For a happy life is nothing more," says St. Augustine,[4] "than the joy which is found in truth; that is, in God, who is truth, the sweet light of our souls, our salvation and our repose." Therefore David[5] excites the just of Israel to manifest their joy, and St. Paul said to the Christians:[6] "Rejoice always in the Lord; I say again, rejoice. What constitutes the kingdom of God is the justice, peace, and joy, which come from the Holy Spirit."

This disposition of the heart enables it to resist the evil spirit, according to the words of Ezra to the Jewish people: "The joy of the Lord is our strength."[7] What can the evil spirit do against a soul whose sole pleasure is to serve God, who has no other solace than to love and praise Him? There is, moreover, nothing which makes so great an impression on the people of the world, as witnessing the interior contentment of a truly good man, which is seen in the serenity of his countenance. This is, according to St. Augustine, what compels them to admit that they themselves have not true joy, but that is reserved for God's servants.[8] What could have been said of St. Francis and his brethren, ever happy and joyous, though worn down by austerities?

It was not alone by the ardor of his zeal, and the tenderness of his affection, that the holy founder led on his brethren, but by a wonderful discretion and prudence in the government of his Order. Although he used

---

[2] 2 Cor. 7: 10.

[3] Prov. 15: 15.

[4] St. Aug., Conf., lib. 10, cap. xxiii.

[5] Psalm 31 (32): 14, et alibi, passim. Esdr. 8: 10.

[6] Phil. 4: 4; Rom. 14: 17.

[7] Esdr. 8: 10.

[8] S Aug. in Psalm. XCVII, n. 19.

every endeavor to induce his religious to live austerely, he, nevertheless, recommended them to be guided by moderation; and he did not countenance indiscreet penances.

Brother Sylvester, the first priest in his Order, having fallen into an illness of languor, brought on by excess in his mortifications, had a wish to eat some grapes: Francis, having been informed of it, hastened to procure him this relief. He took him, as well as he could, into the vineyard of one of his friends, which was near the convent, and, having made him sit down near a plant of vine, he blessed it, and ordered him to eat the grapes, and ate some with him. As soon as the sick man had eaten of them, he found himself perfectly cured, and he frequently afterwards related the circumstance to his brethren, with tears in his eyes, as a proof of the love the holy father bore to his children; it was, also, an effect of his discretion, for, disapproving of Sylvester's excessive austerities, he chose that he should take this sort of remedy, which nature seemed to call for, and it pleased God to render this the subject of a miracle.

This prudent and charitable father came to know, one night, that one of his children who had fasted too rigidly, could not take repose, in consequence of the hunger which oppressed him. Not to leave him in so dangerous a state, he sent for him, offered him some bread, and pressed him to eat of it, eating some himself first, to give him confidence. The religious got over the shyness he at first felt, and took the nourishment he so greatly required, being well pleased to have been relieved from the peril his life was in, by the prudence and kindness of the saint, and to see so edifying an example. In the morning, Francis assembled his brethren, and having told them what had occurred in the night, "Brethren," he said, "take a precedent from this, not as to what I ate, but that I had recourse to what was charitable." Then he pointed out to them that virtue should always have discretion for its rule and for its guide; not that discretion which the flesh inspires, but that which has been taught by Jesus Christ, whose most holy life is the finished model of all perfection.

"Let each man," he continued, "have regard to his constitution. If some of you are strong enough to support life well, while eating very little, I do not wish, on that account, that one who requires more nourishment, shall imitate them in this respect: such a one might give his body what is necessary for it; for, as in eating we are obliged to avoid whatever is superfluous, which is hurtful to the body and soul, so also we must guard against excessive abstinence, and the more so because the Lord requires mercy rather than sacrifice. This is what God says by the Prophet Hosea,[9] which means that He prefers the practice of works of mercy to our neighbor, to the exterior exercise of religion, and that this worship which must be rendered Him, is not pleasing to Him without mercy."

Now, as we are commanded to love our neighbor with a love of charity, St.

---

[9] Hosea 6: 6.

Thomas teaches us, as does St. Augustine,[10] that the same love obliges us to have a similar regard for our own body; from whence it follows that, this charity not being found in immoderate abstinence, God does not approve of the sacrifice. To this we may add, that it is sometimes the devil who instigates a person to undertake immoderate fasting, in order to render that person incapable of spiritual exercises, and for other evil intentions.

The holy founder cautioned his brethren to avoid excess in fasting, even more than excess in eating, because he knew that they were all animated by the spirit of mortification. Their fervor was so great that, in fasting very rigorously, they at the same time wore iron girdles, coats of mail, coarse hair-shirts, and took severe disciplines, which brought on frequent illnesses. For this reason he often recommended discretion to them. "My brethren," he said, "if a servant of God gives his body what is reasonable for its nourishment and for its repose, and that the body is nevertheless sluggish, lazy, sleepy at prayer, in watchings, and other good works, it must, then, be chastised, and treated as a horse that refuses to work, or an ass that won't go on, although they are well fed. But, if the body is deprived of its real wants, it is disabled from bearing the yoke of penance, and performing the functions required by the soul; it has, then, every right to complain."

We shall, perhaps, be surprised that St. Francis, who preaches discretion so admirably to his brethren, should have carried his own austerities to excess; but we must bear in mind that he was a man guided in all things by the Holy Spirit, in whom God was pleased to show the abundant riches of His grace, and whose prodigious penitential exercises were to draw down an abundance of mercy on sinners. Thus, what appeared excessive in his mortifications, arose from his perfect fidelity to the extraordinary impulse he received from above; and this was true prudence.

Fervent persons are occasionally found who would wish to imitate the fastings and other austerities of the saints, but this is presumption, unless they are called thereto by God, and that this vocation has been well sounded and approved by legitimate authority. The general and safe maxim, in cases of austerities, is not to undertake anything extraordinary, without the consent of superiors and confessors. Before granting any permission of this nature, the constitution and character of the person must be carefully examined, and inquiry minutely made whether the applicant practices regularly the ordinary mortifications, and if he is as zealous in controlling his passions, and acquiring the virtues requisite in his station, as for the maceration of his body; for it is often found that those who solicit extraordinary penances, neglect those which are ordinary and common, and who, in mortifying their bodies, do not take sufficient pains to purify their hearts, to become humble, obedient, mild, and charitable.

---

[10] S. Aug. de Doct. Christ., lib. I, cap. xxvi; S. Thom. 2a, 2ae. quest. 25, art. 5.

The lessons which St. Francis gave on the subject of discretion, are of no great use in the world. There, it is rather requisite to repeat these words of our Savior: "Be careful of yourselves, lest your hearts be weighed down by intemperance;"[11] and those of St. Paul: "Present your bodies a living sacrifice, holy, pleasing to God."[12] Those even who endeavor to mortify themselves, often experience the truth of what the apostle says: "No man ever hated his own flesh, but nourishes it, and takes care of it."[13]

St. Augustine[14] found it very difficult to satisfy the wants of the body, without giving somewhat unto sensuality; and he says that he had daily combats with temptations of that kind. St. Bernard[15] admits that we owe it to our body to preserve it in health; but he adds that, on the score of health, sensuality lays dangerous snares for us, and that in so artful and subtle a manner, that it is difficult for us to preserve ourselves from them, and sometimes even to perceive them. We must, therefore, as St. Francis remarks, not have that false and dangerous discretion which is inspired by the flesh, and flatters the senses.

It may not, perhaps, be believed that the holy patriarch carried his discretion and condescension even to the buildings and the habits, he who advocated extreme poverty on these two articles. He had carefully recommended to his brethren to build only small, low houses, surrounded only by hedges, in remote and solitary situations; but, as his own companions tell us, he admitted that in towns, and near towns, it was proper to act otherwise; that, in consequence of the number of religious who were there for the service of the faithful, it was necessary to have the convent surrounded by walls.

The multiplicity of vestments greatly displeased him; he could not bear stuffs that were soft and downy; he said[16] that coarseness and roughness in their habits were necessary for his Institute, and for preaching repentance. Nevertheless, besides allowing two tunics by the rule, and giving permission to wear shoes in cases of necessity, he enjoins the ministers to provide carefully for the clothing of the other brethren, as they may deem it requisite, taking into consideration the time and place, and cold countries, and, for this purpose, to have recourse to their spiritual friends; that is, to say, as has been already remarked, to persons in good circumstances, friends of the Institute, whom they may solicit to pay for the material which they may only receive as an alms. This was a measure to which he was greatly adverse, because of the dislike he had to money in any shape, and he only permitted it for the wants of

---

[11] Luke 21: 24.

[12] Rom. 12: 1.

[13] Ephes. 5: 29.

[14] S. August. Confess., lib. 10, cap. xxxi.

[15] S. Bern, de Divin. serm. 6, n. 21.

[16] Reg. Fratr. Min., cap. ii. et iv.

the sick, and the clothing of the brethren; and this is a proof of his discretion, which is shown even in the ardent love he had for poverty It would be impossible to form a more correct idea of it than from this.

His companions also say that he allowed those who required it, to wear a softer and warmer tunic; on this sole condition, however, that the outward garment should be very poor, to keep up the spirit of humility, by the contempt the world entertains for such as are poorly clothed. Finally, the same authors testify that, although he was very austere from the moment of his conversion to his death, with a constitution very delicate and weak, yet he prudently moderated the austerities of his brethren; and that many things which he rigidly refused himself, he allowed to the others, from discretion and from charity. This, indeed, is characteristic in the saints: severe and inflexible to themselves, they spared their neighbors, and were indulgent in their regard; while hypocrites, such as the Pharisees, and certain heretics, who resemble them,[17] put heavy burdens on the shoulders of others, which they are unable to carry; overwhelm with austerities those whom they direct, often for the most trifling faults, while they themselves live in comfort and at their ease.

The discretion of St. Francis was apparent in every part of his conduct. Bernard de Besse, one of the writers of his life, and secretary to St. Bonaventure, says that he never spoke to his brethren but in terms of moderation and mildness; that he compassionated the weak, and encouraged the young in the practice of virtue; that he had great respect for old age; that whatever faults a priest might commit, he never reprimanded him but in private; in fine, that he had proper consideration for all those whose birth, merit, or dignity required it.

Brother Guy, who was beatified by the Holy See, and of whom we have before spoken, begged the saint to allow him to build a cell in the fissure of a rock which was opposite to the convent of Celles, near Cortona, in order that he might live there in great solitude, and give himself up to contemplation. Francis, who knew that Guy, although he was only in the novitiate, had the virtue of the ancients, and would raise himself up to an eminent degree of sanctity, permitted him this peculiar retreat, but upon this condition, that it was not to prevent him from attending all the offices said by the community, in order to preserve the uniformity of the observance, and to obviate the illusion which might mix itself up with unusual practices. This was also what the saint himself practiced; he quitted regularly his contemplation, to join in singing the praise of God in community.

One of the brethren asked him, in his last illness, why he had given up the government of the community, and why he allowed many things contrary to what he had taught his first companions. The question was displeasing to him, but he gave this answer:

---

[17] Matt. 23: 4.

"Some are surprised that I do not correct the defects which exist in the Order, and they wish to know the reason of it. May God pardon them, for they oppose me; they pretend to put a task on me which concerns me no longer. As long as I was the superior of my brethren, and that they continued firm in their vocation, I was sufficient for them by my example, by my exhortations, and by my minute attentions, although, from the beginning of my conversion, I was very weak. But when I saw that God had permitted them to increase in number, and that there were some whose fervor diminished, and who began to pursue other ways, without paying attention to my example or to the engagements they had entered into, I gave up the guidance of the Order to God and to the ministers.

"At the general chapter, I pleaded my infirmities, as the motive of renunciation; however, if all my brethren had wished to conform to my views, and had also desired, for their benefit and consolation, not to have any other superior than myself until my death, I also would have wished it, on account of the advantage it would have been to them and to me. It, likewise, would give me so much pleasure that, even in the bed to which illness would have confined me, I would have applied myself to everything which could have been satisfactory to them: there is no great trouble in guiding inferiors who are very submissive. The post of superior is an employment wholly spiritual, which consists, as to what respects evil, in preventing it, or in correcting it by example and by cautioning. If these be insufficient, I will not have recourse to measures of rigor, as the powers of the world. I have, nevertheless, that firm confidence in God, that He who punishes in this world and in the next, by invisible enemies, will make use of them to punish lukewarm and sluggish brethren: inasmuch as those who execute the Divine justice, will stir up worldlings to reproach them with their lukewarmness, and induce them, by the shame and confusion they will be made to feel, to return to their duty. As to myself, I shall not cease, to my last breath, to instruct them by my example, to advance in the path the Lord has pointed out to me, as I have already taught them by my actions and by my words. If they do not profit by this, they are inexcusable, and I shall no longer have to give an account of their conduct to God."

The complaints of the saint regarded Elias, and some of the provincial ministers, who followed his spirit of relaxation in what regarded poverty. The remedy which it seemed feasible to adopt for the evil, was to depose Elias, and the ministers who were his adherents; but, besides that the holy patriarch was too infirm to have it in his power to act, God had revealed to him that he was to place Elias as Vicar-General, and leave him in that situation. It was a surprising and impenetrable decree of Providence, but one which His servant was bound to adore, and act up to. In this situation, prudence did not permit him to do more than caution, exhort, threaten, give good example, and implore the aid of heaven.

He said most truly, that worldlings are incited, by invisible enemies, to censure religious for their relaxations. In fact, generally speaking, they are the most worldly who speak with greatest bitterness of the faults of religious persons, and we may well imagine that it is at the instigation of the devil; for they only speak of these faults to spread them, and to disparage a state of holiness, which, of itself, bears witness to the irregularity of a worldly life. They attribute to the whole Order whatever they deem blamable in any one of its members; they magnify everything, and often fancy evil where none exists. The broachers of new opinions do the same, in respect to the religious, who expose and controvert their unsound doctrine, as the Friars Minors have done for the last six hundred years, and still do on all occasions. But what is only sheer malice in the devil, in worldlings and in heretic must be considered, in the dispositions of Divine Providence, as a means of making known to all religious that motives of decorum, of honor, and of edification, are joined to those of the love of God, and of their own salvation, to bind them faithfully to fulfill the duties of their state of life.

The earliest authors who wrote the life of St. Francis, have recorded one of his answers, which shows to what a degree he possessed the art of governing. They spoke to him one day of some of the provincial ministers, who, animated with the spirit of Brother Elias, arrogated to themselves the government of the provinces, as a sort of hereditary tenure, and pretended to perpetuate themselves therein, so that they could not be brought back to the condition of an inferior, without giving them great offense, and putting it in their power to give the community great trouble. "Let them live as they like," the saint replied, angrily; "a time will come when they will repent it: the loss of some is a lesser evil than the loss of many. If it was attempted to depose these ministers, they would excite great disturbance, and that would be a scandal to the good religious, who now obey simply and peaceably."

Deposition is certainly what these provincials deserved, since, according to the maxims of the holy fathers, it is sufficient to take steps to attain ecclesiastical dignities, and even merely to wish for them, to be rendered unworthy to hold them. Moreover, to pretend to hold an office of right, and to keep it in perpetuity; to take measures for always being in command, and never obeying, in a profession which is profoundly humble, is something absolutely monstrous. We must, nevertheless, admit that St. Francis was extremely prudent in not deposing these ambitious ministers, in order to avoid trouble and scandal. St. Augustine[18] says that we should put up with certain evils, when they can only be remedied by a greater evil; as in the case of the husbandman, who would not permit the tares to be eradicated, lest in so doing the wheat should be injured. Such is the course pursued by superior minds, who follow the promptings of prudence, and are guided by the principles of

---

[18] S. August, contra Epist. Parmen., lib. iii., cap. ii., n.13, et seq. et alibi. Matt. xiii., 29.

good government. Little minds, who are zealous, and are in possession of authority, wish, at any cost, to do away with everything that is evil; and, not satisfied with what is good, they insist upon having something better, without reflecting that amongst men there are inevitable evils which must be submitted to patiently, and that sometimes, by indiscreetly insisting upon having what is better, the good itself is destroyed.

These words of St. Francis on the governing provincials are very remarkable: "Let them live as they like; a time will come when they will repent of so doing;" as if he had said: "I let them do this, because I cannot hinder them, and I have no hopes of converting them. They follow now the desires of their heart, but they will one day appear before God, and the sentence which will be passed upon them will be followed by a bitter, but fruitless, repentance." In fact, the pride which gives birth to ambition is one of those vices of the mind of which the prophet says, that "it ascends continually;"[19] and St. Thomas says that it removes us extremely from God. This is the reason why the heretical innovators, who only dogmatize through pride, are seldom converted. The conversion of the ambitious is equally rare. Whenever pride induces them to love dignities and honors, they never cease from longing for them, to seek for them, and to flatter themselves that they are more deserving of them than any others, to procure them and retain them till their last moments. Now, if the Holy Spirit assures us that, in general, "a more severe judgment shall be for them that rule; that to him who is little, mercy is granted, but that the mighty shall be mightily tormented;"[20] what a dreadful consideration is not this, in particular for those who acquire command through ambition, to whom, what the Council of Trent says as to churches which are governed by bishops: "They are onerous places, capable of making angels tremble."[21] It would be very useless to repeat in hell with those sinners of whom the wise man speaks: "In what has our pride served us? All has passed over as a shadow."[22]

The holy patriarch, being on his death-bed, was asked his opinion as to the qualifications which his successor ought to have, and he explained himself as follows:

"My dear children, I see no one who has all these qualifications requisite for being the leader of so large an army, and pastor of so numerous and widely spread a flock. But I will draw a portrait, from which you will see what sort of a person such a chief and such a pastor should be.

"He should be a man of serious character, very discreet, of good repute; exempt from any particular attachments, lest the friendships he might have for

---

[19] Psalm 73 (74): 24; 2a 2ae. quest. 73, art. 5.

[20] Sap. 6: 6 et 7.

[21] Conc. Trid., sess. 6, cap. 1., de Reform.

[22] Sap. 5: 8 et 9.

some might give scandal to others. A man of prayer, devoted to this holy exercise, yet who so distributes his time, that he may have certain hours for himself, and others for his flock. In the early morning he should offer up the holy sacrifice of the Mass, and employ a considerable portion of time in soliciting the protection of the Almighty for himself and for his flock, with the deepest sentiments of piety. After his prayers, let him receive all persons, and answer for all things, but let him make no distinction of persons, and let him pay as much attention to the most simple, as to the learned and wise. If he himself has the gift of knowledge, let him, nevertheless, be simple in his conduct, manifesting much patience and humility; let him encourage these virtues in others, as well as in himself; let him continually exercise himself in them, and lead his brethren to their practice, more by his example than by discourse.

"As to what concerns money, let him hold it in execration, for there is nothing that can sooner introduce corruption into our Order. Never let him make a bad use of any purse, he who is the head, and should be the model to others. Let him be satisfied with one habit for himself, with one book in which he may register the affairs of the Order, with one inkstand, and a seal to affix to the documents he may have to send out. He must not be anxious to collect many books, lest, in giving up too much time to reading, he should take too much from the duties of his office.

"Let his heart be full of compassion for the afflicted; let him afford them every consolation, since he is their last resource: if he did not hit on some remedy for their miseries, weakness might throw them into despair. If he meets with insolent and unruly spirits, let him humble himself, in order to soften them; and to gain their souls to Jesus Christ, let him give up some of his rights. The bowels of his compassion should be opened for such as have left the Order, as for sheep that have strayed, without ever refusing to treat them with mercy, considering that the temptations which have led to such falls must have been very great, and that if God were to permit him to be similarly attacked, he might himself fall down a still greater precipice.

"I should also wish that all the religious should honor the general, as holding the place of Jesus Christ in their regard, and that they provide for all he may require, according to the decorum of our Institution. But he must not take pleasure in being so respected, nor care for the honors which may be rendered him, no more than for the insults which may be offered him; so that the honors shall not make any change in his character, unless, perhaps, for the better. In case his infirmities should require more nourishing food than the rest of the community, let him not take it in private, but publicly, that the others may have no scruple of having recourse to similar indulgence, when their infirmities may require it.

"His principal employment is to penetrate into the secret of hearts, and to extract the truth from its most hidden recesses. In the first place, he must look with a suspicious eye on all accusations, principally when those who bring those accusations forward are great talkers; he must not be eager in listening to them much less in believing them, unless, after careful investigation, it shall be found that the accuser has spoken truth. The strength of his mind should be such, that no desire to retain the place he fills should induce him to violate the rules of firm and inflexible justice, nor even to relax them in any degree; but he must so order his decision, that excessive rigor shall not cause the loss of any souls, nor useless lenity, nor irresolute indulgence encourage tepidity, or enervate discipline; thus, that he may make himself feared by all, and be beloved by those who fear him. All this must make him feel that his office is even more burdensome to him than honorable.

"I also am desirous that the general may have very virtuous companions, enemies of all sensible pleasures, courageous in all difficulties, and full of compassion for those who have fallen into any errors. They should love all the others equally, nor receive anything for their labor but what is absolutely necessary to support life, not longing for anything but the glory of God, the good of the Order, merit for their own souls, perfection and salvation for their brethren. They should be complaisant and obliging, and should receive with a holy joy all those who come to them, so that by purity and simplicity they may exhibit in their persons the model of evangelical observance, of which they make profession in the Rule of the Order. Such, then, should be the general and his companions."

What they had asked the saint as to the general, gave him an opportunity of stating his wishes as to the provincials. "My brethren," he said, "it is my will that the provincials should be mild and kind, even to the lowest; and that they should have so much benevolence, that those who have fallen into faults should have no hesitation or fear in casting themselves on their charity. I should also wish them to be very reserved as to giving orders, easy in pardoning offenses, and more inclined to lend their aid to sinners than to load them with censure; that they should be declared enemies to vice, but that they should be as physicians to the vicious. In fine, I would wish them to be such, that their lives should be to the others a true image of regular discipline. But I require, also, that all the others should have for them great respect and affection, as for those who bear the weight, and anxieties, and labor of the community, believing them to be worthy of a great reward before God, if they govern on these principles."

Do we not see herein the exalted ideas which St. Francis entertained of every sort of perfection; the great knowledge he had of the human heart, of morality, and government? The penetration, solidity, and even the delicacy of his mind, his discretion and his consummate prudence, in the midst of evangelical purity? We might imagine that he had read all that the holy fathers, and St. Gregory in particular, had written so forcibly on Christian morality. The portraits he puts before us may serve as lessons to all who have authority in the Church. There is no regular superior who will not find in it an excellent rule of conduct, and those of the Friars Minors must consider it as a special favor that God had been pleased to permit them to be instructed in their obligations by their most holy patriarch himself. We should be glad to put on record all his other instructions, which are not less sound, nor less spiritual; but we must confine ourselves to those which he gave on learning and on preaching, with the last letter he addressed to the religious of his Order, shortly before his death.

St. Bonaventure says that some of his religious asked him one day if he thought it proper that such persons as were already learned, when they were admitted into the Order, should continue to study the Holy Scriptures? To which he replied: "This is very pleasing to me, provided they follow the example of Jesus Christ, whom we find to have prayed more than He seems to have read, and do not neglect the exercise of prayer; and provided they do not study so much to learn what they are to speak, as to practice what they have learnt, and to induce others to practice it also. I wish my brethren to be disciples of the Gospel, and that they should progress in the knowledge of truth, at the same time that they increase in simple-mindedness, thus joining, according to the method of our Divine Master, the simplicity of the dove to the prudence of serpents."[23]

A novice, to whom the Vicar-General had allowed the particular use of a Psalter, came to solicit Francis' confirmation of this permission, and this is the reply he got: "Charlemagne, Orlando, and other great captains, rendered themselves illustrious by their exploits; the martyrs are celebrated in the Church by their sufferings and death; but there are others who aspire to glory by the sole reading of the feats of these persons." The saint intended to give him to understand that no one is estimable unless by his actions and conduct, and that there is nothing more vain than a reputation grounded on fruitless science.

The novice, who did not rightly understand the drift of the answer he had received, came back, some days after, to ask again for the Psalter, when Francis said to him: "When this shall have been granted to you, you will next want a Breviary, and then other books; then you will ascend the pulpit as a great doctor, and you will imperiously require to be served by your companions." His zeal excited him. He took some ashes, and, rubbing the novice's forehead with them, he repeated several times, with great animation: "A Psalter for me! a Psalter for me!" and, for the instruction of the young man, who was in great astonishment, he added: "My brother, I also was tempted as you are, on the subject of books. In order to know the will of God, I had recourse to prayer, and I opened the book of the Holy Gospels, in which I found this sentence: 'To you it is given to know the mystery of the kingdom of God; but to the rest in

---

[23] Matt. 10: 16.

parables'."[24] The application he made of this was, that the truths of the Gospel are better known by those who practice them, than by those who know them, and do not put them in practice. From thence the two beautiful maxims which were familiar to him: A man has no knowledge or eloquence, but inasmuch as he acts up to what he knows and says. We see many who take great pains to acquire the other sciences, but happy is he who is satisfied with knowing Jesus Christ crucified.

Doubtless the holy patriarch wished his brethren to have Psalters and Breviaries, since they were obliged to say the Divine Office. He knew, also, that books were necessary for them, to enable them, by study, to be enabled to instruct their neighbors, according as their vocation required, and he himself read the Scriptures. But he did not approve that any one should have a book for his own peculiar use, either fearing that an idea of having property in it should be mixed up with it, or because he remarked too great a desire for knowledge, of which he feared that the consequences might be in opposition to simplicity, humility, and devotion.

The study which is entered upon more through vanity than piety, and less to gain souls to God than to gain for themselves the praise of man, was his abhorrence. He said of those whose desire for learning was out of curiosity: "In the day of tribulation, they will find nothing in their hands. It would be better that they should labor now to improve themselves in virtue, in order to have the Lord on their side at that time; for the time will come, when books will be thrown aside as useless. I do not choose that my brethren shall be curious in learning and books; what I wish is, that they be well grounded in humility, simplicity, prayer, and poverty, our mistress. It is the only sure way of their salvation, and for the edification of their neighbor, because they are called to imitate Jesus Christ, who followed and pointed out this path. Many will forsake this path, on pretense of edifying other men by their knowledge; and it will turn out that understanding the Scriptures, by which alone they fancied themselves filled with fight, devotion, and the love of God, will be the cause of their remaining cold and empty. Thus, in consequence of having, in pursuit of vain and useless literature, lost the time which ought to have been given to living according to the spirit of the state they had embraced, they will not have it in their power to return to their primitive vocation."

St. Francis looked upon the ministry of preaching as the most agreeable sacrifice which could be offered to the Father of Mercies; this is also the grand idea which St. Paul entertains of it,[25] when he says: "God has given me the grace that I should be the minister of Jesus Christ among the Gentiles, sanctifying the Gospel of God, that the oblation of the Gentiles may be made

---

[24] Luke, 8: 10.

[25] Rom. 15: 16.

acceptable, and sanctified by the Holy Spirit." St. Chrysostom[26] concludes from that, that preaching is a sacrifice; that the preacher is the priest; that an attentive and devout audience is the victim; that the Word of God is the sword which immolates, spiritually, and the grace of the Holy Spirit the fire which consumes. What exalted sentiments must not a preacher entertain, in exercising this sort of priesthood; and with what sprit of devotion should not those attend who are thus holily immolated!

The blessed father had another beautiful idea as to the ministry of the Word, and St. Bonaventure has made a particular note of it. He compared the evangelical ministers to those who, in the Ancient Law, raised up posterity to their brother defunct, who had not left any.[27] According to him, this brother defunct is Jesus Christ crucified; and when a preacher makes any converts, they are the children he raises up for Him, and of whom he takes care. From this we see that the holy man made profound reflections upon passages in the Holy Scriptures, which seem less appropriate to moralists, and that he found in them most edifying spiritual sentiments.

The ardor of his love for Jesus Christ, and his great zeal for the salvation of souls, made him esteem all preachers very venerable. His intention was, that some of his Order should be brought up to that duty, and that they should be respected by the others, because it is they who instill life, who combat the infernal enemy, and who enlighten the world. But he desired that they should exercise their ministry in a spirit of charity, even more by example, by prayers, and tears, than by eloquent discourses.

"I desire," he said, "that these ministers of the Word of God should apply themselves solely to spiritual exercises, and let nothing turn them from them; for, as they are chosen by the great King to declare His will to the people, it is requisite that they should learn, in the privacy of prayer, what they are to make known in their sermons; and that they should be interiorly warmed, in order to make use of language which shall kindle fire in the hearts they address. Those who make use of their own lights, and who savor the truths they preach, are very praiseworthy; but it is a bad division when all is given to preaching, and little or nothing to devotion. As to those who sell their labors for the oil of approbation, such as those excite our pity."

He also said that "it was a deplorable thing to see the state of a preacher, who seeks, by his discourses, not the salvation of souls, but his own glory, or who destroys, by his example, what he had advocated by his doctrine. A poor brother, simple and without eloquence, who, by good example, induces others to the practice of virtue, is to be preferred to him. 'She that was barren,' says a prophetess, 'has become the mother of many children; and she who had many

---

[26] Chrys. Homil. 29, in Epist. ad Rom.

[27] Deut. 25: 5.

children, finds herself barren.'[28] The barren represents the poor brother, who, not performing the functions of the minister who gives children to the Church, will, nevertheless, have many at the day of judgment, because then Jesus Christ, the Supreme Judge, will honorably attribute to him those whom he now converts by his prayers, which he offers up in private. She who had many children, and will now find herself barren, is the representative of that vain preacher who has nothing but words. He rejoices now in having begotten many children to Jesus Christ, by the eloquence of his discourses; but he will then be made aware that they belong not to him."

The holy man continued thus: "Many employ themselves solely in acquiring knowledge, deviating from humility and prayer, dispersing themselves and dissipating themselves within and without. Where they have preached, and find that some persons have been edified and moved, they raise themselves up, and become proud of the success, without reflecting that God has granted that success to the prayers and tears of some poor, humble, and simple brethren, who do not themselves know this result; for God chooses that they should remain ignorant of it, in order that they may have no temptation to be proud. These are my true brethren, whom I call Knights of the Round Table, who hide themselves in solitary places, to have better opportunities of devoting themselves to prayer, and whose sanctity, well known to God, is sometimes unknown to men, or even to their brethren. One day they will be presented by angels to the Lord, who will say to them: 'My beloved children, here are the souls that have been saved by your prayers, by your tears, by your good example. Receive now the fruit of the labors of those who only made use of their learning for this object. Because you have been faithful over a few things, I will set you over many.'[29] They will thus enter into the joy of the Lord, loaded with the fruit of their virtues; while the others, who have employed themselves in studying the way of salvation, in order to teach it, without following it themselves, will appear naked and empty-handed at the tribunal of Jesus Christ, having on them marks of grief and confusion.

"Then will be known, exalted, and glorified the true merit of holy humility, simplicity, prayer, and poverty, in which consists our vocation. It is now controverted by the actions and discourses of those men who are puffed up with the wind of learning, who treat truth itself as falsehood, and blindly persecute those who walk in the ways of truth; but their erroneous notions, which they endeavor to pass off as truths, and by which they blind many, will, in that time, tend only to their shame and affliction: they, with their gloomy ideas, will be cast into exterior darkness, there to associate with the spirits of darkness."[30]

---

[28] Reg. II: 1.

[29] Matt. 25:29.

[30] Ibid., 8: 12.

All that St. Francis says against vain learning, a learning which is ostentatious and void of devotion, is founded on the beautiful words of our Savior: "Many will say to me on that day, Lord, Lord, have we not prophesied in Your name? And then I will profess unto them, I never knew you, depart from me you that work iniquity;"[31] and on these of St. Paul: "If I speak with the tongues of men and of angels, and have not charity, I am become as sounding brass, or a tinkling cymbal."[32] "I chastise my body, and bring it into subjection, lest, perhaps, when I have preached to others, I myself should become a castaway."[33]

But it may not be concluded from this that the holy patriarch had any wish to prevent his brethren from studying and becoming learned; for, 1st, he was not unaware of what St. Augustine teaches on that head.[34] That learning is good in itself; that it is a gift of God; that it is most useful, when charity employs it; that it serves as a guide to piety; and that, when it has the Holy Scripture for its object, it powerfully excites to the love of God. How many learned men there are in whom humility, simplicity, and all the other virtues, are combined with deep reading! 2nd. He positively declared, as has been reported upon the evidence of St. Bonaventure, that he was well pleased that his brethren should study; it was his wish that schools should be opened in his Order, and he himself, as has been already noticed, instituted St. Anthony of Padua lecturer in theology. 3rd. He wished to have his brethren apostolical men, employed in the holy ministry for the salvation of souls, and he had inserted in his Rule a chapter which solely relates to the instruction of preachers. He desired, in consequence, that the Friars Minors should acquire the learning requisite for fulfilling their functions, which, in the ordinary course of things, is impossible without study.[35] "It was, certainly, his intention," adds St. Bonaventure,[36] "that his brethren should apply themselves to the study of the Holy Scriptures, for, one day, having but one copy of the

---

[31] Ib., 7: 22 et 23.

[32] 1 Cor. 13: 1.

[33] Ibid., 9: 27.

[34] S. August, de Grat. Christ., cap. xxvi.; de Doct. Christ., lib. 2, cap. vii.; Epist. 55, ad Januar. alias 119, cap. xxi., n. 37.

[35] This is what Mabillon has established on the clearest grounds in his "Réflexions sur la Réponse fait à son Traité des études Monastiques," by Abbé de la Trappe, who pretended that Saint Francis had forbidden his religious to study; although he says, in the same work, pages 135 and 136, "I don't mean to speak of those religious whom the Church is accustomed to employ in her ecclesiastical functions." The learned Benedictine shows that the Friars Minors must study, to render themselves capable, by their learning, of duly performing the sacred functions of the ministry; that Saint Francis approved of their studying, provided they attended to their studies with piety; and the facts brought forward by the abbé do not prove the contrary. We have not alluded here to the celebrated dispute of these two eminent men on the subject of monastic studies, except to say that it ended like those lawsuits in which each party gains and loses something. —Réflexions sur la Réponse, p. 62, et seq.

[36] St. Bonaventure, Opuscul. de trib. quest, ad Magist.

New Testament, he divided it into leaves, which he distributed among them, that all might read and instruct themselves at the same time." The holy doctor maintains,[37] in another place, that there are no religious who, by their position, are more employed in preaching than the Friars Minors; and he adds that, as St. Francis required them to be correct and accurate in their discourses, it is clear that he himself obliges them to study, since, without such application, it is impossible to be correct. If the blessed founder has spoken more of humility and piety than of learning and study, it is, in the first place, because he well knew that, naturally, persons are more prone to learn than to practice; and, secondly, because the virtues which purify the heart, are gifts more precious and necessary than learning, which only enlightens the mind; and, in the third place, because he knew that St. Paul says that "knowledge puffs up,"[38] that a learned person easily becomes proud and presumptuous, if charity does not keep him in humility, and in mistrust of himself.

Finally, let not his words be misconstrued to give color, under pretense of piety, to laziness and ignorance. He preferred, to vain and sterile learning, the humility and simplicity of the poor brethren, who spent their time in prayer: this was no more than right. "A rustic holiness," St. Jerome remarks,[39] "is more valuable than vicious learning and criminal eloquence." But the blessed patriarch only spoke of the lay-brethren, who were not intended for the sacred ministries, or of those clerks whose talents were not equal to being employed in them, and whose occupations were limited to prayer and labor. In respect to the others, who, by study, might render themselves capable of serving their neighbor spiritually, he certainly would have censured them, had they continued in ignorance, even under the pretext of prayer and manual labor; he who had adopted, as we have seen, the maxim that "nothing is preferable to the salvation of souls."

He well knew that all the brethren did not resemble some among them whom God had supernaturally enlightened, and who, without any other aid than that of prayer, had sufficient light to be able to announce the Word of God. St. Jerome says,[40] that if a man of talent must not persuade himself that holiness consists in the beauty of his composition, and in the ornament of eloquence, so also a simple and unpolished man must not imagine that his ignorance constitutes him a saint. This is even still clearer, when this man must not be ignorant. Now, it is maintained that a Friar Minor, clerk, or priest, is obliged, in conscience, according to the talent he has received from heaven, to study carefully, in order to be competent to fulfill properly the ministries of preaching and the confessional, because the spirit of his vocation, and of his

---

[37] Id. Expos., in cap. 9, Regul. Fr. Min.

[38] 1 Cor. 8: 1.

[39] S. Hier. Epist. ad Nepot., 34 alias 2.

[40] Ibid., supra.

Order, is to labor for the salvation of souls. But he must always have before his eyes what his blessed father wrote to St. Anthony of Padua: "I agree that you should teach the brethren sacred theology, in such manner, however, that the spirit of holy prayer be not extinguished, either in yourself or in others, according to the rule of which we have made profession."

CHAPTER VI

THE SIMPLICITY OF ST. FRANCIS

He commands animals, and is obeyed—He performs many other miraculous actions—The great honors which were paid to him—His character and appearance—In what sense he was simple.

E HAVE BEFORE observed that, when St. Francis was at Sienna, in his last illness, he fell into an alarming state of weakness, so that it was feared he was about to breathe his last, but that, when that had passed over, he dictated a letter to his whole Order; this is the tenor of it:

"To the Reverend and very amiable Brethren, the Minister General, and other Brethren of the Order of Minors, Brother Francis sends greeting, in Jesus Christ:

"Since it is true that he who comes from God, hears the word of God,[1] we must, consequently, my well beloved brethren, we who are destined to render to the Lord a purely spiritual worship, not only hear and practice what He says; but also, in order to give a sublime idea of the majesty of the Creator, by a profound submission to Him, give particular attention to all that is contained in any of His words. It is for this that I call upon my brethren, and I exhort them, in Jesus Christ, to attend to His divine words with all the respect in their power, wheresoever they may find them written; and if they were not in a decent place, or if on the ground, to pick them up, and put them, as much as it may be in their power, in convenient places. It is in order to pay due reverence in these words to the Lord, from whom they emanate, for there are many things which are sanctified by the word of God; and it is by virtue of the words of Jesus Christ, that the sacrament of the altar is completed.[2]

"I add, to this admonition, the confession of all my sins, which I make to God the Father, the Son, and the Holy Spirit; to the Blessed Mary, ever a virgin,[3] and to all the saints in heaven and on earth; to the Minister-General of

---

[1] Joan. 8: 47.

[2] 1 Tim. 4: 5.

[3] What could be the intention of the author of a new form of Breviary which is printed in a foreign country, at least if we may give credit to its title-page, and circulated clandestinely in Paris? He has omitted, in the first part of the Confiteor, the name of the Blessed Virgin Mary and the saints. He will, doubtless, answer that it was to return to ancient precedent. But, had not the Church the

the Order, as to my true master; to all the priests of our Order, and to all my other brethren, blessed by God. I have committed many faults, of which I acknowledge myself very guilty, inasmuch as I have not kept the rule, according to the promise which I have made to God; inasmuch as, by my negligence, or pretext of my infirmities, or because of my ignorance and want of talent, I have not said the Divine Office as the Rule prescribes.

"I entreat, in every possible way, the Minister-General, my master, to take care that all keep strictly to the rule, that the clerks celebrate the Divine Office with devotion, as being in the presence of God, in order to please Him by the uprightness of their hearts. Do not let them affect to utter sounds which are pleasing to the ear by the softness of their voices, but let them take care that the voice shall be in unison with the spirit, and the spirit with God. It is what I promise[4] to put strictly into practice by His grace, and I shall recommend it strongly to my brethren who are with me, as well as the observance of the other rules. Those who will not adhere to this, I shall not consider as Catholics, nor as brethren, and until such times as they shall have done penance, I will neither see nor speak to them. I say the same thing of those who take useless journeys, to the contempt of regular discipline. They ought to remain in obedience to their superiors, since our Savior suffered death not to fail in obedience to His most holy Father.

"I, Brother Francis, a vile and unworthy creature of God, declare, in the name of our Lord Jesus Christ, that the Minister-General of our Order, and all his successors, the provincials and the guardians, present and to come, must be in possession of this writing, keep it carefully, and observe, and cause to be observed, what it contains. According to the good pleasure of Almighty God, all you who shall faithfully put these things in practice, be ye blessed now and ever, as long as the world shall last, and may the Lord be with you eternally. Amen."

---

power, when it deemed it expedient, to make addition to the formula of public confession; and has any individual a right to leave out what it thought proper to add? Moreover, our present formula is not one of recent date. Cardinal Bona says that he had seen similar ones in very ancient manuscript missals, and in many which are earlier than the thirteenth century: it is found in its present state in a missal printed by order of Pius V. The confession made by St. Francis is an additional proof on this head. It is strange enough that in these days people consider themselves wiser than the Church; that they have the rashness to censure her discipline, set aside her usages, change her rites, and even say Mass differently from what she prescribes: this is the unfortunate consequence of that spirit of error which caused the alteration of her dogmas, and the rejection of her decisions. If it is wished to know who has made this alteration in the Confiteor, it is only necessary to apply to the Bishop of Evreux, who, by the depth of his learning, and his zeal for the faith, does honor to the Holy See. —Bona de Rebus Liturg. lib. ii., cap. 2, nn. 5 et 7." See, also, the 4th Tome of D'Achery's *Spicilegium,* in which he notices the usages of the monastery of Cluny, according to which the public Confession was made to God, and to all the saints: lib. ii.,, cap. 30.

[4] He expressed himself thus on his death-bed, because he was sincerely resolved to recite the Divine Office, as he directed his brethren to recite it, had he lived several years longer.

1. It must be remarked, in this letter, that the holy man often and strongly insists on the attention requisite, not to let any papers be scattered on which the name of God occurs, or any holy words, but to have them collected, and placed with care in appropriate places. This sentiment arose from a lively idea of the greatness of the Sovereign Being, and of the homage which vile creatures are bound to render Him.[5] If we reflect that holy and terrible is the name of God; that the Supreme Majesty has condescended to speak to us, and that we have His own words in writing, could we see such a name, and such words, in indecent places, and leave them there? Is it not scandalous that the Holy Scriptures and works of piety are bought and sold for profane uses? They ought to be properly taken care of, or burnt.

2. The humility evinced by the holy patriarch, in confessing his sins, in writing, to his Vicar, and the whole Order, in terms of the greatest contempt of himself, exemplifies the truth of this saying of Wisdom, that "the just man is the first to accuse himself."[6] St. Ephrem, St. Augustine, Pope St. Gregory,[7] and many others, accused themselves publicly of the faults they had fallen into, or that they thought they had committed in the service of God, and which great tenderness of conscience magnified in their eyes. This is a great subject of confusion to those who cannot bring themselves to admit that they have been in the wrong, even when their fault is palpable and apparent; whom we hear bitterly complaining of being obliged, by their religion, to accuse themselves of their sins in the tribunal of penance, and who only accuse themselves, while excusing what they have done. "Confession," says Tertullian, "is instituted to humble and pull down the pride of man,"[8] because there is only a contrite and humble heart that can appease the wrath of God. The priest and the people confess, alternately, their sins before the Introit of the Mass, and pray for each other, in order to celebrate and hear it more worthily, being thus prepared, by humiliation and contrition. It is likewise a method of expiating ordinary offenses, which is adopted by all the religious orders, who publicly accuse themselves of the faults they have committed.

3. What Francis notices in his letter on the subject of the Divine Office, is a complete proof that, as early as those times, punishment was in use; and this is confirmed by a regulation made in the general chapter of 1249, against those who changed the usual chant used and approved by preceding chapters-general. But the blessed founder desired that they should not sing in a soft and

---

[5] Psalm 110 (111): 9.

[6] Prov. 13: 17.

[7] St. Ephr. repreh. sui tom. I., pag. 6 et alibi, edit. Antwerp, 1669. St. Aug. Confess., lib. x., cap. 30, et seq. St. Greg. Mor. in Job, cap. ult.

[8] Tertull. de Poenit., cap. 9 et 10. Psalm. L. et xi.

effeminate style. St. Bernard,[9] sending to the religious of Montiers-Ramey the office he had composed for the feast of St. Victor, required a similar condition. "If they sing," he said, "let the chant be full and grave, without softness, and without harshness; let it be melodious and fluent, without being light and precipitate; let it be pleasing to the ear, so that it may reach the heart, drive away sorrow, and calm the passions; and that, instead of weakening the sense of the words, it may give them additional strength. For, to be deprived, by the music, of the fruit which is derived from attention to what is sung, and to apply one's self to modulations of the voice, rather than to give force to the things to which the voice gives utterance, is no small loss of spiritual benefit." This is a just idea of plain chant, and altogether of church music, which must be very different from that of profane assemblies, not wholly to give pleasure to the ear, when the principal is to excite devotional feelings in the soul. St. Augustine was so nice on this point, that, when he heard a psalm sung by a beautiful voice, he was fearful of being more moved by the sound, than by what was sung.[10] However, the Friars are not confined to plain chant by their rule, although it is prescribed to them to perform the Office according to the usage of the Roman Church, because the one is not bound by the other. Those who use it, do well; and those who do not sing it, do well also; both the one and the other have good reasons for their respective practices. Each one must conform to the usage of the place where he is, and bear in mind these words of the common father: "Let the voice be in unison with the mind, and the mind with God."

4. As to what the holy patriarch declares, that he will not hold for Catholics, or for brethren, those who will not recite the Divine Office as he prescribes, and who will not conform to the other regulations, it must be understood as in his will given above, which, he says, was only made, in order that the rule should be better kept in a Catholic manner. He means to say, as the faithful do not consider those as Catholics and brethren who break in matters of faith that unity of spirit which animates all the members of the Church, so he does not hold as Catholics, nor as brethren, in the regular observances, those who lose that spirit of uniformity which all the members ought to have, of which a religious order is composed. We might, nevertheless, say that he took the word Catholic in the sense which concerns faith, because he feared that those who would not recite the Divine Office in the spirit of the Church, who would refuse to submit to the regulations of an Order approved of by the Church, and which they have entered, must have in their hearts some sentiments hostile to the purity of the faith, or were disposed to adopt such. At least, experience teaches us, and it is seen at this day, that those who censure the discipline and usages of the Church, are the authors or the

---

[9] St. Bernard., Epist. 398, n. 2.

[10] St. Aug. Confess., lib. x., cap. 33.

supporters of the doctrines she condemns.

The other instructions of St. Francis, which are neither less solid nor less affecting, are found in his works, which have been collected and given to the public. No one must feel surprised that he was able to give instruction on so many different subjects. Although he had studied little when in the world, says St. Bonaventure, he had subsequently acquired much information, not only by means of prayer, but by reading. He appropriated some time for reading the holy Scriptures, besides which he was very talented, had great judgment, and was very quick; his memory was so good, that what he had once learnt he never forgot; and the more so, as he continually impressed it on his heart, by tender and affectionate devotion. The divine truths which he expressed in his conduct, by a faithful imitation of the virtues of Jesus Christ, and the constant application he gave to prayer, had rendered his mind so pure, and so free from any darkness, had attracted to it such brilliant rays of eternal light, that he penetrated the profoundest mysteries with surprising judgment. The Holy Spirit, whom in his heart he cherished, instructed him by a plenitude of unction;[11] the love of God carried him into those sanctuaries into which other masters cannot penetrate, but remain at the door. It is thus the holy doctor speaks of him.

While the holy patriarch was ill at Sienna, a religious of the Order of the Friars Preachers, who was a doctor of theology, and a truly learned man, put several very difficult questions to him: he answered them so learnedly, and so clearly, that the doctor was quite surprised, and spoke of the circumstance with admiration. Truly, said he, the theology of this holy father is an eagle, which soars to a great height; it is raised up, as if with wings, by the purity of the heart, and by contemplation, while our knowledge is as that of animals which crawl on the ground.

Thus, according to St. Athanasius, the great Anthony,[12] who was illiterate, showed admirable knowledge in his controversy with the heretical Arians, and in his replies to pagan philosophers who strove to puzzle him. So also, according to the testimony of Sulpicius Severus,[13] no one explained the Holy Scriptures more clearly than the celebrated Bishop of Tours, St. Martin, who had never studied.

Another Friar Preacher asked St. Francis how he was to understand these words of the Savior to the Prophet Ezechiel: "If you do not speak to the impious that he may be converted from his wicked way and live, the same wicked man shall die in his iniquity; but I will require his blood at your hand."[14] The humble father having at first excused himself, that he should

---

[11] John 2: 17.

[12] Vit. S. Anton., n. 69, et 72 apud S. Athan.

[13] Alp Sev., Vit. S. Mart., no. 29.

[14] Ezech. 3: 18

apply to learned theologians to learn the sense of the Holy Scriptures, but, as the religious urged him, nevertheless, to give his opinion, and expressed a great wish to have it preferably to that of others whom he had consulted, he gave him this answer: "I believe these words, if taken in the full extent, to mean, that the servant of God must be by holiness, and the good odor of his life, a torch which burns and enlightens, in order that the splendor of his example may be as a voice which censures the impious; for this is the way to warn and reprehend them all: if he act otherwise, and scandalize his neighbor, he will not escape the punishment of heaven."

St. Francis was not ignorant that the literal and immediate sense of this passage is, that pastors, and all those who are in authority, are obliged to instruct, warn, censure, and correct those who are committed to their charge; and they become guilty of the loss of souls, if they are silent when they ought to speak. He himself, faithful in the mission he had received from God and the Holy See, never ceased from exhorting his brethren to sanctify themselves, and from urging sinners to be converted; but he found in the above passage a more extended sense, and one of greater moral influence, which was, to preach by example; and he adhered to this for many reasons: 1. Because words produce small effect when they are not backed by example. 2. Because there are a greater number of superiors who instruct and censure, than of those who edify by example. 3. Because the number of persons who have no right to instruct and reprove, is the greater, and it is good that they should know that God will call them to account for the good example which it was their duty to have given, which might have contributed to the conversion of sinners. All this shows how solid and proper the saint's reply was.

We have also reason to believe that he was instructed in the canon law, since we have seen that he quoted some of its decrees, and that he consulted a talented barrister for the affairs of his Order. As to the subjects of morality which he has treated of, as we find similar thoughts and expressions in them to those of the fathers of the Church, it must necessarily be admitted that he had read some of their works, or that God had given him similar lights. On the mysteries of religion he always spoke with correctness and theological precision; and we may have remarked that he employed against the heretics the strongest proof we have for invincibly establishing the real presence of Jesus Christ in the Eucharist.

His style is plain, because he formed it on the Gospel, from which he would not in any degree deviate; besides that, his was not the age of elegant Latinity; but in all that he has written we do not find anything that is not clear and intelligible; there are even passages insinuating and persuasive. We have also reason to admire some parts which are beautiful from their simplicity. Let the cleverest men read his description of the rich sinner on his death-bed, and he will be obliged to admit that it would be impossible to draw a more natural or more striking portrait.

He had so completely the talent of persuasion, that neither popes, cardinals, nobles, nor any other persons could resist his appeals; whatsoever he wished, they complied with. It is not easy, for the sake of piety, to persuade to that which is contrary to the interests of a family: nevertheless, St. Francis succeeded in this. The following is an example, which, relating only to a very common subject, we, notwithstanding, select, because it contains wholesome instruction:

The saint was one day sweeping out a country church, according to his usual practice, when a man, whose name was John, and who was ploughing in an adjoining field, came and took the broom from his hands, and after having swept the whole church, he said to him: "Brother, what I have heard of you and of your brethren, has inspired me with an idea of serving God as you do. I did not know how to come to you, but, since it has pleased God that I should find you here as I had wished, I offer myself to you: do with me as you please." Francis, knowing by an interior light, that this man had been sent him by the Lord, resolved to receive him into his Order, and after having instructed him in the Rule, he said to him: "If you resolve upon joining this Institute, you must renounce all you have, and give it to the poor." John went immediately to his plough, unyoked the oxen, and brought one to Francis, saying: "I have been long in the service of my father, and I maintain the family by my labor; I think I may take this ox for my reward, and do with it as you shall direct me." He immediately went home to take leave of his parents, and desired them to take care of the plough.

The parents, alarmed when they learnt his intention, ran in despair to the church, where Francis still was, and conjured him not to take a man from them who was so useful to them, and earned their means of living. He replied mildly to them, and told them that he should come and dine with them, and sleep at their house, and would endeavor to console them. He went, and after dinner, addressing himself to John's father, he said: "My dear host, your son wishes to serve God, and it is God who has inspired him with this thought. This ought not to give you any displeasure; on the contrary, it ought to be gratifying to you, and you should give God thanks that He has been pleased to select one of your family for His service. This will be no small gain to you; for, for this son whom you give up, you will gain as many children and brethren as there are religious in the Order he is about to join. Moreover, your son is one of God's creatures; and if God has destined him for Himself, who shall dare to resist His will? Who shall say to Him, 'Why do You do thus?'[15] He is all-powerful, and He is also just. He only asks for what belongs to Him. May His will therefore be done, and may His mercy be extended to your son, whom I cannot and ought not to refuse to receive into the house of God, which he so anxiously wishes me to do. All that I can, and will do for you, is to desire him to leave

---

[15] Esther 13: 9; Job. 9: 12.

you the ox he had destined for the poor, according to the Gospel, and that, abandoning to the world what belongs to the world, he come stripped of everything, to throw himself into the arms of Jesus Christ."

This reasoning was so convincing to the parents, that they assented willingly and cheerfully to their son's leaving them, whom before they thought they could not part with. Human prudence will not fail to say that he ought to have remained with his parents, to provide for their subsistence by his labor; but will it say that James and John,[16] being called by Jesus Christ, ought not to have left Zebedee, their father, who was poor, and whom they maintained by their fishing? Our Lord, in calling them, desired that they should obey His voice, and leave to Providence to provide for the subsistence of their father. St. Francis well knew that, under any other circumstances, this laborer would have been bound to work to provide for his parents; but, as he knew that his call was from God to a religious state of life, he wisely judged that the Lord would assist the family by some other means, and that the vocation ought to be followed. The reasons he gave were opposed to the tender[17] affection of those parents who prevent their children from consecrating themselves to God; and although he laid them before them in a simple and unartificial manner, they were not the less calculated to make due impression on the most enlightened persons, as well as on the ignorant peasants who bowed to them.

In his sermons he took no pains to polish his language, and cared as little as the apostle did who was reproached for not making studied discourses;[18] but we are not, therefore, to conclude from this, that he preached without eloquence. A man who has considerable genius, judgment, and quickness, gifted with an excellent memory, a strong, sonorous, and agreeable voice, penetrated with the great truths of religion, and with the most tender sentiments of piety; who speaks with ease, naturally and persuasively, with all the vehemence and all the fire, the effect of ardent charity, employing everything that can move and instruct his auditors, is not such a man eloquent? Well, such a one was St. Francis.

Many people form to themselves a false idea of eloquence; they make it

---

[16] Matt. 4, 21 et 22.

[17] St. Jerome says that it is a sort of piety in a child to be cruel to parents who endeavor to prevent him from sacrificing himself to God, but that it is only in such circumstances that it is permitted to him to be so. —Epist. 5, alias 1, ad Heliod. St. Augustine teaches us that a child whose parents wish to retain him in the world, when God commands him to leave it, must deaden in his heart by the sword of the spirit, which is the word of God, that carnal affection, in order to give life to sentiments of Christianity. —Epist. ad Laet. 243, alias 38, n. 5.; St. Bernard addressed these words to a young man who refused to consecrate himself to God out of tender affection for his mother: "If you have great affection for your mother, leave her for your own sake and for hers, otherwise she will perish by causing your loss." There is impiety in despising one's mother; but in despising her for Jesus Christ, there is great piety. He who has said, "Honor your father and your mother," has also said, that "he who loves his father or his mother more than me, is not worthy of me." —Epist. 104., n. 5.

[18] 1 Cor. 2 et 4; 2 Cor 11: 16.

consist in a happy choice of words, the brilliancy of thought, the harmony of the number and measure of the periods. But all this is the smallest part; it is only that which pleases, in order to attract attention, and it must be used with precaution, particularly in evangelical discourses. "The principal object," says St. Augustine,[19] "is to instruct well, that those who listen may understand every word that is said to them; and to excite such feelings in them as may lead them to adopt the view which is laid before them." These are the dispositions to be created, which the holy doctor calls the triumph of eloquence. He admires them in the prophets and apostles; he thinks that by them the sacred writers joined naturally to their innate sagacity the most beautiful ornaments of the art, without seeking them, and he adduces various examples. "Since," he adds, "it is true that the rules of the oratorical art are drawn from the mind, are we to be surprised that God, who forms those minds, shall imprint on some, without study, the same rules, and that, from time to time. He sends forth such chosen men to announce His word? It is, indeed, with this description of eloquence that the word of God should be announced; by speaking great truths, propounding them clearly, endeavoring to introduce them into the heart; and not making use of the force of language, or other beauties of rhetoric, but inasmuch as it is necessary for instructing and enforcing them."

The polish of language which St. Francis neglected, was wonderfully compensated by divine virtue. St. Bonaventure says that the Holy Spirit, from whom he had received his unction and his mission, inspired him with abundance of words to preach His holy doctrine, and continually assisted him; and that Jesus Christ, who is the strength of the Father, came invariably to his aid; that, indeed, he had recourse to the ornaments of human eloquence in his discourses, but that inspiration was very perceptible; that his preaching was a great fire, which penetrated quite to the bottom of hearts, with so much efficacy, that the most obdurate were softened, and had recourse to penance. Men and women, young and old, nobles and plebeians, flocked in crowds to see and hear this extraordinary man, whom God had sent them. He seemed to them, in fact, to be a man from the other world, when they saw him, with his eyes elevated to heaven, with the view of drawing them thither; and, as soon as he spoke, they felt their hearts moved to compunction.

All that he said against the public scandals, was received with respect; those whose crimes he censured, whatever confusion they might feel from it, did not dare complain, not even those in the highest station. Some of the learned were likewise noticed amongst his auditory, and they, more than any others, admired the powerful influence of his discourses, knowing him to be a man who had not gone through any course of study. In short, the public was so charmed by hearing him, that, after preaching one day at Cortona, and

---

[19] S. Aug. de Doctr. Christ., lib. 4, cap. 12, 13 et 14.

wishing to return to the convent of Celles, the guards at the gates of the town would not let him pass. After having preached for three successive days there he only got leave to go, after the strongest entreaties, and after having promised to leave Brother Guy there, whose sanctity he assured them would free Cortona from many evils. God punished, in a most frightful manner, an insolent young girl, who was making a noise with a sort of drum during the saint's sermon; he had called upon her three times to be quiet, but she laughed at him, and he was then inspired to say, in a loud voice, "Devil, take what is your own." At the same moment the girl was raised up into the air, and she was seen no more. By this dreadful example, God proposed to teach them the respect they were bound to have for the instructions which His servants teach them, as once He taught the faithful not to lie to the Holy Spirit, by the deaths of Ananias and Sapphira,[20] which followed the reproach which St. Peter had made them.[21]

The supernatural and miraculous gifts which St. Francis had received from God, gave great weight to his preaching. A man who casts out devils, who raises the dead to life, who cures the sick, whose prophecies are verified, who discovers spirits, who commands animals, and makes them obey him, a man who performs these prodigies, and many others, is listened to as if he were an angel, when he speaks. We may have noticed, in the life of the saint, how authoritatively he drove out devils from the bodies of those who were possessed. We have seen the dead brought to life, under extraordinary circumstances, and a great number of sick cured.

The Holy Spirit had bestowed on him the grace of cures to such a degree, that it not only gave its virtue to his hands, and to the sign of the cross, which he usually made, but to everything which he had touched. "The cord with which he girded himself," says St. Bonaventure, "fell into the hands of a man who went from house to house where there were any sick, soaked it in water, and made them drink it, which effected their cure." The legend which was composed by order of Pope Gregory IX, immediately after the death of St. Francis, states that infirm persons were placed before him, in the public squares, in order to their being restored to health by him; and he was requested to bless bread, in order that it might be a cure for sicknesses which might supervene.

The holy doctor assures us that the gift of prophecy appeared in our saint with great splendor; that not only did he foretell things to come, but also spoke of those things which were happening in his absence, as if they were present before his eyes; that he penetrated to the bottom of hearts, and saw the most

---

[20] Acts 5: 5 et 10.

[21] St. Jerome says that it was not St. Peter who put them to death, nor who called for their death; that by a spirit of prophecy he only declared the judgment of God upon these two persons. So, also, it was not St. Francis who delivered the girl, who was so insolent, to the devil; it was God Himself, by the mouth of His servant —Epist. ad Demetr.

secret recesses of consciences, so that it might have been said that he inspected the mirror of eternal light, and that its admirable splendor discovered to him what was most hidden. We shall only add here to what has been related on this head, some anecdotes which may be useful.

God revealed to him, in prayer, the loss of one of the religious, who had the reputation of being a saint, but who was so peculiar in everything, that, in order the more rigidly to keep silence, he usually confessed by signs. The blessed father having come to the convent in which this religious was, he saw him, and spoke of him to the others, who were loud in their praises of him. "Brethren," said he, "cease all these praises, and give them not to inventions of the devil; know that all this is but a temptation, and an extraordinary illusion." The brethren could not persuade themselves that so many marks of perfection were but covers to imposture; but, a few days after, this pretended saint left the Order, which proved that St. Francis had probed to the bottom of his soul.

He knew, in the same manner, why another, who seemed to be adorned with every virtue, had thrown off the habit of the Order; and he replied to his brethren who expressed their surprise at it: "Do not be astonished, my brethren; this wretch is lost, because he was not grounded in humility, and in the fear of God. Believe me that, without this foundation, it is fruitless to endeavor to become virtuous."

Of two religious who were returning from the Terra di Lavoro, he saw in spirit that the senior did not by any means edify his companion. On their arrival, he asked the younger what had occurred on the road; the other replied, that all had gone on well. "Take care," answered Francis, "take care, and don't say what is false, on pretense of humility. I know, I know; but wait a little, and you will see." In fact, the giver of scandal abandoned his vocation shortly after.

The charitable father received, with great kindness, one of the brethren who had apostatized from the Order, and now returned; he even gave him the kiss of peace. But, pointing out to him the gallows which was on a height, at some distance, he said: "If the devil induces you to leave the Order a second time, he will lead you to be hanged on the gallows which you see from hence." This weak penitent did not profit from this warning, but left the Order again, and led a libertine life, was taken up for a robbery, and hanged on the spot pointed out. St. Francis might have said of those, as St. John did of the apostates who left the Church, "They went out from us, but they were not of us; for, if they had been of us, they would no doubt have remained with us."[22] That is to say, that they were not firm in the Christian religion.

If religious who renounce their profession, are not always punished in this world, by coming to a tragical end, what judgment must they not expect from God, who cannot endure that, putting the hand to the plough, they shall only

---

[22] John 2: 19.

cast a look behind?[23] But what punishment must not those solitaries have to dread in the next world, who have revolted against the authority of the Church, and against the superiors of their holy orders, for the support of errors which had been condemned, who had made the faithful weep at the sorrowful scene of their scandalous apostasy in 1725?[24]

In the opinion of St. Bernard,[25] it is likewise an apostasy to abandon the austerity of his rule, to adopt one which is milder, without cause, or for an insufficient cause, after having obtained a dispensation upon representations unfaithfully made. He notices, also, another, which he denominates an apostasy of the heart, which comprises a wish to return into Egypt, as the people of Israel did; so that, under a religious habit, the mind is wholly secular, and it is sought to obtain for themselves the vain consolation of the world.

Among many persons who appeared to be firm in a virtuous life, St. Francis, according to St. Bonaventure, predicted, with certainty, such as would fall; and, among the wicked, those who would be converted. It is one of the most singular inspirations which God gives to His servants; for persons only fall by their own free-will, and they are only converted by a free cooperation with grace. God knows infallibly, without any interference with our perfect liberty, in what way the human will will make its choice on these two points; but how can that be explained? This is the difficulty of theologians, and in which they have to avoid precipices.

The knowledge of the human heart belongs to God alone; even the angels have it not, unless imparted to them by His light,[26] and He was pleased to communicate that light to Francis. We have had several instances of this, but we must add the following: The blessed father, being at the hermitage of Grecio, two of his brethren came, from a great distance off, urged by a strong desire to see him, and to receive his blessing, which they had long been desirous of. Unfortunately, they reached the hermitage when he was retired to his cell, from which he did not come out to receive visits, and they could not see him. As they were going away, greatly disappointed, he came out, contrary to his usual custom, called them, and blessed them in the name of Jesus Christ, and made the sign of the cross upon their foreheads, as they had wished. Humanly speaking, he could not have known that they were come, but he knew it in spirit, as well as if he had seen them.

Having restored peace, and performed some splendid miracles in a town, he left the place early in the morning, without having taken leave of the bishop, who had given him a most honorable reception. At a spot where three

---

[23] Luke 9: 62.

[24] The author here refers to the formation of the Jansenist schism in France and the Netherlands. —Editor's note.

[25] S. Bernard. Epist. 313, n. 5. Apol. Ad Guillel. Abb. Cap. 13, et in Psalmo Qui habitat., Serm. 3, n. 5.

[26] 2 Paral. 7: 30; Jerem. 17, 10; S. Chrys. homil. 4 in Matt. I: 20.

roads diverged, he did not know which one he ought to take, and desired Brother Massé, who was his companion, to turn round and round, no doubt to put his obedience to the test.[27] When he began to be giddy, he ordered him to stop, and to follow the road which was before him. Massé went first, and said to himself, "How uncivil! how simple! He not only has not taken leave of the bishop who received him with so much kindness, but he makes me turn round and round as a child." This interior murmuring did not last; these reflections followed: "How could I have so much pride as to despise a man who is so evidently beloved by God? Fool that I am, I deserve to go to hell for daring to censure the actions of Francis, through whom the Lord works such wonders, and whom I ought to look upon as an angel. And, after all, what reason has he given me for censuring him? He left the town without having taken leave of the bishop, but it was to avoid fresh honors being shown him; he made me turn round and round, but he made me take the right road." Then Francis exclaimed: "Ah, Brother Massé, how different are these feelings from those first entertained! From whence do these come, and from whence did those others arise?" Massé, seeing that his thoughts were discovered, threw himself at the saint's feet, and solicited his pardon.

A particular gift which Francis received from God, was the control of animals. He gave them his commands, and they obeyed him, they did whatever he pleased; it was, moreover, noticed that they showed a sort of affection for him, and applauded what he did in their way. Upon which two observations occur. The first is taken from St. Bonaventure, who says that the state of innocence was represented in the power which God gave to His servant over animals. Adam, just and innocent, had absolute control over them, and he exercised it in giving to each of them its proper name, when God made them pass before him, as we read in Genesis.[28] His sin caused him to lose this privilege, with all the others which had been attached to this happy state; and we experience, as he did, the revolt of the animals, in punishment of his having disobeyed God. But when an eminent sanctity has brought men more to original justice, and has, in some measure, reestablished them in a state of innocence, it has sometimes pleased the Almighty to restore them to some of the privileges which man enjoyed in those times, and, in particular, this control over animals. This is what is seen in well- authenticated acts of many saints, and in what St. Bonaventure relates of St. Francis, on the testimony of ocular witnesses, as well as on the evidence of facts which were of public notoriety.

The second thing which deserves notice is, that, when this holy man

---

[27] In this he imitated the holy fathers of the desert, who, as Cassian relates, sometimes ordered their disciples childish and seemingly unreasonable things, to teach them the holy folly of the cross, by caking on them to renounce their own will, their own opinions, and the wisdom of the world; and God sanctioned this by many miracles. —Cassian, de Instr. Renunt., cap. x., 24 et seq.

[28] Genes. 2: 19, 20.

compelled animals to obey him, and when they appeared to be attached to him, it never occurred but when it was to give authority to the word of God, to do some good to a neighbor, to give a salutary lesson, or to excite to the practice of some virtue, as we shall now see. It is another proof that these marvels had their source in God, who proposes, in all He does, some end worthy of His wisdom; from which we must conclude that heretics could not have turned these things into ridicule, but through a malignity which is both irreligious and foolish.

Francis left Assisi one day, to go to preach, not having any longer a doubt but that he and his brethren were called for the service of souls, after the mission they had received from God, and from the Supreme Pontiff, which was confirmed by supernatural lights, as we have seen above. Being near to the town of Bevagna, he saw on a particular spot a number of birds collected, of various species, and he went up to them, and said: "My brethren, listen to the word of God; you have great reason to praise your Creator; He has covered you with feathers; He has given you wings wherewith to fly; He has placed you in the air, where the breathing is so pure; and He provides you with everything which is necessary, without giving you any trouble." While he was thus speaking and saying other similar things, the birds remained where they were, turning towards him, and those which were perched on the branches of trees, bending their heads, as if to listen to what he said. It was a curious thing to observe the joy they appeared to feel and make known by their motions; they stretched their necks, they spread their wings, opened their beaks, and looked anxiously at the zealous preacher, who walked about in the midst of them, and sometimes touched them with his habit, without any of them stirring. They only took to flight after he had given them leave, and made on them the sign of the cross, to bless them.

It was God's intention to honor the ministry of the saint, in the eyes of his companions, by this miracle, which they witnessed, and the circumstances of which they communicated to St. Bonaventure. It was also to show the attention which ought to be given to the truths of salvation; and this is the reason why Francis, in turning to them, said, with admirable candor: "I am very neglectful in not having as yet preached to the birds." He observed, by this apparent simplicity, which was full of good sense, that men often fail to listen to the preachers, as the birds had seemingly listened to him; in the same sense in which St. Martin had said, when complaining of the insensibility of the men of his times: "They do not attend to me, though the serpents obey me."[29] This means that, with the aid of reason and grace, they will not do what unreasonable animals necessarily do, by the impulse of divine power.

But why preach to birds? will the sages of this age ask; but why did David say what the Church repeats daily in her Divine Office? "Whales, and all that

---

[29] Sulp. Sev., Dial, iii., n. 12.

move in the waters, bless the Lord. All ye beasts and cattle, fowls of the air, bless the Lord."[30] The three young men who were in the furnace at Babylon, said the same thing. A heart full of love and gratitude would wish that all creatures should have hearts and tongues, to glorify the Author of their being; he knows that even the beasts praise Him by the marks they bear of His power, wisdom, and goodness; in seeing them, in speaking to them, he commemorates His sovereign greatness.

On leaving Bevagna, Francis went to preach in the borough of Alviano, and not being able to make himself heard, in consequence of the noise the swallows made, who had their nests there, he spoke these words to them: "Swallows, my sisters, you have made yourselves heard long enough; it is now my turn to speak. Listen, then, to the word of God, and keep silence while I preach." Immediately, as if they had understood what he said, they ceased their noise, and remained where they were, to the end of his sermon. The fruit of this miracle was to revive the fervor and piety of the assembly, who glorified God, and listened to the preacher with wonderful deference. The circumstance was soon spread, and produced everywhere a similar effect.

St. Bonaventure, who gives us this anecdote, adds that, some time afterwards, a scholar at Paris,[31] who was of good conduct, having been interrupted in his studies by the chirping of a swallow, said to his companions: "This is one of those who interrupted the blessed Francis in his sermon, and which he silenced;" having then addressed the swallow, he said, with great faith, "In the name of Francis, the servant of God, I order you to be silent and to come to me." It was instantly silent, and came to him; in his surprise he let it go, and was not again troubled by it. It was thus it pleased God to honor the name of His servant.

Other examples are found in the saint's life, of the power he exercised over animals, when, by their noise, or by any other means, they interrupted his sermons or prayers, as on his return from Syria, near the Lagunes of Venice, where he saw a great number of birds which were singing. He went into the midst of them to say his office, with his companions, but the noise the birds made prevented their hearing each other; Francis, upon that, ordered them to cease singing, till he had finished his office, and, in fact, says the holy doctor, the author of his life, from that moment they ceased their chirping until, the office being finished, he gave them leave to resume their song, which they did, as before. He took this opportunity to settle some of his religious there, to celebrate the praises of the Lord, as has been before noticed. St. Ambrose[32] speaks of a circumstance as well known to all the world, that some of the

---

[30] Psalm 14 (15); Dan. 8:3; Psalm 104 (105); Dan. 3.

[31] S. Bonaventure, who had the degree of doctor at Paris, and had lived there a considerable time, who wrote while there, and at Mantes, the life of St. Francis, had every means of verifying this fact.

[32] S. Ambr. de Virginibus, lib. iii., cap. 3, n. 14.

faithful, having been assembled in a spot where the croaking of the frogs greatly disturbed them, a priest commanded them to be quiet, and to show respect for holy things, and that they immediately ceased from making any noise, and that these irrational animals respected what they were incapable of understanding.

We have already seen that when Francis was at Grecio, he freed the country from the wolves which had ravaged it. At Gubbio, he tamed one in an extraordinary manner. He took it into the public square where he preached, and having pointed out to his auditors that God sends sometimes these carnivorous animals to warn sinners to return to their duties, he addressed the wolf, and made an agreement with it, the clauses of which were, that the inhabitants should find it food, and that the wolf should do no injury to any of them. This was faithfully attended to on both sides. During two years the animal came to the town to feed, and did no injury to any one.

The holy man had tamed, in a similar manner, at Carinola, a fox that stole all the poultry of a poor old woman, and from which she received no injury afterwards. Similar traits are found in the lives of many saints, whose acts are admitted to be authentic and certain, by the most talented critics. St. Athanasius[33] remarks, in the life of St. Anthony, that wild animals causing great damage in a field which he cultivated, he took one gently, and said to all the others, while speaking to the one he had caught, "Why do you injure me, who never did you any harm? Go, and in the name of the Lord, never come here any more." The holy doctor adds, that from that time they were never again seen in that place, as if they had been afraid of disobeying him. Sulpicius Severus[34] relates of St. Martin, that he had an extraordinary control over all animals, that, resting himself one day with his disciples, on the bank of a river, he saw a snake swimming over, and he ordered it in the name of the Lord to swim back again, upon which it was seen to return with as much speed as it had come. James, who wrote the life of St. Columban,[35] given by the learned Father Mabillon, after Surius, states that the crows and the bears obeyed him, and that all the beasts of the field came at his call, in the same manner as those which are domesticated. It was in order to teach men to esteem and imitate a virtue which the Lord caused to be respected, even by dumb animals.

The obedience which irrational animals rendered to St. Francis was frequently a sensible stimulus to the practice of virtue. The language which pagans imputed to them, and from which they drew axioms of morality, had nothing in it but what was fabulous; but truly did God confound the avarice and criminal subserviency of Balaam,[36] by opening the mouth of the ass which

---

[33] Vit. S. Anton., n. 50.

[34] Sulp. Sev., Dial, iii., n. 12.

[35] Vit. S. Colomb., n. 25, 27 et 30, inter Act. SS. Ord. S. Bened.

[36] Numb. 22:28 et 30; 2 Petr. 2:16.

spoke to him.[37] We should have no more difficulty in believing that God, by an act of His power, had made some animals perform some instructive actions which were commanded them by one of His most faithful servants, than we have in crediting the above, especially when we have so faithful a reporter of the fact as St. Bonaventure, who had received them from ocular witnesses.

St. Francis, when at Rome, in 1222, had always with him a little lamb, to remind him of the Lamb of God, who chose to be sacrificed for us. When he was about to leave the eternal city, he confided the little animal to the care of the Lady of Septisal, the illustrious widow of whom we have often had occasion to speak.

The little lamb, as if it had been trained to spiritual exercises by the holy man, followed this lady to church, stayed there, and returned with her, never leaving her. If she was behind her usual time of rising in a morning, it would go to her bed, where, by bleating or striking the bed with its head, or other motions, it seemed to call upon her to rise, and offer her grateful prayer to God. The lady was much attached to this lamb, and took care of it, says St. Bonaventure, as a disciple of Francis, which had become her instructor in devotion.

A present was made to the holy father, at St. Mary of the Angels, of a sheep; he received it thankfully, because of the innocence and simplicity of which it was a symbol, and he said to it, as if it could understand him, that it was necessary it should assist at the praises of the Lord, without incommoding the brethren; the sheep obeyed with great punctuality. When the religious went to the choir, to sing the office, the sheep went of itself to the church, placed itself at the foot of the altar of the Blessed Virgin, bent in its fore-legs, and bleated in a low tone, as if to pay its homage. It did the same at Mass, when the Host was elevated. St. Bonaventure remarks, that this animal, by the respect it manifested during the celebration of the sacred mysteries, taught the Christians the deep reverence with which they ought to assist at Mass, and at the same time passed a deserved censure on those who are irreverent or indevout during its celebration. How many worldly persons are there who assist at Mass as if it was a profane assembly, staring about with immodest airs, and in unbecoming postures? They chatter and converse, as if they were anywhere else, and scarcely do they bend a knee when the sacred body of Jesus Christ is elevated, in order that they may adore it. How criminal! how scandalous! without adverting further to the outrages of mind and heart which are offered to the Son of God, in this August sacrifice. Where is their faith?

---

[37] S. Augustine says, that God made no change in the nature of this animal, and only made use of it as an instrument to produce the sounds and words which He intended to convey to the wicked prophet. Qaest. in Numb., 48 and 50. This was neither more miraculous nor more difficult to believe than what we read in the same book of Numbers, chapters xxiii. and xxiv., that Balaam blessed the Israelites three times, whom he desired to have cursed, and that his tongue was moved by a very different spirit from that which possessed his heart.

where is their religion? Did the pagans ever show a want of respect, when they sacrificed to their false gods? How shameful is it that the worship of the true God should be so disgraced! What punishments are prepared for such profanations![38]

The smallest things raised the heart of St. Francis to God, and he made use of them to create similar feelings in the hearts of his disciples. The chirping of a grasshopper, which was on a fig tree, near his cell, inspired him with fresh fervor; he called it, and it came to him directly, and he made it sing on his hand, which it began anew, whenever he required it. At the end of eight days he said to his companions, "Let it now go; it has excited us long enough to praise God;" at the very moment the grasshopper flew away, and was seen no more.

One day, as he was about take his collation with Brother Leo, he felt himself interiorly consoled, on hearing a nightingale sing. He begged Leo to sing the praises of God alternately with the bird; the latter having excused himself, alleging the badness of his voice, he himself responded to the bird, and continued to do so till night, when he was obliged to give over, acknowledging that the little bird had beaten him. He made it come upon his hand, and praised it for having sung so well, fed it, and it was only after he had desired it to leave him, and given it his blessing, that the nightingale flew away.

In the impression which the power of God affected upon animals, in favor of St. Francis, there was this further circumstance, which was marvelous: that they seemed to have an affection for him, and appeared pleased when they saw him. It is St. Bonaventure who gives several examples of this.

The servant of God, going to Sienna, passed near a flock of sheep which were feeding in a meadow. He greeted them, as was his custom, with an air of kindness, and immediately the sheep, the rams, and the lambs, left their pasture, came to him, lifted up their heads to greet him in their manner, which was greatly wondered at by the shepherds and by his companions. Hares and rabbits were presented to him, which had been caught alive; they were put before him on the ground, and they immediately sprang into his arms. Although he gave them their liberty, they remained with him, and he was obliged to have them removed far off into the country, by some of his religious, and put in a place of safety.

On the banks of the lake of Rieti, a fisherman gave him a live water-fowl. After having kept it a little while, he tried to make it fly away, but in vain. He then raised his eyes to heaven, and remained for more than an hour in a state of ecstasy, after which he mildly ordered the bird to go away and praise the Lord, and he gave it his blessing. The bird showed signs of pleasure by its motions, and flew away. On the same lake, a large fish which had been just caught, was presented to him; he held it for some time in his hand, and then

---

[38] See Bourdaloue's sermon on the Mass, for the Monday of the fourth week of Lent.

put it back in the water. The fish remained in the same place, playing in the water before him, as if out of regard for him; it could not leave him, and did not disappear till it had received the saint's leave, together with his blessing. Something similar is found in the life of St. Columban.[39] One of his disciples affirms, that in his solitude he often called to him birds and wild beasts, and that they came on hearing his voice; that he caressed them with his hand, and that they returned his caresses, as little dogs do those of their masters.

The first time that St. Francis went to Mount Alverno, he was surrounded by a multitude of birds, which lit upon his head, on his shoulders, on his breast, and on his hands, evincing by their beaks and wings the pleasure his arrival caused them, which he noticed to his companions, as a mark of the will of God that he should remain in this mountain. When he came thither, and received the Stigmata there, the birds greeted him in a similar manner; and a hawk, which could only have come thither by a supernatural impulse, attached itself peculiarly to his person. When the hour of the night drew near, at which Francis rose to pray, the bird did not fail to come and make a noise at the door of the cell. This punctuality was very pleasing to the saint, because it caused him to be watchful; but when his infirmities were more severe than usual, the bird, well taught by Him who controlled his movements, did not come to wake him till sunrise, and even then did not make so much noise as usual. St. Bonaventure considers these marvels which God operated for his servant on Mount Alverno, by means of birds, as a divine foreboding of the great favor he received some few days after, when, being raised by the wings of contemplation, the winged and crucified seraph appeared to him, and imprinted on his body the wounds of Jesus Christ.

The Lord bore witness to his sanctity until the very day of his death, by the affection which animals seemed to have for him. It is once more St. Bonaventure who affords us the proofs of this. When St. Francis was ill at Sienna, a gentleman sent him a live pheasant which had been just caught. As soon as the bird saw the saint, and heard his voice, it attached itself so intensely to him, that it could not bear to be away from him; it was often taken to the vineyards, to induce it to fly away, but it always flew quickly back to the father. It was put into the hands of a worthy man, who often came to see the sick man, but as long as it was away, it would not feed; but on being brought back, and seeing the father, it showed signs of pleasure, and fed greedily. On the day of the saint's death, which happened on the 4th of October, a multitude of larks hit upon the roof of the convent, although it was at nightfall, and they dislike the dark; they sang for a long time, and their warbling, which appeared to have something peculiar in it, was an evidence as pleasing as it was convincing of the glory of the servant of God, who had so often invited them to praise their Creator.

---

[39] Vit. S. Colomb., n. 30, inter Act. SS. Ord. S. Bened., sec. 2.

It has been thought, for many reasons, that in giving his life to the public, these extraordinary occurrences should not be suppressed: *1.* Because St. Bonaventure, who was so prudent and eminent a divine, has thought it right to give them a place in his legend. *2.* They are warranted by precedents, in the examples given by St. Athanasius, St. Ambrose, Sulpicius Severus,[40] and several other grave authors, whose works have merited the esteem of the learned. *3.* Some passages in the Holy Scriptures may be adduced in favor of their credibility. In the Third Book of Kings, God says to the Prophet Elias: "Hide yourself by the torrent of Carith. I have commanded the ravens to feed you there,"[41] and the sacred author adds, "and the ravens brought him bread and flesh in the morning, and bread and flesh in the evening, and he drank of the torrent." The prophet Daniel, in the lions' den in which he was, replied to King Darius: "My God has sent His angels, and hath shut up the mouths of the lions, and they have not hurt me, forasmuch as before Him justice hath been found in me."[42] Our Savior placed among the number of miracles, that those who believed[43] would perform many in His name, such as taking up serpents, handling them, and killing them without their doing them any injury.[44] Is it, then, incredible that God, by His power, should have made impressions on various sorts of animals, to render them obedient to the voice of His servants? *4.* We have paid little heed to a handful of unbelievers, and some wise worldlings, enemies of anything marvelous, where religion is concerned, who exert their talent for raillery more on what is sacred than on what is profane; but, in order to pander to their malevolence, or to avoid their false and dangerous prejudices, it has not been thought reasonable to deprive the faithful of the instruction given them in the obedience and respect given to the saint, even by animals. Venerable Bede[45] teaches us, that our Lord shows us by that the state in which we should have been, had we not disobeyed Him, which is a reflection which should cause us to sigh, and to submit, in a spirit of penance, to the punishment, which is the chastisement of sin. St. Bonaventure says, that all creatures were submissive to St. Francis, because he had brought his flesh entirely under subjection to his spirit, and his spirit to God. Now, according to St. Augustine,[46] it is in this twofold submission that the whole order of a Christian life consists; by that wild beasts are spiritually controlled by restraining the passions, since, in the opinion of St. Gregory and St.

---

[40] As above.

[41] 3 Reg. 17: 3, 4 et 6.

[42] Dan. 6: 22.

[43] It does not follow from this that all those who have faith must work miracles. This gift has been promised principally to the Church in general, for certain occasions, where it might be necessary for her, and we have seen its fulfillment when the good of religion has required it.

[44] Mark 16: 18

[45] Beda in Hex.

[46] In Psalm 143 (144):6

Bernard,[47] to stifle venomous suggestions is to kill serpents. Finally, the empire of saints over animals is an anticipated reward for the innocence of their lives, and for their inviolable fidelity in the service of God; and does not this give us some idea of the infinite good which God has prepared for those who love Him? St. Augustine said, in speaking of the great miracles which were performed by the relics of St. Stephen, in all countries: "Figure to yourselves, my brethren, what God has prepared for us in the land of the living, in the consideration of what He effects in this world, by the ashes of the dead."[48] May we not also say: "If God has given such power to His friends while they were on earth, He now fulfills in their regard what Jesus Christ has promised in His Gospel, that 'the Master will establish the good and faithful servant over all His goods'?"[49] Let us, then, faithfully serve a Master who is so magnificent in His rewards; let us imitate the saints, in order to share with them, not in the gift of working miracles in this world, but in the graces which sanctified them, and in the happiness which they enjoy in heaven.

The life of St. Francis furnishes many other wonders of this nature, the memory of which is preserved in many parts of Italy, and which are inserted in the Annals of Wading. Here, however, are only two examples of the assistance he obtained from God, for the wants of his brethren. At his return from Spain, great numbers of them came to St. Donin, in Lombardy, to congratulate him; they joined those of the convent, and went before him. When they had thus escorted him, it happened that at dinner-time they were short of bread, because no one had remained at home to fetch it. The saint ordered the dispenser to look into the place where the bread was usually kept, and he found there a quantity of new bread, where, a moment before, there had been none. The religious acknowledged the power which God had given to their father, and ate of it with great respect, as a present from heaven.

The other miracle was common to him and to St. Dominic, and has something very singular in it. It is taken from a Spanish manuscript, written by one of the companions of the patriarch of the Friars Preachers,[50] of which this is an abridgment from the original, which is very lengthy: "St. Francis holding a chapter of his Order in a small town, our father, St. Dominic, was near him, as they frequently visited each other for spiritual conversation. There were no provisions in the convent; dinner-time came and there was nothing to eat. The two saints betook themselves to prayer, and feeling that their payers had been favorably heard, they assembled the religious in the refectory, where, after grace had been said, twenty young men of great comeliness were seen to enter the room, with everything necessary for their repast, who, having waited at

---

[47] S. Greg., Homil. 29, in Evang. S. Bern., Serm. 1, in Asc. Dom., n. 3.

[48] S. August., Serm. 317, n. 1.

[49] Matt. 24:27.

[50] Cod. MS., foil. 13, 14 et 15.

table, retired two and two. Dinner being finished, St. Dominic made a beautiful discourse on confidence in God; he was accustomed to preach in the convents of the Order of Friars Minors, when he happened to be there. This was owing to his great intimacy with St. Francis, since God had brought them together." This finishes the narrative of the author; what he relates is much to be admired, but David assures us[51] that the Lord has always His eyes open on them that fear Him, in order to provide for their necessities. He gave a miraculous proof of this to the prophet Elias,[52] causing him to find bread and water in the desert; and to the widow of Sarepta, in multiplying her flour and oil;[53] and in what He manifested in a splendid manner in favor of St. Francis, at the famous chapter of the Mats, where more than five thousand religious were satisfied by the marvelous intervention of Providence, as has been recorded above, by the writings of St. Bonaventure.

An eminent and manifest holiness, accompanied by evident miracles, drew extraordinary honors on the servant of the Almighty. We have seen the consideration in which he was held by popes, cardinals, bishops, kings, princes, nobility, and magistrates. The Sultan of Egypt, even at the time the Christians were making war upon him, treated Francis with a distinction full of esteem and respect. The legend composed by order of Pope Gregory IX mentions particularly, "that, on his arrival in cities, towns, and villages, the clergy and people, the great and the lowly, men and women, went out to meet him, carrying great boughs, and singing hymns of praise and joy. Some kissed the ground on which he trod, others strove to touch his poor tunic, many cut pieces off it, and it was sometimes necessary to tell him that this had been done. Those who could touch him and kiss his feet, esteemed themselves fortunate."

The heretics paid him their homage, by the confusion which his presence caused them; far from having the courage to oppose his mission, they hid themselves, and did not dare to appear where he was. The faithful, delighted, flocked from all parts to see him. His attachment to the Catholic doctrine, and to the See of St. Peter, apparent in the holiness of his life, and the miracles he performed, strengthened them in the belief of orthodox truths; it was a triumph for the faith. In fact, so holy a life can only be found in the true Church, and it is only to her children that God grants the testimony of miracles. The virtue of heretics is counterfeit, for there has never been any true virtue without faith. All the miracles which they pretend have been performed, confirmatory of their doctrine, are false; for God is incapable of authorizing error. It must also be remarked that, in all the honors shown to the blessed father, who was a poor man, meanly clothed, of no show, solely

---

[51] Psalm 32 (33):18, 19.

[52] 3 Reg. 19:16.

[53] Ibid. 17: 16

solicitous to appear contemptible, he became, nevertheless, the object of public veneration, and was considered the wonder of his age. The saying of St. Augustine is verified, that a soul eminent for sublime virtue can no more be hid than a city built on a mountain;[54] or, as the wise man says, "Glory shall uphold the humble of spirit, and humility goes before glory."[55]

The personal qualities of St. Francis attached men to him in a scarcely less degree than his extraordinary sanctity; and the gift he possessed of working miracles, called for their admiration. This is the portrait we find of him in the legend we have before alluded to: "Our blessed father was agreeable to all. Joy, serenity, kindness, and modesty, were perceptible in his countenance. He was naturally mild and affable, compassionate, liberal, prudent, discreet, gave sound advice, was faithful to his word, and full of courage; he was easy in his manners, accommodating himself to all sorts of tempers; he was all to all, he was a saint among the saintly, and among sinners, as if he was one of them; his conversation was graceful, and his manner insinuating; close in his reasoning, energetic and compliant in matters of business; and, finally, simple in his actions and words."

These are qualifications well calculated to make their possessor beloved, particularly when joined, as in the case of St Francs, with the purest morals, with the most ardent charity, the most profound humility, and a countenance which seemed angelical. After the portrait of his mind, we find in the same narrative the following description of his person: "He was of middle size, neither short nor tall, but well shaped. His face was oval, his forehead smooth, his eyes black and modest, his mouth pretty; his hair was of chestnut color, his beard black, but scanty, his body very thin, his skin delicate, his speech pleasing and animated, his voice strong and piercing, but altogether mild and sonorous."[56]

We must receive in their true sense what was understood in saying that "he was simple in his actions and words." The term simplicity has two significations in the French language. It is used to describe a person of little mind, narrow-minded, dull, not well informed, weak and credulous; it is also used to express candor, ingenuousness, and uprightness; to describe a person who is natural, without finesse or artfulness. It is in this sense that it is said that the greatest geniuses are the most simple, enemies of subtlety and trick, which are only appropriate to narrow minds.

---

[54] S. Aug. de Serm. Dom. in Monte, lib. 1, cap. 6.

[55] Prov. 29:23; and 15:33.

[56] We see from this description that the most talented painters have not given us a correct likeness of St. Francis. There is one in the convent of the Recollects, at Paris, which answers to the description which his companions have left us of him, but the engravers have refused to copy it, because it is not by one of the first masters. It would be desirable that some clever artist would work upon the sketch those who had seen the saint have left us of him, and upon what is correct in the bad painting.

The simplicity of the just, in Scriptural language, is true virtue, solid without drawback, purity of heart, uprightness of intention in opposition to every sort of duplicity or disguise; everything that St. Paul calls "the prudence of the flesh; the wisdom of this world."[57] St. Gregory so explains it.[58] This does not exclude prudence, but only malice and double-dealing. Our blessed Lord warns us "to be prudent as serpents, and simple as doves."[59] St. Paul says: "I would have you to be wise in good, and simple in evil."[60] Every Christian must be simple in faith, submitting himself purely and simply to the decisions of the Church, without any endeavor to elude them by crafty evasions, as some do in so scandalous a manner; simple in the intercourse of society, being frank and sincere, doing injury to noone; simple in devotion, going straight to God; following the way pointed out by the Gospel; not resembling those of whom the wise man says: "They go two ways, and have two hearts,"[61] the one for God and the other for the world.

Such was the simplicity of St. Francis, or, to speak plainer, he was simple because he had no other intention in his mind, no other movement in his heart, than to be conformed to Jesus Christ. In order to imitate His poverty, His humility, His sufferings, all His virtues, he did many things far above the ordinary rules of human wisdom; and, as to his language, it was formed on that of the Gospel. For this reason some persons in the world looked upon him as a simple-minded man, who had more piety than strength of mind, more fervor than understanding.

But, in the first place, they do not reflect that what appears little to the eyes of the flesh is great in the eye of faith, by the excellence of the model, and by the magnanimity of the motive. Is it, then, a trifling thing to conform in all matters to Jesus Christ, in order to become agreeable to God; to embrace the folly of the cross, and to put in practice what is recommended by St Paul: "If any man among you seem to be wise in this world, let him become a fool, that he may be wise; for the wisdom of this world is foolishness with God"?[62]

In the second place, it is forgotten that St. Francis performed actions of which even the world, if it judge correctly, must acknowledge the greatness. Renouncing all the things of this world with more reality and generosity than the most celebrated and vaunted philosophers. Poor, alone, without influence, without support, to have undertaken what would have made the richest hesitate—the repair of three churches—and to have succeeded in this undertaking. To have formed the plan of a society of men, destitute of all the

---

[57] Rom. 8:6; 1 Cor. 3:19.

[58] S. Greg, in Job. Lib 1, cap. 1, et lib. 10. cap. 29, alias 16.

[59] Matt. 10:16.

[60] Rom. 16:19.

[61] Eccli. 2:14; and 3:28.

[62] 1 Cor. 3:18, 19.

goods of this world, who were to spread themselves over the whole earth, and have no other funds for their subsistence than the providence of the Supreme Being. With an ordinary parable, and without any intrigue, to have caused this singular plan to be approved by popes, by cardinals, by the greatest and most learned men who were hostile to it, and to carry it into execution with a success which has been the admiration of the universe for the last six hundred years. To have induced worldlings to forsake riches, honors, and pleasures, to place themselves in the center of poverty, humiliation and penance. To make as much impression, by the eloquence of his preaching, upon the nobles as upon the people, upon the learned as upon the ignorant. To have had the courage to pass over seas, to go through hostile armies, to preach to a Mohammedan prince the religion of Jesus Christ; to have convinced, to have moved, and to have compelled that prince to respect the holy truths of the Gospel. To have devoted himself to public utility, to have lived solely for the service of others, to have worked incessantly to reform the morals of the people, reestablished peace and concord, to render men reasonable and Christians: all this is what St. Francis did; and is this not something great? Can the world refuse to admit it to be so?

To act thus, is it not necessary to have talents, judgment, penetration, adroitness, and strength of mind? It is true that the spirit of God gave him supernatural lights and extraordinary strength; but these gifts do not prevent our admiring the qualifications which were in his nature. Let the character of his mind, his talents, and his natural dispositions he carefully studied, and no doubt will remain that he was destined for great things.

He may be compared to St. Anthony, the patriarch of cenobitical life, and to St. Martin, the Bishop of Tours, for these three saints have some peculiar relations to each other, which will be very apparent on reading their lives. Although St. Anthony had not studied, and lived in great simplicity in the mountainous parts of the desert, he had, nevertheless, according to St. Athanasius,[63] penetrating and lively wit, rare prudence, wonderful facility in confounding, by solid arguments, both the pagan philosophers and the Arian heretics. His sanctity did not render him rude and boorish; he was well-bred and polite; his conversation was remarked to be what the expression of the apostle describes,[64] graceful and seasoned with salt. No one can say that St. Martin was deficient in talents. That illustrious bishop, who was so greatly esteemed by St. Hilary, St. Ambrose, St. Paulinus, and other great personages of his age; who governed his diocese with so much prudence; who spoke to princes with so much firmness, and was so honored by them;[65] whose discourses were so convincing; whose conversation was no less remarkable for

---

[63] Vit. S. Anton., no 72 et seq.

[64] Coloss. 4: 6.

[65] Sulp. Sev., Vit. S. M., n. 26. Id. Did 2, a. 10.

its vivacity and agreeableness, than for its gravity and dignity; who was wholly master of the Scriptures; who explained and developed the most hidden mysteries in such choice, appropriate, and energetic terms, that Sulpicius Severus, who was a very learned man, assures us that he never heard anything to equal it, from any other person whatsoever. Nevertheless, St Martin had not studied;[66] he was a man of great simplicity, very poor, and so negligent of his exterior appearance, that it often drew upon him contempt. He was looked upon as weak in mind, and foolish.[67] When it was proposed to make him Bishop of Tours, there were some bishops who rejected him as a contemptible person, unworthy of the episcopate; and, after his election,[68] he continued to wear the same livery of penance and humility, and was desirous of appearing equally vile in the eyes of men.

St. Francis was similarly simple, but he had great qualities of mind and heart; and his simplicity was a perfection in him, not a defect. If it induced him to do things of which human prudence disapproves, it was because he was guided by divine light; it was because he sought to be despised by the world, to render himself more conformable to Jesus Christ. Men of his age were not deceived by it; they discovered the principle which made him act and speak with such simplicity. His constant endeavor to humble himself, and draw on himself contempt, only gave them a greater esteem for his person, and they loaded him with honors. If our age deems itself wiser, what reason has it for not doing similar justice?

FINIS

---

[66] Paulin. Petroc., Vit. S. Mart., lib. 4.

[67] Sulp. Sev., Vit. S. Mart, n. 7.

[68] S. Greg. Turon., Hist. Franc., lib. 2, cap. 1.

Made in the USA
Middletown, DE
15 January 2021